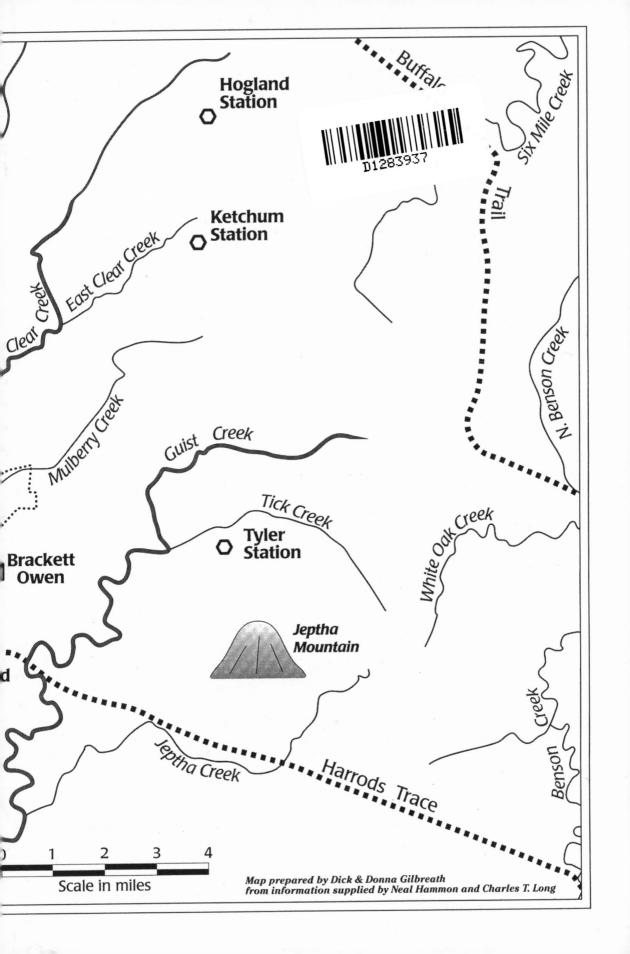

Hogland
Station

Ketchum
Station

Buffalo

Trail

Six Mile Creek

Clear Creek

East Clear Creek

N. Benson Creek

Mulberry Creek

Guist Creek

Tick Creek

White Oak Creek

Tyler
Station

Brackett
Owen

Jeptha
Mountain

d

Benson Creek

Jeptha Creek

Harrods Trace

0   1   2   3   4

Scale in miles

Map prepared by Dick & Donna Gilbreath
from information supplied by Neal Hammon and Charles T. Long

THE NEW HISTORY OF

SHELBY COUNTY

KENTUCKY

View of Shelbyville from the roof of Shelby College, looking southeast toward center of town, circa 1880s.

DEDICATION

FOR THE ORIGINAL SETTLERS WHO NURTURED
AND WORKED THE LAND OF THE PLACE KNOWN
AS SHELBY COUNTY.

WITH GRATEFUL APPRECIATION TO GENEROUS
DONORS INCLUDING
SHELBY COUNTY FISCAL COURT
AND
SHELBYVILLE CITY COUNCIL

CONTENTS

CHAPTER FIVE

CHURCHES 201

Governor Martha Layne Collins

FOREWORD

By Martha Layne Collins

S helby County is a special place. From the days when Indians roamed and hunted the forests, savannas, and waterways of what is now Kentucky to the present day, Shelby County has grown, developed, and changed. Throughout these many years, history has been made which has created the character of this place, influencing its landscape, its people, its economy, its education, the quality of life enjoyed here, and many, many aspects of our daily lives. Several years ago, the Shelby County Chamber of Commerce adopted a slogan, "Good People, Good Land, Good Living." The history of Shelby County is woven tightly into all three of these components.

With roots in Shelby County which date back to the 1790s and growing up in Bagdad, I gained an appreciation at an early age for Shelby County, its people, its natural beauty, its way of life, all of the things that make Shelby County a special place, a great place to call home. And we all know that there is no place like home! Home conjures up images which make us feel secure, reflect our quality of life, and define who and what we are. Similarly, our history provides us with much the same definitive characteristics, yet challenges us to take what we have inherited, to continue to make history that would make our ancestors proud, and to leave a rich legacy and a like challenge to our descendants.

The history of our county is an invaluable source of education. It is a wealth of information for the classroom, scholars, genealogists, and researchers. Most importantly, however, it is a benchmark by which to measure our successes and to identify our failures. History is a precedent for continuing in paths which have led to accomplishment and prosperity. Everyone knows that "hindsight is 20/20," and those who fail to learn from history are doomed to repeat it, so our history teaches us also to appreciate and to learn from the mistakes of the past.

The history of this Shelby County community is a source of interest and inspiration, which creates a desirable place to work, live, raise a family, and a pleasant place for tourists to visit. Shelby County history is a source of community pride, and it challenges us all to give to the future, honor our past by building upon its foundations to maximize our potential, yet preserve the charm and the spirit that makes our county unique.

The Shelby County Historical Society has undertaken the worthy and overwhelming task of compiling this book. This organization is to be commended for its dedication to the preservation of our heritage. Publications such as this capture and save historical information, which is in danger of being lost as the generations pass. As Shelby County continues to grow, as new families choose Shelby County to be their home, as communication and technology continue to make our world a smaller place, this history will give us all a sense of what Shelby County has been, what it is, and what it has the potential to be. It is our duty as readers to learn from it, to share it, and to make it an indispensable tool for education, tourism, and economic development. We must do our part to preserve our history further for future generations. As a native Shelby Countian, I am greatly honored to introduce to you *The New History of Shelby County*.

ACKNOWLEDGMENTS

By John E. Kleber

Geneneral R. R. Van Stockum Sr. and I had known one another for several years when he approached me about editing a new history of Shelby County. Having served as the editor for *The Encyclopedia of Louisville,* and, prior to that, *The Kentucky Encyclopedia,* I did not intend to undertake another editing assignment. But the General was persuasive and, after meeting with the History Book Committee, I decided to take on the task. Now, in looking back, I am grateful to the Committee for its confidence, and for the opportunity to meet and come to know so many wonderful people.

I have read all of the material, and have also suggested additional articles and advised the deletion of others. Other members of the Committee have read the articles and, working together, this book is the result of those collaborative efforts. We are most appreciative of the excellent job of copy editing by Amy Inskeep and Bill Pike, both of Louisville.

It was my good fortune to have worked with Mary Jean Kinsman on *The Encyclopedia of Louisville,* and I incorporated her help on this project. Not only did she bring her professional abilities to the project in the selection of photographs, but she is a native of Shelbyville.

Many people contributed to the illustrations. The Shelby County Public Library has a large and valuable collection of original photographs and copies of historic photographs either donated or shared by their owners. We have used many of these in this publication and appreciate the generosity and cooperation of the owners and of the library staff, especially Deborah Magan. The Filson Historical Society in Louisville provided a number of photographs, including those from the Williams Studio collection. John W. Williams and his son, Otho, were the predominant photographic documenters of Shelbyville and its residents in the nineteenth and early twentieth centuries. The surviving glass negatives, about 300 in number, were preserved by John Williams's granddaughter, Peggy Miller, and her husband, Alwyn, and donated to the Filson Historical Society in 1994. The Kentucky Heritage Council, the State's historic preservation office, shared many photographs from its survey of historic buildings in Shelby County. Staff member William Macintire spent a day scanning photos to be used in the book. Ellis McGinnis was a commercial photographer in Shelbyville in the 1940s and 1950s who recorded scenes and events in the town. His son, Michael McGinnis, donated many of his negatives to the Shelby County Historical Society. Ellis McGinnis also owned an album of remarkable photographs of Shelbyville and Shelby County taken in the early 1900s by an unknown photographer. Michael generously allowed us to use many of those images as well. Other individuals sent us photographs and some writers also submitted them with their articles. The source of each one used is listed in the caption.

Another person I had worked with previously was Kevin Collins. An outstanding researcher and scholar, Kevin spent countless hours in libraries, especially the Shelby County Public Library. He contributed several articles to the book and checked many of the facts presented in other articles. Several people volunteered their time to take articles and scan them into the computer. The willing availability and hearty enthusiasm of the staff of the Shelby County Public Library provided a major boost to the project.

The approach in this history book is topical. The History Book Committee, for the most part, determined what material was to be presented and its choice of authors. Thus, the articles represent the voices and the styles of those who performed the research and put it on paper. These articles refer to the past, but also address the present, and leave a legacy for the future.

Read here, then, the many and varied voices of the special people of a special place, Shelby County, at the beginning of the 21st century and the county's third century. No one can deny the inherent love for place found in each and every article.

In an increasingly transitory age, it is good that some places still attract such loyalty that it is strong enough to prevail to leave a written legacy.

Of such a place is Shelby County.

Book committee seated, left to right: Vivian Overall, R.R Van Stockum, Sr., Emily Thomas and Duanne Puckett. Standing, left to right: Charles T. Long, John Kleber, editor, Ted Igleheart, chairman, William Matthews, and John David Miles (not shown in photo).

INTRODUCTION

By Ted L. Igleheart

T he Shelby County Historical Society existed at one time as the Shelby County Historical Genealogical Society and sponsored the writing and publication of the *History of Shelby County, Kentucky* in 1929, compiled and edited by George L. Willis Sr. For some reason, the Society ceased to exist until an enterprising Executive Secretary of the Shelby County Chamber of Commerce, Joe Tucker, resurrected interest in such an organization in 1963 and attracted a number of hopeful historians to an organizational meeting. Mrs. Purcell Lee was elected its first president, Mrs. Sue Wilson Flowers as vice president, Mrs. Hardin Davis as secretary and Mrs. Willana Brown as treasurer.

One of its first undertakings was the proposal by Joe Tucker to acquire the site of Squire Boone's Station located on the Bayless Farm north of town and develop it into a tourist attraction with reconstruction of the fort. It was apparently too ambitious for success because the owners refused to give or sell the land and the project died with only the members of the Society visiting the area from time to time.

In 1979, *Cemeteries in Shelby County, Kentucky* was published by the Society, spearheaded by Charles T. Long and Martha and Bernice Hedges, who were joined in the hard work of uncovering neglected graves by George Ann Carpenter, Blythe Collings, Frances and Lewis Cottongim, Peggy and Alwyn Miller, Nancy Rives and James M. Todd.

The Society has helped to obtain historical highway markers and nominated city and county homes to the National Register, awarding plaques to landmark property owners in conjunction with celebration of the state's bicentennial in 1992.

The historic home of Governor Augustus O. Stanley, owned by Joe and Kate Casey, was purchased by the Society in 1984 and long hours of restoration were begun by Betty Matthews, Charles Long, Lewis Cottongim and others. Renovation is now completed and period furnishings are being solicited for the use of the house as a museum and meeting place for the Society.

In 1997 I proposed to the board of directors that a new Shelby County history book be published. After obtaining the board's approval, I appointed a committee to help oversee its organization and execution. That committee was composed of Emily Thomas, Gen. Ronald R. VanStockum, Charles T. Long, and John David Myles. Duanne Puckett and Vivian Overall were appointed later. It was called the County History Book Committee of the Society and met at least once a month from 1997 through 2002.

The Committee selected topics based on its knowledge of the county, after reviewing county histories prepared by nearby historical societies. Writers were selected by the Committee after identifying the most knowledgeable individuals. I was gratified that so many talented writers showed such enthusiasm for a new and comprehensive history of Shelby County.

In October of 1999, the Society employed Dr. John E. Kleber as Editor. At his suggestion, Mary Jean Kinsman was also hired as Photo Editor and Kevin Collins was hired as a researcher. Henry Cleveland worked many hours as a volunteer, scanning the articles into the computer so the editor could do his job. Charlene Myles was employed to give technical computer assistance. William Matthews volunteered valuable help to the committee later, rewriting and adding articles in an effort to finish the book. He also provided valuable liason with the publisher.

Harmony House Publishers of Louisville was selected in December 2000 as the publisher after the committee received three bids for the job. Committee members selected various articles to proof read throughout the year 2001 and 2002 to assist the editor before the material was handed over to copy editors and the publisher.

It is the intent of the Committee to compile an accurate, useful reference book that documents the noteworthy people, places and performances in Shelby County from its earliest settlement to date. We trust we have succeeded.

PAST PRESIDENTS OF THE SOCIETY

Mrs. Purcell Lee, 1963-64

Ted L. Igleheart, 1964-65

William Alwyn Miller, 1965-66

Minutes of meetings are missing from 1966-74

Jack Youngman, 1974-75

George Ann Carpenter, 1975-79

William Alwyn Miller, 1979- 82

George Ann Carpenter, 1982-84

Lewis Cottongim, 1984-86

Charles T. Long, 1986-88

Betty Matthews, 1988-93

Charles T. Long, 1993-95

General Ronald R. VanStockum, 1995-97

Ted L. Igleheart, 1997-99

John David Myles, 1999-2001

Jack Brammer, 2001-2003

Sherry Jelsma 2003-

CHAPTER ONE

FRONTIER SHELBY COUNTY

Illustration of a Native American of the Paleo-Indian period. From a poster designed and drawn by Jimmy A. Railey.

Prehistoric Inhabitants

By Ronald R. Van Stockum Jr.

About 12,000 years ago the last great continental glacier, with an ice face towering more than one mile high, began to retreat from its southernmost reach in Indiana and Ohio. Although dating the arrival of humans in the Americas is controversial, the first clear evidence of their presence in Kentucky is between 10,000 and 7,000 BC, a time called the Paleo-Indian Period.

The climate of Kentucky was cooler in the Paleo-Indian Period than in the present time. Small numbers of nomadic Stone Age peoples lived in Kentucky, effectively using flaked stone tools in everyday life. With the exception of pure copper imported from the Great Lakes and pounded into various ceremonial shapes, native Americans in Kentucky never worked or smelted metal ores. They did not develop bronze and iron implements.

The Paleo-Indians carried flintknapping tool kits to fashion their stone implements. These kits included igneous stone hammers imported from outside Kentucky and flaking tools made of hardwoods or antler tips. With these tools they produced distinctive flint stone spearheads such as the fluted Clovis point. They hunted large game with these stone points attached to bone shafts fastened on wooden spears. They hunted animals now extinct in Kentucky such as the mammoth, mastodon, tapir, musk ox, camel, peccary, ground sloth, and bighorn sheep.

The period between 7,000 and 1,000 BC is called the Archaic Period. The human population here became less mobile, spending longer time in centralized base camps and dispersing to rock shelters

Drawing from a poster depicting the Paleo-Indian period. Design and artwork by Jimmy A. Railey.

during the winters. By this time, only deer, elk and bear remained in any numbers as large game in Kentucky. For thousands of years, the human population in Kentucky subsisted on the smaller available game and nuts like those of the hickory tree. Bison returned in the late prehistoric times following the expansions of western prairies in Kentucky during a drying period.

Archaic peoples developed a highly specialized and powerful spearthrower called the "atlatl." This weapon was composed of a short hooked throwing stick weighted down with a "bannerstone." Such a device could propel a short, stone tipped spear with great power and accuracy. They also developed the use of woven baskets tight enough to hold water. Without pottery, these people would cook liquids by heating fist-sized rocks and placing them in baskets of food or into pits dug in the ground.

They developed the grooved stone axe head, which they hafted to a wooden handle. With the use of fire, they were able to work with larger timber and clear forest areas for habitation and game. Trade flourished as flint from Ohio, copper from the Lake Superior area, and seashells from the coasts were traded across Kentucky.

During the Archaic Period, humans in Kentucky often buried their dead in the fetal position and placed tools and food in the grave. During the Middle Archaic Period, primitive horticulture was practiced in the raising of squash for storage vessels. Settlements became more permanent and shifted to the flood plains and terraces above rivers.

Whitetail deer and wild turkey were important sources of meat but bear, raccoon and possum were also hunted. Dogs became domesticated in Kentucky during this time. Hickory nuts were collected and boiled to produce nutritious oil. Oily seeds such as sunflower and marsh elder, and starchy seeds such as goosefoot and maygrass (canary grass) were sought out by Archaic foragers in the forest and field.

The period from 1,000 BC to AD 1,000 is known as the Woodland Period. It is marked by the expansion of horticulture in the cultivation of previously wild populations of sunflower, goosefoot and lambsquarter for seed production. Pottery, which had been developed earlier in the Southeast, spread to Kentucky during this period.

A new ungrooved stone axe known as a celt was developed during the Woodland Period. Instead of being hafted to a wooden handle and tied in place, the celt was shaped in a more narrow point on one end, which was inserted in a hole cut in a wooden axe handle. It was more secure in use and more easily removed for sharpening by grinding.

In the early Woodland Period two societies developed in the upper Ohio Valley, typified by the erection of ceremonial and burial mounds. William S. Webb of the University of Kentucky extensively investigated the Adena culture. The Adena peoples lived in a relatively unstratified society in small-dispersed settlements. The use of textiles and twined fabric developed. They created mounds that were often used as burial sites and sacred earth works.

Between 150 BC and AD 500, the Hopewell culture raised larger, centralized villages where squash, gourds, sunflower, little barley, and a limited type of corn (maize) were grown. During this period, there is evidence that native Americans were exploring Kentucky's caves. Mummified human remains from this period have been found in the Mammoth Cave system containing intestinal remnants of these cultivated plants. Neither Adena nor Hopewell earthworks are evident in Shelby County. However, hundreds of Adena structures were erected in the Bluegrass and upper Ohio Valley. Hopewell structures are particularly well represented in Ohio.

In the late Woodland Period, long-distance trade was greatly curtailed and few mounds were constructed. The bow and arrow was introduced into Kentucky at this time. Most of what are found and described as arrowheads in Kentucky are actually spear and atlatl points. The smaller "bird" points are true arrowheads.

Archaeological discoveries are often made during excavation preceding development. Thus during the 1979 excavation of a softball field in Clear Creek Park in Shelby County, a Late Woodland Period site was uncovered. The time period of this site, 350-750 AD, is called the Newton Phase of the Late Woodland Period and involved seasonal villages located along important watercourses. Wattle and daub houses may have been present but little gardening was performed with the population subsiding primarily on hunting and gathering. Cord-marked pottery, celts and corner-notched spear points were in common use during this phase.

This Shelby County site is composed of two refuse pits fifteen feet apart on a ridge next to Clear Creek. It is called the "Old Bear Site" because one of the pits contained remnants of an old female black bear. Radiocarbon analysis gives a date of AD 510, plus or minus 100 years. The pits were apparently used to roast food and periodically served as refuse repositories. Stone flaking debris and chipped stone tools were also found in the pits.

St. Genevieve Chert (a type of flint) was found in the pits but is not native to Shelby County. The stone was most probably traded from northern or western Kentucky sources. Igneous hammerstones and antler tines probably represent part of a Native American flintknappers kit. Thin walled shards (pieces of broken pottery) with cord marked surfaces and crushed limestone temper were also found.

The many fractured animal bones that were found probably represent marrow extraction. Remains of twenty-five animal species were found, including seven white--tailed deer, three black bear, five raccoons, two wild turkeys, and one individual each of gray squirrel, woodchuck, skunk, wolf or dog, beaver, soft-shelled turtle and terrapin. Plant remains in the pits included squash, honey locust, butternut, shagbark hickory, walnut and acorns. The presence of the broken bones of one adult human near the site is intriguing.

The site was utilized during the fall and winter seasons. Lack of housing remains indicates that the site was probably a temporary one. More permanent summer base camps could have been located in the valleys of larger Kentucky rivers. During the fall, these communities broke into smaller groups, which moved upland to places like the "Old Bear Site."

Another Late Woodland site in Shelby County was discovered during excavations for the Clear Creek Park Amphitheater. Ten pit features were examined. Some of those features served as cooking or storage pits which were filled with refuse after use. Cord marked clay pot shards, flint scrappers, a chert celt, and a stone drill were found. Although the general time period of use overlapped that of the "Old Bear Site," projectile points found at the site ranged from Archaic, Woodland and Ft. Ancient cultures.

Wood charcoal in the fire pits was predominately white oak and hickory. Of interest was the presence of holly wood. The remains of plant food included hickory nuts (representing 90% of nutshells), squash (for seeds), gourds (for containers), maygrass (for high protein and fats seeds) and goosefoot (for starchy seeds and leafy greens). Persimmon, blackberry, sumac and nightshade seeds were also found.

The remains of eleven species of animals were found, predominately deer, bear, turtle and raccoon. Limited elk, cougar and wild turkey remains were also present. Like the "Old Bear Site" fish do not appear to be a significant part of the diet.

You can make clay pots today just as the Woodland Indians did thousands of years ago. Clean wet clay can be tempered with crushed limestone. Pinching a ball of clay with your thumb will form a base for the bowl. The bowl itself is formed by running long rolls of clay in a spiral fashion around the edges of the base, thus building up the walls of the vessel. By smoothing the walls with your fingers you can make the vessel walls thin and taper to make the mouth of the pot. Simply pulling up the sides of a pinched clay base to make the walls causes the clay to crack and break when fired. Using a stick wrapped with rope or twine, cord markings are rolled onto the clay surface as a design. The pot is allowed to dry in the open air and sun for days and then placed in the center of a bonfire to which hardwoods are continually applied until a white-hot temperature is reached. When the pot is finally removed from the cooled fire ashes, the clay has annealed and the pot has become a ceramic vessel. Native Americans in Kentucky did not use glazes, nor were kilns or the potters' wheel developed here.

The Late Prehistoric Period is dated from AD 1000-1700. In Kentucky two cultures developed: the Mississippi culture in the west, as evidenced by the Wickliffe Mound People; and Ft. Ancient cultures in the Bluegrass and eastern areas of Kentucky. It is probable that Ft. Ancient peoples inhabited Shelby County in this period.

This Late Prehistoric Period reflected, for the first time in Kentucky, the greater importance of corn agriculture compared to hunting. As a result, populations in Kentucky increased and more permanent villages formed. Stratified social structures developed, replacing the more equal relationships in the earlier hunter-gatherer societies. Homes were made of sturdy pole frames with roofs composed of grass or reeds. Villages were established near important waterways and were often fortified with stockades. Crushed mussel shells were commonly used to temper clay pots and can be used to generally date potshards to this period.

The Shawnee Indians of Algonquin linguistic stock are probably the descendants of the Ft. Ancient peoples who lived in this area. The explorer Christopher Gist encountered this culture along the Ohio River in Greenup County, in a village called Lower Shawneetown, in 1750.

One survey of recorded archeological locations reported the following sites in Shelby County:

Paleo-Indian, three; Archaic, eight; Woodland, four; and Late Prehistoric, seven. These included one earth mound, two earthworks, one mound complex and 31 open features.

In 1932, the University of Kentucky published Archaeological Survey of Kentucky by W.D. Funkhouser and W.S. Webb. In the section on Shelby County, the authors described the following sites:

1. Several mounds south of Shelbyville.

2. According to tradition the top of Jeptha Knob was fortified by earthworks and was used by Indians up to historical times. Regarding this site Mrs. Luther O. Willis states: "This ancient fortification is situated six miles east of Shelbyville on an elevation two hundred feet above the surrounding country. It is circular in form with a double line of earthworks four to eight feet high enclosing about three acres, now overgrown with large trees. A few graves and Indian relics have been found nearby." Aborigines may well have used this site in defense or lookout purposes, as it commands an excellent view over a wide surrounding area.

3. The remains of an ancient fortification or earthworks on the farm of W.T. Jamison and James Jamison at Clay Village. It should be noted that this site is at the foot of Jeptha Knob. Reported by Mrs. Graham Lawrence.

4. A large mound covering several acres on the farm of T.J. Jones, two miles south of Finchville and about eight miles south of Shelbyville on the Finchville-Olive Branch Pike. This mound has yielded a large number of artifacts and an extension of peculiar form is represented by a tongue of land, which has attracted much attention.

E.H. Igleheart reported a good discussion of Kentucky projectile points found in farm fields along Clear Creek and Zaring Mill Road in Shelby County. Igleheart identified 44 illustrated types including points from Paleo-Indian, Adena and Hopewell peoples.

See Robert Brooks, *The Old Bear Site (155118): An Upland Camp in the Western Outer Bluegrass*, The Kentucky Heritage Council, pp. 110-123, 1985; Charles D. Hockensmith, Kenneth C. Carstens, Charles Stout, and J. Rivers, *The Shelby Lake Site: A Late Woodland Upland Camp in Shelby County Kentucky*, The Kentucky Heritage Council, pp. 121-162, Vol. 5, 1998; Henry S. McKelway, Michael D. Richmond, Robert B. Hand, and Jeffrey Mauch, *An Archaeological Reconnaissance of Proposed Parcels of Kentucky State Highway 55 Upgrade*, and *Phase II Investigation of Site 1551150 Shelby County, Kentucky*, Cultural Resource Analysis, Inc. contract publication series 96-42, 1997; W. D. Funkhouser and W. S. Webb, *Reports in Archaeology and Anthropology*, Archaeological Survey of Kentucky, Department of Anthropology and Archaeology, University of Kentucky, Vol. 2, September, 1932; E.H. Igleheart, *Kentucky Projectile Points, Clear Creek, Shelby County*, The Register of the Kentucky Historical Society, pp. 147-170, Vol. 68, 1970.

GEOLOGY

By Garland R. Dever Jr.

Bedrock exposed at the surface in Shelby County consists of sedimentary rocks that were deposited in marine environments from about 455 to 425 million years ago, during the Ordovician and Silurian Periods. At that time, the part of the North American continent that is now the site of Shelby County was in the southern latitudes, about 25 degrees south of the equator.

About 700 feet of sedimentary rock is exposed in the county. The surface rocks are composed of limestone, dolomite, shale, and siltstone. Drilling in central Kentucky indicates that the area is underlain by thousands of feet of older sedimentary rocks.

Shelby County is on the western flank of the Cincinnati Arch, a north-south-trending anticline extending across central Kentucky. Rock formations in the county generally dip to the west, away from the arch, at an average rate of about 25 to 30 feet per mile. The regional dip causes older rocks to dip beneath progressively younger formations from east to west across the county.

Ordovician rocks (455 to 440 million years old) were deposited mainly in warm shallow seas. They consist of seven formations: in ascending order from oldest to youngest, the Lexington Limestone, Clays Ferry Formation, Kope Formation, Calloway Creek Limestone, Grant Lake Limestone, Bull Fork Formation, and Drakes Formation.

The Lexington Limestone, the oldest formation, crops out along the valleys of Benson and Sixmile Creeks and their tributaries in eastern and northeastern parts of the county. The limestones are partly fossiliferous, containing brachiopods, bryozoans, gastropods, and crinoid columnals.

The Clays Ferry and Kope formations are composed of interbedded shale and limestone, and lesser amounts of interbedded siltstone. Fossil content ranges from abundant to sparse. These two shale-rich formations were deposited in deeper waters than older and younger Ordovician units.

Because of their high shale content, the Clays Ferry and Kope erode to form a distinctive landscape of narrow ridges and valleys, with most of the land in steep slopes. This landscape in the Clays Ferry and Kope outcrop belt of eastern Shelby County is part of the Eden Shale Belt, a geographic region in central Kentucky. Younger Ordovician and Silurian formations cropping out in central and western parts of the county contain lesser amounts of shale and erode to form the rolling landscape of the Outer Bluegrass Region.

The Calloway Creek and Grant Lake limestones and Bull Fork Formation, which are composed of limestone with lesser amounts of shale, mainly crop out in central and western parts of Shelby County. They commonly contain abundant fossils, including brachiopods, branching and subspherical bryozoans, trilobite and crinoid fragments, pelecypods, gastropods, and straight-shelled cephalopods.

Dolomite, limestone, and shale of the Drakes Formation, which are the youngest Ordovician rocks, crop out in the northwestern part of the county. The limestone and shale, deposited in warm shallow seas, contain abundant fossils, including zones of colonial corals. The dolomite, finely crystalline and partly mudcracked, accumulated in shallower lagoons and tidal flats.

Sedimentary rocks of Silurian age (440 to 425 million years old) crop out in northwestern Shelby County and on Jeptha Knob in the eastern part of the county. They consist of three formations: in ascending order, the Brassfield Formation (limestone and dolomite), Osgood Formation (shale and minor dolomite), and Laurel Dolomite (dolomite and minor shale). These rocks were deposited in marine environments, mainly at relatively shallow depths. Fossils preserved in chert residuum on Jeptha Knob suggest that other younger Silurian formations may have been present in the county before being removed by weathering and erosion.

The youngest deposits in the county are the silt, clay, sand, and gravel, which have been laid down in stream valleys during the Quaternary Period, probably within the last several thousand years. These unconsolidated sediments are derived from the erosion of outcropping bedrock and soil.

Jeptha Knob is the most prominent geologic feature in the county. The core of the knob consists of uplifted, faulted, and brecciated Ordovician rocks, which are overlain by nearly horizontal Silurian rocks. The presence of undisturbed Early Silurian rocks overlying highly disturbed Late Ordovician rocks indicates that the event forming the knob occurred in latest Ordovician or earliest Silurian time, about 440 million years ago. Jeptha Knob has been described as a cryptovolcanic or cryptoexplosive structure, but a more recent interpretation proposes an origin by meteorite impact.

Extraction of mineral resources in Shelby County has been very limited. Small quarries, now abandoned, have produced road metal, fill, and dimension stone for local use. The Calloway Creek Limestone was the main source of stone; lesser quantities were obtained from the Grant Lake Limestone and the Drakes and Brassfield formations. Wells drilled in the exploration for oil and gas have encountered only small noncommercial shows of gas and oil, mainly at depths of less than 1,000 feet.

Exploration and Land Grants

By Neal Hammon

T he first white men to leave any record of traveling through Shelby County were those who accompanied the surveyor John Floyd in the early summer of 1774. This party consisted of about eight men who made surveys for Virginia veterans of the French and Indian War. They had just completed surveying about 40,000 acres south of the Falls of the Ohio at the present site of Louisville, after which they surveyed Bullitt's salt lick near Shepherdsville. From there they headed eastward, along the Salt River. One of the men, Thomas Hanson, kept a journal of this trip:

- *12 June, 1774, Sunday*
  We packd up our alls & marched for Salt Lick near Salt River, 12 miles bearing to the South West. We passed a large body of good land well watered & well timbered.
- *13 June, 1774, Monday*
  Mr. Douglass made a survey for Mr. (William) Christian of 1000 acres, round the Lick, then marched off for Salt River. We went five miles & met with a branch & called it Floyd's River. The land is broken and stony.
- *14 June, 1774, Tuesday*
  We proceeded up Salt River 20 miles & found it very crooked, the land chiefly stony hills, except one small bottom.
- *15 June, 1774, Wednesday*
  It rained & thundered, which caused us to stay in camp. Nox & Allen seemed very sullen, & left the camp which made us imagine they had a mind to leave us. But in the evening they returned again dried their blankets & stayed with us that night. Mr. Floyd did not like the land here.
- *16 June, 1774, Thursday*
  We rose early and began our journey up the River. Nox & Allen walked so fast that they left the rest of. the Company, & we never saw them more. Mr. Douglas killed an Elk, therefore we stopped to breakfast. We travelled 25 miles, the land good for nothing.

Daniel Boone passed though Shelby County in the fall of 1775, along with a company that included Daniel Goodman, and Nathan and Thomas Hart. On their way to the Falls of the Ohio [Louisville] the party chanced upon a beautiful spot that they named "the Vinyard." Daniel Goodman claimed the Vinyard, which was a few miles south of Jeptha Knob on a south branch of Jeptha Creek.

Among the other frontier land seekers who visited Shelby County was Daniel's brother, Squire Boone. He deposed that: *"In the summer in the year 1775 I this deponant came to the place where Boone's Station on clear creek was since built I then made a small Improvement about one quarter of a mile North of where the old mill at said Boones Station now stands in the spring of the year 1776, 1 came again to the same place and took a stone out of the creek and with a mill pick picked my name in full and the date of the year thereon, and with red paint 1 painted the letters & Figures all red from which stone this Tract of Land Took the name of the painted Stone tract, the said stone is about one Inch thick and eighteen Inches Long & wide. "*

Daniel and Squire Boone were not the only ones in Shelby County. James Berry arrived in the spring of 1775 to explore Kentucky, accompanied by Henry Tillon [sic, or Tilling], Richard Burk, and others. Burk testified that when traveling along Fox Run, they stopped and raised a cabin "about two rounds high." At the time they saw no other improvements on this creek.

John Smith, who had explored Kentucky in 1773, later gave a deposition about a salt lick that he and others found in 1775 in a cane break along Brashears Creek: *"The Deposition of John Smith of lawful age and being first Sworn deposeth and saith that in 1775. he came to this place from Harrodsburg on his way to the mouth of Harrods Creek on the Ohio in Company with James Harrod, Ebenezer Sevirne and others We then Called this lick within five rod of this place 'Cane lick' in the edge of the Creek, and in 1776 again Came to this place in company with Joseph Bowman, Isaac Hite, Harman Consilla and others. It was Still called the 'Cane lick,' I have not Seen the place since then till now but know it to be the Same and says he knows this is Creek Which was called Brashears's creek in 1776."*

Several men explored what is now Shelby County after traveling down the Ohio, and visiting Drennons Lick. They were unaware that some had already begun using the name Brashears Creek, so they proceeded to name the creeks as they saw fit. Robert Foreman describes his first trip into this country: *"That About the last of February or first of March One thousand seven hundred and Seventy Six he this Deponant came from the mouth of Kentucky to drennons lick And Thence to the dividing ridge between drennons lick Creek And this Creek in Company With Thomas Baird John Porter and Robert Elliot and from the dividing ridge We Came down On the head Waters of this Creek and called it fox Run, in consequence having Killed a fox on the head Waters himsf and We made some Improvements before We Came to this place, and we also made an Improvement at this place."*

John Porter claimed land south of Foreman, and about a mile west of Squire Boone's claim at Painted Stone. Porter later said that *"we found an Improvement Which Were afterwards Informed was Hintons We then Explored Clear Creek and named it clear creek and made some Improvements thereon."*

Bullskin Creek acquired its name because it passed by a well known hunters camp, called Camp Bullskin. This camp was nearly where Interstate 64 crosses that creek.

Guist Creek was first called Gess Creek. According to William Stafford, one of the early Shelby County explorers, in March 1776 he discovered the "brand" (the letter G in a heart) of David Gess on an ash tree about thirty yards from the east bank of that creek, and from that time on it was called by that name. Guist (or Gess) Creek flowed from Jeptha Knob. A south branch of the creek was soon to acquire the name Jeptha, and a northern branch acquired a less flattering name, Tick Creek. Some called Jeptha Creek "Path Fork" or "Trace Fork" because the old trail between Harrodsburg and Louisville ran along this creek.

Although quite a few pioneers managed to visit this area between 1774 and 1779, there were no settlements because it was too isolated and the Indians were on the warpath. But though the country was unoccupied, Squire Boone was looking forward to bringing settlers to the area.

At that time the Virginia legislature finally passed a bill that allowed frontier settlers to acquire western land. The bill provided for commissioners to travel to frontier forts and issue settlement certificates to those who had either lived on their claims for one year prior to 1778, or had grown corn there. Preemption warrants would also be issued to them or to anyone who had traveled west and built a house or hut, or made any improvement on the land prior to 1778. The settlement certificates cost only £2 for 400 acres (ten shillings per 100 acres), and the preemption's £200 for 1,000 acres. Military warrants issued to veterans of the French and Indian War could also be used to claim land. After these men had made their choice, anyone could purchase treasury warrants, which could be used to acquire whatever vacant land was left.

Squire Boone went before the commissioners on November 22, 1779, at the fort at the Falls of the Ohio and requested a 1,400-acre settlement and preemption at his claim called Stockfields on Silver Creek. He also made similar claims for Painted Stone on behalf of his brother-in-law, Benjamin Vancleve.

In 1780, Boone and a group of settlers from Louisville moved to Painted Stone Station, which was about two and a half miles north of the present Shelby County court house. Within a short time there was a wagon road between Painted Stone and Louisville that was generally called Boone's Trace or Boone's Road. But Nicholas Merewether located several of the new settlement and preemption claims on Clear Creek below Painted Stone. During the winter of 1779-80, he marked off the claims of Margaret Pendergrass Wilson, John Porter, George Holeman, Benjamin Pope, Bracket Owens, and Joel Jackson. Merewether started by marking an elm tree beside the creek, about 4,000 feet south of Painted Stone, and running all the surveys from there. It is still possible to see the property lines running in all directions from this tree on an aerial photograph.

Others also claimed land in the area. While the Virginia commissioners were hearing the claims of Kentucky pioneers, a total of 80 men proved they had "improvements" on waters of Brashears Creek, or nearby. These records indicate that most of these were originally made in 1775 or 1776.

Soon after the old settlers and preemptors had made their choice, men began entering tracts in the area on treasury warrants. In fact, in the immediate Shelbyville area more land was surveyed on this type of warrant than any other was.

The largest survey in Shelby County was 30,000 acres entered in the names of James Patton, John Pope, and Benjamin and Mark Thomas. Although the bulk of this land is presently in Spencer County, it was in the original Shelby County, and part of it is north of the present county line. The land was on the east side of Brashears Creek, and included the lower part of Guist Creek.

The next largest survey in the county was 22,000 acres for Captain John Lewis, which extended from Bullskin Creek to Floyds Fork. Captain Lewis (1749-88) was born in Augusta County, Virginia, the eldest son of Thomas Lewis.

Also on the waters of Bullskin Creek were military surveys for William Madison for 2,000 acres and John Madison Jr. for 1,000 acres. James Kemps had a treasury warrant survey of 9,750 acres along Boones wagon road, just to the south of the Lewis survey. Another prominent Virginian who had land here was Peachy Purdy; he had a 3,000-acre treasury warrant survey along Brashears Creek that began at Asturges hunting camp.

Shelby County was not established until 1792, so most of the surveys and grants were originally entered in Virginia counties of Fincastle, Kentucky, and Jefferson.

Some surveys overlapped, because many of the old improvements were too close together. Originally the Virginia legislature had promised frontiersmen 400 acres but a law passed in 1778 allowed them an additional 1,000 acres. The purpose was to raise money to pay Virginia's war debts. Naturally more land was claimed under this arrangement.

By the end of 1785, practically all of Shelby County had been surveyed, and grants had been issued for many tracts. Even so, very few of these landowners lived on their property.

In 1780, the only occupied area within the present Shelby County was Painted Stone. Here the occupants lived in cabins built close together, with pickets between cabins forming a fort. According to Moses Boone, the fort was nearly square and covered about an acre; thus each wall would be slightly over 200 feet long. He also said that those who settled there the first year were "Marius Hansbury, old Mr. Yunt and son George Yunt with their families, Wm. Hall, Abraham Van Metre, Abram Holt, Robert Tyler, John Kline, Philip Nichols, old Robert Eastwood, John Van Cleve, Evan Hinton— and several young men without families, among them were George Hohman [sic, Holman] , Rich'd. Rue, a brother of Philip Nichols, one Leggett, &c. The widow Underwood and family also of the first settlers."

On July 17, Squire Boone's company of militia was called upon to join General George Rogers Clark in his campaign against the Shawnee. Fourteen men were mustered from his station, and several were killed on the campaign.

Following Indian attacks in 1781, the remaining settlers abandoned Painted Stone Station in hopes of finding shelter at one of the six stations along Beargrass Creek in Jefferson County. But Indians attacked them en route near Long Run, killing 7 to 10 in what became known as the Long Run Massacre. The next day John Floyd led a small company of mounted militia to Long Run with the intention of punishing the Indians, but they were outnumbered and defeated with heavy losses. A few days later additional troops were able to evacuate the wounded Squire Boone and the Hinton family from Painted Stone. After they left, the Indians burned down all the cabins at the fort. No white men resided in what is now Shelby County between September 1782 and January or February of 1784.

The following received early land grants: Hezekiah Applegate, John Bailey, Richard Bard, James Beaty, Richard Benson, John Gray Blount, Richard Brashear [Brasheir],Thomas Bull, James Carroll, Richard Chenoweth [Chenoch], George Rogers Clark, Samuel Coburn, James Cruck, Thomas Dagerly, Aniah Davis, James Elliott, Robert Elliott, Henry Failwether, Peter Flin, James Foaker, Robert Foeman, Henry French, William Garrott, Cornelias Gatter, Thomas Gibson, Roger Top, Daniel Goodman, James Hall, James Hannah, James Harrod [Harrods], George Hart Jr., John Helm, William Hickman, Evan Hinton, Peter Hogg, Edward Hoggin, George Holeman, Henry Holeman, John Hunt, Arthur Ingram, John Larue, James Lee, Phillip Lutts, Philip Young McCallock, George McClure, Senica McCracken, John Miller, Edward Mooredock, William Morgan, Thomas O'Bryan, George Paff, Adam Pain, John Paul, Peter Paul , Pendergrass, George Phelps, Benj. Pope, John Porter, Samuel Potter, Richard Rue, George Sitlemore, George Slaugher, Robert Slaugher, Jr., John Soverns, Isaac Sparks, Uriah Stone, Richard Thomas, Charles M. Thruston, Daniel Trabue, Benj. Underwood, Aaron Vancleve, Benj. Vancleve, James Wall, Robert Wall, Adam Whickerham Jr., Aquilla Whitaker, William White, Peter Williams, William Woodard, and James Wright.

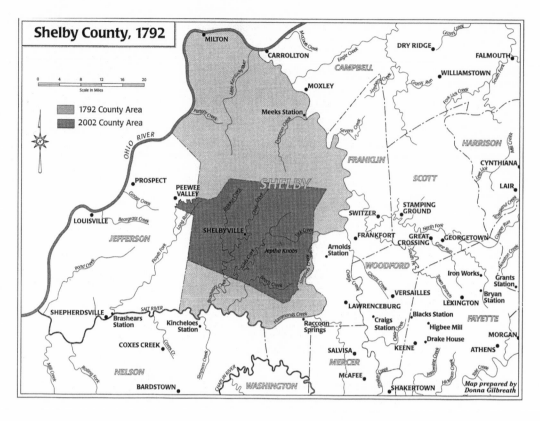

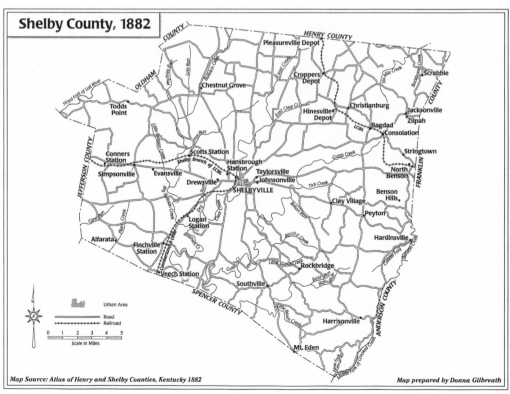

FRONTIER SHELBY COUNTY

By Vince Akers

The frontier or pioneer era in Shelby County lasted from 1776 to 1794. It began when future settlers began making improvements on land so they could claim it. The era ended when General "Mad Anthony" Wayne defeated several Indian tribes at Fallen Timbers in present Ohio. Wayne's victory made much of the frontier safer for whites.

Squire Boone, Daniel Boone's brother, left perhaps the best-known marker of an early land claim in Shelby County. Boone marked his claim to land along Clear Creek in 1776 by painting his name and the date in red on a stone. The marker, which was along a stretch of the Creek between Eminence Road and Burks Branch Pike, is still known as "The Painted Stone."

Guist Creek took its name from David Guess, one of Daniel Boone's men who cut his claiming mark on a tree along the creek. Guess' mark, about the size of the palm of a man's hand, was a capital "G" inside a design that resembled an upside-down heart. "Guess" was later changed into "Guist," giving the Creek its current name.

One of Guist Creek's larger branches became Tick Creek in 1776 after Benjamin Vancleve and others camped near it and named it for the large number of ticks they encountered.

Patrick Jordan, Col. John Floyd and five or six other men established a hunting camp in 1776 along a creek near Brunerstown Road. The men often dried the skins of buffalo they had killed by hanging them in trees around the camp. The place soon became known as "Bullskin Camp," perhaps because buffalo bulls were abundant. Likewise, the creek became "Bullskin Creek."

Squire Boone intended to settle Painted Rock Station (also called Boone's Station) in 1779, but delayed because he feared Indian trouble. He temporarily located his family at the Falls of the Ohio.

However Boone spent the winter of 1779-80 at the station site without meaning to. He and Evan Hinton went there in the fall to make it ready for settlement in the spring. But they couldn't leave due to prolonged bad weather.

Several families joined them in the spring. They built a station with cabins picketed in a square about an acre in size.

The station was not on the south side of Clear Creek, as is often stated. The south side of the creek along the bend above Shelby Lake is a virtual cliff. Squire Boone's sons, Moses and Isaiah Boone, both said the station was on a small ridge on the north bank of the creek.

In addition to the Boone and Hinton families, the original families at Boone's Station included those of William Hall, Abraham Vanmeter, Abram Holt, Robert Tyler, John Kline, Philip Nichols, Robert Eastwood, John Vancleve and Evan Hinton. The settlement also included several single men and at least one widow.

Indian problems were almost immediate. That spring Indians killed a single man known only as Legget and injured Eastwood during an attack some distance from the fortified settlement.

Kentucky received a jolt in June 1780, when the British and Indians captured two stations in Harrison and Bourbon Counties. The captives, 470 men, women and children, were loaded down with plunder from their own cabins and driven on foot to Detroit, a distance of 600 miles. In retaliation, George Rogers Clark led an expedition across the Ohio in August, which was successful in destroying the Indian towns of Chillicothe, Piqua, and Loramie's Store. Squire Boone went along at the head of a company in that campaign. Many of the other men of Boone's Station joined him on the campaign. Colonel Harrod passed through Shelby County along Harrods Trace in July 1780 with about eighty men from Harrodsburg for the campaign.

The number of settlers at Painted Stone during the summer of 1780 can be determined by the size of its militia. Richard and Lewis Collins' 1874 *History of Kentucky* lists 23 Painted Stone men who made up Boone's company: Squire Boone, Alex Bryant, John Buckles, Richard Cates, Charles Doleman, John Eastwood, Joseph Eastwood, Jeremiah Harris, John Hinton, Abraham Holt, Morgan Hughes, Evan Hinton, John McFadden, John Nichols, Peter Paul, John Stapleton, Robert Tyler, Abraham Vanmeter, Adam Wickersham, Jacob Wickersham, Peter Wickersham, James Wright, and George Yount.

With the militia at Painted Stone numbering near 25 during 1780, the total inhabitants of the station surely exceeded 100 men, women and children.

Boone and the Painted Stone settlers were not the only white people in Shelby County in 1780. Brothers James and Peter Sturgus established a hunting camp that year on the east side of Clear Creek. The spot is just off Popes Corner road where Clear Creek nearly touches the road about a half-mile from its dead end. Also in 1780, Peter A'Sturgus established a station on Beargrass Creek near Oxmoor Center in Jefferson County.

Old Shelby County lawsuits involving land claims often mention the six stations along the middle fork of Beargrass Creek in present Jefferson County. Many Shelby County settlers came from the stations, which were established by 1780, or traveled through them. Besides A'Sturgus Station, the others were Floyd's, Hogland's, Dutch or New Holland, Spring and Linn's. Indians frequently harassed the stations, according to letters written at the time.

Painted Stone was 21 miles from Linn's Station, the eastern most of the Beargrass stations. Isolated, Painted Stone was vulnerable to Indian attack. It had two vital links to the other stations: Harrod's Trace, the cross-county road blazed in 1778; and Boone's Trace, blazed perhaps in 1775 or 1776 by pioneers.

Indian attacks accelerated in 1781. In February, Indians attacked Evan Hinton, Richard Rue and George Holeman about three miles from Painted Stone Station. Led by white renegade Simon Girty, the Indians held Rue and Holeman prisoner for three years. Hinton drowned or was killed trying to escape.

On the same day—February 6—the same Indians captured John and Peter Demaree near Painted Stone Station. The Indians held them prisoner for four months until they sold them to the British, who were fighting Americans in the Revolutionary War. The Demarees later escaped from a British jail and returned home.

In April, Indians attacked three men from Painted Stone Station while they were clearing ground. One man was killed, one was taken prisoner and one escaped to the station. Squire Boone and 10 or 12 men gave chase, but were ambushed. Boone was seriously wounded. He recovered, although one of his arms was shattered.

In May, Indians attacked a group from Painted Stone Station that planned to procure salt at Drennons Lick. The Indians killed a white woman and one or two white men. They also captured three African

Daniel Boone in an engraving from a Chappel painting, published by Johnson, Fry & Co.

Americans, who were never recovered. In August, Indians killed Philip Nichols at a spring about 80 yards from the station.

Discouraged and fearing a major attack by the Indians, the settlers abandoned Painted Stone Station on September 13, 1781 for the comparative safety of the Beargrass Creek Stations.

Indians ambushed the fleeing families about eight miles east of Linn's Station where the road crossed Long Run of Floyd's Fork. The settlers were ripe for an attack because they were scattered along the trail. In addition, some refused to fight, rushing instead toward the stations. A running battle about a mile long followed. Militiamen assigned to protect the families were unaware of the attack because they were in the rear, attending a sick man. As many as 15 settlers were killed in the attack, called the Long Run Massacre. Indian losses are not known.

Capt. John Floyd, commander of the Jefferson County militia, and 27 men from the Beargrass Stations sought to avenge the defeat the following day. About 200 Indians waited, knowing the whites would return to the massacre scene to bury the dead. The Indians ambushed Floyd on a ridge between Floyd's Fork and Long Run near Eastwood. Surprised and outnumbered, Floyd's men were quickly defeated. Seventeen were killed or captured. Nine or 10 Indians were killed.

A day or two later, 300 men from Louisville and the stations buried the dead from both defeats in a large sinkhole. The men also went to Painted Stone Station to escort Boone, Hinton and their families to the Beargrass Stations.

Always partial to Shelby County, Boone made another settlement attempt in 1783 after concluding that renewed Indian attacks were less likely. He returned to Painted Stone Station with six or eight families. They had to build a new station because Indians apparently had burned the original station.

An exact description of the rebuilt station has not been preserved. It may have been smaller than the original, but it was the principal fortress in the area for the rest of the decade. In 1784, Boone built a grist and sawmill on Clear Creek. It was the first mill in Shelby County.

Other settlers apparently also believed the Indian threat had diminished. They built several small stations in 1784-85 in Shelby County that consisted of only three or four families and a few cabins connected by a stockade fence.

One of the more unusual groups to settle in Shelby County was the Low Dutch Company, which in 1784-85 bought nearly 9,000 acres in Shelby and Henry Counties. The tract, still known as the Low Dutch Tract, includes North Pleasureville, South Pleasureville, Devoe and parts of Cropper, and Elmberg.

Of Dutch and French Huguenot origin, the Low Dutch immigrated to New Amsterdam (now New York City) in the mid 1600s. Two groups came to Kentucky in 1780, hoping to establish a long-term community where they could preserve their language and religion. Some settled in Mercer County; others tried to settle in Madison County, an attempt that failed due to Indian problems.

The Shelby County Dutch divided their tract into 200-acre parcels assigned to individual families. Their settlement was hardly underway when Indians threatened daily attacks. After initially resisting, many of the Dutch left for Mercer County

Nearly a decade passed before the Dutch could safely return to their land. They developed prosperous farms and spread throughout northeastern Shelby County.

Their descendants include the Bantas, Bergens, Bruners, Brewers, Demarees, Monforts, Shucks, Terhunes, Vanarsdales, Vorises and others.

Shelby County also has presidential connections with Harry S. Truman. Both his paternal and maternal grandparents were married in Shelby County. All four later migrated to Missouri. Robert Tyler, one of the original settlers in 1780 of Boone's Painted Stone Station, was a great-great-grandfather of Harry Truman. Tyler's family ran off without fighting at the Long Run Massacre. He later founded his own station on Tick Creek.

In early 1786 Squire Boone sold his Painted Stone Station to Benjamin Roberts and purchased Samuel Wells' Station, where he moved his family. The Painted Stone Station eventually became known as Lynch's Station. Lynch moved the station to the south side of Clear Creek some fifteen feet above the creek and 100 yards from it on a beautiful bank.

In 1787 Joseph Casman, Vincent Robbins and Aaron Vancleve were hunting buffalo when they met a small Indian party which fired on them. One of Vancleve's fingers was shot off and part of the breech of his gun was shot away. He and Robbins however escaped. But Casman was taken prisoner.

A rescue party found Casman's body mutilated. A leg and an arm had been hacked off and hung up in saplings along with articles of his clothing. The remainder of the body lay in a pool of blood, the head much mangled.

Other settlers besides the Low Dutch had encounters with Indians during the mid and late 1780s. In 1787, Indians killed Maj. James Brenton and a neighbor named Coleman near Drennons Lick. In 1788, Indians killed five members of Bland Ballards' family at their cabin near Tyler's Station on Tick Creek. Such incidents continued into the 1790s, although less frequently. In 1790, Indians killed Betsy Vancleve when she and five men were returning from preaching at Painted Stone Station. The same year, 12-year-old Daniel Cozine was killed in a cornfield by Indians who also scalped—but did not kill—his sister, Sarah Cozine, who was nine years old.

The Treaty of Greenville in 1795 that followed Wayne's defeat of the Indians at Fallen Timbers ended the frontier era—and most Indian problems—in Kentucky. But the era and its Indian problems had started to decline even before then. Kentucky became a state in 1792 and Shelby County was formed from part of Jefferson County. Shelby County originally included all of present Shelby and Henry counties, as well as parts of Carroll, Franklin, Owen and Spencer Counties.

JEPTHA KNOB

By Calvin T. Schmidt

J eptha Knob, the highest point in Shelby County, is about six miles east of Shelbyville between U.S. 60 and Interstate 64. The Knob is horseshoe -shaped, with its western end open. Its top, which is mostly flat, rises to 1,188 feet. The elevation of the surrounding countryside is about 750 feet, while Shelbyville is close to 700 feet.

The formation has intrigued geologists, who have offered different theories about its origin without reaching a definite conclusion. The theories include volcanic action, movement of plates deep beneath the earth's surface and the impact of a meteorite, asteroid or comet. A third theory is the most likely, according to a report published in 1981 by the United States Geological Survey and the Kentucky Geological Survey. The report says: "In summary, the structure of Jeptha Knob is so similar in gross aspect and in many details to impact structures elsewhere that meteoroid impact seems the most likely origin. Nevertheless, enough unanswered questions remain so that Jeptha Knob cannot yet be classified with those cryptoexplosion structures whose origins by impact can be considered as demonstrated."

According to legend, Indians conducted games on Jeptha Knob that could have included archery and tomahawk throwing. Legend also says Indians built earthworks on the knob that could have been used for defense or as outlook posts.

Daniel Boone visited Jeptha Knob in 1775, according to a deposition he gave 20 years later. John James Audubon studied birds on the knob after moving to Louisville from Philadelphia in 1808, according to local historians.

Squire Boone, the youngest brother of Daniel Boone who lived for years in Shelby County, originated the name "Jeptha Knob," according to a deposition by another settler in 1809. Boone, a religious man, may have taken the name from the biblical story of Jephthah, an Old Testament warrior.

THE LOW DUTCH COMPANY

By Vince Akers

The Low Dutch first arrived in Kentucky in 1779, seeking a large tract of land where they could live as a community and preserve their language, customs and belief in the Dutch Reformed Church. Of Dutch and French Huguenot origin, the Low Dutch were clannish, educated and moral. The first Low Dutch in Kentucky lived at stations on Beargrass Creek in present day Jefferson County while they looked elsewhere for enough land to settle. In 1781 they established a settlement with a dozen cabins in Madison County but they never lived there due to the Indian menace.

Some Low Dutch moved later that year to a station they established in Mercer County; however they considered that station a temporary home while they looked for a large fertile tract. Other Low Dutch moved to Squire Boone's Painted Rock Station in Shelby County. Indian attacks and the Long Run Massacre shut down that station temporarily in 1781.

Five years later the Low Dutch seemed to find a home. Organized as the Low Dutch Company, they bought 8,610 acres from Boone for 935 pounds. About 3,500 acres were in Shelby County and about 5,100 were in Henry County. The tract was company property, with 200-acre lots parceled out to individual families.

Dutch families began moving almost immediately to the tract from Mercer County. They stayed only a few weeks because Indian depredations were severe. Nearly a decade passed before the tract could be safely settled. By then, many Dutch families had bought land in Mercer County, creating a split between themselves and the Dutch who settled on the tracts in Shelby and Henry Counties.

The split ended the Low Dutch dream of establishing a colony large enough to protect their ethnic identity from English-speaking people. Their adherence to the Dutch Reformed Church also faded as Low Dutch in both locations turned to the Presbyterian Church, which was similar in doctrine and governance to the Dutch Reformed. Slowly, but inevitably the Low Dutch intermarried with English speakers.

The Low Dutch venture in Kentucky ended with an exodus of Low Dutch to Indiana during the first decades of the 1800s. Cheap pre-surveyed government land attracted farmers who wanted to escape the legal questions that accompanied conflicting claims on tracts of land in Kentucky. The exodus necessitated that the Low Dutch Company begin deeding off farms to individual owners in 1831. The process took 10 years.

SQUIRE BOONE'S STATION (PAINTED STONE)

By R.R. Van Stockum Sr. and Ted L. Igleheart

I n 1775, while exploring the central regions of Kentucky, then a part of Fincastle County, Virginia, Squire Boone, younger brother of Daniel, came upon a beautiful spot on Clear Creek that he felt was a suitable location to settle down. It was located two and a half miles north of the present town of Shelbyville. Boone made the required improvements to claim the land including building a lean to habitation.

The following year he took a stone out of the creek, picked his name and the date 1776 into the stone, and rubbed red paint into the letters and numbers. Thus the site became known thereafter as the "Painted Stone Station," although it was not until November 12, 1779, that Boone obtained a certificate from Virginia in the name of his brother-in-law, Benjamin Van Cleve, for the 400 acre tract on which the station was built. Later, the patent was issued to Squire Boone.

The station was completed in the spring of 1780 and for some two years was the only place for refuge from Indians between the fort at Harrodsburg and the stations east of the Falls of the Ohio. This did not save it from attack, and in April 1781 Indians attacked the settlers at the fort, led by a white renegade named Simon Girty who bragged later that he "made Boone's shirt tail fly" as Boone rushed out of the fort to defend settlers caught outside. Squire was wounded by two bullets and many of the settlers were killed beside trees they were clearing. Boone never fully recovered from these wounds in his shoulder and right arm, which healed finally one and a half inches shorter than his left arm.

In September 1781 the settlers were warned by Bland Ballard that large bands of Indians were searching for forts and cabins to attack. All the settlers at Painted Stone except Squire and the Widow Hinton and her family loaded up and fled for Linn's Station twenty-one miles west near the present town of Eastwood. They were attacked as they crossed Long Run, described hereinafter as the Long Run Massacre.

Revisiting his station in the fall of 1783 with several families who hoped to resettle there, Squire Boone found the cabins and stockade burned to the ground. It was rebuilt the following year and a grist mill and saw mill were constructed. Benjamin Roberts purchased the property in 1786, then sold it to Nicholas Meriwether in 1787. Meriwether, an early entrepreneur in the area, operated the mills and built a residence he called "Castle Hill", presumably after the renowned residence of early Kentucky explorer Dr. Thomas Walker and his wife, Mildred Thornton Meriwether, in Albemarle County, Virginia.

Members of the local Historical Society, assisted by an archeologist from the University of Kentucky, believe they have found the original location of the station on the north side of Clear Creek overlooking a small tributary of the creek and just north of a concrete causeway across the creek. A rock fence on the north now identifies the site and west sides of a one-acre square overgrown with trees and weeds. The site is on the farm known as the Painted Stone Farm on the Eminence Pike and is marked by a D. A. R. monument beside the highway.

TYLER'S STATION

By Betty B. Matthews

Captain Robert Tyler, assisted by his kinsman Bland Ballard and Ballard's sons James and Bland Williams Ballard, built Tyler's Station around 1783. [It is thought the third wife of Bland Ballard was a sister of Robert Tyler]. This station was approximately five and a half miles east of Shelbyville on the south side of Tick Creek near a water supply now known as Cold Springs. Robert Tyler was a well-known participant in the settlement of pioneer Kentucky. He was in Captain William Harrod's company at the Falls of the Ohio in 1780 and later with Captain Squire Boone's company at Painted Stone Station on Clear Creek in Shelby County.

In December 1787 Bland Ballard with his family left Linn's Station to settle at Tyler's Station. Since the station was crowded, Ballard built a cabin across Tick Creek. Here he lived with his last wife, their infant daughter, Elizabeth, a four-year-old daughter, Thursia, and sons, John and Benjamin. Son James Ballard was away at school and son Bland Williams lived with his family in the station. Other families living there were the Robert Tylers, the John Klines, and the Baileys.

In the early morning of March 31, 1788, a party of 15 to 20 Delaware Indians approached the Ballard cabin. John Ballard, who had gone out for wood, was shot. The Indians then attacked the cabin, killing Bland Ballard and his son Benjamin. His wife and their infant daughter were tomahawked. Another daughter, Thursia, was scalped but survived. Bland Williams Ballard was with his family across the creek in the station on the bluff. Upon hearing the shots, he took up his gun and positioning himself behind a sycamore tree fired six shots killing six Indians. The Indians plundered the cabin and left.

Tyler's Station was an important link in the security chain of stations between the Bluegrass forts and those near the Beargrass Creek to the west. After the demise of the station, the logs were used to build a barn along Tick Creek on land known as the Van Young farm.

Robert Tyler died in 1815 at his farm west of the station. Station remains were still evident in the 1840s.

WHITAKER'S STATION

By Clarence Miller

Aquilla Whitaker, one of a handful of pioneers who settled in what is now Shelby County, helped to establish the town of Shelbyville and set the stage for one of the most romantic events in Kentucky history.

Aquilla, the son of John Whitaker, a Baptist minister, was born in Baltimore County, Maryland, in 1755. John Whitaker moved his family to Ft. Dunmore (now Pittsburgh) about 1767. John preached the gospel in that area and did farm work until about 1770, when he, with a large party, embarked on a flat boat down the Ohio River. Their destination was Sullivans Station at the Falls of the Ohio.

Following their arrival, John took his family, including his son Aquilla, to the Salt River region where they cut timber for firewood, which was used in large quantities to fire the kettles at the salt works. When the party exhausted the supply of firewood, they moved further up the stream and its tributaries. The party went up Brashear Creek to a smaller branch later called Clear Creek and established a station there about 1782 approximately three quarters of a mile southwest of what is now Shelbyville.

Whitaker Station was a well-built stockade with an excellent spring and was one of the more important places of refuge for the early settlers. Indians were quite active at the time, and many engagements were fought there. Aquilla's wife is reputed to have shot an Indian at the entrance to the fort. Aquilla bought 650 acres of land surrounding the station from Sam Shannon in 1795 for five shillings.

Whitaker soon became a central figure in the little community and was appointed in 1792, together with Bland Williams Ballard, Peter Bails, and others, to a committee to select a route (road) to the Beargrass settlements near present day Louisville. Later the committee selected a route to Leestown (Frankfort). These two routes are what was called Midland Trail (U.S. 60).

Aquilla was instrumental in establishing the first school in the region and in 1794 or 1795 sold four acres of his land to the Breshear Creek Baptist Church for four shillings. Later, to clear the title in 1810, they paid a Mr. Collier $10.00 for the tract. This tract is located near the sight of Muir's Bridge on the Old Taylorsville Road.

Aquilla, together with Shannon, Winlock, and others, laid out the town of Shelbyville, which was established in 1792. Aquilla, along with Bland W. Ballard, Joseph Winlock, Squire Boone, and others, all under the command of George Rogers Clark, made many forays into the Shawnee villages on the Little Miami River in what is now Ohio. Their purpose was to punish the Indians for their incessant attacks on the Kentucky frontier. Later Aquilla set out an apple orchard at Whitaker's Station. The orchard did so well that in the fall the ripening fruit cast a red glow to the landscape. In time Whitaker's Station became simply "Red Orchard." In fact the name became associated with the whole area of Muirs Bridge on the Zaring Mill site. And so it remains to this day.

Tragedy overtook the illustrious pioneer, for in 1807 he stabbed and killed Joseph Simpson in a barroom brawl. He was arrested and lodged in the log jail. Seven guards were appointed to watch over him, but he escaped that night with a trusty slave. They made their way down Clear Creek, Brashear Creek, Salt River, and the Ohio. He settled in Vincennes, Indiana, and later took on another wife. He later moved to West Florida (Louisiana) where he died in 1812.

Whitaker left a good legacy, for his son Wallace became county clerk in the new county of Shelby. His grandson Brigadier General Walter Childs Whitaker, of the Union army, was a commander at the Battle of Lookout Mountain.

LONG RUN MASSACRE
(BOONE'S DEFEAT) AND FLOYD'S DEFEAT

By Vincent J. Akers

The foundation for America's claim to the Northwest was laid by George Rogers Clark's conquest of the Illinois country in 1778-79. The prize so daringly won by Clark's small force was held throughout the Revolution and for years after in the face of a British policy designed to drive the American pioneer from the West.

From their post at Detroit the British directed the full brunt of Indian hostility against the Kentucky settlements. Raiding parties swept across the Ohio superbly equipped with British guns and staffed with British officers. The Long Run Massacre and Floyd's Defeat are typical of the resulting Indian incidents.

George Rogers Clark realized that Detroit held the solution to Kentucky's problem. Run the British out of Detroit and the Western Indians would make peace. He returned east to Virginia, and by late 1780 had sold the governor on his Detroit solution.

The events, which would culminate nine months later, in the Long Run Massacre and Floyd's Defeat were officially set in motion on Christmas Day 1780. On December 25, 1780, Governor Thomas Jefferson of Virginia penned a long letter of instructions to Clark authorizing a giant campaign to drive the British from Detroit the next year.

A force of 2,000 men was to rendezvous at the Falls of the Ohio under Clark's command. One thousand pounds of rifle powder and 1,500 pounds of lead were to be taken on 300 packhorses overland to the Falls. Men and horses along with four tons of cannon powder, camp kettles, rations, tents, medicine, and clothing together with cannon and artillery were to be floated down the Ohio from Fort Pitt on 100 barges.

Unfortunately the giant 1781 Detroit campaign was not to be. In the end, provisions, ammunition, artillery and boats for an army of 2,000 were collected and taken to Kentucky. But the men needed to fight the campaign could not be raised.

From Wheeling on the Ohio, August 4, 1781, Clark sent a letter of bitter frustration to Thomas Jefferson. Plans for Detroit were abandoned. He would float down the Ohio with the some 400 men. With additional forces from Kentucky, "something cleaver" might yet be done. Otherwise, he would "dispose of the publick stores to the greatest advantage and quit all farther thoughts of enterprise."

Clark waited several days near Wheeling for additional men being raised by Col. Archibald Lochry. Finally, assuming that Lochry's recruitment efforts had been unsuccessful and finding his own men deserting, Clark started down river. The timing was a fateful accident of history.

On August 8 1781, Archibald Lochry arrived at Wheeling with over eighty men. After an overland march of six days, they had missed Clark by only 12 hours! That narrow failure to make connection would prove fatal. Lochry reluctantly and fearfully followed down the Ohio behind Clark's army.

Meanwhile the British desperately tried to organize the equally reluctant Ohio Indians against Clark's army. From New York, the British Superintendent of Indian Affairs had sent his most trusted and successful Indian warrior into the Ohio Valley. This was none other than the celebrated Mohawk chief Thayendanegea, better known as "Captain" Joseph Brant.

In August 1781 Brant gathered a crew of about 100 Indians from several Western nations. Each tribe had its own chief while Joseph Brant was ostensibly commander-in-chief of all the Indians on the expedition. The nations all spoke a different language. This made communication difficult even with the use of interpreters.

Joseph Brant's Indians were far in advance of a much larger British and Indian force slowly being collected to meet Clark. Brant arrived on the Ohio ahead of Clark's passage and inspired his Indians with the notion of attacking and repelling the famed George Rogers Clark as his much larger force passed on its journey down river. The Indians seemed ready and willing for the action as they busied themselves making bark canoes and other preparations. The expectation of large reinforcements at any time no doubt contributed to the initial enthusiasm.

Brant's plans fell victim to Clark's mystique. The Indians held a special awe for the twenty-eight year old Clark and his military character. As preparations turned to waiting, this awe began to play on their imagination. Their runners continually brought notice of his approach. There was simply too much time to talk and consult about the attack. The closer Clark approached, the more discouraged the Indians became. As he moved down the river, Clark occasionally fired his artillery, the ominous noise echoing up and down the heavily wooded valley. The firing of his cannon and the beating of the drum and fife struck such a terror in the Indians that in the end they utterly refused to attack. They let Clark pass during the night of August 17 without firing a single shot. Brant was exasperated with the cowardice. He soon determined to push them against Lochry's smaller force trailing several days behind Clark's army.

On the morning of August 24, Lochry's group landed on the north shore of the Ohio to cook breakfast and feed their horses. They were at the mouth of a creek now called Loughery Creek, about eight miles below the mouth of the Miami River from which the present-day Indiana and Ohio state line runs north. Scouts immediately informed Brant who was just down river waiting. The Indians rushed forward and attacked from the advantage of the high wooded banks. Lochry's men made only a slight resistance before Lochry ordered surrender. It was a total defeat. Not a single man of Lochry's party escaped. Without a single loss on the Indian side, about thirty of Lochry's men had been killed and all the rest were taken prisoner. More were to die following the surrender. In all, 101 men were killed or captured with Lochry's Defeat--37 killed and 64 taken.

A few days later, Brant was joined by 100 white men—"Butler's Rangers"—commanded by Captain Andrew Thompson and 300 Indians under the direction of Captain Alexander McKee. On August 28, this loose force of nearly 500 Indians and British proceeded down the Ohio toward the Falls. It was now little more than two weeks before the Long Run Massacre.

Clark's arrival at the Falls in late August was a welcome relief to Kentucky. The militia's ammunition was entirely exhausted. Food and clothing were scarce and everywhere were signs of a coming Indian invasion.

To discover the willingness of the country to support an expedition, Clark summoned the militia officers of the three Kentucky counties to Louisville on September 6, 1781. Clark addressed the council as follows: "I wait as a Spectator to see what a Country is determined to do for itself when reduced to a

State of Desperation; I am ready to lead you on to any Action that has the most distant prospect of Advantage, however daring it may appear to be.".

However, the country was not determined to do very much for itself. After considerable disagreement, the council concluded the next day with only a recommendation to erect a strong fort at the mouth of the Kentucky River. That was an ironic conclusion, for as Clark's council met at the Falls the Indians and British waited, listened, and held their own council at the very spot the Kentuckians proposed to fortify. They had arrived at the mouth of the Kentucky River on September 5.

The Indians were hardly any more anxious for real action than the Kentuckians. They lost all enthusiasm after scouts returned with prisoners who informed them that no expedition was to be carried on that season against their villages. The already indifferent Indians quickly broke off into small parties; some going home others fanning out to attack isolated cabins and steal horses. The British Rangers also returned home. But somehow Brant and McKee were able to keep together an Indian force numbering 200, too small to attack Clark at the Falls, but entirely adequate as McKee observed "to cross the country and attack some of their small forts, or infest the Roads." Squire Boone's Station presented the closest and easiest target.

No station could be considered more exposed in 1781 than Painted Stone. It had been finished in the Spring of 1780 on the north side of Clear Creek, two and a half miles north of present-day Shelbyville. In 1781 the station occupied a central position in an otherwise unoccupied region. It was over twenty miles due east of the Beargrass stations, its closest neighbors, and about the same distance west of Leestown, a deserted landing on the Kentucky River near present-day Frankfort. The Kentucky and Ohio Rivers formed a vast triangle of uninhabited territory that stretched north of Painted Stone. Beyond the Ohio was enemy country. Rather than serving as a barrier from attack, the Ohio offered the Indians a convenient entry and escape route for their raids.

And raid they did! Painted Stone suffered continual harassment from small Indian raids throughout 1781. By late summer there was a marked increase in Indian sightings. With this obvious and growing concentration of Indians, the inhabitants ultimately decided to abandon the isolated station.

Squire Boone sent a request to the Beargrass stations for a militia guard to aid and escort the evacuation. General Clark ordered out twenty-four light horsemen under Lieutenant Thomas Ravenscraft. Colonel John Floyd ordered out the Jefferson County militia from the Low Dutch Station under Lieutenant James Welsh. Preserved among the Clark manuscripts are receipts signed by Lieutenants Welsh and Ravenscraft at "Boons Station" on September 13, 1781, for corn supplied by Marius Hansbury for their horses.

It became imperative to get the families evacuated before a general siege of the station developed. All were ready to leave except Squire Boone and the widow Hinton's family, who remained behind only because there were not enough packhorses to carry all their belongings. The militia agreed to return for them the next day. Squire Boone gave permission for his nine-year-old son Isaac to ride along with the fleeing families on one of the packhorses.

The evacuation caravan left Painted Stone early in the morning of September 13. The march would be agonizingly slow. The women and children rode packhorses, loaded down with household goods. The men led the horses and drove the cattle along the road. There were twenty-one miles to travel that day to reach Linn's Station, the eastern-most of the Beargrass stations. Boone's Wagon Road was the escape route. Only the year before had trees been cut and the trace widened enough to bring a small wagon into Painted Stone. Along this dark wooded trail the families fled. Unfortunately, they became scattered along the trail. The packhorses moved one behind the other along the narrow trail making a long string. It was impossible to concentrate the families or their protective escort at any one spot.

Their feeble force was further weakened by the loss of a large part of the militia escort after they had proceeded only nine miles. Here, at the ford of the first branch of Long Run, Lieutenant James Welsh became violently ill and had to turn off the trail until the sickness passed. Some ten to twenty of the militia guard remained behind with him. They would try to catch up as soon as Welsh was able to move.

The fleeing families and their remaining escort proceeded on a little more than three miles. It was now just after midday and the scattered group had completed more than half their trek. Those in front were approaching the main ford of Long Run approximately where present-day U.S. 60 now crosses the creek. Suddenly the Indian attack commenced.

Robert Tyler, great-great-grandfather of President Harry S. Truman, was in front with his family and a few other men with their cattle. At first fire Tyler at once dismounted, but several others in front ignored the agreement to shelter themselves behind trees and make a fight. They cut loose their pack loads and darted off without making a stand. The remaining men might have handled the Indians had this loss and the loss of their militia guard in the rear not weakened them.

The other women and children dismounted as ordered and took shelter. Most of the men acted bravely in their defense. But seeing that the horses were getting very alarmed and realizing that the Indians were too numerous, they concluded that they had better remount and make a run for Linn's Station some eight or nine miles west.

With the retreat, the massacre began. The men were able to keep the Indians somewhat in check just long enough to get the retreat moving. Packs were cut and families remounted as they moved along. But many of those killed were shot as the retreat commenced and they ran along exposed to the enemy fire. This soon turned the retreat into a hopeless rout. The large number of women and children made for a truly desperate situation. Confusion and panic reigned as people were shot down. The heaviest casualties fell upon the women and children. There was simply no way to adequately protect them under the circumstances. As Bland W. Ballard sadly summed it up years later, "Many widows and orphans were made" that day.

Most of the men put up a brave resistance. Some engaged in single-handed combat with Indians who had fired their guns and then rushed on the families with their tomahawks. Thomas McCarty fought bravely and was severely cut by three enemy shots. Two of his wounds were in the face, but he was able to make his escape.

Bland Ballard succeeded in getting outside the Indian lines where he used his rifle with some effect. He killed one Indian certainly and thought more as he was able to get off three good shots. Sergeant Muckano, one of the guards who stayed with the settlers, shot and broke an Indian's neck, but soon was killed himself.

The attack continued for a mile and the packs were scattered along the trail most of that distance up to the ford. To some extent this aided the families in making their escape since many of the Indians lingered behind cutting open packs to get at the plunder rather than pursuing their prey. A few were nevertheless persistent in their desire for scalps. The running families had to cross Long Run where the water was knee deep or more, swollen by recent rains. Young Letitia Van Meter was nearly drowned. Her mother heard her strangling and thought it was an Indian. She wheeled around just in time to see Letitia's head pop up out of the water. She reached in and caught the girl by the hair and drew her out. They made it safely to Linn's Station that evening.

Floyd's Fork also had to be crossed a little over two miles west of Long Run. It too was swollen from the recent rains and its waters were quite deep. Benjamin and Aaron Vancleave, ten and twelve year old brothers, had been running along on foot following the people on horses. When they reached Floyd's Fork, they each seized hold of a horse's tail and held on until safely across.

Bland Ballard hid in the bushes at the ford of Floyd's Fork until he saw an Indian on horseback ride into the creek pursuing the fugitives. As the Indian ascended the bank near where he hid, Ballard shot him and caught his horse with which he made his escape to Linn's.

The militia guard with Lieutenant Welsh were so far behind on the trail that they did not hear the firing of the guns and were unaware that the attack had taken place. They had just renewed their march when a horse was caught running back toward Boone's Station. Their worst fears were soon confirmed when cattle came running from the same direction. They turned off the trail a few hundred yards and cautiously continued on. Soon they stumbled upon two Indians holding eighteen year old Rachel Vancleve and her infant sister Sally prisoners. As the Indians dashed off without their captives, one aimed a blow at the young woman, but fortunately missed.

Rachel Vancleve was overjoyed at the fortunate rescue. Her sister had begun to cry and fret and the Indians were ready to kill the child when the guard rode up. The militia made a long circuit to avoid Boone's Wagon Road and the Indians. They got in safely to Linn's Station that night.

The ambush of the fleeing settlers was generally referred to as "Boone's Defeat." Although Squire Boone was not present, it was obviously a defeat for his station. The more descriptive "Long Run Massacre" seems to be a fairly modern title for the incident. The term "massacre" is fitting... for the word conjures up all the instant feelings of dreaded surprise, panic, hopelessness, and wanton slaughter which were part and parcel of the unfortunate affair. "Long Run Massacre" is particularly descriptive since the Long Run location was ever after closely connected with the massacre. One early deponent in an 1809 land suit summed it up, saying, "The crossing of long run was a place of Notoriety on account of the Women and Children being Killed Near the ford..."

The Long Run Massacre was one of the largest and certainly one of the bloodiest massacres in Kentucky history. A fairly complete list of the victims can be pieced together. There were no more than fifteen killed. Tragic as this was, most accounts grossly exaggerate the number of victims. For example, the Kentucky Highway Marker along U.S. 60 near Long Run records in bronze for the passing motorist that the Indians "killed over 60 pioneers."

The Indians responsible for the Massacre were a party of over fifty Miami who had separated from the larger group under Brant and McKee. The main body of Indians had started across country to strike at Squire Boone's Station. On their way they fell in again at Boone's Wagon Road with the jubilant Miamis only a few hours after the Massacre. The united Indian force now again numbered 200. Brant and McKee decided to delay the intended attack on Painted Stone and, in the words of McKee "take possession of the Ground they had drove the enemy from and wait their coming to bury their dead." They did not have long to wait. As soon as the first survivors of Long Run straggled into Linn's Station, runners were sent out to spread the shocking news to the other Beargrass stations. Colonel John Floyd was particularly distressed by the report.

Floyd had been commissioned as Jefferson County Lieutenant early in 1781 after George Rogers Clark recommended him to Governor Thomas Jefferson as "the most capable in the County. A Soldier, Gentleman, and a Scholar whom the Inhabitants, from his actions have the greatest confidence in."

No doubt Floyd was chagrined upon hearing of the ineffective part played by the militia guard which had been sent to Painted Stone specifically to escort its inhabitants to safety. As county lieutenant, Floyd was charged with the defense of Jefferson County and the overall command of its militia. Floyd hurriedly collected what men he could muster at his station and the nearby Low Dutch and Hogland's Stations. A shortage of horses was a problem. Earlier that same day, twenty-five horses had been stolen from the Dutch Station by Indian raiders.

Somehow Floyd managed to quickly mount a small force which he rushed to Linn's Station, fearful that it might be under attack. Linn's was in a dangerous position, being relatively isolated about three miles east of the other Beargrass Stations. His small party arrived at Linn's after sundown and found it free from attack but in an extreme state of alarm. The full particulars of that afternoon's carnage at Long Run were now absorbed first hand from its terrified survivors. Floyd was determined to take the offensive. The remainder of the evening was hurriedly spent preparing for an early march the next day.

It was a small party, which rode out of Linn's Station under Colonel John Floyd early Friday morning September 14, 1781. The party numbered only twenty-seven men, all mounted. Many of the militia who had been at Long Run the afternoon before were unable or unwilling to venture out again. East of Linn's Station the men were divided into three columns. Colonel Floyd commanded the center column, which marched in the road. Captain Peter A'Sturgis commanded the right, and Lieutenant Thomas Ravenscraft commanded the left column. In this position they quickly marched east along the wagon road. They were headed for Painted Stone with all possible speed fully expecting to find it under siege. Unfortunately scouts were not sent ahead.

The British and the Indians fully intended to set up an ambush, correctly guessing that the Kentuckians would organize a burial and relief party. They miscalculated, however, the speed with which Floyd would organize and advance. Accordingly, Floyd came riding through before the Indians were posted to receive him. The Indians were busy that morning collecting and sifting through the plunder of the prior day's massacre instead of setting their ambush. This alone saved Floyd from the total defeat which almost certainly would have befallen his small party had 200 Indians been lying ready in wait. Even so, the whites were unanimous in the conviction that they had fallen into ambush. Certainly it must have seemed so for the terrain and numbers were grossly in the Indians' favor. Floyd's men were riding fast along a stretch of Boone's Wagon Road between Floyds Fork and Long Run. The road here lay along a dividing ridge. They did not discover the Indians until they received their fire. Floyd's men forever after assumed the Indians had been lying in wait, had let them ride through, then closed in behind and had them surrounded. Although not so well planned, the effect was similar. The Indians had simply to pull back from the road and the ridge and shoot down as many of the whites as possible. The nearly one mile stretch of old U.S. 60 follows the ridge and nearly the identical route of Boone's old wagon road. It was along this stretch at the site of the present-day Eastwood Cemetery that the defeat occurred.

Out of the twenty-seven men who rode out from Linn's Station that morning, only ten escaped from the defeat. Seventeen were either killed or captured on the spot. Captain A'Sturgis died somewhere between Floyd's Fork and Linn's as they retreated. Again the Beargrass stations were shocked by the new horror story told by the survivors of Floyd's Defeat as they came in that morning. One woman later recalled Floyd's own words of frustration to her father, "'Worse and worse,' said he to my father. 'Worse and worse, Mr. Campbell." Colonel Floyd immediately sat down and dashed off the following dispatch to George Rogers Clark at the Falls:

Friday 14th 1/2 past 10 0 Clock

Dear General

I have this minute returned from a little Excurtion against the Enemy & my party 27 in number are all dispersed & cut to pieces except 9 who came off the field with Cap t Asturgus mortally Wounded and one other slightly wounded. I dont yet know who are killed. Mr Ravenscraft was taken prisoner. A party was defeated yesterday near the same place & many Women and Children Wounded. I want Satisfaction.. do send me 100 men which number with what I can raise will do. The Militia have no goodpowder do send some. Iam

Jn Floyd I cant write guess at the rest.

The day after Floyd's Defeat, a force of 300 men from the Falls and Beargrass made a long rapid march in the hot weather to rescue the families of Squire Boone and the widow Hinton at Painted Stone. At the sites of the two defeats, the Falls troops performed the gruesome task of collecting and burying bodies now bloating in the September sun. At Floyd's battle ground, bodies were buried in a sinkhole with stones and tree limbs placed on top. Names of the dead were carved on a nearby beech tree.

It was a humiliating defeat for Colonel John Floyd, but not totally without some benefit. Despite their surprise, Floyd's men had succeeded in inflicting several casualties on their Indian attackers. Among those killed was the chief of the Hurons, their principal warrior. He had been a great supporter of the British efforts to keep the Indians organized.

After Floyd had been driven off, Joseph Brant and Alexander McKee vigorously proposed that the Indians follow up their success by taking Squire Boone's Station on their way back or at least, as McKee said, "endeavor to draw them out, destroy their cattle and other ways distress them." But the Hurons were so discouraged by the loss of their chief that they wanted only to return north of the Ohio as soon as possible. With the Hurons, all of the Indians turned homeward.

THE DEATH OF MERIWETHER LEWIS

By Ted L. Igleheart

In the year 2003 we celebrate the bicentennial of the famous expedition ordered by President Thomas Jefferson to discover and explore a route to the Pacific through the Louisiana Territory. Jefferson's secretary, Meriwether Lewis, invited William Clark, at Louisville to hire a crew and so, in October of 1803, the intrepid explorers, Lewis and Clark, launched their keelboat from the Falls of the Ohio on their historic westward journey.

Upon their return in November of 1806, historians hailed their successful trip amid hostile Indians and daunting hardships as the most famous exploring venture in the history of America. However, tragedy was to follow.

Jack Brammer wrote in the *Lexington Herald-Leader* in a 1998 story:

"In late October 1809, Clark, his wife, Julia, and their infant son, Meriweather Lewis Clark, visited relatives in Louisville and were heading home to Virginia. While in Shelbyville, eating lunch, Clark read in a Frankfort newspaper,

The Argus of Western America, that said Lewis had killed himself by cutting his throat 17 days ago" apparently in Nashville, Tennessee. Clark wrote a heartfelt letter that night to his brother, Jonathan Clark in Louisville, about the newspaper article.

The distraught Clark wrote: 'I fear O! I fear the weight of his mind has overcome him, what will be the Consequence?' The two and a half page letter was found in 1998 in a cache of personal letters in a Louisville attic.. James Holmberg, Curator at the Filson Historical Society, which is owner of the letter, deemed it a historical treasure. It went on to say: 'I fear this report has too much truth, tho' it may have no foundation—my reason for thinking it possible is founded on the letter I received from him at your house.' The two explorers had last seen each other only a few weeks earlier.

Clark penned the letter to his brother at Shannon's Tavern in the tiny community of Graefenburg in eastern Shelby County.

Letter from William Clark to his brother, Jonathan Clark, 28 October 1809.

Courtesy of The Filson Historical Society.

Main Street, looking west from Fifth, Shelbyville, KY

CHAPTER TWO

COMMUNITIES

View looking east on Main Street from near Tenth Street. Note the arc lamp streetlight.

COMMUNITIES: AN OVERVIEW

By Sally B. Roach Nicol

The first small stations in Shelby County didn't have time for the niceties of life, for their concerns were survival and safety. This was the focus for many years, but Indian attacks had mostly ceased throughout the state by the time Shelbyville was founded in 1792.

None of the early stations grew into a permanent community, but they formed a near circle around what was to become the town of Shelbyville. The town began to grow quickly after the first county court session in Brackett Owen's house. By 1814, a mere 22 years, four public wells had been dug, both eastern and western additions to the town had been laid out, and the first newspaper was reporting the arguments pro and con for paving the main street. The pros won, and those who were not in agreement could have their property confiscated and sold to pay for their part if they did not go along with the plan.

Churches got off to an early start too with the First Baptist Church meeting at Owen's house in 1785. Eight members were recorded, though the meeting was not repeated for two more years due to troubles with the Indians. Schools were in session almost immediately as well, and by 1825 Mrs. Julia Ann Tevis and her husband opened Science Hill School, a decision they made before traveling from Virginia to Shelbyville.

Mrs. Tevis's words are worth repeating for they express the spirit that built Shelby County: "Our extended view rested upon cultivated farms and intervening woodlands. South of us was the dear, quiet little town. Cheerfulness is perhaps the word that best describes the appearance of the sunny little village, …clean, airy, orderly and comfortable. Shut out from the busy mart of men, no malarious surroundings to engender disease or foster epidemics, it is decidedly a healthy place. This, combined with its rural beauties, renders it a desirable location for a school. Monday, March 25, 1825, our school opened with eighteen or twenty pupils."

Widespread settlement followed the formation of Shelby County. The Low Dutch settlements included the present-day towns of Cropper, Pleasureville, Elmburg, and Defoe.

Finchville grew around the Baptist church and school began there in 1799, its solid gentry settling into excellent farms that would be handed down from one generation to the next. Its proper name came from Ludwell R. Finch's blacksmith shop and store in 1876. Simpsonville, named in 1816 for Capt. John Simpson, evolved as the biggest stagecoach town on the Midland Trail (U.S. 60), named in 1816 for Captain John Simpson. Bagdad was established in 1845 on a high point between Lexington and Louisville. Mount Eden was established in 1846 and Graefenburg in 1850. Waddy grew quickly around its railroad station after it was built in 1886.

True to the early Shelby County pattern, each of these communities held fast from the very beginning to the formula of home, church, and school. Agriculture was at the heart of the economy and the people were independent and largely conservative in their views.

BAGDAD

By Julian Wood

W hen the first white settlers came to northeast Shelby County herds of buffalo roamed the woods. Buffalo smoothed down a large area of several acres by licking the salt and minerals in the soil. On that site today stands Buffalo Lick Baptist Church, just a few miles from the community of Bagdad.

With the arrival of the settlers, huge oak, ash, beech, cherry, and other trees were cut down to make room for cabins and crops. Walnut trees reportedly were four feet in diameter and 40 feet to the first limb.

Shortly after the Revolutionary War the small village of Consolation sprang up in northeastern Shelby County. Many of its early settlers were Revolutionary War veterans who had received land grants for their military services. The land grants were allotted according to a person's rank and length of war service. Most of these early settlers were of Anglo-Saxon origin and 90 percent were from Virginia.

These early settlers in Consolation were used to hardships. They had lived in the backwoods of the eastern states, had fought Indians, and were mostly self-sufficient. The community grew to be a fair-sized village. There were general stores, a wagon maker, a harness and saddle maker, a hat maker, a blacksmith shop, a distillery, a drug store, and all the necessary businesses to support a small town. A post office was established on September 27, 1849.

A railroad was built near the community in 1850. In order to receive train service, the residents of the village had to travel west about a mile to a tiny settlement. Gradually, the businesses and people moved to where they could receive service. Eventually, Consolation was abandoned.

Residents at the new village, that actually was founded during the second quarter of the nineteenth century, soon needed a post office. When the postal service required a name for the community, Bagdad was chosen. Richard Radford was the first postmaster. As the town grew, other nearby post offices consolidated with Bagdad.

The origin of the name is unclear but theories abound. One says a railroad man was called "Daddy Bags." Another says the son of a local miller with a speech impediment said "Bag dad" when a customer entered the store.

The railroad brought many changes and benefits to the community. Before the railroad, a trip to Shelbyville or Frankfort took all day on horseback. Journeys farther away were seldom made. All roads were poor and almost impossible to travel except in summer. With the railroad, supplies and provisions could be brought in from far away places. Pens were constructed in Bagdad so farmers could send their livestock to market. Milk and cream were sent to markets in Shelbyville or Louisville. Salesmen, called drummers, would ride the train to Bagdad. There they rented a room, a horse, and buggy and called on merchants in other communities.

Like settlers throughout the country, the early citizens of Bagdad were interested in an education for their children. The first public schools had only one room and one teacher. These schools were usually poorly equipped with homemade furnishings and generally overcrowded. In 1870 George Thomas

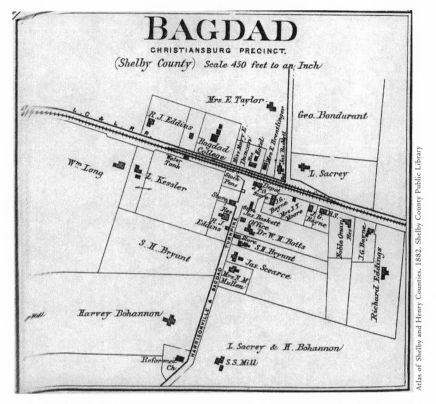

Map of Bagdad in 1882. The Louisville, Cincinnati & Lexington Railroad ran through the town and the map shows houses, several stores, a doctor's office, depot and post office, a hotel, and the Bagdad College.

established a private academy in the community. It flourished for about two generations and offered courses comparable to those in the high schools of the day.

As the need for a high school became greater and as more emphasis was placed on education, Bagdad, in keeping with the trend of the times, built its first high school in 1912 on land donated by George Sacra. Later, R. L. Harrison donated more land. The first building had only four rooms. Here, for six years, an elementary and a two-year high school were conducted, first under the leadership of a Mr. McGowan. In 1918 the third year of high school was added.

In 1920, while Charles I. Henry was principal, construction was started on an addition to the school building. It continued as a four-year high school until 1960 when a consolidated high school was built for the county. During World War II, a very successful cannery was constructed on the school grounds where farmers and housewives could can the fruits and vegetables they raised. Bagdad High School graduated 631 students during its forty years of existence.

On November 12, 1945, under the direction of the Veterans' Administration, Fred Trammell began a class on farming for returning servicemen. This was the first in the United States of several thousand such classes. Here numerous veterans received valuable instruction in all phases of agriculture.

Living conditions in Bagdad and nearby communities were much different in the early days. Wagons and buggies could be driven over the roads only in dry conditions. Peddlers, carrying large packs on their backs, walked through the country, selling cheap clothing, tin items, and trinkets. Hucksters traveled through the country trading produce such as coffee and sugar for eggs, hides, chickens, or butter.

The farms supplied nearly all the simple needs of the people. They made most of their clothing and raised or hunted almost everything they ate. There was very little money, and the first bank in Bagdad was not established until 1888. Many families had a small distillery, which was legal in the early years.

There were few doctors in the area and they had little medical education. People relied on home remedies and herbs. Some of the remedies were worse than the ailment. For example, a common treatment for an abscessed tooth was to hold a red-hot nail or wire to it for a few seconds. An examination of early records shows consumption, fever, flux, abscesses, and pneumonia were common causes of death. Many children died of diphtheria or whooping cough. Childbirth was very dangerous. Records show that one out of four pregnancies resulted in death of the mother. Many diseases were due to unsanitary conditions. The cabins had no screens and were infested with flies, roaches, and other insects. Most of the wells and cisterns were contaminated, and typhoid fever was common. The entire state of Kentucky had a severe epidemic of cholera in 1830. It is said that one quarter of the citizens of Kentucky died, and entire families were wiped out. Bagdad was no exception and lost many lives during this period. A serious outbreak of typhoid occurred in 1915. The Spanish flu hit the town in 1917.

When a person died, the neighbors and family members prepared or laid out the corpse. Burial was in a wooden box usually made by neighbors with internment in a family or church graveyard. Often the body was buried first and at the next visit of the circuit-riding minister the funeral was preached. The Bagdad cemetery was started in 1872.

Freed slaves suffered at the hands of whites following the Civil War. Violence was endemic in the county due to the activities of the Ku Klux Klan, and many African Americans moved away. A community of ex-slaves settled between Bagdad and Hatton. This little community, composed of a church and several cabins and houses, was called Stringtown. The area around Stringtown became known for its lawless and brazen acts against blacks. There, occurred the noted murder case involving Hiram Bohannon and Addison Cook, both alleged KKK leaders. Bohannon was charged with killing Cook after disputes over some Klan activities. This crime aroused such feelings among the population that it threatened the peace and harmony of the community.

Early in 1871, due to the daily Klan threats, the U.S. Army's 7th Cavalry commanded by the well-known General George Armstrong Custer was sent into Kentucky and headquartered at Elizabethtown. He was to maintain law and order throughout the state.

Troop I of the 7th Cavalry was sent to Bagdad and stationed in the Bagdad Christian Church. On the night of October 16, 1872, a group of the Klansmen attacked Stringtown. They killed James Magruder and permanently crippled Lawson Johnson and beat and abused many of the inhabitants. Several buildings were burned and much property was destroyed. This incident was known as the "Stringtown Massacre." The Klansmen responsible for the attack included men from the area's prominent families.

Some of Custer's soldiers and others, who enlisted with him in Shelbyville, were still in the troop when he led his men to disaster at the Little Big Horn River in Montana on June 25, 1876.

Military tradition is strong in Bagdad. During every United States war, Bagdad has had soldiers in all branches of service. At the time of the Civil War, both the Union and Confederacy had soldiers from

Bagdad. The community was proud of all of them, but was a little more proud of the Confederate soldiers. During World War II an amusing story was told of a local soldier stationed in the Holy Land. He wrote home, "Here I am in Bethlehem where Christ was born. I wish to Christ, I was in Bagdad where I was born."

One of Bagdad's proudest distinctions is being the birthplace of Martha Layne Hall Collins, Kentucky's first woman governor (1983-87). Other notables from Bagdad have included L.W. Botts, who was president of the Columbia Trust Co. in Louisville and a vice president of the Louisville & Nashville Railroad; William T. Baskett, former city attorney of Louisville; and Col. Lawrence Long of the U.S. Army.

Businesses in Bagdad prospered when the trains stopped there. Located in a good agricultural region, much business was done by railroad in carrying grain, tobacco, and livestock. But the town depot burned in 1936, and a new one was never built.

Businesses in the town have included a flour and feed mill built by James Bayne and his three sons—James, Samuel, and Robert. Bagdad Roller Mills is still in operation. A corn-planter factory, operated by J.M. Denton, thrived for a time. Among the long-established businesses was the undertaking establishment of G.W. Sacrey and Son.

General stores have supplied the needs of the citizens through the years. Their operators have included James Baskett, J.M. Denton, A.A. Bailey, Victor Bohannon, S.H. Bryant, B.D. Estes, Lee Long, J.W. Hieatt, Garnett Newton, and Lewis Young.

The community still has a post office and a bank. The largest church in town is Bagdad Baptist, founded in 1889.

Courtesy of Alice Barnett

1899 Bagdad Roller Mills

CHRISTIANSBURG

By Jeanette Thurman

Settlers from Pennsylvania known as the Low Dutch searching for rich farm land settled in Christiansburg before 1792, the year in which Kentucky was admitted to the Union as the fifteenth state. A few log homes were built. The area quickly became populated as an agricultural center. Some of the earliest settlers included William Jones, Henry Roberts, William Metcalf, William Tool, Joseph Lewis, Abraham Cook, John Miles, John Clark, Sarah Lewis, Obedience Clark, James Mullican, and Leonard Mullican. Settlers by the names of Robert Miller, David Thompson, Seth Cook, William Cook, Margaret Hacket, John Metcalf, Isaac Metcalf, William Teague, Mary Teague, Elizabeth Jones, Fanny Metcalf, Prudence Metcalf, Moses Loughland and families such as Ashby, Shidmore, Maddox, Skelton, Davis, and McCoy migrated to Christiansburg.

History has not recorded exactly how Christiansburg got its name. One story has it that a train conductor shouted every morning as the train stopped at the town "All out for Christiansburg, where all the good people live."

Map of Christiansburg in 1882.

In 1799, a church known as Six Mile Baptist Church was established in a small log building owned by William Tool. It was contiguous to the community cemetery. The community northeast of Bagdad grew up around the Baptist church. It vies with Finchville Baptist for the honor of being the oldest church in the county. The late historian Rufus Harrod said there was an Old Christiansburg and a New Christiansburg. The Old Christiansburg was located on the Frys-Oldburg Road and New Christiansburg about a mile to the west of the original settlement along Ford-Davis Road. New Christiansburg was originally known as Hinesville.

The church house was also a community center. A school was soon built nearby. A debating society was formed in Christiansburg in 1827 and used the church as its meeting place. The Temperance Society also used the facilities. There were times, however, when the community's use of the church building caused some difficulty. It became necessary, for instance, for the church to instruct its trustees in 1829 "to prohibit the selling of spirituous liquors as far as possible on the Meeting House lot!"

Roads were built such as Christiansburg Turnpike, Bagdad Road, Christiansburg Depot Turnpike and Christiansburg-Demaree Turnpike.

The location of the Louisville, Cincinnati & Lexington Railroad, later the Louisville & Nashville Railroad, in Christiansburg brought businesses by the middle of the 19th century. At one time, Christiansburg boasted of a depot, a hotel, seven stores, two saloons, a harness shop, wool carding shop, two physicians and surgeons, four churches, and a distillery. However, with better roads and transportation, the small local businesses became obsolete and one by one were closed. A community grocery existed until the last decade in the 20th century.

Christiansburg had divided loyalties during the Civil War. Prior to the war, a new brick Baptist church was constructed in 1856 across the road from the first meetinghouse. Following the Civil War the African American members left to start their own church, the Centennial Baptist Church, which continues to flourish.

By the middle of the 20th century changes were occurring rapidly in Christiansburg. Due to the availability of water lines and industrial growth in the county, family farms were subdivided and new homes were built along almost every county road. The number of farmers decreased and men and women commuted to work in Shelbyville, Frankfort, Lexington, Louisville, and Georgetown.

As the 21st century begins, Christiansburg, which started as an agricultural center for settlers, has become a diverse community of a few large farms, several small farms, factory workers, retired people, professional people, modern homes, older stately homes and two churches still at its center.

MEMORIES OF CHESTNUT GROVE

By Bobby Shannon Phillips

S On Dec. 7, 1941, the Japanese bombed Pearl Harbor. Four months and 17 days later I was born on a farm in the Chestnut Grove neighborhood owned by Mr. Jim Ray. Dr. Willis McKee came to our house and delivered me, which is something that would not happen today.

Later, Dr. McKee was drafted into the service and was captured by the Germans. At the end of the war, he returned to Shelbyville and became a very successful surgeon.

My very first memories in life are of Chestnut Grove and the people who lived and worked there during World War II, and the years after the war. We moved away from the neighborhood when I was in the first grade at Gleneyrie School in 1948. Naturally, I don't remember the war, but I think the older people talking about it subconsciously influenced me. I remember seeing some ration stamps that my mom had left over from the war years.

I was only three years old when the war ended. I do remember my dad's brother, Edwin Scott Phillips, coming home. He had been wounded twice during the war, first during the invasion of Normandy, and later in France. He was a sergeant in a tank crew which ran over a German mine. He was the only survivor.

No one, including my sister, Shelby County Clerk Sue Carole Perry, knows how Chestnut Grove or how the Marshall Doaks voting precinct got their names. My theory about the first name: there were a lot of American chestnut trees there when the community was first being developed.

When we lived at Chestnut Grove during the 1940s there were two grocery stores and seven or eight farmhouses. Wilbur Lutz owned the "big" store on the south end of town on Highway 53. Mr. Lutz and his wife Estelle had a slot machine which my dad warned me about. But, most importantly, he had the first television set in Chestnut Grove. In those days TV was in its infancy, and they were far too expensive for hardly anyone to own one. There was only one TV station within our viewing area, WAVE, and the programs each night lasted four hours. Mr. Lutz easily paid for that set by selling Cokes and snacks to all the folks who came to the store to watch.

Families or names which I recall from that era include Phil Raymond, Ida Mae and John Cummins, Ollie Garfield Nation, Irvin and Lilly Mae Moore, Woodrow Mitchell, Mr. and Mrs. Luther Parker, Sam Rutledge, and Lee Schooler.

Another interesting person associated with Chestnut Grove was Harry Lancaster, who coached basketball at Gleneyrie High School during the 1940s. Later, he became a legend as Adolph Rupp's assistant at the University of Kentucky.

Occasionally, I recall those happy days at Chestnut Grove. But those nostalgic times are gone forever. Like the rest of Shelby County, Chestnut Grove has changed dramatically. All those caring people and the lifestyle of the 40s have been replaced by a new generation that lives a much faster pace. Some of us hardly know the people two doors down. Is all this change progress?

CLAY VILLAGE

By Duanne Puckett

Clay Village, a community east of Shelbyville, perhaps got its name after statesman Henry Clay paid a visit there around 1839. It consists of a cluster of homes and farms along U.S. 60 near Jeptha Knob..

The town was laid out in 1830 and incorporated on February 18, 1839. Legend has it that Henry Clay, who spent the night in the then-unnamed community, named the town. The next day he suggested to the local farrier that it be named after him. By 1842, there were fifty-six inhabitants with ten dwellings, five shops, two dry-goods stores, a factory and a public house. In 1847, the population increased to 184, with three dry-goods stores, sixteen shops three groceries, two factories, a seminary, two doctors, and one law office.

The population was 117 in 1860 but fell to 88 in 1870. The population continued to decrease which brought changes. The Henry Clay School, which first housed a high school and later elementary grades,

Shelby County Public Library, from Mrs. Roy Collings, Jr.

Students at Clay Village Academy about 1899. Front row, left to right, Laura "Lollie" Vannatta,
Beulah Newton, ?, Stella Brooks, Grace Clark, ?, Susie Serber, Charley Grant Jones, Owen Sleadd, Ollie Clark, ?.
Middle row, l. to r., George Kent, ____Serber, Mattie Lee Vannatta, Earl Clark, Elmer Serber, Lynn Serber.
Back row, l. to r., Will Davis, Harry Serber, ?, Grovene Snook, Teacher ?, Ben Davis, Marshall "Toad" Clark.

closed in 1989. H.V. Tempel served as principal for many years. The school became a junk-car lot. The Greyhound bus station, a white structure with an arched overhang, is now a home. A cherry furniture shop, once nestled alongside the hillside in the town,
has been demolished.

Activity in the town can be found primarily at the churches, a Christian school, an auto mechanic's shop, a service station, and a quick-stop food market. The other commercial site sells concrete ornaments.

The Baptist Church at Clay Village was originally called the Bethel Missionary Church in 1845 when Josiah Leak was pastor. It was a spin-off of the Bethel Church, a short distance from the community at Cross Keys, where a large inn once stood and where the brick church is now a home. The missionary church bought a lot in Clay Village in 1848 and changed the name officially to Clayvillage Baptist Church in 1850. The first pastor was Smith Thomas. A second building was dedicated in 1887 with B.F. Hungerford as pastor. A third building fund was started in 1942 with the present structure dedicated 10 years later. An educational building with fellowship hall was dedicated in 1972.

Living Waters Christian Church moved to the Clay Village community in 1982 with Joel League as its founding pastor. In 1984, a Christian school opened in the facility. There are about 200 students in kindergarten through twelfth grade from Shelby and surrounding counties.

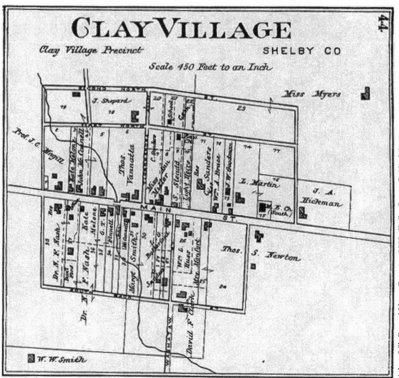

Clay Village in 1882

CONNOR STATION

By Betty B. Matthews

The name of Connor Station is associated with a road that runs south from old U.S. 60 one mile west of Simpsonville over the railroad tracks and ends at KY 148. The origin of the name goes back to 1871. Lemuel Conner (sometimes spelled Connor), who owned over 1,000 acres of land on South Long Run and Bullskin and Little Bullskin creeks, conveyed a half-acre of land to the Shelby Railroad Co. for a station. In return the company agreed "to stop at least one Train each way per day when flagged at Conner Station. If the Company reconveys the half acre they are to pay Lemuel Conner or his heirs the cost of the Station House not exceeding $80 and they will be released of all obligations to stop Trains at said Station."

Lemuel Conner died in 1892 and is buried with members of his family in the Conner cemetery near the railroad tracks and east of the road named for his railroad station.

The station probably ceased to function because automobiles made it easier to get produce and people to their destination. Today there is no sign of a station along the railroad in either direction where the Connor Station road crosses the tracks.

CROPPER

By Duanne Puckett

The town of Cropper is located in north central Shelby County. The first man known to have settled in the area was John H. Nevel. He was a direct descendant of the first Dutch who came to North America. He obtained a grant from Patrick Henry and settled between what became known as Cropper and Elmburg. In 1776, another Dutchman, Joseph Spriggs, was granted a tract of land and settled near Nevel. Other Dutch followed him. Abraham Banta purchased land from Squire Boone for the Low Dutch Company. One of the tracts became Cropper. The name originated from one of those settlers, James Cropper. He was the first person to build a house there and became the first postmaster. He also built and operated the first store.

In 1807, a new group of settlers came from Virginia. Things remained quiet until 1855 when the settlement was thrilled to see the railroad. On August 10, the first train came huffing and steaming through town while a large crowd gathered to witness the event. As the community grew, the Winestock family built a store and dwelling house that later became a hotel.

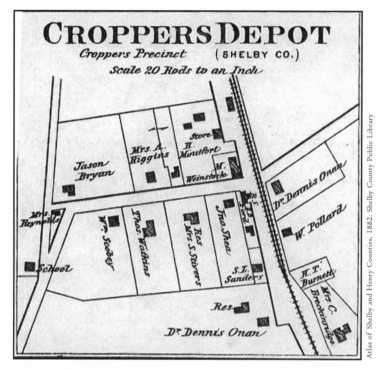

In 1882 Cropper was known as "Croppers Depot," according to this map.

The town grew and was incorporated on April 7, 1890. Herbert Perry was the first and only police judge. There was even a town marshal and a jail.

A lodge meeting took place February 15, 1898, on the night the battleship *Maine* was sunk in Havana harbor, precipitating the Spanish-American War. The first church was known as Union Grove since it was a union of all denominations in the community. In 1855, a new church was built for the Christian and Methodist congregations. The Baptists were in such great number that they built their own structure in 1902. A number of Presbyterians organized and built a church at Mulberry. When that closed, they joined with Shelbyville First Presbyterian.

Ben Allen Thomas Sr., a prominent dairy and tobacco farmer in the area, was the president of the only bank, which opened in 1905 and closed in 1921. Other buildings were a store built in 1917 and, indicative of the coming automobile, a garage in 1920. By 1932, a gravel road was replaced with KY 43 from Shelbyville to Frankfort, followed six years later by a road from Cropper to Pleasureville. The once tree-lined roads, sprinkled with fields of daffodils, have changed with continued development. The former dairy known as Birdland Farm has been transformed into Bluegrass Bison, which has altered the terrain and surrounding acreage.

Activity in the heart of the town surrounds the Christian and Baptist churches, the Ruritan Club's monthly meetings, the Bagdad Volunteer Fire Department sub-station, and programs at the former school, known now as the Shelby County Education Center.

DREWSVILLE

By Maureen Ashby

The events that led to the formation of the African American community of Drewsville began on Christmas 1866, when George Drew, a black man, bought 27 acres of land from Euclid and Harriet Hickman. The tract, along Dry Run, was on the north side of the Louisville-Shelbyville Turnpike two miles west of Shelbyville.

Drew paid $1,000 down, with another $1,000 due by December 1871. In October 1867, Drew began selling lots of one to three acres. Among the buyers were Hiram Chin, William M. Blackwell, and Peter Smith.

In 1869, Chin sold his two acres, which had cost $160, to David Dale for $550. The price increase indicated a house had been built on the property. In 1907, James and Harriet Dale and other heirs of David Dale sold a strip of their land to the Louisville and Eastern Railroad for the interurban line between Louisville and Shelbyville. The strip was 212 feet long and 50 feet wide. It fronted the turnpike.

In 1887, Blackwell granted part of his lot to the trustees of Colored Common School No. 14 for construction of a school for African American youngsters.

Peter Smith sold an acre of his land for $37.50 to the trustees of Drewsville Baptist Church.

In 1917, Patsy Middleton bought the Dale property and in 1920 she acquired more land from Harrison Roman. A restaurant called Maple Moo was built, along with Middleton Heights subdivision. Many African American residents moved to Martinsville in northwest Shelbyville. The move allowed former residents of Drewsville to be nearer their jobs in the Middleton family's general merchandise store on Main Street.

FINCHVILLE

By Charles T. Long

The Finchville community is located about five miles southwest of Shelbyville on a broad gently sloping ridge that is drained by Bullskin and Brashears Creeks on the north and east and by Buck Creek on the south and west. The town is laid out along KY 55 which is the original road that led south from Shelbyville to Taylorsville in Spencer County and from there to Bardstown in Nelson County. The land in the area is characterized by gentle to moderately steep slopes with narrow to fairly broad ridge tops. The soil is mostly of the Lowell type with six to eight inches of brown silt loam topsoil over a thick layer of silty clay, which in turn rests on hard limestone. Crops are cultivated mainly on the upland ridges and gentle slopes although some bottomland is also used. The steeper slopes are best suited for hay and pasture. In general, well-managed farms in this part of the county are highly productive.

It was the land, well watered and heavily wooded with red oak, black walnut, beech, hickory, yellow poplar, ash and sugar maple trees, that attracted settlers. As early as 1774 survey parties entered Shelby County making improvements that would later give them or their sponsors a legal settlement claim. It would, however, require two things before people began to permanently settle on the land—a clear procedure for granting land titles and an end to Indian raids. In 1779, the Virginia legislature improved the title or patent process by establishing a land court in Kentucky and defining more completely who was eligible for vacant land and the terms under which it would be sold or granted. People began to move into the county, first settling at fortified stations, and then, after the Revolutionary War ended in 1783, spreading out onto their newly acquired land.

The first settlement in the neighborhood was on Buck Creek. It was located where KY 148 crosses the creek about a mile west of Finchville. Although the community that grew up alongside Buck Creek was never very large, it was for many years a gathering place for the people in that part of the county. It contained, in addition to a few houses, a store, a blacksmith shop, and a schoolhouse. The Rev. William E. Waller established the Buck Creek Baptist Church there on July 31, 1799, where it remained until 1891 when it relocated to Finchville.

The first school in the Buck Creek community was a log structure built about 1800.

During a large part of the 19th century there were many small schools on area farms that served children from the immediate neighborhood. There were schools on the farms of Caleb Doyle, Alex B. Veech, John Melone, Tinsley Hazelrigg, and Thomas V. Loofborough.

It is said that Joseph Winlock studied at the Loofborough School. Winlock went on to graduate from Shelby College in Shelbyville in 1845 and was immediately offered a professorship in mathematics and astronomy at that institution. He taught there until 1852 when he moved to Cambridge, Massachusetts, where he took part in the computations for the American Ephemeris and Nautical Almanac. In 1857, he was appointed Professor of Mathematics at the Naval Academy at Annapolis and during the next few years served as Assistant at the Naval Observatory in Washington, Superintendent of the Nautical Almanac, and head of the Mathematics Department at the Naval Academy. When war broke out in 1861 he was again made Superintendent of the Nautical Almanac and remained there until 1865 when he accepted the positions of Phillips Professor of Astronomy at Harvard College and Director of the Cambridge Observatory. In addition to his work for the Navy, Professor Winlock is credited with numerous improvements in astronomical instruments and methods. He also established tables on the perturbations of Mercury and introduced a new method for calculating the diameter of the sun.

Another graduate of the area schools was Alice Polk, daughter of Daniel and Elizabeth Polk. She completed her education at Science Hill Female Academy in Shelbyville and in 1868 married William C. Hill of St. Louis. In 1871, the couple moved to Denver where he opened a dry goods store and she entered the newspaper business. Known for her beautiful prose and poetry she was appointed the poet laureate of Colorado and is the author of a pioneer history of that state. She also organized a number of clubs in Denver including the Denver Press Club, the Daughters of the Confederacy, and the Round Table Club.

In time the focus of the community's commercial and educational life moved east locating along the road leading to Shelbyville. In 1841, Ludwell R. Finch came to Shelby County from Woodford County

Courtesy of The Filson Historical Society, Doolan Collection

Thomas Doolan's school, Shelby Academy, at Finchville, ca. 1890.

along with his wife Georgia Ann Lovell. Between 1842 and 1848 Ludwell Finch (known as "Lud") purchased about 200 acres of land from the several heirs of William Wall on which he established his farm. Finch built his own blacksmith shop and store and the locality became known as "Finch's Shop." When the government established a post office in 1876, the name Finchville was adopted.

The first post office was located in a general merchandise store run by Samuel O. Mitchell and William H. Veech and on March 17, 1876, Mitchell was appointed the first postmaster. The first Rural Route out of Finchville was established in 1903 with Yoder Furgerson as the rural carrier. Today there is still one route operated out of the post office. He was suceeded by William H. Veech in 1883, by Henry Hedden in 1899, Frederick S. Robertson in 1908, William Robertson in 1947, Charles L. Emington in 1980, Paul Briscoe in 1984, and Lillie M. Lawson in 1990. The Robertsons were father and son and they operated the post office out of their general store of the same name. About 1960 the post office moved next door to a small brick structure that once housed the Bank of Finchville. The building is still standing and is a part of the Robertson family's country ham processing business, known as Finchville Farms Country Hams. In 1980, the post office moved to a new building at the corner of KY 55 and KY 148.

In 1856, Benoni S. Newland purchased from Claggete Stout a tract of land on the southern edge of what was to become Finchville. He and his wife operated a private boarding school there for several years. In 1867 he sold the residence and school to Thomas J. Doolan and his wife, Rowena.

The farm that Thomas Doolan purchased contained a little over 52 acres on which there was a handsome two story Greek Revival brick home built about 1857. The Newland School was on the left side of the house and Prof. Doolan moved it into a four room building on the right side. He also constructed a separate music room and a row of stalls alongside the road that led from Finchville east to the Olive Branch neighborhood. The Doolans named their school Shelby Academy and the house they called Sylvan Shades.

When it opened on September 9, 1867, there were 108 students enrolled. The majority came from Shelby County but about 25 percent lived in Spencer County. The students who lived some distance away boarded at the Doolan home or with other families in the neighborhood. The school was in operation for 21 years, closing after the first public school opened in Finchville. For the remainder of his life Doolan devoted his time to farming and stock raising. He was president of the Shelby County Agriculture and Mechanical Association for four years, served as a deputy county clerk, and worked as a land surveyor.

The first public school in Finchville was erected in 1886 on the site of what is now Finchville Farms Country Hams. Miss Sophia Stanley was the teacher. In 1893, the school was moved a half mile south to the lot where all the local public schools have since been built. The new school was a three-room frame building painted red, with a separate music room. On September 6, 1896, high school instruction was added. The local school board was composed of J. A. Stanley, William T. Weakley, and James Taggart. W. T. McClain was principal. A new two-story brick schoolhouse was dedicated on December 23, 1915, replacing the frame building. The new school was financed by a tax voted by the people of the Finchville school district. It had eleven classrooms, a library, and an office for the principal. There was central heating and electric lights but indoor plumbing did not arrive for another 25 years. A stable was provided for the use of students and teachers. In 1931 an auditorium and gym building was added.

The wave of school consolidations, which occurred in the last half of the twentieth century, fell early on the Finchville school. In 1949, it graduated its final high school class. After that year students in the upper grades were transported to Simpsonville High School and, in 1960, to the new consolidated Shelby County High School one-mile east of Shelbyville. The last middle school class graduated in 1968 and the final primary class when the building closed in May 1975. The school was torn down soon after. In 1984, the school lot and gym were sold to the Finchville Baptist Church and in 1991 by them to the Finchville Ruritan Club. Today the building and grounds are used for community meetings, the Finchville Fall Festival, and a summer recreation program for children.

For more than 70 years, a railroad passed through Finchville beginning in 1880 when the Louisville, Cincinnati and Lexington Railroad Co. installed a line from Shelbyville to Bloomfield that connected with the main line of the Louisville & Nashville. The L&N, which acquired the LC&L in 1881, operated the Bloomfield line until 1952.

The Bloomfield branch of the L&N was important to Finchville. At a time when it was often difficult or impossible to travel by road, the railroad supplied reasonably efficient passenger and freight service. It provided a means by which the production of area farms could be sent to market and in turn brought in the coal, lumber, fertilizer, farm machinery, and other goods the community needed. For example, the development of the dairy industry in Finchville would not have occurred when it did without the dependable connection the railroad provided to the Louisville market. There were seven stops along the Bloomfield branch in Shelby County to pick up milk and a depot in Finchville. The stops were Gathright, Logan, Taggart, Finchville, Pickett, Veech, and Cottrell. In Finchville the depot was located on the east side of the Shelbyville-Bardstown Road where Finchville Farms Country Hams is now located. There was a set of pens next to the depot where stock was held for shipping.

During the height of operations, the L&N ran as many as six freight and passenger trains each day from Shelbyville to Bloomfield. After World War I traffic declined as a result of the competition from automobiles and trucks. As the volume of traffic declined the L&N reduced the number of runs until, toward the end, there were only two round trips per week from Louisville to Bloomfield.

A system of state and county roads connects Finchville to other parts of Shelby and surrounding counties. The major north-south route is KY 55 which is a two-lane road running from Carrollton to Cumberland Lake, passing through Shelbyville, Finchville, and Taylorsville. The main east-west connector is KY 148. This road replaced the old meandering highways that connected Finchville to Jeffersontown and Louisville on the west and Ky. 44 on the east. The Shelby County portion of Hwy. 148 was built just prior to World War II and was part of a larger plan to built a new connection from Louisville to Lexington via Jeffersontown, Fisherville, Finchville, Mt. Eden, Lawrenceburg, and Versailles. The needs of the war apparently stopped construction and the road never went further east than Hwy. 44. When Interstate 64 was built through Shelby County an interchange was constructed on Hwy 55 just 3.5 miles north of Finchville and this easy access has led to an increase in housing in the Finchville area.

Another result of the construction of I-64 has been an expansion in commercial development on the west end of Shelbyville and along the KY 55 / US 60 corridor north of the interstate. The rise of chain groceries and general merchandise stores in this area has not only increased competition for small merchants in Shelbyville but has also affected retail outlets in nearby towns. Today there are no grocery stores or service stations in Finchville. This has been a recent development. During most of the twentieth century Finchville had one and often two stores selling groceries and other merchandise, as well as a service station.

In the center of Finchville there is a two-story frame building that was for many years known as Riester's store. However, the first owner was Henry Hidden whose initials "H.H." and the year 1909 can be found in the sidewalk in front of the building. Albert and Rosa Riester moved to the Finchville area in 1902 and bought the store in 1923. In later years Alberta Riester Yancey and her brother Leo Riester operated the business. The Riesters sold the building in 1968 to Hubert and Clara Mae Travis who operated it as Travis' Grocery. In 1971, they sold it to Donald Ray and Ruby Slaughter who renamed it the Finchville Country Store and operated until 1977. The old store sat empty and neglected for years until it reopened as an antique shop named Homestead Treasures in 1994. In August 2001 the shop closed and the building is once again empty.

The Robertson Country Store was operated first by Fred Robertson and then his son Bill. It was located on the east side of the Shelbyville-Bardstown Road a short distance north of Riester's store. Today the building is a part of Finchville Farms Country Hams, operated by the Robertson family. The Robertson Country Store continued in business until Bill Robertson closed it about 1955.

Another long lasting enterprise was Lynn Flood's service station, hardware, and feed store. He opened the business shortly after World War I and operated it next to the railroad depot until 1960. His long time employee Claude Taylor Jr. continued the service station for several years after Mr. Flood retired.

In 1904, the Bank of Finchville was chartered with J.W. Hardin as its first president and W. C. Winlock as cashier. It was housed in the little brick building in the middle of town that would later become the post office. It merged with the Bank of Shelbyville in January 1931, the victim of drought and the Great Depression. The officers of the Bank of Finchville at the time of the merger were G. T. Duvall, President,

Shelby County Public Library, from Augusta Rhodes.

The interior of Riester & Co. general store in Finchville, ca.1933. Alberta Yancey is at the far right, Leo Riester is second from right, and Gilbert Hardesty is third from right.

Dr. Evart Hankins, Cashier, Gilbert M. Veech, Vice President, and Directors Joe Russell and Albert Riester. When it closed the bank had assets of about $84,000.

In recent years, others have tried to make a go of it selling groceries and gasoline in Finchville. In 1977, Charles and Nancy Davis constructed a building across from Riester's old store in which they operated the Country Store both by themselves and under lease until 1989 when it too closed. In 1992, the building was sold to the Bethesda Church of God.

Today there are only two business in Finchville—Finchville Farms Country Hams which traces its beginnings back to 1947 when Bill Robertson began curing country hams, and the Finchville Furniture Co. owned by David Robertson which restores and sells antique furniture. Both market almost entirely to customers from outside the area.

The most constant presence in the life of Finchville has been the Finchville Baptist Church. For over two hundred years the church has devoted itself to the people of the community and they in turn have supported the church. Most of the people living in Finchville, especially the old families, are Baptists and for them the church is both the physical and the spiritual center of the town. The ties that bind the church and Finchville are so complete that when one is thought of, the other comes immediately to mind.

However, there have been other churches that have had an impact on the community. Two of these were established, flourished for a time, and then disappeared. A Christian Church was organized in Finchville in 1887 across the road from the Baptist Church. It disbanded and its building was sold in 1925. Presbyterians attended Plum Run Presbyterian Church, which existed between about 1840 and 1890 at the community of Alfarata west of Finchville where the road to Jeffersontown crosses Plum Creek. In later years the community was known as Needmore.

Methodists in Finchville usually attended the Olive Branch Methodist Church, which was first located just east of Brashears Creek about two miles from Finchville. In 1860, it moved to the intersection of the Olive Branch Road and the Zaring Mill Road. In recent years two new congregations have been established, the Shiloh Old Regular Baptist Church of Jesus Christ and the Bethesda Church of God.

Although Finchville is no longer a center of commerce and education, it retains a closeness and sense of community that others would envy. It has accomplished this despite never having been incorporated or having established any form of municipal government. There has never been a mayor, police or fire department, city council, or city taxes, and Finchville does not seem to have suffered much from the lack of them. Residents, whose family connections often go back many generations, do things in the town, working together to meet whatever need arises.

An example of this spirit is how "city" water got to Finchville. In the early 1950s Robert Doyle and his neighbors decided that the community needed a safe source of drinking water. Mr. Doyle, a civil engineer, dug a lake on his farm at the edge of town and constructed a small treatment plant. The neighbors all got together and installed the water distribution lines and by the mid-1970s there were some thirty houses and businesses using Mr. Doyle's system. It is doubtful that the water works ever earned much of a profit and, when it became evident that he was no longer able to expand his system to new customers, Mr. Doyle took the lead in 1978 in helping Shelbyville build a line into Finchville. Over the last twenty years a plentiful water supply has led to the expansion of housing on Parent Lane and along Hwy. 148 and an influx of new people into the community.

The biggest change that has come to Finchville is the decline of agriculture. Once recognized as an important dairy farming area, only a few dairy herds remain. Low milk prices and a lack of farm labor are part of the reason. Another is that dairy farming is very confining work.

Tobacco production is also in decline. It has been the main cash crop for farmers in Shelby County for over a hundred years, and its anticipated demise has already resulted in young men leaving agriculture as a profession. It would be hard to overstate the impact of tobacco on every aspect of the economy of a community such as Finchville. Tobacco has bought the farms, educated the children, paid the taxes, and secured the old age of nearly every grower in the county. The standard of living on farms and in farming communities will undoubtedly go down as tobacco production declines or ends.

The result is that farms are being divided into tracts and sold as residential lots to families moving from adjoining Jefferson County. While the subdivision of farms into building lots increases the price per acre that the owner receives when he sells, high prices make it almost impossible to acquire enough land to start farming. Some land in the area has been converted to raising and training horses, particularly American saddlebreds, and some farms are surviving by increasing the production of feeder calves and cattle. In looking ahead it seems likely that the trend toward converting land to residential use will continue. Interstate 64 and good secondary roads leading to Jefferson County have made western Shelby County an easy commute to Louisville.

Yet for all of this, Finchville and its people retain a sense of history and place that grows out of living where their parents, grandparents and great grandparents were born, raised their families, and are buried. It is an attachment that has withstood a lot of challenges in the past and will not be easily broken in the years ahead.

GRAEFENBURG

By Duanne Puckett

G raefenburg is located 13 miles east of Shelbyville on U.S. 60 in the far eastern corner of Shelby County. Originally called Hardinsville, it was incorporated on December 18, 1850, and named for a landowner and applicant for incorporation, Wesley Hardin. Families' names still prominent in the area are Finnell, Pemberton, Jenkins, Boyce, and Darlington.

The town's name was changed to Graefenburg several years after incorporation by the Post Office because of its confusing resemblance to the name of a town in Breckinridge County. The origin of the name Graefenburg is unknown.

Its population in the 1870 census was 88. In 1874, it was located at the junction of the Louisville, Frankfort, and Harrodsburg turnpikes, which explains why the town prospered for so many years. It had two churches, two stores, a tavern, and several mechanics' shops in 1874. Today, there are three churches--Baptist, Christian, and Methodist. The Baptist church's claim to fame was having Grady Nutt as pastor. Nutt was a well known "Minister of Humor" on the former television show "Hee Haw." A scholarship is named in his memory at the church for a graduating high school senior.

Small homes are clustered on either side of the road through Graefenburg. There is a general store in a curve that has survived numerous mishaps with automobiles. Unlike some communities, it has become quieter over the years.

Shelby County Public Library, from Ann B. Collings.

Blythe's General Store in Graefenburg about 1912. The people in front are not identified.

MONTCLAIR

By Maureen Ashby

A "colony of free men" in Shelby County, now known as Montclair, was first called Hickory Run, and then Evansville. It is located east of Veechdale Road near Simpsonville. Henry and Nancy Lyon originally owned about 138 acres of land on Hickory Run. At Henry's death, in 1853, his land was divided into eight lots (totaling about 97 acres) and a dower portion (of about forty-one acres). The eight lots were conveyed to his heirs, five of whom sold their lands to Basil H. Crapster. Crapster's five-lot purchase totaled about fifty-two acres. Nancy Lyon held the dower portion until her death in 1865, whereupon her heirs then divided, for the purpose of sale, those acres into seven lots.

Between 1868 and 1871 all the lots were sold to freed men. William Firman bought lots one and three (about fourteen acres), Jerry Bullitt and his son-in-law, Lindsey Johnson, bought lot four (seven acres), Charles Edwards, William Todd, Robert Cole, Harvey Jones, and James Evans bought lot Five (about five acres), Adam Kelser (or "Kelsey" or "Kelso") and Sanford Way bought lot six (about five acres), John Edwards and Mary Canady (or "Kennedy") bought lot seven (about six acres). Also at that time lots six, seven, and eight in the original division of Henry Lyon's land were sold. Wilkerson Bullitt bought lots six and seven (about twenty-nine acres), and Henry Jones bought lot eight (fifteen acres). By 1871, the Bullitt family owned the most land in this newly developed community (thirty-six and one quarter acres), and although James Evans owned the least amount (three-quarters of an acre), the community of Hickory Run thenceforth became known as Evansville.

The original lots were again sub-divided and sold. Lewis and Angeline Logan, George and Mary Washington, David Alexander, Anason (or Anderson) Clark, Washington and Eliza (Harris) Swingler, Beverly King, Harrison Reid, William O'Bannon, Wyatt Harris, Allen Martin, William Calbert, Mary Fields, George and Jack Ballou, Adam Owsley, Albert Lancaster, and Gruber became land owners and residents of Evansville.

In 1872, William and Mary Firman laid off part of their land, which was on a hill (now south of the railroad tracks), for a burial ground. A government marker made by the Vermont Marble Company notes the resting-place of William Fields, a former slave, who, in Louisville on April 12, 1865, enlisted in Company "A", of the 123rd U.S. Colored Infantry. The period of enlistment was for three years, and Fields was forty-seven years old at the time. After military service, Fields boarded with the Ballou family on Dry Run road and worked as a farm hand. He died March 12, 1888. The marker was placed on his grave thirteen years later in March 1901, the same year (in October) that the Ku Klux Klan lynched two black teenage boys from the Chesapeake and Ohio Railroad trestle in Shelbyville. The last burial in this graveyard, Beard Brown, occurred about 1980.

The remembrances of Mary Richardson, made at the age ninety-two, place a log schoolhouse in Evansville, with a class of between eight and fourteen children. Some of the early teachers recollected were Sherman Smith, William Calbert, and Maggie Smith Sawyers. In time, a two-story concrete-block school replaced the log structure, to be followed, still later, by the Lincoln Model School. Finally, the

Students in front of the concrete block Montclair Elementary School.

Montclair school was converted into apartments, which were eventually destroyed by fire. In the 1930s, Clarence Calbert taught adult education in Evansville. Classes were held in a house later owned by the Reverend Charles Davis.

In 1946, under the leadership of the Reverend Clay Weaver, the Negro Baptist Church of Simpsonville (founded in 1869) moved to Evansville. They purchased three lots in Booker T. Washington Court to build a church. For the first two years, until the construction of the church was completed, they congregated in a school building across the street. This was the first church building in Montclair. Located today at 223 U.S. 60, the church is named the New Greater First Baptist Church.

The Louisville & Southern Railroad, in 1887, laid track through the southern part of Evansville, on land owned by Henry Jones, Wilkerson Bullitt, Harvey Russell, and William Firman. The land cut off, however, was never developed as part of the community. Today, this area serves as a graveyard for junked cars and trucks. It is also a final resting-place for some of the original settlers.

When the interurban trolley was built early in the twentieth century Evansville was renamed Montclair. The neighborhood of Montclair exists today on the outskirts, about one mile south and east, of the town of Simpsonville. Present-day streets are named Montclair School Road, Montclair Road (the country road), Davis Street (to honor the Reverend Davis), Evans Road (to honor James Evans), Clairview Drive, and Bullitt Road (to honor the original Bullitt family, owners of all the land east of the country road and south beyond the railroad tracks).

MOUNT EDEN

By Duanne Puckett

Incorporated in 1846, Mount Eden is partly in Shelby County and partly in Spencer County. Governments in both counties cooperate to provide services. Mount Eden's first trustees were Al Harcourt, James Long, M.L. Hudson, and George Hickman.

A strong Dutch and German element is part of the town's early history. The early days were prosperous for Mount Eden which reportedly got its name from a scenic hilltop view. Early settlers grew hemp and later tobacco. There was a newspaper called the *Mount Eden News*. Many businesses were located along Shelby Street. Entertainment could be found in five rum shops, a distillery, and a "quart house" where distillery products were sold. Tobacco sales generated income, especially prior to 1940, when sales moved to larger areas.

The County Line Restaurant in the 1990s was located in an old bank building. One general store has been converted into apartments, but the other remains open. Pockets Game Room offers billiards and Rook. Peoples Bank of Taylorsville has a branch in Mount Eden, alongside the Mount Eden Volunteer Fire Department. There is also a post office, funeral home, and cemetery, as well as an electrical repair and installation firm, a carpet and furniture store, a beauty shop, a vineyard, and a Masonic Lodge. The Masonic brotherhood has long been associated with the town and retains an active membership.

An early elementary school educated students through the eighth grade. In the 1920s it acquired a high school, graduating its first class in 1924 or 1925. The high school was lost to consolidation and the elementary school eventually closed as well. The Kentucky Horseshoeing School took over this property. The 10,000 square foot training facility is designed to teach farriers.

Another notable business in the Eden area is Bauer's Candies, a family-owned firm producing Modjeskas. The candy, which originated in Louisville in the late nineteenth century, consists of caramel-covered marshmallows and is sold in fine gift shops across the state.

A crossroads town north of Mount Eden called Southville is home to Carriss' Grocery where farmers and city folks gather for noonday meals and conversations. This has been a tradition at the store for more than 50 years, dating to when the Skeltons first operated it. The idea of a rural general store caught the attention of the federal government, which sent a film crew to tape a day in the life of the store and evening activities in the neighborhood. The film, "The Country Store" was made in 1949 by the U.S. Army's civil affairs division to show occupied countries of Europe how an average rural America community functioned. A short distance from the store is Salem Baptist Church, noted for its towering evergreen trees in the front yard and quaint cemetery. A congregation began meeting at the town in 1811.

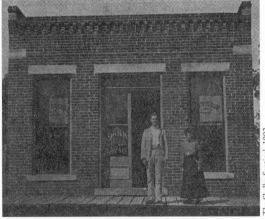

The Mount Eden Bank opened on July 20, 1900.

SHELBY COUNTY

By R.R. Van Stockum Sr.

Shelby, the twelfth Kentucky county in order of formation and the third created after Kentucky was admitted into the Union, occupies 383 square miles in north central Kentucky. It is bounded on the north by Oldham and Henry Counties, on the east by Franklin and Anderson, on the south by Spencer, and on the west by Jefferson. It was created from a portion of Jefferson County on June 28, 1792, and named in honor of Kentucky's first governor, Isaac Shelby. The county seat is Shelbyville. The 1800 census gave the population as 8,191; in 1820 the population was 21,047, but by 1870, through emigration to other parts of the West, it had dropped to 15,733, of whom 10,350 were white and 5,383, African American.

The streams of the northeastern part of the county, Benson and Six Mile Creeks, flow into the Kentucky River; the streams of the much larger southern and western watersheds, Clear, Beech, Guist, Brashears, Bull Skin, Fox Run, Plum, Long Run, and Floyds Fork, join and flow into the Salt River. The land is gently undulating and in a high state of cultivation. The soil is based upon limestone with red clay foundation and is black, friable, and remarkably fertile. Jeptha Knob in eastern Shelby County, named by Squire Boone, is a unique feature, considered by geologists to be a cryptoexplosion structure or a Silurian-age meteor crater. The Sixth-class City of Simpsonville, established in 1816 and named after Captain John Simpson, is located six miles west of Shelbyville.

Squire Boone, Daniel's younger brother, established the first settlement in Shelby County, the Painted Stone Station, along the banks of Clear Creek, about three miles north of present Shelbyville. In the spring of 1780 he brought thirteen families to this tract. As captain, he organized a small company of militia. The station was abandoned temporarily in September 1781 because of Indian attacks, and the settlers were attacked enroute to Linn's Station, twenty-one miles distant, in what has become known as the Long Run Massacre.

Shortly after Squire Boone reestablished his station in the winter of 1783, early Holland Dutch settlers, represented by Abraham Banta, purchased from him 5,610 acres about six miles northeast of the Painted Stone Station on the headwaters of Drennon's and Six Mile Creeks. Here on land that by 1786 included 8,610 acres, they established a Low Dutch Colony. Indian attacks continued to take a toll during the early settlement days in Shelby County.

Harrod's Trace, blazed by James Harrod about 1778 from Harrodsburg to the Falls of the Ohio, passed through Shelby County about two miles south of Shelbyville. The first significant dirt road originated in Maysville and passed through Lexington, Frankfort, and on through Shelbyville to Louisville. In 1825 it became Kentucky's first big macadamized stagecoach road. With the advent of the motor vehicle it was the state's first blacktop thoroughfare and long the most traveled of any in the state. It was later known as the Midland Trail and subsequently as U.S. Hwy. 60. Cross Keys Tavern, no longer in existence, was built by Adam Middleton about five miles east of Shelbyville about 1800. It was a popular inn and stagecoach stop located on this historic turnpike. In the early 1960s, as the interstate highway system was expanded, the principal motor route though the county, paralleling the earlier routes, became Interstate 64.

In the 1850s the railroad from Frankfort to Louisville passed through Christiansburg in northeast Shelby County. In 1870 the Shelby Railroad Co. built the line from Anchorage to Shelbyville. Both routes later became part of the Louisville & Nashville Railroad system. An 1895 extension from Shelbyville created a shorter route from Louisville through Shelbyville to Frankfort and points east. With the addition in 1887-88 of the Louisville Southern Railroad route from Louisville to Lexington that passed through Shelbyville, and the construction of interurban lines, Shelby County, by 1910 enjoyed fine transportation facilities for passengers and freight.

Important early settlers included Major William Shannon (c. 1740-94), commissary for George Rogers Clark, who became a large landowner in the county, and donor of the land upon which the Shelby County Courthouse was built. Captain Bland Williams Ballard (1761-1853) joined the militia upon his arrival in Kentucky in 1779 and was present at the Long Run Massacre in 1781.

Colonel John Allen (1771-1813), a successful attorney in Shelby County, was elected to represent his county in the General Assembly in 1800. He served in the Kentucky House until 1807 and in the Senate until 1812. In December 1806 he and Henry Clay acted as defense attorneys in Aaron Burr's trial in Frankfort. Commanding the First Rifle Regiment of the Kentucky Militia against the British and their Indian allies, Allen was killed on January 22, 1813, while rallying his troops at the Battle of the River Raisin. He was one of more than 400 Kentuckians to die in that defeat. Three states—Ohio, Indiana and Kentucky—named counties in Allen's honor. Colonel Abraham Owen (1769-1811) was the son of Brackett Owen who made his home available as the first meeting place of the Shelby County Court at its first term on October 15, 1792. After coming to Kentucky in 1785, Owen became a distinguished military leader and political figure. He served as a lieutenant in Arthur St. Clair's defeat in Ohio in 1791, receiving two wounds in that engagement, and in General Anthony Wayne's successful campaign against the Indians. He was killed on November 7, 1811, while serving as an aide-de-camp to General William Henry Harrison in the Battle of Tippecanoe in Indiana. He served in the State legislature representing Shelby County and shortly before his death was a member of the Kentucky Senate. Owen County, Kentucky, established in 1819, was named in his memory.

Dr. John Knight (1751-1838) emigrated from Scotland about 1773 and subsequently participated in many engagements of the American Revolution as a surgeon's mate. He joined Colonel William Crawford at the Mingo town on the Ohio River in May 1782 and proceeded with the army to the plains of Sandusky, where Crawford's command met a disastrous defeat. He witnessed the agonizing death of Colonel Crawford, who was burned at the stake, but was able to escape before receiving similar treatment. He survived to become one of the original town trustees of Shelbyville and a practicing physician.

General Benjamin Logan (1743-1802), frontiersman, distinguished military leader, and legislator, participated in the spring of 1775 in establishing the Kentucky settlement called St. Asaph, and subsequently in the building of a fort there, often called Logan's Fort. Shortly after coming from Lincoln County to Shelby County in 1795, he was chosen to represent Shelby in the General Assembly. In 1796, as one of three candidates for governor, he received the highest number of electoral votes. However, the electors, believing that a majority was required, called for a second ballot, in which James Garrard was the winner. Logan represented Shelby County during two additional terms in the lower house of the general assembly and in 1799 was a member of the convention that drafted Kentucky's second constitution.

The Allen Dale Show Herd at a fair in Atlanta, Georgia, in 1918.

Courtesy of R.R. Van Stockum Sr.

The county was the birthplace of Governor Martha Layne Collins (1936-), Whitney Young Sr. (1897-1975), and Whitney Young Jr. (1921-71) director of the National Urban League. Young Sr. was associated with the Lincoln Institute, opened in 1912 to educate young African Americans. Located on 444 acres near Simpsonville the school closed in 1966. The Whitney M. Young Jr. Job Corps Center occupies the facility.

Agriculture and livestock were the basis of the county's wealth. Corn, hemp, and wheat were the primary Shelby County crops before the Civil War. In 1870 the county produced the following crops: corn, 1,108,605 bushels (highest in the state); hemp, 308,200 pounds; tobacco, 239,450 pounds; wheat, 175,996 bushels; hay, 4,188 tons; and barley, 1,156 bushels; livestock inventory in 1870 was: hogs, 22,089 (highest in the state); cattle, 11,804 (fifth in the state); horses, 6,690; and mules, 1,484.

In the early twentieth century, the *Jersey Bulletin*, noting that there were 450 imported and 1,500 Jersey cattle in the county, including the prize herd at Allen Dale Farm, claimed Shelby County to be the Jersey Isle of America.

Tobacco, corn, soybeans, hay, beef, and dairy cattle are now the principal farm products. Shelby County in 1996 was first in the state in the production of burley tobacco and third in the production of dairy products. It is also well known for its alfalfa hay grown in deep, limestone-shale-embedded soil. Estimated crop production for 1996 was: burley tobacco, 9,560,000 pounds; alfalfa hay, 36,480 tons; all other hay, 92,000 tons; winter wheat, 210,000 bushels; soybeans, 533,800 bushels; and corn, 1,530,000 bushels. Estimated livestock data for 1996: Average number milk cows, 5,500; total milk production 60,000,000 pounds; all cattle and calves, 49,000; hogs and pigs, 11,000.

In 1992 there were 1,640 farms in Shelby County, with a total acreage of 229,838. In 1995 the county's cash receipts from farm marketing totaled $60,641,000, ninth in the state.

The American Saddlebred is the only horse that Kentucky claims to have originated. The American Saddlebred Horse Association in 1891 registered the first horse of this breed from Shelby County. The breeding and training of Saddlebred horses has become particularly important in Shelby County since the establishment in 1958 near Simpsonville of a prominent training stable. Based upon the number of Saddlebred horses bred and trained in the county and the success of these horses in international competition, Shelby County claims to be the Saddlebred Capital of the World.

Industrial enterprises are principally near Shelbyville, where fifty manufacturing firms employed 5,648 individuals in 1998. Shelby County's largest employer is the Budd Co., with 675 employees manufacturing metal parts for automobiles. Second is Leggett & Platt, which employs 424 in the manufacture of swivel chairs, sofa beds, and reclining chair mechanisms in Simpsonville. The Purnell Sausage Co., which employs 300, is also in Simpsonville. Other industries employing more than 100 in Shelby County include Alcoa-Fujikura, Atlantic Envelope, Black & Decker, Curtis Industries, Ichikoh Manufacturing, Johnson Controls, Katayama American, Lawson Mardon Packaging, Ledco, Louise's Fat Free Potato Chips, Ohio Valley Aluminum, Omega Plastics, Owens Corning, Roll Forming, and Shelbyville Mixing Center.

Tourist attractions include the Wakefield-Scearce Galleries, known throughout the country and abroad for its antique English furniture and silver; the Old Stone Inn, once a stagecoach tavern near Simpsonville; Science Hill Inn Dining Room; and Claudia Sanders Dinner House, established by Colonel Harland Sanders. Thousands each summer attend the Shelbyville Horse Show, which has been voted the No. 1 Saddlebred horse show in America.

Clear Creek Park, which includes Lake Shelby, a fishing lake, is an extensive recreational area of about 200 acres for picnicking and outdoor sports. Fishing, water skiing, and camping are available on the larger Guist Creek Lake. A Clear Creek Trust has been recently established for the maintenance as a tourist attraction of Clear Creek, which meanders through Shelbyville and Shelby County. Tourism expenditures in the county totaled over $1.1 million in 1996.

The population of the county was 18,999 in 1970; 23,328 in 1980; 24,824 in 1990; 28,836 in 1997, and 33,337 in 2000.

SHELBY COUNTY POPULATION BY RACE

YEAR	TOTAL	WHITE	BLACK SLAVE	FREE BLACK	AFRICAN AMERICANS
1790	NA	NA	NA	NA	
1800	8,191	6,681	1,487	23	
1810	14,877	11,721	3,114	42	
1820	21,047	15,796	5,158	93	
1830	19,030	13,015	5,920	95	
1840	17,768	11,256	6,355	157	
1850	17,095	10,289	6,617	189	
1860	16,433	9,634	6,634	165	
1870	15,733	10,350			5,383
1880	16,813	11,258			5,555
1890	16,521	11,744			4,776
1900	18,340	13,642			4,698
1910	18,041	14,050			3,991
1920	18,532	15,266			3,266
1930	17,679	15,042			2,637
1940	17,759	15,201			2,558
1950	17,912	15,586			2,324
1960	18,493	16,010			2,479
1970	18,999	16,546			2,432
1980	23,328	20,666			2,628
1990	24,824	22,218			2,454
2000	33,337	28,874*			2,942

*Note The data for race in the 2000 Census is not directly comparable to race data for the 1990 and earlier censuses because of changes in the way the data was categorized. For the first time a new racial category called "Some other race" was added to the five traditional races. In Shelby County 798 people chose this racial category and in Shelbyville, 503. The vast majority (90% or more) of them were Hispanics and for racial purposes should probably be counted as members of the white race.

2000 CENSUS FIGURES SHELBY COUNTY

Community	2000	%change	1990	%change	1980	%change	1970
Pleasureville	105	228.1%	32	-146.9%	79	27.4%	62
Shelbyville(city)	10,085	61.7%	6,238	14.6%	5,329	27.4%	4,182
Simpsonville(city)	1,281	41.2%	907	29.2%	642	2.2%	628

SHELBYVILLE

By Charles T. Long

Shelbyville, named in honor of Kentucky's first governor, Isaac Shelby, is the county seat of Shelby County, and a fourth class city. Shelbyville is governed by a mayor and a board of council consisting of six members elected at large from the city. The town was founded in October 1792 at the first Shelby County Court meeting, when William Shannon offered to lay off fifty acres into town lots and provide the county with an acre of land for public buildings. The town was established on the west side of Clear Creek, opposite the mouth of Mulberry Creek, and close to where the road from Louisville to Frankfort crossed Clear Creek.

The General Assembly appointed trustees in December 1792 and the first lot was sold in March 1793. The town trustees required each lot owner to build at least a one-and-one-half story hewed log house with a stone chimney, and by 1795 there were some forty of these structures. Soon thereafter, brick buildings were constructed. The second court house, completed 1798, is an early example. The population in 1800 was 262 and new town lots were platted in 1803, 1815, and again in 1816.

Shelbyville came to be located nearly in the center of Shelby County as the legislature, in the process of creating new counties, reduced Shelby to less than one-half its original size. The town was the principal provider of goods and services to surrounding farms and functioned as a point of sale and distribution for crops and livestock. In the period before the Civil War there was some local processing of agricultural products, such as flour and corn milling and, on a smaller scale, rope making, cotton and wool mills, tobacco processing, and lumber sawing. The 1850 census reveals a community in which most people were employed in direct or indirect support of the farm economy. Merchants, saddlers, wagon makers, blacksmiths, carpenters, masons, cabinet and chair makers, tailors, and shoe makers were all represented, as well as physicians, lawyers, teachers, and ministers.

Schools and academies were organized from the earliest times. The Shelbyville Academy, founded in 1798, operated for many years at Eighth and Washington Streets before moving to College Street. In 1836 it became Shelby College. Five years later the Episcopal church took control and, under the presidency of Reverend William I. Waller, constructed several buildings, including a classroom building that had on its roof an astronomical observatory. Professor Joseph Winlock, who had taught at Shelby College and was a Shelby County native, returned in 1869, along with some of his colleagues from Harvard University, to observe the total eclipse of the sun that occurred on August 7. Dr. Waller apparently resigned the presidency of Shelby College around the end of the Civil War. Under the name St. James College, it continued to operate—primarily as a school for boys—until declining enrollment forced it to close in 1871. The city took control, removed the observatory, and operated a grade school in the building until 1939, when it was replaced by a new structure.

The best known of the Shelbyville schools was Science Hill Female Academy, founded in 1825 by Julia Ann Tevis. Tevis and her husband, the Reverend John Tevis, a Methodist minister, operated Science Hill as a Protestant boarding school for girls between 12 and 16 years of age. Located on Washington

Street, it drew pupils from all over Kentucky and the southern states. Day students from the town attended, including boys and girls not old enough to enter the academy. The mission of the school was to "make an elegant, cultivated, refined woman for society, and fit for the higher duties of home life,..." (Tevis; *Sixty Years in a School Room*, p. 463).

Discipline was strict and moral and religious principles emphasized. In addition to the usual classes in music, composition, orthoepy (the study of correct pronunciation and dictation), elocution, penmanship, and mathematics, Mrs. Tevis, believing that young ladies needed a sound background in the natural sciences, included astronomy, chemistry, and geology in the curriculum. In 1879 Science Hill was taken over by Dr. Wiley T. Poynter, who developed it into a college preparatory school. After his death in 1896 his widow, Clara M. Poynter, became principal and, together with her daughters Harriet and Juliet Poynter, operated the school until her death in 1937. Science Hill School closed in 1939.

The Shelbyville Female Seminary was founded in 1839 by Reverend William F. Hill. In 1846 he erected a building at Seventh and Main Streets that would house the boarding school for the next 57 years. In 1849 he changed the name to Shelbyville Female College. The Reverend David T. Stuart purchased the school in 1851. It operated in association with the Presbyterian church. After his death in 1868, his son, W. H. Stuart, assumed control and continued the school under the name Shelbyville Female College until 1880 when the name was changed to Stuart's Female College. In 1897 it was sold to J. E. Nunn who renamed it Shelbyville College and operated it as a Baptist school until it closed in 1903.

During the Civil War the town was harassed by Confederates. Early on the morning of August 24, 1864, a group of Confederate guerrillas led by Shelby native Captain Dave Martin attacked the courthouse in an attempt to seize muskets stored there. They were driven off by heavy gunfire from townsmen Thomas C. McGrath, a merchant, and J. H. Masonheimer, a tailor. Three guerrillas were killed, along with a black man by the name of Owen who was on the street at the time of the raid and was ordered by the guerrillas to hold their horses. Martin missed the action. He was at the jail in the rear of the courthouse being upbraided by the jailer's wife, Mrs. Henry Burnett Sr., for endangering the lives of innocent civilians, including his own wife and children then living in town.

Shelby County Public library

Four buildings in 400 block of Main, North side

This 1865 photograph shows the blockhouse near the public square on Main Street.

Courtesy of Charles T. Long.

As a result of the raid, the town trustees in January 1865 ordered a log blockhouse, about fourteen feet in diameter, built in front of the courthouse at the intersection of Fifth and Main Streets. Every white male in the town over eighteen years of age was enrolled as a police guard and a watch was kept, with the blockhouse serving as the headquarters.

On January 25, 1865, in a driving snow storm, thirty-five Union soldiers herding government cattle to Louisville were killed in Shelby County just west of *Simpsonville* by Confederate guerrillas believed to have been led by Dick Taylor. That night the Spencer County courthouse burned. About this time, William Clarke Quantrill, the Confederate guerrilla leader who had been operating on the Missouri-Kansas border, moved into Kentucky and began raids in Spencer, Mercer, and Nelson Counties. In an effort to stop Quantrill, General John Palmer, in command of Union forces in Kentucky, placed Captain Edwin Terrell of the Shelby County Home Guard and thirty of his men on the federal payroll on April 1, 1865. Along with Lieutenant Harry Thompson, Terrell led his men through Shelby and surrounding counties, hunting down Confederate guerrillas and intimidating Southern sympathizers. He and his men were welcome in Shelbyville and the town trustees encouraged them to stay by paying their bills at local hotels.

On May 10, 1865, Terrell and his men caught up with Quantrill's raiders at a barn near Wakefield in Spencer County. In the ensuing fight Quantrill was mortally wounded and his guerrilla band broken up. A few days later Terrell rode into Shelbyville to the cheers of its citizens. There was at that time a regiment of Col. Buckley's Union soldiers camped at the fairgrounds and a company of black soldiers quartered in the Court House. On May 19, 1865, one of the soldiers shot and killed Thomas A. McGrath who was trying to prevent him from breaking up his farm machinery for fire wood. Terrell seized the soldier and was in the process of hanging him from the second floor balcony of the Court House when Buckley's soldiers intervened. The Union army paid off and disbanded Terrell and his men on May 24, 1865, and a month later the trustees of Shelbyville stopped paying for their room and board. With the war over and the threat of guerrilla attacks ended, the blockhouse was torn down in

September 1865 and the police guard removed a few months later. Ed Terrell and Harry Thompson, however, continued to make trouble. On August 25th while in Shelbyville they murdered and robbed William R. Johnson, a stock trader from Illinois. They were arrested and tried for the crime in March of the following year but the jury could not reach a verdict. Terrell was transferred to the jail in Taylorsville to await trial there for another killing. He escaped and, with two companions, returned to Shelbyville on the evening of May 26, 1866. While he and his friends were drinking at the Armstrong Hotel, Town Marshall George W. Caplinger organized a posse. When Terrell came out of the hotel he rode a short distance east and stopped to talk to hotel keeper Merritt Redding. As he turned to leave, a volley of shots rang out. Terrell was wounded in the spine and his kinsman, John R. Baker, killed. Merrett Redding was also wounded in the crossfire and died a month later.

Terrell was taken to Louisville but because of the seriousness of his wound he did not stand trial. He returned to his home in Harrisonville in October but his health did not improve. He determined to return to Louisville for an operation to remove the bullet from his back. The surgery was not successful and he died sometime before the end of 1867 at the age of twenty two. The date and place of his death and the location of his grave are not known. Meanwhile, his friend Harry Thompson escaped from the Shelby County jail on October 23, 1866. Local tradition says that he went to Texas where he became a prosperous farmer, using the name Henry T. Grazian.

The half-century between the Civil War and World War I was a period of unprecedented commercial and residential development in Shelbyville. The city limits, little changed since 1816, were expanded to the east and west along Main Street. Nearly all the buildings in the central business district between Fourth and Seventh Streets. were replaced by larger structures designed in the Italianate and Classical Revival styles popular at the time. Some of the new construction was caused by a disastrous fire that struck the business district in 1909. The city expanded its firehouse and city hall on the public square in 1912 and the county completed the present courthouse in 1914. The four oldest banks in Shelby County were all organized at this time, despite the financial panics of 1873, 1893, and 1907. Along west Main Street the town's merchants, bankers, and mill owners built large two-story brick and frame houses.

In January 1895 a public water system replaced the community wells that had served the town for one hundred years and were the cause of recurring cholera epidemics. The Shelbyville Water and Light Company also provided the first electrical light service to the city's streets in December 1884. Telephone service also began in 1895 and a Carnegie Library opened in 1903. The King's Daughters built the city's first hospital on Henry Clay Street in 1906.

The growing prosperity of Shelbyville was directly related to agriculture, which had evolved from a more or less subsistence level before the Civil War to one of increasing production and surplus. Burley tobacco, the most important cash crop grown in the county, was marketed through warehouses in Shelbyville. Wheat and corn were sold to local flour and meal mills. Hemp continued to be grown, particularly on farms close to the town's supply of day laborers. Purebred beef cattle, mules, and saddlebred horses were raised and sold throughout the nation. The dairy industry, which depended on quick and reliable delivery to the Louisville market, grew to become an important part of the economy.

Improvements in transportation played a major role in the growth of Shelbyville and its commercial development. The Shelby Railroad Company constructed a line from Anchorage in 1870, thereby joining the town to the main line of the Louisville, Cincinnati & Lexington Railroad, which was later the Louisville & Nashville Railroad and then CSX Transportation. The Louisville Southern Railroad, later the Norfolk Southern, built a line through the town in 1887-88. The Cumberland & Ohio Railroad had a section of line from Shelbyville south to Taylorsville and the Shelby division of the Louisville & Interurban electric railroad operated in the area between 1910 and 1934. These transportation links, together with the replacement of toll-gate roads with county and state roads, enabled the products of Shelby County farms to move quickly to major markets. Shelbyville lay at the center of that network of roads and railroads.

African Americans did not participate in the growing prosperity. The population of the town in 1870 was 2,180, with 44 percent being black. Those that lived in Shelbyville were mainly day laborers in town or on farms in the vicinity. The average wage was $10 or $12 a month. On January First of each year, the anniversary of Lincoln's Emancipation Proclamation, African Americans from all over the county would gather in town to celebrate and to hire out for the coming year. Most of the black citizens of Shelbyville lived in a section called Martinsville, in rented houses owned by whites. The Ku Klux Klan, centered in the eastern part of the county, created an atmosphere of intimidation, coercion, and occasional violence. In 1901 and again in 1911, white mobs entered the county jail and lynched blacks. These conditions, together with low wages and the lack of real opportunity, led to a decline in the county's black population from 5,383 in 1870 to 3,266 in 1920. The population of Shelbyville in 1920 was 3,760, with 1,224, or 32 percent, being black. Although the number of blacks in the town increased from 1870 to 1920, there was a twelve percent decline in their numbers relative to the white population. In 1990 blacks represented 23 percent of the population of the city.

The period from 1917 to 1945 can be characterized as a time when Shelbyville survived rather than prospered. The two world wars did not generate much economic growth, except for a few industries associated with processing agricultural products. The town participated mainly by providing manpower to the military and reducing civilian consumption in order to free up supplies for the war effort. The Great Depression had an impact on farm commodity prices, together with the problems imposed by the breakdown of the banking system. The decline threatened to lead to the collapse of local lending

A view from Henry Clay Street toward Main Street in 1909. A fire had destroyed much of the block between Fourth and Fifth Streets, including the First Baptist Church.

Main Street in Shelbyville looking east from the southwest corner of Sixth and Main, ca. 1896.

institutions and retail businesses. Measures taken by the federal government to support farm prices by cutting the production of tobacco and milk, along with loan programs and relief projects, helped stabilize the local economy but did not lead to recovery.

The ten years following World War II continued the low rate of growth set in the first half of the century. Manufacturing jobs in Shelby County in 1950 numbered only 448. However, by the mid 1950s conditions began to improve. A new county hospital was dedicated in 1954 and in 1957 the Shelby County Industrial and Development Foundation was formed to recruit industry and provide prepared sites. Three years later the interstate highway system arrived with Interstate 64 crossing the county two miles south of the city. A system of good highways and railroads, adequate utilities, suitable plant sites, and a traditionally non-union work force drawn from Shelby and surrounding counties set the stage for the movement of industry into the area.

In the years since 1960 more than forty-five companies employing more than 5,000 people have established plants in Shelby County. Most of the new plants have been built in three industrial parks located on the western edge of Shelbyville. The city built a new fire and police station in 1960 and new administrative offices in 1996.

Residential developments and commercial centers were created both east and west of the city. Many of these areas were incorporated into the city because of the availability of public sewers and the fact that the sale of alcohol was permitted in the city but not the county. Shelbyville grew in size from 1.6 square miles in 1960 to 7.4 square miles in 1997 and, during the same period, from a population of 4,525 to an estimated population of 8,299. Its population was 4,182 in 1970; 5,329 in 1980; and 6,238 in 1990; and 10,085 in 2000.

SIMPSONVILLE

By Hobie Henninger and Sherry Jelsma

Simpsonville is on the western edge of Shelby County, eight miles west of Shelbyville, thirty miles west of Frankfort and twenty-three miles east of Louisville. The town was established in 1816 by order of the Shelby County Court of Sessions at its October term on the motion of Isaac Watkins. More than 33 acres constituted the territory he guaranteed for the site of the town. The title was vested in the appointed trustees, George Smith, Benjamin Bridges, William Hunt, Abraham Goodknight, and Conrad Pence. Andrew Holmes and John Newland endorsed the petition of Mr. Watkins in the sum of 1,000 pounds, which guaranteed that the title of the land was free, and in legal compliance with current requirements.

The new town was named for a war hero and respected citizen, Captain John Simpson. Born in Virginia, Simpson was a prominent lawyer in Shelby County from 1800 to 1812. He served as the Representative from Shelby County in the state legislature from 1806 to 1811 and was elected Speaker of the House in 1811. Although elected to the U.S. Congress in 1812, he never served this term due to his death at the Battle of the River Raisin in 1813.

Simpsonville was the first big stagecoach town between Shelbyville and Louisville after the stage began running on the Midland Trail (now U.S. 60) in 1825. An inn, now known as The Old Stone Inn, served travelers between Louisville and Shelbyville.

Sixteen years after its founding, the town was incorporated in 1832. In November the county court was asked to make alterations in the Simpsonville road so that it might pass through the town, not behind it. This was done and the stage traveled through town on what is still called Main Street. There was a stop at Minnie and Margaret Bell's Tavern to change horses or let them rest. The long porch at Bell's Tavern faced the road and was attached to a large barn where the stage horses rested before continuing on to Louisville.

The Louisville & Nashville Railroad, now the CSX system, came through on the north side of town in 1875. The Norfolk Southern Railroad runs about one mile south of the L&N and was built in the late 1800s through a small settlement called Veechdale. Both railroads went into Louisville and Shelbyville. Shelbyville had the L&N depot and Veechdale the Norfolk Southern depot. During the early years of the twentieth century an interurban rail line ran along Main Street and was used until 1934. The Bells' Tavern building served the street-car line at this time. In the 1940s the rails were removed for scrap metal for use in the World War II effort.

For more than 175 years Simpsonville was considered an agriculture community with dairy, tobacco, cattle, and hogs the primary sources of income. At the beginning of the twenty-first century the city had two manufacturing plants. Leggett and Platt, with 424 employees, makes swivel chairs, sofa beds, and reclining chair mechanisms. Purnell Sausage Company produced several types of sausage, gravy, and chili mixes. The new Kingbrook Commerce Park and the Business Center are bringing both industry and residents to Simpsonville. The horse industry is well represented. There are veterinary clinics and one animal hospital, which nurtured the first horse in the world that, bred to a zebra, birthed a horse/zebra.

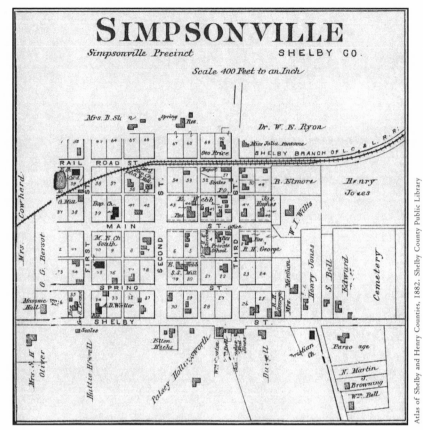

Map of Simpsonville in 1882

Riding schools, saddlebred breeding farms and at least one thoroughbred farm have given the name "Saddlebred Horse Capital of the World" to Simpsonville. The Shelby County Flea Market was the first indoor flea market in Kentucky and one of the largest in the eastern United States.

The town has grown to more than 300 acres in 2001. It is bounded on the south by Interstate 64, the east by county road 1848, the west by CSX tracks, and about a half mile past the CSX tracks on the north. During the 1820s Simpsonville boasted a stagecoach stop, tavern, drugstore and a post office, all located on Main Street. Now Main Street is residential. U.S. 60 is a mixture of residential and commercial. There are 34 commercial and service businesses. In 1999, there were more than 350 residences and three apartment buildings. The Rolling Ridge development is one of many residential complexes. Cardinal Club Estates, Todd's Station, and The Oaks are other developments that offer more than 500 units. The population in Simpsonville has increased 41 percent over the last ten years, growing from 907 in 1990, and 1,281 in 2000.

During the early years, several one-room schools were built and by 1895 the area had four private schools. But the town didn't have a high school until 1912. Simpsonville High School was constructed that year and a new gym was built later with funds from the Works Progress Administration. In 1958, Shelby County voted to consolidate its high schools and Simpsonville High became an elementary school. The last classes were held in the school building in 1987. It was auctioned in 1989 and purchased by the building corporation set up by the Simpsonville City Commission. It now houses a city library among other city offices, The gym is used for Lion's Club Youth Leagues, private rentals and meetings. The elementary building, remodeled in 1991, is called the Generation Center.

The Lincoln Institute, located in Simpsonville, was known throughout the state. In 1910, aided by a $200,000 donation from Andrew Carnegie, a Berea trustee, the president and trustees of Berea College raised enough money for a school for African Americans and formed the Lincoln Foundation to run it. Land near the Simpsonville city limits was purchased and the Lincoln Institute was built. It provided a high school education for African American youth in Kentucky and offered vocational education and some college-level courses as well. There were dormitories on campus for students and houses for some of the staff. In 1947, it became a state supported and accredited high school. In 1966, it closed due to lack of enrollment resulting from the 1954 Supreme Court ruling ordering desegregation of public schools. From 1968 to1970 it was used as a school for gifted and disadvantaged black youth of Kentucky. In 1972, it became the Whitney M. Young Jr. Job Corps Center. A private contractor for the labor department runs it and the property is controlled by the Lincoln Foundation in Louisville.

SIMPSONVILLE BUSINESS REFERENCES.

W. B. RYAN, Physician and Surgeon.

P. A. SHELY, Physician and Surgeon.

A. D. WALLER, Dealer in all Grades of Live Stock.

F. A. BYARS, Dealer and Breeder of Pure Southdown and Cotswold Sheep, from best imported strains. Also Breeder and Dealer in Short-Horn Cattle.

J. C. BYARS, Dealer in and Breeder of Fine Sheep, Cattle and Horses.

BOHANNAN & COOPER, Proprs. of Saw Mill Custom work solicited. Dealers in Lumber of all kinds. Walnut Lumber a specialty. Mill located 2½ miles N. W. of Todd's Point Ky.

McDOWELL BROS., Proprs. of Saw Mill and Dealers in all kinds of Hard Lumber. Clear Oak Lumber a specialty. Mill located one mile west of Simpsonville, Ky.

W. L. HAMMOND, Blacksmith. Does General Custom Work. Horseshoeing a specialty. Give him a trial. You will be well satisfied with his work.

FAIRVIEW MALE AND FEMALE SEMINARY. Session begins First Monday in September. A select course will be taught by the Principal. The best of Teachers are employed to teach in the Primaay and Music Departments. Board in good families can be had at $1.50 to $3.00 per week. The best of discipline will be kindly and firmly maintained. No pupil will be retained in school who cannot be induced to prepare their lessons or refuse to obey the Teachers. Examinations are thorough. For any other information, address in person or by letter, H. F. Jordan, Principal.

E. WEBB, Prop'r of Saw Mill. Dealer in all kinds of Lumber. Also prop'r of Blacksmith and Wagon Shop. Custom work solicited.

D. C. CALLAHAN, Auctioneer, Todds Point, Ky., solicits sales of all kinds in Shelby and adjoining counties, and guarantees satisfaction in all cases. Terms reasonable. Orders left with Neel & Ballard, Shelbyville; John Caseldine Eminence, or Geo. W. Coleman, Simpsonville, will receive prompt attention. Also dealer and breeder of fine Horses, Cattle and Sheep.

W. B. MONTGALL, Dealer in Confectioneries Notions, Staple and Fancy Groceries, &c. Prices reasonable. Give me a call.

LEONIDAS WEBB, Dealer in Fine Cattle and Sheep.

R. B. WINLOCK, Physician and Surgeon.

MISS SALLIE DOBYNS, Teacher.

W. P. RAY, Surveyor and Teacher. Well versed in Latin and Greek. Would accept a situation as Principal of some good school.

Atlas of Shelby and Henry Counties, 1882. Shelby County Public Library

List of Businesses, 1882

The Masonic Lodge was established in the town in 1847, and the building, which is still used, was completed in 1848. During a skirmish between Union and Confederate soldiers, a group of Confederate refugees hid under the building for some time. The dead from this skirmish were buried along U.S. 60 and their graves are marked with blank stones. The Masons were deeded their cemetery from the Odd Fellows Lodge in 1879 for $1.00. In this cemetery is a rare "witch's broom". This strange phenomenon is a small tree growing from the top of a larger tree.

Simpsonville is a fifth class city. The mayor and four commissioners form the city commission, each having one vote. The city employs a city administrator and six other full or part-time employees as well as a full-time police officer, who works closely with the Shelby County Sheriff and the state police. All offices are located in the Community Center.

SOUTHVILLE

By Tony Carriss

A small town located eight miles south of Shelbyville on KY 53, Southville lies at the crossroads of Highway 44. Southville was founded sometime before 1800, and by 1882 the community was a thriving business center. The name came from its location south of Shelbyville.

Some of the original families were Gray, Eggen, Russell, McClain, Shelburne, Carriss, Ritter, Snider, Bootie, Figg, Coots, Shipman, Simnons, Burnett, Sturs, and Freeman.

An 1882 map shows that C.G. Freeman was the undertaker and dealer of all kinds of furniture who stocked a full-line of burial cases. J.H. Carriss was the proprietor of the sawmill and feed mill. H.C. Carriss was the magistrate of the Southville and Mount Eden area. J.L. Eggen was physician and surgeon who made house calls. In the early 1900s a Dr. Dorsey also had an office. A tollhouse, run by the Carriss family, was located across from Salem Church. A Masonic Hall was located at Southville as well as a post office. A one-room schoolhouse also served as the voting place.

The gem of the community is the Salem Baptist Church, which was founded in 1811 and rebuilt after a fire in 1896.

During many years of the twentieth century, Dr. W.E. Morris treated Southville residents in a tiny office located next to the community sign that greets drivers

In 1949, the federal government made a movie called "The Country Store" at Southville. It was used in foreign countries to promote trade and give the people a sense of what rural America was like. A crossroads general store has served the community since 1882. The store has been run by the Heiden, Ratcliff, Skelton, and Carriss families. Jay Carriss died of a heart attack January 19, 2003 defending the store from burglars. It has been a gathering place with conversation about crops, hunting and politics, which reflects the closeness of the community.

Southville businesses in 2000 included farming, cabinet making, automobile repair, feed and fertilizer sales and livestock shipping.

The Carriss Grocery

TODD'S POINT

By Charles T. Long

T odd's Point is located in the northwest corner of Shelby County some five miles north of Simpsonville on Aiken Road (Hwy. 362). The village is strung out for almost a mile along a wide ridge that is the highest point in the immediate neighborhood. Hunters Lane and D. I. Cooper Lane lead north from Todd's Point stopping just short of the Oldham County line. The land is drained by Junkins Run and Miller Branch which flow north to join Floyd's Fork Creek. Todd's Point was named for a family that settled in the area and was probably given the name when a post office was established there on April 18, 1867. Thomas A. Fountain was the first postmaster. The post office closed in 1913 and the town was served thereafter by the post office in Simpsonville.

In addition to several grocery and dry goods stores, Todd's Point has been served over the years by at least two blacksmith's shops, one run by Eugene Bryant and another at a later time by Alex Streible. There was a wagon shop, a saw mill operated by Louis Beatty, and a broom factory. A tomato canning factory was located on Hunter's Lane surrounded by fields of tomato plants. Todd's Point also had a grist mill on a tributary to Little Bullskin Creek at the intersection of Anderson Lane and the Todd's Point Road where the Todd's Point Grocery was later built.

The Mount Pleasant Baptist Church was organized here in 1863 with about forty members and remains today the only church in the community. Although it has been remodeled over the years, it still sits on its original foundation. The first pastor was W. W. Foree. The lumber used in the building was probably milled by Louis Beatty who donated some of the land for the church. It was hauled to the site by Eugene Bryant's father, Thomas Bryant, who was a teamster. Thomas Bryant also delivered the mail to Todd's Point each day from Simpsonville. At one time, Todd's Point had a Baptist church attended by blacks located about a mile west of town where David Cain lives now. The church was blown down by the tornado that struck the area January 18, 1929.

During the early part of the 1900s there were two schools in the Todd's Point neighborhood where students attended the primary grades. They were Long's School located west of town and Rough and Ready School to the east on Aiken Road. They were replaced in 1921 when the county Board of Education purchased 2.5 acres in the middle of town on which was constructed a brick building called the Todd's Point School. Two teachers taught the primary and middle grades. High School students attended Simpsonville High School. In 1940 the school was closed and all students transferred to Simpsonville. One of the teachers, Fanola Atkinson, and her husband E. O. Atkinson, purchased the building and turned it into a residence. Mr. Atkinson ran a store next to Fairview Cemetery. Miss Gladys Mave also taught for a time at the Todd's Point School. There was also a school attended by blacks adjacent to their church. It was moved off its foundation in the same storm that demolished the church.

For many years there was a store selling groceries and gas at the junction of Todd's Point Road (Hwy. 1848), Anderson Lane, and Aiken Road (Hwy. 362). The frame building was constructed in 1938 by Walter and Kathryne P. Maddox on an acre of land given to them by Walter's father Ben Maddox. The business was sold to Gilbert S. and Ann Morrow in 1946, by them to James O. and Evelyn Price in 1955, to Clayton and Sarah Rutledge in 1971, to Tommy and Ruby Porter in 1976, to Grover and Louise Jesse in 1978, to Richard and Katie Thompson in 1986, and finally to Terry and Marcia J. Pinnick in 1987. The Pinnick's called their business the Todd's Point Country Store and in addition to gas and groceries they conducted a soup and sandwich business that could serve about fifty customers at a time. The specialties were potato soup and country ham sandwiches and there was always a crowd at lunch. Once a reporter for the *New York Times* stopped by and wrote an article about the food including a map and directions. For many months afterwards travelers came in off the interstate highway, map in hand, to eat at the store. Finally, in 1996, Marcia Pinnick decided to pursue other interests, the business closed, and the building was converted to apartments.

Across the road was Smith's Shop, a blacksmith shop run for many years by Alex Streible. In 1959 the shop was torn down and Mr. Streible moved his business into a garage built for him by J. O. Price behind the Todd's Point Grocery. Todd's Point is also the home of Fairview Cemetery which was established in 1886 and still operates as a not for profit cemetery company.

Today there are no stores or businesses in Todd's Point and only one church. Over the last twenty-five years the area has experienced a fair amount of residential growth which followed the installation of water lines by the North Shelby Water Company. For the most part Todd's Point remains what it has always been, a quiet area of homes and small farms, peaceful in its solitude.

WADDY

By Bob Spencer

T he town of Waddy resulted from rapid railroad development during the late nineteenth century. In 1886 the Southern Railway expanded east from Louisville. Former confederate Maj. W. L. Waddy, and J. W. Martin, both prominent landowners in the area, agreed to give land for the railroad right-of-way. The railroad was built primarily through the labor supplied by convicts. In 1888 Major Waddy sold one acre to the Southern Railroad at the crossing of the Harrisonville and Bagdad Turnpike for a depot. The $1.00 price included the stipulation that the depot be named "Waddy." This depot location offered entrepreneurs opportunity for success. In a short time, Waddy was the second largest town in Shelby County.

Also in 1888, the first private commercial building was built. It was a blacksmith shop. A flourmill was built in 1890, operated for ten years, burned down, and was never rebuilt. The post office, which seemed to have been in every public building, opened in 1890; the first postmaster was Tom Waddy. In 1900, a rural free delivery was started with J.B. Carpenter as the first carrier. Carpenter traveled a distance of 21 miles and served 75 boxes. His route included Harrisonville, Pea Ridge, Southville, and

Hempridge. The present post office was built in 1967 and currently has two carriers with 850 combined boxes including some in Anderson, Franklin, and Spencer Counties. Mrs. Charles (Peggy) McCormack served as Postmistress from 1936 through 1976 and notable carriers were Walter Cassidy and Middleton Jesse.

Along with every community is a general store. Stores came and went, and at one time Waddy boasted five, each doing good business. At present, Waddy has two stores, Linda's Grocery at the corner of KY 395 and McCormack Lane, and the Waddy Mini-Mart located at the intersection of KY 395 and Fairview. Both of these stores are at sites that have contained stores since the town's beginning. Other early commercial enterprises were the drug store, a canning factory, creamery, and millinery shop.

Prior to Waddy's establishment in 1888, the religious needs of the area were served by Pigeon Fork Baptist (1825), Mount Vernon Baptist (1845), and Beech Creek Baptist. In 1890, Waddy Christian Church was founded and two years later Waddy Baptist Church was built. In 1916, Hempridge Baptist was erected. With the exception of Beech Creek Baptist, all of these churches are active. Additionally, Sunrise Valley and New Life Baptist have joined the community of churches.

Elm Hill and Lone Oaks schools provided the educational needs. Citizens of the community, seeing the need for better schools, banded together and organized stockholders to raise funds for a building. The stock company was composed of Dr. C.P. Johnson, R. R. Sandusky, Joe Campbell, W.T. Snider, A.M.D. Middleton, T. M. Waddy, G. W. Waddy, George W. Scott and George W. Robertson. The school began in 1890 in a two-story building. John W. Withers was chosen as teacher. The course of study was based on a preparatory ten weeks college term. It remained in operation until 1892 when Withers resigned. In 1896, R. A. Burton purchased the property and became president of the Central Normal Academy. He served in this capacity until 1902. Additional buildings were erected and from 1903 until 1911, Professor E. J. Paxton was president of Central Normal.

In 1915, Shelby County erected a new school combining Lone Oak and Elm Hill. Paxton was its principal. This wooden structure burned and in 1920 a new brick school was built. In 1922, Paxton was named Shelby County Superintendent and his replacement was W. R. Martin. "Mister Roy" Martin was principal for 40 years. Among teachers at the school were Posey Brown who served in the Shelby County School system for 51 years, Kitty Garrett, Emma Sanford, Joe Donavan, Bill Hedden, Nancy Bohannon, Mitchell McFarland, and Christine Neblett.

The Shelby Sentinel, 1902.

The Bank of Waddy, the Post Office at left, and the Christian Church at right.

The Shelby Sentinel, 1902.

Solomon's Store was established in Waddy by Joe Solomon in 1900.

About 1894, Waddy was incorporated. The trustees were L.W. Ditto, Dr. J.F. Jesse, John W. Sullivan, H.A. Campbell, J.F. Mahoney and J.S. Downs. The initial office holders were Mayor E.B. Nash, Police Judge E.J. Paxton, Marshall C.T.Tucker, Clerk E.R. McCampbell, and Peace Officer Shelby McClain.

The newspaper *Waddy Enterprise* began in 1894, with the motto, "Push and Progress." The paper was dedicated to the news and business interests of the community.

In 1890, the Waddy Deposit Bank was opened with George W. Waddy as president and R.R. Sandusky as cashier. When the bank burned in 1897, a new bank was started with L.W. Ditto as president and Boyd Hancock as cashier. Due to financial problems, it did not succeed. In 1903, the Citizens Bank was organized as a branch of the Citizens Bank of Shelbyville with W.H. Tipton as president and C.E. Frye as cashier. This bank operated for six years and then was made a private bank under the name of the Citizens Bank of Waddy. E.W. McCormack was elected president and E.E. Frye, cashier. A new brick-veneer building was erected in 1920. In 1955, the bank was merged with Shelby County Trust Bank and following that institution's merger with the Commonwealth Bank, the branch at Waddy was closed in 2003.

The boom years of the 1890s and early 1900s gradually declined and Waddy became a rural, as opposed to commercial, town. Farming became the primary source of income. Tobacco and dairy were the two stables of the community.

In 1951, a fire burned the Smith and Garrett Store and Waddy Christian Church and threatened nearby homes. Shortly afterward, the East Shelby County Volunteer Fire Department was established, with James Sampson as chief and headquarters at the Peytona Garage on U.S. 60. The department still serves Waddy, while Waddy formed its own volunteer fire department in 1967. B. Shouse was chief.

Probably the greatest impact on the area was another large transportation project. That was the construction of Interstate 64 one-mile north of Waddy. The portion of I-64 in the Waddy area was started in 1958 and completed in 1961. The effects of the new road rendered both Louisville and Lexington and cities in between very accessible. As a result, the area has had a housing boom. Much farmland has been turned into residential housing, but Waddy enjoys a small town atmosphere, with many of the original homes and businesses still standing.

WHO'D' A THOT IT HILL

By Sally B. Roach Nicol

Who'd'a Thot It Hill took its name from the presumed reaction of long-ago travelers on Jail Hill Road to a house on a hillside. "Who'd'a thot to build a house there?" they supposedly said at the sight of the little house precariously perched above Clear Creak. Built in the 1880's, the house was 40 feet long and 15 feet wide, with a rock foundation.

Occupants of the house are lost to history, except the final one, a bootlegger who was chased away. The house toppled over around the end of World War I.

Who'd'a Thot It Hill was included in an early 20th century novel called *Sandy* by Alice Hegan Rice, a Shelbyville native. The late Bennett Roach, editor and publisher of the *Shelby News*, used the name "Who'd' a Thot It" for his weekly column on local history, opinion and events. Who'd'a Thot It Hill is also known as Jail Hill.

Jail Hill bridge over Clear Creek, looking down "Who'd a Thot it Hill." This iron bridge replaced the earlier wooden covered bridge.

Shelby County Public Library, Williams Studio photograph, from Peggy and Alwyn Miller.

A tobacco field at James Guthrie's farm, early 1900s.

CHAPTER THREE

FARMS & FARMING

CATTLE

By B.J. Nethery

The raising of cattle has been a major part of Shelby County's growth and economic well being for more than two centuries. The early cattle, mostly "mongrels" that accompanied settlers, were valued for milk and draft purposes. Little importance was attached to their meat value because wild game was plentiful. The shift toward commercial livestock production began about 1794.

Early marketing was a challenge, however. Professional drovers herded cattle and other livestock to markets in the east and later to southern outlets. These early cattle needed speed, hardiness, long legs, and plenty of bone to trail hundreds of miles to market.

The first significant dirt road in Kentucky originated in Maysville and passed through Lexington, Frankfort, and Shelbyville, to Louisville. Drovers frequented this route, allowing smaller producers to sell to or acquire stock from them. Bourbon Stockyards, opened in 1834, was one of several that operated in Louisville. Until its closing in 1999, it provided producers a close terminal market for their livestock.

In the early nineteenth century, Shelby agriculturist Col. Charles S. Todd encouraged others to plow less and establish grasses as a forage basis for supporting a cattle herd. Stock bloodlines improved with imports of purebred Shorthorns and Herefords later in the century.

By 1870, Shelby County had become a leading agricultural county with farms diversified in livestock and crops. Cattle numbered 11,804 (fifth in the state); hogs 22,089 (highest in the state); and corn 1,108,605 bushels (highest in the state). Early local farmers learned that beef cattle and swine enterprises complement each other in balanced feeding. The cattle utilized the dry forages (hay and cornstalks) and pastures, whereas the hogs were fed the corn.

Beef companies, an alliance between neighbors, slaughtered cattle in the cool months and divided the meat among the members. Before refrigeration, this was a means of utilizing the meat in a timely manner. However, the advent of the railroad, especially in the 1880s, revolutionized this small-scale local operation. Now cattle and milk could be transported to market in a timely manner. Many drove their cattle to nearby depots for shipment, generally to Louisville.

The creation of the University of Kentucky's Extension Service in the 1920s led to improved farming practices and advanced livestock production. In 1925, the Dairy Herd Improvement Association (DHIA) was formed. This allowed dairymen to weigh milk and sample butterfat of individual cows. The record-keeping program resulted in improved production, breeding, and efficiency in the dairy industry. The records provided purebred breeders a tool to market cows and bulls from high producing dams.

The introduction of alfalfa in 1910, Korean Lespedeza in 1925, and Kentucky 31 fescue in the 1940s advanced the forage base and production of both beef and dairy cattle. Four-H and Future Farmers of America club members have had an impact on the introduction of purebred cattle genetics into their familys' herds. Many a Shelby County club member has used that first 4-H heifer calf to build a foundation for his herds. All breeds have enjoyed the benefits of improved veterinary medicine and preventive health practices developed throughout the 20th century.

Robert Samples with his Hereford 4-H Club project in the 1960s.

Beef cow numbers (14,000) outranked dairy cows (13,700) for the first time in 1980. The mass exodus from dairying in the county in the 1990s is reflected in the 1998 figures: beef cows 17,000 and dairy cows 5,000. Many dairies simply changed their operations to beef cattle. Some have bred their dairy cattle to beef bulls and used the resulting progeny for their foundation beef herd.

Nature often worked against the cattle farmer. The droughts of 1984 and 1999 were disaster years for Shelby County farmers. The winters of 1977, 1978, and 1996 are long etched in the minds of those who endured the freezing temperatures and battled snowdrifts to feed cattle.

In the new millennium, cattlemen must produce beef that fills consumer demands in quality and consistency. Composite breeds are the wave of the future. In spite of that, the dairy and cattle producers who derive their sole income from the family farm are becoming the rarest breeds in Shelby County.

SADDLEBREDS

By Redd Crabtree and John David Myles

Shelby County has played an integral part in the history and development of the American Saddlebred Horse, the only breed of horse Kentuckians claim to have originated in the Commonwealth. Today's Saddlebred evolved from the family "using" horse that trotted the family to church and social gatherings before the advent of the automobile. Saddlebreds provided the basic form of transportation for peddlers, military men, doctors, farmers, and business men who had no other form of transportation.

The custom of showing horses grew from individual pride of ownership, natural to men and, as it relates to horses, especially natural to Kentuckians. As time progressed, neighbor began competing with neighbor for the right to boast about his good horse. Over time, the competitions grew to include horses from other counties and states. To fill their transportation needs and succeed in competition, early horsemen developed the stylish, high-headed, strong, sure footed, easy gaited American Saddlebred Horse.

Shelby County was home to several pioneer Saddlebred breeders. One of the original foundation sires, Davey Crocket, stood stud here from 1840 to 1845 for the Richard and I.W. Moody family. Col. Henry T. C. Giltner and Lewis S. Ellis were other early breeders. The early importance of Shelby County breeders, traders, trainers, and horses is reflected in the listing of Shelby County horses as the Number I stallion and mare when the National Saddle Horse Breeders Association Register was established in 1891. The Number I stallion was Monte Christo, owned by Jake Crenshaw and bred by the Hopkins brothers. W. P. McCorkle's Bellaire was the Association's Number I mare.

Ed W. McCormack's Chester Dare was perhaps the most famous locally. McCormack, of Waddy, purchased him from J. C. Graves of Woodford County after the four-year-old won the Grand Prize at the St. Louis Fair in 1886. The St. Louis event, established in 1856, was the first national show for saddlebreds. Chester Dare, a mahogany bay, 15.3 hands high, was reported by The Shelby Sentinel in 1902 to be a sire in the combined class "without an equal in the world." He was listed as Number 10 in the Association Register.

The National Saddle Horse Breeders Association was the first horse breed association established in the United States. The name was changed in 1899 to the American Saddle Horse Breeders Association. The early records of the Association are now maintained in the American Saddlebred Museum at the Kentucky Horse Park and the Association has its offices in Lexington.

At the beginning of the twentieth century, Col. Harry Weissinger and his son established Undulata Farm and raised the prominent stallion American Born. During the ownership of the Meyer family, World's Champion Stallion Beau Gallant stood stud at Undulata and sired Gallant Guy, a four time World's Champion who stood stud at Hayfield Farm. Charles Cook of Shelbyville was considered a great trainer. He developed the 1926-29 World's Champion Three Gaited Mare, Jonquil, which is considered the original three gaited American Saddlebred show horse. Oscar Gibbs and Gilbert Phillips were also noted trainers.

Shelby County Public Library, *The Shelby Sentinel*, 1902

Chester Dare, 1902

Shelby County native Robert Alexander Long had a major impact on the breed at the national level. After leaving Kentucky, he amassed a considerable fortune in the timber industry in Louisiana, Texas, and Washington. He settled in Kansas City, Missouri, and established an extravagant horse farm there. He exhibited his horses at the Shelby County Fair and in Louisville and owned World's Grand Champion Chief of Longview and other fine horses. He was interested in Hackney Show Horses and imported a number from England.

Although the Charles Hedden family had established Twin Springs Farm at the northeast corner of the Mount Eden and Hooper Station roads in 1950, it seemed that Shelby County's glory days as a saddlebred center were waning in the Mid-Twentieth Century. However, in January 1957, Helen and Charles Crabtree and their son, Redd, opened their original stable on Old U.S. 60 west of Simpsonville. Over the years since, Crabtree Farms has grown in both size and reputation along with the saddlebred industry in Shelby County. Three time World's Grand Champion Yorktown was foaled at Crabtree Farms. 1976 World's Grand Champion Will Shriver was trained there. In addition to 28 World's Champions, six other World's Grand Champions— Beacon Hill, Belle Elegant, Cora's Time, Glenview's Mandala, Ronald Reagan, and Supreme Airs—are associated with the farm. In addition to filling their trophy cases, the Crabtrees have worked tirelessly to expand Shelby County's role in the saddlebred industry nationwide and to recruit others to establish farms in the county. An early recruit was New York artist Ralph Hunt Sidway who established Falconwood Stable on Taylor Wood Road south of Simpsonville in 1968. Copper Coin Farm, north of Shelbyville Road near the Jefferson County line, was established in the same year by Midge Waggoner. Over the years, notable trainers Don Harris, Jack Nevitt, and John Biggins operated from the farm. Other trainers, owners, and riders from other distant places such as California, Kansas, and Louisiana have been drawn to the unique environment of Shelby County.

In 1975, Marilyn Fields MacFarlane established Walnut Way Farm on Shelbyville Road west of Shelbyville at the old Petrou farm. The farm not only boasts fine saddlebreds but also Hackney/Harness ponies and Friesians. Ms. MacFarlane was the first woman to win the World's Grand Champion Roadster to Bike Class in 1995 with Shining Brightly. She has trained World Champions in every performance division of the World's Championship Horse Show and has instructed riders who have won World's Championships in every equitation division from 8 & Under to Adult. Some twenty-two World's Champion horses have been associated with the stable over the years.

Ed "Hoppy" Bennett entered the saddlebred business in Shelby County in 1971 at Bennett Farms on Taylorsville Road. In 1980, he relocated to the south side of Shelbyville Road near Scott's Station. In 1999, he relocated yet once more to Undulata Farm where he has undertaken the Herculean task of returning it to its glory days.

Hoppy's brother and sister-in-law, R. H. and Leslie Arbury Bennett, have also been part of the circuit since 1980. R. H.'s company, Richfield Video Productions, has brought modern technology to the show circuit, making videos across the country for trainers and owners. Leslie's specialty is developing young horses,including World's Champion Undulata's Perfect Gift. Along the way, the Bennetts have been instrumental in building the Shelbyville Horse Show into a nationally recognized event.

Don and Stan Harris opened their stable at Hayfield Farm west of Simpsonville on Shelbyville Road in 1977 and in the following twenty years compiled an enviable record on the show circuit. Don rode Imperator to the Five Gaited Grand Championship in 1980, 1981, 1985, and 1986. He repeated the achievement in 1993 with Protegé. He guided Gift of Love to the World's Three Gaited Championship from 1975 through 1978 and repeated that achievement in 1982 and 1983 with Sultan's Starina. In 1997, Harris moved his stable to the Charles D. Smith farm east of Simpsonville on Shelbyville Road.

After working at Copper Coin, John Biggins established his own stable in 1982 on the Noland Pike north of Simpsonville. Over 25 World's Champions have been trained at the stable. John's wife, Renee', is a highly respected equitation instructor, having had Tate Bennett, Hoppy and Jane Bennett's daughter, and Rebecca Crabtree, Redd and Helen Crabtree's granddaughter, among her outstanding students. Koller Stables, established in 1985, is located nearby. From there, Jim Koller has trained World's Grand Champions Buck Rogers, Onion, and Garland's Dream.

The grandest saddlebred operation in Shelby County is Golden Creek Farm, home of Mary Gaylord. Located east of Simpsonville on the south side of the Shelbyville Road, the farm features a white-columned ante-bellum house and white barns and run-in sheds dotting its rolling, manicured acres. It is the very vision of a Kentucky horse farm.

The property was purchased by the Gaylord family of Oklahoma in 1985 and Mary took up residence in 1988. Mary's family owns Gaylord Communications and she first became enamored with Shelby County through the Crabtree family at whose farm she kept her horses until 1996. Since that time, she has shown under the banner of Premier Stables.

Mary holds the record for the most wins of the Ladies' Five Gaited World's Championship.

She has won the Open Five-gaited Mare Stakes twice riding Santana Lass with whom she is immortalized in bronze across from the Shelby County Fairgrounds. In addition to saddlebreds, Golden Creek has had ten World's Champions among its string of Hackney, Harness, and Roadster ponies.

In addition to their work with Mary Gaylord, Rob and Sarah Byers have developed Premier Stables into the dominant teaching and training operation in the county. Riders under their tutelage regularly show at the American Royal and the National Horse Show finals in addition to the World's Championship in Louisville and have won virtually every riding championship offered. Jill Brainard, Kelly Gilligan, Kate Harvey, Nancy Orschein, Matthew Williams, and Adolph Zell have won World's Grand Championships in Senior Saddle Seat Equitation, Mr. Zell having achieved this honor twice. Their stable, originally part of Hayfield Farm west of Simpsonville on the north side of Shelbyville Road, has also been home to the great Five Gated Mare, Face Card, winner of the Open Five Gated Mare Stake at the World's Championship.

Numerous other stables are located in the county and hundreds more horses dot the landscape and provide pleasure to the their owners, riders and passers-by alike. The stables have a major impact on the local economy and provide national recognition to Shelby County. They serve as a continuing reminder of the county's agrarian past. It may well be that as the Saddlebred Capital of the World, Shelby County, through an industry it helped create, may be able to cling to an important part of its past.

Courtesy of Jamie Donaldson, photographer, and Undulata Farm.

Undulata's Perfect Gift, with Leslie Bennett riding at the Indiana State Fair in 1996.

SANTANA LASS

By John David Myles

The equestrian statue located at the convergence of Shelbyville's Main and Washington Streets at the entrance to the fairgrounds was created by Bluegrass sculptor Gwen Reardon. She is hardly a stranger to rendering the horse in bronze. Her depiction of a thoroughbred race in Lexington's Thoroughbred Park features seven horses with jockeys barreling toward the finish line. For Shelbyville, she has created a portrait of Mary Gaylord's Santana Lass.

Santana Lass had quite a show campaign. Trained and shown at various times by Mary Gaylord and Redd Crabtree, she won the first of her twelve world championships in 1988. In 1990, 1991, and 1992, she was Reserve Grand Champion at the Kentucky State Fair. She is ridden by Mary Gaylord in full show habit topped, appropriately enough, by a Derby hat. Unlike her more monumental predecessors, Santana appears caught in mid stride, as if in the show ring. She is holding her left front foreleg in the exaggerated arch of her breed. Her head is high and her tail flows in the breeze.

The statue was cast by the lost wax method at the Shidoni Foundry in Tesuque, New Mexico, near Santa Fe. For Shelbyville's statue, Reardon prepared a clay model or maquette approximately three feet tall. The foundry then made a full sized model with a steel armature covered in clay. Once completed, the model was covered with a rubber compound and plaster. When removed from the model, the sections of plaster formed the mold for the final product.

When reassembled, the interior of the plaster mold was coated with melted wax. The plaster was then removed, and the wax model was covered inside and out with a liquid ceramic solution and dipped in fluidized sand. This process was repeated until the sand was approximately one quarter inch thick. At this point, the mold was placed in a burn-out furnace to melt the wax, leaving a hollow shell. Molten bronze was then poured into the cavity from which the wax was lost, hence the name. Once the bronze cooled and hardened, the piece was assembled, burnished and finished.

If this sounds time consuming and complicated, it is and this brief description omits mention of the spruels, vents, and funnel necessary to ensure that the bronze reaches every portion of the mold. Also, a statue the size of a horse will be cast in a number of pieces (sixteen in this instance) which must then be assembled into a seamless whole. However ancient and time-consuming, this is still the process best able to replicate artistic detail in a medium able to withstand the elements for centuries. When one goes to this much trouble, one wants it to last. Thanks to the generosity of the Gaylords, Santana will be announcing that Shelbyville is saddlebred country long after the internal combustion engine has been supplanted by the next great technological innovation, whatever it may be.

World champion Santana Lass was owned by Mary Gaylord. Bronze sculpture by Gwen Reardon.

Photograph by John David Myles.

Tobacco

By Roy V. Catlett

Burley tobacco was named for the Burleigh family of Maryland on whose plantation the first strain was grown. Tobacco was first grown in the Jamestown Colony in 1612. Records indicate it was grown in Kentucky near Owensboro in 1832. Writings from Ben Allen Thomas II, indicate that it was first grown on the Thomas Farm in Shelby County in 1882, with yields of 1,000 to 1,500 pounds per acre.

The marketing of tobacco prior to 1900 was done mostly in hogsheads in Louisville. It was hauled to Louisville by rail after having been picked up at several sites along the tracks. Companies started buying tobacco on the farm around 1900. They paid the grower a flat price for all of the tobacco in his barn. Mr. Thomas remembered a sales price of 6 cents to 8 cents per pound for an entire crop.

The first loose-leaf auction system in the state was in 1906 in Lexington. Different sources indicate that the first sales held in Shelbyville were either in 1909 or 1911. In 1911 or 1912 a group of farmers organized a small corporation and built the Star Warehouse at the site where it is located today. It was destroyed by fire a few years later and rebuilt by Cliff Walters and D. T. Long.

Local tobacco farmers did reasonably well during World War I. The 1919 crop sold for an average of 35 cents per pound with some being sold for $1 per pound. However, the large crop of 1920 averaged just 13 cents per pound with some as low as 3 cents per pound.

Because of these extremely low prices, Judge Robert Bingham of Louisville, owner of the *Courier-Journal* and the *Louisville Times*, spearheaded the organization of a marketing cooperative known as the "Old Pool" in 1921. There was no particular place in the law for cooperatives, so it was organized as a corporation. The "Old Pool" was also called the Burley Cooperative. However, this organization proved unsuccessful due to strong negative efforts by the tobacco companies. Their efforts were seen locally in Shelbyville markets by decreasing pounds sold in 1922 to 5.61 million. This was considerably lower than the 12.2 million pounds sold in 1916 before the operation of the "Old Pool".

This also marked the beginning history of the Western District Warehousing Corporation. Mr. Ben Allen Thomas, II was elected president of the Association. The Burley Association signed growers to five-year contracts. When this period was up, there were not enough signatures to continue operation. Western District and other organizations were given the task of cleaning up the operation and working out financial affairs. It has been operated in Shelbyville since that time and is the last remaining tobacco warehouse operating in Shelby County. Other efforts at farmer marketing organizations over the next few years were also unsuccessful.

Records from the County Agents Office show that Shelby County farmers began working to improve production practices soon after the office was located in the county. Agent John W. Holland reported that in 1928 Roy Smith participated in a test plot on which 1,000 pounds of fertilizer per acre were applied—a large amount compared with usual practices at that time.

Land used for tobacco gradually changed from hillsides ("new" ground) that produced a lighter weight, brighter leaf to flatter ridge land that produced a heavier bodied leaf. Yields were in the 1,200 to 1,500 pounds per acre range.

Shelby County Public Library, from Loula M. Guthrie.

Bidders gathered for tobacco sales at the Farmers Tobacco Warehouse (later the Globe Tobacco Warehouse), between 11th and Kentucky Streets, ca. 1930s. W. Henry Maddox is at right rear standing above and behind the others; Lucien Harbison is at the far right, wearing a bow tie; Sam Skinner is the tallest man at left of center in profile wearing a hat.

Practices adopted by local growers in the 1930s were the use of coke stoves for curing, ridge ventilators for curing barns, an increase in plant population, and the stripping of tobacco into grades.

The Agricultural Adjustment Act of 1938 brought about the beginning of the modern era of burley production. This act authorized the production control-price support system that, with modifications, is still in effect today. The system went into effect in 1940 and was still operating at the beginning of the twenty-first century. It brought about a renewed interest in tobacco marketing. The Shelbyville Tobacco Board of Trade was organized in 1941 to coordinate local marketing efforts. Warehouses included Star, Big Shelby, Globe, Planters, and Growers. New Burley joined the group in 1950 and Big Top in 1953. The first 4-H and FFA Tobacco Show and Sale was held in 1941 at the Star Warehouse. It was discontinued in 1996.

The first officers of the Board of Trade were John Lincoln, president; H. T. Herndon, vice-president; and F. E. Ballard, secretary-treasurer. Fulton Smith was hired as the first sales supervisor. Other presidents have been John D. Dale, Robert Parrish, Jack Thurman, Sam Crawford, Wayne Ashby, Glenn Floyd, Jimmy Nichols, and George N. Busey. Other sales supervisors have been Lindsay Batts, G. Murrell Middleton, Auldon Edwards, Dean Ellis, John A. Young, Harry Wills, and Duncan LeCompte.

Tobacco production has always required significant labor input—250 to 300 man-hours per acre. World War II decimated the county's farm labor supply. In 1942, 218 "mountaineers" were brought to the county to work in tobacco cutting and housing. German prisoners of war were also briefly used, along with local women and children. Labor continued to remain a problem, and in the late twentieth century

Hispanics became important in the county. Large numbers of workers from Central America and Mexico entered Shelby County to take up the task of cutting, housing, and stripping the tobacco. Many of these people stayed on after tobacco season. Some entered other businesses, such as the opening of new restaurants.

The insecticide toxaphene came into wide use about this time as insect problems increased. The College of Agriculture of the University of Kentucky began an active variety development program after World War II to produce varieties that were disease resistant. Local grower Louis Payne worked closely with the college for many years on this project. As a result, the 1948 Agricultural Agent's report indicated that with good management a grower could expect to produce a yield of 2,000 pounds per acre using 1,500 pounds per acre of a complete fertilizer.

In 1949 methyl bromide gained use as a product to kill weed seeds, reducing the labor involved with weeding plant beds. The early 1950s saw the use of aerial application of insecticides and the use of irrigation of tobacco fields. Farmers began using MH30 to control suckers in the late '50's. This resulted in considerable labor savings.

A few years after the one billionth pound of tobacco on the Shelbyville market was sold in 1966, a significant change in the tobacco program occurred in 1971. Shelby County growers joined with others across the belt to approve shifting the burley program from acreage to a poundage control. Price supports remained in effect and the lease and transfer of quotas was instituted. The lease program began a trend of fewer growers growing larger crops. Several growers now produce over 100,000 pounds each.

Possibly the greatest labor saving practice in tobacco history occurred in the late 1970s. University of Kentucky agricultural engineer George Duncan and others developed the method of baling tobacco to replace hand tying. Among local growers testing baling on their farms in 1977 and 1978 were Sam Rutledge, Bill Lancaster, Bob Hornback, Bruce Langley, and LeGrand Thompson. Farm Bureau strongly supported and promoted baling. It became totally accepted by farmers in about three years, saving growers and warehousemen a large number of dollars in labor.

Another drastic production practice occurred in the early 1990s. This was the change from growing tobacco transplants in outdoor plant beds to grwoing them in greenhouses.

Cooperating with the University of Kentucky tobacco specialists and County Agents in the field, test plots have been important over the years. Cooperators have included Sam Crawford, Terry Davis, Bob and Paul Hornback, Slathiel Snyder, Sam Rutledge, Harry Lee Morris, Scott LeCompte, John Rothenburger, Glenn Floyd, Doug Langley, Philip McCoun and Gary and Mary Sue Rutledge.

Over all, these improvements have meant that yields have gradually increased to an average of 2,500 pounds per acre with some growers producing over 4,000 pounds per acre. The value of tobacco production to Shelby County farms has grown to over $20 million annually at the end of the twentieth century. Over 2,500 individuals in the county own tobacco quotas.

Growers received a 21 cents per pound payment in 1999 from money awarded to state government through a settlement with tobacco companies. With strong attacks against tobacco companies continuing, tobacco farmers face a very uncertain future. Most of the crops are now sold by private contract with a tobacco company, instead of at auction in a warehouse.

BURLEY TOBACCO 1935-1998

Year	Acres Harvested	Yield Per Acre	Production (Pounds)
1935	7,340	865	6,349,000
1940	7,900	1,205	9,520,000
1945	10,730	1,050	11,266,000
1950	7,470	1,173	8,762,000
1955	5,590	1,435	8,022,000
1960	5,330	1,680	8,954,000
1965	4,790	2,230	10,682,000
1970	3,650	2,900	10,585,000
1975	4,520	2,510	11,345,000
1980	4,740	2,545	12,055,000
1985	5,060	2,500	12,655,000
1990	4,570	2,355	10,769,000
1995	4,310	2,150	9,273,000
1998	5,530	2,305	12,750,000

BURLEY TOBACCO SOLD ON SHELBYVILLE MARKET 1916-1998

Year	Million Pounds	Avg./100 LBs
1916	12.2	$16.94
1920	16.5	14.07
1925	5.8	20.50
1930	24.3	14.32
1935	15.2	18.86
1940	23.3	15.52
1945	24.4	38.81
1950	19.9	48.90
1955	20.3	60.89
1960	22.1	63.94
1965	25.6	65.02
1970	23.1	72.69
1975	29.0	108.98
1980	36.0	166.18
1985	31.7	160.06
1990	31.4	175.85
1995	27.0	185.62
1998	31.9	189.26

THE THOROUGHBRED INDUSTRY

By Jane C. Hinkle

The Thoroughbred industry has become one of Kentucky's premier industries, and, in fact, the popularity of Thoroughbred racing around the world had reached an all-time high as the 21st century began.

Though no longer needed as a means of locomotion, the horse has come to signify beauty, power, endurance, and romance to the American public.

The eye of the Thoroughbred has also come to reflect dollar bills as breeders and other judges of horse flesh and potential converse on Keeneland twice a year to bid ever increasing amounts for four-legged creatures which have yet to win a race. In fact, many never will.

Riding clubs exist for the young and old alike in every state in the union. And while Thoroughbreds are rarely the horse of choice for these riders, there are some clubs which have adopted this breed for pleasure and racing.

Looking back at the Shelbyville Tobacco Festival, a now gone, but long ago annual tradition which celebrated Kentucky's No. 1 cash crop, upwards of 200 riders paraded year after year down Main Street. These were not Thoroughbreds on parade, but, rather, pleasure horses of various breeds which helped build the momentum making Shelby County one of the top horse-breeding and training counties in the nation.

And while we're paying homage in this article to the Thoroughbred, we would be remiss if we didn't mention that there are many in Shelby County and the Bluegrass whose greatest thrill comes from the Standardbred. These trotters and pacers thunder around the Red Mile in Lexington, matching their riders and bikes in a succession of heats to win a race. All dream of winning the biggest prize, the Hambletonian.

Still, the Thoroughbred continues to stand out as the king of all equine breeds. The Thoroughbred daily delights (and sometimes saddens) the throngs of players and touts who follow their favorites at racecourses all over the world.

Breeding and racing Thoroughbreds has become an industry whose potential riches would be unfathomable to the "hardboot" of yesterday. Virtually everyone loves a sporting atmosphere, and enjoys living in a community or environment where horses have come to symbolize more gracious living.

A community such as this which draws people like a magnet is Lexington, still bursting at the seams with the dramatic growth of industry in the mid-1970s. Here at one time was an oasis of Bluegrass fields, Thoroughbred horses, and tobacco. Today, however, this land of beauty and charm has been done in by the forces of industry, and the Bluegrass fields have been covered over with vast acres of concrete, and usurped by people whose interest in horses is close to zero.

"Timely Tip," owned by Dr. A. L. Birch, ran in the 1954 Kentucky Derby and finished fourteenth.

Since the drastic change has come to the horse capital of the world, horsemen have been on the move. Some have gone south to Florida, Texas, and Arkansas, while others have moved "up east" and to other locations.

Fortunately, some of these Thoroughbred fanciers have discovered or rediscovered Shelby County, and this county has emerged as one of the top horse breeding, training, and sales centers in the world. The Saddlebred has emerged as the county's No. 1 horse, but many other breeds are being enjoyed by record numbers of riders.

Shelby County has always been known for its Thoroughbred livestock, and a colorful local history surrounds this breed. Shelby County was once known as the "Jersey Isle of America," but did not confine its livestock to purebred cattle alone.

Champion saddle horses were bred and trained here such as the world-renowned "Chester Dare" and "Monte Cristo". Scott Newman's "Karalma" was kept only a mile from Shelbyville, and one of the champion standardbred breeds of all times, "Corinne", was bred, foaled, and trained in Shelby County. Owned by John L. Hopkins, "Corinne" was sold to John Madden of Hamburg Place in Lexington. From that famous barn "Corinne" was sent to Italy where she and her daughters reigned supreme on all the racecourses of that era.

Thoroughbred horses were being raced in Shelby County long before anyone ever thought of the Kentucky Derby. At one time the most noted race in the United States took place at the Shelby County Fairgrounds. Thus, the "Sport of Kings" was a reality in Shelby County, while at Lexington horses were still being raced on the commons.

That big race in 1838 at the Shelby County Fairgrounds, which were then located four miles west of Shelbyville, pitted "Black Maria" against "The Tiger". Racing fans poured into Shelbyville for what up to that time was the most famous match race in U. S. history for a purse of $25,000.

Early Thoroughbred racing history was made at a beautiful little race course in a remote wooded area on the Shelbyville-Eminence Road, about 10 miles from Shelbyville and just inside the county line. This track was part of a national circuit which included New Orleans, Lexington, and Louisville. The local track was known as the home race track for "American Eclipse" in his latter years. "American Eclipse" was the "Man O War" of his time.

When his owners, Gilson Yates and Col. Tillett Drane, brought "American Eclipse" to Shelby County, he had previously won one of his major races at Union, Long Island. This was a match race run in May 1823, and he won two out of three heats. He ran the 12 miles in 23 minutes 50 seconds, establishing his reputation as the finest Thoroughbred in the world. He won $20,000 for his owners at Union, and for years afterwards he was bred for substantial stud fees not only to Thoroughbreds, but also to saddle and trotting mares.

"American Eclipse" died in 1847 at the age of 34, and his fame lives even today through his progeny. It is believed that "American Eclipse" is buried somewhere near the old racetrack on what was then the Drane property. But his grave has never been found despite prodigious effort to locate it.

Shelby County is known for its "Good Land, Good People, Good Living." And, according to events then and now, we might add "Fine Horses."

ALLEN DALE FARM

By R.R. Van Stockum Sr.

In 1795, Robert Polk Allen (1767-1834) arrived in Shelby County with his family, including his mother Ann Polk Allen and three brothers. They had left Frederick County, Virginia, the year after the death of Robert's father John Allen. Robert Polk Allen founded Allen Dale, now a 473-acre farm about four miles south of Shelbyville on Zaring Mill Road. John Allen's descendants have owned Allen Dale continuously since its establishment, aided by several court decisions favorable to the family.

Robert Polk Allen's brother, Washington, settled about eight miles from Shelbyville on the same road, but about four miles farther south. Two other brothers, Thomas and John Allen Jr., settled on adjoining tracts about 10 miles southwest of Shelbyville on Plum Creek, near the Old Plum Creek Church. During the early settlement days in Shelby County, three of the Allen brothers, Washington, Thomas and Robert were appointed to the prestigious positions of justices of the peace.

The first legal test to the title of Allen Dale Farm took the form of an ejectment action filed in 1815, based upon overlapping and interfering land patents. In 1825, a court-ordered consent decree required Robert Allen to give up the land in question in exchange for an equivalent parcel of land to the north. Allen had long before anticipated this conflict of title to his original tract and in 1803 had purchased a 250-acre tract to the south, which contains the core of today's Allen Dale Farm, including the farmstead and main residence.

Allen mentioned "the School House situated at the commencement of said Allen's farm" in a petition in 1832 in Shelby County Court involving an alteration in the Shelbyville-Bardstown Road (now Zaring Mill Road.) The Red Brick Schoolhouse of two rooms was well known in the community and stood on the road leading from Shelbyville to Taylorsville, five miles south of Shelbyville. In 1841, Able Harwood from New England brought his bride to teach at the school; Mr. Harwood taught the older children, and his wife taught the younger. This was before the time that public schools existed in the county, and the school attracted pupils from outside the neighborhood who wanted to attend college. Mr. Harwood's successor was Marion C. Taylor, a young man from Ohio County, Kentucky, who taught for three or four years before studying for the law. He subsequently had a successful career in law and politics. In 1850, he participated in the first filibustering expedition to Cuba, known as the Cardenas Expedition. He also served as a colonel in the Union Army during the Civil War.

When Allen died on March 16, 1834, he left all his estate, real and personal, to his son James W. Allen, subject to a one-third interest to his widow Deborah who died in 1841. He was buried in the Allen burial ground close to his mother, Ann Pollock Allen, who had died in 1805.

On September 5, 1836, Deborah and James W. Allen sold the farm for $4,439 to Robert Polk Allen's nephew, John Polk Allen (1810-87). This intra-family transaction transferred the central parcel of the Allen land, subsequently to be called Allen Dale, into the line of Robert Polk Allen's youngest brother James David Allen (1782-1859). Col. James David Allen, who arrived in Shelby County in 1798, was the great-grandfather of Sue Henning of Allen Dale Jersey cattle fame. Col. Allen was also the great-grandfather of Maj. Gen. J. Franklin Bell of Shelby County, who served as Chief of Staff of the U. S. Army from 1906 to 1910.

Two years prior to his purchase, John Polk Allen had married George Ann Baylor, daughter of Judge George Wythe Baylor and niece of Judge R. E. B. Baylor who founded Baylor University. He had commenced a successful business career at the age of eighteen and at one time owned three hemp factories including one in St. Louis and one in Shelbyville.

Bettie Allen, daughter of John Polk Allen, was born at Allen Dale on August 10, 1839. On July 12, 1864, Bettie married Thornton Meriwether, son of Richard Meriwether and his second wife, Susannah Thornton. Thornton Meriwether was the grandson of Nicholas Meriwether (1749-1828), an early Kentucky land locator, entrepreneur and settler. On September 5, 1859, Kentucky Gov. Beriah Magoffin commissioned Thornton Meriwether as "Aide to the Governor with rank of Colonel." Thornton died intestate on March 12, 1868, at the age of forty-three in the fourth year of his marriage to Bettie.

In a deed dated October 1, 1872, John P. Allen and his wife sold to their son George Baylor Allen for a sum of $17,271.62 "a certain tract or parcel of land lying in the County of Shelby on the waters of Meadow Run containing Two Hundred and Forty six acres and One Hundred and Eighteen poles...." This tract was Allen Dale, as constituted at that time, having developed from Robert P. Allen's 193-acre tract. Together with the associated deed of a forty-one and three-quarter-acre tract to his wife George Ann, who thereby relinquished her dower interest, John Polk Allen effectively divested himself of all of the real estate he owned. This deed did not, however, convey unrestricted title to George, for it was necessary for him as part of the transaction to execute notes to other members of his immediate family to assure equitable distribution of his father's estate.

This seems to have been a reasonable action by John Polk Allen, then 62 years old, who by this deed could assure that his farm would remain in the family. His son George Baylor Allen had just married Anna Robinson, a wealthy young woman from Texas, and had brought his bride to Allen Dale. On January 22, 1885, George Baylor Allen asked for Bettie's acquiescence in his plan to mortgage Allen Dale for about $3,500 or $4,000 for a period of three years, expressing his rationale as follows: "I know it is best for us both . . . it will take over three thousand dollars to pay my Bank paper that you are security—now Bett this relieves you & will make me feel proud to get even with the stinken [sic] banks."

On January 24, Bettie, disturbed despite George's assurance that he would dislike doing anything contrary to her wishes, spoke to her brother in Shelbyville. She informed him that she had read his letter and "would never consent to a mortgage going on the place to anyone but me." George directly refused her offer to accept his mortgage.

On January 27, Bettie proceeded to Louisville where she met her brother and informed him that she had come to settle the matter and if necessary to buy the property. George's response was that he had just sold Allen Dale to his wife. Convinced that her only recourse was in the courts, she immediately proceeded to the Louisville Chancery Court, accompanied by her attorney, Alex P. Humphrey, and brought suit against her brother. The next day she amended her petition to include Anna Allen as a defendant.

In her petition she alleged that her brother had not honored notes associated with his 1872 purchase from their father and owed her $7,843 plus unpaid interest (at 6%) of about $2,300, a total of about $10,143. These several notes had been signed and delivered by George Baylor Allen to Bettie, his father, his sister Drue (Drusilla), and his mother George Ann. By the time of the filing of Bettie's petition, her mother and sister had both died. Her father had endorsed his note and delivered it to Bettie. As administrator of the two estates, he also had endorsed and delivered to Bettie the note originally made out by George to Drue as well as two notes made out to George Ann. Thus, Bettie, the petitioner, had become the owner of all the unpaid notes associated with the sale.

Nearly four years after Bettie Meriwether had initiated her suit against her brother, litigation was finally completed with a decision of the Kentucky Court of Appeals taken December 1, 1888. The Judge of the Louisville Chancery Court, William S. Pryor, issued a judgment, entirely favorable to Bettie Meriwether.

A printed handbill was posted at the courthouse door in Louisville and at two public places on the property described offering Allen Dale (246 acres, 118 poles) for sale in order to satisfy Bettie's notes. A public auction took place at the Shelby County Courthouse door at 11 A.M. on February 11, 1889. Bettie Meriwether, by A. P. Humphrey, bid the sum of $8,500 and became the purchaser.

Meriwether lost no time in claiming her ancestral home. On February 11, 1890, she sold half her property at Tenth and Main Streets in Shelbyville. She sold the remaining half and her residence on March 24, 1891. She was thus free to move back to Allen Dale by the summer of 1891. It was not possible, however, for her to return to the original homestead, her father's place where she had been born. That residence, built by Robert Polk Allen, had burned down on June 28, 1885, six months after Bettie had initiated suit against her brother. Bettie's property at this time consisted of the basic Allen Dale tract of 246 acres, the 159-acre Rothchild Farm to the north which she had purchased in 1880, and the 41 3/4-acre dower tract adjacent to the Rothchild Farm which her mother had left her in 1884.

Bettie Meriwether's move back to Allen Dale in 1891 took place about four years after the marriage of her daughter Sue to Will Henning, son of James Williamson Henning of Louisville. In establishing the Henning household in New York City, where Will Henning became a stockbroker, Sue had contributed to her family's financial liquidity by disposing of most of her land in Shelby County. She sold property inherited from her father Thornton and from her uncle Richard Meriwether, who died a bachelor, including a 537 1/4-acre tract for $25,000 on November 25, 1893, and nine lots in Christiansburg, Shelby County, on October 17, 1895.

The Hennings were in a position to enjoy the better of two worlds: the world of finance and New York society on Wall Street and in Tuxedo Park N.Y. And the world of gracious country living centered about Allen Dale. Putting to good use the initiative and talent he had amply demonstrated as a young man in Louisville, Will Henning prospered not only as a stockbroker, but also as a dealer in office buildings and hotels in New York and Chicago.

However, internal stresses had developed in the marriage, perhaps fostered in part by Will Henning's single-mindedness in driving for success. Also it became apparent to Sue that her mother, aging and in poor health, operating a large stock farm with no family member present to help her, needed support and assistance. Thus, Sue shifted her focus of attention from New York to Kentucky and Allen Dale. This change of focus was reflected in 1904 by the decision to build the new Allen Dale residence.

This residence, built on the lines of an old English manor house, replaced the 19th century house that had burned. Constructed of limestone quarried on the farm, it has as a distinguishing feature: a porte-cochere, which leads through the body of the house to the gardens and service area. The Allen Dale farmstead, including the main residence and two large barns, is listed on the National Register of Historic Places. On March 24, 1905, the Shelby Record reported that, "Mrs. J.W. Henning of New York is expected here...to see her mother, Mrs. Meriwether, and their handsome new summer home which is fast approaching completion."

Courtesy of R. R. Van Stockum, Sr.

The house at Allen Dale Farm, built in 1904 for Mr. and Mrs. James W. Henning.

Susanne, the Hennings' only child, was raised in Tuxedo Park and had developed into a beautiful and popular young lady. Like her parents, she was no stranger to Europe where she demonstrated curiosity, fortitude, and endurance. In 1902, for example, under the heading "DARING FEAT OF FAIR ALPINIST", the New York Herald reported that Miss Suzanne (sic) Henning of Tuxedo Park, aged 14, had ascended La Diavolezza, an alpine peak.

In the spring of 1908, while at the home of her parents in Tuxedo Park, Susanne had met a Frenchman from a revered military family. Marquis Antoine (Tony) de Charette de la Contrie was the only surviving child of Gen. Baron de Charette, legendary hero of France, and Antoinette Polk from Tennessee, niece of Gen. Leonidas Polk, the Confederate's famous "Fighting Bishop."

The acquaintanceship between Tony and Susanne developed quickly into romance. By the spring of 1908 Sue Henning had become alarmed. She wrote Tony's mother, Antoinette Polk de Charette: "Your son tells me he has yours and his father's permission to pay his addresses to my daughter, Susanne." She observed that Susanne was very young, inexperienced, and not ready for marriage: "Having been brought up with every indulgence, her father's failure in Wall Street a year ago found her little prepared to meet the change of fortune."

Sue Henning became adamant in her disapproval of the impending marriage, feeling that because of her husband's straitened finances such a marriage was not economically viable. Nevertheless, Susanne traveled to France where on her 21st birthday, July 29, 1909, her engagement to Marquise de Charette was announced at La Basse Motte, the family's chateau in Brittany. Sue Henning refused to attend this event and expressed her disapproval of the engagement. She subsequently refused to attend the wedding, a noteworthy social event, held at St. Patrick's Cathedral in New York City on November 11, 1909.

From 1907 to 1928, Sue Henning was owner and breeder of a prize-winning herd of registered Jersey cattle at Allen Dale. In October 1907, Mrs. Henning imported 80 head of registered Jersey cattle from England at a reported cost of $100,000. Accompanied by W. L. Scott, a Jersey cattle expert, Sue visited the Isle of Jersey where each animal was selected after personal inspection and examination of their pedigrees. Two of the herd, purchased from Baron Rothschild, had never failed to capture prizes in cattle shows in England. Mrs. Henning and Mr. Scott accompanied the animals on their ocean voyage to assure their safe passage.

About 1907, Henning had asked Lexington horseman James Ben Ali Haggin if he could recommend someone to take care of her horses. He recommended Ernest Powell, an African American, who had been groom to Salvator, his famous racehorse from his Elmendorf Farm, holder of the world's record for the mile. That year, or in 1908, Powell brought his wife Carrie and his three children to Allen Dale where they lived in a beautiful eight-room log cabin close to the main residence. Ernest and Carrie would live at Allen Dale for more than twenty years, seven more children being born there. Several of their children, having had successful careers, have visited Allen Dale to provide additional insight into the operation of Allen Dale Farm and the personality and managerial philosophy of Sue Henning.

In 1914, Allen Dale's Raleigh became the national grand champion Jersey bull at the National Dairy Show. Under the direction of Henning, who became the first woman to serve on the board of the American Jersey Cattle Club, Allen Dale Farm became nationally and internationally renowned. Yet, Sue Henning, although winning many prizes in state and national competition, possessed insufficient capital to continue this expensive operation. The failure of her husband on Wall Street in 1911, and the death in 1921 of her supporter C.I. Hudson, a New York City financier and owner of a prize Jersey herd himself, hastened the farm down the road toward insolvency.

In 1923, Mrs. Henning mortgaged her life interest in the farm, which had been left to her by her mother Bettie Allen Meriwether. In 1924, following a decision of the Shelby Circuit Court, which awarded her a fee simple title, she mortgaged that interest also. Then in 1926, the Court of Appeals of Kentucky, in a landmark decision overruled the Shelby Circuit Court, holding that Sue Henning did not own the fee simple title. Thus the farm itself, as opposed to the life interest, was protected from creditors and preserved for the heirs. Henning was required by her creditors to leave Allen Dale in 1928, vowing until her death in 1933 that she was "going back to Allen Dale." She was never allowed to return.

Upon her mother's death, Susanne Henning, Marquise de Charette, acquired life interest in the 406-acre main tract of Allen Dale Farm and title in fee simple to the northerly adjoining 67 1/2-acre Meriwether tract. Returning from France, she lived for several months at Allen Dale, subsequently leasing a Park Avenue apartment in New York City where she lived with her life-long supporter and benefactor Lulie Henning, her aunt. In January 1964, she deeded the acreage that she owned outright to her only child, Susanne, who had married Brig. Gen. Ronald R. Van Stockum, U.S. Marine Corps. On her mother's death later that year Susanne Van Stockum acquired title in fee simple to the rest of the farm and in 1970 took up residence at Allen Dale with her husband and family. At the time of this writing Allen Dale Farm remains in the family, with the title ultimately resting in the hands of Sue Henning's great-grandchildren, all directly descended from Ann Pollock Allen who died in 1805 and lies buried on the property.

BOOKER BROOK STOCK FARM

By Frederika Clore

Booker Brook Stock Farm is on Clore-Jackson Road, formerly known as Ballardsville-Christiansburg Road and renamed in the early 1990s. It has been owned continuously by the descendants of Joseph Hornsby from England, who was a settler of Williamsburg, Virginia. Joseph Hornsby married Mildred Walker, daughter of Dr. Thomas Walker, a Kentucky explorer. They had five children, one of whom was Joseph Walker Hornsby. After the death of his wife, Joseph Hornsby came to "Grasslands" in Shelby County, with his family.

His son, Joseph Walker Hornsby was married in 1808 to Cynthia Allen. They accompanied his father Joseph Hornsby to "Grasslands." They had ten children, one of whom was John Allen Hornsby.

John Allen Hornsby married in 1838 Julia Ann Booker, the daughter of Col. Richard Booker, an officer in the Black Hawk War of 1832. Booker's land grant included what became Booker Brook Stock Farm and the Giltner farm on Smithfield Road, Highway 322. In 1845, he deeded the farm to his son-in-law, John Allen Hornsby, and daughter, Julia Ann, who had six children, one of who was Thomas Lewis Hornsby.

In 1882, Thomas Lewis Hornsby married Mary Louise Baskett. He inherited his share of his father's farm in 1886. He then bought the rest of the farm from his sister Cordelia H. Calloway in 1887 and from his sister Cynthia H. Hudson in 1890, bringing his total land holdings to over 400 acres. Thomas L. Hornsby and Mary L. Hornsby had five children, including Nan Baskett Hornsby.

Nan Baskett Hornsby was married in 1925 to Thomas L. Clore. They inherited a portion of the farm from her mother in 1958 and purchased the remainder from Nan's sister, Louise H. Harris and brother John A. Hornsby. They had two children one of whom was John A. Clore.

John Allen Clore married Frederika Garriott Gillespie. In 1968, they and their one son, K. Alan Clore, acquired the farm. Frederika and K. Alan Clore are the present owners.

Courtesy of Frederika Clore.

Southdown ewes at Booker Brook Stock Farm in 1931.

Thomas L. and Nan H. Clore are buried at Cave Hill Cemetery in Louisville. John Allen Hornsby, Julia Ann Booker Hornsby, Thomas Lewis Hornsby, Mary Louise Baskett Hornsby, and John Allen Clore are buried in the Eminence, Ky. cemetery.

The farm includes Hornsby Bridge, which spans Fox Run Creek. Built in 1903 of limestone with a concrete base, the bridge is unusual in that its three self-supporting arches were built diagonally to conform to the flow of the creek.

BROWNLEA FARM

By Mona Brown

The Cameron Brown Farm, better known as Brownlea, holds a distinct place in the history of Shelby County. This fertile land lies about three miles north of the county courthouse along KY 55 and Clear Creek.

Cameron Brown, the son of John Cameron Brown and Sarah Ann Waters, was born May 6, 1856, in Shelby County and died January 27, 1944. He married Mary Brown King, daughter of Edwin Pierce King and Mary Chenault Brown, on December 14, 1881, at the Baptist Church in Shelbyville. The King family owned substantial land acreage some two miles up the road toward Eminence from Brownlea.

Mary and Cameron built the present house at Brownlea, and it was there John Edwin Brown was born and lived his entire life. He spent a great deal of time in Shelby County farming and commuted for years as a banker to Louisville. John married Sarah Elizabeth Logan of Danville, Ky., daughter of Frank T. and Mattie McDowell Logan, on May 24, 1911. They had one son, Edwin Logan Brown, born February 16, 1916, at Brownlea where he lived his life and died on June 15, 1985.

Logan was married to Mona Bosworth Lewis, daughter of William Miehe Lewis and Stella M. Highsmith, in 1945 in Texas. He had completed his tour of combat missions in England during World War II. They had two sons, E. Logan Brown Jr., born February 16, 1947, and William Lewis Brown, born July 31, 1948. Lewis now owns and operates Brownlea, approximately 700 acres, and is also a practicing attorney. Logan Jr., is a real estate broker in Texas.

The Cameron Brown Farm is on the National Register of Historic Places and is a Shelby County Landmark. The house and 40 acres, with many old barns and various buildings, is still a working farm.

John and Logan Cameron at one time farmed 1,800 acres, including land from the King family and "Stockdale," formerly owned by the Todds. The operation included livestock, tobacco, corn, soybeans, wheat, and commercial mule production

Shelby County native Tom Wallace, editor emeritus of *The Louisville Times*, wrote about the Brown family in the newspaper in 1952: "Most of Kentucky farming families, which constituted a serene revival aristocracy and who depended upon land for their generous way of life, endeavored to continue with certain unavoidable modifications that way of life.

"A canon of the class forbade plowing a pasture between house and a highway. The Cameron Brown family reflected cultural ideals transplanted from Europe when John, after graduation from college, was sent on a European tour more or less like that of Lord Byron, for completion of his education."

With the demise of tobacco, the main cash crop for farming, and the encroachment of people and industry, the farm life as it was is no longer possible. An era of rolling farmland and farm life is fast coming to an end.

CHENOWETH FARM

By Ben Allen Thomas and Paul Latimer

Chenoweth Farm has 3,322 acres on the east fork of Clear Creek off Cropper Road north of Shelbyville. The traditional access to Chenoweth Farm is a tree-lined drive, known as "The Avenue," which is off KY 43. The catalpa-lined Avenue extends a half-mile into the east end of the farm to the historic manor house and complex of farm buildings. Chenoweth Farm remains one of the largest single-tract farms in the county and was for a hundred years at the center of agricultural development in the region.

Chenoweth is a traditional Kentucky family farm owned by the Thomas family whose ancestors built it from many smaller tracts. The original tract was a 300-acre parcel bought in 1833 by Wilson Thomas, great grandfather of the current owners. Wilson's grandfather, Morris Thomas, immigrated to the Pennsylvania colony from Wales. His son Oswald moved to the frontier outpost of Harrodsburg, Kentucky. He was successful enough to be able to buy a farm on Fox Run in Shelby County, on which he built a house and raised a large family. He soon acquired 1,400 additional acres on Fox Run, but did not expand his personal holdings beyond that. In keeping with the practice of the times, he helped his sons buy land in their own names. In this way, the Thomas family acquired several thousand acres of land and became one of the founding farm families of Shelby County.

Times changed and one of the sons, Wilson Thomas, saw that a collection of disconnected, individually owned farms was not the way to be successful in the rapidly developing region. In 1833, he bought a 300-acre tract on the east fork of Clear Creek and began the process of building Chenoweth Farm by acquiring additional land downstream. His sons, Wilson John and Ben Allen, followed their father's precept. By 1900 they had acquired over 3,000 continuous acres of land along Clear Creek downstream from the original tract. W. J. and B. A. Thomas, as they were known, were the true builders of Chenoweth Farm.

Most Kentucky family farms of the early and mid-19th century did not have formal names. They were usually referred to by the owner's name, i.e., "the Thomas farm." By the end of the century, the owners of some large farms began naming them in the manner of English estates or Southern plantations.

A dependable spring at the east end of Thomas farm had become know as "Chenoweth Spring" by vague association with an early Kentucky settler whose wife had survived a dramatic scalping. W.J. Thomas's wife Mary began using the name "Chenoweth Spring Farm," which soon turned into "Chenoweth Farm."

The only heir to this large holding was Ben Allen Thomas II, who took over management of the farm around 1920. The principal cash crop was tobacco. Tobacco had in fact funded the expansion of the farm. Growers had already suffered decades of exploitation by the tobacco monopolies when the market in tobacco collapsed after World War I. The farmers survived and eventually prospered, in large part because of the co-operative movement. Ben Allen was a leader in the agricultural co-operative movement in Kentucky, and later applied the technique to wool production and dairy farming. He spearheaded rural

The Ben Allen Thomas house at Chenoweth Farm. L. H. Gruber & Sons, architects.

electrification and served as director of several banks that financed Shelby County agriculture. Under Ben Allen Thomas's ownership and management, Chenoweth Farm became the major agricultural producer and employer of Shelby County. At its peak, it supported three dairies, a prize-winning herd of shorthorn cattle, herds of beef and dairy cattle. More than 1,000 acres of corn were raised to feed these herds. It grew hundreds of acres of tobacco. Several families lived on the farm, some of which worked under partnership with the owner.

After World War II, Ben Allen's sons, Winford and Ben Allen III, took over management and eventually ownership of Chenoweth Farm, which now produces tobacco, corn, soybeans, and contains one dairy. Although still a productive and profitable farm, Chenoweth is directly in the path of the growth of greater Louisville, which has already turned much of neighboring Oldham County into bedroom communities. Under pressure from developers, Chenoweth Farm is at a crossroad of its distinguished history.

The heart of Chenoweth Farm is the complex of buildings at the end of The Avenue. The two-story Colonial Revival mansion, built in 1900 by W. J. Thomas, was the residence of Ben Allen Thomas II and the administrative nerve center of the farm. It replaced an earlier residence on the same site. The house, which is included in the National Register of Historic Places, was built by Shelbyville designer and architect Lynn T. Gruber & Sons, who built several other large houses in the region. It is also a Shelby County landmark. The house has a root cellar and smokehouse at its rear. On the grounds are the remains of tennis courts and daffodil beds, evidence of the pastimes of former owners. To the east of the house is a complex of farm buildings - barns, drying cribs, silos, and workshops of various eras. The house that originally occupied the site was divided in two parts, both of which are still on the property. At various locations on the farm, other historic buildings remain that are at least a century old.

Chenoweth Farm is one of the finest remaining examples of creek land in northern Kentucky. Because it is such a large area of land untouched by development, it is a prime habitat for many species of wildlife. Resident species include red-tailed hawk, great horned owl, screech owl, and kestrel. Ground animals include red fox, woodchuck, cottontail rabbit, and whitetail deer. This land is a stopover for several species of migrating birds, such as the increasingly rare short-eared owl, northern harrier, Cooper's hawk, sharp-shinned hawk, and red-shouldered hawk. There are proposals currently under consideration for protecting this and other fine creek lands in an extension of the park system or a nature conservancy, but if action is not taken soon, this great natural resource will be lost.

CHESTER DARE FARM

By Mary H. Smith

Nine generations ago, Hugh McCormack served under General Nathaniel Green in the American Revolutionary War. He was awarded a large land grant and moved to Kentucky in 1798 with his wife, sons, and their families. They settled near Waddy, Kentucky, east of Hempridge, west of McCormack Road and south of the Louisville & Nashville and Southern Railroads on land rich for the growing of field grains, livestock and tobacco. It was dense with virgin woods of every variety natural to Kentucky.

Through the years many attendant families and laborers were housed there making the farm a showcase. The land was divided between the siblings of several generations until 750 acres remained in one tract owned by Edward Ware McCormack by 1891, when he married Lillie Boswell of Finchville. They lived on the farm for 28 years until 1919. At the death of E.W. McCormack, Mrs. E. W. McCormack moved to Shelbyville with her daughter Sarah Elizabeth. It remained in the ownership of the McCormack family for 188 years. Edward B. Hayes and Casper W. Hayes Jr. sold the farm in 1987.

The Chester Dare Farm was famous among people across the state and out-of-state during a 20 year period, 1890 to 1910, due to the outstanding reputation of the stallion Chester Dare, and E. W. McCormack.

DAVISLAND FARM

By Rosella Y.C. Davis

On September 27, 1902, Squire Davis purchased 309 acres on the north side of Christiansburg-Mulberry Pike (now called Cropper Road-KY 43) from W. C. and Sally Ash. On March 1, 1920, following Squire Davis' death, his widow Isabella Belle Corley Davis sold this farm to three of her children, one being Ernest Malcolm Davis, who purchased land on the east side of the farm. A short time later, E. M. Davis bought from Thomas Connell a small adjoining acreage also on Mulberry Pike. The Davis family lived in the Connell house while a large, brick house was being built. Then barns, corncribs, and other farm buildings were added for livestock. The two sons worked the farm with hired help.

The younger son, Jesse Hardin Davis, enjoyed working on the farm as a young boy, raising a small amount of tobacco and caring for a calf. He took over the farm operation after attending Western Kentucky State Teachers College (now Western Kentucky University). Tobacco, corn, soybeans, and wheat were grown. The farm also had registered Hereford and Angus cattle, sheep, hogs, horses, mules, and chickens.

In 1925, E. M. Davis bought 207 adjoining acres from Mattie Daniel Van Dyke. At public auction in 1936, he purchased 94 adjoining acres opening on the "Bellvue" turnpike from Frederick B. Davis. In 1938, E. M. Davis and J. Hardin Davis had a story and half brick house built for J. Hardin Davis on Eminence Road. On February 3, 1955, this house and 47 acres were deeded to J. Hardin Davis and his wife, Rosella Y. C. Davis.

The parcel of land has belonged to three families. In 1793, Nicholas Meriwether deeded his ground to Coleman Daniel, who in 1796 deeded it to Martin Daniel. Seven deeds passed this tract to other family members. The 1901 deed states that there is a graveyard on the property that is not conveyed but will remain with the Daniel's family. This graveyard exists today, and some tombstones have names of Wilson, Daniel, and Boone.

Following the death of Ernest Malcolm Davis and his widow, Mary Maddox Davis, J. Hardin Davis and Garland Maddox Davis operated Davisland Farm until J. Hardin Davis' health began to fail. Then they leased the farm to William Gallrein Sr. and Jr. Following Garland M. Davis' death, his heirs and J. Hardin Davis divided the E. M. Davis farm with Garland Davis' heirs, taking the main residence and improvements, along with approximately 100 acres. J. Hardin Davis took the remaining property.

From a will probated August 1991, the current owners are Rosella Y. C. Davis, widow of Jesse Hardin Davis, and his daughters, Mary Hardin Davis Stevens and Rosella Malcolm Davis Rogers. They continue to operate this land and adjoining acreage that was a part of the original farm many years ago. The farm was designated a Shelby County Landmark and received a Kentucky Bicentennial Award.

DUNBLANE FARM

By Jana Scott

The Dunblane farm, which belongs to George Simpson, is on LaGrange Road in northwestern Shelby County. Simpson's grandfather bought the 520-acre farm in 1896. According to family lore, the Simpsons came to the United States from Scotland. After traveling to many of the southern states looking for property to purchase, the family heard of this farm in Kentucky.

George Banta built the house in 1876. Clay for the bricks was taken from the farm. Stone bearing his name can still be read on the house today. The other buildings and all the stock barns and sheds were built from trees on the farm. Simpson's grandfather had a log cutter come in and help with the tree selection and cutting for the buildings. A well that was dug on the farm for the water supply cost $100 in the 1800s.

When Simpson was active, he raised cattle, sheep, and hogs and he tended tobacco, corn, beans, and hay. He was quite proud of the orchardgrass hay.

DUVALL FARM

By Margaret A. Nicholson

The Duvall Farm has been in the Duvall family since 1832. The road leading to the entrance is located on Buck Creek Road, 2.2 miles south of the Simpsonville exit of I-64 in western Shelby County. The farm is found about three fourths of a mile east of Buck Creek Road at the end of a gravel road at one time referred to as Coots' Lane. The farm contains 254 acres of gently rolling fields and is bordered on the east side by Bullskin Creek. Since the 1950s, the farm has been known as Streamvue Farm, so named by the Harvey Lee Duvall family, the current owners. Streamvue Farm became nationally renowned for its registered Holstein cattle. Currently, the Duvall family raises Angus cattle, Corriedale sheep, and grass and alfalfa hay.

The Duvall house was built between 1811 and 1815. Mareen Duvall Sr. originally purchased the property in 1832. Frances Cottingim, noted Shelby County historian, theorized that Gen. Benjamin Logan originally built the Duvall house, the Shelby Ware house on Brunerstown Road, and the Hawkins/Haggard house on KY 55, all located along Bullskin Creek, as homes for his three daughters.

Duvall family members who have owned the property include Mareen Duvall Jr., Eugene and Annie Doyle Duvall, Lee Wilson, and Gladys McAlister Duvall. Harvey Lee and Anita Coots Duvall purchased the farm in 1951 from the estate of his father, Lee Wilson. The sixth and seventh generations of Duvall descendants are currently living on the farm.

The house remains in its original state except for a new kitchen, which was built at the rear in 1983. The house is one of 12 houses remaining in Shelby County built in the Federal style of architecture. The walls are 12 inches thick, made of brick fired on the farm. The windows have nine over six panes with beveled glass. Each of the six original rooms has a fireplace and unique woodwork including chair-rail, 12" deep windowsills, and mantels. One of the front rooms has woodwork identical to that found in My Old Kentucky Home in Bardstown. All of the doors are the "cross and open Bible" design, except for the front door which is the "double cross" design. The house has a full basement composed of three rooms with limestone rock walls. All of the original hardware, which was hand crafted, is still used in the house.

Keeping authenticity in mind, the builders of the new kitchen used hand-hewn, exposed, walnut-ceiling beams, which were salvaged, from a farm building over 100 years old. The flooring is solid oak planks salvaged from the same building. The stone fireplace was rebuilt from a summer kitchen originally located behind the house.

The house was listed on the National Register of Historic Places on December 28, 1988. It is also designated a Kentucky Landmark and a Shelby County Landmark. The farm was designated a "Centennial Farm" in 1992 by the Kentucky Department of Agriculture and the Kentucky Historical Society.

Early 1800s farmhouse at the Duvall farm has been owned by members of the Duvall family since 1871.

Courtesy of Margaret Ann Nicholson.

GUTHRIE/GIRDLER FARM

By Ted Igleheart

Originally a part of Squire Boone's land holdings, by the time the Civil War ended this farm consisted of 520 acres extending from Snow Hill to what is known now as the Painted Stone Farm where Squire Boone's Station was located. A buffalo trail left its worn trace from Mullberry Creek beside the Old Eminence Road and ran due north through the farm and on past Boone's Station. It can still be seen behind the houses on the east side of Colony Drive.

Local residents can still remember the farm being called "Guthrie's Woods" when owned by the Guthrie brothers, James and E. Ralph, but tracts were sold off until it consisted of 263 acres. It was a hemp plantation and the old hemp barn is still standing (minus its old cupola) east of the house. It was also well known for breeding and selling mules. Until the 1940s, a 100-stall mule barn stood north of the slave quarters, which is still standing. In 1931, the old house burned and the farm was bought by Andrew C. Cowan, who sold the 263 acres to Walter H. Girdler, owner of Tube Turns in Louisville. He also purchased the adjoining Milton Fullenwider Farm of 119.5 acres on the Burks Branch Road facing Snow Hill (now the Clear Creek Park), making the Girdler Farm 382.5 acres.

A magnificent southern colonial plantation house, resembling George Washington's Mount Vernon home, was built on the Guthrie site and cost $100,000, a tidy sum in the Great Depression. The interior doors are 2 1/2 inches thick on four brass, ball bearing hinges. The beautiful sunburst fan light over the front door and sidelights can be seen from the highway a quarter mile away down Colony Drive. Five fireplaces with elaborate mantels grace the dining room, drawing room, two bedrooms, and the butternut paneled library. Girdler built a mahogany bar in the finished basement and a log cabin with large field stone fireplace where his poker playing buddies and dove-shooting guests were entertained. He died in 1945 and successive owners sold off more tracts until only 139 acres remained.

Hugh J. Caperton and wife Betty Woodruff purchased the farm, then operated as a dairy farm, in 1955. After returning from a tour of Williamsburg, Virginia, the Capertons stripped the wide front verandah and six columns off, removed the rear double deck screened in porch, copper cupola and dormers, and tore down the large garage with servants' quarters ("because it blocked the sunset"), giving the house the "Georgian look." It drastically altered the architecture of the stately house but it is still a beautiful home at the top of Colony Drive, with outstanding landscaping and lawn dotted with tall maples, oaks, beeches, magnolias, hemlocks, pines, firs, spruces, yews, hollys, sycamores, and rare gingkoes.

Libby and Ted Igleheart purchased 32 acres and the home and horse barn in 1964, when the Capertons divided the farm into tracts and sold them. The Iglehearts built a garage back onto the west wing of the house and subdivided the front 22 acres into lots for sale as The Colony Subdivision, retaining ten acres around the house where they fed a few beef cattle and a horse. In 1983, six acres and the house were sold to Dr. Luther Joe Thompson and his wife. The Iglehearts built a new house on the remaining 3.3 acres, which included the horse barn. The Thompsons sold their six plus acres and house after ten years to the present owners, Randall and Rebecca Kirts. The slave quarters, which must be nearly 200 years old, is now the Kirts' herb house, but at one time it housed the Oscar Fister family, tenants on the farm, and included ten children, all raised in the four room quarters. The seven foot ceiling is supported by exposed hand hewn joists with wooden pegs holding the joints together and serves as the flooring for the second level above. This old house has served human habitation for nearly two centuries.

The second house at the Guthrie-Girdler farm was built in the 1930s.

LONE COLUMN FARM

By Millard Jesse and Guthrie Jesse Jr.

Samuel Jesse originally purchased the Jesse Farm on October 3, 1827. The farm is presently owned by Millard Jesse, Guthrie Jesse Jr., and Clara Jane Jesse. Samuel and Kathryn Jesse had 13 children. Two of the children, Warner and Ephraim, were partners in farming and owned 1,200 acres of land. In addition to farming, the brothers operated a factory where they made rope for baling cotton, which was sent to Louisville to be transported south, by boat.

The farm, as it stands now, came through Ephraim G. Jesse. Many heirs had reduced the acreage so that the two sons of Ephraim G. Jesse, Millard Filmore Jesse and S.W. Jesse, were left with 412 acres. Ephraim G. Jesse acquired the farm on December 25, 1838. Millard F. Jesse acquired the farm on March 28, 1883. E.G. Jesse acquired it on February 16, 1925, and Millard and E. Guthrie Jessie Jr. got the deed to the farm on January 15, 1973.

Of the 1,200 acres, only 114 acres have been in the Jesse family since 1827. Seventy acres were in other hands for a few years, but now that acreage is owned by Millard and E.G. Jesse Jr. The only historical landmark remaining on the farm is the Jesse family cemetery.

The farm is located on KY 714, four miles south of U.S. 60. The present address is 4710 Hemp Ridge Road, Waddy, Kentucky. The farm at present contains 183 acres.

E.G. Jesse's diary states that the first Post Office and store in Hemp Ridge were just across the road from the present owner's house, and the postmaster was Warner Jesse. It also states that Ephraim and Warner Jesse were in the purebred shorthorn cattle business and, with the help of William Waddy and George Smith, the Hemp Ridge Fair was held just down the road from the present farm. It further states this was the first fair held in Shelby County.

MARAVIEW JERSEY FARM

By Larry Gravett

Maraview Jersey Farm is located on Antioch Road in Shelbyville and is owned by Mary Ann Gravett. Her grandfather, Robert J. Shipman, originally purchased the farm, on August 19, 1890. Robert D. Shipman, her father, inherited the farm in 1936, and Mary Ann Gravett acquired the farm at the time of her father's death in April 1993.

The original purchase contained 181 acres. The farm at present contains 191 acres, all of which are farmed. The major crops include hay, corn, wheat, and registered Jersey cows. Holstein Cows were added in 1986. In 1997, Mary Ann's sons, Larry and Bob, diversified some acres into the thoroughbred industry.

Originally the farm was known as Locust Dale Farm. Around 1950, the name was changed to Maraview Farm, representing the first initials of Mary Ann, Robert, and Alice Shipman. Since that time Maraview Jersey farm has won many ribbons, trophies and plaques and is known for its grand champion Jerseys not only in Kentucky, but in the surrounding states as well.

The only remaining original structure is the dairy barn, which is now used for storage. One can still see large notched log beams in the center portion. This five-generation farm has three generations living and working here, including the owner and her husband, their two sons and their grandchildren.

MONTROSE HOUSE AND FARM

By Fred D. Trammell and Jerry T. Trammell

Montrose is an historic house and farm about six miles east of Shelbyville on Trammell Road. The Greek Revival house is about 165 years old. Its early history involves the Venable, Crockett and Logan families.

Abraham Venable and his son, Abraham Jr. received numerous land grants from the British crown during the colonial era, including one roughly bounded by Mulberry and Guist Creeks and the present Trammell and Stapleton roads. The land passed from Venable Jr. to his son, James Venable, who died in 1824.

James Crockett owned about 1,000 acres along Trammell Road that bordered the Venable property. In 1828 and 1831, Crockett's son, John Edward Crockett, bought 442 acres from the Venables, perhaps because the land included springs.

John Edward Crockett built the Montrose home during the 1830s with the help of his 16 slaves. According to tradition, Scottish bricklayers laid the bricks, as evidenced by distinctive trowel marks still visible in the mortar. The house was built near a large spring, which is the present source of Andrews Creek. The old Venable Cemetery was immediately east of the house.

When Crockett died in 1845, Montrose passed to his son, John Edward Crockett Jr. One of Crockett's daughters, Maggie Crockett, married Joseph Logan in 1875. Logan's mother was James Venable's daughter.

John E. Crockett died in 1874 and his wife, Lucy, died the following year. It's possible that Maggie Crockett Logan and Joseph Logan lived at Montrose until 1889, when Lewis and Anne VanMeter bought the farm from the Crockett heirs. The Logans bought Woodlawn, the home of Maggie's uncle, Robert Y. Crockett.

The VanMeters sold Montrose in 1904 to George A. Hill, who lived there until he died in 1927. William Herndon Winchester, who was probably a speculator, bought the house and sold it eight months later to Ambrose and Mattie Dudley. After her husband died, Mattie Dudley sold the property for $14,000 in 1938 to Eleanor and Ruben Taylor.

By then, the house and farm had become run-down. Tobacco and hay were stored inside the house, which was no longer used as a dwelling. The farm had been worked to its subsoil and was badly eroded in places.

The Taylors rescued Montrose from ruin, pouring $72,000 into its restoration. The extensive job included adding an ell to the rear of the house and installing electricity, plumbing, a furnace and new roof. The Taylors also built a four-car garage, installed a new drive and a six-room tenant house and restored the slave quarters for their domestic help.

Because the Taylors did not depend on the farm for their livelihood, they were able to restore the land to its original vitality. They were educated and wealthy, with a utopian agrarian vision for Montrose. Ruben Taylor wanted to preserve old methods of farming that were disappearing. For example, plowing on the farm was done with mules or horses, not tractors. Taylor planted bluegrass, on which sheep and cattle grazed.

The Taylors moved in high social circles and routinely held social events and gatherings. Their friends included the Bingham and Belknap families of Louisville. The grounds of Montrose were meticulously landscaped, with an antique pewter fountain and peafowl strutting about.

In 1962, the Taylors sold Montrose to Fred and Virginia Trammell. For several years, Fred Trammell, later superintendent of Shelby County schools, had been in charge of Montrose when the Taylors wintered in Mexico. Ruben Taylor said he sold the property to Trammell because Trammell improved the land by working it. Virginia Trammell maintained the grounds at Montrose until her death in 1999. Fred Trammell made a new name for the farm by producing outstanding Charolais cattle.

Montrose Farm, house built in the 1830s.

Courtesy of Fred D. Trammell.

SANDERLIN FARM

By Kim Sanderlin

J. R. Sanderlin purchased his first farm on the east side of KY 55 North while he was a financial executive at Brown-Forman Corporation in 1943. He started raising tobacco, Hampshire hogs, and registered Angus cattle. Some of the Angus were exhibited at the county and state fairs. He also bred saddle horses. Oscar Gibbs and others trained these in Shelbyville. Sanderlin continued buying farms and established several dairies, milking Brown-Swiss cows. These farms were run on a tenant-landlord basis with Ed Newton as the farm manager.

After retiring from Brown-Forman, Sanderlin moved to Shelby County from Louisville in 1954. In the late '50s Sanderlin dealt with the tenants directly and replaced the Brown-Swiss breed with the more popular Holstein. In 1962, he started a dairy on the U.S. 60 farm where he and his wife lived. Through the '60s and into the '70s this dairy expanded as the other tenant dairies closed and were absorbed into this operation. During the '70s and '80s, the dairy, operated by James and Marshall Reynolds, milked over 400 cows. Sanderlin also had one other tenant dairy that milked 100 cows.

In 1974, Sanderlin's grandson Kim Sanderlin joined the operation to help manage the dairies, crops, and expanding beef-cattle operations. Sanderlin's son, John B. Sanderlin, joined the farm in 1980 and brought the dairies into the computer age. In 1984, J.R. Sanderlin died at the age of 84. In 1986, his son suffered a massive stroke. In February 1994, due to declining milk prices, Kim Sanderlin sold the dairy cows and later sold some of the farms. He continues to run a large beef cow-calf and backgrounding operation. He also raises hay and corn for the livestock and tobacco with the help of the family's longtime employees, Marshall Reynolds, Norman Brown, and David Riddell.

SLEADD FARM

By Sally B. Roach (Fay) Nicol

The Sleadd farm on Hempridge Road was given as a Revolutionary War land grant to Ezra Sleadd in the early 1800s. The family's first home was a large log house set somewhat down on the highest hill as protection from the wind.

An impressive two-story Colonial-style brick home on the top of the hill was completed about 1858. It was unique in its "T" shape as compared to the usual Kentucky "L" shape. This design, prominent in Deep South homes, made the most of summer breezes. The thick logs from the first house were used to construct a sturdy barn behind the new house.

The front of the "T" consists of four 20'x 20' rooms, two up and two down, separated by a large staircase and landing in the foyer in the center. Both the entrance foyer and the upstairs hallway have small outside porches. Brick fireplaces grace each room; downstairs floors, woodwork, and mantels are of oak, and upstairs are of poplar.

The back of the "T" has another hallway and stairs. Upstairs are two more bedrooms and downstairs are a family room and kitchen, all with fireplaces. Separating the family room and kitchen is a thick brick wall for fire protection with a pass-through window for food. Long side porches stretch for the length of the house both upstairs and down on the southwest side.

The foundation of the house is limestone and was reportedly cut and laid by an Irish stonecutter who lived on the place until the work was completed, a custom common at the time. Bricks for the house were baked from clay on the farm, and they are a soft rosy-red color. Slaves owned by Ezra Sleadd did the work. Slaves lived in frame dwellings on the farm, and one such structure was still used as a corncrib in 1968. Also still usable in 1968 was a two-seater outhouse about thirty feet behind the main house.

Ezra Sleadd was getting along in years by the time the large house was completed. His reputation as an outstanding farmer is solidified by the story that he traveled each spring to Pleasant Hill, the Shaker community near Harrodsburg, to purchase all his seeds for the coming year's crops. The farm produced corn, hay, tobacco, and a huge quantity of hemp, which insured his continuing prosperity.

He built a smaller brick home for his married daughter, about one-half mile from the main house. A sitting photograph of Ezra Sleadd was made sometime in the 1860s, and it shows a clear-eyed, bewhiskered old man, proud and confident. Reportedly he was photographed seated because he was self-conscious of his short stature.

After Ezra Sleadd's death, the farm remained in the family until 1968. Evidently there were no direct male heirs. Colonel Philip Sleadd, a great-great nephew, owned the property in the 1940s and kept it well. He grew grapes and added many botanical specimens to the grounds.

In the 1920s, '30s and '40s, the farmhouse boasted a large central furnace, and two railroad cars of coal were purchased each year off the nearby rail line a quarter of a mile away. This same rail line was used to haul milk from the prosperous dairy business on the place.

A romantic story of the early 1900s recounts that one of the Sleadd men from out-of-town visited the Hempridge Road farm often and was enraptured by a certain local belle. Their initials are scratched together on an upstairs windowpane. When it was revealed that the man was already married, she committed suicide.

By 1968, no Sleadd lived in the home, and some eleven heirs owned it. Frances Sleadd of Louisville was the only one who bore the family name. Robert and Sally Fay purchased the property and they restored the house. The property was again sold in 1977 and has had several owners since.

The Greek Revival house at the Sleadd farm.

TWIN SPRINGS FARM

By Lucinda Hedden Coffman

Twin Springs Farm, situated at the southeast quadrant of Interstate 64 and KY 53, has the distinction of being the oldest continuing American Saddlebred establishment in the United States. The main house, an Italianate Victorian brick, was built shortly before the Civil War by a Mr. Tribble from Lexington. He was married to a daughter or granddaughter of Squire Boone. Originally the farm was called Rose Hill and sat directly on the old Mt. Eden Turnpike. The toll cottage for the turnpike sat due north of Rose Hill at a spot now covered by the interstate. The walls are three bricks deep, the floor ash, the downstairs woodwork is walnut and cherry, and the original metal roof is still in good shape.

The house, which had a double central hall, was modified in the 1940s. The back ell was torn down and bathrooms were added. The barn is somewhat later, built by Col. Weissinger when he acquired the property from Tevis Stone, a relative of the Tribbles. The Weissingers used the farm as their saddle horse breeding and training center. A nephew of Col. Weissinger, Muir Sample, occupied the house late in the 19th Century. During that period the two "twin" springs at the back of the farm were enclosed in grotto-like stone work and a stone swimming pool was built below the springs. The springs were a party spot for the Weissingers. Legend has it that Col. Weissinger had his drinking water carried from the springs.

During the 1920s and 1930s Sam Hinkle's father (grandfather of Sam D. Hinkle) trained horses for the Weissingers and the Hinkles occupied the house.

The house was in disrepair when Ray and Mary Ketman bought the farm in the early 1940s. The Ketman's had two sets of twins and renamed the farm Twin Haven. Ray Ketman was a professional horse trainer and Twin Haven became a prominent name on the horse show circuit.

Charles and Virginia Hedden bought the farm in 1951 and it has been in the family since. They replicated the original ell with a two-story addition in 1959. Reduced from its original hundreds of acres to the current 124, the farm continues as a saddle horse establishment.

TUCKER FARM

By Jane Tucker

Mrs. Ray Pemberton Tucker, and her two children, Ray Moss Tucker and Jane Pemberton Tucker, own Homestead Acres. Ray Moss Tucker, Gilbert Ray Tucker and his children, Ray and Joshua, are the fourth, fifth, and sixth generations to operate the farm. It is a Kentucky Centennial Farm that dates back to the original purchase by the family in 1850. It is a Shelby County Landmark and has been listed in the National Register of Historic Places since December 27, 1988. The Joseph Hornsby Cemetery and the Plum creek Watershed Lake are located on the 607-acre farm.

Courtesy of Jane Tucker

The Pemberton-Tucker house at Homestead Acres.

William H. Pemberton, great-grandfather of Ray Moss Tucker and Jane Tucker, purchased 134 acres to begin his farm in 1850. Its log structure and noteworthy ell-shape Greek eclectic style distinguish the 149-year-old house. It was built when he brought the first of his three wives to the original 30 acres before purchasing the 134 more in 1850. He passed the property on to his widow, Mary Elizabeth (Doyle) Pemberton, in 1896. Amanda Pemberton Tucker and Earnis Tucker took ownership of the farm in 1912. Earnis Tucker and his son, Ray Pemberton Tucker, took over in 1933. Three years later, Ray Pemberton Tucker purchased the farm. Ray Tucker's widow, Annie Moss Tucker, and his children, Ray Moss and Jane acquired it in 1971.

The historic farm is located at KY 148 and Clark Station Road near Finchville and has been actively farmed throughout the years. It is used as a Holstein dairy farm and for growing corn, tobacco, and wheat. The old log barn dates back to the Civil War.

A corncrib and open truck shed is near the barn. Also near the house is the "Old Shop" which still has the dirt floor and anvil. The old "Buggy House" is now a garage. The old granary still stands as well as a shelter where the 1939 iron-wheel tractor was kept. Ray Pemberton Tucker was a dedicated farmer who worked with various farm groups, served as chairman of the Plum Creek Watershed Project and received the Soil Conservation Award. He and his wife received the Progressive Farmer Master Farmer Award in 1959. Ray Moss Tucker is married to Sallye Williams Tucker. They have two children, Gilbert Ray and Ann Hankins. His community activities have been numerous, and have included the Shelby County Board of Education and Shelby County Fair Board President.

Gilbert Ray Tucker follows the footsteps of his grandmother, Annie Moss Tucker, by also serving on the Shelby County Zoning Board for twenty years. In addition, he was first appointed to the Cattlemen's Beef Board in 1994 by the Secretary of Agriculture to represent his fellow Kentuckians on the Beef Production Board. He is the first dairyman to serve as an officer of the Beef Board. His wife Marcia Taylor also works on the farm. Ann Hankins Clark, fifth generation, received the American Farmer Award and in 1979 was the first woman to receive the American Farmer Degree.

The northeast corner of Main and Sixth Streets in 1878. George Petry's drugstore was on the corner, later the site of Slaughter and Goodman, and then Hastings Confectionery. Rowland and Heaton's Tin Store was the next store on the right, later Hall's Pharmacy, and under the awning was Randolph & Shea Merchant Tailors, later S. S. Kirk's.

CHAPTER FOUR

BUSINESSES

Shelby County Public Library, from Lou B. Finnell.

BANKS

By William E. Matthews

I n a spiritual and social way it would be difficult to imagine what Shelbyville and Shelby County would be without its churches and schools. In a material and business way, it would not exist at all without its banks.

Shelby County banks have served as landmarks of individual and community progress for more than 175 years. Every deposit is, in fact, a trust fund zealously guarded by these storied institutions.

The earliest record of a bank in Shelby County appears in the *History of Shelby County, Kentucky* by George L. Willis. According to Willis, a statement issued by the Branch Bank of Kentucky in 1850 showed that 1,000 shares of stock in that bank had been issued to Shelby County citizens. William Bullock was the president, and directors included Mark Hardin, B. F. Dupuy, John Newland, Jacob Castleman, George Waller, Isaac Watkins, John Willett, and James Moore. Dupuy was the leading shareholder (160 shares), and the only other shareholders who had 50 or more shares were Newland, John Gwathney, Watkins and the partnership of Steele & Luckett.

BANK ONE

Bank One in Shelby County is a descendant of the county's oldest in continuous operation bank, the Bank of Shelbyville. The Bank of Shelbyville, while dating back to 1869, actually had been a thriving institution for 13 years prior to that. It was then known as the Branch Bank of Ashland, its charter having been approved in 1856. The first president was Josephus H. Wilson. Gordon Logan, J. C. Beckham, Matthews Hall, Richard Randolph, Jack Frazier, and Ruby Stivers Conn followed. Conn retired in 1990. Presidents who succeeded her were Bob Rigney and Bob Taylor.

The Bank of Shelbyville was sold to Liberty National Bank of Louisville in 1988, and Liberty National, in turn, was acquired by Bank One of Indianapolis in 1994. The bank, which had operated on the southeast corner of Sixth and Main Street for so many decades,

The Bank of Shelbyville and Armstrong Hotel at Sixth and Main in 1909.

Ellis McGinnis Collection, courtesy of Michael McGinnis.

had its doors closed for good in 2001, but Bank One retained a branch location on Boone Station Road.

In 2001 Bank One was the fifth largest bank in the nation and the second largest in Kentucky. The bank had 73 offices in the Bluegrass State, including branches in Louisville, Lexington, Richmond, Danville, Elizabethtown, Owensboro, Shelbyville, and Crestview.

CITIZENS UNION BANK

In 1888 the Citizens Union Bank (CUB) was incorporated as the Citizens Bank. Its first president was Charles Kinkel and its first cashier J. C. Burnett. The capital stock was $50,000. Successive presidents included James Guthrie, P. J. Foree, W. H. Tipton, Charles A. Randolph, Stewart McBrayer, Middelton Phillips, John S. Mathis, and Billie Wade.

This bank, whose history is intertwined with that of several other Shelby County banks, was originally located at 527 Main Street in downtown Shelbyville. G. D. Banta of Henry County who had submitted the lowest of several bids constructed the original building. He was also known for building the Presbyterian Church at Seventh and Main Streets in Shelbyville. *The Shelby Sentinel* reported in 1888 that the "building inside and out is handsome and modern, and is an ornament to the town. It has all the promise of a successful career."

In 1973 the main office of the bank was moved to a newly constructed facility at 827 Main Street. This allowed for easier access from both Main and Washington Streets and remained the primary location until 1996.

The bank's current name was developed after its merger with the Bank of Simpsonville in 1970. The latter had enjoyed a long period of service to the citizens of Simpsonville and surrounding area, having begun life in 1902 with $25,000 in capital.

The first directors of the Bank of Simpsonville included Roy C. Smith, Claud Buckley, L. H. Cooms, T. M. Lyons, C. R. Crosby, S. H. McMakin, and Miller Wilhoite. Presidents included Mr. Lyons, Leonidas Webb, and Middelton Philips.

The Simpsonville bank began its operations on Todd's Point Road, and moved to the corner of Todd's Point Road and U. S. 60 in 1960. The old bank building was used at one time as a grange hall, and during the Civil War it was badly damaged by a band of guerrillas.

The Bank of Simpsonville was also one of the first banks in Shelby County to experience a robbery. In 1932 three young men in overalls held up the bank, forced the bank's employees into a vault, and escaped with $2,945. Fortunately, no one was hurt, and the sheriff was notified of the escapade after the employees had been freed.

To meet the requirements of its Simpsonville customers, Citizens Union Bank built a new facility in 1996 at the corner of Veechdale Road and U. S. 60. The bank had grown in 1986 when it was merged with another locally owned financial institution, the Farmers & Traders Bank, which had served its customers at 601 Main Street since 1871. Following this merger, the former Farmers & Traders Bank location became a branch of Citizens Union, serving as a full service facility until 1996.

The bank's expansion also included acquiring a bank in Bagdad from the Republic Bank. This bank had originated as the People's Bank of Bagdad in 1888. The addition of this location in the eastern part of the county allowed Citizens Union to begin offering loan services to the residents of the Bagdad area and customers in Franklin County.

In 1997, Citizens Union dedicated a new central headquarters building on U. S. 60 West. Subsequently, banking facilities were opened within the Walmart Supercenter, two in Louisville, and another one adjacent to the Weissinger Golf Course. In 1998, CUB established banking operations in Spencer County by opening a branch at 853 Taylorsville Road. It also has several branches in Jefferson County.

The original officers and directors of Citizens Union Bank were Charles Kinkel, president, J. C. Burnett, cashier, Thompson Webber, bookkeeper, and directors G. G. Gilbert, James Guthrie, A. P. Carrithers, Luther Chowning, L. W. McCormack, J. M Maddox, J. J. Ramsey, William Bullard, M. R. Walters, and J. W. Hardin.

At the end of 2001, the bank had assets of about $350 million and was conducting business at eleven locations. The directors were Lea McMullan Anderson, Dr. Edward B. Hayes, William H. Borders, Robert McDowell, E. Ryburn Weakley, Stephen H. Solomon, and President and CEO Billie Wade. Tom Barker Jr. had also served as a long-time director prior to his death in December 2001.

COMMONWEALTH BANK & TRUST
(SHELBY COUNTY TRUST BANK)

On April 27, 1887, a group of Shelbyville businessmen formed the first board of directors of the Shelby County Trust Company. They were G. W. Logan, R. A. Smith, J. A. Weakley, Charles Kinkel, W. J. Thomas, J. C. Beckham, Shelby Vannatta, and John A. Middleton. These men recognized the "need for a solvent and continuous, state-supervised fiduciary in a growing and prosperous community." Weakley was elected president, and a small office established at the rear of Chowning's Shoe Store on Main Street. P. J. Foree, J. C. Beckham, and C. S. Weakley succeeded Weakley, in order.

On July 29, 1904, the Wayne lot on the public square was purchased for the trust company's location, just east of the bank's present day main office. The bank's directors decided that the new facility would be built of Bedford Stone. On May 13, 1911, by amendment, the bank's charter was changed to the Shelby County Trust & Banking Company, with new departments for savings accounts and commercial banking.

When C. S. Weakley died while serving as president, W. J. Thomas and then E. B. Beard succeeded him, in order, in 1918. Successive to Mr. Beard was A. C. Long, Dr. W. P. Hughes, Robert F. Matthews, Lloyd Pollard, and Ben G. Matthews, who served from 1970 to 1981.

During the bank's first 74 years of existence, only three men served as cashier: A. C. Long, J. E. Hoodenpyle, and Lloyd Pollard, who began his service on July 1, 1930, and then became president in 1961.

The bank's most difficult years, as was the case with all other financial institutions, came during the Great Depression. During the worst of those terrible years, Ben Allen Thomas, who was to serve as a director for 63 years, personally transported thousands of dollars in cash in a satchel from the federal reserve to the Shelbyville bank to help meet the bank's obligations. Virtually every American had become skittish about the nation's future when President Franklin D. Roosevelt ordered the banks closed in 1933. But when the banks reopened for business following the mandated "bank holiday," there was enough money on hand to reassure depositors.

In early 1955, the bank acquired the Citizens Bank of Waddy to serve the southeastern part of the county. In 1973 the name of that bank was changed to reflect its parent's name. A branch was also opened in Simpsonville in 1975, and in 2000 a branch was located on the Mt. Eden Road just south of town. Also, a branch was located in 2001 in the Kroger superstore on the Eminence Pike. Another branch functions in Shelbyville's west end.

Louisville businessman Darrell Wells purchased a majority interest in the bank in 1981, and from 1981 to 1990 Jack Ragland, Peyton Wells, and John Brenzel directed the bank.

During the 1990s the bank enjoyed the leadership of CEO Perry Day and President Bobby Hudson.

At the end of 2001, Hudson was chief operating officer and vice-chairman of the board. Pat Sullivan became president. The bank had six locations and assets of approximately 200 million dollars. The board of directors included John Brenzel, Frank Goodwin, Frank P. Hargadon, Bobby S. Hudson, Rebecca Irvine, Frank T. Kiley, Betty Baird Kregor, Robert Logan, Sr., Ben G. Matthews, Robert Pearce, W. A. Smith, Pat Sullivan, B. A. Thomas Jr., Ann Wells, and Wayne H. Wells.

Shelby County Trust Bank. at Fifth and Main on the public square about 1909.

Ellis McGinnis Collection, courtesy of Michael McGinnis.

It was anticipated that the Commonwealth Bank would be merged into the Shelby County Bank during 2002. While the merged bank would operate under the Commonwealth Bank name, Shelby County Trust would retain its charter. Wells would be the majority stockholder.

FIFTH THIRD BANK

Fifth Third Bank is a direct descendant of the old Shelby County Building & Loan Co., which had its office on Main Street in Shelbyville between 5th and 6th Streets for many years. D. I. Cooper was its longtime chief operating officer. Shelby County Building & Loan was sold to The Cumberland in the 1980s, and, later, The Cumberland, which was based in Louisville, Ky., was sold to Fifth Third Bank in Cincinnati. Fifth Third Bank was operating about 1,600 branches at the end of 2002. The Shelbyville manager was Greg Jacobs, and the office manager Mary Maynard.

REPUBLIC BANK

Another bank operating in 2001 in Shelby County was a branch of the Republic Bank, headquartered in Louisville. Republic began operating in Shelby County in 1977 with its purchase of the People's Bank of Bagdad, which had three years previously opened a branch in Shelbyville. At the close of 2001 Todd Davis and John Marshall of Shelbyville were serving on the local branch's advisory board. Mike Tipton was the branch manager.

U.S. BANK

U.S. Bank, located on U. S. 60 in Shelbyville, originally came to Shelbyville as Great Financial Federal, a savings and loan institution. Later, Great Financial was acquired by First Star bank, which, in turn, was acquired by U. S. Bank.

At the end of 2002, U. S. Bank, headquartered in Minneapolis, was operating approximately 2,200 branches throughout much of the United States. The Shelbyville branch manager was Ray Weeks.

FORMER BANKS

Shelby County has had several other banks dating back to the late nineteenth and early twentieth centuries. All were important institutions in their day, and, while each case was different, their demise or change in name or ownership was caused, in most instances, either by hard times, merger mania, or the trend toward outside ownership.

THE BANK OF FINCHVILLE

The Bank of Finchville was incorporated in 1904, and closed its doors in 1931 due to the nation's economic collapse. The Deposit Bank of Shelbyville assumed its accounts. The Finchville bank was located in the little brick building adjacent to Robertson's Country Hams. At the time of the bank's closing, Gustavous T. Duvall was president, and W. C. Winlock, grandfather of Steve Howerton Jr., was the cashier.

One of those who remembered precisely the day the bank failed was Jane Veech Parsons, whose parents, Alex and Marguerite Veech, were giving a dinner party that evening. Although a very young lady at the time, she related that she vividly recalled her father bringing home the "bad news about the bank."

DEPOSIT BANK OF SHELBYVILLE

The Deposit Bank of Shelbyville, which had just acquired what few assets were left of the Bank of Finchville, itself failed during the depression due to the embezzlement of bank funds by Otho Vardaman, its cashier, and, until that time, a highly esteemed citizen of Shelbyville. The bank closed its doors the very day that bank auditors discovered the discrepancy. Vardaman was convicted and went to prison but the funds were never recovered. Charles Edward "Skippy" Connell III recalled that his grandfather was president of the bank at the time, and its collapse meant that "Skippy's" own father, Charles E. Connell Jr. had to forego his education at Notre Dame because of the family's financial predicament caused by the bank's failure.

DEPOSIT BANK OF PLEASUREVILLE

The Deposit Bank of Pleasureville, while not located in Shelby County, contributed substantially to Shelby County's progress because of the progressive policies of its longtime president and chief operating officer, William T. Finn. Under Finn's direction, the bank was the first in the area to pay interest on deposits and to offer Certificates of Deposit. Many businessmen and farmers credited him with helping them to overcome difficult times because of his willingness to make loans that other institutions declined.

When the People's Bank of Bagdad, of which Finn was also president, opened a branch in Shelbyville in 1974, he placed Lee Kinsolving in charge. This branch and the Deposit Bank of Pleasureville were sold to Bernard Trager's Republic Bank in 1977. Later, the assets of this bank were merged into the Central Bank in Henry County. Prior to his retirement, Kinsolving became president of Republic Bank's Kentucky Division, which included all of the bank's operations from Paducah to Louisville.

FARMERS & TRADERS BANK

The Farmers & Traders Bank was incorporated on March 20, 1871, and was in continuous operation on the northwest corner of Sixth and Main Street for 115 years in Shelbyville. The original bank building was remodeled in 1943. Using the original available floor space, new fixtures were installed in many areas exclusive of the vault. At that time war demands meant that no steel was available, so it was not until 1949 that a larger and more modern vault was installed.

In 1956, the bank purchased the property directly west of the original property. The Cleveland Barber Shop and Mose Ruben Dry Goods Store were bought to provide space for expansion. In 1972, it expanded again by acquiring the former Alice Hollenbach home (formerly Maidie's Dress Shop) just west of Rubens. The property was actually purchased from the Biagi family. The additional space was used for a drive-through and parking lot.

The first stockholders were J. D. Beard, George Smith, William Waddy, J. T. Ballard, J. W. Downs, J. P. Foree, W. A. Jones, Thomas Hansbrough, and George A. and J. M. McGrath. The first president was J. D. Guthrie. J. L. Caldwell succeeded him.

The initial stock offering was in the amount of $150,000. In 1878, the bank was given authority to reduce the capital stock to $50,000, which was done on April 12, 1900, and on February 13, 1901.

In 1901, the president was John A. Middleton, and the board of directors included Middleton, W. S. Thomas, John Boswell, John A. Thomas, W. T. Wallace, Charles S. Weakley, W. T. Beckham, and Emmett Harbison. W. T. Beckham succeeded Middleton as president. R. A. Campbell, Charles F. Beard, William A. Scearce, Coleman Wright, Elmo Head, J. L. Coots, and Charles F. Clifton followed him.

Clifton was president when the bank's board of directors voted to merge with Citizens Union Bank in August 1986. The directors at the time of the merger were Harold Huber, chairman, Clifton, William P. Thompson, E. Ryburn Weakley, William R. Hickman, Ralph Mitchell, and H. A. Barnett.

The Farmers and Traders Bank, established in 1871, operated in this building on the northwest corner of Sixth and Main for 115 years.

The Headlight, 1899. Courtesy of William Matthews.

THE CITIZENS BANK OF WADDY

The Citizens Bank of Waddy was chartered on August 9, 1909. It was the successor to the Bank of Waddy that was chartered on December 13, 1899, and went into liquidation 10 years later. The names of the incorporators and the first board of directors were E. B. Beard, E. W. McCormack, Estill J. Cline, G. T. Mahuron, Charles A. McCormack, W. H. Tipton, H. S. Samples, T. J. Doss, and J. J. Paxton. The bank's two presidents were E. W. McCormack and E. J. Cline.

The Citizens Bank of Waddy began its career as a branch bank of the Citizens Bank of Shelbyville, but the courts in a test case determined that a branch bank, even one in the same county where the mother bank was located, was not permissible at that time.

THE CROPPER BANK

In 1905, a bank was established at Cropper. After World War I, when Ben Allen Thomas II was president, land prices declined, and the cashier of the bank absconded with much of the bank's funds. The bank failed in 1921.

Under the laws of double indemnity which existed at that time, Thomas and the directors had to put up twice as much as they had invested in the bank to cover the bank's debts. Some of the debtors couldn't repay their loans, so Thomas had to pay off their indebtedness and hence acquired three farms in the Cropper community.

THE PEOPLES BANK OF BAGDAD

The Peoples Bank of Bagdad was the first bank institution chartered in Shelby County outside the City of Shelbyville. The date was 1888. Presidents included J. Baskett, S. H. Bryant, William Connell, B. D. Estes, and James Young. Virgil Samples was a longtime cashier and chief operating officer.

The Peoples Bank of Bagdad was acquired by the Deposit Bank of Pleasureville and, later by Republic Bank. In March 1996, Citizens Union Bank of Shelbyville acquired the bank from Republic. It now functions as a branch bank of Citizens Union.

The Shelby Sentinel, 1902.

The Peoples Bank of Bagdad was established in 1888.

(Some of the information for this article was provided by a number of individuals, including Harriett B. Scearce, Bobbie Totten, Ben G. Matthews, Steve Howerton Jr., Emily A. Thomas, Lee Kinsolving, and Ruby Conn. Other resources included the centennial edition published by The Shelby Sentinel *in 1940, and the special edition published jointly by* The Shelby Sentinel *and* The Shelby News *in 1967 on the occasion of Kentucky's 175th birthday.)*

BRICK MAKERS

By Charles D. Hockensmith

T he manufacture of bricks is one of the earliest but least documented industries in Kentucky. Shelby County is no exception to this lack of historical coverage. The brick industry permitted the construction of the many beautiful historic homes that are enjoyed and treasured today.

Prior to brick homes, log and frame structures were the standard. As brick structures became popular there was a demand for skilled individuals that could make and lay bricks. This trend led to the establishment of the local trades of making and laying bricks.

During the 19th century when horses and wagons were used for transportation, it was not feasible to transport loads of heavy bricks very far. In rural areas, it was once common for traveling brick makers to make bricks from local clay near the proposed structures. The same men would also lay the bricks that they made. In urban areas, small brick yards were established to make bricks for new structures in the cities. These early brick yards were labor intensive operations where bricks were made by hand in wooden molds and fired in crude updraft kilns. By 1880, larger brick yards with brick machines and permanent kilns increased production, and quickly put the small brick yards out of business.

Historical documents about brick making are scant, perhaps because brick making was a mundane job performed by individuals who were not highly educated. Since these people were rarely well-known in the communities and didn't write about their profession, other information must be obtained from the Census of Manufacturing, the Population Census, county histories, newspaper ads, and Kentucky gazetteers. Since information is so scant, it has been decided to include early information about brick layers as well as brick makers.

In his History of Shelby County Kentucky, George L. Willis lists six early brick makers, including I. Clarkes and William Rolling (1800), Thomas Reynolds and Bridgewater (1818), and John Mintor and Richard Mintor (1820). This information is obtained from a letter written by John W. Williamson of Louisville to Absalom T. Matthews of Shelbyville in 1872.

Certainly the most notable brick religious structure was built in 1804 to serve the needs of the Methodist congregation at Mulberry, located several miles north of Shelbyville. A Mr. Talbott superintended the building of a brick kiln, and the brick chapel was built under the supervision of Bishop McKendree, a pioneer minister in Kentucky. This was the first house of worship constructed by the Methodists in Kentucky, and only the second church built of brick by any denomination in Kentucky. Additional brick were used by Mr. Talbott in the construction of a residence for himself in the immediate neighborhood of the chapel. Both buildings are lost to history.

Kentucky's 1850 Manufacturing Census does not list any brick makers in Shelby County. In order to be listed in the census, a business had to earn at least $500 per year. The Kentucky Gazetteer and Business Directory for 1859 lists E. B. Sain as a brick maker living in Shelbyville.

The 1860 Manufacturing Census does not list any brick makers. However, the 1860 Population Census does list two brick makers in the Shelbyville District as well as several brick masons and layers.

The brick makers were John Cemils and George Perry, and the three brick masons were Augustine Barnett, James Barnett, and Micah Schyler. The Simpsonville District had three brick masons, R. C. Rogers, William Leafy, and Jason Campbell. The latter two had emigrated from Ireland.

The 1870 Manufacturing Census listed Thomas and John Neel as operating a brick yard, having invested $100 of their own money in the business. They paid $50 for all the materials they used in one year, and their four male hands earned a total of $600. Bricks were made only during six months of each year. The brick yard produced 100,000 bricks during the season valued at $900.

The 1870 Population Census listed a brick maker and his employees who were living in the same household. Forty-three year old J. O. Johnson of Shelbyville was listed as a brick maker and builder. His crew consisted of six negroes including Charles Lee, Dudley Tilly, George Taylor, Warren Taylor, Thomas Perry, and Josh Baker.

Two other men involved in the brick industry in Shelbyville included Robert Marshall, and Jonathan Gilbert. In Simpsonville, Wilkerson Bullitt, a negro, was listed as working in a brick yard.

Several white brick layers and negro hod carriers were listed for the Shelbyville area. A few other individuals involved in laying bricks were listed in other communities during 1870. In the Clay Village district, James Barnett was a brick layer. Adam Seay worked as a brick mason in Simpsonville, and H. Deiss is listed as a Shelbyville brick maker in the Kentucky State Gazetteer and Business Directory.

Two statewide directories provide information for the 1890s. The Kentucky State Gazetteer and Business Directory for 1891-92 lists the Allen & Bell Company of Shelbyville as brick manufacturers, and J. L. Eben of Shelbyville was listed as a brick manufacturer in the Kentucky State Gazetteer and Business Directory for 1896.

A few brick masons and brick layers were listed in the 1900 Population Census for Shelby County. Samuel Bickley and John Roberts were brick masons at Bagdad; William Perkins was a brick layer at Christiansburg; and Willis Brown, John J. Brown, George Casey, and John Harris were brick masons in Shelbyville.

The 1910 Population Census lists only three brick layers, all from Shelbyville. They were William Harris, John Harris, and Henry Harris, none of whom was related. John Harris was born in Ireland.

A single brick kiln has been documented archaeologically in Shelby County. During the upgrade of state highway 55, archaeologists under contract to the Kentucky Transportation Department discovered a 19th century brick kiln within the highway corridor.

This brick kiln measured about 57.4 feet x 23.8 feet, with 16 flue channels, a rubble filled trench, and numerous fragments of brick. Historically, this kiln would have been on the property of Sampson Moxley in the mid-1880s, and the bricks made on the property may have been used in nearby brick homes.

COUNTRY STORES

I n the 19th and much of the 20th centuries, the country store provided many of the needs of the people of rural Shelby County. Conveniently located at a crossroads or in towns, they were some of the first small business enterprises in the county. Their demise came with improved transportation and they were replaced by convenience stores, mainly associated with gasoline stations. While they existed, however, they provided pills, plows, petticoats, political discussions, a warm place on a winter's day, and a cool porch from the summer heat. Today, only a few remain in the county, such as Carriss Grocery at Southville, where there has been a country store since the 1840s.

BUCKMAN'S STORE

By Sarah Anne Buckman Carpenter

Walton and Edith Buckman ventured into the retail grocery business in 1933. During those Great Depression years, times were tough and money was in short supply. The Buckmans succeeded in large part due to the help of their very good friend, Judge Harry Walters. The store was located in Simpsonville, on Todd's Point Road, approximately two hundred feet north of the Louisville & Nashville Railroad tracks. It was a general merchandise store, which stocked groceries, dry goods, hardware, paint, shoes, clothing, coal, kerosene, animal feed, and many other items.

Supplies for the store were purchased from large wholesale houses in Louisville, such as Belknap Hardware and Manufacturing Company. Belknap boasted that their inventory included 80,000 items; therefore, Buckman's Store could supply customers with a wide variety of goods.

Many of the store's customers were farmers who depended on the sale of tobacco for their income. Buckman's allowed farmers to set up charge accounts, which were carried through the year until their crops were sold, and they had money to pay. Other customers' accounts were payable on a weekly or monthly basis. Offering home delivery to customers was an expected service. Walton and Edith Buckman had one child, a daughter, Sarah Anne (Sally), who, as a little girl, regularly accompanied her father making home deliveries in their family pick-up truck. It is said that she also enjoyed having her pick of the candy that was always in good supply at the store!

Mike Morgan was a valued employee who helped the Buckmans keep the store open from 7:00 A.M. to 7: 00 P.M. during the week and to 9:00 P.M. on Saturdays. World War II took its toll on the store in many ways. Many items became unavailable or were in short supply. The government rationed other items and customers had to use ration stamps to buy them. Buckman, who was known as "Buck," and Morgan were both drafted into the army. Edith Buckman continued to operate the store until her husband was stationed in Ogden, Utah. Edith then closed the store so that she and Sally, then a

16-year-old, could move to Utah. When the war ended in 1945, the Buckmans returned to Simpsonville and reopened the store.

During President Dwight Eisenhower's administration (1953-61), Buckman was appointed the United States Postmaster for Simpsonville. Part of the store was used for the post office for several years until the store was finally closed and the post office took over the entire building.

ELLIS' GROCERY

By Stella K. Lee

In the late 1920s or early 1930s the first African-American owned grocery store was opened in Martinsville by John Martin. Located on Tenth Street, this may possibly be the family from which the community name was derived. Later, Ellis' Grocery opened on the corner of Tenth and High Streets. Alice Edwards was the proprietor, assisted by her sister Helen Wheatly and her son Otis Ellis. From his truck, Otis sold ice, a popular item because electricity and refrigeration were luxuries few could afford. Martinsville wasn't illuminated until after World War II.

The grocery store was a popular place in the 1940s. Men would gather around the small radio in the store to listen to Joe Louis's fights. To African Americans, who had few national heroes in those days, he was it. Louis was heavyweight champion.

HERRICK STORE

By Ermin McKay Herrick

The Herrick stores were built across U.S. 60 from Simpsonville Christian Church. In the 1930s the grocery store burned. It is said that W.A. Herrick dropped a case of matches and that started the fire. He rebuilt the store where the Abbott Realty Company building is now. Eventually the Herrick Store moved next door to the structure that Bailey Newton had built, now known as Barr's.

JACKSON'S STORE, CROPPER

By Mary Thomas Johnson

Although a predecessor had existed between 1914 and 1919, Jackson's Store was established when T.L. Jackson returned to Cropper after running a store in Lockport, Ky. for two years. He took as his partner, J. B. Smith. The land was purchased and the store opened in 1922 and was called Smith and Jackson General Merchandise.

Smith died in 1941 and Jackson purchased the Smith portion the following year. He changed the name to T.L. Jackson General Merchandise in the mid-1940s. It remained in business until 1972. During those years patrons included residents of the towns of Elmburg, Christiansburg, and Bagdad, and adjoining Henry County.

A coal stove furnished heat in winter and ceiling fans cooled the interior in summer. Chairs located around the stove permitted neighbors to visit. The floors were oiled every three to six months. A section was set aside for the "office" containing a roll top desk, safe, bookshelves, and a swivel antique chair. No food was served nor was there ever a pickle barrel or cracker barrel.

Patrons purchased a wide variety of necessities, including home appliances and furnishings, lines from the Carter Dry Goods in Louisville, tobacco products, Datillo (another Louisville business) fruits and vegetables, patent medicines, shoes, clothing, oil lamps and supplies, heating stoves, cooking ranges, electric washers, fence posts and fencing, radios, seeds, fertilizer, and milking machines. The major portion of sales was on credit with accounts being settled when patrons' crops were sold.

A typical day began around 7:30 A.M. and ended at 9:00 P.M. Sometimes the store was closed to permit a dinner or supper break. The store always closed on Sundays and Christmas Day, although Jackson was prepared to open it for emergencies on those days. The store was typical of many that dotted the Shelby County countryside until the late 20th century when ease of travel caused their demise.

MCDOWELL'S STORE

By Bob McDowell

Robert "R.A" McDowell opened McDowell's Store in Simpsonville in 1908. It was a general store that sold not only groceries but also hardware, feed, seed, and bottled gas for cooking. The post office was located there and "R.A." served as Postmaster until his death.

The original building burned on January 3, 1928, and was rebuilt on the same site where business continued through World War II. That was also the year when Herbert S. McDowell joined his father in the business. It then operated as McDowell & Son until R.A.'s death in 1957.

Soon after that the post office was moved, and

Courtesy of Bob McDowell.

McDowell's Store, in Simpsonville, was destroyed by fire January 3, 1928, and rebuilt on the same site.

Maxie Walters McDowell joined her husband in ownership. In the early 1970s they sold it to Chester J. and Frances Bemiss. They continued selling groceries and hardware as McDowell's Store, adding a lunch service for workers at a nearby factory. He retired in 1985. The building now houses a restaurant.

MT. EDEN GENERAL STORE

By Joann Bain

Hallie Watts built the Mt. Eden General Store, located in the center of Mt. Eden, in 1928. Watts' employees lived in Harrisonville and walked to and from Mt. Eden every day until they completed the store building. Watts ran a market truck out of the store two days a week. He would travel from daylight to dark over the country roads to visit the farmers who had no way to get groceries. If the farmers didn't have the money they would use eggs or chickens in exchange.

The front of the store housed groceries. There were long bins with soup beans, butter beans, and many kinds of dried foods. Flour and meal were stacked in a large tin cabinet in the center of the store. Lard cans and everything to cure meat were available. In one corner were dress material, buttons, ribbon, snaps, needles, pins, and thread on large bolts.

The rear of the store was filled with buggies and farm equipment such as bits for horses, hoe handles, and nails. In the basement, James Hardesty operated a cream and egg testing station. If the eggs passed the test, they were sold upstairs. There was a large wood and coal stove in the center of the store with a few church benches around it. The store ceiling was made of tin and remains in good shape today.

A large barn stood a few feet behind the store where horses got food and water while their owners shopped. Chicken coops were on one side of the barn. Farmers traded chickens for other groceries, so they were kept until someone wanted to buy them. It was a custom then to have fried chicken at Sunday dinner, so the chickens didn't last long in the coops.

Hallie Watts and Dove Temple were the first owners; other owners and operators were Gratch Brown and Marvin Hardesty. Present owners are John and Joann Bain, with operators Richard and Jaylayne Watson. The store was destroyed by fire on December 12, 2002, when a truck delivering gasoline spilled part of its load. The fuel leaked into the basement of the building and was ignited by the furnace.

RIESTER'S STORE

Henry Hedden owned Riester's Store in Finchville. In the front sidewalk are the initials H. H. and the date 1909. The Albert Riester family moved to the area in 1902, and bought the store from Hedden in 1923. Helping out at the store was Alberta Riester Yancey, the daughter of Albert, and her brother, Leo. Another brother, Paul, also helped with the store in the beginning. He left to run a milk route. He returned to help when Leo retired. The store was sold in 1968 to Mr. and Mrs. Herbert Travis, who owned the store for several years before selling it to the Slaughter family.

SAMPLES STORE

By Ruby Samples Bohannon

Leslie and Monta Rodgers Samples bought a farm in Shelby County, rented a building in Bagdad, and opened Samples Store. They ran market trucks and sold general merchandise. In 1938, Mr. Samples decided to build his own store. He died in 1941 leaving the store to his wife and children, Ruby, Selbert, and Marvin. Ruby married Clayton Bohannon in 1937, and Selbert married Nell Stratton in 1945. They continued to operate the store with help from Kate Stratton and Emma Johnson. Numerous others ran market trucks throughout the area. The store was first sold to Carl Tindall who operated it several years before selling it to the present owner, Lewis Young.

SEWELL'S STORE

By Mary Frances Sewell Bailey

A landmark in the Scott Station community, Sewell's Store was operated from 1923 to 1974. Eugene and Lula Mitchen Sewell saw a need for a general store to provide for farmers who were unable to travel to Shelbyville for their necessities. A small building was moved from the back of their house to the front of the lot on Scott Station Road. The building was doubled in size with a kitchen in the rear. E. J. White, uncle of Lula Sewell, did the construction.

Dry goods carried included work pants, overalls, and shirts, bolts of fabric, thread, buttons, safety pins, and hosiery. Miscellaneous items were hog rings, kegs of nails, and staples. Smoking items were tobacco in sacks with cigarette papers to roll your own, Prince Albert pipe tobacco, twists of chewing tobacco and more in blocks to be cut with a tobacco cutter.

Flour was sold in 24 and 48 pound sacks and meal in 5 and 10 pound sacks. The flour came from mills in Taylorsville, Smithfield, and Versailles. Lard was bought in large cans and dipped out in trays. Meat came in large sides to be cut according to the customer's demand. Rat cheese was bought in large rounds coated with paraffin. Rolls of sliced bologna were big sellers. Food included many kinds of fruits, vegetables, and meats in cans. Sugar, navy beans, pinto beans, and chicken feed were stored in barrels. A cake rack held boxes of cookies on display under glass. Soft drinks sold for a nickel, bread was nine cents a loaf, and chewing gum a penny a stick. Christmas was a time for big celebrations and new candy supplies, such as chocolate drops, peanut and coconut brittle, and orange slices. Special fruits included grapes, tangerines, oranges, coconuts in shells, and whole stalks of bananas. Farmers ordered bushel baskets of these items for their tenants. Through the 1930s, many homes didn't have electricity and kerosene was in big demand for the lamps; a supply was metered out with a pump from large barrels. As a service for tenant farmers, some were allowed to charge a grocery bill for a year, to be paid when their tobacco crop was sold.

Mrs. Sewell died in 1957. Her husband continued to run the store with occasional help from Lula Moore, Mrs. James Heady, Lillian Wood, Les and Mary Frances Sewell Bailey. Store keeping was not an easy job before everything was prepackaged.

THE DAIRY TRADITION

By Bob Ehrler

Shelby County has a long dairy tradition that began in the early settlement period and continues to this day. In the early days, most settlers kept a milk cow or two to meet the needs of their families for milk and butter. Dairying was not a year-round occupation since the mixed native stock typically calved in the spring and went dry in the fall; butter and cheese were sent to market twice per year.

Milk was stored in springhouses or "dairies" which were constructed to allow spring water to cool milk stored in crocks on stone ledges. As the population increased in Shelbyville and other hamlets, local farmers had greater opportunities to sell to their neighbors in the towns. The dairymen delivered milk in their horse-drawn milk wagons and used dippers to transfer raw milk from pails or cans into jars or other containers presented by their customers. By 1850, Shelby County ranked fifth among Kentucky counties in the number of dairy cattle with 4,646 milk cows. With the extension of direct rail service between Shelbyville and Louisville in the late 1880s, local dairymen were placed in a position to sell milk to the large Louisville market. By the 1890s, dairymen delivered wagonloads of milk to trains making daily stops at Shelbyville, Simpsonville, Finchville, Waddy, Veech, Conner, and Scott Stations. Cream stations were established at the rail stations to weigh the milk, test its butterfat content, and separate milk from the cream.

By 1900, Shelby County ranked second only to Jefferson County in the number of dairy cattle with 5,832 head. With an increase in the number of dairy herds and a growing emphasis on purebred cattle, Shelby County entered a golden age of dairying. In this period, Sue T. Henning, the first woman director of the American Jersey Cattle Club, established the nationally renowned Jersey herd at Allen Dale Farm, which was the home of numerous national champions. As purebred Jersey cattle spread throughout the county in the early 1900s, Shelby County became known as the "Jersey Isle of America." The Shelby

Courtesy of B.J. Nethery.

Derry's Rosa, one of J.F. Middleton's Maple Grove Jersey herd, 1909.

County Fair became highly regarded among Jersey breeders and nationally significant cattle sales were held in the county. Joining the tobacco barn as an emblem of local agriculture, dairy barns and silos sprang up across the local landscape in large numbers. While small gambrel-roofed dairy barns were commonly found at most farms, local dairyman also erected monumental structures including the round barn at Bird's Jersey Dairy in Cropper, the impressive Allen Dale dairy complex on Zaring Mill Road, and the massive Undalata mule barn on Mt. Eden Road which also housed the dairy.

The lack of sanitary containers and reliable refrigeration depressed consumer demand for milk through the early 1900s. In fact, less than 10 percent of the milk produced in Kentucky during that period was sold as such, with the vast majority being processed into butter or cheese. When the glass milk bottle with sealable top became available beginning in the 1880s, retail dairies began bottling milk. Originally, these dairies bottled raw milk, but government standards later required the milk to be pasteurized. The advances in bottling, pasteurization, and refrigeration greatly increased consumer demand for milk. The horse-drawn wagons were replaced by milk trucks, which delivered door-to-door. While hundreds of dairies were established across the state, Shelby County had more than its share. Many of the retail dairies used handsome bottles embossed with their business names and, beginning in the 1930s, some used colorful "pyroglazed" or painted bottles emblazoned with their names, trademarks, and often slogans. These local dairies live on to this day in the form of hoarded bottles and caps which periodically appear: Maple Grove, Bird's Jersey Dairy, Undalata Farm, Green's, Bonnie Brook, Everet Webber, Neil Roach, T.E. Neblett, W.S. Bland, LeCompte, Kemper, Old Masons Home Jersey Dairy, and Marcardin Farm. These dairies gradually disappeared as costs increased due to modern improvements such as pasteurization and refrigeration. However, the Maple Grove Dairy flourished and adapted to the changing times by opening the "Maple Moo" drive-in on Midland Trail. But by the 1960s, all of the retail dairies in Shelby County were gone.

While the local retail dairies disappeared, dairy farming remained a healthy part of Shelby County's economy. Milk produced in Shelby County was transported by tanker truck to Louisville where it was bottled for retail sale or used in production of other dairy products. With its skyrocketing population, neighboring Jefferson County saw much of its prime farmland devoured by commercial and residential development. By 1950, Shelby County had overtaken Jefferson County as the leading dairy county in the state with 17,034 dairy cattle. Milking machines allowed farmers to increase the size of their herds far beyond the numbers feasible in the days of milking by hand. Eventually, mechanized "milking parlors," which shuttled cows in and out on agricultural assembly lines, replaced many of the large dairy barns with their long rows of cattle stanchions. Shelby County became home to some of Kentucky's largest dairy herds, including large herds on the Sanderlin and Gallrein farms. While, by this time, the Holstein breed had eclipsed the others in Shelby County, a number of Jersey and Guernsey herds continued to be found in the county.

Growth from the Louisville metropolitan area increasingly spilled onto the farmland of western Shelby County. The proximity to Louisville, which fueled the early growth of dairying in Shelby County, also planted the seeds of its potential demise. With modest financial rewards, the relentless ritual of twice daily milkings every day of the year grew less attractive to the younger generation. Dairy farms were sold or tracted and herds dispersed as dairy farmers retired or got a job in town. While Shelby County continues to have a significant dairy industry on the eve of the new millennium, it has fallen to ninth place in the state in milk production. Areas which are farther removed from the growth of Louisville, such as Barren County, have claimed the lead in milk production.

Although Shelby County's dairy herds may continue to decrease, the dairy barns and silos which dot its landscape will serve as silent sentinels of the county's dairy tradition. While some of the monuments such as Bird's round barn have fallen, others such as the Allen Dale complex and Maple Grove barn refuse to release their grip on the present. And for years to come, the intriguing bottles and caps of the dimly-recalled local retail dairies will continue to appear in attics and flea markets like the fossilized bones of some long extinct creature.

MEMORIES OF A "MILK RUNNER"

By Ted Igleheart

As a lad 12 years of age, I obtained a job in 1942 with the Maple Grove Dairy, owned by Chalmer Caudill, with the primary duties of a "milk runner." Getting up at 3:30 every morning was daunting enough, but delivering milk by the bottle door to door through town on a dead run from the truck to the door was even more daunting. This went on for about three hours before calling on the restaurants, where we carried milk in by the case, then making it to school by 7:45 for band practice. I rationalized the benefits of running for three hours by concluding that it would keep me in good shape for football and basketball.

Another benefit I remember was the association with my route driver, "Whitie," who was well known in town as a hail fellow, well met but who drove the runners hard with adamant admonitions to "pick it up and move it out!" All the route drivers for the three retail dairies in town were characters. There was Al Wilson, who drove for Bird's Dairy, and Roger Green, who drove for Green's Dairy, and the competition for customers was fierce. There was even a contest sometimes to see how many of the other dairies' bottles we could pick up while delivering our own. I can remember one time picking up some Green's Dairy bottles next to a customer of mine when out of the darkness and from behind a bush jumped their runner. It scared me so bad I dropped the bottles and broke them on the sidewalk.

There is a vivid memory indelibly carved in my mind of carrying a case of milk one morning into Eddie Hall's hamburger place, rounding the counter to the big refrigerator, and, before I could set the case down, Buck Harbison ran a mouse out from behind the counter. It ran up my pants leg and I dropped that whole case of milk in a shattering heap while dancing a jig in frightful efforts to get that mouse out of my pants, much to the hearty entertainment of a counter full of breakfast customers.

Drinking half pints of white and chocolate milk between distant customers made it easy to skip breakfast before school and, incidentally, supplemented my wages of $12.00 a week. The downside was I fell asleep in church during the sermons and often nodded off in school, which didn't help my carefully cultivated image of being a serious student. It was my first experience, though, in learning the lesson that you have to earn your way to get ahead. Leaving that job for a newspaper route two years later increased my earnings to $18.00 a week.

GREEN'S DAIRY

By Roger Green

Clarence Green and his sons owned and operated Green's Dairy on his 250-acre farm located on Fox Run Road, five miles north of Shelbyville. The dairy plant was built and began operation in 1940. There were approximately 80 cows in the dairy herd. They were primarily Jerseys with a few Holsteins.

Green's son Roger was the primary route deliveryman, serving Shelbyville and the surrounding area. His normal workday started at 3:00 A.M. The delivery route in the city took about three hours. Breakfast came after the deliveries were completed, about 6:00 at the White Cottage restaurant near Seventh and Main Streets. After that, it was back to the farm and the bottling plant to get ready for the next day.

The route deliveryman usually had a helper. The first couple of years when Roger Green delivered the milk, his wife Ruby Adams Green worked with him on the truck. Later high school boys worked on the truck including Bobby Kemper, Lindbergh Miller, and Bruner Matthews, Jr. Luther Green and Forest Frazier were also deliverymen.

The dairy operated from 1940 to 1946. During that time the milk plant bottled about 200 quarts of pasteurized whole milk daily, besides the pint and half pints of chocolate milk, orange drink, skim milk, and buttermilk. The dairy also offered cottage cheese, cream, and butter. In 1946, Clarence Green sold the farm and opened a milk-processing plant at Main and Second Streets in Shelbyville. A milk and cheese plant operated at that location until 1965, when the plant, called Cudahay Inc. moved its operation to Harrodsburg, Ky.

Green's Dairy stand at the Shelby County Fair, 1942. Left, Roger Green, Bruner Matthews Jr. at center, Carl Bryant at right. The truck is a 1940 GMC model.

GRIST MILLS

By Charles D. Hockensmith

M any grist mills once operated along the streams of Shelby County. Later, the introduction of steam engines permitted mills to be located in communities away from streams. These mills ground wheat for flour and corn for meal, as well as for producing feed for livestock. Mills provided places where local people could bring their grains to be ground.

Usually, the miller would take a certain amount of the grain as a toll to pay for the cost of grinding. Often small communities grew up around these mills. As local farmers waited to have their grain ground, they were able to socialize and catch up on the news and gossip. These mills met an important need in the lives of people and often became focal points of communities.

As time passed, local mills were gradually replaced by larger urban mills with improved technology. Mills using millstones began to decline as more efficient steel rollers became popular in the 1880s. During the early part of the twentieth century, after most rural mills had outlived their usefulness, these structures began to disappear rapidly from the landscape. Some were torn down while others burned or were converted to other uses.

Today there is little evidence of these once important structures. In fact, only a handful of the old grist mills, which were once common in Kentucky, are still standing.

Undoubtedly, some foundations and mill dam remains still exist in Shelby County where progress has not obliterated them. While these ruins are of interest to the archaeologist and historian, they often go undetected by the average person.

Unfortunately, little history has been recorded on Shelby County grist mills. George L. Willis, Sr., in his *History of Shelby County*, included a one-page chapter on grist mills, and newspaper man Edward D. Shinnick also commented briefly on some of the old Shelby County mills in his various newspaper articles assembled into the 1974 book, *Some Old Time History of Shelbyville and Shelby County*.

The first grist mill in the county, as mentioned by Willis, was built in 1793 by William Helm on Guist Creek, just north of the three mile bridge on U. S. 60. A second mill was constructed about a mile upstream by Robert Tyler about a month later. Within three years, a dozen petitions for mills had been presented to the court. These mills included one operated by Benjamin Logan on Bullskin Creek, Col. Whitaker south of Shelbyville, Elijah Carr on Mulberry Creek, and Samuel Shannon near the Shelbyville Water Works. Another mill mentioned by Willis was that of Moses Hall who transferred his interest in the mill to his son, David Stevenson Hall. Another mill was operated by a Richard Taylor in 1799 on Brashears Creek.

The turnover in ownership of these mills was great, and we have little account of what transpired from the 1790s to the 1840s aside from the ownership changes.

Sometime in the 1840s, according to Shinnick, Messrs Samuel Brittian and John Carver constructed in Shelbyville a modern steam flouring mill. The general superintendent was Benjamin Jackman. The mill could grind from 30 to 40 bushels of wheat per hour, and 50 to 60 bushels of corn per hour.

Other mills constructed during this era were those of Alfred Zaring and T. B. Caldwell.

The 1850s Manufacturing Census for Shelby County listed a number of operating grist mills, including those operated by R. D. Waters Backbone Mill on the Mt. Eden Road, John Carson, Robert Baird, Logan Brown on Jeptha Creek, T. B. Caldwell on Clay Street, G. L. Seamon, J. W. Bung, T. Cardin, A. R. Johnson, and A. R. Zaring.

The 1860s Manufacturing Census shows that Shelby County had six operating mills at the time, including those operated by L. J. Matthews, J. W. and William Sloan, L. Beatty, and Alfred Harrington.

Grist mill activity appears to have picked up in the 1870s because there were not less than 16 mills listed in the census. They included mills of J. W. Zaring, Thomas B. Tacker, Alfred Harrington, Bell and Company, Logan and Company, Henry R. Johnson, Johnson and Shauman, W. F. Maddle, Thomas Wittering & Garland, T. B. Caldwell & Son, Reubens F. Fields, William Sloan, John D. McDaniel, C. M. Sampson, B. M. Campton, and the Gale Factory at Jacksonville.

Simpsonville mills for 1879 included J. W. Horner's steam-powered mill, William Hunt's water-powered mill, and J. Rogers' steam-powered mill. At Graefenberg, James F. Sorts operated a grist mill in 1876, while R. M. Riggs operated a water-powered grist mill in 1879. J. S. Beatty ran a steam-powered grist mill at Todd's Point. The 1880s saw still more changes in grist mills, with several going out of business, and a few new ones coming on line.

James Zaring operated a steam-powered grist mill in Shelbyville. He employed seven males who worked 12 hours a day, six days a week. Skilled workers received $2.53 per day, while ordinary workers got 60 cents for the day.

B. A. Sampson operated a steam-powered mill, and S. N. Bellefonte operated a steam-powered-mill at Harrisonville and paid his skilled workers $2 and unskilled workers made 75 cents per day,

N. D. Scearce ran a water-powered mill on Guist Creek, and his total investment in wages for the year was $100.

Rogers & Russell operated a steam-powered grist mill on Guist Creek, and total income for the year was $25,000.

W. A. R. Logan had the biggest mill in Shelby County in the 1880s, located on Clear Creek within the Shelbyville city limits. The mill operated year round with employees working 18-hour days between May and November and 12 hours a day between November and May. Skilled workers received $1.80 per day, and ordinary laborers 86 cents. During the year this mill produced 10,000 pounds of wheat flour, 540,000 pounds of corn meal, and 730,000 pounds of feed.

Information on 1890's mills is fragmentary because many of the records were destroyed by fire. However, we do know that R. M. Wiggs was operating a mill at Graefenberg, and Squire Brown was still running his mill at Harrisonville. Shelbyville millers included J. D. Guthrie's Sons and Logan and Logan.

The Logan and Logan Company was incorporated as a milling business on April 19, 1904, with its owners being George W. A. R., and John I. Logan. In 1908 A. R. and John I. Logan retired from the Banner Roller Mills, the new name for the company. Harry M. Logan was placed in charge, and John I. Logan was designated to run the firm's operation in Bloomfield. In 1909 the Logan and Logan Company milling property was sold for $8,930 to R. L. Prewitt of Perryville. Later that same year, the

Banner Roller Mills were totally consumed by fire, and Mr. Prewitt decided not to rebuild. The loss was placed at $18,000.

Also in that year an article in the local newspaper noted the passing of Carver's Flouring Mill in Shelbyville, which had flourished at its location on Clay Street on what was known then as South Back Street. The mill had passed through a succession of owners, including Carver & Jones, George Wells, Euclid Hickman, Logan & Bell, and, later, Logan and Logan. The building had been abandoned as a going concern, and been used for the storage of records. R. M. Brown bought the building for $1,500 and tore it down to make way for a new warehouse.

In 1929, according to the Kentucky Natural Resources Industrial Statistical Guide, there were only three mills operating in Shelby County. They were the Climax Roller Mills, which employed 10 white and two colored men, R. L. Harrison & Son at Bagdad, and O. B. Montford at Cropper who was manufacturing meal and feed with only one white employee.

No one knows when the O. B. Montford operation went out of business, but considerable information exists about Climax Mills, no longer in business, and Bagdad Roller Mills, which continues to be a thriving business at the outset of the 21 century.

The Logan & Logan flouring mill in 1899. The Headlight, 1899.

Courtesy of William Matthews.

CLIMAX MILLS

By Betty Matthews and Charles B. Long Sr.

Around 1820 the Zaring Water Mill was located near the Clear Creek Bridge on Zaring Mill Road. In 1874, Alfred Zaring built a steam mill on North Seventh Street in Shelbyville and moved the business there. Zaring later sold it to J.D. Guthrie and Sons who operated it a few years as Guthrie Bros. In 1904, the mill was sold at public auction to Samuel Monroe Long.

Long and his sons, Paul Webber Long, Samuel Monroe Long Jr. (known as Jim), and Charles Benton Long, modernized the establishment. The first new building contained four wooden tanks where the grain was stored. Behind this building a larger one was built later that had eleven steel tanks. Here various grades of corn and wheat were stored. There were five interstices between the tanks. If the temperature of a tank got too hot, which would cause the grain to spoil, the grain was transferred to another tank. A coal operation was also begun. Three concrete tanks were erected south of the main grain tanks near the railroad tracks where coal would be unloaded for storage. The trucks could pull up to the bins and gates at the bottom of the tank would open and the coal would flow into the trucks.

The name Climax Mill was chosen because it signified the best or top quality of flour. The mill was successfully operated almost 80 years as S.M. Long & Sons Climax Roller Mills and later incorporated as Climax Mills. They milled all types of family flours including a seasoned flour known as Belle and their most widely known brand Climax Old Fashioned white corn meal. They milled the flour and mixed the ingredients for Kentucky Fried Chicken.

Paul W. Long left the mill operation and bought Hollenback's ice cream parlor on Main Street. He ran this business until it closed and then he became the agent for the Greyhound Bus line. His wife, Helen, had a gift shop in the station.

Jim Long stayed with the mill until his death. Charles B. Long Jr. and Edwin Monroe Long (Ned) joined their father in running the business, which began to suffer when they could no longer get enough local grain. They sold the mill property to Gaines and Hawkins. It was later condemned in 1986.

Ned Long opened an antique shop in the former warehouse and ran a successful business as the Old Mill Shop. Though he died in March 1992, it continued in business by his sister, Judy, until it burned in 1998.

Filling flour bags at the Climax Mills. Undated photograph.

Shelby County Public Library.

BAGDAD ROLLER MILLS, INC.

By Alice Barnett

Bagdad Roller Mills, Inc., a feed and grain plant located in the northeastern part of Shelby County in Bagdad, Kentucky, began as a manufacturer of flour when built in 1884 by the Bayne brothers--Sam, Will, and Jim. Twenty-four years later in 1908 the mill was sold to Charles Bates. In 1912 or 1913 Guest and Morgan Scobee bought the mill from Bates. Morgan Scobee died soon after the purchase and Guest attempted to run the mill alone. The name of his best grade flour was "Guest's Best." The local wheat crop was so bad he had to borrow money from the bank to have wheat shipped in to make the flour. He was not able to meet this obligation, and the bank foreclosed. In 1914, R. L. Harrison bought the mill. Coleman, his older son, worked with him until Coleman entered the ministry in 1921. At that time his younger son, Miller, joined the firm.

The start of the day at 6:00 A.M. at the mill was signaled by a strong blast from the steam engine whistle. It was repeated at the close of the day at 6:00 P.M. The mill was powered by a three-cylinder generator, which supplied electricity to the townspeople in the evening. The mill supplied surrounding rural areas with feed for poultry and livestock, while corn meal and flour were made for human consumption. There were two kinds of flour--Golden Eagle self-rising flour and Our White Lily plain flour. Farmers brought in their wheat to the mill to be made into flour. They would have a portion of the flour put on deposit for them to pick up as they needed it until the next crop year. Much of the corn meal was shipped to wholesale grocery companies in eastern Kentucky and for the government-subsidized food program.

R. L. Harrison died in 1940 and Miller Harrison continued to run the business. In 1958, he incorporated and served as its president until his death in 1975. At that time, Julian Roberts was made president, Charles Davis vice-president, Alice H. Barnett secretary, and E. R. Weakley treasurer.

The 1970s discontinued the making of flour and corn meal. The mill focused on making poultry and livestock feed in bulk and bags and dealing in local grains, wheat, and soybeans. In 1995, a new bagging line was installed to provide a higher-quality horse feed. The original three-story building still stands amidst a feed mill, a dryer, warehouses, and storage bins, which have been added down through the years.

Bagdad Roller Mills, 1999.

SAW MILLS

by Charles D. Hockensmith

Saw mills were established in Shelby County to transform local forests into usable lumber. As the local population increased, the demand for pre-cut lumber also increased. Saw mills sprang up along suitable streams near mature forests. They used dams to create mill ponds to store water for turning wheels which provided the power to run the saws. In the early days before passable roads were prevalent, the streams also provided transportation for logs cut upstream.

The first saw mills seem to have been an early example of industrial diversification as they used the same power source as the earlier grist mills which provided essential flour. They were able to become independent operations with the advent of the steam engine which allowed moving the mill to the forest rather than the forest to the mill. Although steam saws were invented in the early 1820s, the water saw remained the prevalent form in Shelby County until the 1870s.

The mills replaced the age-old manual method of sawing which required two men to operate a whipsaw. Early steam saws mimicked this operation using sash saws. They were soon replaced with muley or ripsaws which by the 1880s had succumbed to the circular saw which was ten times faster but far more wasteful.

The first written reference to saw mills in Shelby County is found in 1842 newspaper advertisements. By 1850, the Manufacturing Census listed several sawmills in the county. R. D. Waters, John Hopkins, and J. Stone ran saw mills along with their grist mills. C. Clankers, A. Shannon G. Williams, J. Wilson, D. C. Hagerman, T. Gamsat, T. Moore, A. R. Johnson, and Richard Gormy also ran saw mills. The Hopkins and Gormy mills were steam powered. Amounts of capital invested ranged from $300 to $3,000. By 1852, T. B. Caldwell was advertising his combined mill in Simpsonville. Records of the 1860s are less complete but indicate that L. J. Matthews, J. W. & W. Logan, and L. Beatty were operating combined mills and R. T. Marshall, a settler from Maryland was operating a saw mill in Simpsonville.

By 1870, more detailed information was recorded in the Manufacturing Census. It reveals that the Caldwell and Beatty mills were in Simpsonville. Alfred Harrington, Johnson & Shannon W. F. Maddox, Thomas and Garland Wittering, Ruben F. Fields, William Sloan and B. M. Campton were operating combined mills. The Sloan mill was in Simpsonville and Mr. Campton did business in Hardinsville (Graefenburg). Harrington & Barringer had invested $3,200 in a new steam saw mill presumably located on modern-day Harrington Mill Road.

While the Manufacturing Census listed few locations, the 1870 Population Census listed locations of residents and their occupations but did not tell for whom the individuals worked. This census also gave ages and all of the men listed were under 45 years old, presumably a reflection of the hard and dangerous work involved. William H. Harrison, Jas. M. Gibbins, and Lloyd Brown were all 35 and working near Shelbyville. Bluford Sampson and his boarder, John Hedden, ran a mill near Graefenburg. Tillman Johnson and David Shuck worked in Jacksonville. Robert Carlton worked near Clayvillage and J. J. Hanks worked in one of the Simpsonville mills.

The Sampson and Beatty mills were still in operation at the time of the 1880 Manufacturing Census. New competitors included Lewis N. Bellefonte and the Carpenter brothers who had mills in Harrisonville. Nathaniel Scearce had taken over a water powered mill in Shelbyville. John and Charles McDowell were operating a mill in Simpsonville as were Everly Webb and Bohannon & Copper. Clark & Moore ran a steam powered mill on Jeptha Creek in Clay Village. Benjamin Logan was operating a steam mill on Bullskin Creek and Joseph Sansly ran one on Fox Run. The locations of the William & Beckmill and S. L. Sanders mills are unknown.

The 1880s appear to have been the heyday of the saw mills in Shelby County. Subsequent censuses list declining numbers of mills and persons working in them. By 1920, only three men reported working in saw mills. The demise of the local saw mill was likely caused by a combination of factors including depletion of local timber and improved transportation which allowed importation of cheaper and higher quality materials from the south and west. In this manner, the story of the saw mill presaged the later decline of the older grist milling business from which it originally sprang.

SHELBYVILLE NEWSPAPERS

By Sally B. Roach Nicol

Stability and continuity have long been prominent characteristics in Shelbyville's civic personality. No fly-by-night frontier post, families, churches, schools, and businesses tended to quickly be established. The same story fits the city's newspapers, at least for the past 150 years.

The current *Sentinel News* dates back to 1972 and came into being from the merger of its two parent papers, *The Sentinel* and *The News*. The *Shelby Sentinel* was the older, dating back to 1840 or 1865 depending on who is telling the story, and *The Shelby News* traced its beginnings to 1886. Decidedly not new kids on the block, these two papers were an integral part of the community's business, social, and political scene.

Because of this long period of dominance by *The Sentinel* and *The News*, it is difficult to imagine that Shelbyville has had a total of twenty-one newspapers in its history. Some didn't last long, but each had its "fifteen minutes of fame."

Situated on the major highway between the central Kentucky settlement of Lexington and the fast growing river port of Louisville, Shelbyville had its share of itinerant printers who would come to town and start a paper "with a shirt tail full of type." It didn't take long for the crude, heavy presses floated down the Ohio River on flatboats to make their way overland to frontier towns such as Shelbyville.

The trade of journeyman printer was a useful and honorable one, and it served practical purposes. Sometimes it was a doorway to the world of politics or the law (Ben Franklin is the most exemplary). At worst, with such a trade, a frontiersman, with a fair education, could get together a few subscribers or patrons and hack out a living of sorts until he decided to move to greener pastures.

The typical journeyman printer didn't aim for perfection in the field of journalism; his basic use for the type in his cases would have been for job printing such as auction posters, business forms for city and court procedures, sale bills, official stationery, funeral and wedding cards, and even "wanted" posters. The first rural American newspapers grew out of the necessity to publish legal notices and the like for growing communities, and there was very little if any "news" in them at all.

No copy of Shelbyville's first newspaper exists, but an old lawbook, "Littell's Laws," notes that *The Republican Register* was in operation in 1804, presumably the designated local organ to print official advertisements and notices of the state and county.

Shelbyville's second paper, *The Daily Union*, 1809, again has no proof of existence other than being in a listing of Kentucky newspapers published in 1880. So we take these first two largely on faith, but in the clear and certain knowledge that Shelbyville at the time was populous enough to have needed the services they could provide.

The third newspaper and the first with legitimate proof of existence came along in 1814. Called The *Shelbyville Kentuckian*, it is listed in the document section of the Library of Congress. Its motto was "The freedom of the press is the bulwark of our civil, political and religious liberties," and the January 27, 1816, issue (number 29) declared that the paper "shall be printed weekly at $3 per annum or $2 at the time of receiving the first paper." Among the news it noted were the full texts of three treaties between the United States of America and three Indian nations. The Po dancing school was operated by Henry Guibert at Mr. N. Peay's ballroom, giving notice "to the ladies and gentlemen of Shelbyville and its vicinity that he intends to teach his pupils in the most fashionable way of dancing."

In quick succession came *The Kentucky Advocate* in 1827, the *Public Ledger* in 1830, the *Political Examiner & General Recorder* in 1832, and *The Baptist Banner* in 1835. The 1827 *Advocate* and the 1832 *Political Examiner* can boast copies in the Library of Congress and the *Public Ledger* can be found in the Henry E. Huntington Library at San Marino, California.

In 1840, the first *Shelby News* entered the scene as Shelbyville's tenth newspaper, and it lasted until 1865. And also in 1840, *The Shelby Sentinel* was born, destined to become the grande dame of them all, not only surviving but also thriving until 1972.

But was she? Or was she an imposter? But this mystery must wait its turn while the spotlight is turned on the first *Shelby News*.

Its young editors were Morgan Torr and Henri F. Middleton, full of youthful spit and fire and ardent advocates of Henry Clay and his presidential aspirations. The 1840s and 1850s were dominant Whig years in Kentucky politics, and *The Shelby News* was obsessed with it. Clay speeches were reprinted at great length, and there were reports on Clay dinners, Clay societies, detailed descriptions of Clay's travels, and lengthy reports of his views on all public matters.

Though all this Clay publicity seems a bit overdone, there was great public interest in it at the time. Kentucky was operating under its second constitution, but many reforms were being pushed, and pressures were heavy for a new Constitutional Convention so that more modern revisions could be made. And so the paper was filled with news and comment about all these political issues and Mr. Clay's activities in the U.S. Senate.

In 1843, Mr. Clay resigned his Senate seat and announced his retirement to private life at his home in Lexington. The young editors sympathized and assured Clay of the continued confidence and good will of the people of Kentucky.

Clay's retirement put a decided crimp in the purpose of this important Whig journal, but the cruelest blow was the sudden death of young Morgan Torr, senior editor, taken by typhoid fever at the age of 23. This was on March 18, 1842, and his great friend and partner, Henri Middleton, was grief stricken: "We have loved him with all the ties of a brother and a friend: indeed to those who knew him, it would seem unnecessary to add one word of eulogy."

In time Middleton recovered and resumed his signature light hearted and humorous articles. With tongue in cheek he carried on a mock argument with young ladies about their troubles with dressmakers. And while in Frankfort he sent back articles on the Legislature, long, chatty treatises that he addressed to "my old friend, the office easy chair."

Though recovered emotionally from the senior editor's death, Middleton wrestled constantly with delinquent accounts and pleaded: "Those indebted to the News office are respectfully invited to call and fork over the amount of their indebtedness. The death of the Senior Editor renders it necessary for us to square our books. There are many who owe us from the time we commenced business. We will take Shawneetown money at a fair discount; also hams, lard, flour, meal, oats and feathers for moneys due us."

Middleton gave it up in 1865. John T. Hearn purchased the newspaper, changed its name to *The Shelby Sentinel*, and turned its politics to Democratic. And so one is led to the question of the birthdate of *The Shelby Sentinel*: was it 1840 or 1865, and was the first editor Henri F. Middleton or John Tevis Hearn? And why the controversy in the first place? The quandary arises because of the many years of friendly rivalry between *The Shelby News* and *The Shelby Sentinel*. Each claimed to be the city's oldest newspaper. *The Shelby News* begun in 1886 by John P. Cozine could claim to be the oldest by citing that the "first" *Shelby News* was begun in 1840. But *The Shelby Sentinel* claimed the 1840 date by a sort of osmosis whereby Hearn was an editorial extension of Middleton's talents.

The Shelby News office, circa 1890s, next to the Methodist Church.

The Shelby Record newspaper office in an undated photo. At left, William C. Shinnick, at right, Ed. D. Shinnick. Man at center is not identified.

Indeed, the 1965 125th birthday edition of *The Shelby Sentinel* states: "It was in January 1840 that Messrs. Torr and Middleton founded *The Shelby Sentinel* (then called *The Shelby News* and so labeled for something more than twenty years.) Mr. Henri F. Middleton soon became the sole owner of the paper and remained such until 1865, when he disposed of it to Mr. John T. Hearn." And the *Sentinel* then lists all its editors from the beginning to the present, starting with Henri. F. Middleton in 1840.

Another rival began in 1870, *The Shelby Courant*, and it lasted for seven years. Its November 3, 1870, issue lists all the city and county officials, a church directory, a lodge directory, and these practicing attorneys: W.M. Rogers, John A. Middleton, Jr., L.C. Willis, Leonard A. Weakley, Bullock & Davis, M.T. Carpenter, and Charles Brandt.

J. Layson & Co., undertakers, advertised: "We have always on hand the finest burial caskets and cases, and are prepared with horses of the best style to attend all calls and to insure everything to be done satisfactorily for all sizes of Ladies, Gentlemen and Children."

The Courant's editor, Emmett Logan, gave it up in 1877, saying that the publication business "has become so demoralized by an undercutting competition that a living patronage has existed only for those who would obsequiously seek it. We therefore retire honorably from the field."

Hearn at the Sentinel shot back: "The deuce you do. Selling out is not what we would style honorable by any means. Your valedictory is not replete with the real jewel of genuine modesty." Logan later went on to become editor of The Louisville Times.

Confusion has always seemed to afflict the journalism trade: John P. Cozine, founder of the second *Shelby News* in 1886, had been associated with Logan at *The Courant* for its last two years. He purchased Logan's equipment and started *The Republican* in 1887, but it found little support. He shut it down and accepted the offer of foreman and associate editor of *The Shelby Sentinel*, then under the editorship of Alf E. Ellis. Ellis sold to M.T. Carpenter and John C. Cooper, and a Mr. Kinkel replaced Carpenter.

Cooper and Kinkel owned *The Shelby Sentinel* in 1886 when Fletcher Poynter and Charlie Harwood founded *The Shelby Times*. Somehow in the next few months, Poynter and Harwood ended up with the Sentinel and discontinued the *Times*. Cozine then left *The Shelby Sentinel*, and The Shelby News was born. It was a busy and bustling little town.

It was just the *News* and the *Sentinel* from 1886 until 1894 when Republican enthusiasts started their political organ under Gilbert H. Easley, a well-known high school teacher. After a short period of hard work and little money, Easley returned to teaching. His successor was W.S. Kaltenbacher who tried hard also, but the effort went bust.

In 1899 Truman S. Vance founded *The Shelby Record*. It was later taken over by Ed D. Shinnick, a former partner in *The Shelby Sentinel*, and it survived until 1923. Many copies of this paper survive, and Shinnick was noted for some fine historical articles. After 1923, Shelbyville was a two-paper town until the two merged in 1972.

In the county two weeklies made brief appearances. *The Waddy Weekly Enterprise* in 1893 lasted for a while with some local social notes of who visited whom and advertisements from Shelbyville merchants. *The Mount Eden News* of 1904 provided a church directory, death notices and social items from Cropper, Graefenburg and Southville. The failure of these papers was undoubtedly a lack of financial support.

The brief life spans of some of the Shelbyville papers as well can be attributed to poor financing, but some of the blame must rest with those editors who were basically running a job printing shop with the newspaper as a sideline. *The Shelby Advocate* of 1882, for instance, had not one paragraph of local news on its front page; instead there were reprints from other publications, many of the tabloid type.

Another genre of newspaper that was destined for a short life in the 19th century was the "theme" publication. Shelbyville's example was The Pledge, a "dry" paper promoted by the Murphy Movement which campaigned against strong drink. A lady named Frances Murphy traveled from one community to another across the state garnering signatures against liquor sales. In the March 1878 edition, Mrs. Helen E. Brown contributed an article bemoaning that "too many of our daughters have become wives of drunkards." She admonished women not to patronize grocers who also sell liquor, and urges wives not to use spirits in cooking "lest you create a taste for the poison in those who surround your table." Mrs. Brown also observed: "It is almost proverbial in these days that a good cook cannot be obtained who does not drink." This she blames on the prevalent custom of keeping stimulants in the kitchen for culinary purposes," thus furnishing a constant temptation for the untaught and unprincipled domestic almost an invitation for them to be drunk at your expense."

It was not that the theme publication did not have an important message, but the fact that it was always the same message that led to its demise. Advertisers and readers gradually drifted away, and their attentions were diverted elsewhere. The longevity of the *Sentinel* and the *News* derived from one important fact, namely that the editors recognized the value of strictly local news. It was something that their readers would be able to obtain nowhere else.

The fifth issue of John P. Cozine's *Shelby News* describes over most of the front page a fire that began on a cold December night at the Farmer's Home Hotel. Complete details of the fire and the firefighters' efforts are compellingly written, and the entire story is a "good read." The situation seems to have been handled quickly and well for a small community, and there were no casualties. "About one hundred horses and mules in the adjoining livery stable were cut loose and driven out. Where all did so well, it would be an unjust discrimination to mention anyone in particular. The fire engine, in the hands of the Messrs. Gruber, performed nobly. Bob Watts can drink hotter coffee than anybody."

John Cozine's formula worked well, weathering some three national financial panics and never missing an issue. By the turn of the century, Cozine's two sons, Ben and John, were working full-time with their father. John Cozine died in the early 1900s, and Ben Cozine became publisher. *The News* continued under the same family ownership until 1941 when Bennett Roach bought a half-interest from Ben's widow.

During his stewardship, Roach garnered both state and national editorial honors for *The Shelby News*. A special prize was a personal thank you letter from President Harry Truman for the stories done when his daughter Margaret came to inspect the Shelby County homesites of her Truman grandparents: "As fine as anything of the sort I have ever seen written," wrote Truman. As President of the Kentucky Press Association, Roach pushed through the "open meetings" law in the General Assembly. He was inducted into the Kentucky Journalism Hall of Fame in 1988. Roach continued to write his weekly columns "Who'da Thot It" and "Looking Backward" as he had done for fifty years until he was slowed by failing eyesight at age 92. At 94 he played his "best game of golf ever" at the Clear Creek Course he had helped to establish, then died the next day.

Roach's son-in-law, Bob Fay, purchased the remaining half of *The Shelby News*. He ran the paper successfully for several years, steering it into the new realm of offset printing. When he elected to go into the legal profession, his wife Sally Bond (Roach's daughter) took over as editor.

Down the block at *The Shelby Sentinel*, ownership had stayed in the hands of its founder, John Tevis Hearn, from 1865 to 1904. Hearn was not only a fine newspaperman who consistently pumped well-written local articles into his journal; he was a talented and aspiring businessman. After selling the *Sentinel* to Mike O'Sullivan, he migrated south and established *The Knoxville Sentinel* in Tennessee, then became first editor of *The Tampa Daily Times* and later of *The Savannah Press*. This inveterate and tireless journalist also established three other small newspapers in the south before he died at the age of 94.

Michael O'Sullivan was a hard working and talented writer, the son of Irish immigrants who had lived most of their lives in Georgia. His father had joined the Confederate Army and ended up as a captain; after the War he resumed his trade as a tailor and young Mike worked with him until he purchased the *Sentinel*. Adroit with words, he was a colorful character as well. Many an afternoon in spring and fall he could be spotted, voluminous black cape flying, hopping aboard the interurban outside the *Sentinel* office to ride the rails to the races at Churchill Downs. His Irish love of horses never foundered, and he passed the trait along to his son Dan who raised thoroughbreds on his Finchville Road farm. Late in life Dan made his dream trip to Ireland to see the Irish Sweepstakes.

O'Sullivan reported Franklin Roosevelt's sweeping victory over Herbert Hoover in 1932 thus: "The rooster is hoarse. The people must be tired. The tremendous majorities in nation, state and county, by which Roosevelt and all the Democratic nominees won last Tuesday has been told, retold and commented upon throughout the world until the story is threadbare. There ought to be a law canceling the license of any station that broadcasts another political speech for a year. And any mention of politics, candidates or elections inside of six months should constitute a case of felonious disorderly conduct."

In 1935 the elder O'Sullivan died and the *Sentinel* passed to the hands of his two sons, Daniel and James. Its high standards continued with Dan mostly assuming the business end of the paper and James (Buddy) overseeing the mechanical running of the "back shop."

Serving as editor during this time period was noted local writer George Willis, author of the *History of Shelby County Kentucky*. He produced many excellent articles and editorials for the *Sentinel* before dying at the young age of 40.

The most sensational local story may have been the shooting death in 1937 of General H.H. Denhardt in front of the Armstrong Hotel. Guilty were the Garr brothers, revenging the murder of their sister, Mrs. Verna Garr Taylor, General Denhardt's fiancée. At the time he was shot Gen. Denhardt was awaiting commencement of a second trial on this charge.

The Shelby Sentinel newspaper office on Main Street about 1909.

Miss Mabel Oats whose newspaper career spanned more than 50 years solidly manned the "front office" of the Sentinel. Mike O'Sullivan hired her fresh out of high school in 1922, and he taught her everything from bookkeeping to managing the office and writing social items. "He also taught me how to write death notices," she wrote in the 125th anniversary edition. And so "Miss Mabel" eulogized the unheralded of the community.

In 1962 the O'Sullivan brothers sold the *Sentinel* to William E. Matthews, and "Miss Mabel" wrote: "At his request I am still with the Sentinel and I still feel at home."

Now the *Sentinel* under Bill Matthews and the *News* under Bob Fay both took on steam as the two "young Turks" vied with each other for news scoops and advertising. Both papers were vibrant and interesting, taking various stances on local affairs and attempting to cope with the new printing "revolution."

In 1960, *The Shelby News* became Kentucky's first countyseat weekly to be printed by offset or photolithography. Later it had its own modern offset press and moved from its longtime location opposite the Courthouse to Sixth and Main, the old Petry building.

William Matthews met the new challenge for the *Sentinel* by organizing Greater Kentucky Publishers, a printing plant cooperative that began operation in 1966 on Hwy. 55. It was the first central printing plant in the South and eight newspapers were printed there: *Shelby Sentinel, Jefferson Reporter, Louisville Defender, Oldham Era, Springfield Sun, Lebanon Enterprise, Anderson News,* and *Carrollton News-Democrat.* It took only two years for the cooperative to become a corporation, and in 1968 it emerged as Newspapers, Inc.

In 1972 the unimaginable happened when the two old rivals for more than a century, *The Shelby News* and *The Shelby Sentinel*, consolidated ranks to become *The Sentinel-News*. The new paper published twice a week instead of weekly and offered more timely news to readers and wider coverage to advertisers. And for the first time in well over a hundred years the question of which paper was the oldest was settled: the question was now moot, and nobody cared.

The Sentinel-News made a hit with both readers and advertisers with its newly packaged product, and it grew rapidly in its first year. In no time at all it was the star of the Newspapers, Inc. And Newspapers, Inc. was being closely eyed by the Landmark Corporation, a conglomerate of dailies, weeklies, television stations and the big cable television weather channel, privately owned by the Frank W. Batten family. Landmark bought Newspapers, Inc. in 1973 when *The Sentinel-News* was still in its infancy. The Landmark Corporation moved the entire local newspaper operation to its plant on Hwy. 55 and the newspaper joined the ranks of retailers, banks, groceries and auto dealers who deserted the old downtown streets for the suburbs.

Under Landmark's ownership, the *Sentinel-News* beginning in 1976 received hundreds of Kentucky Press Association awards, including at least twelve first place General Excellence awards signifying the state's best nondaily community newspaper each year. Jim Edelen, one of the original eight Greater Kentucky Publishers and Newspapers, Inc. owners from Springfield, serves as *Sentinel-News* publisher from 1975 to present.

Landmark kept its community newspaper division headquarters in Shelbyville and by the end of 1999 owned 38 papers and several printing plants. Area papers owned by the company included those in Oldham, Spencer, Henry, Bullitt, Carroll and Trimble Counties.

KENTUCKY ABOLITION SOCIETY

By Kevin Collins

There is evidence that two abolition societies were organized in Kentucky before 1797, but there is no record of their activities. Most early societies generally proposed to end slavery through legislation as had already been done in most of the northern states. Slaves would be freed gradually and thus be able through education to prepare for freedom. The slaveholders would be compensated by the state for the loss of their slaves.

In 1808, the Revs. Carter Torrant and David Barrow organized the Kentucky Abolition Society. This society was active in advertising the evils of slavery and urging emancipation.

In May 1822 the society established in Shelbyville one of the first anti-slavery newspapers in the United States. The Rev. John Finley Crowe edited the *Abolition Intelligencer and Missionary Magazine*. The paper was published monthly for one year when it was forced to stop for lack of funds. This paper never had more than 500 subscribers. With the death of this newspaper, interest in abolition in Shelby County decreased. By 1827 only eight abolition societies were left in Kentucky. Many slaveholders withdrew from churches that became associated with the society, and the most radical members of the organization often moved north, where conditions for helping blacks were more favorable.

Undertakers and Funeral Establishments

By William Shannon

Bagdad Area

George Searcy (1858-1933) was an undertaker for many years beginning in the late 1800s. In the early years, several others were providing like services, namely Jimmy Banta and Russell Rogers.

About 1932, R. Lee Shannon Sr. of Shelbyville entered the Bagdad area and for a time was assisted by Banta and Rogers. Later on, Everett Hall and Elmo Wise were for a time associated with R. Lee Shannon. Everett Hall left the relationship in 1949.

In 1951, the partnership of R. Lee Shannon and Son took over the Bagdad operation. At that time, a residence located on KY 22 North just before the intersection housed a licensed van and was used for funerals, if requested. The partnership dissolved in 1976.

Russell Rogers was associated with the funeral business from 1927-35. In 1943, at age 42, he went to Whitesburg, Kentucky, and operated a funeral home until retirement and death in 1984.

Waddy-Harrisonville Area

Ralph Catlett was an undertaker located in Harrisonville for a number of years. He was associated with Gordon Funeral Home of Lawrenceburg. No other information is available.

Mount Eden Area

Jim Cleveland started the undertaking business in Mount Eden in 1861. When "Mr. Jim" grew older and needed help, his grandson, James L. "Little Jim" Cleveland, at age 17, began to assist him. At Mr. Jim's death, "Little Jim" continued to operate the funeral service. By that time he had his undertaker's license. For a time, James L. Cleveland was associated with the Greenwell Funeral Home in Taylorsville.

In January 1952, James became associated with Shannon Funeral Service of Shelbyville as a full-time employee, but with a unique arrangement, which allowed him to continue his Mount Eden business.

On August 1, 1961, a decision was made to incorporate Cleveland's Mount Eden business. The original incorporators were James L. Cleveland, President; R. L. Shannon Jr., Vice-President; and William L. Shannon, Secretary-Treasurer. James L. Cleveland died July 2, 1974, after 23 years association with Shannon's.

After Mr. Cleveland's death, his wife became principal stockholder, followed in later years by William L. Shannon and Virginia T. Shannon. On August 1, 1996, the Shannons gifted and sold their stock to James W. Davis (now President) and John S. Shannon (now Secretary-Treasurer). Lucille L. Cleveland remains as stockholder, as of September 1, 1999.

Shelbyville Area

According to the Shelby Record dated February 23, 1917, two undertakers were mentioned as residents. One was John Fulton who was married to Louise Fulton. He was the father of Mrs. S.H.

Brown and was an undertaker and cabinetmaker. The second was J. Layson and Co. Undertakers located in the old frame house next to the corner shop at Seventh and Main Streets. No other information is available at this time, concerning these individuals.

Guy Wells (1863-1936) was in the funeral business for 40 years. He started in Spencer County and moved to Shelbyville, opening for business. On January 18, 1907, the *Shelby Record* recorded that he had an assistant by the name of Mr. Wallace. In the local paper, the firm advertised a horse drawn hearse and a "call buggy." Later, A. B. Weaver became a licensed undertaker and entered into a partnership with Mr. Wells. The firm was known as Wells & Weaver (1933-36). When Guy Wells died on July 19, 1936, his daughter, Margaret Wells Allen, now a licensed funeral director, continued to operate the firm.

In 1937, Mr. Weaver decided to go out on his own with his son, William Weaver, and moved into what is now the "Henderson House" on Main Street between Seventh and Eighth. In 1938, Margaret Wells Allen and D.L. Ricketts, a funeral director of 35 years in Henry and Oldham Counties, entered into a partnership known as Allen & Ricketts at 1105 Main Street.

In 1941, Margaret Allen dissolved the partnership and moved to Louisville. In the same year, A.B. "Buddy" Fendley joined with Mr. Ricketts to form the firm of Ricketts & Fendley, with Thomas Botts as assistant. This firm was dissolved in 1942 at which time A.B. Weaver & Son moved into the 1105 Main Street location. In 1949, the Weavers sold out to a new firm, Hall & Taylor (Everett L. Hall and James Taylor).

G. W. Saffell and Daisy Mildred Saffell established an African-American funeral home at Fourth and Clay streets in 1931. At Saffell's death, Mildred continued on with several different associates until closing about 1990.

After being associated with Saffell's for some time, George Morton and Sam Beckley (with the assistance of Ross Webb) established a funeral home on East Main about 1988. Later, Mr. Webb purchased a home in 1990 at 1144 Main St. and operated as Webb Central Funeral Home, while also continuing to serve Morton-Beckley Funeral Directors for any service call they had.

GROVE HILL CEMETERY

By Betty B. Matthews

The origins of Grove Hill Cemetery go back to the summer of 1853, when John T. Ballard and Marion C. Taylor took a Sunday walk from Shelbyville out Mount Eden Road. Crossing Clear Creek and ascending the bluff overlooking it, they remarked that it would be an ideal location for a new cemetery since the old grave-yard in downtown Shelbyville was running out of space.

In March 1854, by an Act of the Kentucky General Assembly, the Shelbyville Cemetery Co. was incorporated with sixty stockholders. Colonel Mark Hardin, who owned part of the land, agreed to sell 15 acres at a nominal price. Neighboring landowner, Daniel Lively, gave the eastern acreage in return for a burial plot. Josephus H. Wilson, whose land bordered on the south, also deeded land. The Cemetery Company sold 40 to 50 lots in 1855 and 1856 to citizens who desired to help the project. The surveyors were Stonestreet and Ford. Benjamin Groves, an engineer from Louisville, designed and laid out the cemetery.

The first burial was on January 3, 1856, when the Rev. James H. Logan, a Presbyterian minister, was laid to rest. The second person buried was the infant son of Judge Thomas J. Throop.

After the Civil War, the trustees donated 12 lots to the War Department for burial of Union soldiers. Headstones were sent by the government and erected without cost. Later

Chapel at Grove Hill Cemetery, built in 1893, restored in 1998.

Williams Studio photo, courtesy of Duanne Puckett.

Confederate veterans were buried there as well. Over the years more acreage was purchased, and Benjamin Groves was engaged in 1886 to lay out an eastern part of the cemetery.

In 1892, Lewis Henry Gruber and Sons were commissioned to erect a chapel. Stone came from the limestone quarries in Bedford, Ind., with the Louisville firm of Peter & Melcher doing the stone work. Alberts & Lussky designed the stained-glass windows. The chapel was dedicated in October 1893 and used for over 70 years for services until it was boarded up. It was restored between 1996 and 1998 at 10 times the original construction cost, and was rededicated October 11, 1998.

In 1913, the Peter Burghard Stone Company was engaged to erect a stone gateway, and in 1916 the company was commissioned to build a mausoleum similar to, but smaller than, the Paul Jones Mausoleum in Cave Hill Cemetery in Louisville. The same year automobiles were allowed to enter the grounds.

A new road was constructed from U.S. 60 (Main Street) to I-64 in 1962. A new entrance was made from this road to the newer part of the cemetery, and a one-story brick house was built for the sexton with office space in the basement provided later. This house replaced a frame one built in 1871 for the custodian of the cemetery on the old Mount Eden Road.

The first sexton was Patrick O'Brien who held the position for nearly 20 years. He was succeeded by Frederick Moesser, a German considered a little peculiar in his dress and speech, and a bit old for the job. A hard worker and educated, he convinced the board of his ability to handle the position. The story is told that he buried the nine trustees who hired him; he buried the nine that succeeded them; and he buried three of the nine who succeeded the second nine. At the age 94, he retired and relinquished the position to his son-in-law, William Phillip Elwanger, who held it for 26 years until his death. His son-in-law, Spencer Bond, assumed the position and held it 14 years until he died in 1967. Andrew Johnson, sexton at the Bagdad Cemetery, became the next sexton. He retired in 1981 and his grandson, Mark Brooks, became superintendent.

Secretaries of the Cemetery Corporation include Henri F. Middleton, 1854-78; Jacob M. Owen, 1878-79; George W. Riley, 1879--1900; Joseph D. Hall, 1900-01; Augustus M. Webber, 1901-17; Charles Mapes, 1917-35; Richard Randolph, 1935-68; and Guthrie Goodman III, 1968-present.

HALL-TAYLOR FUNERAL HOME

By Stephen L. Collins

The history of the Hall-Taylor Funeral home is intertwined with the history of Shelby and Spencer Counties. Everett L. Hall and James B. Taylor formed the funeral-home at what was then 1105 W. Main St. in Shelbyville. Unwittingly, they became legatees of a tradition of funeral service dating to 1833.

Alvin B. Weaver and his wife, Ruth Durham Weaver, operated the Weaver Funeral Home at the time of purchase. Mr. Weaver was a former business associate and partner of Guy S. Wells, who entered the undertaking business in Spencer County as a partner to Robert Barker. Barker and Wells Undertakers and Embalmers were located on the southeast corner of the intersection of Main and Washington Streets in Taylorsville. Robert Barker had come into the funeral business as a partner to George Kurtz. Kurtz moved to Taylorsville and began his career as an undertaker in 1833. Kurtz died on June 11, 1885. His wife continued to own a one half interest in the business and his son, L. R. Kurtz continued to operate the establishment. It was during this period of time that Guy Wells began his career in the funeral industry.

In those days, most undertaking was done in the home. The undertaker would be notified by the county coroner, doctor, family member, or friend. The embalmer would take all equipment and essentials necessary to prepare the body at the home. If no embalming was done, the body would be bathed, dressed, and placed in a casket. The body would then lie in state in the house or church and the funeral would be held in

In 1922 this Italianate Revival house was built for the Slater family at 1185 Main Street. It is now the Hall-Taylor Funeral Home.

the church or at home. It later became customary to take the body back to the "shop" or undertaking establishment for embalming, after which the body was placed in the casket and usually returned to the family residence or church. Funeral homes as we know them today are relatively new institutions, it becoming the prevailing custom to remove the body from the home or hospital and to attend to all the details, visitation, and funeral in a funeral home in the 1940s.

About 1906, Wells, who was well known, expanded his business to Shelbyville, where he had a funeral home at 616 Main Street. While his business grew in Shelby County, he also continued to serve the families of Spencer County. The business in those days was known as Guy Wells and Son. Y. Bland Wells, his son, was his partner and the heir apparent. But Bland Wells died during an influenza epidemic in 1918.

Guy Wells continued to operate the business and in 1928 formed a partnership with Alvin B. Weaver. Wells and Weaver served Shelby and Spencer Counties as funeral directors and also operated the Nash automobile dealership in Shelbyville and sold picture frames and glass. This partnership was dissolved in 1936, and Guy Wells died soon thereafter.

Alvin Weaver remained active in the funeral industry. He moved his establishment to 111 E. Main St., and from there to 1105 W. Main St. In 1949, he sold it to Hall and Taylor, who changed the name of the business operation to Hall-Taylor Funeral Home.

The new owners of the funeral home, Everett and Mary Hall and Jim and Nancye Taylor, refurbished the house on W. Main St. and continued providing funeral and ambulance services to the community.

Hall was born on June 29, 1909, in Owen County, Kentucky. During his youth, Hall's father kept a store in which he sold caskets. This was Hall's first association with funeral service. Hall's first experience in the funeral business in Shelby County came through assisting Bagdad's funeral director, Russell E. Rogers.

Hall married Mary Taylor on August 19, 1932, after her graduation from Bagdad High School. They became the parents of Martha Layne Hall who grew up in Bagdad, later married Dr. Bill Collins, and became the first woman elected Governor of Kentucky.

Taylor married Nancye Waters, the daughter of John Nathan Waters and Kitty Lee Watts Waters. Mr. Waters, a native of Mount Eden, was an eminent tobacco warehouseman.

In 1960, Taylor sold his interest in the funeral home to his sister, Mary Taylor Hall. Hall-Taylor Funeral Home remained at 1105 W.Main St. until 1961 when it was moved to 1185 W. Main St.

Hall-Taylor Funeral Home remains the home of Mary Taylor Hall. The operation of the business is under the direction of the Hall's grandson, Stephen L. Collins, a funeral director and attorney.

SAFFELL FUNERAL HOME

By Gayle Graham

The Saffell Funeral Home served the African-American community of Shelbyville and beyond. After the black church and possibly the beauty parlor, the funeral home is one of the oldest African-American institutions in existence today in Shelbyville.

Daisy M. Grubbs was born on June 24, 1875, in Louisville. In the 1880 census, her mother's name was listed as Lizzy B. Waters. The only reference to the father stated that his birth state was New York. Educated in the Louisville public school system, Grubbs graduated from Roger Williams College in Nashville, Tenn. and was a renowned pianist.

On March 10, 1897, in Frankfort, Grubbs married George William Saffell, Jr. Saffell was born on May 10, 1876, in Frankfort to Addie and George Saffell. He attended public school in Frankfort. Together they shared a singleness of purpose: to uplift people of color.

In 1898 at Frankfort, Daisy Morgan Saffell, along with 12 classmates, received her degree from the Kentucky Normal and Industrial Institute (now Kentucky State University). She briefly taught in Frankfort. At some point the Saffells moved to Lawrenceburg where she became the principal of the Lawrenceburg "colored" school from 1906-09. Her husband, Professor Saffell, received his degree from the Kentucky Normal and Industrial Institute in 1900 and also taught in Frankfort and Lawrenceburg. From 1907-19 Saffell served as principal for the "colored" school in Shelbyville. The 1900 census listed George W. Saffell Jr. as a teacher and barber.

Daisy began to look for other business opportunities. It is not known why she chose to pursue a non-traditional occupation in funeral service. Traditionally, only family members who were already connected to a funeral home were expected to follow in the footsteps of their forefathers. Daisy Morgan Saffell was the first African-American woman in Kentucky to obtain both an embalmer's and undertaker's licenses. On the national level, George W. Saffell became the first president of the National Funeral Directors and Morticians, Inc. in 1924. He served as president for six years. All African-American funeral directors and morticians appreciate the Saffell's efforts to uplift them in this profession.

The funeral industry introduced legislation in the General Assembly requiring undertakers and embalmers to be licensed to operate within the state of Kentucky. The law was enacted in 1904 and the State Board of Embalming of Kentucky became the agency regulating the industry. Embalmers were required to complete courses provided by an accredited mortuary school. In order to receive an undertaker license the student had to work with an embalmer for a period of time.

Daisy enrolled in the Cincinnati School of Mortuary Science and graduated after completing the three-month course. Within the year, the Saffells moved to Shelbyville and opened the Saffell Funeral Home. The small building was located at the corner of Fourth and Clay Streets. In the beginning, she was the licensed embalmer and funeral director and ran the funeral home. Her husband also obtained his license as an undertaker. Because most families brought their deceased loved ones home for the wake, the funeral home's primary role was to provide a place to embalm. Hence the size of the funeral home was small. Not only did the Saffells bury the "coloreds" in Shelbyville; they also served Eminence, New Castle, Taylorsville, Martinsville, and Bagdad. Within this community, the Saffells were known and respected. The business venture was a complete success.

Daisy was involved with Clay Street Baptist Church, secretary for the Household of Ruth lodge, secretary for the Colored Undertakers, editor of the Kentucky Club Women, and served on many missionary boards. Her involvement extended throughout the community; Daisy M. Saffell Colored Hospital was named for her along with the King's Daughters Amanda Smith circle. On Saturday, October 2, 1918, Daisy Morgan Saffell died. She was buried in the Frankfort Cemetery.

The Saffells had acquired land just north of the city on Seventh Street. After her death, her husband accumulated a total of 30 acres and eventually opened the Calvary Cemetery. The funeral home relocated across the street from its original location at Fourth and Clay. Between 1918 and 1938, he ran the funeral home with a limited staff.

From an undated advertisement.

On October 31, 1939, Saffell married Mildred Stone in Frankfort. Mildred, wanting to know more about the funeral business, chose to attend the Melton Mortuary School in Louisville. Mortuary schools were segregated then and Mildred, Woodford Porter, Kathleen Williams, and Cecil L. Travis were separated from whites, receiving their training in the same building but on different floors. Mildred's embalming skills were put to work right away and she handled the day-to day operations of their business—funeral home, cemetery, and ambulance service. (In earlier times the funeral home also operated an ambulance service. In the beginning the hearse doubled as the ambulance, but as time went on, most funeral homes had a hearse and an ambulance.) When Saffell 's vision became impaired, Mildred ran the entire operation.

On March 22, 1953, Saffell died. Mildred continued to run the business until blindness caused her to leave it. She regained sight in one eye and moved to the Shelby Manor Nursing Home. She too was involved within the community as a member of Clay Street Baptist Church, House of Ruth, Homemaker Club, and other social groups.

Daisy M. Saffell, founder of Saffell Funeral Home.

SHANNON FUNERAL SERVICE

By William Lee Shannon

The present firm of Shannon Funeral Service is the outgrowth of two branches of Shannons. Both of these branches were in the funeral profession before joining together. John W. Shannon, father of R. Lee Shannon, Sr., grandfather of R. L. Shannon Jr. great-grandfather of William L. Shannon, and great-great-grandfather of John S. Shannon established his business in LaGrange, Kentucky, in 1865. During the earlier years of his business, John W. Shannon made most of the caskets he used out of black walnut and cherry wood.

As a young man R. Lee Shannon Sr. assisted his father then went to work for himself and lived in Louisville for a short period of time. He returned to LaGrange in 1893 and took charge of his father's business when the latter became ill. John W. Shannon passed away February 28, 1893. The business was continued in LaGrange by R. Lee Shannon Sr. until the fall of 1899 when he came to Shelbyville and bought the interest of Shannon Reid in the firm of Shannon and Company and became a partner of John S. Shannon of this city, who had been connected with the funeral business here for a number of years.

The other branch of Shannons in the funeral business started in 1884 when the above mentioned John S. Shannon became connected with the firm of S. M. Long and Company, Shelbyville, which was then composed of S.M. Long, John S. Shannon, and Thomas Ellis.

Horse-drawn hearse, 1865, owned by Shannon Funeral Home. Restored by Indiana Amish craftsmen.

For a period of years, several changes took place in the firm:

1887—John S. Shannon formed a partnership of Shannon & Smith.

June 1887—A new firm was started by John S. Shannon with Thomas Ellis as an assistant.

1888—The firm became Shannon and Lowe.

1889—The name changed to Shannon & Company,

1891—The firm then became Shannon & Reid and remained as such until the partnership was dissolved by the death of Mr. Shannon Reid in 1899, at which time as stated before, R. L. Shannon Sr. moved the business from LaGrange to Shelbyville and bought Shannon Reid's interest. The firm's name again came to be known as Shannon & Company. The location of the business was on the south side of the 500 block of Main Street.

The firm of Shannon & Company was continued until 1908 when Edgar Sleadd bought the interest of John S. Shannon. The firm was then called Shannon & Sleadd and continued until the early part of September 1909, when the furniture and funeral directing business was burned out by the fire which also destroyed the First Baptist Church and several other business houses.

SHANNON FUNERAL HOME

MORE THAN 127 YEARS OF SERVICE
Five Generations Under One Family

John W. R. Lee R. Lee William John

Courtesy of Shannon Funeral Service.

Five generations of Shannons have operated the Shannon Funeral Home.

The firm of Shannon Undertaking Company was begun October 1, 1909, by R. Lee Shannon Sr. in the Odd Fellows Building between Fourth and Fifth on Main Street. The last meeting of stockholders of the Shannon Undertaking Company was held April 29, 1935, with R. Lee Shannon, Jr. and Lula M. Shannon (his wife) as stockholders, when the company officially dissolved.

The firm of Shannon Funeral Service, Inc. was organized to continue on with the business on March 12, 1935, with the first meeting of the incorporators held on April 29, 1935.

Incorporators:

R. L. Shannon, Sr.—Chairman

R. L. Shannon, Jr.—Secretary of meeting

Lula M. Shannon—Director

The business was at one point moved to northeast corner of Eighth and Main Street and then was moved to the present location of 1124 West Main Street in 1941. The name Shannon Funeral Service, Inc. continues to this date.

OTHER BUSINESSES

ATLAS & SONS SCRAP-METAL

By Betty Matthews and Isabella Atlas

Atlas Scrap Metal Yard on South First Street in Shelbyville by the railroad track and Goodman Avenue was a fixture in the east end of town from 1914 until it closed in 1968. The history of the Atlas family is a true immigrant success story. Sam and Eta Rosenburg Atlas were newlyweds living in czarist Russia near Riga, Latvia. Not wanting to serve in the czar's army and to escape the pogroms of the Tsar against Jews, they left in 1890 bringing all their worldly possessions in a small trunk.

Passage by steerage was rough with much seasickness, but they landed in Philadelphia where they found a flat to rent. Being unable to read, write, or speak English, Sam Atlas went to night school where he learned the language. Eta was befriended by an Irish woman who taught her English. Sam worked as a shoemaker and saved enough money to eventually bring to America his three brothers, one sister, and Eta's mother and four sisters, each one working to save passage money for another family member to immigrate. Five children were born in Philadelphia to Sam and Eta: Herman, Samuel Jr., Mike, Louis, and Isabelle.

Atlas had an uncle in Paris, Ky., who encouraged him to move from Philadelphia to Paris. He did so and owned a men's store with his shoe making and repair shop on the second floor. While traveling by train from Paris to Louisville, he saw a sign "Shelbyville— Stop and You Will Stick." He decided to heed the advice, moved to Shelbyville in 1914, and stuck until his death in 1945 about age 73. The Atlases lived in the two-story house at the northwest corner of Third and Clay streets for three or four years. Then they bought a house on East Main near First Street from the dentists, T.D. and H.G. Williams. They and their children lived there 51 years until they sold it in 1968.

Sam began a scrap metal yard buying and selling scrap iron, brass, and other metals. Coal was sold until gas or oil furnaces replaced most coal furnaces. Before the days of recycling, the Atlases bought rags and paper. These they baled and shipped to Louisville for resale. Sam was proud that all four of his sons served their country in World War I. Sam Jr. saw limited service. Louis was called to serve but because of the flu epidemic that hit the camps, his service was canceled. Sam Jr. worked with his father until his death in 1930. Mike was an agent for the railroad station in Paris and then Cincinnati. Louis worked in Louisville. Herman ran a tobacco store in Indianapolis. After the death of his wife in 1937, Herman moved back to Shelbyville and went in business with his father. Eta Atlas died in August 1959 at age 90. Louis died in 1959 and Mike in 1968. In 1968, at age 77, Herman retired, closed his scrap yard and sold the property to Marshall Long. Herman and his sister, Isabelle, sold the Main Street home and moved to an apartment across from the golf course where they enjoyed walking around the neighborhood. Herman died in 1990 almost 99 years of age.

BIAGI'S

By Stephen Biagi

Thirteen years old, alone and knowing no English, Annibale Biagi immigrated in 1909 from Lucca, Italy to the United States. He made his way to Shelbyville where he first found work serving ice cream in a local restaurant. He subsequently operated a wholesale produce business, supplying local restaurants with fruits and vegetables. In 1927, he founded The Biagi Company to sell tires and batteries. The store was originally located at the corner of Sixth and Washington Streets, when Sixth Street was a major hub for the town's commercial activity. During the remainder of the century the company would grow under the care of three generations, and eventually evolve into one of the area's largest appliance and electronics dealers.

The Biagi Company's initial venture into appliances occurred in 1937 when the firm began marketing Maytag wringer washers. These gasoline-powered washers were sold on consignment from Maytag, which received the profits from the sale. Biagi's profited only from selling the oil that was needed to operate the washer's gasoline engine. During the 1940s the transition into an appliance and electronics store continued. By then the company had added Frigidaire appliances and RCA radios. In 1948, the company sold the first television set in Shelby County. A crowd gathered at Biagi's on Thanksgiving Day 1948 to watch the area's first television transmission—a broadcast of the Male-Manual High School's football game by WAVE-TV in Louisville. That original 1948 RCA television, with an 8-inch picture tube, is on display at Biagi's.

In 1944, the Biagi Company moved from its original location to its current location at 541 Main Street. The company was growing and needed more room to display its expanding selection of merchandise. In 1954, the building underwent a major renovation. At that time the storefront was completely redesigned and the interior was remodeled, which included opening it up to access to the second floor from within

Biagi's grand opening of their renovated store on Main Street, 1954.

175

the building. Over the years, as the business continued to grow, adjoining properties on Main, Sixth, and Washington Streets were purchased to provide more sales, service and parking areas.

During the 1950s, under the direction of Annibale's oldest son, Vincent, the transformation into a full-fledged appliance and electronics store was completed. By then tires and batteries had become a sideline. Vincent, who had been involved with the home appliance industry since its infancy, would continue to guide the business for over 40 years. During that same time, his brother, Hugh, was responsible for the company's service department. The two brothers witnessed many firsts in the appliance and electronics industry. Items that are now taken for granted were introduced to area households. Refrigerators replaced iceboxes, automatic washers replaced washtubs, and electric ranges replaced wood-burning stoves. They likewise introduced conveniences such as microwave ovens, room air conditioners, color television, video recorders, and satellite television.

A third generation of Biagis- Vincent's sons, Stephen and Robert- began working in the business in the 1970s, and continue at the beginning of the 21st century.

BOHN'S CREAMERY

By Betty Matthews

Frank Bohn Sr., the father of Paul and Frank Bohn, Jr., built Bohn's Creamery, located at the southwest corner of Second and Washington streets, in 1915.

Frank Bohn had a creamery in Crestwood, Kentucky, where the Bohns lived. He traveled for Blue Grass Creamery Co., finding locations and erecting buildings for the making of buttermilk, churned on the place. Bohn married Agnes Roemmele, whose family owned a farm on Clear Creek, reached by Fifth Street across Who'd'a Thot It Bridge. The fertile low land was called "Betty's Bottom." Frank decided to build a creamery in Shelbyville near the Roemmele farm. As the butter business slackened, the demand for ice cream grew, so Bohn installed equipment to make ice cream.

There were a limited variety of flavors--vanilla, chocolate, maple nut, strawberry, peach, and banana, as the fruit came in season. In the late spring, fresh strawberry was in demand. Paul Bohn remembers his father buying fresh strawberries a crate at a time. He would cap them, chop them in small pieces, add sugar and put them in the refrigerator to be used later. Chocolate ice cream was made from a dark brown powdered chocolate with sugar and hot water. This cooled in the refrigerator and the next day was used in the ice cream. People through the years liked the banana ice cream made with fresh bananas. They started in the early spring but the ice cream was better as summer neared and speckled bananas could be bought. These over-ripe bananas were bought and wrapped to be used later to ensure that real banana flavor. In later years, modern refrigeration for the containers made for much less work.

Bohn came to work early and closed before dark. There was such a demand for sundaes, banana splits, malted milk, and milk shakes; the store was kept open at nights. It was often late when it closed.

Because of heart trouble, Frank Bohn Sr. retired in 1954 and Paul took over. There was good seasonal business but seven days and nights took its toil. When Paul retired in 1972, he closed an establishment that had been a favorite spot for Shelbyvillians.

COCA-COLA IN SHELBYVILLE

By Calvin T. Schmidt

Paul F. Schmidt, owner of the Coca-Cola Bottling Plant and a mayor of Shelbyville, in a 1970 photograph.

In 1920 Paul Schmidt began what was to become one of Shelby County's most successful and well-known industries. The son of Fred S. Schmidt, Paul came to Shelbyville in that year to start a Coca-Cola bottling company. Fred had two other sons: Luke who was sent to start a bottling operation in Elizabethtown, and Martin who was directed to take over operations of the Louisville Coca-Cola plant because of Fred's poor health.

Fred Schmidt had begun his career in the soft drink business in 1901 when he and four others had invested their life's savings in a venture which would introduce the new soda fountain drink, Coca-Cola.

Paul was only 24 when he arrived in Shelbyville, having served an apprenticeship in Hannibal, Missouri. He had also recently married Helen Tafel, daughter of a Louisville jeweler.

At that time, Coca-Cola was being delivered by rail in 36-bottle cases or crates. But Paul soon changed that, locating a bottling plant at 623 Henry Clay Street in the basement of a building housing a Main Street business. Paul, with Tobe Sorrels and Arthur Roberts, washed bottles, filled them on a small filling machine, and then delivered the cases via a chain-driven truck. Sales for the first two years totaled almost 27,000 cases of 24 bottles.

Within two years, a brand new bottling plant was built at Second and Henry Clay Streets, but sales were still so seasonal that usually only three people worked through the winter months. It was in this plant that Paul Schmidt began to produce other soft-drink flavors, among them Cherry Blossoms, Orange Crush, Ginger Ale, and Grape Soda. Some other flavors were produced under the name of "Schmidts Sodas."

A third plaint was built in 1937 east of Shelbyville on the east bank of Clear Creek, an earlier location for Hall's Mill. By this time there were 12 employees who produced and sold 140,000 cases of 6 1/2 oz. Coca-Cola per year, and production of other drinks ceased. The success of that operation put an end to competitors' operations at Sixth and Washington Streets, and across Clear Creek at the New Glacier Ice Company in Shelbyville. Other bottling plants in Frankfort and New Castle also closed down; there was a suspicion that several bottlers in the state were buying fountain Coca-Cola syrup and selling it in their own bottles.

Paul and Helen Schmidt became very involved in city activities, and Paul served a four-year term as mayor of Shelbyville. In 1938, to demonstrate his love for his recently-adopted home town, Paul Schmidt bought 351 dogwood trees, white and pink, and had them planted in the yards of homes along Main and Washington Streets, generally three per yard. The only criteria for receiving a tree was an understanding that the homeowner would water and otherwise care for the dogwood. By 1962, Mr. Schmidt had had more than 2,300 trees planted. Unfortunately, many of the trees were weak and subject to disease and other problems. In 1962, it was estimated that only about 25 percent of the trees had survived, and in 2001, there was probably not more than a handful still alive of those which had been planted in 1938.

In 1947, Paul's oldest son, Craig, joined the business, serving primarily in sales. In 1949, younger son Cal also came into the firm, starting in advertising and soon switching to production when the bottling foreman died. In the early 1950s the Shelbyville Coca-Cola plant produced about 60 percent of all soft drinks consumed within the Shelbyville territory which extended roughly 30 miles in all directions from the Shelbyville plant, but not into Jefferson County.

Paul Schmidt's brother Martin died unexpectedly in 1949, leaving a vacuum in the management of the Louisville plant. Paul temporarily assumed the reins of the Louisville plant while also retaining his position in Shelbyville. A few years later, Martin F. Schmidt, Paul's nephew, took over the head position in Louisville.

At this time, Pepsi-Cola was the best selling soft drink in eastern Kentucky, and Royal Crown held a slim lead over all others in western Kentucky. The Schmidt operations in the Louisville area kept Coke out in front in sales. Also, Ale-8 in Winchester outsold every other soft drink in that area, and it became apparent that changes would have to be made to stem the tide of eroding sales and profits.

In 1954, Craig and Cal persuaded Paul to make many changes, and once again the plant started producing and selling "flavors." Tom's Flavors were introduced in 8 oz. bottles and Bubble-Up was added to combat strong competitive sales of 7-Up.

Craig Schmidt left the company in 1958 to pursue a career in financial management. Cal took over as president of the Shelbyville plant, and Paul Schmidt shifted his attention to the national scene. He

The Coca-Cola Bottling Plant on East Main Street, ca. 1950s.

became president of The Coca-Cola Bottlers Association in 1962-63. This organization represented every Coke bottler in the United States, and soon Paul found himself in hot water as the bottlers battled with The Coca-Cola Company in Atlanta over who should have what rights over the control of new drinks and container sizes being proposed by Atlanta to combat the growing sales of Pepsi, Diet Rite, Diet Pepsi, and 7-Up. It was during Paul's tenure as president of the association that the decision was made to introduce Coke's new diet soft drink as "Tab," not Diet Coke, the latter name being reserved for a better formulation.

In 1961, the bottling company purchased several cigarette, coffee and cheese-cracker machines, placing them throughout Shelbyville and Henry County. Sales grew steadily, and in 1964 the full-line vending division of Shelbyville Coke went into full operation under manager Tom Foster, who had served as Coke's route manage. In 1976, the new company was incorporated, separated from the Coca-Cola Bottling Company of Shelbyville, and named Top Star, Inc.

Five employees of the soft drink company and the vending company decided to start Top Star Wholesale Company in 1976 to fill the void left in Shelbyville when Shelbyville Candy & Tobacco closed its doors on Main Street and moved to Frankfort. The company was sold in 1979 to one of its largest competitors in Louisville.

After 1960 the operation of the Shelbyville Coke plant and Top Star businesses in the building on Main Street became increasingly difficult as more space was needed for all the trucks, equipment, and products needed to service the territory. Accordingly, in 1969, Cal Schmidt purchased 18 acres of farm land on Ky. 53, south of U.S 60, and a building was constructed to accommodate the Coke and vending operation. In 1974, all operations were moved to the new building, and the Main Street building was rented to a circular saw manufacturer for a number of years before being vacated.

In 1977, Craig Schmidt re-entered the Coke business, taking over as vice-president of Louisville Coke. His father, Paul, who had started it all in 1920, died in 1978. His tenure was relatively brief, however, as the Louisville operation was sold in 1979 to Bill and Warren Terry of Lexington. Craig retired at that time, and died in 1985.

Cal Schmidt and three others established a mini-warehouse operation on 1 1/2 acres of property owned by Shelbyville Coca-Cola in 1986. Thus, Stowaway, Inc. became Shelbyville's first mini-warehouse operation. Additional units were built as needed, so that in 2001 there were 350 units at the site.

During the 1970s The Coca-Cola Company in Atlanta began acquiring many of the nation's independent bottlers. Until that time the bottlers had been considered to be the builders, investors and salesmen for the soft drink products that the company produced, operating with perpetual contracts in fixed geographic areas. But everything changed as Atlanta began pressuring the individual bottlers and their production and distribution systems such as the one that had been established by Fred Schmidt in 1901 and subsequently run by his children and grandchildren. The Shelbyville plant felt the pressure acutely as it was surrounded and ignored by company-owned bottlers in Louisville, Lexington, and Cincinnati.

Cal Schmidt retired in 1992, but returned to lead the company a few months later and begin the search for new ownership. In 1994, Coca-Cola Bottling Co. of Shelbyville was sold to Coca-Cola Enterprises, a corporation established by and operating in close relationship to The Coca-Cola Company in Atlanta.

The sales agreement left Shelbyville without the presence of a Coke plant for the first time since 1920. Local bottling operations ceased in 1995.

In 1995, the management and owners of Top Star Inc. elected to sell that company, thereby ending its 34-year local operation.

The sales agreement involving Coke and Top Star permitted the group of 24 stockholders to retain ownership of all land and buildings owned by those two companies in Shelby County. In 2001, this group operates Stowaway, Inc. as the surviving corporation, one which rents mini-warehouses, the 65,000 square feet of the former bottling company, various other buildings and houses, and is actively developing the 54 acres of land which it owns along Ky. 53.

Coca-Cola of Shelbyville brought Shelby County its first full-line vending operation when Top Star was created, and its first recycling operation when cans and bottles were bought and recycled by the bottler during the 1970s and 1980s. And Stowaway, Inc. was the first mini-warehouse operation in the county. Paul, Craig, and Cal Schmidt were leaders in the soft drink industry of Kentucky, with Paul leading the national bottlers for two years. With their family counterparts in Louisville and Elizabethtown, the Schmidts were well known leaders of the national soft drink industry for three generations, from 1920 until almost the turn of the century.

CRUME-HUDLEY OIL CO.

By Duanne Puckett

The small white concrete block building on South Third Street is a landmark in the Shelbyville business community. It has weathered countless floodings of Clear Creek and has remained in the same family for three generations, following in the footsteps of the founder, J.W. Hundley Sr.

J.W. Hundley, the founder, was born in 1894 on Emimence Road. He first worked for the Fullenwider Oil Co. on Seventh Street where he met John Hunt Crume. Their meeting became a partnership that led to the Crume-Hundley Oil Co. in 1929.

The two started in an office on Snow Hill before they leased property at Third and Goodman from the Guthrie Goodman Sr. Estate. On that vacant lot, the two men had built a shotgun-style structure for offices and bay area—the same structure that was painted white with blue trim 70 years later and run by Mr. Hundley's grandson, J. W. Hundley III.

Hundley's son, J. W. Hundley Jr, began working full-time in 1947 after World War II and one year before he married Doris Hardesty. When he started, he made $3 a week sweeping floors, washing windows, and pumping gas. His salary after the war was tripled. Hundley's grandson also started with the family business as a youngster, making 65 cents an hour after school, on Saturdays, and during vacations. He started full-time in 1972.

Crume-Hundley had 21 employees at one time when their fuel was used mainly by homeowners for furnaces. The first source of products came in by railroad on tank cars that were unloaded at Joyes Station. The fuel was gravity-fed into trucks by hand with a bucket and funnel.

The company's business changed during the 1950s, when many homeowners began using natural gas to heat their homes. Crume-Hundley began to focus instead on selling fuel to convenience stores and small food marts.

Hundley Sr. died just prior to his 105th birthday in 1999 and before his death prided himself on a keen memory of local tidbits. At the age of 95, he still lived alone in the home he and Stella, his wife of 70 years, had bought in 1920 for $1,900. All three Hundleys were members and one-time deacons at Shelbyville First Christian Church where Hundley Sr., as a little boy, pumped the organ in the original church.

GLACIER ICE COMPANY

By Betty Matthews

On May 8, 1891, George William and Josephine Bell Logan, Alexander B. and Charlotte Bell Logan, and John Ingram and Annie Stuart Logan sold to the Glacier Ice Co. a tract of land adjoining on the west side Banner Roller Mills. This property ran along Main Street and south following Clear Creek 200 feet. The price was $400 in cash.

Four years later the *Kentucky Gazetteer* listed the Glacier Ice Company's officers as R. A. Smith, president, and John I. Logan, secretary-treasurer. Thirty years later, on Feb. 25, 1925, Robert E. Lechleiter and his wife, Lilly R. were listed as the owners of all the capital stock when the company was sold to Jack and Maurice Montgomery, whose father, John Samuel Montgomery, operated the Royal Spring Ice Co. in Georgetown, Ky.

Maurice and Jack paid $30,000 for the company, and renamed it the New Glacier Ice Co. Included in the sale were three auto trucks, five ice wagons, four head of horses, four sets of harness, all tools and office fixtures, and such supplies and coal and ice as were on hand on March 1, 1925.

The plant at that time was steam-operated, with coal burned to produce the steam. In 1932 the plant was rebuilt and changed to diesel power. Horse-drawn wagons were used up until 1929 or 1930 when the company switched to trucks.

The water was drawn from Clear Creek, filtered, purified, and aerated. When the creek ran low, it would be dammed with old ice cans to guarantee a supply of water. At times, the creek flooded the building, necessitating a major clean-up to get rid of debris and mud.

To make ice, the water was first frozen into 200 pound blocks. When the plant was modernized, 300-pound blocks were used. These blocks were in groups of four, with four or five of these groupings set in brine. This brine solution was in a metal-lined wooden tank. The brine was cooled by ammonia pipes through it.

The salt water wouldn't freeze, but the purified creek water would. This got rid of the sediment and discoloration. Tubes with holes were inserted into the water, and air was blown through these tubes to keep the water circulating and clear while it froze. Wooden covers were placed on the cans. A set of four cans would be pulled out with an electric crane, the covers removed, and the cans moved to the dip tank. With normal temperature the ice loosened.

The Headlight, 1899. Courtesy of William Matthews.

The Glacier Ice Company, founded in 1891, later became the Shelbyville Ice Company.

It was then moved to a "dump" where the cans were tilted on a swivel and the ice blocks were dumped out of the cans. These blocks were cut by hand with picks and single-handle ice hooks. The hooks would score the ice in thirds for 100 pound blocks. Later, a scoring machine was used. With this new invention, the ice blocks were dumped into the machine, raised, and vertical saws made two cuts. Then the blocks were lowered and horizontal saws scored down the center. The result was six 50-pound blocks, which then went through a weighted door into the storage room which was refrigerated with ammonia pipes. There was a small room from which ice was sold, and a larger room where the blocks were stacked for four to five months.

The operation lasted from March until the end of October or the first of November. There was enough ice to carry through the winter.

The New Glacier Ice Co. was the only ice manufacturing plant in Shelby County. Along with city delivery service and drive-in retail sales, the company sold ice wholesale almost daily to every town in the area. Trucks came from Mt. Eden, Waddy, Pleasureville, and Bagdad. On hot summer days, cars lined up past First Street to buy ice. People came with carts, wagons, bicycles, and feed sacks to carry ice home. Prices were 100 lbs. for 40 cents, 50 lbs. 25 cents, 35 lbs. 20 cents, 25 lbs. 15 cents, 12 lbs. 10 cents, and 6 lbs. for a nickel.

The ice plant was a great place for football players to work in the summer since the hard labor was considered muscle building. Some of those who worked there included Bill Gregg, Mark Scearce, Frank Ware, Jesse Floyd, Jack and Sammy Gray, and Bill, Byron and Jack Green. Regular employees included Charles Hatchett Sr. and Jr., Herb and Virgil Purvis, Charlie and Clarence Bailey, Bob Miller, Lewis (Red) McDavitt, Johnny Carpenter, Jimmy Shannon., Kenneth Sharp, Sylvester Harlowe, Shelby Landers, Cecil Vannatta, and Fred Tichenor.

Maurice Montgomery, who bought out his brother in 1937, died in 1940. Bill Gray bought one-third of the plant to run for Mrs. Montgomery. When John Ward Montgomery got out of the service after World War II, he, his mother, and Bill Gray each owned a one-third interest in the plant.

During the war electric power replaced diesel power, and city water replaced creek water. With the coming of electrical refrigeration, commercial water coolers and home refrigerators, the ice business deteriorated. The plant was closed in 1954, and sold to Gilbert Barrickman for $11,000. This was a stripped-down plant because Herman Atlas had bought all the metal parts, pipes, cans, elbows, etc. His scrap metal yard had provided replacement parts over the years for rusted equipment, the brine being hard on the equipment.

In its prosperous times, the New Glacier Ice Co. sold wooden ice boxes, later to be replaced with beautiful white enamel boxes. These were top loaders and care had to be taken in depositing the 50-lbs. block of ice. If it were dropped, it just might go through the tin bottom and on to the floor.

Albert Moffett bought the property after various businesses had operated from the building. He tore down the plant.

During its heyday the New Glacier Ice Company was a source of employment, and it also provided what would become enduring memories for youngsters who would attach their bikes to the back or side of an ice truck, and get a free ride around town. Or at least until the driver would yell, "Stay away from the truck."

FINCHVILLE FARMS COUNTRY HAMS

By William H. Robertson

William H. Robertson started Robertson's Country Hams in 1947. At that time he had a country grocery store in Finchville and decided to cure 25 hams to sell. He sold them and each year thereafter he continued to cure and sell more hams. Later his ham business grew to the point that he was able to discontinue selling groceries and focus exclusively on country hams.

Since Robertson was also the postmaster at Finchville, his time to devote to selling hams was limited. He started shipping his hams via the mail, thus beginning a mail order business that continues to this day. Early wholesale customers included the Louisville & Nashville Railroad and the Executive Inn Restaurant in Louisville.

The company has focused on the wholesale business, although country hams are still available to the public at a small retail outlet at the plant. Robertson's son and daughter joined the business and helped to continue its growth. His grandson has also joined thus allowing the company to continue this tradition into the third generation.

Although the company has grown through the years, the hams are still cured and processed using the original recipe. In an age of fast food and artificial preservatives, these hams are cured with only salt, peppers, and brown sugar—all natural ingredients used throughout the centuries to preserve food before refrigeration.

The company changed its name from Robertson's to Finchville Farms Country Hams due to trademark requirements. Finchville Farms Country Hams has won the Kentucky State Fair Grand Championship many times over the years. *The New York Times* and other publications have written articles on the company and highly recommended the hams.

Jewish Hospital Shelbyville

By Tamara Shumate

The momentum that led to Shelby County's first hospital began on December 4, 1903, when a group of local citizens, led by the King's Daughters Christian Service Organization, purchased land on Henry Clay Street in Shelbyville with the intent to build a hospital. Incorporating as a charitable hospital organization seven weeks later, the King's Daughters formally began its process of generating community support and procuring necessary funding for the hospital's construction.

The King's Daughters raised $7,000 for construction and equipment from the local Shelby County community. The original King's Daughters Hospital, which had 12 rooms, opened in October 1906. An announcement at the time noted that, "It is not for any particular race or class, as the plan provides wards for the colored people wholly separated and disconnected from the white." For African-Americans, in 1913, the King's Daughters purchased a building on Tenth Street (now Martin Luther King Street). The Amanda Smith Hospital for Colored was functional by 1916 with financial help from the King's Daughters Circle. The name was later changed to the Daisy M. Saffell Colored Hospital in honor of a prominent African-American undertaker.

Almost immediately, the King's Daughters Hospital's success mandated the need for additional construction. In 1907, a new $500 addition consisting of a kitchen, pantry, and hallway was built. Seven years later $5,000 was raised in only two weeks for a major addition that included an operating room, 10 private patient rooms, a diet kitchen, convalescent room, superintendent's room, and an office. Nurses' quarters were built on an adjoining lot in 1916. In 1919, growth demanded that another hospital building be built east of the original building at a cost of $33,000.

Land-locked and in great need of more patient rooms, clinical service areas, and operating facilities, the King's Daughters looked west in the early 1950s for a new hospital campus on which to build a new state-of-the-art facility. What was then a 12-acre site amidst green rolling pastures off U.S. 60 west of Shelbyville, became home to a new $1.2 million, 76-bed acute-care hospital. The facility opened amidst great fanfare in September 1954.

The next 20 years brought many challenges, including greater accessibility for area residents to Louisville hospitals via the newly opened I-64, increased operational costs, and a greater demand for medical specialists. To meet these

The old King's Daughters Hospital on Henry Clay Street was built in 1906.

Photograph by Ellis McGinnis.

King's Daughters Hospital on West Main St. in 1955. It is now Jewish Hospital Shelbyville and has been extensively remodeled.

challenges, the King's Daughters solicited United Medical Corporation, a for-profit management corporation based in Orlando, Fla., to take over daily management of the facility in 1974. In 1986, the King's Daughters sold the hospital in its entirety to the corporation. After 80 years in the community as the King's Daughters Hospital, the facility now became the United Medical Center-Shelbyville.

Almost immediately, with the hospital's future increasingly uncertain, a group of concerned physicians approached Jewish Hospital Health Care Services, a not-for-profit health care corporation in nearby Louisville, about forging a relationship with the hospital and the community-at-large. Recognizing the need for quality acute-care hospital services in the area and its growing population, Jewish Health Care purchased one-third interest in the hospital from United Medical Corporation in 1988 and signed a contract to manage the hospital's daily operations.

Jewish Health Care purchased the remaining interest in January 1992. With this new ownership, the facility's name was changed to Jewish Hospital Shelbyville.

Honoring the original mission of the King's Daughters organization, Jewish Hospital Shelbyville immediately began looking for ways to improve the facility and restore its reputation as a quality-driven community hospital. Ground was broken in July 1992 for a $3.2 million project consisting of a new Emergency Department/Emergency Heart Center, Cardiopulmonary Department, Rehabilitative Services Center, Nuclear Medicine Unit, community room, and refurbishment of all patient rooms, lobbies and corridors.

Along with capital improvements, major emphasis was given to the recruitment of family practice and specialty physicians to the hospital's campus as well as to its outlying service communities in Henry and Spencer Counties. Capital construction began in November 1998 on a $5.5 million addition and renovation project that included an enhanced Women's Care Center, new Medical Diagnostic Imaging Center, an expanded lobby and patient registration area, new clinical laboratory, and a gift shop. The 15,000 square feet of additional clinical space and 12,500 square feet of renovated existing space assisted in accommodating the growth in volume that the hospital has experienced.

LAWSON'S DEPARTMENT AND MEN'S STORES

By Ted Igleheart

John W. Lawson Jr. and his son, Stanley G. Lawson of Tucumcari, New Mexico, opened a new department store in the Middelton Building on the south side of Shelbyville's Main Street between Fifth and Sixth Streets in January 1914. Eventually they concentrated on women's clothing and built an excellent reputation for having the latest styles. Minnie Scearce, a sales lady at the opening, served for over 50 years.

By the time of its 50th anniversary, it was owned by Stanley's son, John C. (Jack) Lawson and had branched into furniture, carpets, and other floor and wall coverings. At the celebration in September of 1963, between 3,000 and 3,500 people visited the remodeled store, which included an expansion into the old Wadlington's Hardware Store next door.

At the death of Jack Lawson, the store was taken over by his daughter, Eve Lawson Lewis. Competition from new discount stores dealt Lawson's a slow death and it was closed about 1985.

Briggs Lawson, brother to Jack, operated a men's clothing store at the corner of Sixth and Main Streets for many years before joining Pryor Hower in establishing Briggs-Hower in the old Rothchild Building (now occupied by the Bistro Restaurant). His annual sales were widely attended and developed into a community event that attracted customers from surrounding counties.

Both Jack and Briggs were colorful characters in the community, highly active in church and civic affairs. Briggs led the annual crusade for the Rotary Club to raise funds for handicapped children and adults for over 60 years. When he retired, he sold his interest to Tommy Bemiss, but the store closed less than 10 years afterwards.

PEARCE MOTOR CO.

By Bob Pearce

Sometime in 1928 R. Howard Pearce decided that sharing the family farm on Long Run Road was not going to support his new bride and himself, and their impending heir in the manner to which he wanted to become accustomed.

Accordingly, he took a sales job with Butler Ford in Shelbyville. When the stock market crashed, and the depression began, Henry Ford in Detroit was in a serious financial crunch. Consequently, Ford Motor Co. shipped thousands of stockpiled Fordson tractors to dealers and, as was their right by contract, drafted on the dealers' bank accounts.

These tractors were on metal cleats, unlike all of their rival tractors which had already gone to rubber tires which did not tear up the increasingly prevalent paved roads.

Mr. Butler told Howard that, if he would sell all those tractors, he would give him a partnership. By "knocking on every door in about five counties," Howard Pearce accomplished what must have seemed (and still does) a Herculean task.

The good news for Howard was that Mr. Butler signed the papers giving him a partnership; the bad news was that the latter left town abruptly with all of the company's liquid assets. Howard thus became the 100% owner of a technically bankrupt company.

Shortly thereafter he asked the most respected men he knew—Lindsey Logan Sr., Charles B. Long, Sr., George L. Wills Jr., and Robert F. Matthews Sr.—to help him form a new company. Each did his part, and Howard was able to found the new company in May 1930. Within a few years, he was able to buy out each of those men who had helped him get going.

Howard's son, Bob, entered the business in 1953 following a stint in the U. S. Armed Forces. In 1969, he acquired the balance of the stock. Howard died in 1973.

In 2002 Pearce Motor Company is still 100% owned and operated by the Pearce family, with Howard's granddaughter, Mary Cook, serving as an officer and Fixed Operations Manager. Nan Pearce, another granddaughter, is not active in the business, but is a shareholder and serves on the board of directors.

F.B. PURNELL SAUSAGE COMPANY

By Fred Todd Purnell

F.B. Purnell Sausage Company is a family business. It is owned and run by members of the Purnell family and is operated in conjunction with several other families such as the Wises, the Barnes, the Whites, the Netherys, the Martins, the Leakes and others. Shelby County has been its home for over 45 years.

F.B. Purnell started making his "Old Folks" country sausage in Nashville, Tennessee, in the 1930s. In 1950, he moved his family to Louisville and started over in business. He rented a small plant on Mellwood Avenue, in Louisville's Butchertown district, and the family lived in an upstairs apartment just in front of it. After getting established, F.B. bought land in Simpsonville and built a house and plant in 1954.

The original plant was about 5,000 square feet and was financed primarily by the Bank of Simpsonville. The original 1954 building is not visible from the outside anymore. It has been built around several times in order to increase capacity. Purnell hired Robert Doyle to dig a four-acre lake to furnish his own water because it was not yet available from the city. The new plant opened on May 1, 1955, with 14 employees. F.B. ran the business, his wife Clara sewed the sausage bags, their son-in-law Tom Lincoln, daughter Betty, and sons Bob, Fred Jr., and Allen all worked together in the plant and in sales. F.B. retired in the late 1960s from full-time work as he approached age 70. He passed away at the end of 1974.

When the original plant was built, the company had the hogs slaughtered elsewhere and delivered. In 1969, they started their own slaughtering operation. In 1974, the Purnells borrowed $300,000 to change to a more efficient method of making and packaging sausage. It was a very large debt for the small company but it proved to be the step that would enable them to compete and expand. The benefits of the new process include a much longer refrigerated shelf life for the sausage. This combined with their federal inspection gained in 1970, allowed the sausage to be sold in a much larger territory outside Kentucky.

After improving the sausage packaging in 1974, business boomed with Allen in charge of sales, Bob in charge of maintenance, and Fred Jr. in charge of production. Their efforts combined with those of several long-term employees made the company grow. Charlie Coulter started in 1952 in sales, Bill Nethery started in 1963 in production, and Ray Barnes started in 1967 in production.

The 1970s were a period of great change for the company as it grew. Sales started to chain grocery stores such as A&P, Kroger, and Winn Dixie after Allen Purnell had been calling on them for some 15 years. In 1976, Purnell's started making whole beef sausage after Allen's brother-in-law, Charles Miller had to give up pork. This was and is the only whole beef sausage in the country. Burger Queen (now part of Dairy Queen) started serving breakfast in Mt. Sterling in 1975 using Purnell's sausage and Cracker Barrel Old Country Store started using Purnell's "Old Folks" smoked cured sausage in 1977. Bob Sutherland, a Shelby County native, started with the company in 1977, and in a few years became retail sales manager. Under his direction, the sales force grew to some 56 people living in 15 states and serving accounts in 45 states.

During the 1980s Purnell's had two major expansions including the construction of a state of the art sewage treatment plant. Also, in 1983 Fred B. Purnell Jr. sold his interest in the business to brothers Allen and Bob and retired. 1983 also was the first year Purnell's made sausage gravy, which is a viable part of the business today.

The 1990s were another decade of growth for the company. Changes in consumer's tastes and cooking practices led to the company's 1993 expansion. The primary part of that expansion was a new room for precooking sausage and a room for assembling and packaging sausage and biscuits. A new high bay freezer

Purnell Sausage Co. in Simpsonville. Shelby County Public Library.

and two quick chill spiral freezers and new hog pens were also added. Carl Bunch, a long time Simpsonville resident was hired in 1993 to oversee the expansion.

One of the largest contributors to the growth of the company in the 1990s was the 3- pound package of sausage patties. The patties are sold in the freezer case and are kept in the consumer's freezer until eaten. This innovative way to market sausage has made that product the company's number one seller. The sausage and biscuits have been another product group that grew throughout the decade. In 1998, the company started selling turkey sausage patties to appeal to lower fat concerns.

The year 2000 showed no signs of letting up. The company introduced six new items in that one year alone including Chorizo and Smoky Maple Sausage patties and links. Walmart Supercenters put the frozen three-pound sausage patties in all their stores across the United States. Purnell's also went on the Web under www.itsgooood.com. Direct shipments are available for people where the products aren't available. Another milestone was the naming of a new president, Fred Todd Purnell, son of Allen. Allen and brother Bob are still in charge. Fred B. Purnell Jr. passed away at age 67.

The company has a rich history and Shelby County has been its home for most of its existence. Nearly all the company's management is Shelby County natives or long-term residents and the majority of the work force lives in Shelby County as well.

ROTHCHILDS OF SHELBYVILLE

By Alfred S. Joseph, III

The roots of the Rothchild family of Shelby County go back to the middle of the nineteenth century. That was when, like many other Germans, Esther and Herman Rothchild fled the political and social turmoil of their homeland in search of the promise of greater tolerance and opportunity in the New World. Herman Rothchild, the patriarch of the Rothchild family, was born in Wurtemberg, Germany, in 1812. He married his first wife, Barbara Ochs, in 1833. They had three children—Frances, Sam, and Abraham. Barbara died before the family moved to the United States, and Herman married her sister, Ester Ochs. Ester and Herman had five children.

The Rothchilds moved to the Rockridge neighborhood of Shelbyville in 1851, where Herman farmed and ran a small country store. Along with Esther and Herman were eight children, including Abraham, the eldest son. Abraham and three of his own children would become well known to future generations as leaders in the county's civic and business communities.

Abraham Rothchild got his first taste of leadership (and an enduring nickname) during the Civil War. In the fall of 1861, Abraham enlisted as a private in Company B, 15th Ky. Infantry, US Volunteers. Nearly one year later, Abraham distinguished himself during the October 8, 1862, battle of Perryville, Ky., when he was promoted to first sergeant of the company. During the battle of Stone River, Tenn., Dec. 10, 1962, he was promoted to captain. Except when he was wounded at the battle of Chattahoochee River in July 1864, he remained in command of his company until his muster out of his regiment January 14, 1865.

Courtesy of Alfred S. Joseph III.

The Rothchild family, ca. 1898. Standing, from left, May, Bettie, Edwin, and Helen. Seated, from left, Leon, Sallie, Henry, Abraham, and Clementine.

After the war, Abraham Rothchild returned to Shelby County where everybody knew him as "Captain Abe." With less than $500 in cash, he opened a small clothing shop on Main Street near Sixth Street, founding a family business and community institution that would thrive for the next 82 years. In a few years, Rothchild moved his business to 620 Main Street, a location where the Rothchild family served the public for almost 75 years.

Rothchild apparently had more on his mind after the war than just business. In 1865, he married Sallie M. Kiefer, another German native, who came to the United States in 1851. The couple had seven children—Leon, Bettie, Clementine, Edwin, May, Helen, and Henry.

In 1890, Rothchild purchased a home on South Third Street in Louisville. Every weekday morning, he would come to Shelbyville and, after spending the day at his business, would return to Louisville in the evening. According to the Shelby News, April 2, 1903, ".... His frequent travel on the trains added to his already large acquaintance and perhaps no one in this section was better known or universally liked than Captain Rothchild .... One of Captain Rothchild's good qualities was the great interest he took in young men. He knew them all and watched over them with a careful eye, ever ready to give good advice and if necessary assist them to start right in the business world."

Rothchild was a consummate booster. In addition to his mercantile and farming endeavors, he served for 17 years as a member of the Shelbyville City Council and was a promoter of the first Water and Light Company.

The family clothing business had a variety of names over the years. The store was known as A. Rothchild until 1890. The exception was from 1874 to 1876, when John T. Frazier was a partner in the business and the business was called Rothchild & Frazier. In 1890, the original name was changed to A.

Rothchild & Son to reflect the addition of Leon Rothchild to the business. Later, when sons Edwin and May Rothchild joined the business, it became known as A. Rothchild & Sons. A. Rothchild & Sons was sold in January 1947 to Briggs Lawson and Pryor Hower. Two generations later, Helen Rothchild Joseph's grandson, Alfred S. Joseph III would, with Gerald Karem, purchase Village Plaza Shopping Center from Tom Hower, the son of Pryor Hower.

Leon Rothchild followed in his father's footsteps in more ways than one. He not only joined his father in business; he also took an active role in the development of Shelbyville and Shelby County. Leon Rothchild served for two and half terms (a total of ten years) as Mayor of Shelbyville. Reporting on his selection by the Shelbyville Board of Council upon the death of Mayor Lynn T. Gruber, the *Shelby News* wrote November 7, 1912: "The Board's selection is an excellent one and, we believe, will meet the approval of a vast majority of our citizens. Leon Rothchild is a man of considerable executive ability, fair-minded and has the interest and advancement of Shelbyville as much at heart as any man in it. We are confident he can be depended upon to bring our resources and advantages to the front and keep them there." Leon Rothchild died in Shelbyville on February 1, 1943, at the age of 77.

Edwin Rothchild, remembered for his trademark attire, a black and white checked suit with a red tie, was active in the family business. In addition, he was president and a director of the Shelby County Fair for a number of years, a member of the City Council, a director in the Shelby County Building Loan Association, and a Kentucky director in the Burley Tobacco Growers Cooperative Association. Reporting on Edwin's death on June 3, 1947, at the age of 74, the Shelby Sentinel said, "Probably no man in Shelbyville or Shelby County was better known than Mr. Rothchild.... A man of quiet personality, one who loved to joke with his friends and enjoy their companionship, he was indeed a loyal friend. Possessed of great love for his town and its people, he was ever interested in the civic welfare of the community."

The last of the three Rothchild brothers in the business, May, served as a Director of the Bank of Shelbyville for 30 years and played an important role in the development of Shelbyville as a tobacco marketing center. He served several terms as chief of the Shelbyville Fire Department, always refusing to accept a salary for the post. He died in Louisville on July 13, 1956, at the age of 81.

The following is an excerpt from an article in a Shelbyville newspaper that captures the importance of the commercial venture to the life of Shelbyville and the county: "From a very modest beginning the business house of A. Rothchild & Son has grown to large proportions. Starting with a very small stock of men's clothing, they have from time to time added additional lines of men's, boy's and children's wear and a complete line of men's, women's and children's shoes. The shoe department is a store in itself, occupying over 2,000 square fees of space and devoted exclusively to shoes and ladies' and children's hosiery. From the present stock carried by this firm they are equipped to furnish a complete outfit for men, boys and children's wear and shoes for all. They point with great pride to the standard of quality of the different lines represented in their stocks. Each department is represented by merchandise nationally advertised and acknowledged everywhere as the best that can be offered. No inferior or questionable goods are given space in their store."

The business interests of Leon, Edwin, and May were broader than their single establishment and had long term effects on Shelbyville. For example, the Rothschilds financed the establishment of the Lee-McClain clothing factory in a building they owned across the street from the family store.

Bettie, Clementine, Edwin, and May never married. Bettie and Clementine continued to live on the family farm, known as Greenland, at Ky 53 and Mt. Eden Pike, with their mother and brothers after the death of their father.

The youngest two of Captain Abe's children did not enter the family business. Helen Rothchild's life centered on Louisville, where she taught elementary school and was active in the community, including the presidency in 1919 of the Louisville Section of the National Council of Jewish Women. She married Alfred S. Joseph Sr., a prominent Louisville architect who subsequently designed a number of buildings in Shelbyville, including the current Shelby County Courthouse and the Shelby County Fairgrounds. Henry Rothchild moved to Neenah, Wisconsin, where he joined Kimberly Clark Corporation in 1915 and worked there for 42 years.

SMITH-MCKENNEY COMPANY, INC.

By Martha Donavan

Smith-McKenney Co. was located for many years at 512 Main Street in Shelbyville across the street from the Shelby County Courthouse. The company dates to 1825, when Joseph Hall built a small drug store at this location. A drug store was located there until July 1, 1991.

In 1882, L. G. "Pop" Smith moved from Clay Village to Shelbyville, and became associated with the drug firm. In 1889, he took an interest in the firm with J. M. Owen, and upon Mr. Owen's retirement in 1902, Smith, Jesse McKenney, and Sidney Kirk organized the drug firm "Smith-McKenney Company." It soon achieved statewide recognition, doing some wholesale business under Rexall, a nation-wide wholesale drug firm.

From 1884 to 1944 Smith successfully operated the store as a pharmacy and soda fountain. Rexall made a syrup called "5,000 Chocolate" for milk shakes and had a cosmetic line called "Caranome" which the store carried along with other products. Alonzo Jackson and Donald Holland provided free delivery from the 1940s to the early '90s.

When World War II started, it was difficult to get help since both men and women were going into service. Louise Hower, who served as bookkeeper for 30 years, left her job to take a position at Wright Field, in Ohio in November 1942. Martha Donovan was hired in her place and was still working part-time in 1999. In 1943, Smith sold half-interest in the store to a pharmacist named Harold Hogg. Smith and Hogg did not work well together, and so Smith decided to sell the entire store to C. L. Bradbury, in August 1944.

Bradbury started remodeling at once. He remodeled the fountain and installed new fixtures in the prescription room, new floor coverings, and new lighting. In addition, new lines of merchandise were added, especially cosmetics, which were taken care of by Atha Long, and later by Margaret Mathews, who worked for Smith-McKenney for 33 years.

In January 1948, Bradbury decided to incorporate the business and it became Smith-McKenney Co. Inc. He began to sell stock in the corporation and the first stockholders were John Adams, Martha

Drugstore at Main and Fifth Streets in the 1880s where the Hall Building would later house the Smith-McKenney drugstore.

The Filson Historical Society, Otho Williams Collection.

Donovan, Thomas Moffett, and Thomas Watson, a pharmacist. Officers of the corporation were C. L. Bradbury, president; Thomas Watson, vice president, and Martha Donovan, secretary/treasurer. All the stockholders worked in the store full-time, and each had responsibility for a department.

By December 31, 1949, John Adams, Thomas Moffett, and Thomas Watson sold their stock to Mr. Bradbury. Then, on March 1, 1950, Bradbury sold one-half interest to Ray E. Montgomery, a pharmacist from Central City, Ky. and Montgomery became vice president. On July 1, 1953, Montgomery sold his stock; Martha Donovan purchased one-third interest in the store.

Kenneth J. Easley and his wife, Lucy, both pharmacists in the store, purchased interest in the store in 1953: Mr. Easley was vice president. During the 1950s, air-conditioning, a new heating system, shelves, and floor covering were installed.

In June 1960, James Scofield, a local pharmacist whose store had burned, went to work for Smith-McKenney. On July 1, 1960, Easley decided to leave the corporation and Scofield bought stock in the store. In May 1963, Pat Van, a pharmacist from Elizabethtown, was hired. He purchased stock in the corporation but remained only a short time.

In February 1967, Scofield left the corporation as a full-time employee. William Borders, William (Shug) Hickman, and C. L. Bradbury were the pharmacists. Then in January 1968 Scofield returned and sold his stock to William H. Borders and William R. Hickman. Borders, Hickman, and Martha E. Donovan, each owned one-third of the stock.

Prescriptions had always been the most important part of the business. In the late 1960s and early 1970s, more doctors were coming to town and nursing homes were being built, increasing business.

A fire and smoke, caused by defective wiring, ruined merchandise and damaged the store in March 1971. But the wholesale house from whom medications were purchased was notified of the fire and by 9:00 A.M. the next day they had sent enough merchandise that all prescriptions were being filled and delivered. By June the store was refurbished

In 1972, Smith-McKenney leased 5,000 square feet of space in the new Village Plaza Shopping Center at the west end of Shelbyville. Smith-McKenney then had two locations. William R. (Shug) Hickman managed the original store and Bill Borders managed the new one.

In the latter part of 1985, Smith-McKenney opened a Carlton Card and Gift Shop on Main Street, directly across from the original drug store; however, it did not do well and was closed. Shoppers were going to the shopping center where parking easier. Gradually downtown businesses began to close, and so it was with the Main Street store which closed on June 30, 1991. An apothecary then opened on Hospital Drive, which Hickman managed. Along with prescriptions and medical supplies, medical equipment such as wheel chairs, crutches and hospital beds could also be secured.

In January 1993, Martha Donovan sold her stock to the store. At that time, Gregg Hayse, pharmacist, began to buy stock in the corporation. He had started working in the Main Street store in 1973 when he graduated from pharmacy school; but he later worked in the new shopping center store.

On March 11, 1998, Bill Borders and Shug Hickman sold all stock to Gregg Hayse and Marilyn Fister. Fister had worked as a pharmacy technician at the Village Plaza store, shortly after it opened. The apothecary on Hospital Drive was closed in March 1998, when both Bill Borders and Shug Hickman retired from the corporation.

As of 1999 Smith-McKenney Company, Inc. was independently and locally owned by Gregg Hayse and Marilyn Fister and is presently the home for over one million prescriptions.

Smith-McKenney Co. on Main Street, about 1909.

WAKEFIELD-SCEARCE GALLERIES

By C.S. Chewning

In the summer of 1947, when Wakefield-Scearce opened its doors to sell English antiques, the two partners, Mark A. Wakefield and Mark J. Scearce intended it to be a temporary venture. They never anticipated that the business would still be thriving over 50 years later with a respected reputation well beyond the borders of Shelby County. What began as a whim is today the centerpiece of a group of retail businesses and fine dining in the Science Hill complex that serves local residents and draws tourists from around the country to Shelbyville.

It all began on a winter day in 1947 when Mark A. Wakefield, a Shelbyville native then living in Louisville, approached local jewelry store owner Mark J. Scearce with a Louisville Courier-Journal clipping and an intriguing proposition. Would Scearce, financed by Wakefield, go to England and buy items for sale at the upcoming fair sponsored by the British Antique Dealers Association? The fair was being revived for the first time since World War II. Wakefield suspected that prices would be good since the English needed funds to recover from the devastation of the war. Scearce hesitated; he was confident of his knowledge of old silver, but less familiar with furniture and had never traveled overseas. Wakefield returned a week later with an airplane ticket and his guarantee of financial backing. Scearce left the Louisville airport with several letters of introduction and letters of credit.

At the antique fair Scearce made initial contacts with a shipper and met several dealers with whom he established long-standing business relationships and personal friendships. Visits to smaller shops and sales in the English countryside proved to be the best source of antiques for this first-time buyer.

Wakefield and Scearce quickly had to find a location where the imported merchandise could be stored and from which it could be sold. The solution came with the rental of the chapel/auditorium of the former Science Hill School (closed 1939) on Washington Street for $50 a month. Permission was obtained from the building's owners to remove the central front window in the chapel to create an exterior door to the space. What followed was a spring and fall ritual that would continue for several years.

First, railroad carloads of merchandise shipped from England arrived in Louisville where a customs inspector broke the official car seals. He then accompanied the cars to Shelbyville's First Street depot and from there via truck to the lawn outside the chapel where he oversaw the opening of huge wood crates and inspected all items for authenticity as "antiques." Once the new merchandise was marked and arranged, the gallery opened for business in the early summer. Then a fall auction, with local tobacco auctioneer J. Hayden Igleheart officiating, was held in the Science Hill interior courtyard to sell off whatever inventory remained at the end of each summer season.

Advertisements appeared regularly in the Sunday magazine section of *The Courier-Journal* during the season, and customers began to find the gallery. Under the front-page headline "Antique Gallery Opens Monday" the *Shelby Sentinel* of September 9, 1949, reported that there was "nothing like it in Ky. or Neighboring States." Already Queen Anne, Sheraton, and Hepplewhite furniture were being touted.

Large case pieces were arranged in rows in the chapel, and all space on the tops of the chests, tables, and sideboards was used to display a wide array of silver, both Sterling and Sheffield plated wares.

After the fourth season, Wakefield withdrew from the business but encouraged Scearce to continue on his own and to consider making the business a year-round one. Regular hours and two employees (Bess Rogers and Osten Wilson) were the next steps for Scearce. However, he continued to divide his time between the gallery and his jewelry store on Main Street for more than 20 years. The store was sold to Norman Epstein in 1970.

Noteworthy in 1954 was the installation of the two-ton exterior sign that now stands in front of the business. Scearce and Shelbyvillians William Ellis and Albert Ramsey were responsible for its design and execution. It is an exact copy of a Rose and Crown hotel sign from Tring, England, that Scearce had admired in his travels. And a distinctive feature was soon added to the interior of the chapel—a chimneypiece and mantel from the old Norton mansion in Louisville.

In the spring of 1961, Scearce finally became the owner of the property that housed his business, purchasing it from W. Boyd Roe who had owned it for many years with J. Hayden Igleheart. It was incorporated under the name "Wakefield-Scearce Galleries." His complete purchase included not only the chapel but also the entire east end of the Science Hill property with courtyard and restaurant spaces. Science Hill, Inc. was established as the property management agency. The west wing remained in the hands of the Poynter family, last to operate Science Hill School.

When Scearce acquired the property, the former Science Hill classrooms and dormitory rooms were home to 32 resident guests. As the guests declined in numbers, Scearce slowly began to convert those spaces to business use. He immediately embarked on a lengthy renovation of the property, including extensive rewiring and plumbing, tuckpointing and painting the exterior and interior, redecorating and updating the Science Hill Inn restaurant, a leased business within the complex. A columned portico became the new entrance to Wakefield-Scearce; it was salvaged when the adjacent Tevis house to the east was razed.

Early in 1962 an underground silver vault, modeled after those Scearce saw in London, began to take shape as the crude basement under the chapel was excavated and the first floor reinforced. One of Scearce's passions had always been old English silver, and this new space enabled him to show his premiere collection in a setting unique in this country. Also in 1962 a gift balcony replaced the former chapel stage, giving access to the third floor rooms that were outfitted with antiques and accessories. A door from the balcony was created to connect it with the space beyond, particularly the second floor gallery surrounding the interior courtyard. This space was also used for furniture display and has today become the prime space for showing paintings and prints.

The business continued to expand and so did the inventory. A warehouse with Clay Street access (rear of the former town movie theater) was leased to house the overflow from the showrooms. Eventually the building was purchased and outfitted with three floors of storage space; the Main Street frontage of the building is currently leased to another local business.

In the fall of 1975 the Science Hill property was listed in the National Register of Historic Places, giving much-deserved recognition for its architectural and historic significance. The decade of the 1970s was also when restaurateur Terry Gill and Chef Donna Gill began their tenure at

Courtesy of Katherine and Henry Cleveland.

Wakefield-Scearce Galleries on Washington Street in 1973.

Science Hill Inn. Today they are the longest continuous tenants in the Science Hill complex.

Scearce and Misses Harriet and Juliet Poynter had come to an agreement that Scearce would purchase, over time, the remaining Poynter-owned space, the west wing of Science Hill. By the late 1960s this purchase was complete, but the Poynters retained residency rights in the space as long as they lived. Upon the death of the last sister, the renovation of the west wing began taking place during 1981-82. Additional showrooms were added in the west wing, and leased spaces were created. In addition to Wakefield -Scearce, today's tenants in the vast complex of more than 40,000 square feet are Country Lady (women's wear), Cromwell's (men's wear), and Science Hill Inn (restaurant).

Two awards attest to the vision of the founder of Wakefield-Scearce. The Kentucky Heritage Commission's commercial award for preservation of a landmark building was given to Mark J. Scearce in 1980, and, just a week prior to his death in May 1993, he received the Ida Lee Willis Memorial Award for Excellence in Preservation of Cultural Resources (nominations by Mrs. J. Hardin Davis).

In 1999, Wakefield-Scearce operated with 27 full-time employees plus additional part-time regular and seasonal help. A number of loyal staff members had been with the business for decades. Betty Kirby, Wakefield-Scearce's longest tenured employee, began working at Scearce's jewelry store in 1956, moved to the galleries in the 1970s and was still employed by the business as executive secretary. Paul Bradford has been with the galleries for 30 years, supervising shipping and making deliveries of merchandise throughout the United States and Canada. Several buying trips—overseas, to auctions in this country, and to gift markets—are made each year by employees, assuring an updated inventory including English, American, and Continental silver (old and new), English and French antique furniture, English custom-made furniture, 18th and 19th century English paintings and prints, and decorative accessories of all sorts.

The business continues to host its popular Christmas Open House for several days in early November, a tradition begun in 1963 with a one-day event. An estimated 10,000 people attend each year. It has become a community-wide celebration with many other businesses featuring holiday-focused merchandise and events.

Scearce believed strongly in the power of advertising. Wakefield-Scearce has always purchased advertisements in many national periodicals and continues to mail its own brochures, catalogs, and announcements. In addition, many unsolicited features have been written about the business in newspapers and magazines that have helped attract new customers to Wakefield-Scearce and new visitors to Shelby County. Wakefield-Scearce Galleries has prided itself on customer service and a genteel hospitality. "Spend a pleasant day in the country" has been a motto for years. As Scearce, a staunch Shelbyville booster, envisioned, the community and the business have enriched each other. Visitors over the years have included scores of notable entrepreneurs, politicians, actors, musicians artists, authors, and journalists.

The businesses of Wakefield-Scearce Galleries, Inc., and Science Hill, Inc., remain family owned and operated, with the daughters of Mark J. Scearce currently serving as directors and William Patrick Burnett, with Wakefield-Scearce since 1979, serving as President.

CHAMBER OF COMMERCE

By Duanne Puckett

The first meeting of the Shelby County Chamber of Commerce took place July 6, 1926, at the Armstrong Hotel, which was located at Sixth and Main Streets in Shelbyville. There were 42 businesses that agreed to pay the annual $10 membership fees. It wasn't until six years later that the organization was incorporated with Paul F. Schmidt as president, F.E. Ballard as vice-president, Richard Randolph as secretary, and W.P. Deiss as treasurer. The charter members of the Board of Directors also included S.R. Skinner, J.J. Montgomery, Leon Rothchild, Miles E. Lee, Charles B. Long, S.B. Moxley, W.T. Miller, P.R. Beard, Matthews Hall, Stanley Lawson, J. Guthrie Goodman, and Curtis P. Hall.

The objective of the chamber was "Supporting commerce and promoting growth to enhance the quality of life in Shelby County." Fulfilling that objective has taken a host of volunteers over the years.

To assist businesses, for example, the chamber founded an industrial foundation in 1956. Today, it spotlights members on the local radio station, has a Diplomat Club to assist with ribbon cuttings and new business ventures, and coordinates a gift certificate program that helps shoppers at home. To bring shoppers to town, the chamber approached Fiscal Court in 1989 to establish a Tourism Commission.

To spotlight the culinary scene, in the chamber, in 1986, turned its annual meeting into an affair called "Taste of Shelbyville," featuring samples of the majority of restaurants and caterers. Seeing a need to help industries recruit and retain skilled workers, the chamber allocated $1,500 for a college scholarship to a high school senior who did well in vocational and technical courses and who vowed to return home to work after college. The chamber's education committee oversees the scholarship along with others projects such as the Young Leaders Institute that sends eighth and 10th graders on monthly field trips to better acquaint them with the community. Also, Partners in Education matches businesses and industries with schools for personnel and financial assistance.

The chamber created a Leadership Shelby program, patterned after the acclaimed Leadership Kentucky organization. Leaders or potential leaders are selected for the highly competitive class slots. They are exposed to all aspects of community life and what it takes to make the community thrive. At the end of the yearlong participation, the class is charged with adopting a community service project. The program, started in 1993, became so successful that it severed ties with the chamber to relieve it from administrative responsibilities.

The chamber hired its first executive director in 1946, Louis Quinn. Others who have served are Finley Tynes (1947), Auldon Edwards (1949), Dean Ellis (1957), Bill Brynes (1962), Joe Tucker (1963), Ruby Hoskins (1969), Steve Wilborn (1974), Margaret Stucker (1979), Avery Callahan (1986), Kathy Yount (1987), Kelli Borders (1997), and Monica Weakley (2000).

The chamber believes that the county has been fortunate over the years to have leaders with the foresight to bring in desirable industries and businesses. The chamber will continue to work to assist with education and training young people to enter the work force. There will also be a need to assist those in the agriculturalcommunity because tobacco, dairy, and other farm enterprises have become less profitable.This decrease in farming operations will convert farmland into residential, commercial, and industrial sites, thus increasing the population and demands on community resources.

The congregation of Salem Baptist Church about 1895.

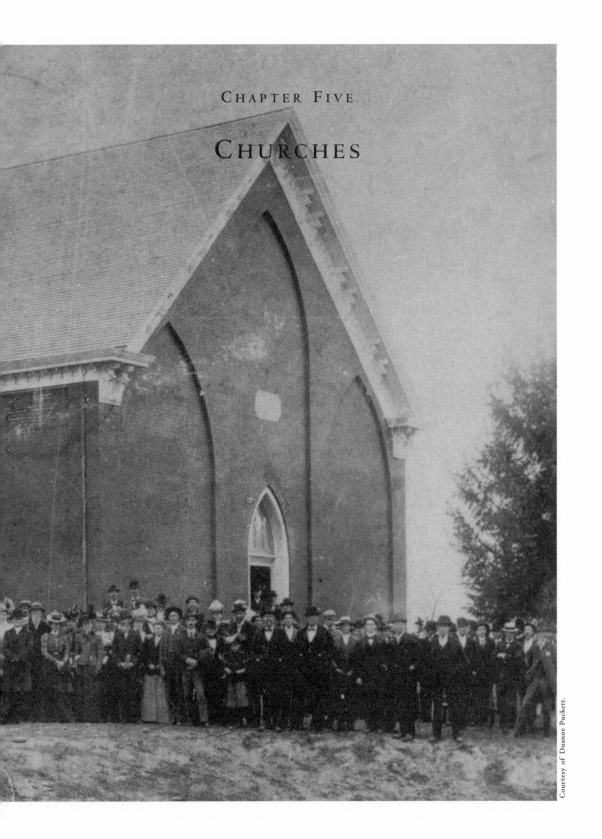

CHAPTER FIVE

CHURCHES

CHURCHES IN THE COUNTY AND TOWNS

by Ted L. Igleheart

Worship services and church life in general here have changed drastically in the last two centuries. Early on, churches may have met only once a month or whenever a circuit riding preacher could visit. Church services often went on the whole day on Sunday with families having "dinner on the grounds" and evangelists sometimes holding protracted meetings for days, preaching "fire and brimstone" exhortations to the unsaved. Now, there is usually an hour of Sunday School and one hour worship services every Sunday, with a choir and other music, and other activities, such as Bible classes and prayer meetings, set during the week. Shut-ins and others can enjoy worship services broadcast on radio and TV.

We are indebted to Ed D. Shinnick, Editor of the old *Shelby Record* newspaper, who researched and wrote articles on the history of the county for the newspaper beginning in 1916. Shinnick says that the first church constituted in the county was in 1794 at Brackett Owen's house 1 1/2 miles southeast of Shelbyville, later constructing a building in 1796 called the Clear Creek Church on the west side of Old Taylorsville Road at Clear Creek. Other sources say the first congregation met at Brackett Owen's Station as early as 1785, calling itself the Brashears Creek Church and merging with the Clear Creek Church in 1843. They were the seeds of Baptists who would later establish many churches in the county.

The first Presbyterian church built in the county was in 1798 on Dry Run about 3 miles southwest of town where the Old Finchville Road now crosses the Norfolk Southern Railroad.

Christiansburg Baptist Church was formed in 1799 as well as the Finchville Baptist Church, according to their records, with members who had been meeting since 1780 in various homes in the Buck Creek neighborhood. The Olive Branch Methodist Church was built in 1800 2 miles east of Finchville on what is now Ky 148 and later built at the intersection with Old Taylorsville Road in 1862.

In 1801 the Methodists built a church called the Brick Chapel 4 miles northeast of town on the Benson Pike and in 1804, they built the Mulberry Methodist Church on the banks of Mulberry Creek. In 1806 the Methodists built a church at the intersection of Rockbridge and Hempridge Roads called the Rockbridge Methodist Church. Also in 1801 the Burks Branch Baptist Church was formed on Fox Run at the end of Burks Branch Road. Buffalo Lick Baptist Church was built in 1805 on the road between Peytona and Bagdad. The first Salem Baptist Church was built in 1811 at Southville, with the present building being erected in 1865. The Dover Baptist Church was formed in 1812 and built a new church in 1887.

The Methodists built the first church building in town in 1810, which was called the Shelbyville Meeting House because it was also used by the Baptist and Presbyterians until they later built churches of their own in town. It was located at the north end of Fourth Street on what was called then North Back Street (now Washington Street).

In 1819 the First Baptist Church was formed at Eighth and Clay streets in Shelbyville, then the building was turned over to the colored Baptists in 1859 when First Baptist built a new church on the southwest corner of the Public Square. Their present building was built in 1969 on West US 60 after collapse of the roof of the old building downtown. First Presbyterians built their first church in 1820 on the lots where the County Library now stands. In 1847 they built on their present lot at Seventh and Main. After fire destroyed a subsequent building, the present edifice was dedicated in 1893.

First Christian Church began in 1832 in a building facing Fourth Street behind a gunsmith shop on east Main. A subsequent building facing Main burned in 1969 and its replacement was sold after a new church was built in 2000 on the Eminence Pike one and a half miles north of town.

Indian Fork Baptist Church was organized in the 1830s west of Jacksonville. In 1830 Simpsonville Baptist Church was formed and moved into its present location in 1923. Graefenburg Methodist Church was organized in 1835 where Goose Creek joins Benson Creek. Simpsonville Christian was first built at the intersection of Antioch and Todds Point Roads, then moved to its present location in 1875. Simpsonville Methodists erected their first church in 1840, then rebuilt in 1876. In 1845 the Mt. Vernon Baptist Church was organized near the village of Harrisonville after a split with Pigeon Fork Baptist. St. James Episcopal Church was organized in 1857 and met in the Episcopal Theological Seminary on College Street in Shelbyville until purchasing its present site at Third and Main Streets in 1871. The Methodists built a new church at Fifth and Main Streets in Shelbyville in 1857, which served for 40 years before a new structure was built in 1897. Fire destroyed the sanctuary in 1978 which was rebuilt and dedicated in 1982.

The Catholic Church of the Annunciation began in 1860 at the corner of First and Main Streets in Shelbyville. In the same year, Clay Street Baptist Church was organized at Eighth and Clay Streets in Shelbyville and they sold an earlier lot on East Clay to the Bethel African Methodist Episcopal Church, which built in 1867. In 1984 Clay Street Baptist moved into a new building on the south side of US 60 West. The New Mount Zion Baptist Church was founded at Clay Village in 1880, later moving to near Waddy, and in 1977 moving to Shelbyville. In 1885 the Cropper Christian Church was formed and in 1889 the Bagdad Baptist Church was organized, followed in 1890 by the Cropper Baptist Church. In the same year, the Shelbyville Church of Christ was begun at the corner of Scotts Station and Harrington Mill Roads as the Shiloh Church of Christ. They built a new church on Washington Street in Shelbyville in 1924 and moved into a new church on US 60 West at Hospital Drive in 1972. Waddy Baptist Church was organized in 1892.

St. John's Methodist Church was built in 1896 on College Street in Shelbyville and at one time was the largest congregation of colored members in town. When the building became unsafe in recent years, a new church was erected on Martin Luther King Street in 2000. Elmburg Baptist Church was formed in 1913 from the Elmburg Union Church which had been meeting since 1906. Hempridge Baptist Church was created in 1911. In 1959 the Highland Baptist Church built on US 60 East after being organized as a mission of First Baptist. They built a new building on the Mt. Eden Road in 1968.

The Shelby Christian Church was created in 1968 and put up its first building in 1970 on US 60 East past the High School. The Living Waters Church was founded in 1981 from some members of the Graefenburg Methodist Church and has added a Christian School to its growing campus in Clay Village.

Recent churches, including the Shelbyville Christian Assembly, Holy Cross Lutheran Church, Church of Jesus Christ of Latter Day Saints, Lighthouse Baptist, New Hope Independent Baptist Church, Seventh Day Adventist, Shelbyville Community Church, Wesleyan Church and Jehovah Witnesses, have been built. As Shelby County continues to grow in population, its churches flourish in membership and services to the communities.

ALLEN CHAPEL UNITED METHODIST CHURCH

By Julia Triplett

The Methodist Church in Finchville was organized in 1876 by a group of men and their families. There were some 50 members and converts. It met in the home of Sanford Allen, which was once a log building.

The Rev. L.W. Miles and Rev. Parrish Fisher officiated; Sornie Henderson, George Smith and Sam Rhodes were appointed laymen and charter members. The first trustees were Sanford Allen, Simpson Wilson, Sornie Henderson, James Allen and Sam Rhodes. Miles was the first pastor and Fisher was the first superintendent.

The congregation worshipped at the place where they organized for four years after which they were able to purchase the present site in January 1880. Reverend Lawrence was the first pastor of the new church. Since that time, the church has been remodeled, and in 1929 a cornerstone was laid to celebrate the 49th year of worship at the site. The men and women of the church have always planned their programs to benefit the church and its ministries. The members all look forward to the church picnic rally day, men and women's day, anniversary, family day, and the Christmas programs. The United Methodist Women give out Christmas baskets to the sick and elderly. Also, all during the year the Women's Society helps those in need.

With the merger of the United Brethren and the Methodist Church, the church took on a new look and became the United Methodist Church. This began in 1964, with the merger completed in 1968. Allen Chapel was merged into the Louisville Conference.

In 1970, the Rev. H.H. Greene came to the Shelbyville circuit (Allen, St. John and Wesley Churches). Dr. Greene's leadership brought knowledge and understanding. At Allen he uplifted the church, bought new stained glass windows, a new oil furnace and carpet, and trained our church leaders. Dr. Greene was at Allen Chapel for 15 years and died in August 1987.

In September 1987, Robert M. Marshall was placed at Allen and Wesley chapels upon the request of Julia Triplett of Allen and Allena Beeler of Wesley. In June 1988, upon finishing pastors' school, Pastor Marshall was officially placed at his present charge. With good church support he has led the church in some major improvements including a new Fellowship Hall, new siding, bathrooms, a gas furnace, replacement of the church entrance, and an organ. Some of the many pastors who have served the church were the Revs. Lawrence, Ward, Hinkle, Breckenridge, Bush, Watson, Holloway, Henry, Asher, Bowling, Price, Hewitt, Henderson, Johnson, Grarp, Roach, and Herndon.

The superintendents were the Revs. Bloomer, Carroll, Redman, Broaddus, Skelton, Hines, Jordan, Haynes, Marbly, and H.H. Greene. The present superintendent is the Rev. Orin Simmerman, Jr.

During the church's history a number of local leaders have influenced the members and community. Some of the men and women who served as stewards, presidents, Sunday School superintendents, trustees, and lay leaders are: George Smith, Sam Rhodes, Sornie Henderson, Isaac Allen, Curtis Sheckles, Oldham Todd, James Ashby, George Ward, Talbert Duncan, Lee White, William Henderson, Sina Allen, Roberta Henderson, Mary Davis, Sara Murphy, Onie White, Estella Davis, Pauline Crumes, Ivory Williams, Vina Ashby, Virginia White, and W.T. Ellis.

BAGDAD BAPTIST CHURCH

By Julian K. Wood

The Bagdad community came into being in the 1840s. For many years there was no Baptist church within its boundaries. Those who embraced the Baptist faith either attended one of the churches at Christiansburg, Indian Fork, and Buffalo Lick, or waited for a visit from the circuit-riding minister. He performed marriages, preached funerals for anyone who had died since his last visit, and baptized those who desired it.

In June 1889 several Baptists joined together to form the Bagdad Baptist Church. Members came from Christiansburg, Buffalo Lick, and Indian Fork. Services were held in the Bagdad College during construction of the present sanctuary on land donated by Lewis Sacrey. In February 1890, J.M. Fowler was called to be the first pastor, and he served until November 1890. First deacons were Lewis Sacrey, Virgil Lewis, and A.J. Pace. Lewis Sacrey was elected the first moderator and Virgil Lewis the first clerk.

The 18th annual session of the Shelby Baptist Association met in Shelbyville on August 15-16, 1889. At that session, Bagdad Baptist Church presented its Articles of Faith and its petition for membership. Bagdad was the twentieth church to join the association. From the very beginning and throughout its history, the church has demonstrated its commitment to the covenant to "contribute cheerfully and regularly to the support of the ministry, the expense of the church, the relief of the poor, and the spread of the gospel through all nations." In August 1889, the first contribution was made to the Orphans Home. This was followed by subscription for missions and support of the China Mission.

The Sunday school Annex was added to the sanctuary in 1924 while the Rev. John L. Stowe was pastor. Under the leadership of the Rev. Robert Smith, the education wing and fellowship halls were constructed in 1954. While the Rev. Harold Bergen was pastor in 1958, the parsonage was constructed. In 1992, under the leadership of Dr. Mark L. Potts, a 5,000 square foot education-fellowship hall was built. The basement also has 5,000 square feet of space and can be utilized when the growth of the church demands its completion. During the construction-planning phase, the church purchased adjacent property on which the new addition was located. The acquisition of the Harrison property, adjacent to the church, has provided additional space for future expansion whenever the need arises.

Bagdad Baptist Church, built in 1890.

Photo courtesy of Julian Wood.

Being close to the Southern Baptist Theological Seminary in Louisville has allowed the church the privilege and opportunity to be a training ground for many of the young men who have served as pastors. They have shaped the ministry of the church, and they in turn have learned from the congregation.

For most of its history, the church has maintained an adequate number of organizations to fulfill its educational, missionary, and worship ministries. A board of deacons, a board of trustees, and 15 other committees support it. In September 1993, the church further extended its ministry by offering a second worship service each Sunday. This exemplifies the commitment that the church has to its ministry. The latest ministry of Bagdad Baptist Church is Bagdad Day Care, opened in September 1994. It is upon a warm, personal plan to provide a place of worship that its members endeavor to extend Christian ministries to the Bagdad community and, as part of the Southern Baptist Convention, to this state, the nation, and the world.

BUFFALO LICK BAPTIST CHURCH

By Helen Poole

In the days before the organization of Shelby County, when buffalo and other animals roamed this country, there was a trail from Drennon Springs in a southerly direction through what is now the Bagdad neighborhood down into Spencer County and on to the salt springs in Bullitt County. About halfway between Bagdad and Peytona was a lick where the animals stopped for days to browse on the bluegrass, to lick the salty earth, and to drink the clear limestone or sulfur water. The trail was plain and the locality was known as the Buffalo Lick neighborhood.

During 1800-02 Shelby County was much larger than it is today, taking in most of Spencer County, part of Anderson, and a portion of Franklin and Oldham counties, with about 8,500 residents. The land was dense woodland with only paths constituting the roads. Travel was mainly by foot or horseback.

Many of the Buffalo Lick community became members of a Baptist church located about six miles away that was known as Tick Creek, which was later changed to Bethel. In the winters of 1803 and 1804, finding it difficult to travel that distance, the members of this community began to hold services in their homes.

In 1805, two men, brothers-in-law, Tarlton Lee and Martin Baskett volunteered to give one acre of land each for the erecting of a "Baptist church; as long as it continued in that function." The church was constituted on the Philadelphia Confession of Faith, with such exceptions as are made by the Long Run Association.

A church was built of logs and completed around Christmas 1805. The first regular meeting of the newly organized church was on June 15, 1805. Philip Webber was selected as moderator and Charles Mitchell as clerk. The name "Buffalo Lick" was chosen for this new church. The newly organized brethren agreed to meet regularly once a month. The following were the charter members: Philip Webber, I. Underwood, Benjamin Boyd, Martin Baskett, Tarlton Lee, Roderick Perry, John Yount, Charles Mitchell, James McQuade, and Moses Scott.

Brother Abraham Cook preached during the first year. For a period of about 10 years he continued to do so irregularly. In 1816, he was chosen as regular pastor and continued in this capacity until 1851, a total of 46 years. Cook was instrumental in establishing not only Buffalo Lick, but also Indian Fork, Six Mile (Christiansburg), Beech Creek, North Benson and other churches.

Buffalo Lick was a member of the Long Run Association from 1806-16. From 1816 to 1871 it was affiliated with the Franklin Association, and in 1871, along with other Baptist churches of the county, joined what is now the Shelby Baptist Association.

By 1826 the members had outgrown the little log church, so it was agreed to build an extension of about 30 feet. This was completed in March 1827. It was decided in 1835 to build a new meeting house of brick and to provide a gallery for the accommodation of the "colored brethren," who continued to worship with the congregation until some time after the Civil War. The actual work was begun in 1836 and in November 1837, the new church was ready for occupancy. The logs from the old church were used in building a barn on a nearby farm and are still in use.

Brother Thomas M. Daniel came to assist Brother Cook in 1846 and in 1851 became the regular pastor and continued until 1881. In June 1889, 27 members from the Bagdad community asked for letters of dismission in order to organize a church of like faith at Bagdad. Brother J. M. Fowler, pastor at that time, resigned and went with them. Thirteen members left in August 1892 to start a similar church at Waddy.

The church building was completely remodeled in 1945. A contract was signed for the construction of Sunday school rooms in June 1946. On the afternoon of June 22, 1956, a strong wind blew down the west end of the main auditorium and over half of the roof was blown off. A hard rain that ruined the floor, pews, and other contents of the church accompanied the wind. The members were very thankful that the Sunday school rooms were not damaged. Worship services were held there until a new church was built.

After much discussion, prayer, and deliberation, it was agreed a new church would be built and it is the one in use today. The new church was ready for use just before Christmas, and the first preaching services were on Sunday, December 23, 1956. Dedication of the new building was held in March 1957.

Courtesy of Helen Poole.

It was voted to erect a steeple on the church, and this was done in the spring of 1975.

Buffalo Lick has been blessed by many pastors who were students at the Southern Baptist Theological Seminary, receiving not only their masters but also their doctorate degrees. Among the former pastors are presidents and deans of seminaries both here and abroad as well as missionaries and pastors of large churches.

The Buffalo Lick Baptist Church was founded in 1805, and the present building was built in 1956.

BURKS BRANCH BAPTIST CHURCH

By Billy Betts

Nine years after Kentucky became a state and Shelby County was formed, 10 people gathered about four miles north of Shelbyville and organized Burks Branch Baptist Church in 1801. These settlers made their livelihood by transforming a wilderness into a farm community. As they labored six days of the week, they came together on Sunday and formed a church where they could worship on their day of rest.

They took the name from the stream that runs nearby. This stream was named for Richard Burk, an Irishman, who came to America to be a soldier for Britain in the Revolutionary War. Burk was captured by American forces and sentenced to be hanged. However, Isaac Shelby and other officers objected to the hanging, and the prisoner was assigned to an American officer. Burk came under the care of Isaac Shelby, becoming his bodyguard. Burk came to Kentucky with Shelby who gave him 750 acres in the north end of Shelby County. Burk made his home inside a large white oak tree and the stream beside the tree would take the name of the eccentric Irishman.

On June 15, 1801, two ordained Baptist ministers from Virginia, William Marshall and David Thompson, constituted Burks Branch Baptist Church. On that day in June, the church had the following 10 members: James Mullikin, Dan Maddox, David Shepherd, Richard Gott, Fraky Fish, Susanna Mullikin, Nancy Maddox, Elizabeth Butler, Elizabeth Hall, and Lydia Gott. In September 1802, the church called its first pastor, Charles Webb.

The church has met in five different buildings during its history. The first was constructed from logs and used until 1811. This meetinghouse was replaced by a frame building, which for a short period of time also housed the Burks Branch School. In 1835, the members built another building. However, problems with the roof of this structure led to the construction of the fourth structure, which was

Courtesy of Billy Betts.

The fifth building to house the Burks Branch Baptist Church is pictured here. It was completed in 1953.

dedicated on June 17, 1901, and cost $1,500. On July 24, 1951, at 1:00 PM lightening struck the steeple and burned the main part of the church to the ground. A new church building was dedicated on March 23, 1953, and it is this structure that serves the church at present.

Burks Branch Baptist Church has had many years of service in the community, state, nation, and world. The church has sponsored missions under the leadership of the Women's Missionary Union and through the Cooperative Program. The church has sent missionaries to serve throughout the world.

PASTORS

Charles Webb	1802-05	J.A. Barnhill	1919
George Waller	1805-48	J.W. Palmer	1922
Andrew Broaddus	1849-52	L.M. Roberts	1922-26
M.S. Stembaugh	1852-55	D.T Foust	1926-29
Thomas Vaughan	1855-58	W.A Wiggins	1929-34
A.B. Knight	1858-82	Reed Polk	1934-36
J.N. Prestridge	1882-84	Norman Price	1936
Carter Jones	1884-85	Clel Rogers	1938-40
H.P McCormick	1885-86	C.B. Love	1940-42
J. W. Loving	1886-88	John Trantham	1942
W. S Splawn	1890-92	Jack Manly	1942-46
B-.B Bailey	1892-94	J.L. Monroe	1946
J.H. Julian	1894-96	Lewis Searcy	1946-47
H. Dement	1896-99	Lyndon Collings Jr.	1947-51
F.C. Humphries	1899-01	John Hall	1952
W.J. Mahoney	1901	Fred Richardson	1952-54
J.C. Robillard	1902-03	Eugene Hamilton	1954-57
H.C. Davis	1903-07	James Prewitt	1957-61
J.H. Blythe	1907-09	Emory Register	1961-64
J.H. Padfield	1909-10	Maury Fisher	1964-66
S.A. Cooper	1910-12	Bob Wiggins	1966-68
W.C Moffett	1913-14	Bob Vickers	1968-69
P.M. Bailes	1914-16	Ken Clayton	1969-72
W.RYolkely	1916-17	Vann Knight	1972-73
C. S Wroten	1917-18	Bill Blackburn	1973-76
		Paul Duke	1977-80
		David Hull	1980-83
		Mark Sorrells	1983-88
		Coy Still	1988-93
		Kent Ulman	1993-95
		Billy Betts	1995- Present

CATHOLIC CHURCH OF THE ANNUNCIATION

By J. Quintin Biagi

The first documentation of a Catholic in Shelbyville was Kean O'Hara. He came to America around 1798 and was one of the most distinguished of Kentucky educators. Tradition says he was invited by Governor Isaac Shelby to teach in the state. Sometime before 1802 he taught in Shelbyville.

Around 1800 the Rev. Stephen Badin, a pioneer missionary priest in Kentucky, made a visit to Shelby County. The next mention of the clergy in Shelbyville was in the summer of 1830 with a visit and speech by the Rev. Geo. A.M. Elder and Bishop Flaget.

Before the Catholics built a church at Shelbyville there were a number of that faith that lived outside of the city. At Bagdad there were Ned Connell, Ben Morey, Jerry Cotter, the Aherns and others whose spiritual wants were attended by Father Lancaster of Frankfort. Patrick O'Connell and John Goghegan, of Eminence, and others of that vicinity went to Frankfort or Pewee Valley; John O'Mullane and Malachi Donohue went to Taylorsville. The O'Donnells, the Heffernans, and others who lived near Cropper went to Frankfort, but all of them later became working members of the Shelbyville congregation.

Catholics were scarce in those days, in the rural districts, and to reach them meant hardships and privations. Nothing daunted Father Bekkers who obtained permission from his bishop to make frequent trips to the county. In 1855, he made his first trip to Shelbyville. His presence there soon became known to the handful of Catholics, and the announcement that Mass would be celebrated the next morning at the home of Mr. and Mrs. Shinnick was received by them with pleasure. A comparatively large crowd was present at this first celebration of the sacrifice of the Mass in Shelbyville.

Bekkers continued to come to Shelbyville every three or four months, always encouraging Catholics in their hope of being able to have a chapel or church of their own, and a resident priest, promising them material assistance in the future. In 1859, Jane Campbell gave impetus to the hopes for a new church by giving the land on which the present church is located. The construction of the church started shortly thereafter.

On January 1, 1860, Bekkers accepted Campbell's deed to the church lot. Strenuous efforts on the part of the members, supplemented by liberal donations on the part of Bekkers' friends in Louisville, made the prospects of a Catholic Church in Shelbyville promising indeed.

Excavations for the foundations were made as early in 1860. Every member of the church became enthusiastic, all of them contributing as liberally as possible, both in money and work. Ed and John Brady made the bricks for the church. The foundation was laid under the supervision of James McCarthy, assisted by Peter Lee, Thomas Fox, Thomas Gernert, Joseph McGann, Will McFadden, John Harris, Michael Harris, John Lyons, and others. All of them vied with each other in their efforts to do what they could for the good cause, and none took full pay for their services, and those who could afford it took nothing. The carpenter work was done by Watts & Wells of Shelbyville, the bricklaying by a man named Campion, and the plastering by a man named Nolan, the latter two of Louisville. Herman Deiss of Shelbyville did the dressed stone work. Michael Brown mixed the mortar used later in plastering the church.

The work progressed rapidly, and by fall the walls were up and the roof on, but all of the money that was available had been spent, and to continue work on the church to its completion was impossible. It was determined, however, by Bekkers that the best thing to do was to have the church dedicated. This was done and the church was given the name Church of the Annunciation, as the records show, on October 2, 1860, the feast of the Holy Angels. The Rev. M. J. Spaulding, Bishop of the diocese of Louisville, was present and officiated at the ceremonies.

In March 1861, Father Lawler, before his appointment to the pastorate, went from Louisville to Eminence on the train and from there across country on horseback, to take a look at the charge which had been offered him. What he found here was enough to discourage one of less energy and determination, but he returned to Louisville and accepted the pastorate of the Shelbyville, Pewee Valley, and Taylorsville churches. Two months later he and Father Bax drove up the pike from Louisville.

Lawler immediately began to complete the interior of the church. The walls were not plastered inside nor painted outside. The glaziers had done nothing, and no pews had been provided. Not even a start on an organ loft had been made, and a bell to summon the faithful to services had not been purchased. The foundation, the walls, roof, floor, and a temporary altar were there. Fortunately, they were all paid for and since the lot had been donated there was no debt, but there was an immense amount of work to be done. Members of the congregation appreciated the situation and with the assistance of neighbors and others, they were able to have the church plastered, the windows put in, a church bell hung in a temporary belfry in the back yard, and crude improvised benches, instead of pews, put in the church. It was about one year from the time the church was dedicated until the first Mass was said in it. The organ loft and balcony were constructed in 1865.

Shortly after he had begun housekeeping, Lawler began making arrangements for a rectory, or priest's house, on a part of the lot on which the church stood. By the middle of December the house was completed and a few days afterwards Lawler moved into it.

The Sisters of Third Order of St. Francis moved from Mount Olivet to Shelbyville in 1874 and stayed there until 1890. There were as many as 15 nuns at one time. They operated a boarding school on property across First Street from the church, which was known as the convent property.

The Rev. D.F. Crane, during his second assignment as pastor, had the 65-foot bell tower erected in 1890 at a cost of $1,400. The Rev. James Donohue was pastor from 1892 to 1894 during which time new stained glass windows in the nave of the church, new pews, and Stations of the Cross were installed. Father Riley was pastor from 1906 to 1918, during which time the rectory was expanded and the church was enlarged with an extension consisting of a new sacristy and sanctuary.

One of the early festive occasions of the church was the celebration of the Rev. John Henry Riley's silver jubilee. A large banquet was held with Governor A.O. Stanley as toastmaster.

The next major remodeling was under Father Manger's pastorate, when the existing wood floor was replaced by terrazzo flooring. At this time additional property, on which the educational building is found, was obtained. The highway department widened First Street, removing a decorative wrought iron fence that had surrounded the church property.

Father Joseph A. Lyon was pastor from 1965 to 1969, during which time the educational building was constructed. At the same time the church was remodeled, including removing the old plaster back to the

Courtesy of the Kentucky Heritage Council

The Church of the Annunciation was built at Main and First Streets in 1860-61.

brick and replastering, while new pews, altar, tabernacle and pulpit were installed. Father Bowling was pastor for 15 years, the longest of any pastor. During his stay a new rectory was built.

The original property of the church consisted of the lot given by Mrs. Campbell and was 106 feet wide along First Street at Main Street. Over the years the church made a number of additions to the property so that in 2001 the church property consisted of the entire block between First and Second streets. The property at the corner of Main and Second streets, originally a service station, was converted to the Centro Latino. The church has also acquired property across Main Street which has been converted into the youth center.

In 1996, the parish embarked on Project Gabriel, a three phase 15-year long-range plan consisting of new sanctuary space, education building, and a parish hall. The first phase of the creation of a new sanctuary space added to the existing church was completed in the fall of 1999.

CEDARMORE

By Rev. Marvin M. Byrdwell

Oscar L. Moore was born in Versailles, Kentucky, on September 26, 1884. Shortly thereafter, his father moved to Moore's Ridge near Bagdad into a small log cabin (where the band shell at Cedarmore is now located). Six generations of Moores had lived there since Revolutionary War times. There he grew up and, at a very young age, became a printer's devil. He was associated with the printing industry for the rest of his life. He moved to Chicago in 1916, where he eventually established "O. L. Moore Printing and Publishing Company," later incorporated as "Moore Forms Incorporated," an international printing and publishing business. He became a very wealthy man.

Moore, while a young business man, was moved by imagination and dreamed of a place he could come to rest from his business and entertain his family and friends from all over the world. In 1930, Moore reacquired all of the property which had been included in a 900 acre land grant to his forefathers and had surrounded the cabin where he grew up. Moore turned his boyhood environment into a memorial to his ancestors. He created a private estate on 415 acres of the farm land, naming it "Cedarmore" because there were so many cedar trees. The two farm houses were remodeled and the barns were preserved. At the entrance he built a 10-room house, constructed of native stone around logs salvaged from the original cabin, a swimming pool, and a two-car garage with living quarters above. He built a hydroelectric dam to provide electricity to his property, thereby impounding a lake four miles long, ranging from 200 to 500 feet in width and up to 20-feet deep. A pump house on the lakeside supplied a water system serving the buildings and swimming pool. He later added a five-room lodge made of northern pine logs and a fishing lodge overhanging the lake. Other work included five miles of internal roads. He beautifully landscaped the entire 415 acres incorporating such amenities as a nine-hole golf course, many small bridges on the course, two pavilions, a band shell, twin boat docks and a barbecue pit with stone tables. He spent over $300,000 improving the grounds.

Moore 's development stopped in the late 1940s but apparently not from a lapse of imagination on his part. He said it became impossible to get dependable help, so in the fall of 1949, he put Cedarmore and his other land up for sale. The Long Run Baptist Association of Louisville purchased Cedarmore from Moore for $43,000 to be used for their camp and assemblies.

The Association needed someone to come and develop this fine estate into a ministry of camps and assemblies. They asked Marvin Byrdwell and he accepted. Byrdwell and his wife, Violet, moved to Cedarmore on December 1, 1949. He immediately asked Long Run to appoint a committee to work with him to plan programs. With the help of this committee, they were able to have twelve weeks of camps and assemblies in 1950.

That first year, camps for young boys started the last week in May and lasted to the third week in June with attendance of 430, and 114 decisions for Christ. Girls' camps started the last week of June and ran until the third week in August with attendance of 472, and 122 decisions for Christ. The one week of young people's camp had an attendance of 55, and six decisions for Christ. An adult program had an attendance of 93 with visitors to the program for one day increasing that number to 246. In addition, they had many visitors, picnickers, and fishermen bringing the total registered attendance for all purposes to 5,654.

After that first year, the Kentucky Baptist Convention purchased Cedarmore from the Association and moved the statewide camps from Clear Creek to Cedarmore. The Convention asked Byrdwell to remain and to lead them in developing Cedarmore into one of the best and most efficient camps and assemblies in the South. The planning and developing of Cedarmore was done by Dr. W. C. Boone and Byrdwell along with a Kentucky Baptist Assembly committee appointed by the State Board of Kentucky Baptists. Mr. J. H. Potts, an architect, was added to the committee and gave us much good advice as we planned.

In 1951, Kentucky Baptist Assembly had their first camp by improvising with the existing buildings, using tents, etc. The attendance for the camps was 962 boys and girls with other programs and activities bringing the total of persons enjoying the facilities to 5,447. Because of limited facilities, large numbers of people were turned away who wanted to come to Cedarmore.

The committee and Byrdwell had set priorities for facilities to be constructed. They had remodeled two of the barns into dormitories, dubbed "Barnmore" and "Oakmore," the latter still in use. A dining room was first constructed that seated 400 people and had staff quarters underneath. It had a modern kitchen, bathrooms and a long porch. In later years, the dining room was turned into a Conference Center and it since has been renamed "The Byrdwell Conference Center" in honor of the Byrdwells. Other construction included a prayer garden, a tabernacle that seated 600 people, four motel buildings with four units in each, four cottages that house eight people each, a swimming pool with bath houses, and a fishing dock for boaters. Four miles of the road were rebuilt and blacktopped. The investment made was now $240,217.45.

By 1954, attendance of boys and girls at the camps reached 2,221 and the attendance for the adult programs was 3,032 for a grand total of 5,253. In spite of all the improvements, people were still being turned away. In 1955, the largest attendance for one day was 3,275 when Brotherhood men from all over the state arrived in 400 automobiles.

In 1962, the state board commissioned architects to make a study of Cedarmore to see how best to develop it so that it could increase its capacity. The resulting recommendation was to build a hotel-type lodge at a cost of $440,000 that would accommodate 300 people with dining facilities. On December 11, 1962, the Executive Board of the Kentucky Baptists voted to carry out this recommendation. Construction began in February 1963 and was completed by September.

In the following years a separate, self-contained facility was constructed for the boys camps having pioneer-type wagons for shelter and its own dining room and swimming pool located across the lake from the main campus. A similar self-contained camp, having log buildings for shelter, was constructed for girls on the opposite side of the main campus . A Youth Camp on the edge of the main campus was constructed to facilitate spiritual retreats and programs for smaller groups of young people and others. The Ferguson-Jaggle Conference Center consisting of four facing buildings within easy walking distance from the lodge expanded the utility of the lodge for many programs.

In 1971, it was reported that 5,600 people had made a decision for Christ at Cedarmore during Byrdwell's twenty-two years as manager. At his retirement that year Cedarmore was left in the hands of good people and, more importantly, in God's hands.

CENTENARY UNITED METHODIST CHURCH

by Ted L. Igleheart

The first annual conference of the Methodist Church met in Fayette County in 1790 at Masterson's Station and shortly thereafter formed the Salt River Circuit, which included the counties of Jefferson, Nelson, and Shelby. It is believed that the Rev. Barnabus McHenry was the first Methodist preacher in Shelby County. The Shelby Circuit was formed in 1796 and Rev. Jeremiah Dawson was assigned to preach here, followed the next year by Rev. William Kavanaugh, father of Bishop Kavanaugh.

The first Methodist Church in the county was formed in a log house on the Fielding Neel farm on Rockbridge Road. It was named the Rockbridge Church from many charter members having come from Rockbridge County in Virginia. A church building was built in 1806.

In 1804, a brick chapel was constructed on the Benson Pike, about four miles northeast of Shelbyville, where the Methodists of the town worshiped when not meeting in their homes or at the early courthouse. It was called the Mulberry Methodist Church, taking its name from the Mulbery Creek which ran nearby. The first members were George Cardwell, Sarah Cardwell, Moore Weaver, Dresilla Weaver, Elizabeth Talbott and Edward Talbott, who oversaw the construction with the supervision of Bishop McKendree.

Methodists built the first church in town around 1810 on Lot No.9 donated by John Bradshaw at the north end of Fourth Street. In 1816, they purchased from John Bradshaw Lots 10 and 11, located on the north side of Washington Street between Fourth and Fifth Streets and built what was called the Shelbyville Meeting House, later turning the first building over to a black congregation. The Baptists also used the Meeting House until they built their own church at Clay and Eighth Street in 1819. The Presbyterians also worshiped at the Meeting House until they built a church in 1820 where the County Library is now located. Thereafter the Meeting House was called the Methodist Church. It was enlarged in 1824 and along with the Brick Chapel became one circuit, with Rev. Richard Corwine as pastor. The Kentucky Conference met there, presided over by Bishops McKendree and Roberts. Officers of the church were: William Owen, George Robinson, John Bradshaw, Isaac Pomeroy, William Cardwell, Jacob Cardwell, Robert Bull, Edward Talbott, Nathaniel Talbott, Hardin McGruder, Adam Winlock, Richard Waters, and Robert McGrath.

In 1845, Pastor H.H. Kavanaugh, later bishop, presided over a crucial controversy in the church regarding slavery, which was dividing Methodists nationally. As a result, the Methodist Church here changed its name to Methodist Episcopal Church, South.

In 1857, with Rev. J. W. Cunningham as pastor, a new brick church was built at Fifth and Main Streets on a lot given by Rev. John Tevis. He bought the brick from the old church building and built the north wing of the Science Hill School which he founded. The officers of the new church were: William Winlock, Jacob Owen, John Robnson, John R. Beckley, Fielding Neel, Daniel Polk, Dr. B.P. Tevis, Judge Thomas Wilson, T.B. Cochran, Dr. Robert Winlock, and Judge Martin D. McHenry. At the dedication, in which Bishop Kavanaugh preached the sermon, it was announced that the building had cost over $15,000 and $3,800 was still owed. A collection was taken, raising the sum of $4,100, which paid off all the church's indebtedness. It served the congregation for 40 years.

Growth of the congregation to 250 members and the encouragement of Dr. W. T. Poynter, who had purchased the Science Hill School, resulted in a decision in 1896 to build a modern church on the same site. It was to be called Centenary Methodist Church in that it was the hundredth year of the Shelby Circuit. On June 4, 1897, the corner stone was laid in which a copper box was placed containing the history of Methodism in Shelby County. Several hundred attended. With continued growth, by 1960 an educational annex had been built on the east side of the church.

In 1968 the Evangelical United Brethren Church merged with the Methodists and the combined denomination was then called the United Methodist Church.

Centenary was placed on the National Register of Historical Places in 1978 and the church underwent extensive renovations

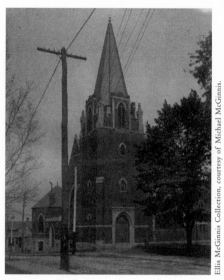

Centenary Methodist, built at Main and Fifth Streets in 1897, in a photo from 1909. This building burned in 1978 and was rebuilt on the site.

and repairs at a cost of $80,000. The Christmas Eve Candlelight Service was not only a celebration of the birth of Jesus but a celebration of the beautiful sanctuary and building repairs and renovations. Pride was turned into grief four days later, however when early on December 28, 1978, flames were observed shooting into the sky too late to save the 81 year old building from almost complete destruction at the hands of a burglar and arsonist. The Education Annex suffered smoke damage, but the main sanctuary was gutted by the fire leaving only the brick shell and some of the beautiful stained glass windows. As tearful members stood in the cold viewing the smouldering ruins, many expressed their intent to rebuild on the site.

Church was convened the following Sunday morning in the Circuit Courtroom by Board chairman, Ted Iglehart. Later, meeting at the old Shelbyville High School, a majority of the membership voted to rebuild downtown on its existing historic site. With insurance proceeds of $645,000, plans were drawn for rebuilding, keeping most of the brick shell but supporting the roof by wood columns inside. With the leadership of Rev. Harold Hunter, long hours of decisions by the rebulding committee, the bankruptcy of the original contractor, vigorous fund raising, favorable interest earned on funds, and many prayers,the restoration was completed in just over four years at a cost of $1,200,000. Over 600 attended the Consecration Service on October 24, 1982.

Seven years after the disastrous fire, on December 29, 1985, the remaining note of $175,000 was burned in the pulpit by the Rebuilding Chairman Joe Burks, and the debt free, restored building was rededicated to the glory of God.

In 1979, the four lots adjoining the church on its northeast side were purchased and made into parking space. In 1993, the office building next door was purchased for classrooms and the Youth department. The dilapidated store buildings east of the Youth building were purchased in 2000, after being condemned by the city, and long range plans called for future additions to the church. They were removed in 2001.

Centenary United Methodist church, nearly 700 members strong, launches its mission into the 21st century as a growing family of believers of Jesus Christ established through God's grace: nurturing our congregation in love, serving our community and world, and asking God to lead our future.

PASTORS

Richard Corwine	1823-24	Joseph Rand	1874-78
Richard D. Neale	1824-25	F. W. Noland	1878-80
John Tevis	1825-27	John R. Deering	1880-82
George C. Light	1827-28	Edward L. Southgate	1882-86
Edward Stevenson	1828-29	James Scott Sims	1886-89
George C. Light	1829-30	Thomas J. McIntyre	1889-91
Jonathan Stamper	1830-32	Alexander Redd	1891-92
Marcus Lindsay	1832-33	James Rector Savage	1892-96
George W. Bush	1833-35	W. F. Taylor	1896-1900
Benjamin T. Crouch	1835-36	Thomas W. Watts	1900-04
and Henry VanDyke	1835-36	O.J. Chandler	1904-07
Richard Corwine	1836-37	Horace G. Turner	1907-11
Silas Lee	1837-38	William Owen Sadler	1911-12
Henry E. Pilcher	1838-39	J. P. Strother	1912-16
Richard Tydings	1839-40	O. B. Crockett	1916-20
Thomas N. Ralston	1840-43	Walter V. Cropper	1920-25
George W. Fagg	1843-44	M. T. Chandler	1925-27
Hubbard H, Kavanaugh	1844-45	B. Orland Beck	1927-29
John Miller	1845-47	Walter V. Cropper	1929-33
John C. Harrison	1847-49	J. L. Clark	1933-36
Lorenzo D. Huston	1849-50	B. Orland Beck	1936-39
George W. Bush	1850-52	J. E. Savage	1939-43
John S. Bayless	1852-54	L. D. Rounds	1943-47
William C. Dandy	1854-56	Lloyd F. Moody	1947-52
John W. Cunningham	1856-58	Robert L. Anderson	1952-56
John H. Linn	1858-60	S. C. Rice	1956-61
Daniel E. Stevenson	1860-62	William Edward Hisle	1961-67
W. G. E. Cunningham	1862-64	Virgil J. Fryman	1967-76
Henry Clay Northcutt	1864-65	Earl Tudor Curry	1976-78
David A. Beardsley	1865-66	Harold G. Hunter	1978-83
Hugh A. C. Walker	1866-68	Edward G. Coleman	1983-91
George L. Staley	1868-69	Samuel R. Clark	1991-94
Edmund P. Buckner	1869-71	Steve Drury	1994-97
D. B. Cooper	1871-74	Robert Gipson	1997-99
		Lowell Ogden	1999-

CHRISTIANSBURG BAPTIST CHURCH

By Douglas Sturgeon

The little town of Christiansburg is not only a pioneer town of Shelby County, but also one of the oldest in the state. The area was settled by the Low Dutch around 1792. They emigrated from Europe because of religious discrimination and first settled in Pennsylvania then migrated to Kentucky.

Sometime in 1799, the last year of George Washington's life, during the presidency of John Adams, the settlers established Six Mile Baptist Church (renamed in 1845 after the community of Christiansburg). The earliest records of the church date from August of the year of its founding and contain the names of 13 members. By 1803, when it joined other churches in establishing the Long Run Association, its members numbered 108. The church met in a log meetinghouse until the present building was constructed in 1856 at the cost of $2,154.49.

From the very outset of its ministry to the people of the community, the church strove to be careful to embrace and articulate the message and doctrine given in the Scriptures. In July 1800 the church adapted its Articles of Faith, Discipline and Decorum which set forth a Trinitarian understanding of the godhead, a very high view of the Scriptures, the universality of the sinful condition of humanity, and the gracious and willful provision of God to remedy that condition as expressed in the fourth article: "We believe in the Doctrines of Eternal and Particular Election and Redemption, Effectual calling, Justification of the saints by the righteousness of Jesus Christ imputed to them, Sanctification by and through the Holy Spirit, the final Perseverance of the Saints in Holiness, resurrection of the Dead and general judgment."

When, in the early 1800s, a doctrinal crisis of vast proportions swept through Baptist churches in Kentucky, the church took a strong stand to remain steadfast in the doctrines founded in the Bible and to resist the introduction of the new teachings being proposed and embraced by many. In July 1830, in Frankfort, Kentucky, a meeting of Baptists was called which one church historian has labeled "the most important called session of any association ever held in Kentucky." William W. Ford, longtime member of the church, who had served as deacon, clerk, and was then pastor, served as moderator of this meeting, where, for the first time, Kentucky Baptists took a strong stand to stem the tide of the new doctrines which stressed salvation gained by works, and which contained very anti-missionary views.

An issue, with which this church struggled, along with many others, was in the area of race relations. From the very beginning, the church welcomed black members; of course, most, if not all of them in those early years were slaves. In 1860, prior to the Civil War, the church voted to allow "the coloured brethren" to meet once a month, as long as two white members were also present at the meetings. One of the tragic changes brought about by the war was the increased separation between black and white members. By 1868, the black members were allowed to hold their own business meetings and thus, in effect, establish their own separate congregation.

The Civil War was, of course, a significant crisis in the history of the church, especially since there was no consensus as to the sentiments and loyalties of the congregation. The membership lists record the deaths of young men in both the Union and Confederate armies. Prior to the actual outbreak of war in

1861 the Christiansburg community was beset by violent disagreement. The situation grew so tense that in late 1860 the church voted that "no political meetings be allowed in this house in future." Despite decreasing attendance and giving during the War years, the church struggled on, attempting to minister as best it could amidst strife and discord.

The church maintains a pioneer cemetery which pre-dates the church's founding. Veterans of the War of 1812, the Mexican-American War, as well as the Civil War, are buried there. The cemetery also has the grave of William Truman, the great-grandfather of President Harry Truman.

In the 20th century, Christiansburg Baptist Church participated with other Baptist churches in the beginnings of real cooperation in missions and ministry. From the first steps of such cooperative efforts of funding missions, the church's participation had grown to the 1999 level of over $18,000 given to missions and other benevolent causes. The church is an active member of the Shelby County Baptist Association, supporting its efforts to reach the people of Shelby County, including our growing numbers of Hispanic neighbors, with the gospel of Jesus Christ. With a desire to move forward beyond the divisions of the past, the church gladly holds annual joint worship services with Centennial Baptist Church, an African American church located nearby.

As the church looks back in awe at two centuries of ministry, the members also look expectantly to the coming days with this hopeful purpose: "Beginning a third century of exalting the Christ in Christiansburg."

CLAY STREET BAPTIST CHURCH

By Maureen Ashby

The First Baptist Church of Shelbyville was constituted on Saturday January 23, 1819. The charter members were 20 in number, 11 men and nine women. It appears that this group proceeded at once to erect a house of worship. The site chosen was a lot on First South Back Street, now known as Henry Clay Street. On the fourth Saturday in November, the group met in their new house of worship.

At a business meeting held early in 1821, the church resolved to commune twice a year, in April and September. In 1825, there were 126 whites and 111 blacks who paid tithes. The tithe was a tax levied only on males over 16 years of age. At the close of 1855, the church had 309 members, 181 of whom were black.

In 1858, the church reported preaching three times a week, with prayer meeting twice a week, and Sunday school every Sunday morning. The number of Sunday school scholars was 65. Membership consisted of 147 whites and 143 blacks making a total of 290. There was a time before the Civil War when this church had more blacks than whites. In 1859, a lot at the corner of Fifth Street and Public Square was purchased and a new church was erected.

In 1859, the Colored Baptists were organized. A lot was purchased from George Adams by Simon Grisby's Committee for the Colored Baptist Church of Shelbyville located where the Bethel A. M. E Church is now located. This was known as the Stray Pen Lot. A building was never constructed because

The Clay Street Baptist Church on U. S. 60 West was built in 1984.

the white Baptist church sold the colored Baptist church the structure and land at Eighth and Henry Clay in 1860. The remains of their dead that had been buried on the lot were removed to private burying grounds or Grove Hill.

According to Shinnick's History of Shelbyville, their structure burned in March 1863. From 1863 to April 1867, the record is obscure. It is thought by some local historians that the people may have worshipped with the whites again at the Public Square Church until another structure was erected. In April 1867, the Colored Baptist Church group filed a list of elected trustees with the city. These persons were Daniel Lawson, John Cole, Wyatt Roe, and Chairman Simon Grigsby. On April 20, 1867, the Colored Baptist Church sold the Stray Pen Lots to the A. M. E. Church.

From 1870 to 1888, the records are again very obscure. In 1888, after a fire had destroyed all or a portion of the building, a new or restored building was completed under the leadership of Rev. Moses Allen. Since its organization in 1860, the church has had the guidance of 11 Pastors—the Revs. Simon Grigsby (the founder), Clark, W. W. Brown, Moses Allen (built the present structure at 723 Henry Clay Street), A.A. Russell, R. T Huffman, H .W. Jones, W.M. Brown, R. Jackson, Claude Taylor, and Ronald Holder.

In the early 1980s, five acres of land on U.S. 60 West was purchased for the purpose of building a new sanctuary. A groundbreaking ceremony was held and the sanctuary was under construction for one year. On June 3, 1984, members marched from the old site on Henry Clay Street to the new site. The mortgage was paid off on June 6, 1993. On June 23, 1995, the old structure at Henry Clay Street was sold to Clay Street Out Reach Ministry.

In 1997, the church embarked on another building venture. The Marnel C. Moorman Family Life Center was built. Marnel C. Moorman was a trustee, active church member, Brotherhood Member, and educator in Shelby County. This center houses Childtown Day Care Center along with a gym, additional classroom space, a computer lab, choir room, exercise rooms, a walking track, and additional office space. There are five associate ministers: the Revs. Robert Thomas, Donald Massey, Terry West, Harold Stateman, and Michael Hickman.

CROPPER BAPTIST CHURCH

By Fred Porter

On June 17, 1900, 14 women and two men separated themselves from the Union Grove Church to form the Cropper Baptist Church. The church began its long affiliation with the Shelby Association of Baptists in the summer of 1901.

On January 17, 1903, the first official building that housed the congregation was completed. An organ was purchased and a choir was organized in 1914. That year marked Cropper's change from Saturday to Sunday meetings.

During the ministry of Tucker N. Calloway, full-time services were started. The Mountain Movers, a mission organization of young people, was organized in June 1943. The group met weekly to pray for those who had problems and to write them letters of comfort.

The first educational space was completed and dedicated in August 1957. The sanctuary received considerable remodeling in 1971. New pews, pulpit, furniture, and a communion table were added. A new church parsonage was dedicated on December 1, 1955. On September 13, 1987, the church voted to purchase the adjoining property in order to construct a multi-purpose building. On March 5, 1989, the Cropper Baptist Church Christian Life Center was dedicated to the service of the Lord. In addition to the building a baptistery was installed. A van ministry among the Cropper community began in 1997.

On June 7, 1987, the Cropper Baptist Church adopted its first constitution and by-laws. The church became officially incorporated on November 30, 1988.

In June 2000, the Cropper Baptist Church commemorated a century of service to the Lord and the community of Cropper.

Courtesy of Fred Porter.

Cropper Baptist Church, built in 1903 and remodeled in 1971.

CROPPER CHRISTIAN CHURCH (DISCIPLES OF CHRIST)

By Bonnie Slaughter

The sanctuary in the present church structure dates back to the original building. It was built by the community for four denominations to worship—Presbyterians, Methodist, Baptists and Christian, or Campbellites as they were called in 1885.

Cropper's first church was known as the "Union Grove Church." The name was changed in 1967 to the Cropper Christian Church (Disciples of Christ).

The Thomas family, of Shelby County, has played an important part in the history of the Cropper Christian Church. It has given spiritually and financially from the very beginning.

The Christian Women's Fellowship and Christian Men's Fellowship have played an active role. The women have made quilts, gowns, lap rugs, first aid kits, and fruit plates over the years. The C.W.F. and C.M.F. have strongly supported Disciple causes throughout the state, country, and world where there has been a need.

This small church in the country goes forward with the same optimism into the 21st century that the beginning forefathers had when the church doors were opened in October 1885.

On October 5-6, 1985, the congregation celebrated its centennial of worship and service to the Lord. Former ministers and members, present members, and good friends came to join in the celebration.

Cropper Christian Church members and Sunday school classes in 1911 on the first anniversary of Rev. Joel Jones, pastor.

Shelby County Public Library, from Mary David Myles.

DOVER BAPTIST CHURCH

By William Fleming

The Dover Baptist Church was constituted in 1812. It is located on Dover Road in the northwestern part of Shelby County. The preachers who organized the church are uncertain. George Waller, who was then pastor at Burks Branch Baptist Church, was probably in the organization. William Keller, pastor at Licks Branch, now LaGrange, was perhaps present. Benjamin Allen was the first pastor. Dover became a member of the Long Run Association.

The constituents are not all known. James Neal and wife, Daniel McCalister Sr. and wife, Samuel Ellis and wife, are six of the 13 entering into the organization. Billy Williams was probably a constituent member. James Neal and Daniel McCalister were messengers to the Long Run Association in 1812, which met with Burks Branch Church.

To James Neal, Dover owes much for faithful work performed during his connection with the church. The church stands on land that was donated by Neal. He was ever ready, able and willing. His daughters, Polly Lancaster, Adeline Price, and Jane Hanna, like their father, were strong supporters of the church.

The name of the church is evidence of the remembrance of the membership of old Dover Church of Virginia, from which many of them came. From one meeting are found the following minutes: "Resolved that we build a new meeting house and that the following be appointed a committee to solicit funds and ascertain the probable cost: Adam Hanna, W. H. Allen, T. A. Price, and Sisters Virgie Guthrie, Fannie Sandford and M. C. Hamblin." In April 1887, the finance committee reported $1,006 subscribed. A building committee consisting of the following was appointed: S. T. Sandford, Taylor Lancaster, Adam Hanna, T. A. Price, C. Varnarsdale, and S.S. Vincent. This committee was empowered to dispose of the old building and supervise the erection of the new. The result of their labors is the present structure. The church was dedicated in September 1887. The membership at that time was about 95.

In 1938, the first electric lights were installed. Coal oil lamps had been used for most, if not all, of the previous years. For a few years prior to this, some "Aladdin lamps" had supplemented the coal oil lamps but they were very unreliable—sometimes leaving the pastor in the middle of his sermon in complete darkness.

In July 1948, there was much discussion of moving the church to a new location. However in February 1950 the minutes reflect a unanimous vote to raise the existing structure by building a basement. In May 1950 a contract was made for all labor and materials except windows for the cost of $4,000. In March 1951 a furnace was installed and the basement was partitioned off into eight rooms for a cost of $1,324. A special fund, promoted through the Sunday school for several years, led to the building of an educational annex to the side of the auditorium containing five Sunday school rooms, inside rest rooms, a kitchen and a fellowship hall. This building was dedicated debt-free in June 1970.

In 1955, a parsonage was added to the grounds. In the summer of 1974 a new parsonage, in the form of a double mobile home, was placed on the church grounds for a cost of $17,000. In February 1989 the church was faced with either remodeling or improving the old parsonage, at a cost of $23,000 or

Photo courtesy of William Fleming.

Dover Baptist Church, built in 1887 and remodeled in the 1950s.

building a new one with an estimated cost of $58,000 to $60,000. The church voted to build a new parsonage. It was dedicated on September 17, 1989.

From 1860 to 1883 Dover was a member of Sulphur Fork Association. Then it joined the Shelby County Association at the meeting with Mount Vernon Church in the Association's 12th session, August 16, 1883. It is interesting to note that the church brought a letter of dismissal from the former association, in the same manner that the church today grants letters to its individual members.

Until the early 1870s preaching services were held only once a month, with a preaching service preceding the business session on the last Saturday of every month. In 1870, it was decided to hold preaching services twice a month (weather permitting). It was not until the early 1920s that roads leading to Dover were passable during many late fall, winter, and early spring months. Records show that Olivet Presbyterian Church was used part of the winter of 1907 and again in 1913 or 1914, but there were often Sundays when no services were held due to the weather and poor road conditions. The 1916 minutes show that for a few months the church voted to have preaching services every Sunday, but the next year shows the pastor being paid for preaching only twice a month. In 1935, under the leadership of the Rev. D. H. Daniel, the church began a full-time ministry of worship each Lords' Day and continues so.

The organization for training church members was first called Baptist Young People's Union or better known as BYPU. The first organization at Dover began in 1915. There is a reference in the church minutes to a Ladies Aid Society before 1912, apparently the forerunner of our present WMU. The Brotherhood is the "baby" organization of the church, starting in 1954 with fourteen members. The work of sponsoring the Royal Ambassadors (RAs) was given over to them by the WMU in 1955. The Brotherhood encourages tithing among the men and boys and urges giving to all mission causes.

Throughout the years the mission and objective of Dover Baptist Church has best been expressed in words excerpted from the Constitution and By-laws and reflect ARTICLE III: "The object of this church shall be the worship of God, the preaching of the Gospel of Jesus Christ, the administration of the ordinances of the New Testament, the religious training of its youth, the Spiritual development of its members, the conversion of the world to Christ through systematic support of missions and the furtherance of the Kingdom of God through such activities and organizations as may seem necessary."

ELMBURG BAPTIST CHURCH

By Julian K. Wood

In the 1880s the community of Elmburg came into being. Several houses and a general store had been built around the crossroads located in northeastern Shelby County about one mile from Henry County. The people of this small village petitioned for a post office about 1890. The residents wanted the village to be named Oakdale, but since there was already an Oakdale in Kentucky, another name was selected. There was a large elm tree growing in a nearby field, so the little community named itself Elmburg.

There were churches within a few miles in any direction, but none in the immediate area. Those who attended church found it necessary to travel several miles on horseback or by buggy. The population was of mixed Christian faiths, and no denomination was of sufficient strength to build and support a church of its own. After much deliberation, the four denominations of Christian, Methodist, Presbyterian, and Baptist constructed a church at Elmburg about 1906. Louis Ethington donated the land with the understanding it would revert back to him or his descendants if the structure ceased to be a church. This church was known as the Elmburg Union Church. Sunday school was held jointly by all four denominations, and each denomination had a minister of its own preach one Sunday each month.

In the spring of 1913, there were 10 Baptists who were under the watch of the Baptist Church. These ten were Sallie Weakley, Mattie Wood, Leslie Beckley, Susie Beckley, Jennie Bohannon, the Rev. A.B. Morgan, Belle Thompson, Silas Beckley, Sudie Bohannon, and Dora Smither. This small group of Baptists asked Morgan to become their regular minister. Morgan, who lived in Defoe, accepted this call on a part-time basis.

On November 16, 1913, a meeting was held with Morgan as moderator for the purpose of organizing a Baptist Church. Several members from Union, Indian Fork and Cropper Baptist Churches were invited to help with the organizational meeting. A.B. Moore was the clerk at this meeting which resulted in the organization of Elmburg Missionary Baptist Church. With the 10 charter members and the 14 who joined during an August revival, the church now had 24 members. Rev. A.B. Morgan was unanimously elected pastor and served three more years until November 17, 1916. Oscar Beckley, Leslie Beckley, and I.S. Bohannon were selected as the first deacons of the newly organized church. After Morgan resigned, the Rev. C.B. Austin accepted the call as pastor and served about one year.

Elmburg Baptist Church, built in 1918.

Two additional members, J.T. Parks and M.M. Bohannon, were selected as deacons on May 18, 1917. These two along with the original three were ordained as deacons by Reverend S.J. Ezele, a visiting minister, on June 14, 1917. On this same day, the church voted unanimously to withdraw from the Union Church and to build a church separate from the other denominations. This action met with disfavor from the other denominations, but the Baptists were fully convinced this was the time to withdraw.

A lot was purchased for $400 from Sam Wood. A building committee awarded the contract to Mr. Sanford, who along with other carpenters constructed the church on the lot where it now stands. The building was completed in May 1918 at a total cost of $4,000 for labor and materials. By the time it was completed, all but $800 had been paid. The dedication service for the new building was held on October 19, 1919. By the day of the dedication, the $800 debt had been paid and the new church was off to a good start with a debt-free building. In addition to the 24 original members, 127 others had come to make this their church home. From this number the young church had lost nine members by death, three by letter, seven excluded, leaving a total membership of 132 on the rolls in October 1919.

Additional building was done on the church in 1951. Under the leadership of the Rev. Burrell Lucas, Sunday school rooms were constructed, a basement with cooking and dining facilities was added, a pastor's study was completed, and the main auditorium was redecorated. The old coal stove was replaced with an oil furnace. The total cost was $13,795 about three and one-half times the cost of the 1918 original building.

The Union Church steadily lost members by death and relocation; finally, all services were discontinued and the building was abandoned in the 1970s. Several potential buyers were interested in purchasing the property, but were unable to do so. The original deed states that it would revert to the original owner or his heirs if the building ceased to be a church. The heirs were widely scattered and some were deceased. Others could not be found, so a clear title could not be made. The building stood there and began to deteriorate. Finally in 1999, it collapsed. It is sad to view what was once a fine building serving the spiritual needs of the community.

FINCHVILLE BAPTIST CHURCH

by Ted L. Igleheart

Records kept by First Baptist Church indicate that its origin can be traced back to 1780 when settlers of the Buck Creek, Plum Creek and Elk Creek area met in their cabins for worship services. According to George L. Willis' History of Shelby County, and material put together by local scholar, Richard Todd Duvall, the church was formally organized in 1799 by William Edmund Waller, a distinguished Virginian, who had arrived in the neighborhood in 1789. By 1800 a log church and schoolhouse had been built. The church was called Plum Creek Church first, then Plum and Buck Creek Church, and in 1807 it was contracted to Buck Creek.

Waller was its first pastor and the charter members were: John Patterson, George Davis, Sarah Patterson, Johnston Patterson, Theodore Davis, Priscilla May, Elizabeth Breedon and William Mackensen. At the death of Waller's wife, he returned to Virginia after serving only four years and later died there. He was succeeded by his son, George Waller, who served the church for forty years, during which time its membership went from 8 to 342.

Finchville Baptist Church

Dr. Wayne Ward, a later pastor and distinguished professor at Southern Baptist Seminary, wrote in his history of the church that the first fifty years witnessed many instances of members brought before the business meetings for failing to attend meetings, using profane language, drinking too much, dancing, attending races, cock fighting and other disorderly conduct. Fist fights broke out over being charged with an offense or over lawsuits filed in land title disputes. Shots were even exchanged on church property. Anyone found guilty was excluded from the church.

Trouble arose in 1849 between the new pastor and the congregation which divided the membership into two factions, each claiming to be the original Buck Creek Church. The Long Run Baptist Association brokered an agreement whereby the "Waller side" was to have full use of the building on certain days and the other side had the remaining time. 140 members adhered to the pastor while 72 formed a new organization, both factions using the same building for ten years. In 1860 they reunited as the Buck Creek Church, which continued until 1891 when the brick building was razed and its material used in the erection of a new church in the center of Finchville, according to Willis. Thus, the Finchville Baptist Church was born. In 1992 an addition to the building was dedicated.

A number of pastors are remembered by the congregation today. Rev. John E. Owen began his ministry at Finchville in 1974 and Rev. Leslie Hollon in 1978, along with his wife, Vickie, who was a gifted musician. Rev. William Clay Smith came in 1985. Rev. Mark Johnson began his service in 1989, followed by Dr. Ken Murphy in 1994. Rev. Scott Patton and his wife, Janet, who came in 1997, led the church into its bicentennial celebration in 1999. Rev. Tony Smith and his wife, Lisa, came to the pastorate in 2000. Beth Dunn, a graduate of the seminary and National Teacher of the Year, carried the burden of interim pastor at times while serving as church musician and youth leader. She was later ordained as a gospel minister, a first for Finchville Baptist Church.

Finchville Baptist represents the center of religious life in the Finchville community. Its long history and proud tradition are evident in the simple but elegant architecture of the building.

FIRST BAPTIST CHURCH OF SHELBYVILLE

By Zena B. Jesse

On January 23,1819, 20 people met at the Shelby County courthouse to form First Baptist Church. They entered into a covenant with God and adopted a constitution.

The story of First Baptist Church really began in the 35-year period prior to 1819. In 1784, only a few hardy pioneers lived in what would become Shelby County. They were settled in small communities called stations. It was in the station established by Brackett Owen that eight charter members constituted the first church in the area in 1785. It was named Brashear's Creek Church and was the 14th church formed in what would later become the Commonwealth of Kentucky. It was located out what is now known as Mt. Eden Road.

In a sense, Brashear's Creek Church is the mother church of First Baptist Church and perhaps other Baptist churches in Shelby County. In 1843, the Brashear's Creek Church was renamed Clear Creek Church and in 1858 it ceased to exist. The members voted to give the church property to First Baptist Church and become part of First Baptist or other county churches.

The Methodist Church built the first church building in what would become Shelbyville in 1814. This building was located at Fourth and Washington(then known as North Back Street) and was known as the Meetinghouse. Methodists, Presbyterians, and Baptists all used this building for services. In 1819, First Baptist built a framed church building on the northeast corner of Eighth and Clay Streets, which was later replaced with a brick building.

The early 1830s proved to be a trying time for young First Baptist. During these years the church suffered financial reverses due to severe droughts. A number of church members died in a smallpox epidemic that swept Shelby County. It was also during those years that the church lost 20 members to the Alexander Campbell movement.

However, the years 1835-47 were ones of tremendous growth. The membership more than doubled and the church thrived under the leadership of four capable pastors.

The 20-year period from 1848-68 was a time of increased controversy and bitterness that took the United States down the path to the Civil War and into the difficult period known as Reconstruction. In 1848, First Baptist Church had 400 members, but by 1868 there were only 208 members. However, the church did not stand still during those troubled years. It was during that period that the first Sunday school was organized in 1858 under Pastor S. F. Thompson. Bible study on Sunday mornings is still an important part of the church program.

Also, during those painful years, a new church building was constructed on the southwest corner of the town square at Fifth and Main Streets. This was an imposing brick and stone structure and was dedicated in the midst of the Civil War.

The years between 1879 and 1900 were years of steady growth. First Baptist Church entered the 20th century with approximately 458 members. The church grew and avoided any calamities until September 3, 1909, when the building was destroyed by fire. The most destructive fire Shelbyville had ever experienced

Shelby County Public Library.

The fourth building of the First Baptist Church, shown in a postcard, was built in 1911 on the site
of the third building at Main and Fifth Streets. That building had burned in 1909.

wiped out most of the block between Fifth and Sixth Streets. All the church's records and furnishings were also lost. Under the able leadership of Dr. B. B. Bailey, the church resolved to rise from the ashes and lost no time in making plans to rebuild. Even without a house of worship for two years, the church membership increased. The new church, built at the same location, was dedicated on October 22, 1911.

On March 1, 1926, Dr. C.W. Elsey began his pastorate. Under his leadership the church started a mission church on the corner of Bradshaw and Second Streets. This very successful mission church eventually became Highland Baptist Church.

On May 10,1937, the church began holding an annual vacation bible school under the leadership of Mrs. C.W. Elsey. This endeavor was so successful that the Southern Baptist Sunday School Board in Nashville, Tenn., recognized it as one of the best in the South. During the years of Dr. Elsey's tenure the church outgrew the building. Some Sunday school classes had to meet in the courthouse and other surrounding buildings because of lack of space. Under Dr. Elsey's leadership, the church purchased five and one half acres of the Bayne property on the western edge of town with plans to eventually build a new church building.

Dr. Elsey retired January 1, 1957, and Reverend Raymond was called as the new pastor on May 19, 1957. On April 18, 1958, the ceiling of the church collapsed into the sanctuary and the entire building was pronounced totally unsafe. Had this happened two hours later or on a Sunday morning, scores of people would have died. As a result, the present educational building was completed and put into use October 4, 1959.

Dr. Fred T. Moffatt, Jr. became pastor of First Baptist Church on February 10, 1963, and he served until 1974. The present sanctuary at 1516 West Main was built under his leadership. Eight hundred and sixty-seven people attended the dedication service on May 25, 1969, 150 years after those dedicated Christians vowed together to be God's people in this place.

In 1981, the educational building was renovated, creating the Elsey Memorial Chapel and an enlarged music suite. In 1993, the front of the sanctuary was redesigned to accommodate the choir and organ, which originally were located in the balcony. In 1998, the church installed a new entrance in order to make the buildings handicapped accessible.

Missions and ministry have always been important. A new mission church was started in 1963 at Third and Bradshaw Streets and was named Clear Creek Missions. The Rev. Lyman Austin served as the first pastor. Northside Mission Church was started and met in Northside Elementary School on College Street sometime in the 1960s. Dr. Fred Moffatt Jr. led the worship service.

In 1985, First Baptist purchased a building at 715 Main Street for the purpose of expanding its ministry. Friendship House clothing ministry was moved there, which was named Henderson House. Ministries there have grown to include Sunday school and morning worship every Sunday, Wednesday night learning activities for families, a food pantry, and ministries to families in need. An organization for older church members was started and named Young at Heart. This organization ministers to the needs of older church members as well as residents in the local nursing homes.

Early in the 21st century, the church had grown to 1,039 resident members who were shepherded by Dr. Edward Erwin, the 30th pastor.

FIRST CHRISTIAN CHURCH (DISCIPLES OF CHRIST)

By The Rev. Howard Griffith

The Restoration Movement on the western frontier was planted in Shelbyville in 1830 when, according to the minutes of the Long Run Association, 20 members of the Shelbyville Baptist Church left by consent. That same year that exact number of persons became charter members of a new reform church in Shelbyville called The Church of Disciples of Jesus Christ.

There were 20 persons who were charter members. They were members of the family of Thomas B. Caldwell, Thomas Chiles, Achilles Chinn, Hamilton Frazier, Dr. George W. Nuckols, William Standiford, William Smith, Travis Wilson, and James S. Whitaker. Although they first met in homes, the congregation began to grow rapidly.

The congregation later took the name First Christian Church. It became a part of the denomination known as the Christian Church (Disciples of Christ). The first leader of the newly organized congregation was Dr. George W. Nuckols. The church was one of the first newly formed congregations to organize under the direction of Alexander Campbell. Campbell, who made several visits to Shelbyville, is recognized as the founder of Christian Church (Disciples of Christ).

The first church building constructed by the congregation in 1832 faced Fourth Street because much of Shelbyville was east of Fourth Street. Later as the village grew, it became apparent that the city would grow west of Fourth. Subsequent church buildings were constructed to face Main Street.

In the early days traveling evangelists served the newly formed church. While the evangelist would preach and teach on weekends, the local elders would provide the daily shepherding of the congregation. The first resident Disciples of Christ pastor in Shelbyville was the Rev. William Morton. While in Shelbyville, Morton worked with Dr. Lewis L. Pinkerton and John Johnson to establish the Midway Female Orphan School in Midway, Kentucky. The school now is known as Midway College.

By 1839 the congregation was known as The Christian Church in Shelbyville. In 1864, it had outgrown its building space. The last service in the old building was a funeral for the man who had been the driving force in its founding, Dr. George W. Nuckols. Two weeks after Gen. Robert E. Lee surrendered his Confederate troops at Appomattox, Virginia, the dedicatory sermon for the new church building was preached on April 25, 1865, by one of the denomination's most distinguished preachers and authors, William T. Moore of Cincinnati. For 10 years after the new church was constructed, the congregation grew rapidly. In 1874, under the pastoral leadership of J. W. Ingram the Ladies Aid Society was organized. One of their first projects was to buy a parsonage. In one year they succeeded in raising enough money to buy a small cottage on Main Street, between Third and Fourth Streets.

The congregation continued to grow at the turn of the 20th century with the calling of a new pastor, the Rev. Hugh D. C. MacLachlan in 1901. His ministry was characterized by his attention to organization and detail. Church services were held at precisely 11:00 A.M. Prayer meetings, Sunday evening services, Ladies Aid meetings, Church Board meetings and other regular weekly or monthly events were established. MacLachlan established regular office hours.

The interurban streetcar was running to Louisville, automobiles were beginning to make an appearance, phone service was available by 1904, and railroads were running full steam across the state. The church phone number in 1904 was 266. In 1917, with America's entry into World War I, the pastor, the Rev. David Walker, chose to resign his ministry and go to France to serve with the Young Men's Christian Association as a chaplain. Later he returned to serve for another 12 years. In the early 1920s, a new electrically powered pipe organ was installed. Because it was one of the largest pipe organs in the region at that time it sparked renewed interest in great church music.

With the coming of the Great Depression in 1929 came difficult times. The building fell into some disrepair. The roof leaked, the furnace needed repair, the walls cracked, and the bell tower began to lean dangerously. The church, like the rest of the nation, was in debt. Yet the congregation continued to grow in the face of hard times. With the passing of the depression and World War II, more prosperous times began.

When the war began the Rev. Thomas M. Giltner was pastor. With the outbreak of the war, he resigned to accept an appointment as a chaplain in the U. S. Army.

The church called a new graduate of the College of the Bible, Rev. Wayne H. Bell, to be the next pastor. Under Bell's leadership many improvements and additions were made to the building. Bell resigned in 1951.

With the soldiers coming home from the war, a baby boom developed in the late 1940s, requiring the construction of additional space for church-school use. In 1948 and again 1979 expansion doubled the amount of space available in the church's first 148 years.

On May 20, 1951, the congregation met its new pastor, J. Edward Cayce, and his wife Martha. "Brother Ed," as he was to become known in the community, served First Christian Church for 25 years.

The First Christian Church, in the Italianate style, was built at Fourth and Main Streets in the 1860s. It burned in 1969.

In 1957, the first live radio broadcast of a service was transmitted over the local radio station. That live broadcast has continued. On August 7, 1969, First Christian Church caught fire and burned to the ground. The sanctuary building was rebuilt and dedicated in 1971. Brother Ed retired in 1976.

The Rev. James Lee Collins answered the call to become pastor in 1977. Under his ministry, Childtown, the first day-care center in Shelby County was started.

On August 21, 1986, Dr. James Howard Griffith became the pastor of First Christian Church. Since 1986 the congregation has re-organized its functional structure, developed a stronger financial foundation, expanded staff, and been involved in the formation of several community ministries. With the addition of associate pastor David Pilkinton in June 1988, the new ministry team led the way in organizing a Habitat for Humanity chapter in Shelbyville. In 1992, the ministry team moved the congregation toward a contemporary blend style of worship.

The congregation, through its pastor, was also involved in organizing and supporting Operation Care, a local ecumenical street ministry in 1990.

The Rev. David Pilkinton has brought a special gift for music, worship, drama and Christian Education to ministry at First Christian Church. Through his leadership the Chancel Choir has presented many outstanding musical concerts.

An important and dynamic decision was to relocate from its present address at 400 Main Street to the end of Boone Station Road (KY 55 and KY 43) where a new first phase building was constructed in the year 2000 on 15.9 acres of land.

MINISTERS

Started	Name	Years	Capacity	Served
1830	George W. Nuckols	1830-64	Elder	34
1833	Philip S. Fall	1833-36	Itinerant (1st Bldg.)	3
1836	William Morton	1836-42	1st Pastor	6
1839	Dr. Lewis L. Pinkerton	1839-40	Itinerant	1
1842	Robert C. Rice	1842-49	Pastor	7
1850	Sam Pinkerton	1850-52	Itinerant	2
1850	Sam Kelly	1850-52	Itinerant	2
1852	George Waller	1852-53	Pastor	1 1/2
1854	William Crawford	1854-	Itinerant	1
1854	William Rogers	1854-56	Itinerant	1 1/2
1858	James Henshall	1858-59	Pastor	1 1/2
1860	Richard C. Rickett	1860-64	Pastor (Civil War)	4
1865	C. K. Marshall	1865-66	Pastor	1 1/2
1866	George Mullins	1866-	Itinerant	1/2
1866	C. B. Chandler	1866-68	Pastor	2
1868	W. T. Oldham	1868-71	Pastor	2 1/2
1872	George Taylor	1872-74	Pastor	2 1/2
1874	J.W. Ingram	1874-77	Pastor	2 1/2
1877	Curtis Smith	1877-78	Pastor	1 1/2
1878	C. W . Sewell	1878-80	Pastor	1 1/2
1880	D . W . Case	1880-86	Pastor	6
1886	George Combs	1886-94	Pastor	8
1894	Walter White	1894-96	Pastor	2
1896	Hugh McLellan	1896-1901	Pastor	5
1901	Hugh D.C. MacLachlan	1901-08	Pastor	7
1908	Thadious Tinsley	1908-09	Pastor	1 1/2
1909	Homer Carpenter	1909-16	Pastor	7
1916	David M. Walker	1916-30	Pastor	14
1930	John Hardy MacNeil	1930-36	Pastor	6
1936	Thomas M. Giltner	1936-42	Pastor	5 1/2
1942	Wayne H. Bell	1942-51	Pastor	8 1/2
1951	J. Edward Cayce	1951-76	Pastor	25
1976	Arthur Landolt	1976-77	Iterim	9 mo.
1977	James L. Collins, Jr.	1977-86	Pastor	7
1984	Bruce Merton	1984-86	Pastor	18 months
1986	J. Howard Griffith	1986-	Pastor	

FIRST PRESBYTERIAN CHURCH

By Betty Buntin Matthews

Presbyterians of Shelbyville first met in homes with the Reverend Archibald Cameron as minister. He also ministered to the Fox Run and Mulberry Presbyterian Churches. In 1807, the communicants numbered twenty-five. In November 1809, Robert P. Allen, Singleton Wilson and Moses Hall bought lot 83 from the trustees of the town for six pounds fifteen shillings. Not until 1819 did the Shelbyville congregation proceed to construct a house of worship on the lot. By the fall of 1820 a church was erected, but was destroyed by a violent storm in 1823. It was replaced by a sturdy brick church with a burying ground for members as well as others. It is now the county library site.

In 1824, the church roll numbered fifty-eight. As the town grew, so did the congregation. In 1828, the year of the local great revival, membership grew to 143, and by 1839 there were 236 members. Because the congregation outgrew its building, in 1847 Samuel Shannon, as trustee, purchased lot 32 on the northeast corner of Main and Seventh Streets. The old church property was sold to the Associate Reformed Church for $600.

The style of architecture for the new church was Grecian with four very large Doric columns supporting the pediment. The pipe organ was the first used in any church in Shelbyville. The belfry contained a bell that the sexton rang for every service until the fire in December 1891 destroyed it.

The Civil War years brought discord, not only in the country, but in the churches as well. First Presbyterian Church in Shelbyville did not escape the dissension. In 1866, the Reverend William C. Matthews, who had been pastor since 1847, and around fifty members withdrew and formed the First Assembly Presbyterian Church USA They met in the College Chapel until a new church was built at Ninth and Main Streets. It was dedicated in December 1871. The remaining congregation stayed in the existing sanctuary and affiliated with the Louisville Presbytery US (Southern). The Reverend J. S. Grasty was called to be the minister.

The last service in the Grecian-style Church was March 5, 1888. The church was torn down and the congregation met in Layson Hall while a new church was being built. By December 1888 the church Sunday School rooms were ready for occupancy. The building was not completed until June 1889. The cost of the furnished church was $20,000. Communicants numbered 160.

A calamity occurred Sunday morning around 1:00 A.M. December 27, 1891, when the church caught fire--the cupola's flames illuminating the country around for miles. Everything in the building was lost, including the Reverend D.E. Frierson's extensive library. The members arriving for church that morning found only the walls remaining. While the burned church was being rebuilt, the congregation met in the unused Episcopal Church. On June 3, 1893, a new church was dedicated and membership then numbered 178.

After eleven years, the Reverend William E. Byce asked to be released from his ministry to accept a call to a pastorate in Iowa. The church found itself without a minister until late 1907 when it called the Reverend J. Rockwell Smith. Communicants numbered only fifty-four at that time. In January 1909 the

Session considered reuniting with First Presbyterian Church US. It was approved and the Reverend Smith offered his resignation effective April 1909. First Presbyterian Church minister, the Reverend David M. Sweets, terminated his ministry in March 1909. The joint congregation then called the Reverend W. A. Anderson. The First Assembly Presbyterian Church and lot were sold and half the proceeds were given to the united church. The other half of the proceeds were given to the Presbytery of Louisville of the Synod of Kentucky USA.

The Presbyterian Church has occupied this building with a few modernizations. In 1950, with the closing and demolition of Mulberry Presbyterian Church, an addition was built with the Good Shepherd window removed from the Mulberry Church now serving as the focal point of the extended sanctuary. The tower bell still tolls.

Over the years the church was blessed with inspiring ministers, dedicated elders and deacons, and a loyal congregation that in 2000 numbered around 350. A milestone was reached in 1996 when Dr. Lynn Williamson was called to be the first woman minister.

Ellis McGinnis Collection, courtesy of Michael McGinnis.

The First Presbyterian Church, shown in a circa 1909 photograph, was built in 1888 at Seventh and Main Streets.

PASTORS

Rev. Archibald Cameron	June 2, 1796 - Jan. I, 1835
Rev. Joseph Huber	Jan. I, 1835 - April I, 1837
Rev. Simeon H Crane	July 1837- Sept. 1837
Rev. W. W. Hill	June 10, 1838 - Sept. 1842
Rev. James Green	Feb. 1843 - Feb. 1844
Rev, James Smith	June 1845 - April 1848
Rev. William C. Matthews	Nov. 25. 1848 - 1866

withdrew with 50/80 members to form Assembly Presbyterian Church

Rev. J. S. Grasty	Sept. I, 1867 - Dec. 12, 1874
Rev. S. M. Neel	Oct. I, 1875 - Dec. 6, 1888
Rev. D.E. Frierson	Dec. I, 1889 - Mar.20,1898
Rev. David M. Sweets	Oct. I. 1899 - Mar.1909
Rev. W.A. Anderson	1909 - 1920
Rev. Carl S. Matthews	1921 - Oct. 1928
Rev. Angus N. Gordon	June 1929 - Jan 1941
Rev. (Dr.) Glover Daniel	April 1942 - July 1963
Rev. (Dr.) William Gardiner	Feb. 1964 - Mar. 1966
Rev. Gayle Threlkeld	Sept. 1966 - Dec. 1982
Rev. J. Roy Sharpe	Nov. 1983 - Aug.15. 1995
Rev. Kenneth Armstrong (Assoc.)	Nov. 1986 - Feb. 1989
Rev. Gary Pennington (Interim)	1995 - 1996
Rev. (Dr.) Lynn Williamson	Oct.13. 1996

GRAEFENBURG UNITED METHODIST CHURCH

By Mrs. Luther Stivers

The Graefenburg United Methodist Church, located about halfway between Shelbyville and Frankfort just off U.S. 60, was established in 1835. Although the congregation has been small, many church members have gone into full-time Christian service

Most outstanding was Bishop Urban Valentine-William Darlington. Darlington was born August 3, 1870, at Graefenburg. He received his early education in the Shelby County public schools and later attended Kentucky Wesleyan College, where he prepared for the ministry. Later the college conferred upon him the honorary degree of doctor of divinity. Bishop Darlington served for 22 years as pastor of leading Methodist churches in Kentucky and West Virginia. He also served two years as president of Morris Harvey College in Barbourville, West Virginia, before being made a bishop in May 1918 at Atlanta.

His first assignment as a bishop took him to Europe for eight years, following the devastation of World War I, where his leadership in church relief work won wide acclaim. He later served several areas in the United States, and for many years was in charge of the Kentucky Conference. He retired from active service in 1944 but was called back two years later when another bishop died, and continued until 1949. On June 6, 1944, the Kentucky Conference honored him in a celebration at his home church, Graefenburg. Many dignitaries of church and state, including the governor and lieutenant governor, were present for this occasion at the little white church where Darlington was first licensed to preach nearly 50 years earlier. A commemorative tablet was dedicated on that date and now stands as a memorial to him in the churchyard. Darlington died of a heart attack on October 1, 1954

Several of the present members of Graefenburg Methodist Church represent third, fourth and fifth generations of church members. With the great example set by Darlington and others, the present members are proud to be a part of this little country church. The church celebrated its 165th anniversary on August 19 and 20, 2000. Many former pastors and members were present for the occasion.

HEMPRIDGE BAPTIST CHURCH

By Ann Ruble

The Hempridge Baptist Church originated from a Sunday school held in the Wolf Run schoolhouse. After four months of preaching by T. N. Fontaine the group met on October 4, 1913, to organize. The Rev. O. M. Huey of Crescent Hill Baptist Church in Louisville was elected chairman and Brother Fontaine secretary. The members were: J. W. Newton and wife Ira, Abe Raisor and wife Ida, Nannie Green, Charlie Green, Ramsey Neal, Winford Neal, Gilbert Neal, Lawrence Pulliam and wife Roberta, Margaret Gains, Garnett Morris, Maggie Shropshire and children, Virginia, Dara, Ola, and Raymond, Allen Howerton, and Susie Green.

Fontaine was called as pastor, Lawrence Pulliam was elected church clerk, and John Newton and Don Calvin were elected deacons. They were ordained January 1914. The church voted to build a house of worship on ground given by Ben Perkins.

In 1917, a revival was held in a nearby barn. E. H. Blakeman was the evangelist. Thirty-five members were added to the church. In 1918, the church building was erected. Brother Steele, Mrs. Maggie Shropshire, Mrs. Omer O'Nan and others led work. On August 31, 1919, the building was dedicated to the Lord's service. The first revival was in August 1919. The Shelby County Association was held in the new church August 1923.

The sanctuary was used for Sunday school classes as well as for worship services. Each class had its corner and cloth curtains were used as dividers. The heating system was two cast- iron pot-bellied stoves and the lighting came from hanging kerosene lamps. The accompaniment for the singing was a pump organ. At that time preaching services were only held twice a month. In 1937, progress brought electric current and Hempridge began to make needed changes.

By the late 1940s the membership and attendance was growing. With full-time worship services, there was a need for Sunday school rooms. After much deliberation and hard work the addition of the rooms were approved. By 1949 they were completed and ready for use. Since 1950 improvements and changes have been made a little at a time. In 1964, the members voted to buy the Raymond Jesse house for a parsonage. The Rev. Mike Darrow was the first pastor to live there. After a short period of time this debt was paid and it was agreed to build a cistern, kitchen and rest rooms. These were completed in 1968.

Since the beginning of Hempridge Baptist Church, it has been served by 38 pastors as of September 1999. All the pastors have been students of the Southern Baptist Theological Seminary. Most have gone on to larger fields of service.

HIGHLAND BAPTIST CHURCH

By Allen Clark

Since 1949 Highland Baptist Church, 511 Mount Eden Road, has been offering ministry programs and service to Shelby County. In May 1941, the First Baptist Church of Shelbyville began a mission at Second and Bradshaw Streets. This mission, called the Baptist Chapel, held worship services and Bible study for eight years before organizing into a church. On Sunday, February 13, 1949, the Baptist Chapel was organized as the Second Street Baptist Church, calling John A. Hatcher as pastor.

The Charter members of this newly formed church were: Nellie Bramblett Adcock, Ellen Bramblett, Elizabeth Brewer, Shirley Brewer, Vivian Brewer, Allie Catlett, Carolyn Catlett, Lillian Catlett, Louise Catlett, Quenna Catlett, Justice Childs, Mrs. Albert Clark, Betty Clark, Charles Clark, Mrs. Charles Clark, R.S. Clark, Elizabeth Corn, Lettie Cummins, Lillie Mae Cummins, Charles Ford, Jesse Irvin Frazier, Lois Garrison, Louise Garrison, Ethelda Goins, Marion Goins, Brenda Gordon, Estill Gordon, Jane Gordon, Ronnie Gordon, Virginia Gordon, Jesse Hatcher, John Hatcher, Irene Herndon, Lorrian Herndon, Martha Herndon, Romona Herndon, Mrs. Hildebrandt, David Hortenberry, Frances Hughes, Katherine Hughes, Oscar Jones, Mrs. Oscar Jones, James Martin, James Mattin, Mamie Mattin, Betty Melear, Mrs. Nally, Lydia Price, Dean Raltson, Christine Robinson, Calvin Rucker, Porter Rucker, Emma Sallee, Margie Taylor, Ellis Simpson, William Simpson, James Taylor, Jennie Townsend, Prentice Turner, and Charles Whitman.

On February 21, 1951, the church bought a lot in the Highlands, on U.S. 60 east of Shelbyville, for $1,600. At that time the church adopted the name Second Baptist Church. That same year, it became self-supporting and requested that financial aid from the mother church, First Baptist, be discontinued. By September 1951 the church began construction on its newly purchased lot. Many members worked on construction, decoration, and financial aspects of the new building. The name Highland Baptist Church was chosen on October 8, 1958.

Highland Baptist soon outgrew its building, requiring it to conduct overflow services at Shelbyville High School. This allowed for two Sunday schools and two worship services each week. To meet its growth, the church purchased 9.6 acres on Mount Eden Road in 1964.

Highland Baptist Church on Mt. Eden Road. The new sanctuary was built in 1985.

In January 1965, a planning and surveying committee was chosen to aid in the selection of a church plan and to promote building fund offerings. In 1965, a barn was relocated to the newly purchased lot and remodeled for worship and Sunday school space. Overflow services were relocated to this structure. The church continued to conduct two worship services and two Sunday schools for many months. In May 1967, the church appointed a building committee. Groundbreaking ceremonies were conducted on May 21, 1967, and the church began meeting in its new building in 1968. The cornerstone was laid on Easter Sunday, March 29, 1970.

Highland Baptist Church continued to grow. In November 1981, a study committee was formed to explore the possibility of building a new sanctuary. The new building finance committee was appointed in August 1983 and the new sanctuary addition was completed in 1985.

Early in its history Highland sponsored a mission church that met on Thursday nights in the overflow building on the church property. This mission was called the Mission of Light.

Over the years Highland has sponsored numerous mission teams that have gone to various parts of Kentucky, Ohio, and Illinois to share the message of the Gospel through word and work. Highland was among the first churches in Shelby County to minister to Hispanics coming into the community. Highland provided fellowship meals with devotionals in Spanish and translated weekly services into Spanish. Members of Highland led in the formation of Shelby Baptist Association's Hispanic Ministry.

Throughout its history, 12 men have served as pastor of Highland Baptist Church. Those men are: John Hatcher (February 1949-August 1950); Ray Alexander (September 1950-March 1954); Marshall Phillips (May 1954-June 1961); Earl Wilson (July 1961-April 1965); Gene Puckett, Interim (April 1965-August 1965); Ray Bateman (September 1965-March 1968); Noah Benningfield (April 1968-January 1969); H. Douglas Olive (January 1969-August 1971); Norman Shands, Interim (September 1971- March 1972); Phillip Basinger (April 1971-October 1976); J.C. Nuckols, Interim (November 1976-May 1977); and William A. George (June 1977-).

INDIAN FORK BAPTIST CHURCH

By Julian K. Wood

Jacksonville is located in eastern Shelby County about one mile from the Franklin County line. Jacksonville came into being in the 1830s and was named in honor of Andrew Jackson. Jackson was admired as an Indian fighter, as a general who fought the British at New Orleans, and as president of the United States.

Jacksonville had at least two general stores and a two-room school. The small post office of Zilpah and its postmaster, G.F. Montgomery, served the people until the post office was consolidated with Mitchell on August 30, 1902. Jacksonville is a crossroads community with a small cluster of homes. Most of the people in the area are farmers.

Just west of Jacksonville is Indian Fork Baptist Church. The Rev. Abraham Cook who came from Virginia organized it in 1803. The church is located at the mouth of Indian Fork Creek and was named for the creek. Early settlers had found a dead Indian in a fork of a tree on the creek, thus the name Indian Fork. Many of the charter members came from Tick Creek Baptist Church.

The first building was constructed of logs cut in the area. It stood until a brick building was constructed in 1889. The bricks were fired from the clay from the nearby Indian Fork Creek. Like all early churches, Indian Fork operated somewhat differently than most churches of today. A business meeting was held each Saturday afternoon, preaching services were each Sunday, and the sermons lasted until 2:00 or 3:00 P.M. Church members were brought before the church for infractions of the rules. These included dancing, cussing, lying, reading novels, working on Sunday, playing cards, and many other "sins." Those brought up on charges had to discontinue these habits or be put out of the church.

Once a year a meeting was held to pledge provisions for the minister. Because there was little money, members would pledge corn for his horse, shoes for his family, salt pork, a new saddle, homemade

The third building of the Indian Fork Baptist Church, built in 1947.

furniture, cornmeal, and some even pledged whiskey. Whiskey was not looked upon as unfavorably as it is today. It would seem that nearly everyone drank, which was all right as long as no one got drunk. It is reported that some of the deacons once accused Reverend Cook of drinking too much and had to hold onto the pulpit to keep from falling during two Sunday services.

In 1880, the Shelby County Association meeting was held at Indian Fork. It was attended by 4,500 people and lasted one week. People came in wagons and entire families attended. As many as four speakers would preach at once. Each one had his own stump and little group of followers. Others were engaged in horse-trading or other activities. Before the week ended the whole area was in a very unsanitary condition.

In April 1944, the entire back end of the church collapsed while some work was being done to the building. For several months, church services were held in various places until a new building was constructed in 1947. This made the third building Indian Fork Baptist Church has had.

There is a cemetery on the church property. There rest many of the pioneer settlers of this area. The church has served the community for almost two centuries and continues to be a beacon to anyone who needs its services.

LIVING WATERS CHURCH

By Duanne Puckett

In March 1981 a group of about 100 people met at Henry Clay School in Clay Village for worship services. At that time Living Waters Church was born from a vision of God in the hearts of those families from several surrounding counties and different denominations. Kent Sullivan, a fellow graduate of Asbury Theological Seminary and pastor in the Bedford, Ky. area, joined Joel League, pastor, in full-time ministry that same year. Sullivan was called by the church not only to preach to the congregation, but also to fulfill an awesome responsibility of starting a Christian school in Shelby County and reaching out to the surrounding areas of Franklin, Anderson, and Henry Counties.

One year later, the congregation moved across the road on 6 acres of land and into a new building. By this time the church had grown to around 200 members. The multi-purpose building served not only for the weekly worship services but all of the activities of the church and school.

In fall 1984, Kent Sullivan took the helm and guided the formation of the Christian school, equipping it with teachers, materials and students. Living Waters Christian School (now Cornerstone Christian Academy) began with an enrollment of 35 students. The first year was a labor of love for the teachers who gave of their time and teaching skills without pay.

By 1989, the cramped spaces used for church and school facilitated a new addition of ten classrooms, youth room/lunch room, and much needed office space. The sanctuary was renovated to seat 350 and later remodeled to seat 500 worshippers.

Through the years Living Waters Church has continued to reach out to families in the surrounding areas through youth and children's programs, vibrant contemporary worship, and missions, local and foreign.

Courtesy of Duanne Puckett.

Living Waters Church was built in 1982 and enlarged in 1989.

Living Waters Church would be considered charismatic by most; however, members think of themselves as simply one expression of the Body of Christ in this Kentucky area. There is a definite flavor of free worship and a balance between contemporary cutting edge worship and the great hymns of the faith. In addition to a great emphasis on worship, the congregation is committed to the centrality of the living Jesus and the Word of God. The pastors insist that the congregation be students of the Bible and believe that the spirit and the Word must agree.

In May 1999, 36.4 acres of land were purchased, two miles east of the old location in Clay Village. Looking to the future, Living Waters Church planned to build a new activity center with gyms and a new school on the site.

MOUNT VERNON BAPTIST CHURCH

By Jeff Brown

The Mount Vernon Baptist Church was established on March 29, 1845, as The United Baptist Church of Christ at Mount Vernon. It was constituted that day in the house of William Taylor on Catridge Creek. The specific circumstances surrounding the organization of the new church have been lost. What is known is that Mount Vernon was started by a group of members from the Pigeon Fork Baptist Church (established 1825) after some disagreement concerning the fourth article of faith. That article deals with the way of salvation. The pastor of the Pigeon Fork church, Vint Ash, led the founding. A portion of the membership eventually requested and gracefully received permission to withdraw in order to constitute a new fellowship. Eventually, both churches concluded that it would be best if the exact nature of the disagreement were removed from their individual minutes. Their fellowship has been pleasant ever since.

The church began construction on its first building in April 1845. Land was obtained and a design chosen for a building. This structure was completed on the site of the present facilities sometime in 1849 and used until August 1939. The current church building was completed and dedicated on December 17, 1939. In 1943, the church received a house and land in Harrisonville from the estate of Smith T. Watts for a parsonage.

By 1892 the name of the church was reduced to The Baptist Church at Mount Vernon. The church, affiliated with the Southern Baptist Convention and the Kentucky Baptist Convention, has had approximately 47 pastors in its 150-year history. Since the late 1930s, the majority of pastors have come as students of the Southern Baptist Theological Seminary in Louisville.

Mount Vernon's history, like that of any other church, is marked with times of highs and lows. The highest membership was 437 persons in 1950. The greatest years of evangelistic outreach, as reflected in baptisms, were 1893 when 44 were baptized, 1910 when 41 were baptized, and in 1940 when 38 were baptized. Financially, the church's budget has increased slowly over the present century. Its greatest financial progress has occurred between 1983 and 1998 with gifts to the church and missionary causes doubling in amount.

Mount Vernon continues to work for the glory of God. Outwardly, associational involvement missions giving, and evangelism remain high priories. Inwardly, Biblical preaching, children's ministries, and ministry to shut-ins have become a primary focus of fellowship.

PASTORS

Sandridege Arnett (1845-48)	E.M. Thompson (1934-36)
Benjamin F. Keeling (1849-55)	L.D. Stucker (1936-38)
James A. Peters (1855-56)	Thomas J. Tichenor (1939-43)
Vincent Ash (1857-58)	Roy O Beaman (1943-45)
David Bruner (1859-60)	Stephen Cloud (1946-47)
James Smith (1861-64)	L.M. Hamilton (1948-51)
James T. Hedger (March 1865)	Prince Claybrook (1952-54)
James A. Peters (July 1865)	Robert E. Brown (1954-57)
S. S. Perry (1867-74)	Edward Ferrell (1957-59)
John Harrington (1874-77)	B.B. Boaz (1959-61)
J.T. Adkins (February 1878)	Harold Smith (1961-64)
Jerome T. Sampson (1879-85)	J. W. Rogers (1964-67)
S.S. Perry (1886-89)	Mack T. Harris (1967-1970)
Jerome T. Sampson (1889-91)	Carl Hogue (1970)
W.E. Powers (1891-96)	Darrell Stone (1971-74)
Samuel Wilson (1896-99)	Grant O'Dell (1975-77)
W.E. Powers (1899-1908)	David Byrd (1978-79, int.)
E.H. Blakemen (1908-1914)	Ray England (1979-82)
J. Sam Kirby (Feb. 1915)	Tom Harrington (1983-84)
Elmo Royalty (1916-19)	Steven D.C. Corts (1984-1990)
J. Samuel Wilson (1919-23)	Bernard Perry (1990, int.)
Coleman Harrison (1923-24)	Mark T. Bowen (1991-94)
Walter Walker (1924-26)	Jonny W. Collett (1995)
Cecil Sheets (1926-27)	Jeffrey D. Brown (1996-present)
E. S. Summers (1927-34)	

MULBERRY PRESBYTERIAN CHURCH

By Betty Matthews

In 1796, a Presbyterian church was organized on the headwaters of Mulberry Creek with the Rev. Archibald Cameron as minister. The Presbyterian congregations on Six Mile Creek, known as the Low Dutch, and on Tick Creek were reduced in number and chose to merge at this location because it lay between the two settlements. Cameron was a native of Scotland and came to Nelson County, Kentucky, at an early age with his parents. After being ordained, he preached at Fox Run, Shelbyville, Six Mile, and Mulberry Presbyterian Churches. He was pastor for almost 40 years until his death in 1836. Many early Shelby County families worshipped at Mulberry Church—Venable, Miles, Crockett, King, Allen, Hope, Brown, Bird, Buford, Lyle, Glass, Graham, Morton, Hanna, Logan, and Van Meter.

The first church was an 18-by-20-foot log house. During the great revival in 1828 membership doubled. Then it dropped in 1835 with migration to Indiana and western territories. By 1838, the log church had been succeeded by a commodious brick building. This structure stood until 1852 when a larger brick church at a cost of $2,298.50 replaced it. About this time the Session voted to give Centre College $500 for a perpetual scholarship available to a member of the church.

The Rev. J.D. Paxton (1839-55) succeeded Rev. Cameron, after several moderators. Again moderators served the church until the Civil War brought discord. The Louisville Presbytery withdrew from the General Assembly of the USA and formed a new Presbytery. Mulberry Church joined the new Presbytery, and Dr. Samuel McPhetters was called to minister to the congregation. He had been dismissed from his large church in St. Louis for his southern support. An invalid, he preached from a couch that is now in the First Presbyterian Church, Shelbyville. Dr. McPheeters died in 1870 and again moderators filled the pulpit until 1872, when the Rev. William Irvine was called. He served until 1890.

In 1896, the Louisville & Nashville Railroad condemned the church property for a right of way. Following a suit in Shelby Circuit Court, the church was awarded damages in excess of what the L & N had originally rejected. With the imminent danger going to and from the church from the railroad and trains scaring the horses, the congregation voted to take the $3,525 court award and build a church on the Mulberry Pike north of the present building. The new church was erected for $3,401.23 and dedicated on June 23, 1897, with the Rev. J. 0. Sullivan as minister. Subsequent ministers were the Revs. John B. Gordon (1898-1903) and A. H. Doak (1906-12).

World War I and the following years created financial and ministerial problems for the church. Membership dropped while membership in the Shelbyville Presbyterian Church increased due to the automobile making it easier for Presbyterians to travel. Supply ministers filled the pulpit from 1924 to 1937; then seminary students served until 1946. The church closed in 1948 and the 19 remaining members moved their membership to the First Presbyterian Church in Shelbyville.

The property was sold to Dr. K.E. Ellis and his wife who found it impractical to convert the building into a residence. It was torn down and much of the material was used in building their home. The fireplace is made from stones from the church, the mantle is a large stone from the church, windowsills are from the church and concrete forms from the church can be seen on the patio. Reuben Taylor bought many of the bricks and used them to build an addition to his old home on Logan Road (now owned by Fred D. Trammell). The small stained-glass windows were bought by Henry Brown and placed in the Highland Baptist Church. The large stained glass window called the Good Shepherd Window was set in the exterior wall of the addition to the Shelbyville Presbyterian Church in 1950. The pews were given to the Rev. Robert A.Craig to be used in the Church of Christ on Washington Street. Though Mulberry Presbyterian Church is gone it lives on in these various buildings.

NEW MOUNT ZION BAPTIST CHURCH

By Rev. Kilen Gray

In the year 1880, under the leadership of the late Rev. Tibbs, with the officers and trustees, a church was organized at Clay Village on U.S. 60. After a while, the members began to move away and the membership became so small that the church decided to move, this time to Benson Creek about 1.5 miles from Waddy.

There the Revs. George Butler and Thomas Butler helped with the service. Many people joined the church, but later they too began to move away. This forced the church to move again. Since there was no ground to build, Brother Claude Wade talked to Tom Waddy who gave the church about one acre on the Waddy Road near the railroad. A tent was put up for services and the first basket meeting was served in 1906. Much work was involved in building the church. Lumber had to be hauled from the church in Benson. After the building was finished, the Rev. Owens worked with the people and many members were added to the church.

The Rev. Bryant laid out a mission on June 6, 1975. Under his pastorate 31 members joined. In April 1977, the church moved from Waddy to Shelbyville. When the Rev. Bryant died, the Rev. Samuel Mack took over as interim pastor until the Rev. Derrick Span was called in 1983. The Rev. Span started the nurses' guild and the orientation seminary to familiarize members with the doctrine, Teachings of Faith.

The Rev. Kilen Gray was installed, September 29, 1985. He reorganized the youth department and outreach, improved the music department, and purchased a church bus. Under his guidance a spiritual awakening began and the church has continued to grow.

The church family purchased 10 acres of land on Harrington Mill Road and paid it off on March 21, 1996. On April 6, 1997, the church adopted a 5-year strategic plan; and on April 15, 1997, it signed a contract to begin a master plan to develop the land for a new church building. On June 6, 1999, Sister Thosha Alexander was the first female to deliver a trial sermon at the church.

MINISTERS

Rev. J. A. Baker	1919-20	Rev. Weaver	1943-45
Rev. Roberts	1921-28	Rev. Boggs	1946-47
Rev. Lloyd	1929-31	Rev. Young	1947-70
Rev. Owens	1932-33	Rev. L. Brown	1971-75
Rev. Brisco	1933-35	Rev. Bryant	1975-82
Rev. Humphrey	1939-40	Rev.Span	1982-85
Rev. Sullivan	1941-42	Rev. Gray	1985-

OLIVE BRANCH UNITED METHODIST CHURCH

By Sadie Igleheart

In 1800, the Boswell, Taylor and Figg families moved from Culpeper County, Virginia, and settled near Brashears Creek on the crossroad between Zaring Mill and Taylorsville Roads about two miles east of where Finchville now stands. They soon built a frame church on land owned by the Barriger family. About a half mile away, a spring flowed toward the church, splitting in two, and flowing around both sides of the building. Because of the abundant water surrounding the little church, they were reminded of the scriptural account of the great flood and the faith of Noah in following God's directions. Thus, they named the church Olive Branch Methodist Episcopal Church South, memorializing the return of the dove with an olive branch, indicating that the waters had receded and God's promise had been fulfilled.

By 1860, after a great revival at the church and many new members, the old church building was inadequate. Warner T. Figg donated an acre of land on the Zaring Mill Road near the corner of the crossroad, now known as KY 148. They fired the brick about a quarter mile from the site. The building was dedicated in 1862, led by the Rev. J. E. Strother. The congregation continued to grow and in 1885 had over 200 members, which was considered to be the largest church in the county.

The church was part of the Shelbyville circuit (which at various times included Taylorsville, Graefenburg, Clayvillage and Rockbridge Methodist Churches) and for many years held services once a month. By 1935, services were held twice monthly and by 1944 weekly services were held. In 1946, a basement was dug and Sunday school classrooms were added. Two stained glass windows were installed. In 1949, a new parsonage was built next door. A centennial celebration was held in 1961 and many former ministers attended. In 1979, ground was broken for an educational annex, which was dedicated on November 22, 1980, as Thanksgiving was celebrated. In 1981, a bus ministry was begun with the purchase of a 45-passenger vehicle and many members and visitors without transportation were brought to the services.

Courtesy of the Kentucky Heritage Council.

Olive Branch Methodist Church, on Zaring Mill Road, was built in 1862.

PASTORS

J. E. Strother, Anselin Minor, W. H. Winter, Robert Hiner, W. H. Vaughn, J. H. Henderson, D. B. Cooper, T. B. Cook, J. T. McIntyre, George Froh, J. J. Johnson, T. J. Godby, M. T. Chandler, J. W. Simpson, E. K. Pike, P. J. Ross, J. E. Wright, C. H. Caswell, R. R. Rose, E. W. Ishmael, A. G. Stone, J. R. Whealdon, F. D. Simpson, O. S. Gardner, J. W. Parrish, E. E. Ashley, Harold Gardner, G. O. Miley, Harold Brooks, Julian Simpson, David Finch, Graham Abbott, Robert L. Meyers, Clayton Klingenfus, Walter Rhodes, Roger Herman, Sam Glenn, Stephen Hallman, Tom Brewer, Robert Bradley, Stephen Boggan, Tom Holman, Steve Pearson, Fred Wiles, and Jerry Shelley.

ROCKBRIDGE UNITED METHODIST CHURCH

By The Rev. Bob Nalley

Rockbridge United Methodist Church was established in 1806 at a location directly across Rockbridge Road from where the church is now located at the junction of Rockbridge and Hempridge Roads. The original church was a small log structure that was used until around 1811 when a fire destroyed the original church. The members evidently had planned to build a larger church eventually and had already purchased the two-acre present site. A copy of the original deed shows that the site was purchased from Benjamin Fry for the sum of $2.00 ($1.00 per acre), and dated June 20, 1808. Fry requested that the property be used to build a church of worship for members of the Methodist Episcopal Church and that they would permit any minister from the Church of England, passing through the country, to use the facilities to expound the word of God, if the church was not otherwise in use.

The church was a vital part of the community in the 19th century. At times the church would be filled to capacity and the overflow crowd would surround the building and listen to the sermons while sitting in their buggies. Things went well for Rockbridge Church until World War II, when the younger generation began moving away. Attendance dropped so that by the 1950s the church was opened part-time and in the 1960s it closed.

In 1978, a group of people, largely composed of some of those who attended there as children, decided that it was wrong for Rockbridge Church, with all its history of doing God's will, to be closed. The group, with help from the community, began a restoration program that took over two years to complete. Rockbridge United Methodist Church reopened in July 1981. A fellowship hall/education building was built in 1988. Since reopening, Rockbridge Church has purchased an adjacent house for a parsonage and purchased the 2-acre lot across the road for further expansion.

The Rockbridge United Methodist Church was built in 1808.

SAINT JOHN'S UNITED METHODIST CHURCH

By Eunice Marie Payne Reed

The Methodist Episcopal Church was established in America in 1784. By 1845, the slavery question had caused divisions in the church and the southern Methodists formed the Methodist Episcopal Church South. Negro Methodists separated in 1870 into the Colored Methodist Church, of which St. John's was a part.

In 1894 and 1895, Reverend George Smith led a campaign to construct a new church building and the land was acquired on College Street in 1897 from David H. Wayne by the trustees: L. Coleman, Charles Davis, Alfred Buss, Peter Gordon, Davis Riggs, F. Mason, Lazarus Howard, Henry Wilson, Jr., and W. M. Stewart for $125.00. The lot is 225 feet by 50 feet. Church services were being held in the Lodge Hall up the street and were conducted by Reverend John Russell. The new structure was completed in 1896 at a cost of $3,000.00 and contained 30 beautiful stained glass windows, double entrance doors, spacious seating, a high ceiling and a tall steeple with one of the largest bells in town. It was the largest Negro church in Shelbyville with a membership of over 200. Reverend Booker presided at the dedication.

Some of the pastors who have served St. John are: Rev. Charles White, Rev. John Roach, Rev. W. H. Bloomer, Rev. Rusaw Down, Rev. R. E. Hines, Rev. Samuel Chenault, Rev. R. Jones, Rev. Donald Herndon, Rev. Bradford, Rev. Greer, Rev. Crawford, Rev. H. H. Greene, Rev. H. J. Johnson, Rev. J. M. Bell, Rev. J. W. Robinson, Rev. Steve Boom, Rev. C. H. Brower, Rev. Norman White, Rev. W. H. Henderson, Rev. Kevin Edmonds, Rev. J. W. Crook, and Rev. Robert Marshall, Sr.. Rev. George Cottrell, Sr. has filled in between pastors.

Many improvements were made over the years. In 1979, under the leadership of Rev. H. H. Greene, carpet was replaced, new pews were purchased, new altar drapes, pulpit and baptismal font, communion table, hymn books, clock, table linens, vases and screens were purchased. The ceiling was lowered and new lights were installed, uplifting the church's spirit and morale. It was rededicated November 11, 1979. Aluminum siding, new roof and ceiling fans were added in 1982.

The Reverend H. H. Greene was a legend in the Methodist Church. He preached first at St. John's in 1926. He was a grandson of a previous pastor, Rev. W. H. Bloomer, who served from 1906 to 1909 and returned later for another year's service. Rev. Greene was ordained in 1929 in the Lexington Conference and came to St. John's after a division in the membership in March of 1969 while Rev. John Roach was pastor. The prayers of the faithful were answered when Rev. Greene arrived and pulled the church together again with many members returning.

Special mention must be made about special people who have made an impact on the history of St. John United Methodist Church: Dr. John W. Robinson, who was born in Shelbyville, was ordained into the Lexington Conference and served as District Superintendent. He later served St. Mark in Chicago and St. Mark in New York. Mrs. Zora Clark, aunt of Rev. H. H. Greene, was the first Negro woman in Shelby County to receive a nursing degree. T. S. Baxter was the first Negro to be elected City Councilman here and was a member of the County Republican Executive Committee. William Baxter was a restaurant operator and well known pianist. He served as the church pianist and traveled with a band for many years. Mrs. Verna Chinn was the first Negro woman to establish a kindergarten in the county. She served as Sunday School Superintendent. Mrs. Rebecca Smock Tilley, wife of civil war veteran Joseph Tilley, was an educator and Superintendent of the Sunday School. Beulah Roland was the church organist for many years and was succeeded by her sister, Dollie Roland Miller, a fine organist also, but moved to Chicago. Ethel Dirks served as President of the Choir for many years and also as Trustee. Lula Rucker Thomas taught elementary school at Finchville for many years, then operated a catering business and restaurant here. William H. Payne, Sr., was Chairperson of the Administrative Board for 35 years and a member of the Board of Trustees and Choir. He also served as Chairman of the Board of Education for the Colored School before integration of the schools. He is now in charge of the Building Fund, which is engaged in raising funds for replacement of the present church building. Ollie Murphy was Secretary of the Finance Commission, Trustee and church treasurer for many years. Julia P. Wilson was President of the Choir for 15 years, Trustee, Building Fund Chairperson and Communion Steward. Mary White served as Communion Steward for 30 years and served on the Finance Committee. Etta Roland was president of the choir for many years and a leader in the Church School. She also put on the Christmas pageants for years. Bessie Fleming was recognized as the county's Mother of the Year with seven children, twenty-five grandchildren, and fourteen great grandchildren. She is also the mother of attorney Willie C. Fleming, who was the first black lawyer graduated from the University of Louisville.

Arthur Ashby, Jr., was the first black electrician in the county. Malinda R. Baxter and her husband, Willie Baxter, operated a general store and integrated restaurant for more than thirty-five years. She was church secretary, trustee, and member of the Finance Committee. Nettie Hawkins was president of the choir and chairperson of the Finance Committee. Rev. George Cottrell, Sr., has come forward in hard times when we have not had a pastor and has filled the pulpit with his generous spirit. He is now Assistant Pastor. Rev. Robert Marshall, Sr., has served as our present pastor through difficult decisions on rebuilding, relocation and renewal. He has responded to God's call in humble obedience to His Will and carries the responsibility of pastor also to Allen's Chapel near Finchville and Wesley Chapel at Chaplin in Nelson County. He continues to be a life saver. Five members have been honored with scholarships to college by the generosity of Harriet Poynter, late member of Centenary United Methodist, who left funds in her estate for the education of black musicians and other scholars. Those receiving scholarships have been Angela White to Eastern University, Jackie White, Rhonda Hicks and Darlene Marshall to University of Louisville, and George Cottrell, Jr. to Kentucky Wesleyan College.

Our members have been taught that a full, free and present salvation is the gift of God to every man and woman through faith alone in Jesus Christ. The Methodist doctrine of regeneration is through repentance and faith in our Lord, Jesus Christ. Sanctification is through the saving truth spiritually received and applied by faith and obedience to God.

SALEM BAPTIST CHURCH

By Ernestine Jennings and Patricia Skelton

Sitting majestically atop Salem Hill on Mount Eden Road (Highway 44) behind two towering pine trees and beside a well-kept cemetery, Salem Baptist Church has served as a lighthouse to Shelby County and the surrounding community since 1811. Guided by Christ's command to "Go ye therefore and teach all nations" (Matthew 28:19), Salem has maintained a strong focus on missions while being sustained by a dedicated nucleus of members.

Led by Moses Scott, pastor of Beech Creek, and James McQuade, a pioneer circuit rider, a group of 19 charter members constituted a Baptist church at the Southville home of Sarah Dugan on January 19, 1811; largely from the membership of old Beech Creek, the church was served by circuit-riding preachers until 1818. Originally called Beech Ridge Church, the institution was renamed Salem in 1823 for an unknown reason.

Cutting logs and using rocks close at hand, workers laid a foundation and built the first meeting place, a log structure with a big fireplace for heating and a pulpit on the side. It was located approximately 100 feet southwest of the present church, an area which is now used as a cemetery, with the grave of the first "official pastor," Rev. John Holland, under the former pulpit. While there is no proof, the structure is believed to have been built in the summer of 1811 or 1812. This site became the property of the church on May 17, 1817, when John Fisher, agent for the heirs of Robert Slaughter, deeded 17 acres of land to Beech Ridge Church for $1.00, which was a gift. The land was to provide plenty of wood for the church.

This building was used until 1836 or 1837, when it was replaced by the first brick structure, which was located just west of the log structure. Bricks made nearby proved to be of inferior quality, and a new place of worship had to be constructed in 1857 or 1858. Being moved west approximately 50 feet, this structure was erected on the present site. Contractors, who lived in the old church while the new one was being constructed, were paid in part by being given the old brick building. The congregation, which included slaves, was to be allowed to worship in the old house until the new one was completed. For some time after the new building was completed, tramps and campers used the old structure so freely that the contractors complied with the church's request to move it. In November 1894, this third meetinghouse burned, and the present structure was erected on the same foundation with largely the same walls.

Beech Ridge Church was a part of the Long Run Association from 1812 at which time it reported 35 members. In July 1837, the church affiliated with the Middle District Association, which was organized that year. Sending five messengers, the church reported 217 members. Representatives from six churches attended the association meeting hosted by Salem on July 30, 1840, and reported their membership: Bethel, 245; Beech Creek, 123; Moriah, 148; Pigeon Fork, 75; Bethlehem, 37; and Salem, 280.

As the association met from time to time, the churches seemed to have enjoyed prosperity until about 1848, when Bethel reported 156 members; Beech Creek, 129; and Salem, 302. A year later, Bethel had no report, Beech Creek reported only 50 members, and Salem, 328. Near this time, circuit riders were finding their task arduous; some suggested giving money to the laity rather than expecting them to bear their own expenses with only meager support. Although some churches became only memories, Salem continued to flourish. Accepting the association's emphasis on missions, Salem demonstrated its missionary zeal. It remained a member of the Middle District Association until 1872, at which time the Shelby County Association was organized at Salem.

While the exact date of Salem's Woman's Missionary Union is unknown, it apparently began around 1913. Records show, however, that ladies have been supporting specific mission endeavors since 1889 with children and the poor receiving special attention. Since a missionary to Brazil spoke at Salem in 1905, many opportunities to host similar speakers have been sought. In 1919, Salem set a goal of $10,000 for missions over a five-year period. The minutes show that before the end of November 1919, "the campaign closed with the pledges amounting to $12,576.75."

Having organized a Sunday school in 1919, Salem later entered a building program, which resulted in the first classrooms being opened in October 1935. Receiving $10 from a joyful elderly gentleman who was baptized in 1953, the Rev. Oscar Smith placed this money in a building fund. In 1961, under the leadership of the Rev. Wendell A. Romans, the current education building was erected. At that time, the facility successfully served more than 200 in Sunday school. Discipleship training, mid-week prayer services, Brotherhood, Mission Friends, Royal Ambassadors, Girls in Action, and Acteens, as well as three groups of Women on Mission, minister to members and provide opportunities for growth and service to those outside the church.

The mission effort has extended beyond meetings, speakers, and donations; in the early 20th century, some members taught a Sunday school lesson once a week at Sunnyside School and assisted other churches in various ventures, paying particular attention to "relief of aged ministers and orphanages and for the education of young preachers" (Ratcliff). Throughout many decades, several of Salem's members have held association offices, and at least five ministers have been ordained. The budget for 2000 designated 17 percent of regular offerings to the Cooperative Program and 2 percent to Associational Missions with sizable amounts being given to special offerings for Kentucky, North American, and International Missions, as well as monthly projects to benefit local organizations and individuals.

While caring for others, members have upgraded the church's facilities. Having owned housing in Shelbyville for ministers, church members sold the parsonage in 1948 and purchased a house a few hundred yards from the church. Another parsonage was built in 1974. For decades, Salem used a nearby creek and ponds for baptismal services with as many as 34 being baptized at one time in 1937. A vote was taken to build an outdoor baptistery in 1949. In later years, Salem used baptismal facilities at First Baptist Church until the opening of the current education building in 1961, the 150th anniversary of the church. Less than a decade later, extensive redecoration of the sanctuary occurred.

Nearing her 200th anniversary, Salem, which now has slightly over 400 members, has experienced many changes and undertaken innumerable projects and programs. A mission, which was begun in 1979, was constituted as Salem Baptist Church of Nelsonville, Ohio, in 1985. Although it has since closed; many were introduced to Christianity through its teachings. As conflicts have occurred, a nucleus has remained faithful, recognizing that trends and programs come and go, but God's Word and His guidance are eternal. Contacts with former pastors and casual encounters with myriad people who say, "I was once a member at Salem," bring accolades as they speak fondly of the light of spiritual growth and nourishment emanating from those touched by the majestic edifice which sits atop Salem Hill.

PASTORS

1811 - 18	"Traveling Preachers"	1923 - 27	Rev. W. W. Davidson
1818 - 41	Rev. John Holland	1927 - 32	Rev. E. M. Gash
1841 - 46	Rev. George Bristoe	1932 - 34	Rev. L. M. Polhill
1846 - 51	Rev. Nimrod Beckham	1934 - 43	Rev. R. B. White
1853 - 61	Rev. William G. Hobbs	1944 - 45	Rev. M. P. Delaney
1861 - 70	Rev. Thomas M. Vaughn	1945 - 48	Rev. D. R. Bennett
1870 - 74	Rev. B. F. Hungerford	1949 - 51	Rev. Quentin Lockwood
1875 - 83	Rev. J. S. Gatton	1951 - 52	Rev. Arnold Williams
1883 - 84	Rev. O. L. Hailey	1952 - 53	Rev. Oscar Smith
1885 - 88	Rev. J. B. Tharp	1954 - 55	Rev. Vernon Sisco
1888 - 1901	Rev. H. C. Davis	1955 - 59	Rev. Robert Holland
1902 - 04	Rev. U. S. Thomas	1959 - 63	Rev. Wendell A. Romans
1904 - 06	Rev. A. J. Foster	1963 - 67	Rev. H. Dallas Sugg
1906 - 07	Rev. J. S. Wilson	1968 - 80	Rev. A. J. Hensley
1907 - 13	Rev. A. R Willett	1981 - 85	Dr. R. Trevis Otey, Jr.
1913 - 17	Rev. D. T. Foust	1986 - 90	Rev. Tex T. Selph
1918 - 20	Rev. G. C. Greenway	1990 - 95	Rev. Claude "Skip" Alexander
1920 - 23	Rev. E. W. Mason	1996 -	Dr. Derek Coleman

SHELBY CHRISTIAN CHURCH

By Rev. David Hamlin

The Salt River Christian Men's Fellowship decided in 1967 to establish a new congregation known as the Shelby Christian Church in Shelbyville. This congregation would believe in duty and the Lordship of Christ, the inspiration of the Scriptures, and the autonomy of the local congregation. It would adhere to the basic principles of the Restoration Movement, believing in Baptism by immersion for the forgiveness of sins, assembly for worship on the first day of the week, and observance of the Lord's Supper weekly. They would seek the unity of all believers in the teachings of the Scriptures, which is their rule of faith and practice.

Kenneth L. Shouse was extended a call to become the first minister in June 1968. Shouse immediately set up an extensive calling program and spoke in the supporting Christian Churches in the Salt River area through the month of June. The date of July 7 was set to begin the new congregation. Four hundred people assembled in the former Highland Church building across from the Old Mason's Home for the opening services. Fourteen people became the charter members of the church on opening day.

A committee was set up to search out for the availability of land to construct a future building for the congregation. Four and one half acres of land was found in October one half mile east of the Shelby County High School. Construction began in September 1970. An educational building was completed in 1976.

Again, growth of the congregation demanded more facilities. In 1985, plans were made to construct a new multi-purpose building and to blacktop the parking lot. Construction was completed in February 1986. As growth continued, 1995 became a year of great excitement and anticipation as well as a year of transition. With the purchase of additional land, the church constructed a Family Life Center. This facility with 17,000 square feet brought with it the addition of an extensive activity ministry to the church and the community. The center has a fully equipped high-school gymnasium and walking track, large game room and craft room, full-service kitchen and meeting room, as well as new preschool rooms.

Along with the addition of the activities ministry came the addition of a preschool ministry under the direction of Diane King. The Shelby Christian preschool has morning opportunities for 3 and 4 year olds and kindergarten children. With the addition of these ministries, the mantle of senior minister also changed. Kenneth Shouse, after 28 years with the congregation, went into semi-retirement and David Hamlin assumed the role. Hamlin became the senior minister after being the former associate minister and former youth minister. Hamlin came to Shelby Christian in May 1987 to serve the youth. After encouragement from Shouse and the church, Hamlin began preaching on Sunday nights and became the associate minister in 1993.

The continual growth of Shelby Christian Church can be attributed to the longevity it has been fortunate to have in its ministers, as well as its focus of doing everything with excellence. In 1999 the church had over 800 members and three Sunday morning services.

Shelby Christian Church was built in the 1970s and 1980s.

Courtesy of Rev. David Hamlin.

SHELBYVILLE CHURCH OF CHRIST

By C. Thomas Craig

Around 1830 a movement commonly known as the Restoration Movement took hold in Shelby County. Many folks from various other religions subscribed to this movement, and a church was located at the corner of Main and Fourth Streets in Shelbyville. About 1890 another church under the name Shiloh Church of Christ was established. Its building was located at the intersection of Scotts Station Road and Harrington Mill Road. In 1921, property was purchased at 704 Washington Street and a building was erected in 1924. After the church moved into this building, its membership began to increase. Additions were made until it could no longer accommodate the growing numbers. In 1972, land was purchased at 1512 Main Street and a new building constructed. The church is currently located at this site.

The charter members of the Shiloh congregation were: R. A. and Laura Craig, Alfred Stephen Harrington and family, Hollie and Lydia Morris and family, James and Jennie Morris and family, Nell Wilson Swenney, Fulton Wilson, John and Bell Wilson, and Mary Wilson.

Robert (Bob) Craig was the first full-time preacher. He attended Freed-Hardeman College from 1913-15 and was appointed as an evangelist missionary for the Haldeman Avenue Church of Christ of Louisville in 1918. While serving as the full-time preacher for the Shelby church Mr. Craig also established nine churches in the surrounding counties.

The Shelbyville Church of Christ is involved with various local and remote ministries. It supports missionaries to India and Latin America. Local benevolent works include assistance to the needy with food, clothing, and shelter. Emergency aid is supplied to those on an as needed basis. The church has an active out-reach program, sponsoring "In Search of the Lord's Way" on the local television cable. This program is nationally known and acclaimed by numerous religious groups. Various revivals, meetings, seminars, Bible schools, and other learning opportunities are also offered each year by the church, and are open to the public.

In 1999 three elders led the church: C. Thomas Craig, Barry Leake, and Glenn Wooters. Barry Leake also serves as the pulpit minister.

SIMPSONVILLE BAPTIST CHURCH

By James Carpenter

On April 22, 1830, the Simpsonville Baptist Church was constituted with 43 members and was a member of the Long Run Association. At that time, the church met in the homes of members and later met in a building on Main Street. In the beginning the church met on the second and fourth Sundays, but in 1919 it began meeting every Sunday. In 1868, the African American membership withdrew and formed a church of its own sponsored by the church family. At that time, there were 242 black members and 174 white members.

The first Women's Missionary Society was organized in 1879. In May 1923, the present building was begun and finished in June 1924 at the cost of $32,394.64. In June 1957, plans were made for an addition to the original building. It consisted of six classrooms, a choir room, rest rooms, a baptistery with dressing rooms, and a pastor's study. In 1961, the church adopted the Caney Mission in Knott County and in 1975 the church began a mission of ministering to the young men at the nearby-by Whitney Young Manpower Center. In 1967, the parsonage was built. The renovation of the sanctuary was dedicated on April 26, 1981. Further growth prompted the need for additional space and in December 1988 a new annex building was completed. This addition is used for fellowship hall, adult Sunday school, preschool department, offices and rest rooms. The membership in 1999 was in excess of 550, with a church budget exceeding $165,000.

The pastors of Simpsonville Baptist Church have been: John Dale, S. Thomas, Wm. Fore, T.R. Palmer, T.M. Palmer, A.B. Knight, M.T. Lowry, I.W. Bruner, A.W. Graves, J.S. Gatton, S.C. Humphries, Auston Crouch, H.S. Hanington, J.J. Farmer, D.J. Evans, W.R. Cooper, E.L. Andrews, G.W. Duncan, W.E. Denham, W.B. Harvey, O.M. Huey, E.J. Trueblood, Harold Tribble, Austin Stovall, Paul Horner, George Cummins, Findley Edge, L.T. Daniel, Louis Ader, Mark Osborn, Noah Benningfield, Eugene Cotey, W.D. Sharp, Thomas Caudill, James Bruton, James Atchley, Thomas R. Kinman, Steve Carreker, Hal Poe, Scott Pittman, and Steven D. Boyd.

The Simpsonville Baptist Church was dedicated in 1924.

SIMPSONVILLE CHRISTIAN CHURCH (DISCIPLES OF CHRIST)

By Rev. John M. VonAlmen

The Simpsonville Christian Church had its origin in a rural congregation, the Antioch Church of Christ founded in 1839. It was located 2.5 miles north of town at the intersection of the Todd's Point Road and Antioch Road. As the congregation grew the members decided to move the church to Simpsonville. In 1870, meetings began in the lower part of the old Masonic Hall in Simpsonville. Rev. Jackson Willis, Wallace Tharp Sr. and John Smith, known throughout Kentucky as Raccoon John Smith, a very old man at that time, preached for the church.

In 1875, the congregation decided that it was strong enough in number to erect a building and support a pastor. A committee composed of Harrison Walters, William Graves, and Miller Fields was given the task of selecting the site and overseeing construction of the new church. The present lot was purchased in the spring of 1875, ground was broken, and the foundation laid for the new meeting house. The bricks were burned in a kiln erected on the back of the lot, the logs used to fire the kiln being brought from Taylor woods. A belfry was built and "a bell of lovely tone was hung from its rafters and could be heard far out in the country." The bell would be rung twice; the first was the signal to get ready and come to church, and the second was the signal for service to begin.

The church was completed and dedicated in October 1875. The Rev. J.W. Ingram of the Christian Church in Shelbyville delivered the dedication sermon. Scott Willis, later to enter the ministry, used the tuning fork and the Rev. Jackson Willis led the singing. A basket dinner was served in the yard. The congregation called the Rev. G. G. Bersot as the first pastor, and he served the church for about eighteen years. In the early years "preaching" was held twice a month when the minister would come to participate in worship. On the other Sundays the elders of the church would talk to those attending Sunday School and communion. Calien C. Lewis wrote in her early history of the church that "these talks were inspiring and as good as any sermon delivered by a minister."

The old Antioch church building was torn down in 1883, but several relics were purchased for use by the Simpsonville church, including the marble topped communion table and the silver chalices. The silver communion set was eventually sold when the first individual service set was purchased, but the old table, originally purchased for the Antioch church in 1838, is still here. A Ladies' Aid was organized soon after the church was built, but it was abandoned during the 1890s. About 1902 it was reorganized, and Mrs. Maxie Walters was selected as President. The Ladies' Aid was reorganized as a Missionary Society in 1906 becoming part of the Christian Woman's Board of Missions.

In the early days only men were allowed to teach in the church, but eventually the members became a little "broader minded," and women soon began teaching Sunday School classes as well. In 1934 a woman was allowed to preach from the pulpit. An organ was installed in the church in 1895. Mrs. Will Johnson was the first organist and played until 1938. Youth ministry began in 1900 with the establishment of the Christian Endeavor Society by the Rev. H.D. McLaughlin. In those days Simpsonville also had a YMCA, and the young men involved helped all the local churches with their " young people's organizations."

Courtesy of the Kentucky Heritage Council.

The Simpsonville Christian Church was built in 1875.

Records indicate that several of the ministers during the early years of the twentieth century were affiliated with Transylvania University or the College of the Bible, either as students or professor. The educational building was built in 1948 and dedicated on February 20, 1949. At that time the first baptistery was also installed. Prior to that all the Sunday School classes met in the sanctuary. The men's class (Allen Frazier Class) met at the back of the west side of the sanctuary. In the middle of the same side was the Julia Frazier Class (one of the ladies classes), which has been combined with the Allen Frazier Class, and so are back in the sanctuary where they began. Two more women's classes met on the east side of the sanctuary, and the two youth classes met in the "old choir loft" and in the balcony. The parsonage was built in 1953. The Rev. Douglas Bell was the first resident pastor, being called in April of that year. He followed "Brother Highfield" (the Rev. J. T. Highfield), the last non-resident pastor, who had resided in New Castle and commuted during his long ministry (1939-52).

The church celebrated its centennial on October 12, 1975. A week of activities preceded the homecoming celebration that day. Many members came to worship in vintage dress. A large dinner on the grounds followed worship. A time capsule containing items of the period was buried and a concrete monument erected to mark its spot on the front lawn of the church. Those gathered for worship also made a pilgrimage to the site of the Antioch Church.

SIMPSONVILLE METHODIST CHURCH

By S.K. Zimmerman

The time is 1838 and the place Simpsonville, a peaceful, serene little settlement located in a fertile area among wooded slopes. One might observe a young man riding horseback slowly along the lanes and trails. He has followed the old Wilderness Road, coming into the Simpsonville community. He was a dedicated man, a vibrant personality, filled with the desire to serve God. A Methodist Circuit Rider, his name was W. B. Kavanaugh. He found a cordial welcome in the homes of these good people. In these homes he conducted family altars, prayer meetings, and led in hymn singing.

The first Methodist Church on record in Simpsonville was built in 1840. James G. Byars was received into this church in 1839. In 1840 Henry Webb was received by Kavanaugh who was pastor of the church from 1838 to 1840. The historical records of the "Western-Cavaliers Redford" say that at a meeting in 1842 there were thirty-two individuals who joined this church. At that time the Shelby Circuit was under the ministry of Napoleon Lewis and John W. Fields. The church continued growing for thirty-six years, necessitating the building of a larger church.

The church, built in 1840, was brick, painted white, having double front doors. The altar and pulpit were in the front, the congregation seated in elevated seats, facing the pulpit and the front doors. The ceiling was rather low with hanging lamps. This church was on the present location, but at that time the church yard extended farther to the north and south. In the yard were rows of hitching posts, and near the road was a large stile block made of heavy stones, on which the ladies dismounted from their horses. This present church building was dedicated by Dr. R.H. Rivers and cost approximately $7,500. The establishment of this church in 1876 was made possible by: L. S. Wright, John Adams, Francis Asbury Byars, James Dillard Byars, Preston Owen, F. C. French, James W. French, Francis Wright, George W. Wright, Dr. H. Harding, Henry Webb, Mary Carpenter, John Morlan, Thomas McCormick, Bushrod Taylor, Thomas Smith, D. C. Waller, and Nancy Owen. These names with others previously listed represent the very human foundation of the Simpsonville Methodist Episcopal Church, South.

During the pastorate of Rev. W. D. Welburn (1923-25) the present building was remodeled and redecorated. George W. Knorr presented a sum of money for the Primary Department, as a memorial to his wife. The influence of Rev. E. C. Watts was far reaching. He was a great scholar and a Christian gentleman who ministered untiringly. After his retirement, Rev. Watts, with his family, came back to Simpsonville and purchased the old Methodist parsonage He lived here until his death, serving not only the church but the community.

During the early period of the church, there was a circuit including Simpsonville, Hebron, and Eastwood (Tunnel Hill). Hebron was combined with Shelbyville, but until 1946 Eastwood shared the circuit with Simpsonville. In 1943, the Shelbyville District became the Frankfort District.

In 1940-41 evidences of re-organizations and progress were noted when the Women's Society of Christian Service assumed more responsibilities and activities. The Wesleyan Service Guild was organized in January 1949, and became a group of dedicated young women with many worthy

Courtesy of the Kentucky Heritage Council.

The Simpsonville Methodist Church was built in 1876.

accomplishments. The church had also had a Methodist Men's Organization.

The Simpsonville Church was made a station in 1946. The new parsonage adjoining the church lot was built and completed December 1950.

In 1954, plans for an Educational Building were formulated. In the same contract was the remodeling and restoring of the sanctuary. The building was opened formally in October 1955 in a service presided over by Rev. W. A. E. Johnson; the speaker was Dr. E. L. Tullis. In 1964-65, the bricks were painted and the exterior of the sanctuary repaired. Memorial stained glass windows were installed in 1964.

ST. JAMES EPISCOPAL CHURCH

By Gilbert M. Ellis

St. James Episcopal Church of Shelbyville was organized in 1857 by a group led by the Rev. Jno. Trimble. The first services were held in the chapel of the Episcopal Theological Seminary, formerly known as Shelby College located on College Street, between Eighth and Ninth Streets. The original communicants were descendants of Anglican settlers of Virginia who migrated to Kentucky following the Revolutionary War.

Seven members of the Vestry and the Rev. Trimble purchased a portion of Lot No. 163, located at Third and Main Streets in September 1867. They then raised $1,100 to purchase the lot and construct a building. A report by the Rev. A.E. Freeman said that money was needed to finish the church, as it was without a Vestry room and were using oilcloth instead of sash and glass. However, by 1871 the church was reported as having seats and furnishings and out of debt, but with only thirty-two communicants and no clergy. The present Gothic Revival Church is an elegant and graceful structure with walls three bricks thick laid on a massive hewn-stone foundation. The vaulted interior has five decorative trusses framing the roof. Exquisite stained glass windows back the altar and alternate in each of the bays that separate the roof trusses. The antique cherry pews seat over one hundred persons.

St. James had full-time Rectors from 1868 to 1923, after which the church was under the auspices of the Bishop, who would send a canon or lay reader to conduct services for Ash Wednesday, Easter, Thanksgiving, and Christmas.

St. James declined during the 1930s and remained open due to the extraordinary efforts of Judge and Mrs. Charles Marshall, Mr. and Mrs. Hart Wallace, Miss Bessie Todd, Mrs. Charles Randolph, Mrs. Clarence Barrickman, Mrs. Hugh Collins, and Mrs. Jesse C. Owen. Through their efforts, broken glass panes were replaced and a coal burning pot-bellied stove was installed. St. James was revitalized and services began again when the Rev. Sheppard Musson was assigned in 1938 to conduct services as a part-time Vicar.

Other part-time diocesan clergy helped to maintain some worship regularity until 1958, when the Rev. Musson returned to St. James to conduct services part-time. Because so many St. James' clergy were part-time, recognition is given to a number of laymen who, as licensed lay readers, faithfully conducted services for extended periods due to the absence of a priest. Among them were Lyndon Everbach, Florian Wood, Dan Ross, and William Giltner. The administrative affairs of the church were looked after by Andrew Johns and Wade Edwards.

On the 100th anniversary of St. James in 1968, the Rev. Musson dedicated the "Bessie Todd Parish Hall" and its cloister garden. The new hall with rest room facilities and kitchen enabled the congregation to begin church school classes on a regular basis. A two-story Victorian style house adjoining the church

Courtesy of The Sentinel-News.

St. James Episcopal Church, at Main and Third Streets, was completed in 1871.

property at the rear was purchased in 1975 and named "Barnett Hall." Soon, St. James was serving the community by hosting Alcoholics Anonymous and Al-Anon groups and conducting social and educational church functions.

St. James celebrated its 125th anniversary in 1983. The Rev. Henry Pinkerton was part-time Vicar and part-time chaplain at the University of Louisville. He served until 1987. Again, St. James was dependent upon lay readers or visiting clergy. William Giltner again served as lay reader and was licensed by the Bishop to deliver sermons.

A fire in the furnace/air conditioner areas destroyed much of the church interior in mid-1985. Punching a hole in the roof and ventilating the heat and smoke gases from the interior saved the precious stained glass windows from ruin. Regular services were held in the Bessie Todd Parish Hall during the reconstruction. The renovation was completed in time for Christmas services.

Bishop David Reed appointed the Rev. John Trager as Vicar in 1989. He served until December 31, 1999, when he retired. St. James grew substantially and moved from a mission to a parish status by action of the Diocesan Convention in February 1993. The Rev. John Trager became Rector of St. James parish. Following Rev. Trager's retirement in 1999, the Rev. Ken Thompson became interim Rector. The Victorian house was completely renovated for church school and parish functions. St. James is the eastern-most parish of the Diocese of Kentucky, which extends as far west as Paducah.

WADDY BAPTIST CHURCH

By Helen McKinny

Waddy Baptist Church was organized on September 21, 1892, by a small group of people in the Waddy community. Pastors from nearby churches met that day to complete the organization of the Missionary Baptist Church at Waddy. The church was created with twenty-eight charter members. The first officers were: E. R. McCampbell (Moderator); C.D. Martin (Clerk); William Snider (Treasurer); and deacons Thomas Brown, William Bullard, Craven Garrett, and John Walker Martin. The land and parsonage lot were donated by Mr. Martin.

Four months after it was organized, on January 14, 1893, regular business meetings were held in the church's own building. The structure was only partially completed and without furniture. The present sanctuary was completed and dedicated on the last Sunday in April 1893. J. R. Pentuff answered the call to be the church's first pastor.

It was decided by the founding fathers that the first Sunday in each month be designated for preaching services. Sunday school classes were also incorporated into the first church service. In 1894, the church voted to hold regular meetings on the first weekend of each month, with a business meeting held on Saturday and church services held on Sunday. With the church organized, the members embarked upon their first missionary effort, a collection for the Louisville Orphan's Home. Contributions to missionary funds were solicited and yielded $6.45 and four barrels of flour. These first efforts sparked an ongoing contribution to missions that has remained constant throughout the church's history.

Waddy Baptist Church has had thirty-eight pastors, most of whom attended the Southern Baptist Theological Seminary in Louisville. Brother B. F. Hungerford, pastor from 1906-08, accepted the position only on the condition that there would be preaching twice a month. Brother E. A. McDowell, pastor from October 1927 to June 1931, extended preaching services from twice a month to every Sunday. Brother David Q. Byrd, pastor from October 1946 to October 1949, went on to become Dean of Boyce Bible School in Louisville in 1978. Don W. Dixon, pastor from February 1987 to April 1990, along with his wife Billie, served as missionaries in Brazil.

On September 25, 1901, a group of women from the church decided to organize the Women's Mission Society. Since these women were limited in their finances, it was decided that their annual dues would be five cents a month. They also gave birthday dues—one cent for each year. The Waddy Baptist women started two circles—the B. J. Davis Circle, named after a former pastor, and the Mildred Fann Circle, named after a missionary from the church.

In 1905, the church hosted the Shelby County Association for the first time. The Association returned in 1929, 1952, and 1978. In 1917, the Sunday school was graded. A new organ was installed in 1920. Ten years later, Sunday school rooms were built. On July 2, 1940, the church authorized the addition of a pastorium. The first resident pastor was Brother Ralph Acree. During the 1940s a basement was dug. It was also during this decade that the six clear glass windows were replaced with stained art windows.

Twenty-nine years after they were built, the Sunday school rooms were torn away to make room for a new annex in 1959. The annex contained classrooms, rest rooms, a nursery, kitchen, and fellowship hall. It was at this same time that the baptistery was added. By 1952, the building had been completely renovated, with the exception of the original sanctuary. The walls were painted and new carpeting was laid in the auditorium. The original pews were restored and air conditioning was added. Late in the decade, the parking lot was paved.

Courtesy of Helen McKinny.

The Waddy Baptist Church, organized in 1892, completed this building in 1893.

The Shelby County Public Library was built in 1903 with funding from the Carnegie Foundation. The architect was Val P. Collins of Louisville.

CHAPTER SIX

EDUCATION & SCHOOLS

Ellis McGinnis Collection, courtesy of Michael McGinnis

SHELBY COUNTY SCHOOLS

By Duanne Puckett

By the time this area was officially declared Shelby County in 1792, a private educational system was well established. These private schools provided mostly secondary instruction, relying on boarders from inside Shelby County and out-of-state to fill their enrollments. Teachers, for the most part, were imported from the East where they had received formal training.

The few schools in the less populated, rural areas were attended by children whose parents saw the need for education. Those teachers were usually literate members of the community or traveling instructors. The state passed legislation establishing a system of public education in 1838. Three years later, Shelby County was divided into fifty-three school districts. Only twenty-one held elections and only six adopted the provisions or actually had schools in operation. Based on school census records, Shelby County was entitled to $946 as its share of the state's School Fund.

In 1844, there were 2,429 children between the ages of 5 and 16 in Shelby County schools. By 1850, only 1,123 children attended on an average basis, despite the compulsory school tax.

When C.J. Hinkle became the county commissioner in 1866, he visited every school district to talk to patrons about raising the school tax. Summer institutes were also held to advance teachers' training.

By 1899, Shelby County had 48 white and 19 black school districts, three white high schools, two white colleges, a Normal Training School (for teachers) at Waddy, and nine district librarians.

With the passage of the County Board Bill, reorganization took place in 1908 of the white and black sub-district schools under one county board. The local boards established its own standards and policies rather than adopt those of the state. One, adopted in 1909, was the "duplication plan" which had the board match any amount of money raised. This provided a strong incentive for the communities to build and improve schools and to pay teachers in the low enrollment schools comparable salaries to teachers in the larger enrollment schools.

In 1917, the board adopted a policy that eliminated any school with less than 60 percent of its census children in attendance. Teachers were hired with this understanding, so also were the truant officers. Eventually, consolidated schools became the focus. The introduction of federal funds aided the consolidation movement by providing funds through the Public Works Administration. With the state's New School Code law in 1934, further consolidation occurred, reducing the number of county schools from 28 white and 10 black schools, to 10 white and seven black schools by the end of the decade. This trend continued in the 1940s when the eight county high schools were consolidated into three in order to maintain state accreditation. In 1954, the state passed the last piece of major legislation, which encouraged or mandated consolidation by sharing transportation costs with school districts. This was also the year the U.S. Supreme Court ruled dual systems of education for blacks and whites to be illegal.

Financing was always a problem for Shelby County schools. In this regard, the county was typical of the lack of statewide support. New community groups emerged to seek financial support for the school

Courtesy of Guthrie Zaring.

The Shelby County School Board meeting at Gleneyrie School about 1915. Jacob Lawson Zaring is third from the left, the others are unidentified.

system, yet no new taxes were passed until 1959 when a central high school was built, Shelby County High on U.S. 60 East. The school buildings in the outlying communities remained as elementary sites off and on through those early years. In recent times: Finchville Ruritan Club transformed the old school gym into a Community Center. Simpsonville City Commission used economic development funds to renovate the school and gym into a Community Center, library, and City Hall. Bagdad Ruritan Club tore down the school and built a new Community Center. Waddy School burned. Mount Eden School became the Kentucky Horseshoeing School. Henry Clay School houses a used car lot. Cropper's school building has remained part of the school system as an alternative education center.

The last schools to close were Bagdad, Cropper, and Henry Clay. The consolidated school is named Heritage Elementary and is located near Peytona.

A capsule look at the Shelby County Public Schools system indicates:

Shelby County Preschool Center serves children who are 4 years old by October 1 and whose family qualifies for the federal free lunch program; 4-year-old children with developmental delays, which may include speech and language, hearing motor skills, vision or cognitive delays; and 3-year-olds who have a disability. Classes are held at the center at Painted Stone Elementary and also at Heritage Elementary.

The Primary Program replaced kindergarten, first, second, and third grades in all elementary schools in 1990 under the Kentucky Education Reform Act. This program recognizes that children develop different abilities at different rates and in a holistic manner. It also builds on the idea that schools should give young children more encouragement and opportunities to be successful.

Southside Elementary was built on South Eighth Street in 1957 for children in grades 1 through 6. Since 1990, it was a true example of the Primary Program at work. In 2002, it was reconfigured to accommodate grades 1 through 5. Non-graded classes worked in teams of two or three, allowing 6-, 7- and 8-year-old children to learn from not only the teacher but from each other.

Painted Stone Elementary opened in 2002 for grades 1 through 5. It is located on land next door to West Middle off LaGrange Road, just north of town.

Northside Elementary was erected in 1939 and houses the original school bell from an earlier academy that stood on the same site as Northside on College Street.

Simpsonville Elementary is located on Shelbyville Road on the edge of Simpsonville and was built in 1988, replacing a six-building complex that dated back to 1918. The new school also has a strong physical fitness awareness program and an outdoor classroom called Wyatt's Woods, plus a garden.

Heritage Elementary's name reflects its past since it is the result of consolidating smaller community schools. Located on U.S. 60 East in Peytona, the school was built in 1990.

Wright Elementary is named for former Circuit Judge Coleman Wright, a strong advocate of education in this county. The school on Rocket Lane was built in 1980 and offers an after-school care program that is both recreational and educational.

East Middle started as Upper Elementary in 1968 and was expanded in 1999 by 14 classrooms to house 750-student capacity. It provides educational opportunities for students from Heritage, Southside and Wright Elementary.

West Middle moved into a new building off LaGrange Road in 2000. Once located in Shelbyville's Historic District on West Main, it had been housed in what was Shelbyville High School. That school closed with the merger of the city and county school systems in 1975. West serves students who come from Painted Stone, Southside and Simpsonville.

The Shelby County Education Center is for students ages 11 to 17 from both Shelby and Henry County schools who have not been successful in the regular classroom setting. These students are referred by teachers or parents or are court-ordered to the program. The school offers extensive counseling and individualized instruction. The students can return to regular school after successful completion of the "phase" program.

Shelby County High School offers courses to guide students along the right paths to college and careers. In addition to academic departments, there are classes in horticulture/agriculture, business, family, consumer science, and technology, as well as opportunities through the Junior ROTC unit. Additional vocational programs such as pre-nursing are available at the Shelby Area Technology Center at the rear of the high school.

The Shelby County Area Technology Center is located at 230 Rocket Lane. It offers technical training to qualified high school students from Shelby and surrounding school districts. Adults from Shelby and six surrounding counties may enroll on a quarterly basis for entry-level skill training. Employees in business and industry are also trained in specific designing programs.

An ABE/GED program is offered at Henderson House on Main Street with day and night classes.

Courtesy of The Filson Historical Society

The class of 1924 at Waddy High School.

ABE allows adults to work on skills to assist them in obtaining the GED or simply to upgrade their skills. GED is for students 17 years or older who have dropped out. Individual tutoring is available.

The intent of the Family Resource & Youth Service Centers (also developed through the Kentucky Education Reform Act) is to enhance students' abilities to succeed in school by assisting children, youth, and families in meeting some of their basic needs. This is done by providing services at the center or by linking families to agencies in the community. The centers are commonly referred to by their acronym FRYSC, which is pronounced FRISKY. The centers are open year-round, even on days when school is out. Enrollment in Shelby County Public Schools in the 2002-2003 school year was:

Heritage - 542

Painted Stone - 546

Simpsonville - 505

Southside - 499

Wright - 491

East Middle - 578

West Middle - 637

Shelby County High - 1505

Cropper Center - 62

The Jefferson Community and Technical College opened in the fall of 2002 west of the County High School.

*School Board members--(since 1989) Bob Darby, Tish Wilson, Alma Hardesty, Margaret Perry, Edgar Vaughan, John Doyle Wilson, Linda Scearce, Eddie Mathis, Brenda Jackson, Allen Phillips, Marc Rucker, Jim Henson, Leo Young, Eugene Peete Jr., Sam Hinkle. *Superintendents--G.M. Money (1897-1914); L.H. Gregg (1914-18); Mrs. N.L. Hall (1918-24); E.J. Paxton (1925-38); Al Townsend (1938-40); George Giles, (1940-61); Fred Trammell, (1961-74); William Jesse Lacefield, (1974-84); Otis Reed, (1984-88); Ed Smith, (1988); Dr. Leon Mooneyhan (1988-).

SHELBYVILLE SCHOOLS

By Duanne Puckett

Then and now could be the theme when evaluating the history of education in our community because early minutes from the Board of Education show similarities to what has occurred in recent years including building projects, teacher salaries, tax and bond issues, mergers, and community involvement.

Involvement was always the key and continues to be because parental involvement in a child's education is critical, just as involvement from the business sector is critical to the financial well being of a school system. No one likes taxes and early school records show tough times when schools were forced to close because of limited resources. Support of education today, though, is much improved as society has determined the best schools, the best tools, the best teachers can help produce the best students who can become the best employees, the best leaders, the best citizens of tomorrow.

The Shelbyville Graded School was the first place of learning, located on the lower floor of the Masonic Lodge between Sixth and Seventh Streets. Its continued operation was contingent upon subscription and tuition fees from its patrons. It was free from taxes and reflected ideologies and policies of their founders and financial supporters.

Faculty at the old Shelby Graded School, ca. 1900. Seated, left to right: Prof. Logan, Prof. Sampson, Angie Willis, Kathleen Kirk, Ora Hunt. Standing, left to right: Lillie Hedges, Virginia Bird, Ola Figg, Willie Harbison, Mary Blakemore, Sallie Tevis, Rose Randolph. .

The Land Endowment Act or Academy Plan was enacted in 1798 and was Kentucky's first attempt to establish a system of education. Shelby County took advantage of the plan, with the aid of a group of concerned citizens, and replaced the Graded School when it erected Shelby Academy on what is now College Street in Shelbyville. It apparently suffered the same fate as most academies—lack of funds and poor management by trustees—so in 1836 it was reorganized as Shelby College.

In 1842, Shelby College property was transferred to the Bishop and trustees of the Episcopal Church and its name was changed to St. James College. In 1870, St. James fell victim to financial woes and its property was transferred to the city. A special charter was received from the Kentucky General Assembly to operate the Shelbyville Graded School in March 1871, which the voters approved the following May.

A five-member Board of Education established and implemented policies, certified and employed teachers, determined curriculum, and informed the City Council of problems and financial needs.

The five-member Board that oversees the Shelby County Public Schools only establishes and implements policies from that early list of responsibilities. It is responsible for the financial management of the schools under the Kentucky Education Reform Act of 1990. The hiring of employees is the responsibility of the superintendent with input from the School-Based Decision-Making Councils, which also handles curriculum matters with input from Central Office administration.

Poor test scores and inadequate pay scales for educators were key issues in the reform. The Commonwealth Accountability Testing System evaluates students in Kentucky and labels each Novice, Apprentice, Proficient, or Distinguished—with Proficient being the ultimate goal for each student by 2014. Based on the belief that all students learn at different levels and at different paces, innovative and hands-on instructional techniques are emphasized at all grade levels.

That wasn't the case in 1873 when records showed the high school students receiving "opportunities to pursue a higher course of English, Math, Latin and Greek." Enrollment that year in Grades 1-12 was 288. Enrollment in 1999 in Grades 1-12 was 4,800.

Students were dismissed from school in 1909 when outbreaks of smallpox and contagious diseases reached epidemic proportions. An ordinance was passed by the mayor to keep children off the streets, and a contract was made between the city school and local physicians to have children immunized against smallpox. School was closed again in 1910 for an outbreak of scarlet fever, in 1912 for an undisclosed disease that forced the building to be fumigated, and in 1917 for the flu epidemic that affected schools throughout the nation. The hiring of a health officer in 1918 evidently curtailed further closings.

In 1914, arrangements were made to rent the Colonial Hotel at the northwest corner of Main and Seventh Streets as temporary headquarters for Shelbyville High School. Two years later, a special election was called to vote on a $50,000 bond issue that would enable a new school to be built. It passed 457 to 64 and land was acquired from J.T. Logan on West Main for $12,500. Construction began in October 1916 and students started classes there the following fall.

That building served as Shelbyville High School until 1975 when the city and county school systems merged. SHS became known as West Middle, serving sixth, seventh and eighth grades. The building was declared surplus in 1999 when construction got under way for a new West Middle off LaGrange Road, north of Shelbyville. It is being renovated to serve as the school system's administrative office.

The financial strain of the Great Depression affected the city school system. The School Board was forced to trim its operating budget and be satisfied to simply meet, not exceed, state standards. However, when Mrs. Willie C. Ray became superintendent in 1930, she provided practical solutions to problems and unselfish devotion to the school and its patrons. Throughout the three decades she was superintendent, she initiated and implemented ideas which saved the district money, involved local residents in the school's operations, and provided new programs for students and for the community.

Four years into her tenure, the New School Code Law was passed, which made the city school system responsible for all schools within a two-and-a-half mile radius. This area included what was known as the Colored School. The city schools drew up a contract in 1936 for all black students wanting a high school education to be provided transportation to Lincoln Institute, an all-black school on the outskirts of Simpsonville. Shelbyville, Shelby County, Henry County and Eminence school systems were involved in this arrangement.

Three years later, the Colored School was upgraded using Public Works Administration funds and a 90-cent general school tax, which also paid for a four-room addition at the high school, a stadium at the athletic field at the high school, and a new graded school on the College Street site.

Community involvement was high in the 1930s with the first mention of a Parent-Teacher Association and of the city's recreation department using both the high school and the graded school as community centers.

The war years emphasized the need for skilled recruits and provided the impetus for the federal government to pour funds into the school district for specialized training. The Colonial Inn was transformed into a vocational department that offered woodwork, electricity, and engine work. The high school even offered a course called Victory Corps along with nutrition, retail selling, and auto mechanics. Home economics was added in 1943, and was even offered in the evening. Teachers had the chance for extended education with federal funds paying for a civilian pilot training school. The high school building itself was used for war efforts with a canning facility opened and operated by the students.

After the war, it was business as usual with a concentrated effort made to secure funds for a new Colored School since its building was destroyed by fire in 1945. A replacement was built on lots at Eleventh and High Street in the Martinsville neighborhood.

The 1950s brought years of overcrowding without a solution in sight because of increased enrollment from county students wanting to attend city schools, the issue of desegregation, and discussions about consolidating the city and county school systems. No new students outside city school lines were allowed to attend. A committee of three blacks and three whites examined integration. And any talk of consolidation was put on hold.

The Gradual Integration Plan was revealed to the public in August 1956. It gave African American students in the first through seventh grades the option to attend the white school or the Colored School. A year later, a new elementary to be called Southside School was built off Eighth Street where a limited number of black children attended classes with the white students. The former Graded School on College Street took on the name Northside.

A pivotal year was 1956 due to the launching of Sputnik by the Russians. Federal matching funds were secured to buy equipment to improve math, science, and foreign language courses. Special education classes were also started to comply with federal law.

Mrs. Ray ended her 30-year term as superintendent in 1960 when William A. McKay replaced her. Enrollment at the time was 1,454—increasing to 1,681 by 1969 when the city schools were forced to go to double sessions.

The problem increased in 1966 when the U.S. Office of Education deemed the so-called Freedom of Choice desegregation plan unacceptable. High Street Colored School and Lincoln Institute were closed, thereby completing the integration process.

To alleviate the overcrowding, plans were made in 1968 to add six rooms to Southside and to acquire 45 acres for a new high school. The plans never became a reality when voters failed to pass a 48-cent school building tax in 1970. Two years later, another sets of plans were designed for a middle school to be converted to a high school.

However, a group of citizens, referred to as the Better Education Committee, filed suit against the city and county school board, demanding consolidation. The city school officials sought a waiver from the suit so it could move forward with its building plans. When the waiver was denied, discussions began about double sessions and using the educational building of First Baptist Church.

By 1973, the City School Board was ready to resume talk of consolidation with the County School Board. The county rejected negotiations so the city appealed to the state to merge the districts according to law. Proceedings were held in Frankfort December 10 and the last meeting of the Shelbyville Independent School Board was held December 20.

Fred Trammell resigned as county superintendent in 1974, succeeded by William Jesse Lacefield. The two high schools merged in 1975. Shelbyville High became West Middle; Upper Elementary became East Middle, both serving students in grades six, seven and eight.

By 1976, records no longer indicated any reference to the former school system as separate and distinct, suggesting that merger was finally complete.

Shelbyville High School, built in 1917 on West Main Street.

*City School Board Members:

1906-09: Joseph D. Hall, A.L. Harbison, Emmett C. Harbison, J.C. Bright and Dr. R.D. Pratt. Dr. Pratt died in office and was succeeded by Ernest VansArdale then by Dr. W.G. Buckner.

1910-19: Joseph D. Hall (resigned), A.L. Harbison (resigned), J.C. Bright, Ernest VansArdale (resigned), Dr. W.T. Buckner, Emmett C. Harbison (resigned), Pryor R. Beard (resigned), Dr. E.B. Smith, Fielding E. Ballard, W.T. Layson, Charles W. Guthrie, A.F. Heinrick, Stanley G. Lawson, C.P. Hall, George W. Thompson and Henry Maddox.

1920-29: Stanley G. Lawson, Fielding E. Ballard (resigned), C.P. Hall (resigned), George N. Thompson (resigned), S.D. Hinkle (resigned), Henry Maddox, George S. Chowning, M.A. Wakefield, Allen M. Bond (resigned), Dr. Clarence C. Risk, P.R. Beard, J.G. Maddox and J. Guthrie Goodman.

1930-39: Stanley G. Lawson, George S. Chowning (died in office), Chalmers B. Caudill, J.G. Maddox, Henry Maddox, J. Guthrie Goodman, Charles Long and Paul Schmidt.

1940-49: Paul Schmidt, Charles Long, Dr. Clarence C. Risk (resigned), Chalmers B. Caudill, J. Guthrie Goodman (died in office), Howard Pearce, Mark Scearce, Dr. A.D. Doak and the first woman, Mrs. D.L. Green.

1950-59: Charles Long, Mrs. D.L. Green, Pryor Hower, Dr. A.D. Doak, Dr. Donald Chatham and Mark Scearce. Mr. Scearce resigned in 1958 and his vacancy was filled by Cal Schmidt.

1960-69: Charles B. Long, Dr. Donald Chatham, Mrs. D.L. Green (resigned), Elmo C. Head, Cal Schmidt, Dr. A.D. Doak (resigned), Mark Scearce, John Paul Martin, C.T. Craig (resigned), Tom Cobb, William Shannon, Robert J. Stratton and Rev. Fred T. Moffatt Jr.

Superintendents: B.A. Logan (1906-12); T.A. Houston (1912-15); H.H. Elliott (1915-18); J.T. Hazelrigg (1918-21); Mark Godman (1921-23); J.H. Muntz (1923-27); E.E. Bratcher (1927-30);Mrs. Willie C. Ray, (1930-60); William McKay, (1960-66); Sam Potter (1966-73).

(Source: Research papers belonging to Shelby County Public Schools by Nancy Hapgood)

SHELBY COLLEGE

(SHELBYVILLE ACADEMY/ST. JAMES COLLEGE)

By Kevin Collins

In 1798, six years after the founding of Shelbyville, the Kentucky General Assembly granted a school charter to the trustees of "the Shelbyville Academy." Shelbyville had had a school as early as 1796, but the charter granted to thirteen trustees on December 22, 1798, gave the community additional financial aid to educate its children. With the charter came a grant of 6,000 acres of land lying south of the Green River in what was then Christian County (today Christian and Livingston Counties) as well as permission to raise by lottery the sum of $1,000. A form of civic fundraising in lieu of taxation, lotteries were regulated by the General Assembly and were commonly used to support community endeavors—churches, schools, medical institutions, etc- throughout the state.

The sale of approximately half the land-grant and the addition of some minimal proceeds from the lottery raised sufficient funds to begin school construction in 1810. In 1806, the trustees had acquired lot eighty-four on the northeast corner of Seminary (today Eighth) and Washington Streets (adjacent to today's Public Library) from the estate of Brackett Owen. In the years between 1805 and 1810, before the Academy schoolhouse was completed, school was held in the lower floor of the Solomon Lodge Building on Washington Street.

In 1815, Kentucky Secretary of State Joseph C. Breckinridge recommended the Rev. John Finley Crowe to the trustees of the Academy. Crowe, a Presbyterian minister and teacher, was also a man

Shelby College with its observatory atop the building ca. 1875.

deeply committed to the plight of slaves and, as such, was an advocate of gradual emancipation. While at the Academy he consulted with the influential slaveholders of the town for permission to teach a Sunday school for slaves and was given their approval "if it could be done without arousing opposition." In addition to his duties as a teacher and a minister in several Shelby County churches, Crowe also edited the antislavery publication, *The Abolition Intelligencer and Missionary Magazine.* The magazine lasted only one year, from May 1822 until April 1823, before it ceased publication for lack of funds. In 1823, following threats to his life "for inciting slaves to rebellion," Crowe moved to Hanover, Indiana, where he helped found Hanover College. Crowe taught only one session on the school grounds and then was told by the trustees to cease. By 1816, the Academy had acquired a second teacher and an enrollment of fifty or more students in regular attendance.

In 1836, Shelbyville Academy, ever bedeviled by financial concerns, was reorganized and re-chartered as Shelby College. In the ensuing years the school relocated to College Street, between Eighth and Ninth Streets (site of the present-day Northside School), and by 1841 the old Shelby Academy schoolhouse had been raised, the land graded and consecrated to the task of a graveyard. In 1840, still plagued by weak finances, the trustees of the school approached the Protestant Episcopal Church, which was then considering plans to establish its own college. An agreement was reached, and in January 1841 the legislature granted the trustees of the Episcopal Church a charter for Shelby College. In May 1842 the church chose the Rev. R. B. Drane as president and classes began on September 7. At that time the school's campus consisted of eighteen acres, a brick school building, and a house for the president. Sometime after the charter, a theological seminary was added to the college's course of studies.

Members of the Harvard Astronomical Expedition when they came to Shelby College to observe the solar eclipse of August 7, 1869. Some townsfolk of Shelbyville are also in the photograph. Numbers can be seen on some of those photographed: 1. Dr. Otho Miller, 2. Capt. W. C. Winlock, 3. Miss Eliza Winlock, 4. Mrs. Belle Winlock, Cambridge, Mass., 5. Dr. R. F. Logan, 6. Miss Anna Powell, 7. Capt. Marion Taylor, 8. Frank Adams, St. Louis, Missouri, 9. John Tate, 10. Hon. James S. Morris, 11. R. C. Tevis, 12. Prof. Joseph Winlock, Cambridge, Mass., 13. Ed. D. Shinnick, 14. George A. Armstrong, Jr., 15. Prof. Roy Pierce, Cambridge, Mass., 16. Samuel Wayne, 17. Possibly the servant and cook in the family of Judge Fielding Winlock of Shelbyville.

The conditions of the contractual agreement between the church and town were such that, should the church discontinue or remove the college, ownership of the property and buildings would revert to the trustees of the town of Shelbyville. In 1846, spurred on by local dissatisfaction with the school's small enrollment the church, after a special convention, renewed and energized its commitment to the college. The presidency of the institution was then offered to and accepted by the Rev. Dr. William Waller, who began his tenure in September 1847.

By May 1848 the Rev. Waller, an energetic and ambitious educator of some personal wealth, had submitted a plan for the construction of additional school buildings at a proposed cost of $6,500. He also championed a telescope for astronomical observations to be purchased in Munich, Germany, at a cost of $2,500. With approval of the trustees it was bought and the work begun on the buildings. However, by 1850 a church audit revealed that the original estimates had been faulty and, with work still unfinished, the outstanding debt had risen to $26,000. The attempted resolution of these intractable financial problems would plague the college throughout its history and ultimately be the cause of its demise.

The Rev. Waller, with the concurrence of the trustees, advanced the cost of part of this new construction from his own personal funds and secured his loan to the college with a mortgage against the lottery grant that the state had previously given to the institution. This grant, or permission to hold a lottery, was in principal good for eighty or ninety years, and all parties thought it sufficient to cover over time and by partial payments any present and proposed future indebtedness. This arrangement ended in chaos and litigation in 1866. Waller claimed to be owed an additional $50,000 in added construction costs, deferred salary, interest, and currency depreciation. The Board rejected these claims and pressed a contract reached with Waller in 1859 which they said settled the possibility of all future claims. The lottery in turn did not perform as expected, came under attack, and, to raise needed cash, sold its rights to a company that would shortly afterwards go bankrupt. The disposition of these disputes and confusions finally culminated sometime around 1867-68 in Rev. Waller's departure from Shelby College and by 1871 the college failed.

The use of the lottery, heretofore a principal device used to raise funds for the beleaguered college, came under increased attack in Kentucky and throughout the nation. Some in the Episcopal Church found the support of a seminary school by the proceeds garnered from gambling to be untenable. The General Assembly, responding to growing pressure that gambling was immoral and degrading and that lotteries were open to corruption and fraud, proposed in 1852 to bar all lottery privileges within three years and to make the participation in the promotion of a lottery a criminal offense. In response to this new law, Waller, who prior to 1852 had executed his mortgage and lien on the lottery's charter and privileges, commenced legal action. In 1859, in Gregory's Executrix v. Trustees of Shelby College, the Kentucky Court of Appeals ruled in Waller's favor. The court, in a decision that became an important precedent in Kentucky lottery history, overturned the 1852 law, finding that it violated Waller's rights. This decision effectively secured Waller the right to conduct a private lottery.

Lotteries were still being held for the benefit of Shelby College as late as 1865. The firm of T. Seymour & Company, with offices in Lexington and New York, advertised a "Havana Scheme" lottery to be drawn March 31, 1865, offering prospective winners hundreds of cash prizes of diminishing amounts. The prizes, of course, came from the proceeds of the sale of the tickets. Ticket sales were not limited simply to the state of Kentucky and, in such a far-flung effort the possibility for abuse and mismanagement existed. There is no extant record of how successful any of these schemes were in raising funds.

Sometime after Rev. Waller's departure Shelby College became St. James College. St. James functioned primarily as a school for boys, but, with attendance in decline, closed its doors in 1871. In 1872, the president's house, vacant for a number of years, succumbed to fire.

Under the provisions of the agreement reached in 1840, the ownership of the school and grounds reverted to the Board of Trustees of the town. In March 1871, the General Assembly granted the trustees of the town the authority to establish a graded public school on the site of the former St. James College. The Graded School functioned until 1939, when it was razed to accommodate the construction of the Northside School.

Despite its baleful financial history, Shelby College nonetheless achieved notable educational successes. It offered preparatory education to students ten to sixteen years of age. A theological seminary was established with, as noted in the school's 1849 catalogue, "an extensive theological and classical library." The school catalogue of 1851 listed eighty students from Kentucky, Florida, Mississippi,

Louisiana, New York, Iowa, Texas, Virginia, North Carolina, and Missouri. Instruction was offered in modern and ancient languages, history, mathematics, religious study, chemistry, philosophy, astronomy, mechanics, optics, geology, and debate. By 1854, under the auspices of Colonel E.W. Morgan, vice president of the college and also a civil and railroad engineer, courses were taught in surveying, civil engineering, apothecary science, and medicine. By 1860 a course in military tactics was offered by a Major Moore. Joseph Winlock, born in Shelby County in 1826 and an 1845 Shelby College graduate, was one of the school's more renowned personages. Winlock taught astronomy and mathematics at Shelby College for about ten years after graduating and went on to become the head of the department of mathematics at the U.S. Naval Academy. In 1866 he was named Phillips Professor of Astronomy and Director of the observatory at Harvard College, where he specialized in spectroscopic studies of heavenly bodies.

The *piece de resistance* of Shelby College was, undoubtedly, the observatory and telescope housed in the cupula atop the main building. In its day the telescope was acknowledged to be one of the three best in the United States. On August 7, 1869, some twenty years after its purchase, it was in position to observe a total eclipse of the sun. Although total eclipses of the sun occur fairly regularly, they can be observed only from a narrow region of the earth's surface, and, in those limited regions where the phenomena can be observed, any one place experiences a total eclipse only about once every 360 years. On August 7, 1869, that very narrow region of both the earth's surface and infinity's time included the skies over Shelbyville. Astronomers from across the country, including a contingent from Cambridge, Massachusetts, led by Professor Winlock, traveled here for that amazing event. The sky was perfectly clear and the assembled astronomers were jubilant over their success in being able to secure eighty-five timed photographs of the event. In their report *Harper's Weekly* on August 28, 1869, focused the nation's attention on the campus of Shelby College, and the Courier-Journal described the local heavens as follows;

"One of the most important discoveries made by Professor Winlock with the spectroscope was eleven bright lines in the spectrum of the protuberances of the sun, only five having ever heretofore been determined. He also observed a shower of meteors between the moon and the earth. . . . During the partial obscuration the beautiful red flowers or solar protuberances were visible to the naked eye. Bailey's beads, as well as the dark and dismal shadow of the moon sailing away through the air, were plainly noted by a party of amateurs stationed on the top of Shelby College."

AFRICAN-AMERICAN EDUCATION

By Kevin Collins

The history of African-American education in Shelby and other Kentucky counties is one chapter in Kentucky's educational history that has not been thoroughly explored. Although state and local school records do include much of the same basic information on black and white schools, the volume of information about each system is vastly different. The information is also written from the perspective of white educators who had very little actual contact with the black schools or black communities.

The earliest state records regarding education for either black or white schools in Shelby County began in 1841, three years after a system of public education was introduced to Kentucky. At the time, most blacks in the county were slaves, and not included in the public education system.

It was not until after the Civil War that laws addressed the issue of educating blacks. The first of these laws, passed in 1866, levied a $2 poll tax to "support colored paupers and educate colored children." Initially these revenues were divided equally between paupers and school children, but by 1868 the same funds were used to support paupers first, with only the residue used for school children.

The first reference to black schools in Shelby County was in the 1866 county commissioner's Epistolary Report to the state. Commissioner C. J. Hinkle reported that "the trustees would do nothing towards reporting the colored children of the county." This statement, coupled with a more general indictment of trustees who had "little interest in their schools," reflected a common theme among educators throughout the state, and led to the numbers and powers of trustees being reduced over the years.

Records regarding Shelby County's schools were very sporadic from the late 1860s to the turn of the century. Two black schools were reported in operation in 1875; seven in 1880; 1885 reported twelve schools in a separate "Colored Report." Most of the early black schools were held in churches, the length of term usually between three and five months. There were, however, two black schools taught for eight months in 1885. The only reference to curriculum in the black schools came in 1885, when it was reported that "branches were taught in reading, writing, spelling, geography, arithmetic, and grammar." In the same report, teachers received "only the public money," suggesting that no taxes were levied.

By 1891, the number of black school districts had increased to eighteen, all of them taught for five months or more. The school census was 2,282 with 962 children enrolled and an average daily attendance (ADA) of 570. Five men and nineteen women made up the teaching force. The average wage was $44.76 a month. The school building situation had changed somewhat, with only six churches used as schoolhouses. There were 2 log schoolhouses, 7 frame, and 1 brick. Another school was considered for condemnation. This was the first year that the County Superintendent reported having visited any of the black schools. It was also the first mention of money being collected through taxation or subscription in the black school districts. The $64.85 raised was used for repairs and to buy brooms, buckets, and other equipment.

By the mid 1890s considerably more information was available regarding black schools, though most records were simply statistics about census figures, ADA, salaries, type of school buildings, and information which indicated whether or not the school districts were complying with state mandates and "encouraging legislation." Other records included whether a teacher institute was held in the county, the number in attendance, and who conducted the session. A three-member County Board of Examiners held separate teacher institutes for blacks and whites, as were the examinations of teachers, usually conducted in May and June.

The 1898 Census records from Shelby County Fiscal Court provided the following information about each black school district, its location, and the number of school age children in each district. These records refer to black districts by letter (to distinguish them from the white school districts which were listed by number), although this designation was not carried throughout the records. District A, Shelbyville, was the only black school district which provided more than one teacher and separate grade levels for students. It was also the only black school district in the county with its own facilities and governing board.

District Letter	Community	# of Students	District Letter	Community	# of Students
A	Shelbyville	731	K	Harrisonville	55
B	Simpsonville	86	L	Benson, daddy	57
C	Chestnut Grove	94	M	Clarks Station	61
D	Christiansburg	86	N	Drewsville	81
E	Stringtown	36	O	Logans Station	37
F	Olive Branch	74	P	Evansville	83
G	Todds Point	85	Q	Bagdad	52
H	Southville	19	R	Clayvillage	53
I	Scotts Station	52	S	Rockbridge	45
J	Buck creek	67	T	Clear Creek	71

After passage of the County Board Bill in 1908, black schools came under the jurisdiction of the county board. Since the governing board was composed entirely of whites, "colored supervisors" were appointed in individual black districts to take the census and, according to County Superintendent G. M. Money in 1909 "to see after the wants of his school." The only mention of county school board members having direct contact with black schools was when they met in black communities to evaluate a prospective school site or to check on building construction.

Most references to black schools from 1909 to1919 concerned tuition and transportation contracts the county board had with Lincoln Institute and with the black graded school in Shelbyville, and refurbishing or building schools for black students. The county board provided the same incentive to black school districts as they did to white districts, that is, to "duplicate" or match any funds raised within the district for the purpose of schooling. Through the board's duplication policy, three new school lots were purchased at Christiansburg, Buck Creek, and Clarks Station and new buildings erected. Also a new floor was put in the Olive Branch Colored Church indicating that the board gave churches the same consideration as other school buildings in providing matching funds for improvements.

Interestingly, it was the black schools, which first experienced consolidation. Six schools were consolidated into three in 1911: Clay Village with Rockbridge, Harrisonville with Waddy, and Scotts Station with Todds Point. In April 1915, Evansville was consolidated with Simpsonville. However, the building program previously mentioned increased the number of black schools to ten by the end of the decade.

References to black schools in the 1920s were similar to previous years, noting hirings, tuition contracts with Lincoln Institute, Shelbyville Graded School, and the Kentucky Normal and Industrial College (now Kentucky State University). These contracts reflect the county board's concerns for providing secondary instruction, which was mandated by the state in 1910. Shelby County was fortunate in having several schools within its borders, which provided high school instruction for black students, so more blacks had access to higher learning. The close proximity to secondary schools also meant that the county board had less transportation costs and logistical worries than some of Shelby County's neighboring school districts.

Other records from the 1920s indicate that a $200 lot was purchased and a $1,600 school constructed at Chestnut Grove. Waddy school was enlarged to accommodate students who were consolidated from Harrisonville, and old schools at Clay Village and Olive Branch were sold at public auction. A new school was built at Bagdad for $939. While it was under construction, the board paid $3.45 per pupil per month to transport Bagdad's black students by train to the Christiansburg school. During the decade the board also duplicated on the costs for extending the school term at the Model School in Simpsonville.

Most references to black schools or black education in the 1930s had to do with transporting students. In 1936, a delegation from Mulberry requested that students be transported to Christiansburg. The board agreed to pay so much per pupil per month though there was no mention of the price, the means of conveyance, or by whom. However, other references suggest that transportation was contracted with individuals for anywhere between $1 per pupil per month and 10 gallons of gas to a flat $40 per month

Shelby County Public Library, from Ann Patterson.

Students and teachers at the Lincoln Model School in 1918. It was located at Lincoln Institute and built by the Lincoln Institute Carpentry Department. Theodore Patterson and his brothers are on the right, front row.

fee. Other transportation contracts were made with the Shelbyville Graded School and with Henry County to transport students to Lincoln Institute. By 1938, the county board signed a $100 a month contract with the Shelbyville Independent school district to transport the county's blacks to Lincoln Institute.

Records suggest that in 1935 Lincoln Institute took over the operation of Lincoln Model and reorganized the grades so that a high school was offered for Shelby County's black students. The same year John Ellington signed a contract with the board to install a broom factory in the basement of Lincoln Model. By 1938, records indicate that the county board rented Lincoln Model for $60 a month to operate a graded school for grades 1-8. Other references to black schools in the 1930s indicate that in 1936 Harrisonville was declared an emergency school, which normally meant enrollment was below the state prescribed minimum. Clarks (formerly Clarks Station) and Todds Point schools were rebuilt, Bagdad painted, and an addition built at Scotts.

The decade of the 1940s saw major consolidation of black schools and the accompanying problems of transporting students further from their community of residence. The board began purchasing buses rather than contracting for transportation, which increased their expenses considerably.

In 1940, Lincoln Institute announced plans to dispose of the Lincoln Model School. Black patrons requested that the county board purchase a lot and build a new school at Montclair to house students from Lincoln Model. An agreement was made whereby the National Youth Administration (NYA) would provide the labor to build the school using Lincoln Institute employees and the county board would provide construction materials and would transport the laborers to the Montclair site. After further negotiations on the type of building materials and the cost, a two-room school was built at Montclair. By the end of the decade there were only three black elementary schools serving the black students in Shelby County.

Clark Station School students in 1925. Students are not identified. Mrs. Bessie Overstreet, teacher, is at the far right.

High Street Elementary School students and teachers in two undated photographs. Students are not identified. Teachers are, left to right: Mrs. E. Byrd, Mrs. D. Dale, Mrs. R. Radcliffe, Mrs. J. Dale, Mrs. V. Purdy, Mrs. H. Taylor, Mr. M. Moorman, Mrs. M. Brown, Mrs. F. Stone, Mrs. W. Mathis, Mrs. H. Thomas.

There were very few references to black schools in the 1950s. The only school mentioned in 1950 was Montclair, which underwent expansion to provide more playground space and lunchroom facilities and to upgrade its sanitary facilities. In 1951 the board refurbished the old white school at Mulberry for blacks to use, but when the white school at nearby Cropper burned in 1953, Cropper's students were moved to Mulberry and the Mulberry students provided for at the High Street Elementary School.

In 1954, the Supreme Court ruled against dual systems of education for blacks and whites. The following year a delegation of blacks and two attorneys asked the county board to state their plans for immediate desegregation. The board responded that they intended to "effectuate total desegregation as soon as possible" but added that the overcrowded conditions within white schools, particularly at Simpsonville (which would house the largest number of blacks) and at Gleneyrie would make any attempt at immediate integration impossible. The board added that "to force it (integration) would imperil opportunities for blacks and whites, and impair relations between races, and deter an ultimate orderly desegregation program."

By 1956, desegregation was still not "effectuated," due in part to black and white patrons who wanted to maintain the existing educational system. At an April board meeting, the County Superintendent shared the results of a survey, conducted by Whitney Young, of all black families with students attending Lincoln Institute. The unanimous consensus of these families was to keep their children at Lincoln Institute.

County board records regarding black schools in the 1960s dealt primarily with planning for integration and complying with the 1964 Civil Rights Act. Ironically, at a time when the issue of integration was at its height, references to black schools and black education was sketchier than in any previous decade. In 1962, a committee was formed to study attendance and transportation problems associated with integration. The following year a survey of redistricting was done to determine if existing facilities could accommodate integration. The board agreed to begin integration in the 1964-65 school term, though there are no records to substantiate what their plans entailed or their timetable for completion. Records do indicate that Montclair was closed in September 1965 and its pupils integrated into Simpsonville school. In September 1966 a special meeting of the board was held to discuss integrating Lincoln Institute students into the Shelby County High School. However, a 1967 entry allowing Lincoln Institute the use of county buses and another entry in 1969 discontinuing this practice suggests that integration was still incomplete by the end of the decade.

The only references to black schools or black education in the 1970s was in 1974 when the board received a letter from the Kentucky Civil Liberties Union, and in 1980 when the NAACP educational chairman requested that the board adopt a minority recruiting plan. When the superintendent presented a proposed Affirmative Action Plan that was unacceptable to the NAACP chairman, the chairman requested that citizens' committee or task force be formed. The task force presented its plans to the board in October 1980, which was the last reference to black schools or black education in county school board records.

In considering the question of dual systems of education in Shelby County's school system, there are four distinct impressions about the operation of black schools. First, the early board minute records contained a much more complete picture of black schooling than those for later years, despite the fact that there were fewer references to black schools. Second, the black schools trailed behind the white schools in being upgraded or provided with needed equipment by at least a decade. The only time black schools experienced a "trend" sooner than the white schools was in the case of consolidation. Third, where increasing attention was paid to modernizing white schools and offering diverse curricular and extracurricular activities, there was virtually no indication that black schools had any organized sports program or a curricula other than the most basic. This was particularly apparent from the mid-1930s to the 1960s, when the influx of federal and state money provided a steady stream of curricular and extracurricular programs. Fourth, the steady decline of patron requests from blacks over the years strengthens the idea of blacks becoming more "invisible" within the school system infrastructure as concerns about equalizing education between blacks and whites became more visible.

Much remains to be discovered about the quality and content of education for blacks in Shelby County and in counties throughout the state. The hope is that the quest for information will continue and that these relatively invisible schools will soon become a more visible part of the history of education in Kentucky.

LINCOLN INSTITUTE

By Duanne Pucket, Vivian Overall and Betty Matthews

Lincoln Institute was opened in 1911 to educate African American students in Kentucky. On July 1,1904, the Day Law, sponsored by state Representative Carl Day of Breathitt County, mandated segregation in both public and private schools in Kentucky. The bill passed 73-5 in the House and was approved 28-5 by the Senate. It remained in effect until the U.S. Supreme Court invalidated it in 1954. Aimed primarily at Berea College, which was committed to the education of black and white students, the Day Law was fought unsuccessfully by the administration of Berea College.

When the Supreme Court ruled against it, administrators decided to fund a new school for black students, which was required to be at least 50 miles from Berea. Andrew Carnegie gave $200,000, which was matched equally with other gifts by 1909. The original site was Anchorage, Kentucky, but serious objections by area residents that land values would be lowered and black families encouraged to move into the area changed the location to Simpsonville. The new site in Simpsonville contained 444.4 acres made up of three farms. The school was designed for students to commute or board and was strategically placed in the heart of central Kentucky, easily reached by students from every section of the state.

Five individuals were mainly responsible for establishing Lincoln Institute: Dr. A.E. Thomson, the first principal of the school, two graduates of Berea College, James Bond and Kirke Smith, the former a member of Berea's board of trustees and the latter to become dean of education at Lincoln, and the Rev. William E. Barton, former Berea student who later became a member of the Berea board of trustees and Lincoln Institute's board. The fifth supporter was William G. Frost, president of Berea College. The Institute was founded October 16, 1909, and incorporated January 17, 1910.

Chosen for the design of the school were African American architects William Tandy and G.W. Foster of New York City. The mayor of Shelbyville, Lynn T. Gruber, was awarded the construction contract. This helped alleviate some of the fears and criticisms by local residents. Gruber died before the project was complete and his widow made a satisfactory settlement so that the job could be finished.

Academic studies for students began on October 1, 1912, with 13 full-time employees and a student body of about 85. Students paid a $17 monthly fee. Some paid a portion of the amount and worked off the remaining balance at 15 cents an hour.

The curriculum focused upon vocational education: home economics for girls, and agriculture, building trades, and maintenance engineering for boys. Normal training was available for those interested in becoming teachers. To gain experience in farm management, the students planted and cultivated crops and operated a dairy. Kentucky's top cash crop, tobacco, could not be raised because the students could not use tobacco products.

Woodworking and shop classes at Lincoln Institute in 1932.

Shelby County Public Library, from Arletta Shouse.

A track team at Lincoln Institute in 1931. Standing, left to right: William H. Stone, Dewey Allen, Charles H. Payne, James Griffin, Eugene Thomas, James P. Miles. Middle row: Clay Grey and John J. Douglas. Front row, Edward Foster, John Dupee, Jr., Clifford D. Whiteside.

Thomson served as principal 16 years before resigning and being replaced by Dr. Benjamin E. Robinson, a former missionary to China for 15 years. From 1927 to 1935, Lincoln would have four different principals due to decreasing enrollment and the decline in donations. In 1935, the trustees voted to close the school. However, Dr. Whitney M. Young, an African American, and Mansir Tyding, a white man, persuaded the group to keep the school open. They developed a recruitment campaign which resulted in the enrollment of 125 new students. Within two weeks of the Young-Tyding Faith Plan, an African American man from Lexington, William Henry Hughes, left the school $10,000 in his will. Contractual agreements were then established with both the county and independent school districts, so other funds could be accepted.

A newspaper article in 1940 reported the chief assets of Lincoln Institute as being 19 buildings, a dairy herd of 35 Jersey and Holstein cows, and a vocational high school department with 13 teachers and 295 students. The objective was to limit enrollment to some degree to give students individualized instruction. Of the 25 classes that had graduated by 1940, Lincoln produced three college deans, one college president, 76 teachers, three preachers, six lawyers, 26 businessmen, 21 farmers, three doctors, four dentists, 14 engineers, 58 trained domestics, 10 government employees, 10 carpenters, five nurses, 11 insurance agents, and the only African- American postmaster in the state.

In 1946, all physical properties of Lincoln were deeded to the state with the stipulation that the site was to be used as an educational center for state youth, or the Lincoln Foundation would receive $250,000 from the state. A fire that destroyed one of the boys' dormitories triggered this agreement.

Dr. Young became the first African American president of the newly formed public school and remained in that position until the school closed in 1966. His wife, Laura, became the first African-American postmistress in Kentucky, operating the post office established at Lincoln Ridge, the community named to house the Lincoln Institute.

During the late 1940s and 1950s, groups of Girl Scouts from Louisville camped in a wooded area south of the Lincoln Institute where there were frame cabins that stood on railroad tie foundations. With the construction of I-64 in 1956, about 35 acres of the area was divided from the rest. This inaccessible land was sold and was no longer available for the scouts.

The campus became the Lincoln School after the last class graduated in 1966. For two years the new facility was an integrated educational facility for students who were both gifted and economically disadvantaged. In 1968, it became a federal job corps center bearing the name of Whitney M. Young Jr., son of the former president. Young had attended Lincoln Institute and had become director of the National Urban League. The job corps center is operated under the guidance of the U.S. Department of Labor and the Lincoln Foundation in Louisville.

FINCHVILLE SCHOOL

By Richard Duvall

Finchville was first known as Buck Creek. The village was located in the neighborhood now known as Gadsville. Between the residences of Walter Purdy and Ernest Doolan was erected the first Buck Greek Church. Nearby about 1800 the first schoolhouse was built. It is thought the first teachers were a Mr. and Mrs. Burbank from Boston, Massachusetts.

Between the years 1823 and 1838 this schoolhouse was supplanted by Buck Creek Seminary, a brick building situated on land owned by Archibald Collins who inherited it from his father-in-law, Nicholas Ware. This building was near Bull Skin Creek in the neighborhood of a farm owned by a Mr. Van Dyka. The house now occupied by Joe Lyons was at that time owned by a family named Hazelrigg, who boarded students attending this school. The old Winlock homestead and the farm of W. C. Winlock and W. L. McMillan probably comprised the farm of Thomas Loofborough on which this school was located. The brick cabin in the yard of W. L. McMillan has been thought for many years to be a part of the original brick school building. Among those who attended this seminary in 1849 were Mary F. Davis, Eliza Wailer, John and Kate Beckham, James Pickett, Dock Davis, William and George Thatcher, James and Louis Malone, James Carnine, Lou and Sarah Turnham, Fannie and Lou Davis, Mandy and Cynthia Doyle, Anne Thatcher, Susan Whitaker, and Georgia Newland.

At the intersection of Parrent Lane and Olive Branch Road in 1863 stood a log schoolhouse. The old well belonging to the schoolhouse is still there. This log schoolhouse was the first school attended by Mrs. J. A. Stanley, sister of Mrs. Crawford Jones. Among the teachers were Miss Mary Goodman and Miss Sallie Cruss.

Near this school about the same time Benoni Newland ran a boarding school. He was a botanist and left books and specimens of great value. He made several trips to Europe, and it was from there his wife, Amelia Froman, came. Students from various places came here and every resident in the neighborhood took students to board. The Newlands also maintained a Sunday school.

The Finchville School in a 1909 photograph.

Ellis McGinnis Collection, courtesy of Michael McGinnis.

Shelby County Public Library, from Helen Gee.

Finchville High School, built in 1915.

Newland sold his school and home to Thomas J. Doolan. Mr. Doolan opened his school September 9, 1867, with an enrollment of one hundred eight—twenty-six of whom were present and were the following: James Wakefield, Joseph Wakefield, Julius Melone, Sol Smith, John Myers, George F. Shockney, Eddie Heady Beard, Thomas Boston, Silas Jones, Don Benefield, William Mareen Duvall, Robert M. Smith, Lewis R. Polk, George Salem Boswell, J. A. Stanley, James D. Middleton, William T. Weakley, John Marshall, W. H. Campbell, Joseph T. Smith, John Smith, Gus Duvall, Everet Boswell, James Thomas Allen, Henry Gray, and Drury Lee Melone. The Doolans taught here for 21 years assisted principally by eastern teachers.

The village of Finchville obtained its name from Ludwell R. Finch who came to the neighborhood in 1841 and bought land. A blacksmith's shop owned by Mr. Finch was known as Finch's Shop and the village was known thus until the building of the Bloomfield branch of the Louisville & Nashville Railroad when it was given its name Finchville.

The first public school in Finchville was established in 1886, and Miss Sophia Stanley was the teacher. This school was a three-room framed, red building with a separate music room.

On September 6, 1896, the Finchville High School began. The board of officers were J. A. Stanley, William T. Weakley, and James Taggart. The faculty consisted of W. T. McClain, Principal; Miss Fannie White, intermediate department; Miss Lula White, primary department; and Miss Lillian Davis, music. The tuition for one year for the primary department was $18, the intermediate $22.50, and the high school was $27. Pupils of the primary and intermediate department living in the Finchville district paid no tuition the first year.

Finchville High School was built in 1915. In 1931 an auditorium was added to the structure and still stands today.

HOME SCHOOLS

By Mary Elizabeth Thomas

The origin of the Shelby County Home School Group began in the spring of 1993. Kim Havard, a new resident of the county and also a home-schooler, found out about the numerous home-schoolers in the county. There was no established connection between these families. After a great deal of research and advertising, the first meeting was held at the Havard's home. The guest speaker was Don Wollett of the Christian Home Educators of Kentucky (CHEK), a statewide group for Christian home-schoolers. Among other functions, its leadership helps to develop local support groups. That meeting was attended by over forty people, and was the beginning of the Shelby Area Christian Home Educators (SACHE). The group grew in two years to over fifty families and 200 children. Activities ranged from science and art fairs, to field trips, to an organized weekly YMCA program for home schooled children. Families from both Shelby and Franklin Counties along with other neighboring counties were a part of SACHE. In the spring of 1995, with the increased number of home schools, this group split and Shelby County now has its own support group.

CORNERSTONE CHRISTIAN ACADEMY

By Duanne Puckett

The school, located on Frankfort Road in Clay Village, opened in 1984. At that time it was called Living Waters Christian School because it was located in the Living Waters Church. Plans were announced in 1999 to build a separate complex with athletic facilities to meet the growing needs of the private student body. The name change also came in 1999.

Most students and parents choose Cornerstone primarily because of a religious conviction. Parents may also want a smaller, more traditional educational environment. Faith is a key component to the philosophy of Cornerstone Christian Academy. Faculty members use the Bible as a textbook and instill Christian behavior in the students from kindergarten through twelfth grade. Christian education is intertwined with other aspects of curriculum. For example, in history, students may study characters of biblically strong men and women or in spelling the list may contain the books of the Bible or characters from the Bible.

In 2000 there were about 170 students enrolled in the school, which attracted pupils from Shelby, Anderson, Spencer Oldham, Franklin, and Jefferson Counties. Extracurricular events involve athletics with the boys and girls advancing to state championship competition in 1999, and two key players were nominated for Miss and Mr. Basketball among the Christian schools in Kentucky. Classes are formatted accordingly to make the students competitive for college scholarships.

THE MORSE SCHOOL OF TELEGRAPHY

By John E. Kleber

The invention of the telegraph may rank as the greatest of humankind. It permitted the immediate transmission of messages over distance thus altering forever the spatial-time dimension. All subsequent modes of communicating information are but a variant of the telegraph.

Samuel Morse constructed a rude operating model of an instrument in 1835. Within a few years it had been perfected. In the United States the first telegraph line was strung from Baltimore to Washington in 1844. By 1860 it had been strung across the continent and now Maine could instantaneously communicate with California. The value of that communication was questioned by no less a luminary than Ralph Waldo Emerson who doubted the value of what they had to say. Emerson's concerns notwithstanding, in 1901-02 the number of telegraphed messages reached their peak. That year, there were 1,200,000 miles of telegraph lines in the United States. And in that year Shelbyville could boast a school to teach the use of the apparatus and its accompanying international code consisting of a series of dots and dashes encompassing the alphabet.

The heavy load of telegraph messages meant a paucity of operators at the beginning of the twentieth century. It was reported that operators along the Baltimore & Ohio Railroad were working both day and night. To meet this demand the Morse School of Telegraph had begun in Shelbyville in 1884. In 1901, it joined with the Ross College of Lexington and they combined their resources in Shelbyville in what was described as "a commodious building and beautiful surroundings." To facilitate the consolidation the school acquired the old convent building at First and Main Streets. The Shelby News of January 17, 1901, noted that it was quickly being renovated and that the Morse School was expected to open there by February 1. By January 31 the school was in full operation with an enrollment of about sixty students.

The old convent building at First and Main Streets where the Morse School of Telegraphy was located in 1901.

The Shelby News observed that they were "a quiet lot of gentlemen and are well behaved. They are not attending school for their health, as is the case with many students at the higher colleges, but on the contrary, are preparing themselves to take positions on railroads and in telegraph offices to make a living. We believe that this class of students are the best for a town and we gladly welcome them to our midst."

To recruit students, the school emphasized the increasing need for telegraphers. From 50,000 in 1889 the number had increased to 250,000 by 1901. Each year 40,000 new telegraphers were needed, and the Morse

School was there to meet that need. Telegraph offices always remained open. In addition, salaries were good. A farm laborer could receive $10 to $25 a month and board, but a telegraph operator's salary was $40 to $125 a month.

Men and women were enrolled in the school. Men were preferred although it was noted that "the Western Union Telegraph Company alone employs thousands of them (women), having on average, two lady operators to every gentlemen...." It discouraged women from getting into the railroad business, however, noting "few lady operators are employed on railroad lines." Telegraphy was well suited to women's' skills, and the school catalogue noted that "many telegraph officials claim that in any commercial telegraph office ladies can perform the same duties as gentlemen, and are considered more steady in their duties and hours." Fifteen women were accepted at any one time and no more since "calls from the Commercial Telegraph Companies are infrequent for ladies." Students ranged in age from 4 to 60, although 18 to 22 year olds predominated.

The school prepared both railway and commercial operators. Its curriculum worked closely with railroads in its preparation of graduates. The daily program of study included railroad accounting, typewriting, Western Union Telegraph Company rules, Standard Railway rules, messages and reports for same, freight and ticket reports, station account current, train orders, train reports, train signals, market and board of trade reports, and press reports. Classes began daily at 8:00 and ended at 4:00. School amusements included a military drill every Saturday, Edison Debating Society, M.S.T. Orchestra, and a school prize spelling contest.

The Morse School prided itself on having an actual railroad located in miniature in the second floor classrooms. With two terminals, and eight intermediate stations, each room was supplied with train order signals, semaphores, switches, sidings, etc. Fifteen to twenty trains were moved daily. Students were placed in charge of the two offices with its wires and were held responsible for the condition of said station. In such a way students became "familiar with the movement and operation of trains by telegraph, so as to be conversant with all the duties they may be called upon to perform when in charge of an office." The school touted this practical experience for all who enrolled.

The school's catalogue called Shelbyville a perfect college town. In addition to its healthy location, it was a place where all vice and immorality were strictly prohibited. Therefore parents could safely send their sons and daughters "with the assurance that they will be benefited morally as well as intellectually, by their surroundings." Shelbyville was a town of churches, a public library, and "innocent amusements."

Shelbyville was also described as easy to reach over four railroad lines and had two telegraph companies— the Western Union and Postal lines. It warned students to be careful of fraudulent schools that promised much but delivered little. And to show its cooperative spirit, it offered students the opportunity to learn bookkeeping and shorthand at the Shelby Commercial College.

In 1901, the new president and general manager of the consolidated Lexington and Shelbyville schools was Prof. J.H. Shulkey and Prof. W.J. Ross was vice-president and secretary. Shulkey had been an operator with the Northern Pacific Railroad. Ross owned and ran a successful telegraph college before moving to Lexington and subsequently joining with the Morse School. An article in the Shelby Record of January 1903 noted that the school was under new management. Ten citizens of Shelbyville bought out the old proprietors. Those who purchased it were: Jno. Logan, J.C. Burnett. L.C. Willis,

L.G. Smith, A.L. Harbison, Geo. S. Chowning, Pryor R. Berd, W.M. Owen, D.C. Alexander, and S.S. Kirk. Assurances were given that the school would continue to be a home affair of great pride.

In time the demand for telegraph operators declined, generally to be replaced by the telephone. The great optimism with which the school changed hands in 1903 disappeared. At the time of its founding, it was truly believed that "an educational institution of this character can do better work and accomplish more good in a city of this size than in a large city, on account of the many temptations and draw backs to be contended with in a large place." As the century progressed many small towns saw their school close or move to those larger cities.

MYLES KINDERGARTEN

By Mary David Myles

Myles Kindergarten held its first class in the fall of 1966. At that time, there were no kindergartens in the Public Schools in Shelbyville or Shelby County. Two private kindergartens were located in Shelbyville and the need for another was great. With help from Mr. and Mrs. Ted Igleheart, the necessary information for starting a kindergarten was requested from Mr. Harry Sparks of the Department of Education in Frankfort.

The first class was held in September 1966 in the home of Mr. and Mrs. Jack Kimbrough who lived on Southlawn. The large room used for the class was on the lower level of their home. There was also a large backyard for playing. Sixteen children enrolled. Classes met on Monday, Wednesday and Friday mornings from 8:30 to 11:30. Contact was kept with Mrs. Lillian Sorrel, a First Grade Teacher at Southside Elementary School about material the children should know before starting the first grade.

At the start of the second year, the kindergarten moved to its permanent home at the residence of Mr. and Mrs. Edmund Myles on U.S. 60 West about 3 miles west of town. A two and one-half car garage on the ground level of their home, which had been built according to the Fire Code of Louisville, was transformed and used as a classroom. There was a very large adjacent play area. The square footage allowed for 16 children. In twenty-one years (school closed in June 1987) approximately 350 children passed through Myles Kindergarten. So popular was the school that talk around town was to call from the hospital and put a baby's name on the waiting list if one wanted to get in.

Graduating class at Mary David Myles's kindergarten, May 1, 1970. Front row, left to right: Dean Logan, Angie Smith, Dale Poulter, Tony Smith, Freddie Atchley, Cathy Borders, Bob Gravett, Karen Yount. Back row, left to right: Virginia Shannon, Brian McMullan, David Vaughn, Susan Purnell, Carla Trumbo, Nancy Todd Threlkeld, Lucie Anne Logan, Philip McAtee. The teacher, Mrs. Myles, is behind the back row.

Courtesy of Mary David Myles.

RHODES SCHOLARS

By Duanne Puckett

Clusters of crimson-colored bushes are planted in a star-shape in the rear of Clear Creek Park north of Shelbyville. Among the bushes are five trees from Oxford University to mark the five Rhodes Scholars who have called Shelby County home.

Winchester Stuart was born in Shelbyville in 1885. He became known as the greatest corporate mortgage consultant of his time and perfected a type of mortgage known as "open end." Stuart graduated from Centre College in 1908 and studied for the ministry at Queens College in Oxford where he graduated in 1911. He rowed with distinction in 25 races for the college rowing team. He lived most of his life in New York City where he worked for the Electric Bond and Share Company. He died in 1967.

Allen Barnett was born in Shelby County in 1888. He taught in New Hampshire, Virginia, and at Georgetown College. Made a Rhodes Scholar in 1911, he served as an officer in the American Expeditionary Force in World War I. He retired to Shelbyville where he taught senior high English at Shelbyville High School in the 1950-60s. He died in 1970.

Edwin Powell Hubble was born in Marshfield, Missouri, November 20, 1889. His family moved to 928 Bland Avenue in Shelbyville. His father, a manager for National of Hartford Insurance, had moved them there from Chicago. After graduating from the University of Chicago, Edwin spent the summer of 1910 visiting his family there. It was from Shelbyville that he left to attend Oxford that year. He gained fame as an astronomer. His scientific discoveries helped make space flight possible. In 1991, the United States launched a telescope named for Hubble that continues to orbit the earth. He was awarded many honorary degrees for his astronomical work. He died in 1953.

Rueben Thornton Taylor was born in LaGrange in 1892. He studied folk songs and sang them while he plowed on his farm near Bagdad. He was made a scholar in 1916. While at Oxford, he became involved in World War I as an ambulance driver in France. He bought a farm in Shelby County in the late 1930s and lived there about twenty years. He died in 1967 in Taxco, Mexico.

John Harrod was born in Shelbyville in 1946. After graduating from Shelbyville High School, he attended Centre College where during his senior year his adviser suggested he interview for the Oxford scholarship in order to prepare for the Woodrow Wilson Scholarship interviews. He was one of 31 Americans chosen in 1967 to be Rhodes Scholars. He dropped out but quickly re-enrolled when faced with being drafted for the Vietnam War. He played basketball and completed the two-year course of studies.

When he returned home, he took up playing the fiddle and traveling the state to meet and record old-time fiddlers. His music acquainted him with his wife, Jane, who also sings and plays. Together, they have performed across the state at various historical, environmental and educational events. They have two daughters.

Harrod teaches in the gifted/talented program in the Frankfort Independent School System after years of working in the same field in the Owen County Public Schools.

SCIENCE HILL SCHOOL

By Rosella Yager Cunningham Davis

"...Yes, provided..." was the reply Rev. John Tevis received when he proposed marriage to Miss Julia Ann Hieronymus. The provision was that he agreed for his bride to open in their home a school for girls to learn to read, write, study Greek, Latin, and sciences like their brothers.

On March 25, 1825, Mrs. Tevis opened Science Hill School in the first room on the left side as one entered the front door of their Shelbyville residence on Washington Street at the end of North Sixth Street. It opened with twenty girls of different ages, and learning abilities from the town. Later, as students came from their homes in the county, they became known as "boarders" since they stayed overnight.

As the enrollment steadily increased, qualified teachers had to be obtained. Classrooms and bedrooms had to be provided. In time three sections were added around an open court and pulled together as one building under a common roof.

Rev. Tevis, a Methodist Minister, soon joined Mrs. Tevis in operating the school until his death in 1861. Mrs. Tevis maintained her connection with Science Hill until her death on April 22, 1880, in her eighty-first year. Both Tevises are buried near the chapel in Grove Hill Cemetery.

Hard times and a cholera epidemic nearly closed the school in the 1830s. However, in 1839 Tevis published a school catalogue that was widely distributed. By 1857 Science Hill boasted 230 students from all over the South, housed in a substantial brick edifice.

Dr. Wiley Taul Poynter and his wife, Clara Martin Poynter, purchased the school on March 25, 1879. For seventeen years Dr. Poynter devoted himself to adjusting its courses of study to modern requirements and the advanced ideas of education for girls. He died on July 30, 1896, and Mrs. Poynter became its principal holding the same high standards of character and scholarship. Classes at Science Hill were small, allowing well trained, and experienced teachers to give individual help to their students. Juliet Jamison Poynter, their oldest child, graduated from Wellesely College in 1905 and returned as the associate principal.

An outsider at the school gave the College Entrance Examination necessary for admission each year. Science Hill was an accredited school of the Association of College and Sec-ondary Schools of the Southern States. Science Hill Scholarship Program allowed some to attend the school during the Great Depression that might not have otherwise.

Upon completion of the necessary requirements for graduation, diplomas were awarded to Graduates of Diploma Course, which is equivalent to one year in college, Graduates of College Preparatory Course (most used for college entrance), or Graduates with Special Certificate (most in English and last given in 1927).

School opened with morning chapel, classical prelude, singing of hymns, Bible reading, and prayer. Bible study was required of all students from freshman through senior classes, which was followed by an examination at the end of the school year. Students attended school on Saturday with Monday as their free day. Sundays were devoted to church services and Bible study. Boarders had a strong Young Women's Christian Association.

Shelby County Public Library, Sue Long Collection.

An unidentified group of students and faculty at Science Hill, 1889. The Poynter family is believed to be in the photograph.

Among the annual highlights of the school year were the Christmas Play "Bethlehem" which included all students; the senior play where all boy parts were played by girls; and the May Day Program. Halloween and Washington's birthday celebrations were a time for costumes, good music, and dancing. Field Hockey was played in the meadow behind the buildings against Louisville's Collegiate, Versailles' Margaret Hall, and the United States Field Hockey Association Touring Team. Other activities included tennis, basketball, badminton, archery, and parlor games in "the court." Springtime in "the court" included interpretative dance and tap dancing.

Science Hill's Primary Departments was located in a little, red, two-story, frame building separated from the main school and was on the hilltop overlooking the meadow below. That was where little boys attended through the fourth grade. Primary Department teachers were Miss Heady Hawes and Miss Katherine Reeves (later on faculty of Cornell University).

Once one completed the fourth grade they were transferred into the main building for individual classes. The much-loved Miss Sue Godbey taught spelling, languages, geography and diagramming. She was known as a specialist in diagramming-preparing students for future English classes. Miss Louise Morse, (later Registrar at Harvard) taught mathematics including fractions and percentages. Miss Beth Atkinson taught mythology and English history. Miss Mary Elizabeth Chinn introduced students to a year of Latin grammar in the eighth grade.

Between 1890 and 1900 twenty-three graduates completed their bachelors at Wellesely and others received degrees from Vassar, Bryn Mawr, Stanford, Goucher, New York University, University of Chicago, University of California, and University of Michigan; three received their M.D. degrees from Rush Medical School, University of Wisconsin and Johns Hopkins and another her Ph.D. from Columbia University.

Among some of the teachers at Science Hill were: Rowena Weakley, who taught mathematics, algebra, geometry, and trigonometry; Sarah Ellen Lilly, who taught French and English; Margaret McGing, who taught English for freshmen through senior classes; Mary Elizabeth Chinn, who taught Latin grammar; Elizabeth Crosby Bridge, who taught Latin; Blenda Thormer taught biology; Katrina Quintus taught chemistry and physics; and Millie Yvonne Fleury taught French. Harriet Rockwell Poynter, the second daughter of Dr. and Mrs. Poynter, headed

Courtesy of The Filson Historical Society, Otho Williams Collection.

Science Hill School buildings, probably in the 1920s.

the Music Department. She taught violin, choral class and Glee Club. Among the piano teachers were Miss Jenny Lemmel of Germany and Bertha Mary Schriber of the New England Conservatory of Music. Private piano lessons were given and individual practice rooms were available. Misses Poynter and Schriber gave concerts over WHAS and WAVE radio stations in Louisville. Piano, violins, voice, operetta and Glee Club recitals were open to the public.

Mrs. Poynter was principal at the time of her death on March 7, 1937. Funeral services were conducted in Science Hill Chapel with burial beside Dr. Poynter in the Lexington Cemetery. Juliet Poynter became principal on March 25, 1937.

Many alumnae and friends were shocked to read in the Courier-Journal that Science Hill School would close at the end of the 1939 school year, after 114 years of continuous operation under the leadership of two families. The Great Depression was taking a heavy toll on the school. Efforts were made to find buyers for the school to continue the high standards of education and dedication that the Poynter family had used. When none could be found, the school closed in June 1939, partly due to the poor health of Juliet Poynter. It was purchased by Lindsay Logan, then sold to Iglehart and Roe Realtors.

On Founder's Day, March 25, 1961, some two hundred former Science Hill students gathered for a surprise appreciation luncheon in the former school dining room. At that time Juliet Poynter announced that Mark J. Scearce had purchased the entire building and over a period of time planned to include it as one unit on the National Registry for Historic Preservation. Poynter closed by saying without any en-dowments and trusts, Science Hill closed without a penny of in-debtedness. In 1966, a Kentucky Historical Marker was placed in the Poynter's front yard at the end of Sixth Street.

Misses Juliet and Harriet Poynter continued to play active rolls in Centenary United Methodist Church and Kentucky Methodist Church Conferences, and social and civic clubs. Juliet died on November 4, 1974, and was buried in the Poynter Family lot at Grove Hill Cemetery. Harriet Poynter continued to live at Science Hill with her niece, Emily Ruth Poynter. On October 26, 1982, Harriet died in the same bed in which she was born at Science Hill School. She also was buried in Poynter's Family lot at Grove Hill Cemetery.

REMEMBRANCES OF A SCIENCE HILL STUDENT

By Martha O'Nan

In the spring of 1934 when I was fourteen, my mother and I went to Science Hill School to discuss enrollment with the principal, Miss Juliet Poynter, who immediately asked how much Latin, French, or German, science, and mathematics I had studied. My mother replied that I had completed one year of high school where there were no foreign languages and only a general science course. Miss Juliet said that students at Science Hill began Latin in the eighth grade and French in elementary school. I felt absolutely inferior but was relieved when she added that she would accept me. However, she would not grant any credit for my high school courses and was certain that I would need four or probably five years for the college preparatory course.

My mother wanted me to complete the course in three years. No doubt the reason for three years was the cost. My parents had planned for me to be a boarder, which in 1999 dollars would be $30,000 to $35,000 per year. Three years, Miss Juliet said, would require my fall schedule to be: algebra (second year), English (second year), Latin (freshman level; eighth-grade Latin was to be made up with a tutor before fall 1934), French (beginning), biology, ancient history, Bible once per week, physical education five times per week, and piano. She reminded us that students who were preparing for entrance into superior colleges had to receive an acceptable grade on national examinations of the College Examination entrance Board.

Boarders had to have items which my mother soon ordered: black serge bloomers, white blouses with buttons to keep tails in, black stockings, and gym shoes which were for physical education and hockey games.

A regulation that made my parents unhappy was that boarders could not return home before Christmas. We lived just eleven miles from Shelbyville. Yet it was impractical to have someone drive me to school every day in our Model A Ford or new Ford V8. Finally, my parents decided to rent an apartment from Mr. and Mrs. Eugene Cowles so that my mother and I could spend schools days in Shelbyville (Tuesdays, Wednesdays, Thursdays, Fridays, and Saturdays). After 1934-35, I had a room at the home of Mrs. Ed McCormack (Lillie Boswell, an 1887 graduate of Science Hill). Jane Veech, her niece, had a room next to mine. We walked to our classes and window shopped at Miss Mary Bloomer's shop on Sixth Street.

Occasionally my mother bought me a dress from Miss Mary's to wear to Louisville concerts attended by Science Hill students and programs in the school's chapel (Jesse Stuart, Carl Sandburg, and Little Philharmonic Orchestra). My school clothes (usually skirts and blouses, sweaters in winter, and Arnold shoes) came from Stewart's, Selman's, and Byck's in Louisville.

Among the graduates were two of my teachers. One was Miss Rowena Weakley who taught me mathematics (algebra, geometry, and pre-calculus). The other was Miss Nette Pullen who taught history and Bible. In her classes, students had to answer orally and rapidly every day. When she called on me, I always suffered stage fright and stumbled on questions such as the causes and results of the three Punic wars.

My other teachers were younger and did not come from Kentucky. My teacher in French was Mille Yvonne Fleury. First-year French had about fifteen students, the largest class I had. A few students were true beginners, but most had studied some French. I struggled with pronunciation, comprehension, International Phonetics, and literary texts. I passed but to improve my chances of success in second year, I had a tutor for the summer of 1935. In English, too, I lacked preparation. My only experience in writing had been true false, multiple choice, and fill-in-the-blanks. My English teacher, Miss Margaret McGing, required me to complete extra work for an entire year. At the same time, I was in her sophomore English class where there were selections from English and American authors. In addition, there was a text for techniques of writing and suggestions for compositions to explain, describe, and persuade. A third text was Woolley's Handbook of Composition valuable for its rules of good English. For the next two years, Miss McGing was my teacher for English and American literature presented by genres. Each year, there was a new text for the many required compositions. In three years, she brought me from "illiteracy" to a high score in English on college entrance examinations. Years later, I learned that her approach to literature was called New Criticism at the University of Chicago and explication de texte in France (role of a line or paragraph in an entire work, lexicon, structure, theme, images, style, and conclusion as to text's impact).

Equally outstanding was my Latin teacher, Miss Elisabeth Bridge. By the time I left her classes, I knew almost by heart Bennett's New Latin Grammar and in college had no difficulty with Livy, Plautus, Terence, Lucretius, Horace, and other Roman authors. In fact, my college Latin professor said that I was the best-prepared student he had ever taught.

Other superior teachers were Miss Katrina Quintus who taught me biology, chemistry, and physics; Miss Elinor Pike who directed gym five times per week (good weather outdoors, bad weather in the court) and who had corrective exercises (posture and feet) with students one by one; and Miss Bertha Schaber for piano.

The success of these teachers came from their outstanding preparation in the subject taught and from students whose goal was to enter colleges of high academic standing and who were willing or forced to spend hours on homework. With few exceptions, 100 percent of the Science Hill graduating class went directly to college where most completed their degrees within four years. This successful high school and college graduation came also from families who stood behind their daughters with financial and academic support. If Science Hill still existed, the degree offered would be the international baccalaureate, a diploma based on five or six years of high school with international tests and standards.

SHELBY COUNTY PUBLIC LIBRARY

By Deborah F. Magan

In January 1810, the following act was passed by the General Assembly incorporating the Shelby Library Company: "Be it enacted by the General Assembly, that Thomas Johnson, Edward Talbott, Benjamin Sharp, William Adams, George Piersey, John Ketcham, Joseph Bondurant, James Ford, and David Demaree, and their successors, duly appointed as is hereafter directed, be, and they are hereby constituted a corporation, to have continuance for ten years, by the style of the trustees of the Shelby Library Company." The corporation was given the power to appoint a librarian, secretary, and treasurer.

In February 1835, an act to establish the Shelbyville Library Company was passed by the forty-third

General Assembly. It stated that "...the Shelbyville Library Company, instead of seven directors, shall, at their next annual meeting, elect only five, three of whom may constitute a quorum to do business." Records of this library have not been found.

The Shelby County Library of today traces its history to 1897. In March 1897 the Woman's Club of Shelby County heard a paper at one of their meeting that was published in the Shelby Sentinel at the club's request. The newspaper editorialized, "The fact that the 'Free Library' is on the program of the Woman's Club of Shelby County shows that the need of the library is already felt and that the women of the community are anxious to share in this modern movement for the intellectual and moral advancement of the people." On December 1, 1898, the Board of Council with Mr. Luther Willis as Mayor passed an order granting the use of the council chamber for a public library. Nothing was to be nailed to the walls, and the rooms were to be heated, lighted, and cleaned without cost to the city. The rooms were located above the old firehouse on the southeast corner of Fifth and Main Streets.

The library opened on June 1, 1899, with 200 volumes on the shelves. The first librarian in the room was Miss Fannie Scearce.

A major development occurred when the city of Shelbyville was awarded a $10,000 grant from the Carnegie Foundation to build a library. However, no funds were provided for an endowment. Shelbyville would provide the site and $1,000 annually for maintenance. The city owned two abandoned lots in the central part of the city, located at Eighth and Washington Streets. The corner lot had been used as a cemetery but was abandoned when Grove Hill Cemetery opened in 1854. The next lot had belonged to the Presbyterian Church but reverted to the city after the church was destroyed by a storm. The library trustees petitioned for this property and it was granted on the condition that the library pay $500 for the actual building location. The money was used to clean the graveyard.

Val P. Collins of Louisville designed the Classic Revival building. The building was completed and ready to open in January 1904. Miss Florence Ballard was the first librarian in the new building. At the Board of Council meeting on May 25, 1905, the management of the Shelbyville Public Library was turned over to a Board of Directors. Miss Katherine Nicholas, who served as head librarian from 1923-77, provided the longest service to the library.

Courtesy of Katherine and Henry Cleveland.

In 1958, the library became the Shelby County Public Library and a member of the Eden Shale Library District, one of sixteen regional libraries. This change made it possible to receive funds from the Kentucky Department of Libraries. The library was integrated at this time. In 1962, Shelby Countians voted to levy a library district tax to support library services.

In 1955, the library got the first bookmobile, donated by Mrs. Archibald B. Young in memory of her

Miss Katherine Nicholas, librarian, in the Shelby County Public Library.

husband, a Shelby County native. Mrs. Howard (Helen) Lawson of Waddy was the first driver. She retired December 31, 1978.

The library expanded in 1969 when a $32,623 wing was added to the north side of the building nearest College Street. In 1979, the building was renovated and an addition to the northeast corner provided rest rooms and an elevator. The renovation cost was $282,000. In 1996, the library board started a major renovation and addition of 7,805-sq. ft. for a total of $1,020,000. A Kentucky Room was opened in 1975 for genealogy research and offers newspapers, census records, family files, and many local history books.

In 2001, the Shelby County Public Library housed over 55,000 volumes. It also offered magazines, newspapers, CDs, audio books, videos, large-print books, adult new reader books, a reference collection, and computer and Internet access. Children's story hours and various programs were held throughout the year. Over 8,000 people were registered users. The bookmobile and outreach program served over 250 users at local nursing homes and daycare centers. The library provided supplemental library service to local schools, and was a member of the Inter-Library Loan Program. The library had six full-time and three part-time employees

LIBRARY TRUSTEES

1899
Mrs. W.F. Thomas, President
Mr. John I. Logan
Mr. J.C. Burnett
Mrs. R.F. Foree
Mrs. L.C. Willis

1905 to 1958
Miss Mattie Harbison
Mr. John K. Todd
Mrs. Will McGrath
Mrs. John Fitch
Mrs. Ed McCormack
Miss Annie Bell
Mrs. Harry Lockridge
Mrs. Garnett Radcliff

Mr. Lloyd Pollard
Judge Coleman Wright
Mr. Hayden Igleheart
Mrs. Lewis Frederick
Mrs. James Hackworth
Mrs. Wilder Lee

1958 to 1999
Mr. Roy Neel
Mr. Mark Scearce
Dr. K.E. Ellis
Mr. F. E. Van Slyke
Mr. Eli Jackson, Jr.
Mrs. Albert Davis
Mrs. Lewis Cottongim
Mr. Charles Clifton
Mr. Bennett Roach

Mrs. Emily Thomas
Mr. Stewart McBrayer
Ms. Irene Duvall
Mr. Charles T. Long
Mrs. Tom Kehrt
Mr. Mike Cowan
Mr. Don Swindler
Mrs. Mary Robertson
Mrs. Betsy Megibbon
Mrs. Laura Moorman
Dr. Carlen Pippin
Mr. Kenneth Hudson
Ms. Vivian Overall
Mr. Roy Weeks
Mr. Phyllis Merchant
Mrs. Alice True

HEAD LIBRARIANS

Miss Fannie Scearce—Library Room
Miss Florence Ballard—Carnegie Library
Virginia Barringer (Baskett)
Jennie Reed Sampson
Annie Bell
Katie Mae Brown (Meehan)

Clay Willis (Lapsley)
Katherine Nicholas 1923-1977
Sherrell Morrison 1978-1989
Martha Rankin 1989-1991
Carol Giese 1991
Pamela W. Federspiel 1991-

STUART'S FEMALE COLLEGE
(SHELBYVILLE FEMALE SEMINARY/SHELBYVILLE FEMALE COLLEGE/SHELBYVILLE COLLEGE)

By Kevin Collins

Professor William F. Hill founded the school later known as Stuart's Female College—perhaps its most famous, if not its longest lasting, name—in 1839. During its initial years the school was first called the Shelbyville Female Seminary. With the significant financial help of the neighboring Presbyterian Church, Hill erected a school building on the northwest corner of Seventh and Main Streets. Conceived as a boarding school, the construction on the new two-story building was completed in time for the school's twentieth session, which commenced August 21, 1848.

On February 24, 1849, the institution was incorporated and its name changed to "Shelbyville Female College," Mr. Wm. F. and Mrs. R. A. Hill Principal and Assistant Principal, respectively. School terms, two per year, lasted twenty-two weeks per term. The institution offered preparatory studies (tuition $10.00), as well as principal instruction (tuition $16.00) in among other subjects, music, art, and modern languages, with "special care and attention" to morals and manners. The accommodations for those students who boarded included sleeping rooms, light and fire included, for $40.00 per semester. In addition to Mr. and Mrs. Hill, the College had an instructional staff of six.

In 1851, Professor Hill sold the institution to the Rev. Dr. David Todd Stuart, a young Presbyterian minister in charge of the Olivet and Shiloh Churches. Hill, a Baptist minister, then set himself the task of rebuilding the fire-ravaged Baptist Female College, located on Main and Second Streets.

Although several accounts of the school's history erroneously report that the Rev. D.T. Stuart then renamed the school "Stuart's Female College," the fact is that it was not until April 22, 1880, that the institution's name was formally changed to "Stuart's Female College." Furthermore, if it might have been the case that locally, at least, the school was informally called "Stuart's," nonetheless all newspaper stories and advertisements for the school up to 1880 refer to the institution as "Shelbyville Female College." In fact, for almost half of the institution's existence it was known as "Shelbyville Female College".

The Stuart family, however, was the guiding force behind the school for some forty or so years. The Rev. Dr. David Todd Stuart, with his capable wife, Olivia Winchester Hall Stuart, was actively in charge of the School from 1851 to 1867, and the College enjoyed steady growth during the period before the Civil War. The 1853 graduating class had only eight students, but in two years time it numbered fourteen and by 1860 there were twenty-seven graduates. Students came principally from Kentucky, but they also matriculated from Ohio, Illinois, Indiana, Texas, Mississippi, Louisiana, and Missouri. The School offered a Primary Department, described in its brochure as "comprising a thorough course in Spelling, Reading, Writing, Elementary Geography, Elementary Arithmetic, an introduction to Natural History, etc." The Collegiate Department curriculum covered four years and thirty-five areas of study, from mental arithmetic through trigonometry; chemistry to zoology; Biblical antiquities to moral science; natural philosophy to logic; English, history, music, and the fine arts.

The years from 1862 to 1867 saw the school's enrollment decline and the number of graduates in each of those years return to the 1853 figure of about eight. In a printed circular for the thirty-third session of the school, beginning the first week of September 1867, the Rev. Stuart had penned, "we regret that the number of our pupils has diminished . . . (but) as sweet peace has returned, we hope that by a little effort on the part of its friends, the College may gain its former prosperity." And, indeed, it did, beginning with an undergraduate class that year of forty-seven students, all but five from Kentucky. Unfortunately, the kindly and impressive Rev. Stuart, known, in the words of one contemporary description, as a man of "energy, ability, purity of character, and noble Christian manhood" died the following year. After his death, Olivia, with the help of her four daughters, who taught music, painting and literature, guided the school's fortunes until her son, Prof. W. H. Stuart, could assume control.

Winchester Hall Stuart received his early education in the schools of Shelby County and his collegiate education at Jefferson College in Pennsylvania. After graduation he spent some time as a private tutor in Mississippi before becoming the principal of Columbia, Kentucky, schools. At the death of his father, Stuart returned to Shelbyville to become head of Shelbyville Female College, a position he held until about 1890. It was he who to honor his deceased father's memory and work petitioned the General Assembly in 1880 to rename the school "Stuart's Female College of Shelbyville."

Married to the former Martinette Chiner of Shelby County, the couple had a large family of sons and daughters. Mrs. Stuart, in addition to family responsibilities, supervised the Boarding Department of the College. The school had a faculty of eight by this time, and ten-week terms of instruction in 1879 cost $50.00 for board and tuition. A tuition addendum of $15.00 was applicable to students studying music, no doubt necessitated by the acquisition of seven new pianos.

In 1890, Stuart left the College to become President of Owensboro Female College. Five years later he departed Owensboro to become the Superintendent of the Bowling Green schools. He died in 1902, the same year that Oxford University, in England, initiated the Rhodes Scholarship—an honor his son Winchester would receive.

After the departure of Prof. Stuart the Board of Directors leased the institution to two sisters, the Misses Lake V. and M. E. Sullivan, late of the Synodical Female College of Talladega, Alabama. Acting as Principal and Associate Principal, respectively, the Sullivans ran Stuart's College until its sale in 1897. Courses of study included ancient and modern languages, composition, the sciences, music and art. The student population at that time included women and men, as well as children from Shelby County families named Logan, Shannon, and Middleton. In 1897, Stuart's Female College was sold to Professor J. E. Nunn, a Baptist minister and former owner of Nunn's Academy in Bagdad.

Professor Nunn, a teacher for more than twenty years and a graduate of LaGrange College in Missouri, formed a stock company to buy the Stuart property and then chartered the reorganized school under the name "Shelbyville College." During the summer of 1897 he renovated the entire building, extending it from two to three stories in height and adding conical roofs to the building's turret-styled corners, but still retained the stately columned portico that fronted Main Street. With Nunn as President and Prof. E. W. Elrod, a recent arrival from Georgetown College, as Vice President, the 1897 matriculating class numbered 109. Of these, 25 were female boarding students and 46 were music pupils studying both voice and instrument. In addition to musical studies Nunn's school offered seven other departments of instruction— English, Mathematics, Natural Sciences, Mental and Moral Philosophy, History and Literature, Ancient and Modern Languages, Art and Elocution. The department of Music was under the direction of Miss Grace E. Motheral, a graduate of the New England Conservatory of Music. A graduate of the University of Virginia, Prof. M. M. Hargrove, taught Latin and French. Co-education lasted until 1902, when Shelbyville College became solely a woman's college. The graduating class of 1902 numbered ten, six recipients of Bachelor of Arts degrees and four recipients of Bachelor of Science degrees.

It seems that Prof. Nunn's commitment to education was offset by stronger acquisitive concerns, and in the fall of 1903 he bought up all outstanding Shelbyville College stock, closed the school and converted the building into a hotel, which he leased to Mr. P. Carney. Carney ran the Colonial Hotel, as it was named, until it was sold in 1910 to a Shelbyville syndicate led by Mrs. L. C. Willis. Nunn, having moved to Texas, subsequently made his considerable personal fortune there in the business of oil wells and telephones. Mrs. Willis' plans for the imposing, structurally sound but antiquated Colonial Hotel called for its renovation with the addition of a heating plant and electric lighting. In 1911, however, the federal government selected the Hotel's lot for a post office building. Between 1911 and 1917, when the venerable, old school building was finally demolished, it served as a boarding house and as temporary housing for Shelby High School. In time the building at 701 Main Street became too small for the post office and it was purchased and renovated by the First Presbyterian Church. It was renamed the Mulberry Building and is presently owned by the Mount Zion Baptist Church.

Shelby County Public Library, Williams Studio photograph

Stuart's Female College was located on the northwest corner of Seventh and Main Streets. The building was built in the 1840s and in the early 1900s housed the Colonial Hotel.

The Shelbyville police force and Mayor Robert F. Matthews in 1940. From left to right: Archie Ware, Sr., "Red" Baker, Rhene Strange, Mayor Robert F. Matthews, Chief Roy S. Jones, "Jake" Brummett, Albert Black.

CHAPTER SEVEN

GOVERNMENT

Courtesy of Archie Ware, Jr.

Shelbyville's city government in 1899. Mayor Luther C. Willis is in the center of the middle row. Other officials are: top row, left to right, T.J. Ramsey, councilman; Dr. T. E. Bland, councilman; W. M. Harrison, police judge; J.W. Bodkin, Jr., councilman. Middle row, left to right, Ben. F. Pemberton, chief of police; Luther C. Willis, mayor; Shannon Reed, city clerk. Bottom row, left to right, M. L. Dubourg, councilman; E. B. Beard, city attorney; P. T. Finnell, councilman.

GOVERNMENT

By Ted Igleheart

H istory does not record how many people congregated on a Shelby County farm on October 15,1792, to decide how the residents of the new county would be governed. The leaders probably were white male wealthy landowners. Their task was to implement a system of governing to follow the law of the new commonwealth. Kentucky had joined the Union as the fifteenth state on June 1 of that year. No longer was Shelby County a frontier void of law and order. A formal government was put in place.

At the county's first court session on that farm, a decision was made for a site for the new county seat town. It was called Shelbyville in honor of Kentucky's first governor, Isaac Shelby.

In just a few months, justices of the peace were named to govern the county. Also named were county clerk, commonwealth attorney, sheriff, and justices of the quarterly sessions, now known as circuit judges. State representatives and senators were elected. Later came county attorneys and mayor.

COURTS AND OFFICIALS

The principal offices of county government in Kentucky and throughout colonial America were Justices of the Peace and the principal institution, which the Justices formed collectively, was the County Court. Englishmen invented the county and the local magistrates that governed it. Virginia adopted the same form of government and Kentucky followed in 1792 with its first constitution. A new constitution was adopted in 1799 enlarging the powers of the County Court, which remained unchanged until a third constitution was written in 1850.

County Court Day in the county seats was the most important day of the month, attracting hundreds to the county seat. Legal petitions were heard by the County Court, deeds were recorded, and crops and livestock were bought and sold. Politiking and speech making, merrymaking, gossiping, drinking and brawling were common activities after one's official business was completed.

Justices of the Peace were appointed by the Governor in each county until 1800 with the advice and consent of the Senate. Besides their duties on the County Court, as individual magistrates they decided petty and criminal cases, took depositions, certified legal documents, impaneled commissions to inspect turnpikes, levied taxes, and performed marriages. Under the second constitution, the senior magistrate was ordinarily commissioned as Sheriff. Magistrates were appointed for life. According to the 1850 census, 80 percent were farmers, 5.6 percent were lawyers, and the rest were businessmen. Magistrates were generally wealthy landowners, active in politics, and highly regarded.

The County Court's powers included judicial, legislative, and executive functions. Most of the judicial business involved probate of wills and overseeing administration of estates. It also had jurisdiction over the emancipation of slaves, fining officials for neglect of duties, taking appeals from decisions of magistrates, and building roads. The administration of taxes and expenses occupied much of its time.

Quarterly Court, consisting of the same magistrates, met four times a year to conduct civil and criminal trials. However, by 1804 the General Assembly abolished the courts of quarterly sessions and replaced them with circuit courts staffed by judges who were not justices of the peace. Appeals of their decisions were taken to the Kentucky Court of Appeals in Frankfort.

The first County Court in Shelby County was held at the home of Brackett Owen on October 15, 1792. It was located where the State Highway Garage is now at the corner of Seven Mile Pike and KY Hwy 53 South. It was presided over by the four Justices provided for by the First Constitution. They were Arthur McGaughey, Alex Reid, James Logan, and Henry Davridge. The first lawyers sworn in as officers of the Court were John Logan, Isham Talbot, Blackburn, and Roberts. The first Clerk of the Court was James Craig.

Numerous attempts to reform the county court system were launched over several decades without success until 1849. Complaints of politics, nonattendance, bargain and sale of office, abuse of power, misappropriation of tax funds, nepotism, and incompetency finally aroused a majority of voters to call a constitutional convention which resulted in the reforms of 1850. A presiding County Judge was provided for, who along with magistrates from districts, would be elected and constitute the County Court. Sheriffs, jailers, coroners, surveyors, clerks, constables, and county attorneys would also be elected.

Delegates to the Constitutional Convention of 1890-91 sought to answer complaints that because the County Judges and magistrates were not required to be lawyers, their attempts to administer justice were inept and corruption and incompetency prevailed. However, only minor changes were made in the county court system. Magistrates were limited to eight in the county. County Judges continued their political control.

A new Constitution was drafted in 1964 providing for major reforms, including stripping county judges and magistrates.of judicial functions. However, under the hue and cry of county officials, the proposed Constitution was defeated at the polls. It was not until 1978 that successful judicial reform was brought about by adoption of an amendment to the old Constitution. It established qualifications, duties, and terms for judges, county attorneys, commonwealth attorneys, clerks, and other county officials. County Courts were abolished and replaced with Fiscal Courts composed of a presiding officer, the County Judge/Executive, and magistrates, who manage the fiscal affairs of the county. All judicial functions were placed in a District Court with one or more District Judges and a Circuit Court with one or more Circuit Judges, all required to be attorneys with certain minimum experience.

The District Courts handle civil matters involving not more than $4,000, traffic offenses, misdemeanors, probate of wills, administration of estates, appointment of guardians and conservators, preside over Juvenile Court and Small Claims Court (not exceeding $1,500), and hold examining trials in felony cases, which can be waived to the Grand Jury where felony charges are heard for indictment or dismissal in Circuit Court.

Circuit Court handles divorces, with custody, child support, and property questions. It handles civil cases involving over $4,000 and criminal cases involving felonies which may result in confinement in the penitentiary. Appeals are from District Court rulings.

A constitutional amendment was passed November 5, 2002, creating Family Courts which will decide all domestic issues exclusively. Implementation in Shelby County has not yet occurred.

Appeals from Circuit Court may be taken to the Kentucky Court of Appeals and on to the Supreme Court of Kentucky under certain conditions.

CIRCUIT JUDGES

By Kevin Collins and Ted Igleheart

Chapter XXXV, section 6, of the Kentucky State Constitution, passed June 28, 1792, established the Court of Quarter Sessions, one of the precursor courts of the present-day Circuit Court. The Court of Quarter Sessions was to consist of three Justices to be appointed from amongst the Justices of the Peace of each given county, with any two of them being sufficient to constitute a Court. In Shelby County, the court was to meet quarterly, in the months of February, April, June, and September. Charged with being "conservators of the peace in their respective counties," this court had jurisdiction to "hear and determine all causes whatsoever, at the common law or in chancery, within their respective Counties," except for criminal cases in which the penalty was loss of life, or other actions that were specifically mandated to some other court, such as the County Court.

Quarter Session Court dealt, inter alia, with escheats (the reverting of property back to the government for lack of heirs), forfeitures, injunctions (court orders prohibiting or demanding some action), writs of Ne exeat, (an order prohibiting a person, or, sometimes property, from leaving the jurisdictional area of a court) and writs of Habeas Corpus (protection from illegal detention or imprisonment).

The first judges in Shelby County were the Justices of the Quarter Sessions. Appointed by the Governor, the presiding Justices from 1792 until 1812 were Alex Reid, D. Demaree, James Logan, Arthur McGaughey and Henry Davridge. Davridge was the first Justice called a Circuit Judge. Succeeding Davridge were James Pryor, Mason Brown, Samuel Cooper, and W.F. Bullock.

The third Kentucky Constitution of 1850 provided for direct election of Circuit Judges. No person was eligible who was not a citizen of the United States, was at least thirty years old, had practiced law for at least eight years, and had resided in the district for which he was a candidate two years next preceding his election.

The first election was held on the second Monday in May 1851. The second election was held on the first Monday in August 1856, and all following elections on the first Monday in August in every sixth year thereafter. Should a vacancy occur during a term, the Governor filled it by appointment if the unexpired term was less that one year or, by issuing a writ of election if the residue of the vacant term exceeded one year. In 1851, P. B. Muir became the first elected Circuit Court Judge. Succeeding him was Thomas H. Throup. In 1867, Throup was followed by George W. Johnstone. After Johnstone, H. W. Bruce was elected. W. L. Jackson followed Bruce to the bench.

When the General Assembly divided the state into twelve judicial districts, Shelby County became part of the 12th District, which encompassed the six counties of Anderson, Henry, Oldham, Shelby, Spencer, and Trimble. At that point, Judge S. E. DeHaven, of Oldham County, succeeded Justice Jackson on the Court. Following DeHaven, Judge W. S. Carroll, of Henry County, held the bench for twelve years. Judge Frank Peak followed Carroll, but he resigned after only two years. When Justice Charles C. Marshall succeeded Peak in 1907, he began the longest tenure of all Shelby County Circuit Court Judges, presiding until 1943, a total of thirty-six years.

The next twenty-eight years, from 1944 to 1972, saw the Circuit Court led first by Judge J. Wirt Turner, of Henry County (from 1944 to 1951), and then by Coleman Wright (from 1952 until the redistricting of 1972).

In 1972, Shelby County, along with Spencer and Anderson Counties, were split off from the 12th Judicial District. A new Judicial District, the 53rd, was formed. During this transitional period in 1972, Three successive judges served—George F. Williamson, of Oldham County, the Governor-appointed Walter Patrick of Lawrenceburg, and, finally, Harold Y. Saunders of Shelby County. Judge Saunders served the 53rd Judicial District for twenty years, from 1972 to 1992. The current Circuit Judge, William F. Stewart, followed Judge Saunders.

The judicial amendment of 1975 established eight-year terms for judges of the Circuit Court, with a term commencing on the first Monday in January next succeeding the regular election for the office. To be eligible for the office, one must be a citizen of the United States, licensed to practice law in the courts of Kentucky, have been a licensed attorney for at least eight years, and be a resident of the Commonwealth and the district from which he is elected for two years next preceding his taking office. Since 1976, candidates for Circuit Court Judge have been elected from a non-partisan ballot, with the hope that the court system would be distanced from political concerns.

Before the amendment of 1975, the 1891 Constitution had specified terms of six years for Circuit Court Judges. Also, eligibility requirements at that time required judges to be at least thirty-five years old and to be practicing lawyers for at least eight years.

Today's Circuit Court, by law, must hold sessions in each county (if there is more than one) within its district; so, Judges of the 53rd Circuit must travel to Shelby as well as Spencer and Anderson Counties.

All felony trials, contested probate, and cases involving monetary values of more than $4,000 begin in Circuit Court. The Court also has jurisdiction over domestic relations as well as appeals from District Court and administrative agencies. As Circuit Court is a trial court, it impanels juries of twelve jurors. Jury verdicts in Circuit Court criminal trials must be unanimous; in Circuit Court civil trials, a three-quarter majority of the jury is sufficient for a verdict. The new constitutional amendment adds a Family Court Judge to the Circuit Court for all domestic issues.

CLERKS OF COURT, CIRCUIT AND COUNTY

By Kevin Collins and Ted Igleheart

CIRCUIT COURT CLERK

The current Kentucky Constitution, having been so amended in 1992, provides that, "beginning in the year 2000, and every six years thereafter, there shall be an election in each county for a Circuit Court Clerk." The term of the office shall be for six years, beginning on the first Monday in January after the election. A candidate for the office must be twenty-one years of age or older, a citizen of Kentucky, and "no person shall be eligible who has not resided in the state two years, and one year next preceding his election in the county and district in which he or she is a candidate." Except for incumbents at the time of the adoption of this amendment, all candidates thereafter were required to first attain a passing grade on a standard examination administered by the Administrative Office of the Courts (AOC).

In addition, there is also a certification requirement by a Judge, a practice that dates back to the first State Constitution of 1792 and has existed in one form or another in the subsequent constitutions of

1799, 1850, and 1891. The first two constitutions required that a candidate had to be certified by a majority of the Judges of the Court of Appeals. Today, a candidate must procure from "a Judge of the Court of Appeals or a Judge of a Circuit Court a certificate that he has been examined by the Clerk of his Court under his supervision, and that he is qualified for the office for which he is a candidate." Judges have rarely, if ever, denied qualification to a candidate for office.

The obligations of the Clerk of Circuit Court are enumerated in a state manual. The manual lists that the office, among its other duties, shall maintain court records, receive payments of fine, issue driver's licenses, schedule jury trials, and record trial proceedings for both the circuit and the district courts. The performance of these duties is monitored by the AOC.

In Shelby County, James Craig was the first Clerk and served also from 1793 to 1816. Craig was followed in office by Robert and Samuel Tevis. The subsequent clerkships of William A Jones, John Robinson, and Richard T. Owen bring us to the year 1884 when T.C. Bailey became Clerk. Following Bailey, W. M. Cardwell, in 1902, assumed the office and served until 1914, when Frank R. Wight took over. Wight worked until 1926, when Rolla Tipton succeeded him. Tipton died within a year, however, and the office was temporarily filled by H. A. Campbell until an election could be held. In 1928, Marian A. Harbison won that election, and served twelve years until the election of Ann Tipton Howser in 1940. Mrs. Howser, who in 1952 became Mrs. Trimble, performed yeoman-like service for the court until 1988, for a total, mirabile dictu, of forty-eight years. The present Circuit Court Clerk, Kathy Howser Nichols, began her clerkship in 1988.

COUNTY COURT CLERKS

The present-day qualifications for County Court Clerk are the same as those mentioned above for Circuit Court Clerk, with respect to age, citizenship, residence, and the certification of competency requirement executed by a judge. But, County Court Clerks are not required to take an AOC examination. However, pursuant to Section 103 of the Constitution, noting that the General Assembly is authorized to require that a County Court Clerk give a bond before taking office, guaranteeing faithful performance of the designated duties, they must post a performance bond.

The Constitution of 1850 made the office of County Court Clerk elective. Before 1850, because the position could be very lucrative, especially in prosperous counties, appointments to the office were often bought and sold, leading to instances of corruption. In 1992, the omnibus executive reform and election schedule amendment provided that at the regular elections of 1998, and every four years thereafter, all county officers would be chosen, including the office of County Court Clerk. The four-year term commences on the first Monday in January after the election.

The office of County Clerk, today, has three primary duties:

1) To serve as filing officer for all land records, deeds, mortgages, liens, and the many other related items in the county, such as the recording of probate documents,

2) To administer all motor vehicle titles and registrations, and the collection of taxes related thereto in each individual county, and

3) To serve as the Chair of the Board of Elections of the county, and as the filing officer for the elections.

In addition to these principal duties, the Clerk's office has, over the years, been given many other miscellaneous duties including the receipt of all delinquent property taxes and the issuance of marriage licenses; the administration of various other licenses- notary public commissions, so-called road house and alcohol licenses, transient merchant and going-out-of-business licenses, veterinary licenses and the like. In addition, in some smaller counties the County Clerk is also the Clerk of the Fiscal Court.

The list, and dates of office, of Shelby County Clerks are as follows:

William Shannon	1792-93	Ernest Tyler	1906-08
James Craig	1793-1816	Luther Black	1908-18
John Newland	1816-18	Ezra Ford	1918-26
James S. Whitaker	1818-51	James C. Ray	1926-33
Hector A. Chinn	1851-58	Lucy L. Ford	1933-41
John T. Ballard	1858-70	Charlton P. Nash	1941-68
John F. Davis	1870-82	Ruth Vawter	1969-77
Andrew J. Stephens	1882-90	Sue Carole Perry	1978 to date
E. J. Doss	1890 - 1906		

COMMONWEALTH ATTORNEYS

By Ted Igleheart

From 1792 until 1798, the duties now performed by Commonwealth Attorneys were exercised by the Kentucky Attorney General. In 1799, legislation provided that an attorney for the Commonwealth could be appointed by the respective courts having jurisdiction as needed. It was not until 1813 that statutory provision was made for appointment to the office by the Governor, with the advice and consent of the Senate, in each judicial district. Then, the Constitution of 1850 made the office elective by the voters. The duties of the Commonwealth Attorney mainly involve presentation of evidence of felonies to the Grand Jury, then prosecution of those indicted before the Circuit Courts in the judicial district, now comprised of Shelby, Spencer and Anderson Counties.

John Logan is believed to be the first Commonwealth Attorney in the county, having been appointed by the Circuit Court for a specific prosecution in 1810. The records in the County Clerk's office do not reveal an elected Commonwealth Attorney until 1904, since there are no County Election records available for the 1800s. Charles H. Sanford was elected in 1904 and served until 1922; H. B. Kinsolving was elected in 1922 and served until 1928; Charles H. Sanford, elected again in 1928, served until 1929; H. B. Kinsolving, elected again in 1929, served until 1946; James F. Thomas of Henry County, elected in 1946, served until 1964; Lucien L. Kinsolving elected in 1964, served until 1982; Ted L. Igleheart elected in 1982, served until 1994; Marquita Shelburne was elected in 1994, becoming the first woman Commonwealth Attorney in the state, and served until 1996, when she resigned under indictment for thefts and tampering with Grand Jury evidence. She pleaded guilty and received a sentence of ten years in the penitentiary. Fielding E. Ballard, III, was appointed by the Governor in 1996 to the vacancy, later being elected to the balance of the regular term, and now serves a regular term.

COUNTY ATTORNEYS

By Ted Igleheart

The Kentucky Constitutions of 1792 and 1799 made no mention of the office of County Attorney. The public prosecutor was the Commonwealth Attorney, who was appointed by the respective courts when the need arose. In 1829, however, the General Assembly provided for a County Attorney to be appointed annually by the County Court to attend to the courts of the county. The appointive method was used until the Constitution of 1850 provided for the office to be elective for a term of four years. The duties of the County Attorney included advising county officials, attending all county cases, investigating claims against the county, and prosecuting all charges of misdemeanors and charges of felonies in an examining trial. He was also required to enforce the laws governing tavern keepers and the collection of taxes.

Every County Court Order until 1850 would have to be examined to learn who the County Attorneys were. And, to make the task more difficult, there are no election records in the County Clerk's office until 1900. However, perusing the County Court records reveals that James Blair was the first appointed County Attorney. James W. Whitaker was serving in 1816, Samuel Tevis in 1817, and C. J. Hinkle 1870. Charles C. Marshall was elected in 1902 and served until 1910; George L. Pickett elected in 1910 served until 1914; E. H. Davis, elected in 1914, served until 1922: C. G. Barrickman, elected in 1922, served until 1926; Robert F. Matthews, elected in 1926, served until 1934; Coleman W. Wright, elected in 1934, served until 1941; William H. Hays was elected in 1941, and served until 1970; Ted L. Igleheart was elected in 1970 and served until 1978; James Hite Hays, elected in 1978, served until 1999. Charles R. Hickman was elected in 1998.

COUNTY JUDGES, COUNTY JUDGE/EXECUTIVES, AND DISTRICT JUDGES

By Kevin Collins and Ted Igleheart

COUNTY JUDGES

From 1792 until 1852, the County Court was composed of Justices of the Peace, with a Presiding Justice appointed by the Governor upon the recommendation of the Representative and Senator from that district. The Kentucky Constitution of 1792 in Chapter XXXV, established the County Court system and stated that County Judges "shall be conservators of the peace, within their respective Counties, and shall have cognizance of all causes of less value than five pounds current money, or one thousand pounds of tobacco."

The act further stated that all judgments rendered "when the amount thereof shall not exceed Fifty shillings or Five hundred pounds of Tobacco, shall be final." Judgments in excess of this amount could be appealed to the next Court of Quarter Sessions to be held for the County wherein the judgment was rendered." In Shelby County the Court of Quarter Sessions was held, as required by law, in the months of February, April, June, and September.

The law required that County Court be held monthly. Its jurisdiction covered, among other things, "all cases respecting wills, letters of administration, mills, roads, the appointment of Guardians and settling of their accounts and the admitting of deeds

Courtesy of William Matthews.

County Judge George L. Willis, Jr. is seated second from the right in this undated photograph. The other gentlemen are not identified.

and other writings to record." In addition, the Kentucky Constitution of 1799 in Chapter X, added to the tasks of the County Courts the duty, whenever necessary "to appoint inspectors, collectors, and their deputies; surveyors of the high ways, constables, and county jailors." It would be accurate to say, then, that the County Court generally performed most of the local civic business of its county. County Court was the nucleus of local government. Among its concerns, in addition to the aforementioned, were the appointment of most other offices of the county, the levying of local taxes, the regulation of local taverns, and providing for the poor.

The third state Constitution, of 1850, provided for the direct election of judges (as indeed, most municipal offices) "by the qualified voters in each county, for the term of four years." It set the following eligibility standards for County Judges—a citizen of the United States, over twenty-one years old, and a resident in the county of election at least one year to the day prior to election.

The final state Constitution of 1891 required that County Judges of quarterly courts and justices of the peace be at least thirty-five years old, but did not require them to be lawyers.

The duly-elected County Court Judge had a myriad of functions. He constituted the probate court (wills) and the quarterly court (which had jurisdiction over minor civil and criminal matters). He was also the presiding member of the court of claims, which conducted the financial and governmental business of the county.

COUNTY JUDGE-EXECUTIVE

The passage in 1975 of the Judicial Amendment to the state Constitution stripped the County Court Judge of judicial functions. The title of county judge was changed to county judge-executive, and the office became responsible, as it is today, for presiding over fiscal court (the former court of claims). The powers and duties (Ky. Revised Statutes 67.710) of the office are complex and imposing, and encompass the responsibilities for the proper administration of the affairs of the county. Today, a county judge-executive is required by law to give a bond guaranteeing the faithful performance of his designated duties before he or she takes office.

DISTRICT JUDGE

By adopting in 1975 the Judicial Amendment to the Constitution, the voters in Kentucky consolidated and unified their judicial system. Among the beneficent results was that the confusing system of trial courts of limited jurisdiction was consolidated into a single tribunal, the District Court. District Courts have limited jurisdiction over felony preliminary hearings; mental inquest warrants; probate; and misdemeanors, including traffic violations, juvenile matters, and civil cases involving disputes of less than $4,000 value. District Court also has a small claims division, which handles disputes, more informally and without a jury, involving money or property valued at $1,500 or less.

Jury trials are held in District Court. Juries are composed of six members, and a five-sixths majority is needed in civil cases to reach a verdict. District Courts in Kentucky annually render final judgments in more that a half-million cases, making it the busiest court in the state judicial system.

District Court Judges are elected for four-year terms. To be eligible, a candidate must be a citizen of the United States, licensed to practice law in the courts of this commonwealth, have been an attorney for at least two years, "and have been a resident of this Commonwealth and of the district from which he is elected for two years next preceding his taking office."

SHELBY COUNTY JUDGES

Robert Doak	1852-56	Edward T. Pollard	1918-26
Joseph P. Foree	1856-60	George L. Willis Jr.	1926-33
James L. Caldwell	1860-70	Harry F. Walters	1933-40
Erasmus Frazier	1870-78	Coleman Wright	1941-52
Joseph P Foree	1878-88	(W. R. Reasor interim term)	
J. W. Crawford	1888-91	Ralph Mitchell	1953-64
W. H. Tipton	1891-1901	Paul T. Ratcliffe	1965-73
Edwin H. Davis	1901-10	Fred W. Bond	1974-77
Ralph W. Gilbert	1910-18		

SHELBY COUNTY JUDGE/EXECUTIVES

Sammy Wood	1978-81
Bobby Stratton	1982-02
Robert Rothenberger	2003-

DISTRICT JUDGES

District #1: Fred W. Bond 1978-98
          Linda Armstrong 1999 to date

District #2: Ollie J. Bowen 1982-86
          William F. Stewart 1986-92
          Michael J. Harrod 1992 to date

SHELBY COUNTY COURTHOUSES

By Charles T. Long

T he first county court was composed of Thomas Shannon, Joseph Winlock, Daniel McClelland and Abraham Owen who were appointed justices of the peace for Shelby County by Governor Isaac Shelby in the summer of 1792. County courts in Kentucky had a wide range of judicial and administrative duties that included probating wills and administrating estates, providing for the support of orphans and the indigent, appointing guardians, approving apprentices, establishing and setting rates for taverns, overseeing the laying out and maintenance of roads and bridges, and providing for public buildings such as courthouses and jails. They also approved the siting of milldams, admitted deeds and other documents to record, administered the emancipation of slaves, and until 1819 tried felony cases involving slaves. County courts appointed officials of the county including clerks, jailers, constables, the county attorney, surveyor, and coroner, and played an important role in the Governor's appointment of the sheriff.. They appointed tax commissioners whose duty was to list taxpayers and assess property in the county for the purpose of collecting state taxes. Most importantly, the county courts set the county levy each year from which county expenses were paid. This tax was collected from all tithable inhabitants of the county—a category that consisted of all males (free and slave) sixteen years of age or older and all female slaves sixteen years of age or older, living in the county.

When the court met for the first time on October 15, 1792, at the home of Brackett Owen, it agreed to locate the town of Shelbyville on land owned by William Shannon in exchange for his offer to donate an acre of ground to the county for public use. When the town was platted the acre was divided into four "squares" formed by the intersection of what is now Fifth Street and Main Street with each square measuring ninety nine feet by one hundred twelve feet. At its meeting in January 1793, the court ordered that a courthouse be built on the northwest corner of the public grounds and on the 15th of that month a contract in the amount of 15 pounds was let to William Shannon for its construction. The court directed "That it be a log house, twenty by sixteen feet, with a cabin roof, one door in the end next the street; a plank floor below, and joists to be either sawed or hewed, and the loft to be laid over with loose planks. A seat for the judges, a place for the jury and a bar made in the way they are usually made but plain." There was to be a window on each side of the bar, each with a plain shutter, and the inside walls were to be hewed down.

At the same time he appointed members to the county court, Governor Shelby named Daniel Standiford the sheriff and Martin Daniel, Benjamin Roberts and Thomas I. Gwin justices of the court of quarter sessions. The court of quarter session, and later district and circuit courts, had jurisdiction in important civil cases and most criminal cases. Both the county court and the court of quarter sessions sat at the courthouse in Shelbyville. In the early years the county court met for one and sometimes two days beginning on the second Monday of each month except during February, June, and September. Today the court meets on the second and fourth Tuesday of each month.

The single story log courthouse that was built in 1793 soon proved to be too small. It had about 250 sq. ft. of interior space and when court was in session there must have been only enough room for the justices with little space left over for clerks, attorneys, or juries. On May 18, 1796, the county court decided to construct a new courthouse on the same site as the original building. John Allen, Benjamin Logan, Adam Steele, Martin Daniel and Isham Talbot were appointed commissioners to oversee the work. The court first ordered that the ". . . courthouse be of brick, 40 x 36 feet from out to out, the lower story to be fourteen feet in height in the clear, and the upper one ten feet, with a sufficient number of windows and three doors, a square roof with a spire and neat pediment front, with "conveniences" becoming a courthouse and that all be done in a good and workmanlike manner." After changing the size of the building at its August term to 40 x 40 feet in the clear the court decided on October 18, 1796, to approve a revised plan submitted by James Hunter. It was further ordered the building be set back 25 feet from the north side of Main Street and that it border the west side of Fifth Street.

The contract was let to Josias Bullock and Winfield Bullock who agreed to do the work for eleven hundred and seventy six pounds (or about six thousand dollars) and to complete the building by October 1798. The best description of the second courthouse that remains is contained in the bond that the "undertakers" filed with the county clerk. "The said courthouse to be built thirty six by forty two feet in the clear, two windows on each side of the door in the front, with the addition of a steeple with a ball spire and weathercock in proportion. The house covered with poplar shingles (to be nailed on inch planks) at least three fourths of an inch at the butt. The foundation to be of stone till it rises to the water table. The foundation to be sunk at least two feet and one half from the surface and the foundation raised two feet above the surface of the earth with stone arranged in the front side and to be twelve feet from the lower floor to the upper floor. The upper story to be ten feet in the clear a pediment over the chief judge's seat, a pediment front door, a modillioned cornice. The windows of the lower story to have thirty five lights, the sash of walnut, the upper story windows twenty four light each. A common

Shelby County Public Library, Williams Studio photograph.

The Greek Revival courthouse built in 1844-45 on the site of an earlier structure at Fifth and Main Streets.

roof to be painted Spanish Brown with a pediment front and Bulls Eye. Each jury room to have a fire place, four funnels to appear through the roof, two at each end. The door and window frames to be made of oak or walnut, the lower floor to be made of tile or oak plank. The whole of the lower floor to be level except where the attorney's bar and jury's feet rest, which is to be elevated nine inches. The said house to be painted where necessary with blue and white, all which is to be done in a neat and workman like manner, and all seats that will be necessary."

During construction the court authorized the commissioners to make several changes. The height of the ceiling on the first floor was made fourteen feet instead of twelve, the second story was cut into three rooms, and a set of stairs built starting at the southwest corner of the building and winding "around the corner so as to end in the passage above." Eighty dollars were added to the contract to cover the additional work. The contractors were paid one half out of the levy of 1796 and one half out of the levy of 1797.

Despite the detailed description in the bond executed by the contractors, it is not clear what material was used in the walls of the building. Although brick was the preference of the court in May 1796, when the project was first proposed, there is no mention of it in the bond. This may be an omission on the part of the clerk copying the bond into the county records. From the architectural details provided, including symmetrical windows, modillioned cornice, pediment front door, roof with a gable front and a steeple, the building was constructed in the Georgian style, and the material most commonly used in this part of the country for Georgian style buildings was brick.

The first clerk of the Shelby County Court was James Craig. He served from the formation of the county in 1792 until his resignation due to ill health on October 16, 1815. For much of that time he did not use the courthouse as his office. County court records indicate that in 1805 a house was rented from Abraham Owen for $50 for the use of the county clerk as an office and in November of that year the court ordered a building erected on the public square for that purpose. However, in October 1806, the justices accepted the offer of the county clerk to give the county part of lot 69, at the south end of Sixth Street where he lived, on which to build the clerk's office. Moses Hall was the contractor and was paid about $500 to construct the 18 x 26 foot building. James Craig died in 1816 and the county sold the property in 1818. In November of that year the county court appointed William G. Boyd and Samuel Tevis commissioners for the purpose of letting and superintending the building of offices for both the Shelby circuit and county courts on the public square in front of what is now the Methodist Church. The clerk's offices remained there until a new courthouse was completed in 1845.

Two of the best references relating to the history of the county are the weekly columns of Ed. D. Shinnick in the *Shelby Record* between 1916 and 1918 and the *History of Shelby County, Kentucky* by George L. Willis published in 1929. Both of these sources refer to a third courthouse that was built according to Shinnick in 1811 and to Willis in 1814. Neither man is able to supply details of the building other than Willis' statement that it had a "hip roof and a belfry in the center." Shelby county court records indicate that in 1813 and in1814 commissioners were appointed to make repairs to the courthouse. Improvements included paving Main Street in front of the building and putting up a post and chain fence around the public grounds. At the November 1815 county court meeting a new group of commissioners, Jos. Simrall, Ben. F. Dupuy, Jon. Newland, John Smith, W. Bullock and Tho. Mitchell, were appointed. Apparently the need for repairs was urgent because the court at its January 1816 meeting ordered that if

The present Shelby County courthouse completed in 1914 and designed by the architectural firm of Joseph & Joseph of Louisville.

the commissioners decided that they needed more money to do the job "...in a proper manner the said Commissioners are authorized to appropriate any additional sum they may find necessary..." By the end of 1816 they had spent about $4,000 including furnishing a bell which was hung two years later.

Did all this work amount to building a new building? Maybe so, but nowhere does the record suggest anything more than extensive repairs. The county court minutes do not include any discussion by the justices of plans for a new building or of arrangements for tearing down the existing building or selling the old material, all of which occurred when other courthouses were built. When the work is mentioned it is referred to as "repairs". There is evidence that the building that was torn down in 1844 in order to clear the way for a new courthouse was made of brick.

The maintenance of public buildings and bridges was a constant concern to county courts. Every year commissioners were appointed to oversee repairs to the various buildings and money was appropriated from the county levy to pay for them. In 1841 the court decided that the building that housed the circuit and count clerks was not safe and appointed commissioners to rent new office space. Two years later the cost of constructing a new building for the clerks was investigated but it was decided that a new building was too expensive.

Then in December of 1843 the court received a petition from the judge and jurors of the Shelby Circuit Court relating to the condition of the courthouse and other public buildings. Commissioners were appointed to investigate and at the February 1844 term it was decided "...that a courthouse and office shall be built and erected upon the plan now presented to the court..." Samuel W. Moore, G. W. Johnston, Win. Kinkade, Robt. T. Robb and William S. Helm were appointed commissioners to superintend the work. The committee moved quickly and by April of that year a contract was let, the old courthouse removed, and temporary quarters found for the Circuit and county courts. The contractor or "undertaker" of the job was Thomas B. Caldwell, the owner of a saw mill in the county, who was paid about $9,500 for the work Prior to the June 1844 term of court, James I. Whitaker, the County Clerk, inserted the following note in the minutes, "The Northeast Corner Stone of the new Courthouse laid the 4th day of June 1844, 62 years after Crawford's defeat." The official laying of the corner stone was held on June 11th in ceremonies presided over by Henry Wingate, Grand Master of Solomon Lodge No. 5.

One year later the building was far enough along for the county court to began meeting there but it was probably not finished until sometime late in 1845. Photographs of the courthouse show a three story rectangular brick building with a flat roof and square cupola topped by a clock turret. There is a flat portico two stories high, supported by four unfluted columns, which extends across a part of the facade. It was constructed in the Greek Revival style and exhibits all of the "mass" of that architectural form but little of its classical detail or sense of proportion. It was a plain utilitarian structure that probably reflected the common sense, no frills, nature of the men who commissioned its construction.

This courthouse served Shelby county for 68 years until it was torn down and replaced by the present building. It was replaced because it was outdated and lacked the conveniences of a modern building such as central heating, plumbing, and electricity. In looking over the plans for the new court house a grand jury in 1913 commended "that the county will have a building suitable for the county's wealth and progress."

The County Judge during the design and construction of the new courthouse was Ralph W. Gilbert. The plans were drawn by the firm of Joseph & Joseph of Louisville with Alfred S. Joseph serving as the supervising architect. By the end of February 1913, the old building was vacated and a contract for $1,200.00 had been let to John and Buck Fawkes to tear it down. The sound brick and larger timbers were sold by the county and the money used to help pay for the new courthouse. County officials obtained temporary quarters in buildings around town, except for the county and circuit clerks. They and their records were housed in two steel buildings which the county purchased and erected on that part of the public grounds known today as Veterans park.

On March 15, 1913, the bids for the new building were opened and the contract for the general construction was let to Falls City Construction Company of Louisville for $87,964,00. Kuhn & Company of Shelbyville received the heating contract for $3,212.00 and the plumbing contract of $1,724.00. The electric contract in the amount of $1,949.00 was awarded to the Marine Electric Company of Louisville. Work proceeded and on June 11, 1913, the corner stone was laid on the northeast corner of the new building. The date chosen was the same as the corner stone of the previous courthouse and once again Solomon Lodge No. 5 was in charge of the Masonic ceremony. The articles placed inside the stone included all the contents removed from the corner stone of the 1845 courthouse along with recent newspapers, lists of various city, county, and school officials, coins, financial statements, and pictures of Shelbyville street scenes.

The building was completed by July 1914 at a cost of $120,000.00, including all interior finishes, fixtures, and furniture. Work on the courthouse also involved moving the public fountain from the center of Main Street to the southeast public square where it remains today. The cost was paid out of two bond issues totaling $100,000, a special tax levy, and the sale of brick and timber salvaged from the old courthouse. When it was finished the Shelby County courthouse was one of the finest public buildings in the state. It was designed in the Beaux Arts Classicism style of architecture developed by the School of Fine Arts in Paris, France and popular in the United States between 1895 and 1920. This style is characterized by smooth, light colored walls, elaborate decorative moldings on walls and above windows and doors and, paired columns. There has been no other public or private building constructed in the county before or since that matches it in grandeur and beauty.

When it was first built the courthouse was large enough for all county and court activities with space left over. Rooms in the basement were rented to attorneys and others to help defray the expense of operating the building. In due course, with the growth of county government and the reorganization of the court system in 1974, all the space in the building became taken up by public functions. In 1992 the Fiscal Court purchased a building at 501 Washington Street and converted it into an annex for the county clerk and the county property valuation administrator.

SHERIFFS

By Ted Igleheart

The Kentucky Constitution of 1792 provided for the election of a sheriff for a term of three years. In 1799 the Constitution provided for the Governor to appoint the sheriff recommended by the County Court for a term of two years from one of a county's Justices of the Peace. In 1850, the new Constitution made the office elective again for a term of two years and a sheriff could succeed himself one time. The Constitution of 1891 provided for an elective term of two years in 1892, three years in 1894 and four years in 1897 and thereafter. The sheriff could not succeed himself. Under the most recent constitutional amendment, the sheriff can succeed himself.

The duties of a sheriff are primarily as a peace officer and legal process server, but the office has attracted many candidates traditionally because of the lucrative commissions for serving as a collector of state, county, and district taxes. He must also serve as bailiff in each of the courts in session.

The records of the County Clerk's office are missing for much of the 1800s, but the County Court Order Book reveals the first sheriff serving in 1804 to be William Johnson. Isaac Ellis Jr. was serving in 1805, Robert Jeffries in 1807, William McClure in 1809, and Jacob Castleman in 1810. H. C. Malone was elected in 1870 and served until 1874; George W. Wells served 1874 to 1878; D. T. Long 1878 to 1882; G. W. Wells 1882 to 1886; H. G. Cardwell 1886 to 1890; A. C. Long 1890 to 1894; H. F. Bohann 1894 to 1898; H. A. Campbell 1898 to 1902; R. A. Briggs 1902 to 1910; Ben Perkins 1910 to 1914; Jack L. Smith 1914 to 1918; Lewis D. Roberts 1918 to 1922; N. A. Campbell 1922 to 1926; John D. Buckner 1926 to 1930; George B. Perkins n 1930 to 1934; Forest Barnes Jr. 1934 to 1938; Alex Green 1938 to 1942; Jesse Swindler 1942 to 1946; Hubert Gordon 1946 to 1950; A. E. Brooks 1950 to 1954; Sammy Wood 1954 to 1958; Thornton Johnson 1958 to 1962; William Stone Proctor 1962 until resigning in 1965 when his wife, Katherine, was appointed to fill out the term; Garnett Shelburne 1966 to 1970; J. B. Cook 1970 to 1974; Sammy Wood 1974 to 1978; Stanley Greenwell 1978 to 1982; Tom Lincoln 1982 to 1984; Fred Ruble 1984 to 1986 to complete Lincoln's term and 1986 to 1990; Harold Tingle 1990, succeeding himself in 1994 and 1998, and was serving until 2002 when Mike Armstrong was elected.

SHELBY COUNTY JAILS

By Charles T. Long

Since the formation of Shelby County there have been seven jails constructed here by county officials. For information on the first two jails we are indebted to Ed. D. Shinnick whose columns in the *Shelby Record* between 1916 and 1918 give a detailed description of the buildings taken from the first County Court Order Book—a record that has since disappeared from the County Clerk's office.

According to Shinnick, the county court at its first term in October of 1792 ordered that a jail be built on a portion of the public grounds donated to the county by William Shannon. Joseph Winlock and Daniel McClelland were appointed commissioners to oversee the project. The jail was completed in December 1792 by Edward Ashby who was paid 93 pounds for his work.

This building, and the one that followed, was constructed on the southeast public square where the Shelbyville fountain is now located. The first jail was a fifteen foot square stone building with a single door and two windows. The walls were three feet thick leaving just 81 square feet of interior space for the prisoners. In August 1797 the court ordered extensive structural repairs to the jail, paying William Butler three pounds for labor and Alexander Reed four pounds, fifteen shillings, and sixpence for the material used.

In November 1799 the county court ordered a larger jail built and Isaac Ellis, Arthur McGaughey, and Adam Steele were appointed to award a contract and superintend its construction. James Logan was selected as the contractor and agreed to do the work for 451 pounds and 17 shillings. The second jail was a square two story building with a stone foundation. The walls were made of two layers of logs, each 25 feet long and one foot square, separated by a one foot space which itself was filled cross wise with short logs. The logs were surrounded on the outside by a nine inch brick wall and the whole structure covered by a wood shingled roof. Access to the jail was by a set of steps that led up from the outside to the second floor and then through a trap door to the room below. Readers interested in a detailed description of the first two jails should consult Ed. D. Shinnick *Some Old Time History of Shelbyville and Shelby County* published by the Shelby County Public Library in 1974.

The location of the jail on the public square in the heart of town, surrounded by private residences and business houses, was not a happy choice. In 1817, the citizens of Shelbyville asked that the jail be removed and rebuilt in another place but the county court took no action. The jail was still there in 1823 when Jefferson King was hanged for murder, the sheriff receiving $5.21 from the court for arranging the execution. Around 1826 the townspeople succeeded in getting the jail dismantled and moved. In November of that year the county court appropriated $400 and directed commissioners Mark Hardin, Joseph Simnall, Charles Mitchell, George Bergan, and Samuel Tevis "to remove the jail in a good and workman like manner without further call upon or responsibility of this court." A year later Robert Logan was paid $120 more for moving the jail.

The new site for the county jail was on the south side of Henry Clay Street between Fourth and Fifth Streets on the lot now occupied by the Bethel AME Church. On the plat of the town this is the east side

Shelby County Public Library.

The fourth county jail was the one-story stone building in this photograph to the right of the brick jailer's house. The stone structure was built in 1849. In 1863 the brick second story of the jail and the jailer's house were completed. The jail was demolished when the 1891 stone jail was constructed on the corner of Washington Street, but the jailer's house still stands.

of lot No. 55. It was at this jail on April 28, 1843, that James McLaughlin killed himself on the day he was to be hanged for the murder of William Patton. Almost four years later, on the night of January 27, 1847, the old log jail was destroyed by fire.

The county court, having just completed a new courthouse, decided to move the jail to the rear of the new building and in August 1847 purchased from William Cardwell and Martin McHenry their individual interests in Lot 25 for $1,350. The court appointed J. H. Magruder, Robert Doak, and Robert T. Robb commissioners to oversee the construction of the county's fourth jail. The contract was let to Edward Sain and he appears from the records to have been paid about $2,410 for the job. The building was a single story structure 34 x 23 feet constructed of stone slabs at least four and one-half feet long and eight inches thick. It was built on the east side of the lot close to the corner of Fifth and Washington Streets. The new gaol was a dark, damp, and unhealthy place but it was fire-proof. It was completed and accepted by the court in May 1849.

Jailhouse number five was a second story addition to the stone jail completed in 1849. On June 7, 1862, the county court ordered that Thomas C. McGrath, J. H. Magruder, and H. Frazier be appointed "...the Building Committee for Shelby County in the constructing and building (of) a brick and iron jail and brick Jailer's house attached thereto according to the plan and specifications adopted by this court marked No. 1 ...." A month later the court changed the specifications so that the hall, the water tanks, and walls of the jail would be all of iron. By May 1863 the construction of both the jail and Jailer's residence was complete and the building committee was discharged with the payment of $100 each. Not much is known about the builders. It appears from the court records that the jail and residence was constructed by Watts & Wells. They were paid about $5,640 for the work, $4,000 out of the county levy for 1862 and the balance out of the levy for 1863. The jailer's house, built in the Italiante style, is still standing and is the oldest public building in Shelby County.

The new jail was fire-proof but it was certainly not escape proof. It had been built a little more than three years when Harry Thompson, an accomplice of Capt. Ed Terrell in a number of crimes during and after the Civil War, escaped through the new brick addition. Others followed over the years including, on the night of January 21, 1891, a couple of safe-blowers named Regan and Beaver and a man named Dalton who was in jail for stealing clothing. They succeeded in breaking out by opening their cell door with a piece of wire. Once in the corridor the prisoners used a corset stay notched like a file to remove some of the iron sheeting and make a hole in the wall.

The safety and unsightliness of the old building, along with the obvious difficulty of securing prisoners, convinced county magistrates to build a new jail. At the May 1891 term of court a plan to construct a stone jail was agreed to and a committee composed of County Judge A. P. Carrithers, W. H. Tipton, and A. V. Weakley appointed to let the contract and supervise the work. The builder was the McDonald Bros. Jail Building Co. of Louisville and the amount of the contract $9,000 plus the material in the old jail. To pay for the building the court ordered two tax levies, the first in 1891 for six and one-half cents on every $100 of taxable property and another in 1892 for six cents.

The new jail was constructed of rusticated stone blocks, each at least three feet in length and ten inches thick. It is three stories high with a castellated parapet, a turret, and two towers rising above the roof. As originally built each floor contained four cells, a hall, and a small vestibule with the vestibule on the different levels being connected by stone stairs. Each cell had about 50 square feet of floor space and contained four canvas bunks attached by lather straps to hooks in the walls. There was a dry pipe in each cell for sanitation and a small window for light and ventilation. The capacity of the building was 48 prisoners all of whom were cared for by a single jailer and his wife. In 1892, after the old brick jail was torn down, a porch was built on the north side of the jailer's house where the two buildings connected.

For 105 years this imposing medieval style building served as the Shelby County jail and today still dominates the corner of Fifth and Washington Streets. There have been escapes from the building and on two occasions, in 1901 and again in 1911, mobs broke into the jail and lynched black prisoners. Readers interested in details of these lynchings can consult George C. Wright *Racial Violence in Kentucky 1865-1940* (1990).

On the evening of Tuesday February 12, 1957, as he was carrying a bucket of coal into the cell

The rusticated stone jail, built in 1891, is shown under construction in October of that year. It was designed and built by the McDonald Bros. Jail Building Co. of Louisville. It is still standing on the corner of Fifth and Washington Streets, although now used for emergency dispatch.

Shelby County Public Library, Williams Studio photograph, from Peggy and Alwyn Miller.

area, Jailer Luther W. Hammond was attacked and beaten by two prisoners who escaped after throwing him down the stone stairs between the first and second levels. Hammond had just unlocked the vestibule door when George Baker and William Thomas Lainhart, both in jail on forgery charges, attacked him. They had gotten out of the cage in the cell area by using a coal poker to pry open the lock and were waiting by the door. Using the door's heavy padlock, Baker struck the 71 year old Hammond in the head fracturing his skull. The other prisoners alerted a passer-by and the police were notified. Patrolman Hubert Gordon arrived within five minutes of the escape and took the jailer to the hospital. Gordon was able to get a brief description of what happened before Hammond lost consciousness. He never recovered and died the following Monday.

Meanwhile Baker and Lainhart fled down Jail Hill and caught a ride to Eminence. They spent the remainder of the night and the next day walking to Bagdad. On Wednesday evening they entered Clarence Harrod's poolroom to get some food but fled when the owner got suspicious. The police were called and began a search and early the next day State Trooper Morgan Elkins and Deputy Sheriff Stallard "Boots" Smith captured the pair outside a deserted house between Bagdad and Hatton. They had been free barely 36 hours. Three months later George W. Baker was found guilty of murder and sentenced to life imprisonment. William Thomas Lainhart, alias Roy Thomas Cook, received a ten year sentence for forgery. Mrs. Luther Hammond was appointed jailer by the Fiscal Court to fill out her husband's term.

As a result of this tragic affair the jail came in for justified criticism. Bennet Roach editorialized in the *Shelby News* that "something will have to be done about our antiquated, badly neglected county jail. It is insecure and obsolete, and will have to be brought up to date somehow, or replaced with a new one." The jail did have its flaws. A critical one was that the design allowed very little separation between jailed and jailer so that in the routine of caring for prisoners the jailer was forced to mingle with the inmates. There was also not enough staff to control violent prisoners or discourage escapes.

Twenty-six years later the jail's outdated design and lack of professional staff would lead to another killing. On the night of Monday April 11, 1983, Deputy County Jailer Charles Wentworth was shot to death by inmate Alfred Hawks using a gun that had been smuggled into the jail by Tamela Bolin and Lesia Bowling when they visited Hawks the week before. Hawks was in jail charged with burglary, receiving stolen property, and trafficking in marijuana. It was Wentworth's third day on the job as a deputy county jailer and he was in the jail alone. Hawks persuaded Wentworth to let him out of his cell to make a telephone call and then shot him once in the chest with a .25-caliber pistol. Hawks then ran out the front door to a waiting car. A jail trustee heard the shot, found Wentworth, and called police. Hawks and Bolin were arrested some three hours later at his mother's home in Muldraugh, Kentucky, and Bowling was arrested at her parents' home on Rockbridge Road early Tuesday morning. On June 1, 1983, Alfred Hawks entered a plea of guilty to capital murder and escape and was sentenced to life imprisonment on the murder charge and 10 years for escape. Tammy Bolin and Lesia Bowling both pled guilty to facilitation to murder, facilitation to escape, and promoting contraband. Bolin received twenty years and Bowling fifteen years.

Once again questions were raised about jail procedures and security. In its investigation of the shooting the Shelby County grand jury found "serious shortcomings in facilities management and operating policies" and criticized the jailer and the staff for lax security. The building had no visitation room so anyone who wanted to talk to an inmate during visiting hours was allowed to go up to the cell and speak through the bars. Female visitors were not searched although pat-down searches were made of male visitors. It was impossible for the lone jailer or deputy on duty to observe what was going on in all areas of the jail and as a consequence it was easy to pass contraband to the prisoners. Staffing remained a problem. Jailer Tom Van Natta was first elected in 1973 and re-elected several times by wide margins. He and his wife Edith operated the jail pretty much alone and lived in the jailer's residence next door. They moved out shortly before the Wentworth shooting. At the same time a new state law required that the jailer or a deputy be awake and on duty 24 hours a day. This resulted in the county hiring several deputy jailers but with no one occupying the jailer's residence there was, during much of the day, still only one man on duty in the building. The new deputies were hurriedly trained and paid the minimum wage of $3.35 per hour.

The death of Charles Wentworth and stricter jail standards adopted by the state forced the Fiscal Court to make physical changes to the jail. Work was begun immediately on installing telephone jacks in each cell, providing a small visitation area where visitors and prisoners could be kept separated, and building an exterior fire escape on the east side of the building. County Judge Bobby Stratton added $30,000 to the jail budget to cover these and other improvements and pledged more if it was needed.

It proved easier to modify the building than to keep the prisoners inside. Before 1983 ended, a series of disasters turned the jail into an embarrassment to county government and an object of derision by local citizens. On June 9 a jail trustee escaped but was recaptured at his home several hours later. Tom Van Natta and his wife, citing health reasons, resigned as Jailer and matron on August 15. Deputy jailer Fred Gee was appointed Jailer partly because of his seniority. He had been hired the previous March and had worked at the jail longer than any of the other deputies.

Then on Sunday August 28, in the most serious escape in the history of Shelby county, five men broke out of the jail. Fred Gee was in the building alone when a prisoner in one of the downstairs cells asked for an aspirin and a new trash bag. When he opened the cell door to exchange bags, Charles Whitten stepped out into the hall with the full trash bag and blocked Gee's path. Another prisoner, Jackie Jordan, threatened the jailer with a brick he had dug out of the wall, took his keys, and forced him into the cell. Then along with two of their cell mates, Carl Dupin and Mark Quire, they went upstairs and released Garland Tipton. All five were in jail on serious felony charges and their escape resulted in a huge manhunt in Shelby and surrounding counties.

On the following Saturday state police trooper Stewart Brumfield and Sgt. Richard Otto, acting on a telephone tip, picked up Dupin and Quire in the woods behind the home of Betty J. McKinney in the Bald Knob area of Franklin County. McKinney's 17 year old daughter was a girlfriend of Mark Quire and both the daughter and mother were charged with hindering prosecution. The four surviving prisoners were quickly indicted by the Shelby County grand jury on numerous felony charges including first degree escape.

The County Judge blamed the jail break on a momentary lapse in procedure by Fred Gee when he did not wait until another deputy was present before he opened the cell door. Gee blamed the Fiscal Court for not hiring more deputy jailers. Police officers began calling the jail "Freedom Hall East." Things got worse in October when two deputy jailers were arrested and suspended for having sex with female inmates.

About midnight on Sunday November 27th three more inmates broke out of the jail after assaulting a deputy jailer. Rodney Stone and Jerry Walker were in jail awaiting transfer to state prison to begin serving sentences for armed robbery. David Rose was awaiting trial on felony theft and persistent felony offender charges. Stone and Walker were in a cell together on the third floor when they called down to deputy jailer Mike Rackley that they wanted him to take a television out of their cell and move it to another room. Rackley, who had been working at the jail for about a month and was alone at the time, went up to tell Stone and Walker that he would not open the door. One of the men reached through the bars, grabbed Rackley's arm, and forced him to the floor. They took his keys and let themselves out. Rackley fought with the inmates but they pushed him into the cell and locked the door. Walker and Stone then went down to the second floor and let David Rose out.

Deputy jailer Rackley alerted police by setting off the cell's smoke alarm which was wired to the fire department. The three fugitives did not get far. Deputy Sheriff Tommy Sampson and Shelbyville police, with the aid of a bloodhound, found them about twelve hours later hiding in the crawl space of a house at 61 Juniper Dr. in Shelbyville. All were charged with first degree escape, a charge now becoming routine in Shelby County.

The Sentinel-News, in an editorial reminiscent of the one in *The Shelby News* twenty six years earlier, stated that "...if it were possible we'd like to get rid of the jail and its problems completely. Thousands of dollars have been poured into that ancient facility with little positive result." In recommending that Shelby consider contracting with another county to house prisoners or join in erecting a regional jail, *The Sentinel-News* concluded by saying "...we hope Fiscal Court and Judge Stratton will seriously consider getting us out of the jail business and out of the jailbreak limelight. Enough is enough." Conditions, however, began to improve in December of 1983 when the building passed a state inspection and the attention of the grand jury and the Fiscal Court turned to upgrading jail operations by adopting a policy and procedures manual.

Having rejected the idea of going out of the jail business, the Fiscal Court in 1987, in a controversial move, authorized the renovation and expansion of the jail rather than building a new one. The plan called for housing most prisoners on one floor, adding more space, and improving security with electric doors and television monitors. Architect Quintin Biagi designed the revisions and Joe James Construction Co. received the contract which amounted to $100,000. Three years later an outdoor recreation area was added by Long Construction Co. for slightly over $20,500.

Jailer Fred Gee lost his bid to succeed himself when William B. Casey won the Democrat primary in 1984. He was followed in turn by Jack Samples, Harold Sutton, and Jack C. Lewis. It was during Lewis' term (1991-97) that the jail once again came in for public scrutiny. The structure was often full to over flowing. Although originally designed to hold 48 prisoners, tougher state standards for housing inmates reduced its capacity to 26 beds. Despite this it was not unusual on week-ends to have 40 or more prisoners in the building. Along with county jails all over Kentucky, the Shelby county jail was not able to meet state and federal physical requirements such as width of doors and ceiling heights. In 1993 the Fiscal Court commissioned a study to review all its options for housing prisoners. That study concluded that it was too costly to renovate the old jail and recommended that a new jail be built on a new site.

In January 1996 the court purchased a 14 acre site on Snow Hill just north of Clear Creek for

$160,000 and in April accepted the plans for a new jail submitted by Paul Brauckmann of Architecture Plus, Inc. The new facility cost $2.8 million and construction was supervised by David Codell and the Fiscal Court jail committee. The new building has a total capacity of 124 beds including eight beds for females and four 24-48 hour holding cells for juveniles. There is a wing containing 40 beds for class-D felons, a category of state prisoner that is allowed to be housed in county jails and for which they receive reimbursement. Devices such as door locks operated from a central control room, video monitors, the physical separation of inmates and visitors, and secure prisoner receiving and booking areas were incorporated into the design. Most importantly, the new jail has a trained staff of thirty full and part time employees including the Jailer Bobby Waits and Administrator Ralph Evitts.

The new jail began operation in September 1997, but before the old jail closed it produced one last embarrassment for the county. In May of that year a Shelby County grand jury indicted two former deputy jailers, Dennis Perry and Ted Moffett, on several charges, the most serious of which was assisting Robert Aguon to escape from the jail three times—two in November 1996 and the third on December 5, 1996. On the last occasion Perry took Aguon on an unauthorized trip to Jefferson county in order for the inmate to get money to buy stereo equipment. Aguon escaped from the deputy and was not recaptured until the FBI picked him up in February 1997 in connection with a bank robbery.

In July Dennis Perry pled guilty to one count of complicity to escape, one count of complicity to tampering with physical evidence, and single counts of tampering with public records, promoting contraband and official misconduct. He received a total sentence of eight years and was placed on probation. Ted Moffett was tried on charges of complicity to escape and tampering with public records. He was convicted by a jury on the tampering charge and sentenced in April 2000 to a year in the penitentiary. Moffett has appealed Judge William Stewart's refusal to grant probation.

The grand jury that indicted Perry and Moffett also issued a report critical of the performance of Jailer Jack C. Lewis stating that he "...lacks sufficient administrative, management and organizational skills to deal with the employment situation of the jail and its staff." The report invited the Jailer to resign and recommended that the Fiscal Court employ a trained jail administrator to run the new facility that was then under construction. Lewis accepted responsibility for the troubles at the jail and resigned on May 9, 1997. Sheriff Harold Tingle and Chief Deputy Sheriff Mike Armstrong assumed the duties of Jailer until June when Fiscal Court appointed Bobby Waits to fill out Lewis' term.

When the new jail opened the old one was not removed. Although it appears somewhat of an oddity standing next to the more architecturally sophisticated court house, the people of Shelby county seem to take pleasure from its familiar, solid presence on Washington Street and the Fiscal Court has never seriously considered taking it down. In fact it is being put to new use. In the summer of 2001 part of the old jail was converted into space for the county-wide 911 dispatch system with the remainder being used for storage.

NOTED CRIMES AND TRIALS

By Ted Igleheart

The crime of murder has always produced the most interest when the subject of crime is discussed. From earliest history it has earned the most severe penalty. For centuries the penalty was beheading, often without trial, then hanging by the neck until dead, which was the commonly accepted penalty in the early history of Kentucky, and continued until supplanted by the electric chair in the early 1900s, and lethal injection later in the century.

Criminal trials, at least in western civilization, rivaled church services as great social occasions. Even minor offenses tried on court days in Kentucky would fill courtrooms with public spectators. Both prosecutors and defense lawyers used the forum to display their oratorical skills, and the best of them eventually ran for public office. Persons charged with crimes usually asked for a trial by jury, even in the most comparatively insignificant cases as well as serious crimes and capital offenses.

In over two hundred years, there have been few capital cases tried in Shelby County. In 1803, a "free negro" called Ned killed a Miss Betty Bean and threw her body down into a hog pen where it became mangled almost beyond recognition. The girl's father had ordered the man off his farm several days earlier, and Ned vowed he would get even for the "insult." The crime was clearly traced to Ned, who confessed after his arrest. It was told that he sold his body to some medical students while he awaited execution. Ned was hanged on a scaffold erected at the intersection of U.S. 60 East and Old Benson Pike. The students had the body flayed by a local tanner who made razor straps from the skin.

The second execution was of Jeff King, a white man convicted of the murder of a black in 1820. He was the son of a respected family west of town and known as the "handsomest and also the worst" young man in the county. He was hanged on a scaffold where the present fairground is located at the corner of U.S. 60 and the La Grange Road.

The third capital conviction occurred in 1843 when a Louisville businessman was tried for killing another man in Louisville. Such anger and outrage arose that the trial was moved from Jefferson County to Shelby. During the trial, McLaughin, the accused, became so enraged at the prosecutor, Nathaniel Wolfe, that he threw a heavy book at Wolfe, knocking him to the floor of the courtroom. Wolfe got up and gave the prisoner a thrashing before being pulled off. The jury took three days of deliberation before finding McLaughin guilty. He made persistent efforts to escape before execution and it was rumored that his influential friends from Louisville would attempt to free him. The militia was summoned to guard him day and night. While more than a hundred soldiers guarded the building, McLaughlin slit his throat to avoid the hanging. When the sheriff arrived to escort him to the scaffold, the prisoner was found nearly dead. Doctors sewed up the throat more than once and each time McLaughlin tore open the stitches until he bled to death.

The notorious guerrilla outlaw Capt. Ed Terrell was charged with the murder of a stock trader who had been reputed to carry large sums of cash. Terrill and a lieutenant decoyed the victim on Clear Creek, shot him, tied strings around his pants, loaded his clothes with stones, and tossed him in the creek, where the body was later found by a fisherman. Terrell was arrested but escaped from the old jail. Sometime later Terrell returned to shoot up the town and took possession of the old Armstrong Hotel. Town citizens were determined to apprehend the outlaw and his cohorts and demanded their surrender. Terrell and the other desperadoes emerged with guns blazing, fatally wounding the proprietor of the Redding Hotel down the street, and wounding many other citizens. Terrell himself was wounded and taken to the jail in Louisville where he suffered for some time before being allowed to return to Harrisonville where he died at 26 years of age. He had been a hero before that for killing another famous guerrilla, Quantrill, in Spencer County.

Next to Quantrill and Terrell, Captain David S. Martin and his band of guerrillas were best known in Shelby County, according to George L. Willis Sr. in his History of Shelby County. Confederate Captain David S.Martin, of very dark complexion, was known as "Black Dave." In one of his raids on Shelbyville, a battle was waged between the Court House and the nearby blockhouse in which three of the guerrillas were killed along with a local Negro blacksmith who was forced to hold the guerrillas' horses.

The blockhouse was an 18 by 12 foot log structure erected in the middle of the Main and Fifth Street intersection, commanding a view from portholes in all directions to protect the public buildings. It was quickly manned by designated citizens with their guns when an alarm was given of approaching trouble. Guards were posted there every night for two years during the Civil War.

The raid began at dawn in August 1864 and was intended to capture arms and ammunition stored in the Court House. As their approach from the Burks Branch Road was observed near Main Street, the alarm spread. Thomas C. McGrath, a merchant next to the Court House, and J.H. Masonheimer, a tailor, began firing, killing four horses and four men. The guerrillas were driven off, but McGrath was shot and wounded in the head.

In May 1865, a regiment of federal soldiers was encamped at the fairgrounds and a company of Negro soldiers was quartered in the Court House. The Negro company decided to also take over the Market House which stood at the rear of the Court House. When the proprietor, Thomas A. McGrath, attempted to stop the rampage, he was shot and killed. A battle ensued between a group of citizens and the soldiers. "Bad Ed Terrell" showed up with his band of guerrillas, joining the citizens against the soldiers, who were subdued. The soldier who killed McGrath was beaten and taken by Terrell to the Court House balcony with a rope around his neck. A squad from the regiment at the fairgrounds rode in and took charge of the prisoner before he could be hanged. He was taken to Louisville, tried by court martial, convicted and hanged for murder.

In 1870, an organized band of lawless men emerged in the county known as the Ku Klux Klan. Its members lived in the vicinity of Bagdad, Consolation, and Jacksonville. They terrorized the community and were suspected of beating a Negro mail carrier to death. Federal troops under the command of George A. Custer were stationed in the county to insure safety of African Americans. However, vestiges of the klan survived for years and made a modern-day appearance in 1977 when a cross was burned and a rally held on McMakin-McMullan Road, south of Shelbyville.

The last legal execution in the county occurred in 1881. A tramp named John Vonderheide escaped from the penitentiary and murdered a 12 year old African American girl named Rebecca Johnson, hiding her body in a secluded spot in the northern part of the county.

HENRY H. DENHARDT

Brigadier General Henry H. Denhardt was educated as a lawyer, then served as Warren County Judge, Lieutenant Governor of Kentucky, and Adjutant General of the Kentucky National Guard. As a sixty year old divorced man, he persistently courted the belle of Oldham County, Verna Garr Taylor, who was reputed to be the most beautiful widow of the county. She operated the family's laundry business in La Grange and the General operated a large farm in the county, to which he had moved since his divorce in Warren County. After months of wooing, Mrs. Taylor consented to marry the General in August 1936, in spite of vigorous opposition from her three brothers, Roy, Jack, and Dr. E.S. Garr.

On November 6, 1936, the couple drove to Louisville, spent some time at the Pendennis Club, stopped at a restaurant where Mrs. Taylor called home to say she would be there too late to chaperone her daughter's dance. Before nightfall they returned to the vicinity of La Grange near New Castle on KY 22, with Mrs. Taylor driving, when the vehicle stalled. While a passing motorist offered to get a fresh battery in La Grange, General Denhardt and Mrs. Taylor remained at the car. The car having been pushed off the roadway to the driveway of George Baker, Baker asked them if they wanted to wait in his house. This offer was declined.

The Bakers had settled down before their fireplace but soon afterward heard their dog barking. Upon opening the front door to investigate, Baker saw Denhardt walking fast back toward his vehicle. Within a few minutes, the Bakers heard a gunshot and before Baker reached the highway he heard another loud noise and observed Denhardt by his car. The General suggested they search for Mrs. Taylor because she had walked up the road to look for a lost glove. At that moment, the vehicle returned from La Grange with a fresh battery. When the group approached the Denhardt vehicle, General Denhardt opened the glove box and exclaimed: "My God, my revolver is gone. She must have taken it. What a pity. She was the finest lady I ever knew". Witnesses noted that he referred to her in the past tense.

After searching, the body of Mrs. Taylor was found 640 feet from the Denhardt vehicle, lying on the ditch embankment of the roadway. In one gloved hand was the other glove. There was a bullet wound above the left breast. A few feet above the body lay a .45 cal. U.S. Army pistol, which the general admitted was his. Denhardt showed no grief or remorse and protested his innocence as the authorities investigated the scene and later interviewed him at his house. A paraffin test revealed no residue on Mrs. Taylor's hand from a pistol firing; however, General Denhardt's hand revealed traces of nitrate, indicating he had recently fired a weapon of the type found near the body. Dr. Garr swore out a warrant charging Denhardt with murder.

Newspaper and radio publicity of the investigation was widespread. Over a thousand spectators attended the coroner's inquest, where evidence was presented that the body had been shot on the pavement and carried away from the stalled vehicle. The coroner's jury concluded foul play. At the examining trial, more evidence was presented and the county judge held the general to appear before the Henry County Grand Jury where he was indicted for willful murder.

The defense team, composed of John M. Berry of New Castle, Rodes K. Myers of Bowling Green, and W. Clark Otte of Louisville, tried to move the trial out of Henry County but the prosecutor, H. B. Kinsolving from Shelbyville, convinced Judge Charles C. Marshall that Denhardt could receive a fair trial in New Castle. As the April 20, 1936, trial date neared, the press moved in from everywhere and filled

Shelby County Public Library, Sentinel-News copy photograph.

The Armstrong Hotel, southwest corner of Sixth and Main Streets, where Gen. Henry Denhardt (a former lieutenant governor of Kentucky) was shot by the Garr brothers in 1936.

all available rooms for rent. Spectators came from all over the state to view the highly publicized proceedings. Food was hoisted by rope to the second floor courtroom as the spectators refused to leave their seats all day. The crowd outside the Court House was entertained by a singer and a snake charmer. Denhardt returned from Florida for the trial tanned and confident.

The trial lasted two weeks. The defense team countered the prosecutor's case with the theory that a despondent Mrs. Taylor had killed herself. Witnesses presented contradictory testimony and experts argued over positions of the weapon and significance of blood samples. When the jury retired for deliberations, it discussed the testimony for a little over one day and reported that it was hopelessly deadlocked. A mistrial was declared and the eleven farmers and one filling station operator were excused. General Denhardt was released on bond and resumed command of the 75th Brigade of the Kentucky National Guard.

A second trial was set and the day before it was to begin in New Castle, Denhardt and his attorney, Rodes K. Myers, registered at the Armstrong Hotel in Shelbyville at the southwest corner of Sixth and Main Streets. A meeting was held with attorneys Berry and Otte after dinner. The general and Myers then went across the street for a beer and, while strolling back to the hotel, the general noticed three men standing by an automobile. He recognized them immediately and shouted: "There's the Garrs!" Denhardt dashed for the hotel, zigzagging to avoid the ensuing rain of bullets. Seven shots were heard, two bullets striking Denhardt in the back and one in the head. He collapsed and died at the front door of the hotel. Myers also ran but was caught by Dr. Garr and released only after his brother, Roy, intervened to save his life. Myers was reported to have begged: "Don't shoot me. I'm just his lawyer" As the Garr brothers stood in front of Blakemore's Grocery next door to the hotel, they were taken into custody by city officer Jeptha Tracy.

County Judge Harry F. Walters denied bail for the Garrs and they were held in jail where admiring visitors brought food and congratulated them on their righteous deeds. J. Ballard Clark of La Grange, who had served as special prosecutor against Denhardt in his trial, now acted as chief defense counsel for the Garrs, assisted by George L. Willis Jr. and former Congressman Ralph Gilbert.

The killing of General Denhardt drew international press and national magazines exploited the surrounding events with sensational exaggerations that embellished Kentucky's image of gun toting violence. In the examining trial, Roy Garr testified that Denhardt had reached for his back pocket and that only then did the Garrs begin firing the weapons they carried. However, the three brothers were bound over to the Shelby County Grand Jury on charges of murder before being released on surety bonds.

The trial of Roy and Jack Garr began on October 1, 1937, in the absence of Dr. E.S. Garr, who had been placed in a home for the mentally ill in Pewee Valley. H. B. Kinsolving withdrew from the prosecution, claiming his friendship with the Garr brothers presented a conflict of interest. Kentucky Attorney General Hubert Meredith assumed the prosecutorial duties, contending that the Garrs had gunned down an unarmed man in revenge for their sister's murder, even shooting Denhardt in the back. The defense team argued that Denhardt was one of the most violent and unscrupulous men of his day, that the Garrs thought Denhardt was going for a gun, and that they only shot in self defense. Many military men testified against the general.

The Judge dismissed the charge against Jack Garr because he had not fired a weapon. Ralph Gilbert closed the case for the defense by condemning Denhardt as a "mad dog" and that Roy Garr had a legal right to shoot down a mad dog. The jury was out only an hour and a quarter before returning a verdict of "not guilty." The crowd of spectators erupted and rushed to congratulate Roy and Jack Garr and their defense counsel as rebel yells were shouted. The charge against Dr. Garr was later dismissed by the state and their pistols were returned to them.

Professor William E. Ellis of Eastern Kentucky University, formerly of Shelbyville, wrote in an article published in the *Register of the Kentucky Historical Society*, from which much of this summary was drawn: "In 1937, the folkways of Kentucky over-whelmingly supported the Garrs' act of vengeance. A half century later, under similar circumstances, would society condone such circumvention of the law?"

A ballad written by George A. Hendon, shortly after the trial, sums up this tragic episode: "The harvest moon was shinin' on the streets of Shelbyville, when General Henry Denhardt met his fate; the Garr boys was a waitin', they was out to shoot to kill. Death and General Denhardt had a date."

VANISSA WAFORD

Vanissa Waford, an employee of Maxie's Shoe Store in Village Plaza Shopping Center in Shelbyville, was found beaten to death at the store on June 25, 1989. Her jewelry and wallet were missing, along with the store's receipts. William R. Stark Jr. was charged with her murder after being arrested (and later convicted) for similar robberies and assaults in Louisville.

The state sought the death penalty but the case never went to a jury. Generating widespread publicity, it was twice delayed by reviews by the State Court of Appeals—once over a change of venue and once over the admissibility of Stark's other convictions. The case was dismissed in 1993 after the defense claimed that Stark, who was black, would suffer from the disproportional conviction rate among African-Americans in Shelby County. The defense also said the charges should be dismissed because of the need to further investigate new evidence and the impossibility of trying the case without further delays.

MARY EVELYN MCKEE

The widow of prominent surgeon, Dr. Willis McKee, 78 year old Mary Evelyn McKee had established a routine of daily walks around her neighborhood between 5:00 and 6:00 in the evenings. On February 21, 1995, her brutally beaten body was found lying between two houses on Plainview Avenue. An autopsy revealed death by multiple blows to the head from a blunt object 24 hours earlier. Her underclothes had been removed and her dress was raised over her head. A violent struggle was indicated to fend off rape and death from her attacker.

After numerous interviews in the neighborhood and lab texts, a fifteen year old juvenile, Billy Jeffries, was arrested and indicted for murder and attempted rape. The victim's eyeglasses had been knocked off and the right palm print of Jeffries was identified on the glasses. Blood from the victim was identified by DNA testing on shoes worn by Jeffries on February 20. Two witnesses placed Jeffries near the crime scene between 5:30 and 6:30 that day. Jeffries had a long history of offenses in Juvenile Court and had been placed on "home incarceration" at his Ashland Avenue home near the crime scene. Under questioning, he admitted being drunk in the vicinity and coming through the crime scene that day and time on his way from a juvenile party nearby but denied killing Mrs. McKee.

A change of venue was granted because of extensive publicity. The trial was moved to Anderson County where the case was prosecuted by an assistant attorney general and defended by a public defender. The jury found Jeffries guilty of murder, recommending a sentence of twenty- five years, and guilty of attempted rape, recommending a sentence of ten years, to be served consecutively for a total of thirty-five years in the penitentiary. A motion for new trial was filed, alleging newly discovered evidence of somebody else confessing to the crimes. After a hearing and allegations from the defense that exculpatory evidence was withheld by the prosecution, Judge William Stewart rejected the motion. This decision has been appealed and is pending.

The extensive publicity and persistent efforts of the victim's son, Dr. Willis McKee of Frankfort, in pursuit of improvements in the juvenile justice system, persuaded the Governor and the General Assembly to adopt tougher juvenile incarceration and sentencing laws, which are in effect today.

The Ku Klux Klan, Lynching, and Shelby County

By Kevin Collins and Charles Long

The history of the Ku Klux Klan and lynching in Shelby County is a complicated and lamentable story. For many years after the Civil War the Klan was active in the rural areas of Kentucky, including Shelby and surrounding counties. The most systemic violence occurred in the years immediately after the Civil War and in well documented hangings in 1891, 1901, and 1911.

According to the *Kentucky Irish-American*, as late as 1925 half of the Shelbyville City Council were members of the Klan (George C. Wright, *A History of Blacks in Kentucky*, p. 85). In the 1930's, according to the memoirs of Lyman Johnson, Louisville civil-rights leader and educator, Shelbyville was, "...one of the most hellish places I ever experienced . . . As bad as any town in Mississippi or Alabama. If a bunch of white people walked down the street, Negroes got off the sidewalk to let them by or they got their heads beat in." Such was the racial divide that existed in those days that many whites either actively supported and abetted Klan activities or were intimidated into silence by their threats.

The Rev. Elijah Marrs, in his autobiography, *The Life and History of the Rev. Elijah P. Marrs*, recounted several instances of the Ku Klux Klan in Shelby County. While teaching school in Simpsonville, in 1866-67, he wrote,

"One day, while the school children were at play, during recess, some one fired a shot among them. I saw the man who did the shooting, and going to him, charged him with the offense. He denied it, and raised a club to strike me, when I retreated to the schoolroom, glad to get away alive, for, though the war was over, the K. K. K. was in full blast, and no man was safe from their depredations . . . I remember an incident that occurred while I was in Simpsonville. One night, while all were asleep, the K. K. K. rode into town, some of them mounted on horses, some on mules, and others on asses. They were provided with tin horns, old tin pans, drums, bells, etc., and made a terrible din. Coming into the yard of the house where I lived, they dismounted and began stripping the trees of switches, as if preparing to come into the house to administer a flogging to every one of us. I stole downstairs, and armed with my old pistol, stationed myself in a chimney corner, prepared to fight my way through should occasion demand it. They made threats or some sort, which I could not hear, but finally rode off, my back was saved, and I felt mightily relieved."

In 1871 Marrs, who owned a home in Shelbyville and intermittently lived here while he taught school in Henry County, wrote, "At that time Henry County was overrun with the K. K. K., and a colored man in public business dared not go five miles outside of the city for fear of assassination."

Also in 1871, Klansmen boarded a mail train at Hatton in northeastern Shelby County and beat a black postal employee. Later, at the trial of several men charged with the offense, it became clear that the person who committed the assault was Addison Cook, and since he was dead, the case was dropped. Nonetheless, Klan turmoil in the Bagdad, Consolation, and Jacksonville areas compelled General George Custer to detach Troop I from the 7th Cavalry, then stationed at Elizabethtown, Ky., and place them at the Bagdad Christian Church. After several months in Bagdad, the company, commanded by Captain

Miles W. Keogh, moved into Shelbyville. They quartered in a livery stable at Eighth and Main Streets owned by James L. Long, and remained here until sometime in 1873. Captain Keogh and thirty eight other officers and men of Company I were killed at the battle of the Little Big Horn on June 25, 1876.

In the summer of 1871, Hiram Bohannon of Bagdad was arrested for the murder of local Klan leader Addison Cook who Mr. Bohannon considered a thief. He was arrested, tried and convicted of the murder by the Shelby County Circuit Court, and sentenced to hang. However, Bohannon's conviction was reversed by the Court of Appeals and the case remanded for retrial. In September of 1872, on motion of the Commonwealth Attorney Phil Lee, the case was dismissed and Mr. Bohannon lived for many years a respected citizen.

Then, on October 16, 1872, a band of Klansmen attacked blacks at Stringtown, a small community of ex-slaves situated between Bagdad and Hatton on what is now Hwy. 1005. Buildings were burned, residents beaten and one man (variously reported as James Magruder, Gabe Flood, or Gibb Magruder) was murdered. Another, Lawson Johnson, was permanently maimed and his barn burned. Today while Bagdad and Hatton survive, Stringtown has long since vanished.

Amid cries from the *New York Times* and the *Louisville Courier-Journal* that the Democratic leaders of Kentucky were refusing to quell Klan violence, and mindful of the fact that the legislature in 1871 had rejected a law against mob violence, the *Times* on November 8, 1972, singled out Shelby County for national attention.

The following is an excerpt from the *The Kentucky Kuklux: Catalogue of recent outrages in Shelby County— a fearful list of murders, arsons and floggings committed by a band of lawless criminals. Correspondence of the Louisville Courier-Journal, Shelby County, Ky., Oct. 30, 1872.*

"As many of your readers are not aware of the many outrages perpetrated in this county and vicinity in the last few years by disguised bands of men known as Kuklux, I propose to give an outline of their atrocities, depending wholly on my own memory and information. That this combination of night-prowlers is a more dangerous element in our midst than many good citizens are aware of I hope to show before I am done writing up this sketch. The first outrage of note I remember to have heard of that can safely be laid at their door was the murder of a man named Onan, living on the Kentucky River. This man's cries and supplications for mercy could be heard in the darkness of night by some of his neighbors, who were afraid to go to his rescue. The whole transaction, as described by those conversant with the facts, was among the foulest murders ever committed in a civilized community. They broke into the house of William Bohannon, and flogged him for no cause whatever. They made a raid on the store of William Balew, and attempted to break into the store, and one of their number came to his death in the act. They hanged Jacob Lighter near Clay village in this county. (Author's note: Lighter, a member of the Klan, was hung by them for making disclosures of Klan activities to Federal authorities while under arrest for being drunk in Frankfort.) This murder has no superior in atrocity yet chronicled by any writer on crime. They broke into the house of Miss Millie Ann Sturgis, who had no protector except an old colored man and his wife, and lynched the old Negro man for nothing; and on another occasion so terrified Miss Sturgis by their foul presence that she escaped to the fields, where she concealed herself the remainder of the night. They went to the house of Miss Elizabeth Demaree under the pretense of "regulating" a colored man in her employ, and shot off the arm of her house-boy (a colored boy fourteen or fifteen year old.)

They broke into the house of a man named Pilcher, and flogged him without mercy, one of the assassins holding the muzzle of a pistol to his wife's head to deter her from screaming.

They dragged a Mr. Claxton from his house and gave him a choice to withdraw a suit he had instituted in a Henry Circuit Court against a citizen of this county or dangle at a rope's end. He agreed to draw the suit, (who wouldn't?) but afterward prosecuted it, as he ought to have done. They visited the houses of three colored citizens near Christiansburg, in this county, and relieved two of them of gun, watch, and other valuables, and wounded the third one by shooting him. They flogged two colored men near Pleasureville and Bellview, and robbed one of them of what little cash he had on hand. They flogged J. I. Connell, breaking into the house of a prominent citizen of this county for the purpose. They lynched a man by the name of Graves, because-as they said-his cow had broken into a widow's garden. They attempted to rape a married woman and her daughter at their home in this county, who escaped by their loud cries of murder. They whipped one Sandford, and an inoffensive man named Bishop. They burned the store of a man named Shannon, in the extreme north-east corner of this county. They robbed James Kessler of about $600, entering his house at night for the purpose. They flogged John Riddle and Henry Hearold. They went to the house of George Lindall, and, with the threat of burning his house, forced him to give up some promissory notes he held against a man in Henry County. They have ridden many farmers' horses till they are temporarily unfit for use, and have stolen their bridles and saddles. In short, they have done everything that freebooters and assassins are capable of doing. The last, but not least, of their outrages were the murder of Gibb Magruder, of color, and the burning of old Lawson Johnson's barn, stored with his Winter provender, farming utensils, etc.

A more diabolical piece of work could not be imagined. The above is but a part of their dark deeds. If a man should take the pains to collect together all the information necessary to write an impartial history of their crimes, and should write them in detail, they would make a large volume; and if traced by the pen of an able writer, the story, for its mingling of romance and horror, would not be exceeded by any history of crimes. The question is frequently asked if politics cut any figure in the Kuklux organization about here? I answer unhesitatingly no! These men have no politics except the polity of the devil. They have no principles. With their brutal carcasses steeped with mean Whiskey, and their corrupt hearts boiling over with malice, they have no humanity. They hate all good citizens. They hate all law. Murder, arson, rapine, theft, blackmailing, flagellation, and, if there be anything else contrary to the laws of God and of man, these are their politics, these are their principles."

In September 1873 the Klan shot to death Sam Smith "one of the most respectable citizens of Clay Village" (Courier Journal Oct. 29, 1874). A grand jury looking into the matter a year later failed to indict any of the suspects in the case and Klan activity resumed in and around Clayvillage. The Courier Journal reported on Oct. 29, 1874, that "...for the past six weeks, but one Saturday night has passed without a visit of the masked scoundrels to Johnson's toll-gate, at the crossroads, two and a half miles above Clayvillage, a point that seems to be their most common rendezvous, as they have been seen gathering in there at once from the four roads that mark the four cardinal points of the compass. Right here they have committed a number of outrages within the past three weeks, such as breaking into Negro cabins, whipping the inmates, seizing and carrying off arms, and in one case attempting to ravish a woman." Johnson's toll-gate was located at Peytona at the intersection of old U.S. 60 and Ky. 395.

This newspaper report details an incident that occurred on Saturday October 24th that forced the Governor to take notice of Klan violence in Shelby County. Sometime after midnight a group of men attacked the home of Walter Huss, a black man, flogging him and all those in his house. They then rode a mile and a half to the farm of Thomas Ford, a white man, where ten Klansmen beat several black men and women living in one of Ford's cabins. Next they broke into Ford's house and threatened Mr. Ford and his wife with death for employing Negroes and ordering them removed. The men knew the Fords by name and were familiar with the house.

After leaving Ford's farm, four of the Klansmen, led by a tall man in a black hat with a feather and his partner, a short man affecting an Irish accent, rode to Jeptha Knobs to the isolated cabin of Chris Barringer which sat on the summit of one of the heavily wooded hills. Barringer, a black man with a wife and six children, was thought to have a musket that the Klansmen wanted. They threatened to burn down the cabin and then fired through the front door. Bullets hit Barringer's fourteen year old daughter Alice in the eye and right shoulder. Reports differ on whether her wounds were eventually fatal.

The wanton violence of the attack caused a public outcry that was led by Henry Watterson, editor of the Courier- Journal, and on October 27th Governor Preston H. Leslie issued a proclamation offering a five hundred dollar reward for the capture of the Klan members responsible. The Governor's statement said, in part, "The local authorities seem too often to forget that the whole power of the county is, by law, placed in their hands, and that on them, and not on the State Executive, rests the first and chief responsibility for the repression and punishment of crimes committed in their jurisdiction....I regret to say that there is reason to believe that to the apathy or, in some cases, apparent sympathy of citizens, and the neglect of their sworn duties by the local authorities, have been mainly due the disgraceful impunity of offenders and the consequent increase of such crimes in our State" (*Courier-Journal* October 30, 1874). Despite Governor Leslie's offer of an reward, the Shelby Klansmen responsible for the attack on Alice Barringer were never brought to justice.

The charge of rape or "detaining a woman" was often the cause of mob lynching of black men. The execution of Sam Pulliam, a black man who lived with his wife and children near Johnsonville, on the eastern edge of Shelbyville, was just such an example. Pulliam was taken from a sheriff's escort by a mob, reportedly numbering about one hundred armed men, and hung from a walnut tree two miles outside Lawrenceburg in Anderson County.

The *Shelby Weekly News* (July 22, 1891) and the Louisville *Courier-Journal* (July 21, 1891) reported the incident in florid detail. The *News* headline, for example, read, "SWIFT JUSTICE—A Cruel Crime and Prompt Punishment—A black brute assaults and rapes a respectable married lady in the broad light of day—After a long chase he is captured and pays the penalty of his dastardly crime at the end of a rope." The following facts come from these two news accounts.

On Monday morning, July 20th, Sam Pulliam approached the home of Mr. Thomas J. Glenn, a young, prosperous Shelby County farmer. Hettie Glenn, his forty year old wife of two years was home alone. Pulliam, who often did work for the Glenns, allegedly told Mrs. Glenn that something was bothering the chickens at the neighboring Boswell farm. Mrs. Glenn then walked there to tell Mr. Boswell. Meanwhile, Pulliam, having gone by another way to the same area, lay in wait alongside the Shelbyville and Frankfort Turnpike (U.S. Hwy 60) for Mrs. Glenn's return. There, in a hemp patch, it is reported, Pulliam sexually assaulted Mrs. Glenn.

After the alleged assault, Mr. George Newton, traveling the road in a buggy, spotted the disheveled and voiceless Mrs. Glenn in ripped clothing, as well as the confused and bewildered figure of Sam Pulliam some forty yards away. As Pulliam ran away Newton gave chase. But, being unarmed, he chose to make discretion the better part of valor and broke off pursuit. Instead he sounded the alarm. In due course, a hundred Shelbyville men, forming into smaller groups, began the search for Pulliam.

According to the *News*, Pulliam was first seen escaping through a hemp field at the rape scene. He reportedly fled, generally speaking, in a southeasterly direction roughly parallel to the Louisville Southern railroad tracks. He was reported to have been seen running on Hempridge road; then, after resting alongside the railroad tracks near Waddy, was thought to have escaped through some woods into Anderson County. After passing through Avenstoke, he was finally apprehended in Wilson's woods (between Avenstoke and Alton in Anderson County). Pulliam was captured by Sam Marrs, tied to a buggy and delivered to the Lawrenceburg jail.

At this point in the narrative the Shelbyville and Louisville newspapers differ. The *Courier-Journal* states that Pulliam was escorted from the Lawrenceburg jail after nightfall, transported and guarded by Shelbyville/Shelby County officers and men - Sheriff A. C. Long, Chief Rutherford and twenty armed guards; that armed men from Shelby County had been arriving in Lawrenceburg throughout the day, and that trouble was imminent; that Pulliam confessed to the crime; and finally, that fifty men of Shelby County were responsible for his death.

The *Weekly News* writes that at ten thirty that night Pulliam was escorted from the jail by Rutherford, W. A. Meeks, and W. P. Hastings; that outside the Lawrenceburg city limits a crowd of one hundred men disarmed the three officers and, despite their pleadings, took Pulliam; that there was not one Shelby County man involved in the lynching, although there were hundreds who would have wished to be; that Pulliam before being hung, did not confess to the rape, but, as was usual in these cases, blamed another black man; that previously, however, Pulliam had, in fact, confessed the crime, stating that he didn't know why he had done it; that the lynches were "all respectable in appearance and quiet and gentlemanly in demeanor" and "all unrecognizable strangers, citizens of Anderson County in Lawrenceburg for Court day"; and finally, that after Pulliams's death Mr. John T. Blumer, of Lawrenceburg, sent the rope used to Mr. Glenn, the alleged rape victim's husband.

The next week the *News* reported that "some one, described as a large man, with a large straw hat pulled well down over his face, went to the hut of the father and mother of Sam Pulliam in Johnsonville, and notified them that they must leave the County within five days, or they would receive a dose of the same medicine administered to the son." Pulliam's seventy five year old father left that night for Louisville and his wife and son-in-law followed the next evening. No one was ever identified, apprehended or tried for the death of Sam Pulliam.

The double theme of sex and murder played a role in the 1901 lynching in Shelbyville of Jimbo Fields and Clarence Garnett. Fields, age sixteen, and Garnett, age eighteen, were taken from the Shelby County jail early on the morning of October 2, 1901, by a mob of forty or fifty men and hung from the Chesapeake and Ohio railroad trestle that crossed Clear Creek north of town. Contemporary accounts from the *Shelby News* (September 26 and October 3, 1901), the Louisville *Courier-Journal* (October 2 and 3, 1901), and the *Louisville Evening Post* (October 2, 1901) supply the following account. Early Saturday evening, September 21st, the unconscious body of William C. Hart, a printer with the *Shelbyville Sentinel*, was found near the house of Ann Fields in the black neighborhood of Bucktown. Hart, twenty five years old and a recent arrival from Lebanon, Ohio, had been in Shelbyville about two months. After a heavy day of drinking he made his way to the Fields house, being amorously involved with Ann Fields. Around nine p.m. his body was discovered in a nearby alley and taken to the police courtroom, where he died, reportedly without regaining consciousness.

Reports say that an argument apparently erupted between Ann Fields and Hart. Some say that she hit him with something and that her son, Jimbo Fields, then ran to get his friend and neighbor, Clarence Garnett. At this point some accounts have the two boys throwing rocks at Hart through a window; others report that Fields and Garnett actually stoned Hart to death. Most reports state that Hart was assaulted inside the Fields' house, then dragged outside. Whatever the facts, within hours of Hart's death, Fields and Garnett were arrested.

The next day an autopsy by three doctors fixed the cause of death as a blow on the top of the head that resulted in a brain concussion. On Monday, a grand jury indicted the two teenagers for willful murder. On Tuesday, the 24th, Ann Fields was also arrested and indicted for murder. An unnamed witness saw her hit Hart, in her living room, with a steel rod.

Threats to lynch the two boys were made immediately after their arrest. Early Tuesday morning, Sept. 24th, a mob of forty or so men attempted to take them from the jail. The attempt failed, despite the fact that the men had a jail key. However, during the effort someone was able to steal, or was given, a second key that insured the success of the subsequent attempt on October 2nd. No thought was apparently given to removing the prisoners to Louisville for safekeeping.

A week and a day later the mob returned at two o'clock in the morning. They took Fields from the third floor of the jail, Garnett from the second, tied their hands behind their backs, marched them a short distance to the trestle and hung them. By nine in the morning hundreds of people, including school children and the visiting delegates of the Kentucky Conference of the Methodist Episcopal Church, had viewed the bodies. They were not cut down and removed until after the coroner's inquest was convened later that same morning.

The coroner's jury issued the following report: "We, the jury, find that Jimbo Fields and Clarence Garnett came to their death upon the Chesapeake and Ohio Railroad trestle by hanging, by parties unknown to the jury." No one was ever identified or arrested. Ann Fields was released from jail and the charges against her filed away.

Nearly ten years later, on January 15, 1911, the last and largest lynching carried out in Shelby County took place. Three men were taken form the County jail and hung from the same Chesapeake and Ohio railroad trestle used in the Fields-Garnett lynching. They were Gene Marshall, 25, convicted of murder, Wade Patterson, 29, accused of detaining two white women, and James West, 25, also accused of detaining a white woman. Again contemporary accounts from the *Shelby Record* (January 20, 27, February 3, 10, and 17, 1911) and the *Louisville Courier-Journal* (January 16, 17, 18, and 19, 1911) supply us with the following material.

Gene Marshall was convicted on February 12, 1910 of the willful murder of Lizzie Spruce Harrington of Shelbyville. Marshall, a married man, had left his wife and persuaded Harrington, who had been living for years with another man, to live with him instead, in Martinsville. The day before her murder, however, Harrington left Marshall and returned to and married her former boyfriend.

Harrington's murder was particularly brutal. Marshall was captured a few days later in the southwestern part of Shelby County. At trial it was established, among other things, that Marshall had threatened to cut the victim's head off, which was, in fact, how Harrington died. The jury sentenced Marshall to death which penalty was affirmed ten months later by the Court of Appeals. At the time he was taken from the jail, Marshall was awaiting an execution date from Governor Augustus E. Wilson. Of the six men lynched during this period Marshall was the only one who had been convicted of a crime and the only one whose victim was a black person.

Wade Patterson's arrest and death is perhaps the saddest of the three cases. Newspaper accounts say that he attacked two white women, a mother and her twenty year old daughter, who were returning home from a lecture given at Science Hill Female Academy.

On December 5, 1910, at nine thirty at night, and in a heavy snowstorm, Patterson was alleged to have slipped up behind the two women and put his arm around the waist of the daughter. When the mother screamed, the newspaper reports that Patterson hit her and ran away. "Indignation was expressed by every good citizen and there was talk of a probable lynching." reported the *Shelby Record* (January 20, 1911). The next morning Patterson, also a married man, was arrested at his home six miles outside of Shelbyville.

On December 18th there was an examining trial before County Judge Ralph Gilbert who set bail and bound Patterson over for a grand jury hearing. Unable to meet the bond of two thousand dollars, Patterson was in jail on the night of his lynching. Later Gilbert would have this to say about the examining trial, "There was little proof against Patterson and I personally do not believe he was guilty of wrong intent. He simply ran into two women late at night and they thought he was bent on criminal assault. It appears that he had just run out of a saloon in a half drunken condition and accidentally ran into the two women without intention" (*Courier-Journal* January 16, 1911).

James West, also married, was arrested for allegedly making unwanted advances to a fourteen year old white girl. West, a chauffeur in the employ of W. C. P. Muir, a retired U. S. Navy Commander, had, while driving Muir home, been told by his employer to offer a ride to the young daughter of Muir's neighbor.

After driving Muir to his home about a mile south of Shelbyville, West proceeded the additional half mile, alone with the girl, to her residence. It was alleged that during this ride he made advances toward the youngster.

This first offense happened in November and was followed, the girl said, by repeated offenses in December, such as West throwing kisses to her whenever they met or telling her to meet him at night. On December 31st, two months after the initial misdeed, the girl reported West's conduct to her father for the first time. A complaint was lodged and West was arrested and bond set at one thousand dollars, which Commander Muir posted. However, when rumor and indignation began to rise in Shelbyville, the bondsman surrendered West to the authorities. West waived his examining trial and was in jail on the fateful night, along with Patterson, waiting for a grand jury hearing.

On January 15, a Sunday morning, at about two a. m., a masked mob of between twenty and fifty men assembled at the jail and in the course of almost two hours broke the three men out of their cells and attempted to lynch them. Marshall, hung with a thick rope, his hands tied behind his back, was the first prisoner to die. Patterson, his hands unbound, and West, his hands loosely tied, were thrown over the trestle at the same time. Both were hung with thinner rope than was used on Marshall.

Patterson's noose broke and with his hands free he fell twenty feet to the shallow creek below. He scrambled through the water to level pastureland on the opposite side of the creek and headed up-stream toward Seventh Street. He encountered a tall barbed wire fence and, instead of returning to the water, attempted to scale the fence. The entire lynch mob, infuriated, crossed the bridge in quick pursuit, and with as many as seventy five shots executed him.

Meanwhile, with the mob's attention on Patterson, West was somehow able to free his hands, slip out of the noose, and jump to the ground. He escaped in the opposite direction. Shortly before daybreak he arrived at the home of his in-laws, Mr. and Mrs. George Bennett. There his wounds were dressed and he was hidden in the house until Tuesday evening, when, with new clothes and money, he escaped Shelbyville.

Rumors surfaced about West's whereabouts over the next few weeks and County Judge Gilbert offered a two hundred dollar reward for his apprehension and return. Judge Gilbert stated publicly that he was certain the lynch mob was from Shelbyville and that West most probably could identify them. James West was never located and no one in the mob was ever attested.

There is no doubt that the events of January 15, 1911, were made possible by the breakdown of law enforcement in Shelby County and Shelbyville. Although Sheriff Ben C. Perkins, Jailer Ed Thompson, and Police Chief Oscar Duncan all denied any prior knowledge of the lynching, it appears from a report in the *Courier-Journal* (Jan. 16, 1911) that it was known in the town some hours before it happened. The cast and crew of the play *The Wolf*, which was performed in Shelbyville on the night of the lynching was told by a stage hand that "…they would see some fun if they would stay up as late as two o'clock." A member of the theatre company also stated "…that the whole thing was framed at a meeting of seventeen men on Friday night, when each man agreed to bring four others with him Saturday night to lynch the three Negroes."

Governor Augustus E. Willson could not have condemned the actions of local officials in stronger terms and he was joined by editorialists at the Courier- Journal. Indeed, the failure of law enforcement officers to do their duty on the night of January 15th is difficult to explain and impossible to justify. During the mob's pick-ax assault on the jail and its locked cells, which took an hour and a half, the jailer, who that morning had sent his wife and child to Frankfort to visit a sick relative, sequestered himself in a back room with the jail keys. His actions did not prove much of an impediment to the mob.

A constable and two policemen, all armed, heard a commotion at the jail around three a.m. Leaving police headquarters they headed toward the jail but were stopped by members of the mob when they had reached the town fountain, then located at the intersection of Fifth and Main Streets. They remained there, chatting with the wrongdoers for twenty minutes, making no attempt to summon help.

The Chief of Police stated (*Courier -Journal* January 17, 1911) that he received a telephone call at about three a.m. from policeman Bennett to the effect that "there's something going on down town". He turned on his porch light, found four armed men sitting there, and answered his officer with, "Let it go on" and went back to bed.

Prisoners Patterson and West had been moved to Louisville after their arrests as a precaution against earlier rumors that they might be lynched. When they were returned to Shelby County is not clear, but the sheriff maintained after the lynching that he was unaware that the men were at the Shelby County jail that night.

On January 19th Governor Willson offered a five hundred dollar reward for the arrest and conviction of each person who was engaged in the lynching at Shelbyville and refused the request of County Judge Gilbert to offer a reward for the return of West. Instead, the County Court offered a two hundred dollar reward for West but nothing for those involved in the lynching. Later that month Circuit Judge C. C. Marshall, in an effort to identify members of the mob, charged the grand jury to "...ascertain who they are and return indictments here, regardless of who they might be" (*Shelby Record* January 27, 1911). However, the only indictment the grand jury returned in this case was one against the missing James West for detaining a woman against her will.

The traumatic events of the Marshall-Patterson-West hanging brought to a close Shelby County's experience with lynching. The Invisible Empire, and the attitudes that allowed it to flourish, although diminished, continued to have influence in county politics for another thirty years. Shelby County's last brush with the Klan was in 1976, when the United Klans of America sought to hold a rally at a site south of Locust Grove Road. The attempt was thwarted.

SHELBY COUNTY FISCAL COURT

By Kevin Collins

Section 144 of Kentucky's Constitution requires that a county have a Fiscal Court made up either of a county judge and from three to eight justices of the peace (also called magistrates), or of a county judge and three commissioners. Voters in each county choose which of these two forms of fiscal court they wish to adopt. Shelby County has opted for the former, as have most Kentucky counties (one hundred six of one hundred twenty), and its fiscal court is comprised of a County Judge/Executive and seven Magistrates.

The County Judge Executive is a member, as well as the presiding officer, of the Fiscal Court. He or she has the same powers as the other members of the court, including the right to vote on all matters coming before the court. In addition to duties on the Court, the County Judge/Executive has extensive executive and administrative duties when the Court is not in session. All residents of the county qualified to vote elect the County Judge/Executive, on a partisan ballot, every four years.

Shelby County Magistrates are elected from seven magisterial districts. Today, unlike the past, these Magistrates have no judicial power, and have few duties outside the Fiscal Court. Relative to county governance, they have official power only as members of the Court, and only when it is in session. Magistrates are elected every four years, also on a partisan ballot, with each magistrate being elected by the qualified voters of his or her district.

The Kentucky Constitution does not address the question of the exact powers and duties of fiscal courts. That task is left to the General Assembly. KRS 67. 080, for instance, permits Fiscal Court to appropriate county funds for lawful purposes, buy and sell county property, supervise the fiscal affairs of the county and county officers, maintain accurate fiscal records, and exercise all other corporate powers of the county. Fiscal Court may also investigate all activities of county government as well as establish appointive offices and define their duties. This statute also requires that the court provide funds for county roads, buildings, and county detention centers. It also directs the Fiscal Court to adopt an administrative code for the county. KRS 67.083 (the county home rule statute) in turn empowers Fiscal Court to enact ordinances, issue regulations, levy taxes, issue bonds, appropriate funds, and employ personnel for a host of public functions. Theses are but two of a number of laws scattered throughout the Kentucky Revised Statutes that form and shape the function of the Shelby County Fiscal Court.

Fiscal Court, today, is solely an administrative and legislative body. However, it is not the only legislative body of government in the county. There is also the Shelbyville City Council and the Simpsonville Town Board. Each of these three legislative bodies is responsible for its respective area's services but they can also, as needed, function in unison. The formation of the Triple S Planning and Zoning Commission is such an example.

Kentucky law mandates that all meetings of the County Fiscal Court be open to the public. Residents may speak at meetings. Meetings are held in Shelbyville, at the Stratton Center, 215 Washington Street, on the first and third Tuesdays of the month.

SHELBY COUNTY JUDGE/EXECUTIVE

Sammy Wood 1978-81   Bobby Stratton 1982-02   Robert Rothenberger 2003-

FISCAL COURT MAGISTRATES

District 1	Bob Walters	1978-02
	Hubert Pollett	2003-
District 2	Jack Frazier	1978-82
	Robert F. Wilson	1982-98
	Hobie Henninger	1998-02
	Michael Riggs	2003-
District 3	Hubert Gordon	1978-82
	George Van Huss	1982-90
	Robert L. Samples	1990-02
	Allen Ruble	2003-
District 4	Roger "Bill" Bailey	1978-85
	Cordy Armstrong	1985 to date
District 5	Edward Masters	1978-82
	Howell Raizor, Jr.	1982-98
	Betty Curtsinger	1998 to date
District 6	James Shaddock	1978-82
	Harold Sutton	1982-86
	James Shaddock	1986-90
	Tony Carriss	1990 to date
District 7	Stuart Demaree	1978-86
	Mike Whitehouse	1986-02
	James Robertson	2003-

Members of Shelby County Fiscal Court, 2001. Front row, left to right: Sue Carole Perry, County Clerk; Betty Curtsinger, Magistrate; Bobby Stratton, County Judge/Executive; Hobie Henninger, Magistrate. Back row, left to right: Chuck Hickman, County Attorney; Bob Walters, Magistrate; Plomer Wilson, County Engineer; Tony Carriss, Magistrate; Mike Whitehouse, Magistrate; Cordy Armstrong, Magistrate; Robert Samples, Magistrate.

SHELBYVILLE CITY GOVERNMENT

By Bobbie Smith, Charles T. Long, Betty Matthews and Duanne Puckett

At the first court meeting held October 15, 1792, decisions were made on the site selection for the town to serve as county seat. It was to be called Shelbyville in honor of Isaac Shelby, the state's first governor.

One of the first actions of the new town was an order in 1793 that tavern keepers should charge no more than 6 shillings per gallon for whiskey; breakfast with tea or coffee one shilling and three pence; and warm dinner, one shilling and six pence as opposed to a cold dinner, which cost only one shilling.

William Shannon offered to donate sufficient ground for the public buildings and square for the town. He made arrangements for town officials to be empowered to sell lots and give deeds for them. These "gentlemen trustees," as they were called, made a rule that every purchaser of a lot in Shelbyville should erect a hewed log house with a stone chimney, not less than one story-and-a half high, otherwise the lot was to be forfeited to the use of the town.

When the construction of the city began, the boundaries extended from what is now Third Street to Seventh. Shortly after the town was incorporated, lots were sold and a Court House and jail built. Old records indicate that by 1794, there were about twenty houses. The town limits were first extended in 1803 by an act of the General Assembly. By 1806, the town tax was 30 cents on each $100 assessed property value and an 80.5 cents poll tax. The receipts from those tax sources that year amounted to $122.27.

An election was held in August 1817 for the selection of five members to the town's Board of Trustees. There were 27 candidates, yet only 81 people voted. Once the Board took office, it began to fine citizens for offenses, such as leaving wood on the main streets for more than 24 hours.

In 1821, the town entrusted its Trustees to create "promises to pay" notes that were printed and signed by the Board chairman. The notes acted as fractional currency. Fifteen-hundred dollars in notes was circulated. It was printed on regular bank paper and when it was mutilated or worn, the authorities redeemed it in good money or new scrip.

In 1830, considerable trouble was experienced in procuring sufficient water for family use. Every spring adjacent to town was cleaned and walled up at the expense of the town for use by the citizens.

In the spring of 1847, the Trustees passed and published 41 town ordinances to force citizens to comply with the requirements of the law.

Official records of city action do not exist before 1894. However, there are references in 1890 to a Dr. Baker as chairman of the Board of Trustees. And the obituary of George Petry, who died in 1889, mentions "he was for a number of years Mayor of the town."

The Kentucky Revised Statutes set the qualifications for the office of mayor as the following: "a person must be 25 years of age or older; be a qualified voter in the city; and reside in the city throughout the term of office." The mayor must be elected by the voters at a regular election. The term of the office begins on January 1 following the election and is for four years.

Shelbyville has a mayor-council form of government, and thus, in keeping with the separation of powers doctrine, the mayor is not a member of the legislative body. The mayor may not introduce legislation nor vote on any issue, except when necessary to break a tie. The mayor is the chief executive and administrative officer of the city, and the principle function is to oversee the management of the city's daily affairs.

Before 1938, Shelbyville mayors were elected to four-year terms by members of the City Council. In that year, the General Assembly passed a law requiring the direct election of mayors. In 1942, Robert F. Matthews Sr. became the first person to win the office in a city-wide general election. From 1910 to 1938, mayoral candidates ran only in their party primary, sometimes together with council slates representing the city wards. Council candidates successful in their primary and the following general election then met in caucus to elect the mayor. Because there were so few council members elected from the Republican party, the selection of the mayor was usually settled in the Democratic primary.

Mayors of the City of Shelbyville were:

John I. Logan - Jan. 1894-Jan. 1898

Luther C. Willis - Jan. 1898-Jan. 1906

Dr. T. E. Bland - Jan. 1906-Jan. 1910

Lynn T. Gruber - Jan. 1910-Nov. 1912

Leon Rothchild - Nov. 1912-Jan. 1922

Curtis P. Hall Sr. - Jan. 1922-Jan. 1930

Paul F. Schmidt - Jan. 1930-Jan. 1934

Robert F. Matthews Sr. - Jan. 1934-Jan.1946

Lewis S. Frederick - Jan. 1946-April 1946

Robert F. Matthews Sr. - April 1946-Jan. 1954

Harold Y. Saunders - Jan. 1954-Jan. 1958

Jesse L. Puckett - Jan. 1958-Jan. 1970

Wyman B. Porter - Jan. 1970-Jan. 1974

Marshall Long - Jan. 1974-Jan. 1982

Neil S. Hackworth - Jan. 1982-Jan. 1995

Donald Cubert Sr. - Jan. 1995-Nov. 1995

David Eaton - Nov. 1995-2002

Tom Hardesty - Jan. 2003-

Curtis Preston Hall was born in Shelby County in 1873. When he was 23 years old, he joined his father, W. H. Hall, in the lumber and coal business in Shelbyville and remained active in it until his death at the age of 74 on April 18, 1948.

W. H. Hall started Hall and Stewart in 1889 and when C.P. Hall entered the business in 1896, the name was changed to Hall & Son, and later to Hall & Davis.

C.P. Hall married Nancy Wilkinson of Nelson County in October 1905. In 1908, they built at home at 720 Magnolia Avenue in a new subdivision called Fairview that had been recently incorporated into the city limits of Shelbyville. Hall was one of the founders of the Shelby County Building and Loan Association, and served as its president from 1926 until his death in 1948. He entered politics during a period when slates of candidates often formed and reformed around various office-seekers. Election contests were spirited and to the winning faction went the privilege of filling city jobs. In 1910, he was chosen by the City Council to represent the 6th Ward after the council redrew the ward boundary to exclude T. S. Baxter, a Black Republican, who had represented the 6th Ward for 18 years.

Hall served two terms on the council. He was elected in 1916 to the Board of Trustees of the Shelby Graded School District on a slate that was in opposition to the old Board's rules concerning the qualifications of teachers. In 1921, he was elected mayor for the 1922-26 term when then Mayor Leon Rothchild broke a tie among City Council factions in his favor. Mayor Hall had to break another tie in 1925 by voting for himself for mayor for the 1926-30 term.

During his two terms in office, C. P. Hall paved Main Street in concrete from Sixth Street to the western city limits, oversaw extension of the sewer system, and reorganized the city debt.

Robert F. Matthews Sr. was born in Shelby County, the son of Benjamin Franklin and Margaret Killgore Matthews. He graduated from Louisville Male High School in 1915 and practiced law after graduation from the University of Michigan Law School in 1920.

While in Michigan, Mr. Matthews attended an Upper Room Bible Class and when he returned to Shelbyville, he organized a class at First Christian Church in January 1925 patterned after the one in Michigan. Under his leadership for 36 years, the Upper Room Class grew to about 125 young men. In his obituary of April 1961, it stated that the class "will ever be remembered as his dream of a united effort to study and worship in memory of some who gave their lives in defense of their country."

Matthews was president of the Shelby County Trust and Banking Company for 25 years. In 1922, he was elected to a two-year term as Shelbyville City Attorney and then served eight years as Shelby County Attorney. He was Mayor from 1934 to 1954, except for a four-month period when Lewis S. Frederick was mayor.

Matthews was described as "a man of strong convictions who strove to uphold what he believed to be right." He served as finance chairman of the Democratic State Campaign Committee. During World War I, he was in the U.S. Naval Reserves. He married the former Zerelda Baxter of Richmond in 1922. They had three sons, Robert F. Matthews Jr., Ben Gaines Matthews, and William Edmund Matthews.

Lewis S. Frederick Jr. was born in Shelbyville in 1895 and attended Shelbyville High School and the Virginia Military Institute. He served as a bugler in the Kentucky National Guard on the Mexican border in 1916 and entered World War I on April 1917 in Company H 1st Kentucky Infantry. His unit sailed for France October 1918 and he mustered out as a First Lieutenant in January 1919. He married Mary Bruce Redd August 25, 1917. They had two children: a daughter, Lynn, and a son, Lt. Col. Lewis Frederick III who was killed in December 1944 in an air crash in England.

Frederick was a prominent tobacco man and served for many years as sales manager for the Shelby Looseleaf Tobacco Co. and the Growers and Globe warehouses in Shelbyville. He also worked in the Maysville and Lexington markets, and in Georgia and North Carolina.

In August 1945, he won the Democratic primary for mayor, defeating Glenn Harris. He was unopposed in the general election in November. He took office January 1946 amid expectations that his administration would soon complete a new swimming pool, city incinerator, and the construction of the Washington Street extension. However, Mr. Frederick's health soon began to fail and he was forced to tender his resignation on April 4, 1946. In his statement to the council, Mayor Frederick stated, "It was my greatest ambition to become a good Mayor of a good town—our own beloved little city."

His main accomplishment was to order a new $9,500 pumper for the fire department. Shortly after leaving office, he moved to Dover in Mason County where he died May 27, 1948 at the age of 52.

Harold Y. Saunders made $50 a meeting when he was mayor of Shelbyville. The six members of the City Council made $10. The city had three police cars, yet one was in need of repair. Nonetheless, during his term of office, he worked with other community leaders to "bring jobs for veterans because employment opportunities had been dormant for a number of years."

One of those avenues was through the Department of Economic Development and the state Chamber of Commerce, which hosted an industrial tour of Shelbyville in 1957. A newspaper article recounts the visit: "An interesting observation was the fact that the out-of-state visitors were just as interested in the schools, stores, recreational facilities and general appearance of the town as they were in the actual plant sites."

Saunders was also proud that the city sold the gas company and bought the water company to provide better services. In 1957, the water connection fee was set at $90, and sewer service increased from 20 percent to 50 percent of a water user's monthly bill. The reason was "dilapidated sewers must be repaired." The recommendations were "heartily endorsed by the bonding firm at the time of the water company purchase and had this been in effect all along, sounder economy would have been realized." A follow-up to the tour was a workshop to discuss problems faced by Shelbyville and five other communities in relation to industrial development.

Saunders also promoted a mobile X-ray unit that visited Shelbyville in May 1957 to help screen citizens for tuberculosis. He was among the first to be X-rayed in the unit brought to town through the Shelby County Health Department. Close to 1,800 took advantage of the mobile unit.

He continued with the plans to extend Washington Street even though some residents objected to the change, which eliminated two-way traffic on Main Street. Intertstate-64 was also started during Saunders' administration.

Saunders, a native of Shelby County, was the son of Nova Young and Clifton Saunders. Both had been teachers, even though Saunders knew the happiest day in their lives was when he became the first family member to graduate from college. He graduated from Henry Clay High School in eastern Shelby County, Transylvania College, and the University of Louisville School of Law. He was a practicing attorney from 1947-70, and served as circuit judge for 20 years.

Jesse L. Puckett was one of twelve children of Egbert Barnabus and Mary Bondurant Perkins Puckett. He was born September 3, 1912, and died April 6, 1995. He owned Puckett's Men's Shop on Main Street when he decided to run for a seat on the Shelbyville City Council. After a two-year term, he cast a vote for himself as Mayor of Shelbyville—a position he held for three terms. He won his second term by one vote over Republican Laban Jackson Jr.—a race that nicknamed him Landslide Puckett for a number of years. When he was defeated for his fourth term by Dr. Wyman B. Porter, Puckett was named City Clerk. He also served as a director of the Shelby County Industrial and Development Foundation since it was founded in 1958. He retired only two months before his death in 1995 at age 82.

During his term as Mayor Puckett built the first city hall called the Municipal Building at 1040 Main Street, which is now home to the Fire and Police departments. It was designed by Shelbyville architect Quintin Biagi. He founded the Shelbyville Housing Authority and opened the first federal housing project, which was named Bondurant Heights after Puckett's mother, secured rights to Lake Shelby for use by the citizens as a recreational site; constructed Guist Creek Lake as the city's main water source with assistance from then Governor A. B. "Happy" Chandler; built the sewer treatment plant on Old Taylorsville Road.

Puckett was named Shelbyville's first Employee of the Year in 1984 by then Mayor Neil Hackworth. Besides his public service, Puckett was a veteran of World War II, a former president of the Shelbyville

Kiwanis Club, member of the Shelbyville Country Club where he scored two holes-in-one, and owner of the men's clothing store from 1949-71 after working as a cutter at the former Lee-McClain Clothing Co.

He was considered a town character because of his nickname "The Old Dog," and was honored for his love of his hometown by the Industrial Foundation when the East End Triangle was landscaped and dedicated in his memory and that of fellow Industrial director Eddie Hall.

He and his wife of 54 years, the former Ella Mae Terry of Clarkson, had three daughters.

Wyman B. Porter served as mayor 1970-74. He was an optometrist in Shelbyville for more than 45 years, until his retirement in 1995. A native of Central City, Porter died at age 75 at a fire in his home November 8, 1998. He was a former Chamber of Commerce president and former member of the City Council. He and his wife, the former Ann Newton, had one son, Scott, and one granddaughter.

During his four years as mayor, Porter did not take a full salary. In appreciation of his generous public service, the Street Department building on College Street was named after him. In 1973, Porter tried to ban the sale of pornography in Shelbyville. Playboy magazine fought the ordinance and had it overturned.

Porter collected antique mechanical banks that lined a shelf in his optometrist's office on Sixth Street. Many were destroyed, though, when a fire in 1985 destroyed his office and heavily damaged four downtown buildings. The structures were eventually torn down, which prompted the city to look at creating an Historic District ordinance to protect future structures from such a fate or from being replaced with buildings not conducive to the historic character of Shelbyville. Porter relocated his optometrist's office to Washington Street where he retired in 1995 due to poor health.

Marshall Long was born in Shelbyville in 1937 and is a graduate of Centre College in Danville. After serving two terms as mayor, he was elected State Representative from the 58th District, a position he held until being elected State Senator from the 20th District in 1998. Among his many citations in the General Assembly, Long was named Most Effective House Member in 1996 and Most Effective Legislator in 1998.

Long was proud of the relationship that was developed between the city and county government during his term in office. "Years ago there was much animosity between the city and the county. I think the merger of the high schools (in 1975) and the joint efforts of the road departments have helped tremendously in bringing the city and county together," he said during a 1978 interview as he began his second four-year term.

He was pleased with the successful push for annexing certain areas of the city and for expanding the city's sewer lines, as well as maintaining a professional police and fire department, building a financial surplus, keeping up building inspections, and renovating the City Hall at Tenth and Main.

He and his family had owned and operated Long Block & Supply while he was mayor, during which time he also served on the zoning board and hospital board. He sometimes was criticized for conflicts of interest in his business life and political life.

One incident that stood out in Long's mind during his time in office occurred in the fall of 1976 when Shelbyville was planning a Bicentennial Parade. The night before the parade, Police Chief Edris Belcher notified Long that he had been told the Ku Klux Klan intended to march in the parade the following Saturday morning. As a precaution, Mayor Long called the Kentucky State Police and asked them to send additional troopers because Shelbyville only had 10 police officers at the time.

Long recalled, "Saturday morning, we were to form up the parade at the Shelby County Fairgrounds, and sure enough, there were about 10 to 15 members of KKK, complete with white robes, masks, guns (so I was told), and their usual low IQs, in the fairgrounds preparing to join the parade. I met with them and carefully outlined that I had no intentions of letting them march, and explained that they were not from Shelbyville and they were not welcome. They began to mouth off about what they intended to do and surrounded me in the parking lot."

Long did not know at the time that the University of Kentucky had a football game that day and that there were no state police available to send to Shelbyville. In addition, there was a large contingency of local African American citizens gathering at Seventh and Main who Long said, "were not very happy, for good reason."

Shortly before the parade was to start, while Long was still arguing his case with the KKK, one state police cruiser pulled into the fairgrounds. The trooper got out of his car, opened his trunk, and pulled out a pump shotgun. "He then pumped the shell into the chamber; a sound you could clearly hear over what suddenly became a very quiet fairground," Long recalled. "At that point, the leader of the KKK decided they would not march and he ordered his cohorts to load up. After a threat to "get me and my kids" and returning to Shelbyville for another parade, they left quietly."

That night, the KKK did return to burn a cross on Old Zaring Mill Road but the Sheriff's Department kept them well away from the city limits.

Long said, "I heard later that the KKK had put out a "wanted poster" with my picture on it. I really hope it was not one with me in my leisure suit. Regardless, the KKK never returned to Shelbyville and in the end we had one great Bicentennial Parade."

He and his wife, the former Claudette Hulette, are parents of Tyler, Matthew, Hannah and David.

Neil S. Hackworth graduated from Shelbyville High School in 1966 and after graduating from Kenyon College received a law degree from the University of Kentucky. He married his high school sweetheart, Sharon Kemper, and they had one son, Will, and one daughter, Melissa.

When he took office in 1982, Shelbyville came under a national microscope as a finalist for General Motors' Saturn automotive plant. Other industrial recruiters took notice and Shelbyville became a hot spot. Several located within city limits. However, much occurred outside the city's boundaries which Hackworth said was "a situation that often led to a demand for increased city services without a corresponding increase in the money needed to help pay for them."

At the same time, downtown Shelbyville was in decline because of its close proximity to shopping malls in eastern Jefferson County. Wal-Mart came to town and a westend shopping center was developed. Later in his term as mayor, Boone Station Road was built and the Hi-Point Center was developed. Downtown began its transition to becoming a home for antique and specialty shops.

An important step was the town's decision to participate in the state Main Street Program and to hire a full-time downtown coordinator. The Historic District was created; the Shelby Development Corporation was formed; and a loan pool was established for downtown property owners to change the face of the area. Hackworth said the centerpiece of this effort was the Shelbyville 2000 Plan completed in 1988.

In the early 1980s, responsibility for services transferred from the federal government to state and local governments. To remain fiscally sound, Shelbyville imposed a 1 percent occupational tax, a levy that became the tax choice of communities across Kentucky.

Another response focused on making local government more entrepreneurial. The city bought a private golf course and converted it into a public course—a source of revenue that ultimately enabled the city to support its parks and recreation services with user fees instead of taxes.

It was obvious the job of mayor was becoming more than could be handled on a part-time basis. So the salary was increased to compensate for the responsibilities. Additional personnel positions were also added to modernize city government and its management practices. Tied in with this was the process of developing a new City Hall.

Hackworth said not all the events during his term as mayor were good news, though. He recalled fires that destroyed Centenary United Methodist Church and a section of buildings on Sixth Street; a tornado at Governor's Square shopping center; numerous floods; and the potential breach of the dam at the country club.

He also recalled race-related issues brought to the forefront by the Rev. Louis Coleman, a state civil rights activist with ties to Shelbyville. "We learned that crumbling school buildings, such as the old High Street School, an all-white city police department, and unsafe housing in predominately black neighborhoods were symbols of racism and segregation that had to be addressed."

When these issues could not be solved overnight, it was sometimes seen as resistance on the part of city leaders. However, Hackworth said solutions were eventually brought about, including adding minority staff members at all levels of authority.

It was also during Hackworth's time in office that area farmers first began bringing migrant labor from Mexico and Central America.

He resigned in 1995 before his term of office was completed to accept a position with the Kentucky League of Cities.

Donald Cubert Sr. was appointed by the City Council to serve as mayor when Hackworth resigned. He did so until an election in November 1995 when he was defeated by fellow council member, David B. Eaton.

Cubert was born in 1928 in Spencer County. He and Tennie Burgin were married in 1952 after which they moved to Shelby County to be near her family. He worked for Joe Davis, who sold automobiles and operated a service station. Cubert took over the station in 1957 and moved it to Eleventh and Main Streets in 1961. He retired and sold the business to his son Donald in 1995. Cubert was inspired to run for public office through his involvement with the Jaycees, which was at that time an all-male club. He also named public servants that he admired and in whose footsteps he wanted to follow (Circuit Judge Coleman Wright, and Mayors Paul Schmidt and Jesse L. Puckett).

He was elected to City Council in 1982 and is proud to have served on practically every city committee. He was a member of the Parks & Recreation Board for ten years, and served on the Boards for 911, Landfill, Tree, and Shelby Development Corporation. During his short term as mayor, Cubert believed he laid the groundwork for improving relations between city and county governments. One key step was starting discussion about the interlocal agreement regarding the occupational taxes.

The mayor and members of the city council in 2001. Standing, left to right: Bobby Hudson, Mike Miller, Tom Hardesty, Charles T. Long. Seated, left to right: Val Owens, Mayor David Eaton, Don Cubert.

After he was defeated by Eaton, Cubert was re-appointed to the Council and was re-elected again when that term expired. Looking back over his years of service, he's proud of the new City Hall and the leap of faith that the city took in buying what was to become Weissinger Hills Golf Course.
The Cuberts have two children.

David B. Eaton began his term on Shelbyville City Council in 1986. Ten years later, following a special election after the resignation of Mayor Neil S. Hackworth, he took over as mayor. Initially, he served part-time since he was a teacher for Shelby County Public Schools. He eventually retired to devote full-time to the city. He announced his candidacy for State Representative for the 2002 election but was defeated by Brad Montell. He and his wife, Donna, have two children. During his years in office, Eaton gave annual reports to the Council and citizens about city business.

1996: The SHARE Shelbyville program was started to encourage people to volunteer for community service in exchange, for the ability to purchase a food package for a nominal cost. City Council meetings were televised on the local access cable TV channel. The first round of a three-year Repair Affair grant was implemented to perform aesthetic work on homes. An interlocal agreement was established between city and county government to alleviate double-taxation for some citizens in relation to the occupational taxes imposed by both governmental agencies. For the city's efforts in working with youth, it received the Kentucky League of Cities' President's Award of Excellence.

1997: Work continued to improve the appearance of Shelbyville, through the Tree Board, the Repair Affair grants, and the Clean Community Program. A highlight was the unveiling of the horse statue and landscaping of the west-end triangle, compliments of Edward and Mary Gaylord. The new City Hall opened its doors. Two award-winning projects were the Streetscape Project for downtown that won the KLC President's Award of Excellence and the Youth Summit that was named by the Partnership for Kentucky Youth as one of three outstanding projects in the state.

1998: Shelbyville received another KLC President's Award of Excellence for its SHARE Shelbyville Program. The city was also named one of five Renaissance Gold Cities in Kentucky. Work was begun on a fire sub-station at Weissinger Hills to serve residents in that area.

1999: More than $1 million in grants was received during the year. The funds helped build a 1 million-gallon water tank, complete another block of the Streetscape design, to rehabilitate some buildings downtown, and upgrade police equipment. Work with the community's youth continued through a Job Fair, Project Graduation, a Summer Youth Program, and the Teen Court Program operated by District Judge Linda Armstrong.

2000: A city police officer was named a School Resource Officer for West Middle School, a collaborative effort with Shelby County Public Schools as a preventive measure. The city started a website: www.shelbyvillekentucky.com. The Sister City Program was revived with Bitburg, Germany— a venture that was started in the 1960s under the administration of Mayor Jesse L. Puckett along with the Shelbyville Business & Professional Women's Club. The Family Activity Center opened its doors at Clear Creek Park, following a cooperative effort between the city, county and citizens/organizations. The center received the Governor's Award of Excellence for parks/recreation. The final crowning event of city/county cooperation was merger of the city sewer system with the county Sanitation District, opening up more avenues for sanitation improvement in the community.

DELEGATES TO CONSTITUTIONAL CONVENTIONS

By Ted Igleheart

The records of the First Constitutional Convention held in Danville in 1792 do not contain a list of delegates. In the Constitutional Convention of 1799, Benjamin Logan and Abraham Owen were elected to represent Shelby County. Andrew S. White and John W. Johnstone represented the county in the Constitutional Convention of 1850. J. C. Beckham represented the county in the Constitutional Convention of 1890-91.

STATE REPRESENTATIVES

By Marshall Long

Disclaimer: errors in this document are due to the condition of its sources. Variation in spellings is actual variations within sources.

There have been any number of parties representing Shelby County in the Kentucky House of Representatives. The first mention of a party affiliation is in 1828 when Henry Crittenden, James Ford and George Woolfolk ran under the banner of the American Party. The Republicans were first mentioned in 1829 when Samuel Shannon, Percival Butler, and George Johnston ran under that banner. In 1830 Butler ran as a Jacksonian, accompanied by Andrew S. White and James C. Sri on that ticket. The Whigs dominated from 1834 to 1853, but there is no further mention of them after that date.

Democrats were elected from 1869 to 1999, a period of 130 years, before Gary Tapp finally claimed the seat for the Republicans. Marshall Long of Shelbyville holds the distinction of the longest serving Representative from Shelby County, serving from 1982 to 1998 when he was elected to the State Senate.

1793-1794	William Shannon and Benjamin Roberts
1794	Benjamin Logan
1796-97	John Knight and Thomas J. Guinn
1798	Benjamin Logan and Bland Williams Ballard
1799	Joseph Winlock and Bland W. Ballad
1800	John Allen and Bland W. Ballard
1801	Alexander Reid
1802	Alexander Reid and John Pope
1803	Bland W. Ballard and James Wardlow
1804	Matthews Flournoy and Alexander Reid
1805	Matthews Flournoy and Bland W. Ballard
1806	John Simpson and Alexander Reid
1807-08	John Simpson and Bland W. Ballard
1808-09	Thomas Johnston and Bland W. Ballard
1809-11	John Simpson, Abraham Owen and Thomas Johnston

1811-12	John Simpson, James Moore and James Young
1812-13	Thomas Johnston, James Young, and Samuel Tinsley
1813-14	Thomas Johnston, Samuel White, and James Ballard
1814-15	Samuel White, James Ballard, and George Knight
1815-16	James Ford, John Logan, and George Knight
1816-19	James Ford, John Logan, and Benjamin Eleston
1819-20	Samuel White, Joseph Knight, and Samuel Oglesby
1820	Cuthbert Bullitt, George Pierce, and William Boyd
1821-22	John Younger, William Logan, and George Pearce
1822	Henry Smith, George Woolfolk, and John Wells
1823	John Logan, Samuel Oglesby, and John Younger
1824-25	Henry Crittenden, Thomas P. Wilson, and James Ford
1826	John Logan, Alexander Reed, and James Ford
1826-28	Alexander Reid, James Ford, and David Wilson
1828-29	Henry Crittenden, James Ford, and George Woolfolk
1829-30	Samuel Shannon, Percival Butler, and George Johnston
1830-31	Andrew S. White, Percival Butler, and James C. Sri
1831	Thomas P. Wilson, Henry Crittenden, and James M. Bullock
1832-33	George W. Johnston and Percival Butler
1833-34	Andrew S. White and Isham T. Underwood
1834-35	James Ford and James C. Sri
1835-36	James Ford and Samuel W. White
1836-37	James C. Sprigg and Samuel Shannon
1837-38	James C. Sprigg and Nicholas Smith
1838-39	James C. Sprigg and William C. Bullock
1839-40	James C. Sprigg and John A. Logan
1840-41	James C. Sprigg and James Ford
1841-42	Walter C. Drake and William Welch
1842-43	William S. Helm and Robert Doak
1843-44	Lloyd Tevis and Fleming H. Garnett
1844-45	James Ford and Martin D. McHenry

1845-46	Shannon Reid and James G. Balee
1846-47	Martin D. McHenry and William L. Jones
1847-48	John Brown and Hartwell A. Baile
1848-49	William L. Jones and Josiah H. Magruder
1849-50	Gideon Mitchell and Tand N. Allen
1850-51	George W. Johnston and Thomas Todd
1851-52	James L. Caldwell and James C. Sri
1853-54	Marion C. Taylor and Thomas Jones
1855-56	Archibald C. Brown and Joshua Tevis
1857-58	James L. Caldwell and Stephen T. Drane
1859-61	Henry Bohannon and Fielding Neel
1861-63	John B. Cochran
1863-65	Henry Bohannon
1865-67	Joseph W. Davis
1867-69	Calvin Sanders
1869-71	John F. Wright
1871-73	P. J. Foree
1873-76	Thomas W. Henton
1877-78	John A. Thomas
1879-80	G. N. Robinson
1881-82	Harrison Bailey
1883-84	J. C. Beckham
1885-86	G. N. Robinson
1887-90	J. J. Long
1891-93	John Botts
1894	Newton Bright
1896-97	P. J. Foree
1898-99	Michael O'Sullivan
1900-03	S. W. Booker
1904-07	J. A. Frazier
1908-09	Elliott B. Beard

1910-13	John W. Holland
1914-15	W. R. Ray
1916-17	George L. Pickett
1918-21	W. T. Beckham
1922-23	John E. Brown
1924-29	E. J. Doss
1930-31	Ralph Gilbert
1932-33	G. Murrell Middleton
1934-35	Ralph Gilbert
1936-39	William T. Baker
1940-47	Harry F. Walters
1948-49	Laban Phelps Jackson
1950-51	W. R. Reasor
1952-53	Dr. Benjamin F. Shields
1954-59	Paul T. Radcliffe
1960-63	Luther F. Morgan
1964-67	Louis T. Peniston
1968-71	Ralph Mitchell
1972-73	Louis T. Peniston
1974-77	David G. Mason
1978-81	Stephen W. Wilborn
1982-98	Marshall Long
1999-02	Gary Tapp
2003-	Brad Montell

Source: Biographical Directory of the Kentucky General Assembly 7:7
Source: 1908 - 1948, Staff, Jim Monsour. 03/02/99 2:19 PM
Source: "ASSEMBLY," this is from a LRC Library document.
C:\Program Files\Microsoft Office\Templates\kystsen.dot

KENTUCKY STATE SENATORS
(REPRESENTING SHELBY COUNTY)

Disclaimer: errors in this document are due to the condition of its sources. Variation in spellings is actual variations within sources.

There is no reference to party affiliation in the record books until 1829 when Samuel W. White ran on the American Party ticket. Two years later he ran as a Republican. The Whigs were the dominant party in representing Shelby County from 1833 to their disappearance just prior to the Civil War. William C. Bullock was the last Whig to represent Shelby County, from 1857 to 1859. The Democrats assumed control of the Senate seat from 1869 with the election of William Johnson. It remained in their control for 132 years, until Gary Tapp was elected in 2002 as the continuation of a Republican take-over of the Kentucky State Senate. In January 2003, Republicans held a majority of 22 to 16. The Democrats enjoyed a three-to-one majority in the State House of Representatives.

1792-95	No record
1796-97	David Standiford
1798	David Standiford and John Poe
1799	No record
1800-05	Joseph Winlock
1806-11	William Roberts
1811-13	Joseph Winlock
1813-14	John Allen
1814-15	Winfield Bullock (resigned) and James Young
1815-19	James Simrall
1819-22	James Ford
1823-31	Samuel W. White
1831-39	William G. Boyd
1839-43	George W. Johnston
1843-47	Walter C. Drake
1847-52	John W. Russell
1852-53	William C. Bullock
1853-54	Martin D. McHenry
1855-58	William C. Bullock

1859-63	Walter C. Whitaker
1863-65	Samuel E. DeHaven
1865-67	Walter C. Whitaker
1867-69	Thomas B. Cochran
1869-74	William Johnson
1875-76	Thomas J. Barker
1877-80	M. T. Carpenter
1881-82	C. H. Harwood
1883-84	J. D. Elliott
1885-88	G. G. Gilbert
1889-92	W. H. Anderson
1894-97	George S. Fulton
1898-01	Newton Frazier
1902-05	W. W. Booles
1906-07	Ben Johnson
1908-09	Sam H. Peters
1910-13	Phil Beard
1914-17	W. W. Booles
1918-19	H. A. Hinkle
1920-27	Newton Bright
1928-33	Percy Gaines
1936-39	Ralph Gilbert
1940-43	Gilbert Wood
1944-45	Martin T. Smith
1946-53	Louis Cox
1954-57	Dr. Benjamin F. Shields
1958-61	James R. Hamilton
1962-65	Marvin Edwards
1966-69	Lawrence Wetherby
1970-73	Mack Walters
1974-81	Tom Easterly
1982-98	Fred Bradley
1999-02	Marshall Long
2003-	Gary Tapp

The old Shelbyville Post Office was completed in 1928 at Seventh and Main Streets, on the site of Stuart's Female College.

An interurban car on Main Street in Shelbyville headed east near Sixth Street before 1920.

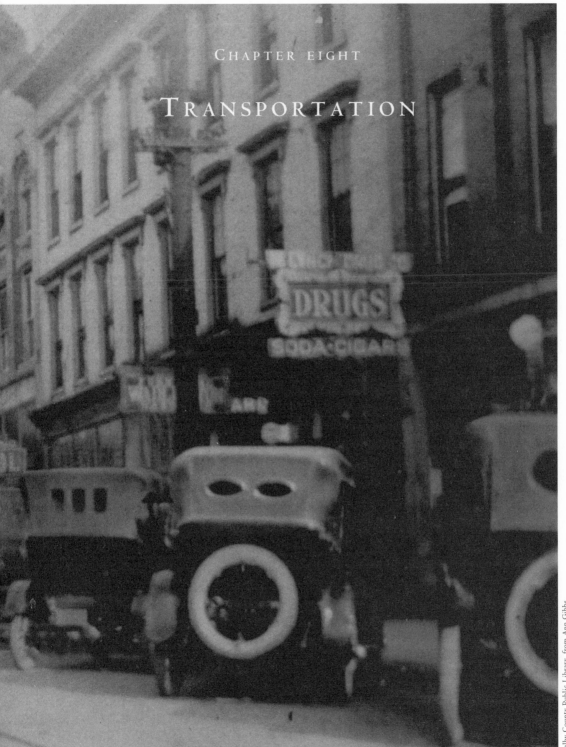

CHAPTER EIGHT

TRANSPORTATION

Shelby County Public Library, from Ann Gibbs.

A reminder of the early days in transportation was the old livery stable that stood at Fifth and Washington Streets.

TRANSPORTATION

By Charles T. Long

In the frontier days of Kentucky, Indians traveled paths worn by buffalo. When the white man came, those buffalo traces, as they were called, became dirt roads for settlers. It is believed that the "big dirt road," the first major road through Kentucky that began in Maysville, stretched southward to Lexington and then westward to the Falls of the Ohio at Louisville, originally followed a buffalo trace through Shelby County. It ran 2.5 miles north of Shelbyville and passed the Painted Stone Station of pioneer Squire Boone. From those humble beginnings came a transportation system in Shelby County that today features numerous roads and a major interstate highway.

Early work on roads was the responsibility of county government. Able-bodied men were expected to give a portion of their time to roadwork. The development of roads in the late eighteenth century was accompanied by the building of inns and taverns to ease the weary traveler. Besides offering rest and refuge, they played a big part in the social and political life of the community.

A big log tavern in Shelby County called Cross Keys Inn served over 10,000 travelers from 1800 to 1825. They came by wagon, stagecoach, and horse, paying 20 cents for a meal, eight cents for lodging, and five cents for a shot of whiskey. Maybe the most prominent tavern in Shelby County started in 1837. The Simpsonville establishment was called Old Stone Inn.

As years piled atop one another, numerous covered and iron truss bridges were built. They gave way in the 1930s to concrete bridges.

In 1871 the 18-mile Shelby Railroad Co. began operating between Shelbyville and Anchorage in Jefferson County. The main rail shipping point for freight in and out of Shelby County was at Christiansburg. The last railroad passenger service ended in 1971. Norfolk Southern today maintains freight service in Shelby County for several businesses.

The early part of the twentieth century saw new forms of transportation in Shelby County in the form of the bus and the interurban line. Bus service was one of the main modes of transportation between Louisville and Lexington from the late 1920s until the late 1990s. The interurban rail line between Louisville and Shelbyville operated from 1910 to the late 1930s. During World War II, its tracks were taken up and used for the war effort.

The construction of I-64 through the county provided an important link east and west and has stimulated development at its interchanges. It must be considered one of the reasons for increased housing developments for people working in Louisville, Frankfort, Georgetown, and Lexington.

AVIATION

By William Shannon

On October 12, 1945, a tract of land between U.S. 60 and Benson Road owned by Mr. and Mrs. Clarence Catlett Sr. was leased by Scharton Flying Service, Inc. to establish the Shelby County Airport. The Scharton Flying Service was composed of R. C. Scharton, president; Virginia T. Shannon, vice-president; and William L. Shannon, secretary/treasurer. With the help of Philip Ardery of Frankfort, the airport was approved by the state. The purpose of the airport was to make available services to transit airplanes, provide a base for crop dusting, make Shelby County better-known, and provide an opportunity to returning World War II veterans to learn a skill.

In that regard, on June 3, 1946, the directors of Scharton Flying service approved a contract with the government for Veteran's Flight Training under a law that provided veterans training for careers in civil aviation. During the next six years, 230 veterans signed up for this program.

Running the operation were the Catlett family, R. C. Scharton, and William L. Shannon. Helping was A. C. Weiss, a mechanic and instructor, Gus Gillette, an instructor, and Mr. and Mrs. B. C. Thacker, who were caretakers, cashiers and record keepers.

The facilities included hangars, a repair shop, an office, living quarters, plus four Aeronca trainers. When R. C. Scharton resigned January 13, 1947, Scharton Flying Service, Inc., was dissolved and a new corporation—Shelby Flying Service, Inc.—was formed. The officers were Clarence Catlett, president; Emma Catlett, vice-president; William L. Shannon, secretary/treasurer. At the death of Clarence Catlett on April 9, 1948, Emma Catlett became president with Virginia Shannon as vice-president and William L. Shannon as secretary/treasurer.

The airport and flying service flourished for the next few years until the Veteran's Flight Training program ended. On February 28, 1953, the directors agreed to cease operation and on March 1, 1953, sold all buildings, stock, and supplies to Emma Catlett. Mrs. Catlett was soon able to lease the airport to Cummins Flying Service of Harrodsburg, Kentucky. This arrangement continued for several years until the airport was closed.

BUS TRANSPORTATION

By Roger Green Jr. and Curtis Hardesty

Early mass transportation began in Shelbyville with the construction of the interurban rail line, which was completed and operational from Louisville to the Shelby Fairgrounds on August 20, 1910. It provided inexpensive transportation and freight hauling to Louisville on a daily basis. The line eventually ran through town along Main Street to Second Street where there was a trolley turnaround and station on the northeast corner of Second and Main Street. During World War II the tracks were taken up and used for the war effort.

The origin of bus service in Shelbyville closely parallels the development of bus service throughout the country. The first bus service from Louisville to Lexington was begun by Harold O. Barnes and his father, James. In 1921, the Barnes Brothers Busline began with two, seven-passenger Studebaker automobiles. These automobiles were not heavy enough to make these continued long runs and were replaced in a couple of years with Fagel buses. In 1928, the Barnes brothers purchased four Yellow Coach Buses, which were nicknamed "the Yellow Birds".

Bus service, via Greyhound Bus Lines, came to Shelbyville in the early 1940s. The station was a commission agency located on Main Street between Fifth and Sixth Streets, in a restaurant operated by Paul Long. The station moved to several different locations in the city. The second location was at the corner of Eighth and Main across the street from Blue Gables Motel. Next the station was moved to the south side of Main between Sixth and Seventh Streets. Again the station was moved to the building containing Green's Bar and Grill at Second and Main Streets. The bus station occupied one side of this building and Green's Bar occupied the other side. Ownership of the agency changed hands during this time, when Paul Hardesty purchased the agency from Paul Long in 1957. The station moved once more

The second Half-Way House restaurant on U.S. 60 in the 1950s.

Ellis McGinnis photograph.

367

to a location on the north side of Washington Street between Seventh and Eighth Streets. Lastly, in the late 1970s it was moved to a service station located on the west side of the Shelby County Fairgrounds. There were also a couple of bus stops east of Shelbyville. The W. A. Smith Sr. family built the Halfway House bus stop on old U.S. 60 by Peytona. The Smiths ran the bus stop until the early 1940s then they went out of business. When U.S. 60 was rebuilt, a new Halfway House was built on the new road. The Shady Rest, later called the Old Colonel bus stop, was built in 1925 or 1926 approximately one-mile east of Clay Village. The Old Colonel bus stop closed in the mid-1950s and was converted into a home.

Bus service was one of the main modes of transportation between Louisville and Lexington from the late 1920s until the late 1960s. The advent of the automobile and the interstate highway system greatly diminished service to the smaller rural towns in Kentucky. But while it lasted, it was a primary means of daily transportation for those persons traveling between Louisville, Frankfort, and Lexington. Scheduled service was approximately once an hour. Tickets could be bought for each trip or as a book of discounted tickets. Each was hand written on a preprinted form and then stamped with a large embossing stamp to verify the ticket for the driver. Scheduled connections, like the railroad, could be made in the larger cities for travel to any part of the country. Greyhound service was the preferred method of short distance travel as the train schedules were not as frequent and more expensive. Like the train service Greyhound enjoyed a large volume of business during World War II, when travel by the military was of primary importance.

Another aspect of bus service, especially Greyhound Bus Lines, was the freight service provided. Beneath the passenger compartment in large bins were carried the passenger baggage and also all manner of freight for local business needing quick delivery from Louisville or Lexington. Many local businesses could have same day delivery from Louisville or Lexington. All manner of freight was delivered from car parts for Pearce Motors to medical supplies for the hospital, as well as the delivery of The Louisville Times evening newspaper. The arrival of the paper was the cause of a gathering of many people each afternoon to get the latest news. This gathering was a social event for all regular customers with much joking and kidding among themselves.

The Greyhound station, while occupying several different locations, was a local business offering many different services other than just bus service alone. The Western Union office was located there and was a very busy place during the time when the tobacco market was in session. Memories of war and the bad news carried by a telegram often gave the Western Union office a morbid reputation, especially among the older generation of the town. In earlier years, it was a restaurant and soda fountain. One could buy a bus ticket to any part of the country, purchase the latest statewide newspaper, send or receive a telegram, ship or receive a package, purchase, in later years airline tickets, and as often happened meet friends there while conducting business. Families and friends were welcomed or tearfully departed on the bus.

In 1980, the Greyhound Lines made only four scheduled stops in Shelbyville at the Shelby Cab Company located on Second Street between Main and Washington Streets. By 1989, one bus ran each way between Louisville and Lexington per day. It made a flag stop in Shelbyville on the highway. In 1990, Greyhound suffered a severe and protracted work stoppage, and some time after that the Shelbyville service was discontinued.

The Shady Rest (later the Old Colonel) bus stop east of Clay Village.

HIGHWAYS, BYWAYS AND BRIDGES

By William "Whitie" Gray

Travel in Shelby County at the beginning of the 20th century was by horseback, horse drawn vehicles, and railroad. Roads were packed dirt or crushed stone and followed the natural lay of the land. Macadam or asphalt paving was non-existent until after the advent and proliferation of the automobile. Horse drawn rollers made of wood and filled with rock were used to compact crushed stone (or snow in the winter) where traffic was heaviest.

Horses could ford most streams in the northern half of the county. Bridges were needed only in a few strategic places. These were mostly wooden beams with heavy wood planks for the deck. More permanent bridges were made with stone arches.

The watershed drainage in Shelby County is ninety percent from north to south. Two of the four largest streams, Clear Creek and Bullskin Creek, join near Logan's Station to form Brashears Creek. Guist Creek joins Brashears Creek in Spencer County. They were deep enough most of the year to require bridges on the most used thoroughfares. Eventually all forty-three of the creeks and wet weather streams had names and roads that crossed them. Some were named for early settlers such as Jeptha Creek and Floyd's Fork (of Salt River), Benson, Lutz, Ballard, Wise, Fibles, Bradshaw, Britton, Long, Waifs, and Jenkins all had streams named for them. Others were named for trees like Mulberry, Beech, and White Oak or animals like Fox, Mink, and Wolf runs. There are Goose, Rattlesnake, and Tick Creeks.

Midland Trail from Louisville to Lexington, which ran west to east through the center of the county and crossed Long Run, Bullskin, Clear, Guist and Benson Creeks, is now U.S. 60. There were wood truss covered bridges over Clear Creek in Shelbyville and Benson Creek at Hardinsville, which is now Graefenburg. The patented wooden trusses had to have a roof to prevent weather damage and decay. The other four bridges were simple stone arches and subject to damage by spring flooding.

The covered bridge over Clear Creek at East Main Street, probably in the 1880s.

The two main turnpikes, Burks Branch and Christiansburg, entering Shelbyville from the north, crossed Clear Creek on Jail Hill Road and at the foot of Snow Hill. These were also covered bridges. The Mount Eden Turnpike out of town to the south crossed Clear Creek at Third Street.

Road building was arduous, using horse drawn (or oxen or mules) drag pans, graders and rollers without the benefit of any of the earth moving equipment that revolutionized highway construction during the second half of the century. No one considered building a road without taking into account where the horse would drink and the size and type of bridges needed. The springs on the Bagdad Road and other roads were walled with rock especially for the horse traffic.

Building the bridges was relatively easy compared to the labor intensity needed to build the abutments. Some of these required the most backbreaking labor of any projects built in this county. The bridge abutments and approaches on the original roads were built of quarried limestone (Kentucky granite) and laid, without mortar, beginning on bedrock or as deep as could be dug by hand. Most of the bridge abutments built for the wooden truss bridges were later used for the iron truss bridges that replaced them. The stone abutments on Jail Hill Road have supported four different types of bridges including a Queenpost Truss, a covered Burr-Kingpost Truss, an overhead iron truss, and a post World War II (WWII) Bailey Bridge.

Some of the early roads and bridges in the county were built by private landowners to access the railroad and ship their produce and livestock. A good example is the Joyes Station Road. Patrick Joyes built the road at his own expense, planting catalpa trees along both sides to shade the horses, and erecting a stone arch bridge over Nash's Run.

The stories of how the roads were built were fascinating, but my keenest attention was drawn to the iron truss bridges. Most of the bridges had been installed before 1930 and had served the county well for fifty or sixty years. They had been the elegant design solution in the earliest days of transition from horses to automobiles. Autos couldn't ford the streams and rubber tires couldn't step over ruts and washes. So better roads were a must and the problem of bridges was perfectly solved by the iron truss.

Firstly, they were light and many times stronger than wood, and secondly, they were easily transportable by railroad and horses and wagon to any remote area of the county. They were pre-engineered for any span or road limit and could be ordered to fit any job or road situation. The only weakness of the iron bridge design was their vulnerability to rust and need for regular maintenance. Over the next five decades this led to their demise. Because of poor maintenance, overgrowth, weather, and oxidation they seemed to fit into the landscape, becoming a part of nature. In time, automobile/truck transportation progressed to the point where the iron bridge was outmoded. Roads had to be built straighter and the bridges had to jump longer spans to make the roads smoother for the increased speeds and sizes of the auto, trucks, and buses.

As the development of the steam engine and the production of steel had been to the Nineteenth Century, so was the development of the diesel engine and reinforced concrete to the twentieth century. The steam shovel and steamroller were used to build the major turnpikes and the interurban. But road building, even with gasoline powered tractors, was slow and labored until the diesel engine was developed for earth moving machines in the 1930s. Some of the first power derricks, cranes, drag line shovels and bulldozers were brought to this county in the 1940s by L. L. Riggs on Ninth Street and D. L. Rice of Taylorsville and in the 1950s by Forrest Smith and John Booth.

Beginning in the 1920s reinforced and pre-stressed concrete had been developed and perfected along with the machinery, technology, and equipment to move, place and handle it. Concrete was no longer just a foundation material used for compression but could handle tensile forces and could soar into our tallest buildings and jump our longest spans in our bridges. The iron bridges of Shelby County started to give way to concrete in the 1930s.

According to an article in the Sentinel-News by Bennett Roach, the concrete bridge on U. S. 60 in Simpsonville replaced a wooden railroad bridge in 1927. The bridge over Clear Creek on Main Street (U. S. 60 East) was one of the first iron bridges to be replaced by concrete. In 1941, it was decided to

Road building machinery in Shelby County, ca. 1909.

Ellis McGinnis Collection, courtesy of Michael McGinnis.

improve the road to Frankfort by paving it with the new Bituminous Concrete (Black Top) and straightening many of the curves. The iron bridge over Clear Creek at Snow Hill was replaced in the 1950s and the old Third Street Bridge had to be replaced in the 1960s. It was the only iron bridge on a highway to have a pedestrian walkway along the outside of the truss allowing access to the sidewalks leading to the Grove Hill Cemetery. Then one by one the iron bridges were replaced or bypassed and removed as the roads were paved and improved. By the 1980s only a few iron bridges were left on the most remote roads. At one time there were 27 iron bridges (large and small), or their abutments, in Shelby County. In the spring of 1998, the last remaining iron bridge was washed off its abutments by a record spring flood. It had survived for 80 years across Brashears Creek on the Old Pickett's Dam Road. With its two-pier approach it was the longest bridge in the county and the oldest.

The iron bridge over Brashear's Creek was washed away in a spring flood in 1998.

INTERSTATE 64

By Charles T. Long

Perhaps the largest public works project ever built in Shelby County was the construction of Interstate-64. In terms of its impact on the economy and the changes it has produced in the lifestyle of the people living here, the interstate rivals in importance the coming of the railroads and the rural electrification of earlier times.

The federal government adopted the concept of a nationwide system of limited access super highways in 1956 when Congress passed the Interstate Highway and Defense Act. The U.S. Department of Transportation paid ninety percent of the cost of the new roads with individual states picking up the remaining 10 percent. Kentucky moved quickly to take advantage of the program, and by 1957 planning for a network of interstate roads totaling over 700 miles in the state was largely complete.

One of the roads was I-64, which was to run from Norfolk, Virginia, to St. Louis, Missouri, following more or less the route of the Midland Trail or U.S. 60. A portion of the new highway connected Louisville and Lexington via Shelby County. Just as important as the new highway to local communities was the location and number of interchange connections to be built. In this respect Shelby County was fortunate in having four access points to the interstate with Simpsonville and Waddy-Peytona each receiving one and Shelbyville two. No other county, except the urban counties of Jefferson and Fayette, had as many. Mack Walters of Simpsonville, who would later serve as a State Senator representing Shelby, Franklin and Spencer Counties, was Rural Highway Commissioner at the time the interstate was being planned and deserves the credit for the extra interchanges the county received.

The interstate in Shelby County was constructed in two parts. A 14-mile section between English Station Road near Middletown and Hwy. 55 at Shelbyville was begun in 1958 and opened on November 3, 1961. The 21.6-mile section from Shelbyville to Hwy. 127 at Frankfort was begun in early 1959 and dedicated less than three years later on December 19, 1961.

Over the years, I-64 has enabled many residents to commute daily to Louisville or Frankfort to work and shop. It has allowed people from other communities to live in Shelby County and still keep their jobs in the metropolitan centers. It was one of the critical factors that led to the growth of industry around Simpsonville and Shelbyville. The interstate gave people more options for where they could live, work, and shop. In breaking down the protection that distance once provided, it also forced Shelby County to change, to confront new challenges, and accept new ideas in its economy, government, and social structure.

Roads and Tunrpikes

By Ted Igleheart

The first major road through Kentucky was called the "big dirt road." It began in Maysville, originally called Limestone, and ran south to Lexington, then west to Frankfort, then west and north of Shelbyville, and onto the Falls of the Ohio at Louisville. It developed into a major thoroughfare because of its commercial traffic, in spite of the earlier Wilderness Trail blazed by the Boones from the Cumberland Gap across eastern Kentucky to the Bluegrass area. That road carried mainly immigration traffic and declined in use as the settlers from Virginia and the Carolinas decreased.

It is generally understood that the early trails followed the buffalo traces and Indian paths. It is believed that the "big dirt road" originally followed a buffalo trace through Shelby County, 2 1/2 miles north of Shelbyville, and passed the Painted Stone Station of Squire Boone. A careful observer may see the well-worn trace of the buffalo from the Old Eminence Road beside Mulberry Creek, through the Colony Subdivision behind the houses on the east side of Colony Drive. This route became known as "Boone's Wagon Road," beginning south of present Graefenburg, running north above Benson Creek to White Oak Creek, then west with Tick Creek, crossing Clear Creek 2 1/2 miles north of Shelbyville to the Painted Stone Station, then west to near Long Run where it passed through present Eastwood. This roadway was cleared enough to permit a wagon's passage in 1781.

In June 1778, however, the first man made road was created through the county when Col. James Harrod led about 60 men from Harrod's Station to the Falls of the Ohio, intending to join Gen. George Rogers Clark for the attack on Vincennes. It became the principal highway from Harrodsburg to the Falls. It branched off from the Wilderness Road at Harrod's settlement, extended northwest along a route similar to that of the present Norfolk Southern Railroad right of way, entered Shelby County south of the Shelby, Franklin, and Anderson Counties' corner, proceeded west through present Waddy, followed Jeptha Creek about six miles, crossed Guist Creek due east of the present junction of Rockbridge and Mount Eden Roads, and crossed Clear Creek south of present I-64. It then followed generally thereafter the path of the interstate highway to Eastwood where it then proceeded along the present U.S. 60 right of way which became the Midland Trail from Frankfort to the Falls.

Fifty years later, around 1825, the Midland Trail was straightened, improved, and became Kentucky's first macadamized road because it was the main stagecoach road in the state. As the most traveled road in the state, it became the first black topped, modern vehicle thoroughfare in the state.

By 1800, other dirt roads were plowed and spaded out toward other county seats, churches, schools, post offices, blacksmith shops, and stores. Citizen work on early roads was abrogated in favor of their privatization. In this way, maintenance would be assured. Toll gates were set up with a heavy pole across the road by individual land owners through whose land the roads passed and tolls were collected for the right of passage in order to recover the cost of improving or macadamizing the right of way. Private companies were also formed under authority of the county courts to improve a roadway, then collect tolls for passage, recovering their costs and making a profit for the stockholders. Only in the last thirty years of the 20th century were the last of the tollhouses torn down on the Old Taylorsville Road (Zaring Mill Road) near Clear Creek and on the Old Eminence Road at the end of Jail Hill Road.

Laws were passed after the Civil War to enable the counties to purchase the roadways from their owners and thereafter maintain them with public funds. Shelby County acquired over 500 miles of roads but had insufficient funds to keep up the maintenance. Magistrates were often elected purely for the purpose of obtaining public funding for improvement of the roads in their district. Deep ruts, mud, steep hills, and potholes kept the citizens in an uproar over broken wheels and axles and getting stuck so they couldn't get to town.

Modern motor vehicles required smoother and more properly maintained roads by the early 1900s, and the state was eventually authorized to take over the main county roads and maintain them. At one time, Shelby had more miles of roads than any nearby county, including Jefferson. With the state taking over the main roads, transportation improved drastically. The Midland Trail became U.S. 60, built with the help of federal funds, and was the most traveled highway in the state before I- 64 and I-75. During the administration of Governor A. B. Chandler (1955-59), a local leader, Mack Walters, was made Rural Highway Commissioner. His accomplishments included black-topping every rural road in the county and securing two access roads from the interstate into Shelbyville, one at Graefenburg, one at Waddy and Peytona, and one for Simpsonville. Under the leadership of county government, the county roads are in good condition and all the old obsolete bridges have been replaced except the Jail Hill Bridge.

Ellis McGinnis photograph.

U.S. 60 (earlier known as the Midland Trail) west of Shelbyville in 1955.

TRAINS

By William E. Matthews

Railroads have been an integral part of Shelby County's transportation system since 1871 when residents of Shelbyville got their first glimpse of a Shelby Railroad Co. locomotive, coal car, and three passenger cars at the 8th Street depot. The train's arrival was witnessed by several thousand citizens from Shelbyville and the surrounding area.

Construction of the Shelbyville-Anchorage branch line, via Simpsonville, had been started shortly after the Civil War. At Anchorage the branch made a connection with the Louisville Cincinnati & Lexington (LC & L), whose track ran north-westward from Louisville to LaGrange. At LaGrange it forked, one line going to Covington and Cincinnati, and the other through Eminence and to Frankfort and Lexington. During the 1970s, the Shelby Railroad Co. was leased by the LC & L which established through freight and passenger service from Shelbyville to Louisville. The LC & L itself became part of the Louisville & Nashville (L & N) through outright purchase in 1881. So L & N's official entrance into Shelbyville was in 1881.

With trackage already existing from Shelbyville west to Anchorage, construction of a new line, to be known as the "Shelby Cut-off", was begun in 1895 from Shelbyville to Christiansburg, approximately 8 1/2 miles east. The junction was made with the L & N's LaGrange-Lexington line.

Completed in 1896, the cut-off shortened both traveling time, and also rail distance by 10 miles from Louisville to Lexington

With completion of the cut-off, the Chesapeake & Ohio began using the tracks under a trackage rights agreement. This agreement continued until the C & O discontinued passenger service through Shelbyville in 1971.

The history of the Shelbyville-Bloomfield Branch of the L & N, a once-colorful, but long-since defunct line, is interwoven into the great railroad-building schedules of the post-Civil War days. In those days, the dreams and schemes involving railroading were many!

The railroad line between Shelbyville and Bloomfield was completed in 1880. When the LC & L was acquired by the L & N in 1881, the Bloomfield line came under L & N control through lease, and, later in 1891, through outright purchase. At one time, the branch went by the imposing name of the Shelbyville, Bloomfield & Ohio Railroad.

Prior to the advent of paved highways, the Bloomfield Branch saw operation of several daily passenger and freight trains. Rural communities such as Bloomfield, Finchville, and Taylorsville depended on this branch line for travel into Louisville, and as an outlet for agricultural produce.

Improved highway transportation in the 1930s cut deeply into the Bloomfield Branch's usefulness, and track service was reduced to a single daily run, except on Sunday. After World War II, train service was further reduced to a "mixed" (passenger and freight service) train on Tuesdays and Fridays.

Another problem for the Branch was the high maintenance costs necessary to keep the line up to standard. There were numerous trestles, 27 bridges, and a tunnel.

The final run for the Shelbyville-Bloomfield train occurred on Oct. 10, 1952. Immediately thereafter all tracks and structures were either removed or abandoned. A small amount of track was left intact south of Shelbyville so that this growing industrial area could still be served

On the occasion of Shelby County's 175th birthday in 1967, Raymond E. Bisha, vice-president of operations for the L & N, reviewed the railroad's "valuable ties" to Shelbyville. He made special mention of the "tobacco trains" which ran from Shelbyville to Louisville, and vice-versa, for three solid months during the sales season at the city's various warehouses. These trains of up to 18 cars left Shelbyville every evening for Louisville and return. Each of the cars contained as many as fifty hogsheads weighing 900 to 1000 pounds each. Overall, the L & N moved up to 600 tobacco cars each year.

The last L & N "local" passenger train which served Louisville and Lexington via Shelbyville was taken out of service in October 1941. However, it was still possible to ride from Louisville to Shelbyville until 1952 when the Bloomfield branch was discontinued

The L & N still serves Shelby County, but under a different name. A series of consolidations, if not mergers, found this railroad eventually losing its identity and becoming a part of the CSX Corporation in 1983. The CSX operates coal and miscellaneous freight trains through Shelbyville, and serves the needs of a growing number of Shelbyville industries.

The last C & O passenger train, The George Washington, came through Shelbyville on April 30, 1971. It operated for many years from Louisville to Ashland and then on to Washington, D. C. via another C & O train arriving from Cincinnati which picked up the passenger cars at Ashland. A companion train, The Sportsman, had been retired from service a number of years previously.

The first Southern Railway train to be welcomed into Shelbyville arrived in 1888 after 20 years of legislative and financial effort.

The Southern Railroad depot in Shelbyville in an undated photograph by Otho Williams.

Shelby County Public Library, from Peggy and Alwyn Miller.

The excitement that the train brought to town was recalled years later in a local newspaper article by James Clements Scott, who sold newspapers and candy and acted as a baggage man on Southern trains for many years after 1888.

According to "Scotty," that first train left the 10th Street station in Louisville and consisted of several grain cars and five cattle cars. The latter were filled with benches for a capacity number of people who were riding free to celebrate the occasion. There was a barrel of ice water, but no food, in each cattle car. "Scotty" remembered that Tom Hanlon of Shelbyville was the conductor on that first train. Other local conductors who worked the train in later years included Henry Kenney, Cam King, Henry Till, Frank and Stanley Hollingsworth, Will Carlin, J. R. Ragland, Len and Hugh Vanarsdale, and John Bryan.

Some of the railroad agents included Fisherville, Dick Bradley; Veechdale, Clarence Wilson; Shelbyville, John Bryan; Hempridge, C. D. Harris; and Waddy, Cad Clark.

The Louisville Southern began construction of a Louisville-Harrodsburg line in 1887, and in January 1888 the company asked for bids on 100 flat cars, 200 coal cars, and 200 box cars. By the end of February, grading was completed on the line, 10 Baldwin-type locomotives had been ordered, and land had been purchased in Louisville for a freight depot and repair shops.

Track laying continued through March and April at a brisk pace, and by April 20, the rails were within eight miles from Shelbyville, and from the other direction had passed through Lawrenceburg. The first train was welcomed by the mayor, city council, and several thousand enthusiasts. The carloads of grain were bound for points in Georgia and Alabama. Col. Bennett H. Young was on the train. He had just been elected president of the railroad, succeeding J. W. Stine who had resigned.

Excursion trains carried about 2,000 people over the road on May 30 to formally celebrate the opening of the line. A huge barbecue was held at Harrodsburg, and a few days later celebrations were held in Shelbyville and Lawrenceburg.

Soon after the completion of the main line from Louisville to Burgin (and a connection with the CNO & TP), the Louisville Southern leased the line to the Louisville New Albany and Chicago Railroad (the "Monon"), and it was operated as part of the Monon system until 1890.

Shortly after the lease was ended by mutual agreement, the Louisville Southern was leased to the East Tennessee Virginia and Georgia Railway. When a network of railroads across the south was organized in 1894 as the Southern Railroad Corporation, the Louisville Southern became a part of this new service.

The Southern Railway and the Norfolk Western Railway were merged in the 1970s to form the Norfolk Southern. This railroad operates several trains daily through Shelbyville, and has become increasingly important in sparking Shelbyville's industrial expansion.

The Southern's last passenger train through Shelbyville was in 1954.

The worst rail accident in local railroad history occurred on the evening of Sept. 8, 1881, when a Shelby Railroad Co. train jumped the track and plunged 30 feet into Floyds Fork Creek. Seven people were killed and 50 to 60 people injured. All of the deceased and a majority of the injured were from Shelby County.

The "mixed" train, which included two passenger cars and three freight cars, left Anchorage an hour late after making a connection with the LC & L which ran from Louisville to LaGrange. As the train approached Floyd's Fork, the headlights picked up a bull standing on the tracks. Frank Honaker, the engineer, decided to speed up in an effort to push the cow off the rails. Later, he told investigators that he was following orders in such emergencies.

But instead of being bowled aside, the cow got stuck under the wheels of the locomotive, causing it to jump the track and plunge 30 feet into the ravine below. The baggage car and both passenger cars followed.

Killed were: Col. Fielding Neel, a veteran of the Mexican War, a former Kentucky state senator, and then a director of the Farmers & Traders Bank in Shelbyville; W. H. Maddox, 34, Shelbyville Town Marshal, who was accompanying a prisoner from Indianapolis; T. D. Jones, Shelbyville shoemaker; Walter Scearce, prominent young Shelbyville businessman and farmer; Sea Captain E. Clinton Wentworth, en route from Boston to Shelbyville to visit his sister, Mrs. L. A. W. Fowler, an instructor at Science Hill; and M. W. Perry and J. L. Hardin, passengers.

More than half of the injured were from Shelby County and they included Capt. George Petry, conductor; Frank Honaker, engineer; Goodlow Hammons, W. H. Bryan and Joe Johnson, brakemen; Willis Pemberton, baggage master; and passengers W. H. Mooney, Sallie Jones, Julia Connelly, Mr. and Mrs. J. C. Beckham and daughter, Annie, Rev. W. H. Jensen, and Charles Jones.

A wave of public indignation followed the disaster. An old-time newspaper clipping headlined its story: "The Floyd's Fork Murder." Lots of wreck photos were made into stereoptican views, and exhibited on screens at the Opera House on Main Street in Shelbyville.

(The author thanks Charles Castner, retired executive with the L & N railroad and a consultant with the University of Louisville railroad collections, for his assistance on this chapter. Also important was the research performed by Bennett Roach, who owned The Shelby News for many years and wrote about local railroads in the 175th anniversary edition published jointly by The Shelby Sentinel and The Shelby News.)

Shelby County Public Library, Otho Williams photograph.

A bridge abutment under construction on the Southern Railroad at the mouth of Liveleys Branch in the 1880s.

Courtesy of the University of Louisville Archives, L & N Railroad Collection.

A Louisville & Nashville freight train passing the Shelbyville passenger station, ca. 1950s. The L&N freight station in the right background was built in 1870.

INTERURBAN

By Bobbie Smith

The first account of the interurban connection for Shelby County seems to be in February 1901. The surprise announcement in The Shelby Record stated that the Secretary of State and the Railroad Commission of the Commonwealth of Kentucky had issued certificates to secure a charter for a new company called the Shelby County Power and Railway Company. Totaling twelve miles in length, it would have the privilege of operating a telegraph or telephone line on or over the railway with the right to furnish surplus power used in operation of the railway to factories, mills, residences, churches, and others in need of power. It would run through Shelbyville to the fairgrounds and north toward Eminence. Stock in the company was to be $100 per share, not to exceed $200,000. The charter was to operate uninterrupted for 99 years unless discontinued by law. The route could be adjusted over time to provide facilities joining with the electric railway being built from Louisville to Anchorage and Pewee Valley.

By November 1901 the line was completed between Louisville, Anchorage, and Pewee Valley. The line was to extend to Shelbyville with a problem area noted at Floyds Fork Hill. Railway officials voted to review the land for the exact routes. By June 1902 the engineers arrived in Shelbyville and told the directors of the Railway Company the results of the land surveys. In late 1902, the announcement was made that the line would be built immediately. From Beechwood, the line would go down the State Pike (U.S. 60) to Simpsonville and Shelbyville.

At the meeting in December, the council passed an ordinance to provide right of way to the Louisville, Anchorage & Pewee Valley Company. It would run from west Washington Street to Second Street, then south to Southern Railway, running parallel with Southern Railway to First Street then again to Second.

In the spring of 1903, the railway company issued a letter to Mayor Willis of Shelbyville that stated the company had every intention of getting the construction underway, and reassuring the public that they would complete their proposed route. However, by May the mayor had come to believe that the company had not been able to sell its bonds and had begun looking at other companies to undertake the railway project.

Later that month, it was reported that the Louisville and Eastern Railway Company had obtained a mortgage on what the Louisville, Anchorage & Pewee Valley Company owned—their rights, franchises, and equipment. The report indicated the purchase was recorded in all four counties in which the line would operate. The route would extend the Louisville and Eastern Company from Beard's Station to LaGrange, from Lakeland to Shelbyville, and from Shelbyville to Frankfort. Though that sounded positive, in December *The Shelby Record* reported that the people in Shelbyville were skeptical about any railway being built. However *The Courier-Journal* reported that within the next few months construction was to begin.

Nothing more was done, and by May 1906 it appeared from the Shelby Record that the project was certainly doomed. The options once held by the Louisville and Eastern Railway had run out. Then on May 3, 1906, an agreement with the city gave the Louisville and Eastern Railway permission to lay tracks through the town, but the work had to be done on or before August 1, 1907, or the contract would become void. The entire ordinance was reprinted in the Shelby Record on May 4, 1906.

The Courier-Journal reported that funds for the completion of the line were available, the material to be used during construction was contracted, and the road was to be built immediately. The Louisville and Eastern Railroad, increasing its capital stock from $300,000 to $2,400,000, filed amended articles of incorporation.

A syndicate of local men purchased property along the proposed route into Shelbyville. They intended to develop residential lots alongside it and were willing to give right-of-way to the city and the Railway Company. By September the right-of-way from the county line to Lakeland had been obtained. By October the line from Shelbyville to Louisville looked more a certainty. In November 1906 the route from Simpsonville to Shelbyville was determined and would follow surveys made two years earlier along the lines of private property owners on the north side of the State Pike. By January 1907, everything seemed to be in place. Mike McCiuskey was given the contract for grading the first six miles west of Shelbyville.

More delays occurred when in April 1907 the Louisville and Eastern Railroad was declared insolvent and work ceased. A judge for the case recommended that the court complete the branch or up to $300,000 investment would be lost. Apparently 18 miles of track needed to be put down between Beechwood and Shelbyville before the Louisville and Eastern could be operated. This extension of the line was the real source of the financial troubles. It seems after half of the line was completed, the money in the treasury gave out and litigation quickly followed.

In May 1907, there was an announcement of more railroad consolidations. The Louisville and Eastern

Railroad merged with the Louisville & Interurban. With the merger work began again. By late June, the final decision was made that the line would in fact come down the center of Shelbyville's Main Street.

In February 1909, the Louisville and Eastern Railroad was officially sold to the Louisville Railway Co. The Louisville Traction Company became the operator as it extended service to Shelbyville. Determined to move ahead with their plans, in June 1910 a fee structure for riding the rail was outlined in the *Shelby Record*. From Louisville to LaGrange was 50 cents one way and 85 cents round trip. The line to Shelbyville was opened on August 19, 1910, just in time for the county fair. But it did not penetrate Shelbyville until 1912. It ended at the western boundary until the city determined where tracks were to be laid.

On September 15, 1912, the railway line was completed through downtown Shelbyville and the depot was placed on the north side of Main Street between First and Second Streets. It was quite elaborate and offered white and colored waiting rooms, indoor lavatories, and a ticket office. The rail cars were painted green and later yellow and were equipped with a coal stove surmounted by an electric blower, which forced hot air back through a duct along the floor. The conductor would come to the seats and collect the fares. At the door at the front of the car was the fare register, which the conductor could operate from any place in the car by turning the indicator pointer to the amount of the fare, then pulling the cord.

The interurban provided prompt and frequent passenger and freight service for people along the line. Local option became of interest, as Shelby County was dry some weeks and wet some others. Rail ticket sales would soar when patrons would pack the cars to travel to the nearest wet county during dry weeks!

Though the original charter was for a period of ninety-nine years, the railway actually existed for a much shorter time span. During 1922, the cars became one-man operations, meaning the motorman, now called the operator, could collect fares at the door and operate the cash register from the front end. At the same time, air-operated front doors and dead-man controls were installed. Dead-man controls meant that if the motorman was incapacitated, the brakes are automatically applied. Such a system is still characteristic of electric cars and light rail, but missing on motor buses. The conversion had the effect of changing the cars from double-end to single-end operations. Double-end cars had controls fore and aft and could be operated from either end. They did not need to be turned around. By the late 1920s and early 1930s, automobiles and improved roadways began to erode the interurban business. Services were reduced and eventually the lines were abandoned. The Great Depression hastened the end, although the line had been running in the red for years. Finally, the decision was made to terminate the operation on May 15, 1934.

TAVERNS

By George Ann Carpenter

In order to get a good picture of the establishment of the early taverns one must let the mind turn backward, turn on your imagination and picture the settlements that sprang up where buffalo trails crossed and where there was a good spring nearby.

During the prehistoric period of Kentucky's history, wild animals, particularly the buffalo, were the road makers. The buffalo roads not only traversed the state but also were transcontinental in extent. The buffalo did not move in a haphazard fashion but with marvelous instinct they seemed to pick out the most direct and favorable routes. Without the aid of the trail blazing buffalo and the path finding Native American, the task of the early explorers and settlers would have been more difficult and the advance of the settlers into the Ohio Valley and the Middle West would have been delayed longer.

Pioneers soon learned that they must band together for safety. In the beginning many made the entire journey on foot or by horseback marching single file with their patient pack horses carrying all of their worldly goods. There were no inns, taverns or camps where they could stop at night. There was often great suffering but these sturdy pioneers made it through all of these hardships.

With the influx of more settlers wagon roads were being opened. The Limestone Road from the Ohio River to Lexington had opened by 1787.

The General Assembly of Kentucky soon saw the advantage of better roads and appropriated money to improve the Wilderness Road. In 1796, it opened to wagon traffic.

Soon there were stage lines, the first being established in 1803. One of the first was from Lexington to Frankfort. There was a stage tavern and halfway house in Woodford County about half way between these two towns.

The early taverns were landmarks from which distances were computed. The weary traveler, recognizing the names a long way off from the picture on the creaking sign, of the Green Tree perhaps, or the Sheaf of Wheat, the White Horse or the Cross Keys, heaved a sigh of relief as he stopped for the night knowing his day's work was done.

It was late and he found the wagon yard already filled with wagons, stagecoaches, pack trains or saddle horses. He removed the feeding trough from the rear of his wagon, fastened it to the tongue, drew provender from a bin in the wagon and hitched his tired horses to it to eat and rest. Then he crossed the long tavern porch being eyed all the time with some suspicion by the group of idlers, tilted back in their homemade chairs, whittling sticks, shifting their tobacco chews from one cheek to the other and contending over politics. The large public assembly room that he entered was always the main feature of the tavern. It had an immense stone fireplace with a blazing back log and comfortable homemade chairs and rough tables. One corner of the room served as a bar where liquors were kept in barrels, jugs, and bottles. Over the bar was the notice required by law giving the prices for board and lodging.

The bar was probably constructed by the neighborhood carpenter of rough lumber. Across the bar were dispensed drinks of whiskey, French brandy, peach brandy, rum, Madeira wine, and cider with prices ranging all the way from 4 1/2¢ to 2 shillings 3 pence. Another favorite drink in Kentucky was Metheglin. The long beans of the honey locust were ground and mixed with honey, herbs and water and fermented. To remind the dilatory customer that he must pay cash there were often signs over the bar. One read like this:

"My liquor's good, My measures just;

But, honest Sirs, I will not trust."

The kitchen in the tavern opened from the main room and the bedrooms were usually upstairs. Sometimes all the beds were in one or two large rooms. If all the beds were occupied when our traveler arrived he would lie down on one beside its occupant, without caring who the sleeper might be. If all the beds were filled when he came in and there was no space left, he went without comment to his wagon, got his blanket, spread it on the floor in the public room, lay down with his feet to the fire and rolled like a human cocoon in his blanket or fur robe and surrounded by other similarly situated companions, heaved a sigh and went to sleep. Often the room was so crowded with the forms of weary men that the late arrival had to explore by candle light and careful steps to find a place to sleep.

The next morning our traveler and the other guests unrolled themselves, bathed their hands and faces in the watering trough outside and passed the towel around with due courtesy. Sometimes there was more than one towel and a slave to offer assistance.

The landlord announced breakfast usually by blowing a horn or ringing a bell on the roof of the tavern. The table was bountifully set with everything in easy reach of the hungry traveler. They ate their fill with no apologies as they discussed the road, the weather, politics and the price of land. There were many personal questions too, such as: Where are you from? What is your business? Were there any fevers where you came from that was a place to avoid? There was an outbreak of cholera in Simpsonville in 1834 and an exodus from Lexington during the cholera epidemic which was a boon to the stage coach lines.

Taverns were an outgrowth of the times. At first there were so few towns and villages that hospitality was shown at every cabin, station, farm, or plantation. Every man's house was an inn and settler a landlord. In general there was no charge to the chance visitor, his stay deemed a pleasure in the secluded life of early backwoods Kentucky.

These early taverns were built mostly of logs and a few of stone. They often had but one or two rooms but with the improvement of roads and the advent of stage wagons these were replaced with more comfortable taverns in the settlements, at the country crossroads, and at frequent intervals in between these points. They were usually situated along the principal stage routes, convenient for the traveler as well as for the relief of the horses.

Taverns were sometimes called ordinaries, universally pronounced "ornaries", which pronunciation probably hit the nail on the head more appropriately than the spelling. The term inn or tavern was employed to distinguish between a mere drinking place and one where meals were served. "Tippling houses" was the term used where only whiskey and other drinks were served. Sometimes the term "inn" was not preferred because it was considered "too English."

Laws governing taverns were among the first to appear on the statute books. In 1793 a law was enacted providing that any person intending to run a tavern should petition the County Court and obtain a license for a period of one year. He had to give bond guaranteeing his good conduct. He had to display in his public room the tavern rates fixed by the Courts at least twice a year. Ten days before applying for a license the owner had to put up four public notices nearby and one upon the courthouse door.

If a tavern keeper overcharged his guests, he was fined 30 shillings for each offense. Special care was taken to safeguard the sobriety of the guests and to see that none drank too deeply of the liquors provided.

Though they did not want to call them inns, the early taverns were patterned after the old English Inns. Abraham Reece ran one of the first taverns out in Shelby County in 1798 at the head of Clear Creek. The Court Order Book of March 1806 said that Jack Davitt could keep a tavern at the place formerly occupied by Abraham Reece on the road going to Henry.

The tavern played a large part in the social and political life of the community. Many were the reasons given to explain and justify attendance at the tavern; one was that often the only newspapers were kept there. This small sheet saw hard usage for when it went its rounds some could hardly read it and some pretended to read. This sign was seen posted over the bar in one taproom. "Gentlemen learning to spell are requested to use last week's Newsletter." People came to hear the local gossip and to learn what was going on in the East. The traveler imparted information that he had gathered on his journey.

The tavern became a civic center. Very often the public room was the only room large enough to hold a public meeting. Frankfort was selected the capitol of Kentucky in Brent's Tavern in Lexington. The sittings of courts were held there. Frequently one found notices posted on the wall offering a reward for a run-away slave. Traders and slave drivers frequented the taverns for gossip and information relative to available human chattel. The tavern was used for assemblages of all kinds—meetings of the town trustees, taking depositions, examining applicants for law licenses, caucus, and town elections. Usually there was a tall rather rough writing desk at which a traveler might write a letter or sign a contract or where the landlord made out his bills and kept books.

The public room at the tavern was the favorite place for performances of all sorts, small shows, fortunetellers, exhibits of dwarfs and freaks, the Siamese twin brothers—the number and variety were legion.

Not only were the taverns used for shows and exhibitions of skill but they were often scenes of brilliant balls and dances, entertainment of distinguished guests and famous visitors as well as concerts of music.

General LaFayette was entertained in a tavern on his way to Lexington. It was the Cross Keys, the best-known tavern in Shelby County. Both Henry Clay and Andrew Jackson were guests. Adam Middleton, a blacksmith from Virginia, built this tavern in 1800. He settled there and for a time plied his trade. Since there was always a stream of travelers pouring down the old dirt "State Road," young Middleton thought a tavern was a good idea. Since the road forked there he hung up two immense brass keys on a tree at the roadside and called his inn "The Cross Keys Tavern." The brothers Adam and Robert Middleton married sisters and for many years successfully operated one of the most enjoyable inns along this route. It was the stopping place for all who journeyed over the turnpike from the Bluegrass to the Ohio River. It was the halfway house between Lexington and Louisville. It is estimated that between 1800 and 1825 it sheltered 10,000 travelers.

The original structure was built of stone and became the center when a wing of logs was added in 1813 and the front with great white columns in 1851. It remained in the Middleton family until 1919 when it was sold at public auction. It burned in 1934.

Another inn was Old Stone Inn in Simpsonville. It is probably the second oldest stone residence in the county. The building was begun in 1792 by Fleming P. Rogers, one of the first Virginia land grant owners. It was nearly completed when it was sold to Isaac Greathouse in 1827; sold again to Philip Johnstone in 1833, who sold it in 1835 to Lindsey W. George, whose son Capt., Richard George, lived there for nearly 80 years. It was a stagecoach inn and tavern, as well as a home for many years.

Another tavern in Simpsonville according to a newspaper story was Bell Tavern, operated by the grandparents of Robert and Minnie Margaret Bell. According to the story it had a long front porch, which paralleled the road, and a large wagon yard. There was also supposed to be a small tavern on Main Street in Simpsonville.

Frequently the license just stated that the tavern was in a house in Shelby County. In some instances it would tell where in Shelby County. In 1838, Daniel Johnson and George W. Johnstone had one in Simpsonville. They applied again in 1843. Joseph Howell and Isaiah Shipman applied for a license on March 8, 1841, to have a tavern in Howell's house; James Hughes and Walter Drake applied on November 9, 1840, for one in Simpsonville; again in Simpsonville, Michael Goodknight and John P. Bailu on May 8, 1843, and on May 13, 1843, it was Goodknight and James R. Ragland. It is unknown what happened to Bailu. On April 13, 1840, Enoch Webb and Michael had applied. George Hudson and M. Goodknight had applied June 12, 1837, not saying where.

The following taverns were licensed in Clay Village.
1. Tyler Elliot & Robt. Saunders, July 10, 1837
2. Albert Saunders & Robert Saunders, November 12, 1838
3. Tyler Elliot & C. Saunders, August 12, 1839
4. Albert Saunders & Robert Saunders, November 11, 1839
5. Peter Minor & Jefferson T. Doss, December 12, 1842
   They also applied for one in Shelbyville in 1844

Christiansburg:
1. Daniel K. Mitchell & Shannon Reed , May 14, 1838
2. W. H. Wilson & James Sprigg, May 14, 1838
3. Daniel Mitchell & John M. Ogden , May 11, 1840
4. John W. Kyle & John R. Beckely, September 4, 1840

Connersville (later Harrisonville)
1. Henry B. Landers and Joseph Hackworth, November 13, 1837
Harrisonville:
1. Robert R. Baker & James Harrison, September 11, 1843

Hardinsville (later Graffensburg)
1. James Hackley & William Bullard, November 13, 1837
2. Richard Pemberton & William Bullard, November 12, 1838

3. Richard Pemberton & Calvin Saunders, December 9, 1839

4. Richard Pemberton & Calvin Saunders, January 10, 1842

Other taverns were in Shelbyville and Shelby County. John Booth applied for a license in August 1806 to have a tavern in his house on the road from Frankfort to Middletown. Henry Atherton had a tavern in Shelbyville in his house in 1807 and again in 1809. Others in Shelbyville were:

1. John McGaughey, July 1809

2. Daniel McClelland tavern in own house October 1805, renewed May 1808.

3. G. Leonard George tavern in house of Daniel McClelland, July1809

4. Wm. Jewel tavern on Main road leading from Shelbyville to Bardstown 12 miles from Shelbyville, May 1807

5. Benjamin Roberts in house on road leading to mouth of the Kentucky River, April 1805

6. George Smith in house in Shelby County, July 1806.

7. Michael Speck in Shelbyville, October, 12, 1807

8. Abraham Smith in house of Daniel McClelland, December 1809.

9. John Shannon in Shelby County, August 1809

10. Isaac Watkins to keep taverns at the house formerly occupied by Mosea Hall, April 1805, again in October 1808 AA Abraham

J. Winston Coleman's book Stage Coach Days in the Bluegrass gives these taverns listed in Shelbyville:

Watkins Inn—Isaac Watkins—1800-20

Eagle tavern—William Hardin—1820-23

Brenham's Tavern—Robert Brenham—1825

Golden Bee Hive Tavern—S. Buckner—1822

Farmer's House—H. S. Hastings—1847

Washington Hall—J. S. Murphey—1849

Redding House—Merritt Redding—1852

Sign of Bee Hive Inn—John S. Robson—1824-26

On one occasion a tavern was the site of tragedy. One John Felty of Jefferson County was granted a deed to Lot 26 on Main Street in Shelbyville on May 21, 1793. Located next to and west of the courthouse, it belonged to William Shannon and was granted by the trustees for 15 pounds on Shannon's behalf.

John Felty established a tavern on this lot. It later became known as the McGrath Block, J. H. Hartford's, and A. Hollenback's lots. In July 1794 William Shannon went into the Felty Tavern for dinner. Shannon and Felty quarreled but were separated by friends. As Shannon was leaving by the front door they quarreled again. Shannon picked up a stone off the street and threw it at Felty. At the same time Felty threw a dirk which struck Shannon and killed him instantly. Felty died of his wound a few days later.

Today's modern hotels and motels are a far cry from the primitive and sometimes dangerous conditions of early taverns. Those of Shelby County were typical of early accommodations for travelers. Not until the post-Civil War years when travel became more convenient with the railroad did improvement occur.

CROSS KEYS INN AND OLD BETHEL BAPTIST CHURCH

By Calvin T. Schmidt

In 1800, 23-year-old Adam Middelton and his wife, Mary Fulton, came to Shelby County from Virginia. Middelton built a blacksmith shop on what was then a halfway spot between Lexington and Louisville. He located five miles east of Shelbyville on the "trail" between Maysville and the Falls of the Ohio at Louisville, picking a site just north of Jeptha Knob. The trail ran between his shop and a small log structure.

The flowing tide of travel past his shop soon gave him an idea, and he bought the log house and extended it into a big log tavern. Beating out two big brass keys, he crossed them, nailed them on a tree, and painted "INN" under them. This was the beginning of "Cross Keys Inn." The inn provided food and shelter to a large number of travelers and local citizenry on a daily basis during its early days. From 1800 to 1825 this inn served over 10,000 travelers who came by wagon, stage, and horse, paying 20 cents for a meal, 8 cents for lodging, 5 cents per drink of whiskey or 37 1/2 cents per gallon.

Running the inn, farm, and other services around Cross Keys kept the young Adam Middelton, his wife, and ten children so busy that they somehow had to have three or four slave families to help them. There were slave quarters located within 100 feet of the inn consisting of a one story section of four log rooms, one being quite large, plus a small stone room. These remained on the property until new property owners bulldozed them in September of 1997.

In the 1830s two of Adam Middelton's sons, Adam Jr., born in 1813, and Robert, born in 1816, inherited the tavern. They married the two Willis sisters, Mary and Letitia, and reared a double family of thirteen children around one fireside. The house was enlarged to form an "L," having two entrances with stately columns and a metal balcony adorning each porch.

In 1797, Joshua Morris or James Dupuy established a church near Tyler's Station. That early church was called Tick Creek Baptist because of its location near the creek of that name. This creek ran its course a bit north and east of Cross Keys.

In 1899, a fine brick church was erected on the south side of the "big State Road," directly across from Cross Keys Inn, probably on the site of the Middelton's original blacksmith shop. This building became known as "Old Bethel Baptist Church," a replacement of the old wooden Tick Creek Church which had apparently fallen into disrepair. An old hewn log, 18 inches or more square and about 50 feet long, had been used to add support to the floor of the new sanctuary, and from its appearance probably came from the remains of the older church. The log remains in its place under the floor of Old Bethel as of 2001.

In its first days, Bethel Baptist was associated with the Elkhorn Association. By 1803 it came into the Long Run Association with 107 members. The Middeltons were members. Sometime after 1831 Bethel's 259 members split over the issue of missionary vs. anti-missionary. At that time the majority of the congregation left to create their own Missionary Church at Clay Village, a short distance east up the "Pike." The small group, which stayed at Bethel, was opposed to the idea of missionaries, and their congregation had few members. The Middeltons followed the larger group to Clay Village. The Bethel

Baptists finally disbanded after many years of struggle, and the brick church building soon became a tenant house for the Old Cross Keys farm.

The Middelton family was one of Shelby County's most illustrious. Cross Keys remained in their ownership until 1919. That year it was purchased by Joe "Buck" Headen, a large landowner of the area. In the late 1920s financial difficulties caused the property to revert back to lending institutions, the Federal Land Bank and the New York Life Insurance Company.

In August 1930, Austin L. Moore, a Shelby County Realtor, put together a complicated land deal. He sold Dr. Ransdell, a local druggist, a plot of the Cross Keys land lying west of the inn and on the north side of "the Trail" (known also as U.S. 60 by then). A Shelbyville doctor, Dr. T. E. Bland, bought several acres on the south side of the road, both men paying about $65 per acre. Virginia Snider and her husband Estes, along with Mr. Moore, purchased 144 acres of the land. A few days later the Sniders conveyed 128 acres to A. L. Moore, including the old Bethel Church and its cemetery on the south side of the Trail where the Middeltons were all buried and about 40 acres north of the inn. The Sniders kept 16 acres on the north side including the inn, along with water rights to a free-flowing spring in front of the church from which they piped water under the road to the inn — just as it had been done since the earliest days of the inn.

Virginia Snider, with her two sisters, Bess (Mrs. Arnold Plues), and Ann (Mrs. Nilsson) worked with their mother, Mrs. James Tinsley, to restore the home to its original use as an inn. For the next four years Cross Keys once again became a popular hostelry and restaurant. The three Tinsley daughters knew how to prepare food and ran a first-class establishment. Then, on the night of May 23, 1934, a raging fire consumed the inn. The sky lit up so brightly that people only miles from Louisville could see the red glow in the sky. All that remained of the inn was the slave's quarters which were not connected to the inn. Mrs. Velena White and her husband purchased the site of the inn some time after the fire.

Cross Keys Inn, east of Shelbyville, in 1921.

Courtesy of The Filson Historical Society, R. C. Ballard Thruston Collection, neg. TC1320.

OLD STONE INN

By John David Myles

In 1939 lunch at Old Stone Inn cost 75 cents and dinner $1.50. According to Thomas Marshall, legendary waiter there for six decades, "You probably got more then than you do now." For a building which always seems to have been there, the Old Stone Inn has undergone many changes. In fact, when Marshall and his friend Willie Sullivan got up at 4 A.M. to feed the live stock, kill the chickens (up to 300 a week), gather the eggs, and milk the cows in the 1920s, the place was already over one hundred years old.

The land upon which the Inn sits was part of a 2,596 acre Treasury warrant granted to Granville Smith. Harrod Samuel Mitchell shows up in the Shelby County tax lists as early as 1799 but is not identified as owning the Inn tract until 1807. He and his wife Lenah sold 74 acres of the tract to Fleming P. Rogers in 1817 for $747.50. Rogers sold the property to Isaac Greathouse for $1,600 in 1827, and he in turn sold it and an additional 77 acres to Philip Johnston for $2,685 in 1833. Johnston sold the property, then consisting of 281 acres, to Lindsey W. George for $5,676.

There is no definitive date for the Inn's construction. However, several factors and long-standing tradition indicate that Fleming Rogers started the building shortly after purchasing the land in July 1817. His deed describes the property as "north of the big road from Shelbyville to Louisville." The town of Simpsonville had been laid out in 1816. The Kentucky General Assembly enacted legislation in February 1817 authorizing turnpike road companies "for the purpose of forming artificial roads." Mr. Rogers apparently knew a good business proposition when he saw one.

The 1817 date is also consistent with the building's architecture. Although 1817 is late for a stone building, the story and a half configuration, the foursquare layout, and the exterior chimneys are closely related in style to Woodstock, the William Hayes house in Fayette County which was constructed in 1812. Woodstock lacked the central hall of the Inn, and this feature is found in another Fayette County house of similar construction, the Cleveland-Rogers House, built around 1819. Thus, while built of a material then losing favor, the plan of the Inn was on the cutting edge of residential design in Kentucky when it was built.

It was constructed of coursed limestone with flat jack arches over the openings. While always five bays wide with a central double door on the front, there was originally a second door to its right. This door is presumed to have entered the tavern room directly and the room had interior access only to the wide hall. These doors with transoms were six paneled and had paneled reveals. There were two windows per story between the paired exterior chimneys on the east and west walls, giving additional light to the first floor rooms and lighting the upper rooms in the gables. Those on the east can still be seen while those on the west have been blocked by later additions. Each of the eight primary rooms had its own fireplace. The most interesting features to have survived are the exterior window and door facings on the facade, which are reeded with bull's eye corner blocks, again attesting the sophistication of the building. It clearly would have been an outstanding building on the frontier even if General

In this photograph from the early 1900s, the Old Stone Inn has an added front porch and only one dormer.

LaFayette had not danced there or Andrew Jackson stayed when commuting from the Hermitage to Washington.

A history of the Old Stone Inn, written in 1947 by The Anchorage Genealogical Society, states that, "A picture of the Stone Inn taken about 1866 shows three original dormer windows and a belfry on the roof where the bell hung that was wrung for the farm hands to call to their meals any travelers who might be staying over night. There were four columns across the front of the porch, and a sun dial in the yard." This picture does in fact document early dormers, which are unusual in construction of this date and very rare in Shelby County. The windows are shown with nine-over-six sash in keeping with the date of construction. The porch, an off center lean-to descending from the eaves line, covers the two doors. It was clearly added well after construction and is supported by four heavy square posts of Greek Revival design. The "belfry" is also there but no bell is showing. One suspects that the reference to the sundial is a typo and instead refers to the four-step stile visible next to the entry gate.

In 1827, Fleming Rogers sold the property to Isaac Greathouse. Greathouse sold it in 1833 to Philip Johnston who sold it in 1835 to Lindsey W. George. George left the best documentary evidence of the building's use as a tavern when he and Thomas Smith posted a 100 pound bond for a tavern license on May 8, 1837. George's will was probated in 1847 and the property eventually passed to his son Richard.

Tradition tells that he continued to run the inn until he sold the property in 1877 to William Hammond and moved to Shelbyville. Hammond was a blacksmith and the Inn became a home at this time. He sold the Inn and 18 acres to Mary Jane Campbell in 1881. She bought the remainder of the tract in 1883 and it remained in her family until sold by her administrator to Leonidas Webb in 1899. A photograph in the Kentucky Historical Society collection shows the property during the Webb tenure. The original shake roof has been replaced with tin and two of the three dormers have been removed. The original windows have been replaced with Victorian two-over-two sash and the four heavy columns have been replaced with three turned posts with brackets.

The Webbs owned the property until 1922 when Jane Shannon bought the building and 6 acres and opened a tearoom known as "Ye Olde Stone Inn." A picture in George Willlis' 1929 History of Shelby County, presumably dating from that period, shows the roof again clad in shake shingles and the front of the house and porch shrouded in a lush growth of vines of some sort. Although she returned the Inn to its original function, she did not stay long, selling in 1924 to J. E. Tinsley and his son-in-law, A. W. Plues. Sarah Tinsley and her daughters, Elizabeth Plues and Virginia Snider, ran the restaurant until it was sold to Mrs. Cecilia O'Neal in 1930, on the occasion of the Tinsley family buying Cross Keys. Mrs. O'Neal continued operation of the restaurant until she sold it back to the Tinsley family in 1934, after fire destroyed Cross Keys. A photograph by J. Winston Coleman in his *Historic Kentucky* shows the Inn as it appeared during the Tinsleys' tenure. It also gives the best indication of how the Inn appeared when built. The missing dormers have been replaced and the porch has been removed. The only items clearly different from the date of construction are the six-over-six sash and the glass panels in the central double doors.

Once returned, the Tinsley family continued to run the Inn until 1969 except for the years during World War II when Mr. Plues was stationed in Chicago and help was otherwise unavailable. One suspects that in those days of rationing even in the county the ingredients for such mainstays as corn pudding and mock oysters were difficult to acquire. Mrs. Snider ran the "front," and Mrs. Plues ran the kitchen. Judging from Marshall's account and the wide reputation the Inn enjoyed, they ran a tight ship. Over the years, the building acquired its flanking wings to accommodate the crowds which flocked to enjoy its hospitality. A small porch was added over the central doors and the old tavern door was converted to a window, giving the Inn a symmetry it had not before enjoyed.

Mr. and Mrs. Snider and her sisters, Mrs. Plues and Ann Nilsson, both then widows, sold the Inn to Kenyon Investment Company, owned by Louisville businessman Lincoln Miller, in 1969. It leased the restaurant, which was managed by Bill Fensterer who was in charge when the Inn was listed on the National Register in 1976, one of the first properties in the county to achieve this national honor. In June 1987, Allen and Robert Purnell bought the Inn and surrounding property which abuts their sausage plant. Joyce and Paul Hutcherson ran the Inn from 1989 until 1997, when Mike Stone began his efforts to return this local institution to its former glory under the ownership of the Tinsley family.

It is now run by young Allen Purnell.

Old Stone Inn, 1934.

The "inner circle" at the Shelby County Fair and Horse Show, 1940.

CHAPTER NINE

CLUBS, RECREATION & SPORTS

Anna McClarty Harbison, founding regent of the Isaac Shelby Chapter, Kentucky State Daughters of the American Revolution.

KENTUCKY ALPHA IOTA OF ALPHA DELTA KAPPA

By Joan Goodwin and Ernestine Jennings

Alpha Delta Kappa (ADK) is a teacher's honorary sorority with headquarters in Kansas City, Missouri. Members of the Kentucky Alpha Iota Chapter of Alpha Delta Kappa are dedicated educators who believe in high standards of education and actively pursue these ideals through community support, altruistic activities, teaching, and fellowship of women educators.

The Chapter was established on June 10, 1980. Ruth Ramey, George Ann Carpenter, and Liz Kimbrough initiated the first meeting and enlisted twenty-eight. Active today are Dottie Adams (Byars), George Ann Carpenter, Patty Delk (Thomas), Nellie Druin, Pat Ellis, Carla Foster, Ernestine Jennings, Liz Kimbrough, Mary Ann Phillips, Lillian Sorrels, Lynda Tharp, Elaine Waits, Anne Webb, and Charlotte White.

Eight women educators have served as president of this altruistic organization since its charter: Lillian Sorrels, 1980-82; Eleanor Busey, 1982-84; Ernestine Jennings, 1984-86; Barbara Blair, 1986-88; Dottie Adams (Byars), 1988-90; Carolyn Chesher, 1990-92; Patricia Skelton, 1992-94; Carol Beth Mooneyhan, 1994-96; Dottie Byars, 1996-98; Patricia Skelton, 1998-2000; Maggie Nicholson, present.

The Kentucky Alpha Iota Chapter is part of the Central District of Kentucky, which includes Jefferson, Franklin, Hardin, and Shelby Counties. Every three years the ADK chapters from the Central District may apply for the State Altruistic Award. Shelby County received the award in 1995 and presented $1,000 to Theresa Hardin of Operation Care.

The annual Christmas Trims & Whims, a Kentucky Alpha Iota tradition, brings together the talents of multiple craftsmen from diverse areas and Alpha Iota sisters who host a tearoom. This event funds numerous altruistic activities, including an annual senior breakfast in honor of the graduates and two scholarships presented annually to students who plan to pursue a career in education. Given in memory of Eleanor Busey, a charter member of Kentucky Alpha Iota, and Susan Fields, an honorary member of Kentucky Alpha Iota, these scholarships are among the many ways in which Alpha Iota sisters build bridges "from the best of the past to the best of the future."

BUSINESS AND PROFESSIONAL WOMEN'S CLUB

By Cecilia A. Piccini

Shelbyville's Business and Professional Women's Club is part of The National Federation of Business and Professional Women's Clubs/USA (BPW/USA). BPW/USA is the world's preeminent organization of working women and the leading advocate for working women. Founded in 1919, it promotes full participation, equity, and economic self-sufficiency for working women through legislative advocacy, member training, support programs, and communications. A Kentuckian, Lena Madesin Phillips, was instrumental in founding the national because of the need to correlate women's skills and activities during World War I.

The BPW Foundation was established in 1956 by the members of BPW/USA to promote the goals of the Federation through education, information, and research. Kentucky BPW was founded in 1921. The Shelbyville BPW was founded in 1948 to address the needs of working women in Shelbyville and Shelby County. Its mission is to achieve equity for all women in the workplace through advocacy, education, and information.

Since its organization, Shelbyville BPW has been recognized for outstanding achievement on the regional and state levels for programs, public relations, and community service. While many of its officers have moved into positions of leadership on regional and state levels, the central focus remains helping women of Shelby County become better prepared women. It provides opportunities for leadership experience, career development, personal improvement, legislative involvement, business contacts, and networking. Scholarships and grants for research and continued education to upgrade skills are offered not only through Shelbyville BPW's scholarship to a graduating Shelby County High School student, but also through the Kentucky Foundation and BPW/USA.

CHAUTAUQUA CLUB

By Zena B. Jesse

The Shelbyville Chautauqua Club was organized on October 4, 1912, with sixteen members. This club was formed as a study club under the guidance of the Chautauqua Literary and Scientific Circle which is a part of the Chautauqua Institution located in western New York state. The Chautauqua Literary and Scientific Circle (C.L.S.C.) organized Chautauqua clubs in small towns all across the United States and provided courses of study and directed reading programs organized under college professors. Originally the Shelbyville club followed the C.L.S.C. course of study but eventually decided to choose its own programs.

While this club has its roots in the Chautauqua Institution, other groups, with no connection to that organization, have sought to emulate the magic of Chautauqua and have used the Chautauqua name. One such group was the traveling Chautauquas that brought culture and entertainment to small towns all across the country. Shelbyville was fortunate to be one of the towns on the circuit beginning in 1913. For seven days each summer, Shelby Countians flocked to hear the

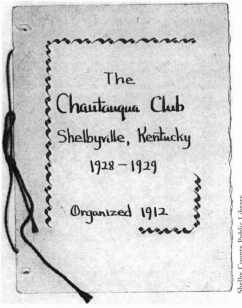

Membership booklet of The Chautauqua Club in 1928-29.

greatest assortment of public performers the world has ever known. However, by 1927 hard times and changing interests brought on the demise of the traveling Chautauquas.

Through the years, Chautauqua Club members have presented programs on many varied subjects. Programs have looked backward to learn from the past and forward to catch a glimpse of the future. The club has taken arm chair trips to foreign lands and looked in on famous people and families. There have been programs about Kentucky and Shelby County and many musical occasions.

The ladies of Chautauqua are very patriotic with programs on our four freedoms, country inns of America, and great American cities. During both world wars the Chautauqua ladies suspended study to help with the war effort.

At the beginning of the 21st century, the Chautauqua Club is the oldest continuously meeting club in Shelby County.

CHAUTAUQUAS

By Zena B. Jesse

In 1868, James Redpath, who was a reporter for the New York Tribune, attended a lecture given by Charles Dickens. There he learned of Dickens' difficulties and exasperation trying to set up lectures as he traveled about the United States. Redpath decided to establish a clearinghouse to smooth the travels of distinguished speakers and artists, relieving them of the tiresome job of negotiating dates, train schedules, and fees. From this came the Redpath Bureau that organized summer performances called Chautauquas.

Artists and speakers with the Redpath Bureau traveled to small towns all across America. Charles Harper wrote in his biography of Redpath, *Strike the Tents*, that in 1921 nearly one hundred traveling circuits were reaching 9,597 communities in the United States and Canada and forty million people. Shelbyville was fortunate to be on the Redpath Circuit beginning in 1913. For seven days each summer, the people of Shelby County flocked to the big, brown Chautauqua tent set up on the grounds of what is now Northside School, to hear the greatest assortment of artists and public speakers the world had ever known. A Chautauqua week was about one-third lectures and two-thirds music and drama. There were three performances every day with four performances that were especially for children.

Inside the big tent, Shelby Countians heard orators praising or condemning socialism, the protective tariff, Wall Street, rural coops, the vote for women, and free verse. They were treated to inspirational lectures on self-improvement and how to succeed. It was on the Chautauqua circuit that millions of Americans first heard impassioned pleas for a federal income tax, slum clearance, free schoolbooks, world disarmament, and prohibition of child labor and dozens of other social issues.

Adults were treated to a variety of concerts such as the Russian Cathedral Choir wearing beautiful choir vestments and quaint peasant costumes, the well-known Cavan Welsh Singers and the Royal Hungarian Orchestra to name just a few. Edgar Bergen and Charlie McCarthy traveled the Chautauqua circuit, as did Hughie Fitzpatrick, the clown and comedian. Characters from storybooks were portrayed to the delight of Shelby County's children.

Each year several opera companies performed and there were stage productions of current plays. George M. Cohan's musicals were always favorites. Another favorite was the original musical production of Stephen Foster by the Dumond Concert Company. During the years prior to and during World War I there were many patriotic concerts and productions prompting President Woodrow Wilson to pay tribute to the traveling Chautauquas as an integral part of the national defense.

Teachers, preachers, explorers, scientists, statesmen, orators, and politicians were involved in these summer performances. One speaker who traveled the circuits was known to managers and crew boys as "Old Dependable". This gentleman, who ran unsuccessfully for president of the United States three times and served as Secretary of State under President Woodrow Wilson, was none other than the great orator William Jennings Bryan.

Weathering the years of World War I, the circuits carried on until 1927 when attendance began to decline. Banks were failing in small towns all across the nation. Hard times on one side and changing times on the other brought on the demise of the traveling Chautauquas. At the end of the 1933 season the big, brown Chautauqua tents were struck for the last time.

SHELBY COUNTY COMMUNITY THEATRE

By Frances Smith and Bill Matthews

The idea of a community theater germinated in the mind and heart of Robert C. Shy who returned to Shelby County High School after serving five years as director of education and programming at Kentucky Educational Television. He brought with him the belief that a community theater has the power to bring people together from all walks of life in a way that enriches lives. He believed that amateur musicians, actors, dancers, set designers, and writers who opted for traditional careers could now express their artistic leanings and, in so doing, create something very special for their friends and neighbors.

The creation of the Community Theatre came less than two months after the organization was formally chartered on June 30, 1977. When the curtain went up for "The Music Man" on a very steamy night in August, nearly 200 volunteers had been involved in the staging of that popular musical. At the same time that the hammering and scene blocking was going on for that show, the board of directors was busy launching a membership drive and raising funds to support this substantial undertaking. Then, in 1978, the production of "Reynard the Fox" revealed the theater's potential for enticing youngsters to showcase their budding talents.

It was an easy decision to move the theater from its temporary status to a formal organization with new directors, each serving staggered terms. The original incorporators were William R. Hickman (President), Bruce Sweeney, Ryburn Weakley, Annabel Lewis, June G. Davis, and Carolyn Giltner. The original board faced the risks of uncharted waters, but the ongoing board had to deal with how to keep a good thing going. Under the leadership of Presidents June Davis, Quintin Biagi, John Sanderlin, Calvin Schmidt, Mary Helen

Miller, S. K. Zimmerman, Jim Smith, Jon Jacoby, Bob Giltner, Carolyn Peterson, Gary Steinhilber, Mark Burks, and Pat Wetherton, the next generations of board members proved equal to the task.

As the reality of the undertaking set in, the Board was confronted with the departure of the founder of the theater when Bob Shy moved out of the area. Then there was the need to build a solid financial foundation for the organization, and the troupe of actors bumped up against increasing logistical problems with the staging of production in facilities where the theater was a "guest." Producing "Anatomy of a Murder" in the Shelby County Court House, "The Odd Couple" in the Floral Hall at the Fairgrounds, and "Fiddler on the Roof " at East Middle School meant carting construction materials from place to place and tying up space that belonged to someone else for several weeks.

True to its heritage of a community effort, solutions to these problems came from many corners. The director's void was filled by several volunteers who graciously stepped forward. Later, Zerelda Matthews expressed concern regarding the demands on a director's time during productions, and urged the Board to consider paying directors with training and experience in the theater. She contended that amateur actors needed professional direction if they were to do their best. Enter Eugene Stickler, a drama teacher and stage master with the Jefferson County Public School System. During his nineteen-year association he has not only been a stage director, but a set designer, confidante to the Board, and has utilized his many skills in every way imaginable to benefit the theater.

Ongoing financial security for the theater got its first and continuing major boost from an idea advanced by Else Matthews. She believed community supporters would respond well to an annual ball, and suggested that it could be held in the Floral Hall at the fairgrounds. With the help of dozens of volunteers, Floral Hall was transformed into a virtual spring flower garden, and the first Fantasy Ball, named by Ann Porter, became a huge success in 1977. With many individuals and local and regional businesses donating products and services of great value, the silent and live auctions at it raised more than $10,000. Over the next 20 years it was to raise more than a quarter-million dollars. Jean Logan was highly instrumental in the success of the Fantasy Ball, and of the theatre itself.

The Fantasy Ball was important in helping end the vagabond existence of the theater. But there are many other people who deserve to be mentioned in helping to put the theater on permanent financial footing. In the fall of 1979, June Davis, Nancy Crabtree, and Frances Smith traveled together to Morehead, Kentucky, for a meeting of statewide community theater board members. On the drive back, Davis expressed his overriding thought, "If the theater is to survive, it must have its own home." Obsessed by the conviction, and with the backing of highly regarded architect and board member Quintin Biagi, Davis called an emergency board meeting. There was a building at the corner of Eighth and Main Streets available for purchase. Acting with Board approval and a line of credit from local financial institutions, the building was secured for $30,500, on October 27, 1979, as the theater's permanent home. Mrs. Helen Schmidt contributed $30,000 toward the building's purchase.

When the lights went up for "Oklahoma" in August 1981, filled-to-capacity crowds electrified the air. After eight sell-out performances and two holdover shows, director Gene Stickler proved that, "Yes, a big musical can be successfully staged in an area smaller than an auditorium." Musical performances moved directly into the spotlight in 1982 when the artistic committee initiated the Command Performance. Envisioned by Frances Smith and developed by producer-director concert pianist Betty

Jean Chatham, the Command Performance showcased local vocalists and musicians whose talents had not previously been extended to countywide audiences.

A major theatrical offering to the children's theater was the creation of the Pop Corn Theater in 1985. The key person in developing this newest offering by the local theater was Harolyn Sharpe. Sharpe recognized the interest of children in acting lessons and began Saturday morning seminars, followed by productions where their newfound skills could be shown off. Sharpe's other, most important, contribution was moving productions into state and regional contests. She directed "The Dining Room" locally, and, after a successful run, took the performers to competitions where they won the Kentucky Theater Association award and advanced to regional competition. In 1993, director Dan Herring from Louisville Children's Theatre entered the Shelby County Community Theatre's world premier production of "And the Tide Shall Cover the Earth" and won awards in both state and regional competition. Quite happily, the performers were rewarded by being named number one in both contests. Herring and another troupe of local performers repeated the feat in 1994 with "Quilters" and with "The Dining Room," a 1999 encore production.

Over the years the theater has endeavored to encourage the use of its facility to promote the arts. This includes childrens' and adults' art classes, acting workshops for all ages, dancing recitals, concerts, and individual musical performances. Since 1997 the theater has hosted the highly competitive Arts on Main annual juried show which draws acclaimed artists from all over Kentucky and neighboring states. The theater also works with the public schools to bring in children for enjoyment of the childrens' productions.

In 1987, the theater was able to purchase the adjoining property on Main Street. The goal to create local opportunities for involvement in the arts was realized when the theater backed the work of local director turned playwright, Eugene Stickler, who collaborated with local composer, Betty Jean Chatham, to create a musical around the local historical landmark Science Hill School. Entitled "Science Hill 1919," it got rave reviews and a waiting list for all nine performances. That reputation for excellence is certain to grow as the theater enters a new millennium.

A scene featuring Hazel and her "Hazelnuts" from Radio Gals, performed in May 2001.

SHELBY COUNTY FAIR

By Duanne Puckett

Shelby County Fair and Horse Show, 1940

Library of Congress 55201-S #226581

October 1, 1842, was the first date that a Shelby County Fair was held in Shelbyville. Running the event was an association of gentlemen who called themselves the Shelby County Agricultural and Mechanical Association. The president was N. Owsley while Henri F. Middelton served as secretary. The first premiums issued to winners that year were not silver cups but standard agricultural and other books. They were given for horses, jacks, cattle, hogs, sheep, agricultural implements, and domestic manufacturers. There were fifty-one premiums awarded costing $81. The largest premium was a treatise on the horse, valued at $3.

Almost regularly thereafter a similar fair was held each fall and on an increasingly larger scale. The only years that a fair did not take place were during the Civil War in 1862, the Great Depression in 1933, and World War II in 1942.

The Shelby County A & M Association was officially incorporated December 18, 1858, to "encourage and improve the breeding of stock of all kinds, also the more successful propagation of fruits, vegetables, etc." Officers were: A.B. Veech, president; I. S. Todd, vice president; John A. Middelton, secretary; J.M. Owen, treasurer; and W.O. McMakin, George Smith, John Robinson, T. Merriweather, S.H. Miles, N. Howell, A. Middelton, W.L. Waddy and F. Neel as directors.

The board immediately purchased a 15-acre tract of land and contracted to erect an amphitheater in time for the fair the last week in August 1859. During the presidency of Adam Middelton, the contract for the building of Floral Hall was given to Layson Bros. for $1,950 on June 16, 1871. The hall was circular and two stories in height. A new amphitheater was built in 1898 on the same site as the old one. The new one had a seating capacity of 5,000. Its use was short-lived, however, because fire destroyed it, Floral Hall, and the ladies' cottage in April 1903. Even the shade trees that surrounded the amphitheater were destroyed. The origin of the fire was never known.

A contract went to Thomas Clark of Clay Village who pushed to get a new amphitheater in place the last week of August. The new structure, costing about $9,000, had a three-story bandstand. The new Floral Hall had four wings—one to display poultry, another for a ladies' dining room, and the other two for the display of vegetables. The entire second story was to exhibit the ladies' fancywork, pictures, etc. This amphitheatre burned in 1968, but a beautiful new amphitheatre with pavilion, is now in place. Floral Hall was demolished in the 1970s and replaced with a blue metal building that also serves as a site for other community dances and events.

Ellis McGinnis Collection, courtesy of Michael McGinnis.

The grandstand, at left, and Floral Hall at right, Shelby County Fairgrounds, ca. 1909.

There were no intoxicants sold and no games of chance allowed on the grounds. And a report in 1916 boasted "An abundance of ice water is always where it can be found without trouble or cost." The Board of Directors that year were: J.L. Zaring, president; J.H. Fullenwider, vice president; T.R. Webber, secretary; Eugene Harbison, treasurer; and E.W. Young, Edgar Vaughan, W.S. Gibbs, S.D. Hinkle, C.A. McCormack, Stanley Smith, R.B. Donaldson, Roy Mitchell, E.L. Stout, W.N. Nash and W.P. Johnson as directors. They were described by Ed Shinnick, editor of the Shelby Record, as "a class of progressive, straightforward, energetic men who give credit and standing to any community."

They and the directors before and after them, work to make the reputation of the Shelby County Fair known throughout the state for being "the best county fair in Kentucky." The motto became fact in 1994 when the A & M Association started receiving recognition from the Kentucky Association of County Fairs:1994 All-Kentucky Fair, 1995 All-Kentucky Fair,1995 Most Progressive Fair in Zone 3, 1996 All-Kentucky Fair, 1997 All-Kentucky Fair, and 1998 All-Kentucky Fair.

Popular events at the fair are the horse show, tractor and truck pulls, livestock exhibits, and the crowd-pleasing Baby Show, Little Miss Contest, and Fair Queen Contest. The community still takes an interest in Floral Hall with 615 entries reported in 1999 when $24,378 in premiums were awarded.

Officers and directors for 1999-2000 were: John Miller, president; Don Baker, vice president; Bob Wilson, secretary; John Rothenburger, treasurer; and Carla Gravett, executive secretary. Directors were R.H. Bennett, J. T. Clemmons, Tom McGinnis, Bobby Moore, Doug Langley, Ray Tucker, Hite Hays, Larry Gravett, Jack Coots, Jack Lewis, Harold Sutton and Paul Hornback. Associate directors were Audrey Armstrong, Mike Armstrong, Edward R. Bennett, Jonathan Blank, Johnny Bohannon, JR Bradley, George Brinkhaus, Woody Briscoe, Paula Brown, Bobbie Brenner, Duvall Burk, Mike Casey, Roy Catlett, John Early, Pat Hargadon, Tom Ingram, Paula Moore, Dennis Newton, Mie Sloan, Christine Tapp, Rob Wilson, Gil Tucker and Mike Whitehouse.

FOUR SEASONS GARDEN CLUB

By Else J. Matthews

The Four Seasons Garden Club was established in 1965 by a group of mostly novice gardeners who were motivated to increase their knowledge of horticulture and help beautify the community. The first meeting was held at 1108 West Main Street in the home of Mrs. William E. Matthews with about 12 individuals in attendance for the organizational meeting.

At the start of 2002 the club had grown to approximately 20 regular members, and the meetings continued to be held in members' homes. The club meets monthly from September through June, except during the month of December.

Over the years the club has hosted many outstanding speakers, not only from Shelby County, but from Louisville, Lexington, and surrounding communities. Field trips have extended as far as Indiana and Ohio. The principal fund-raising effort of the club has consisted of a biennial French Picnic which encompasses an auction of unique garden and craft items, including some created by the members themselves.

Over the years club funds have been used to support the Fred Wiche Park in Simpsonville and provide a sign for the Simpsonville Community Center; help pay for playground equipment at the Shelby County Park on Snow Hill; pay for plantings at the Shelby County Community Theater, the Veterans Park across from the courthouse, and Northside School; pay for an out-of-town speaker who addressed Southside School children on how not to litter; and buy 60 trees in 2001 which were planted at the Shelby County Park.

HOP CLUB

By Bobby Webb

According to the Shelby Record of November 1904, the reorganization of the Shelbyville Hop Club (a club for society bachelors, age 18 or older) was preparing for its 45th Annual Ball to be held at Layson Hall (on the south corner of Seventh and Main Streets). The ball was postponed to February 26, 1905, due to the condition of Layson Hall. Officers who were elected were: Henry Moxley, president; William Harbison, vice-president; and A.M. Webber, secretary-treasurer. To join, one's name was submitted and if an individual was not "black-balled," he was in.

The Shelbyville Hop Club was known to have the best dances. The other surrounding clubs located at Harrodsburg, Frankfort, Lexington, Louisville, and Eminence received blanket bids and thus provided the stags for the dances. Young ladies were invited and delighted to attend. There were usually three dances a year; the Christmas Dance, a June dance, and one at the time of the Shelby County Fair in August.

For many years the overseer of the dances and organization was Temple "Pete" Bird, dressed in his tuxedo, waltzing Ann Hollenback around the floor, with Ben Staples checking at the door to see that one had been properly invited and was appropriately dressed.

In the early years the dances were held on the second floor where Lee McClain had a factory. There was dancing in the area with chaperones and spectators watching from the balcony. At intermission everyone would cross the street to go to Hollenbach's Hitching Post (Briggs-Bemiss). In the late 1920s and 1930s, the dances were held at the Elk's Club (south side of Main, between Eighth and Ninth). In the 1940s and '50s, they were held at Shelbyville High School Gym or the skating rink (Clay Street).

When the Hop Club started, tails were the dress; then came tuxedos and in summertime, white dinner jackets. In summertime Bermuda shorts, black or blue knee socks, with madras jacket and matching cummerbund were worn.

As to the nature of the dances, there were six on a card and each gentleman had first and last with his date and traded with another couple for the other dances. The dances began with a Grand March. In the early 1950s the "Cliff Butler Band" always played "When the Saints Go Marching In," and "Dixie," and the dance closed with "Goodnight Sweetheart." By that time the hat was passed in hopes of collecting enough money so that the band could play for another hour or two. During Shelby County Fair Week, dances started at 11:00 P.M. and lasted until 5:00 A.M. One of the last big events was when Sam Batts (1962) had the Ralph Materri Band (which was playing in Lexington) to come on Thursday evening so his band could play at the Big Top Warehouse with 500 to 700 in attendance.

COTILLION CLUB

By Bobby Webb

Betsy Gilbert and Virginia Frances Mowry formed the Cotillion Club in the mid-1930s. Girls' names were submitted at age 16 to become members and were voted on for membership. On becoming a member, they were members until they married.

The Cotillion Club had two dances a year to which the girls asked their male friend to be escorts. The young ladies were always dressed in their beautiful gowns with white gloves to the elbow and gents wore their tails; they did not soil the gloves of the ladies, as the gents also wore gloves. When without gloves, the gentlemen took a linen handkerchief from his pocket and placed it in his hand so that he would not soil the ladies' glove.

The dances were held at either the Shelbyville High School gym or the skating rink. The Cotillion Club continued into the 1970s and became defunct, as did the HOP Club, in the 1970s.

THE INTERNATIONAL ORDER OF THE KING'S DAUGHTERS AND SONS

By Lillian Sorrels

In January 1886 in New York City ten women founded a ministry known as The Order of The King's Daughters. The chosen motto represents the attributes of faith, hope, and altruistic service of this interdenominational society that reaches worldwide.

"Look up and not down,

Look forward and not back,

Look out and not in,

And lend a hand."

The King's Daughters of Shelbyville had its beginning in 1898 when Mrs. Will Jefferson, state president, came and organized the Handmaiden Circle at the home of Miss Mary Hill Ross. Present were Mrs. Eugene Cowles, Miss Florence Ballard, Miss Nannie Utterback, and Miss Willie Harbison.

This band of dedicated women, working with a zeal only found with such women, began the task of building a hospital. Another circle, for which no name can be found, was started in October 1901 at Chestnut Grove. Mrs. J.C. Price was leader; Mrs. George Raymond, vice leader; Linda Allen, secretary; and Mrs. L.Y. Browning, treasurer. A 1902 account states there was a small temporary medical treatment center somewhere in the city. A lot located at Tenth and Clay Streets was purchased in 1903 for $700. The circles paid $300 and the remainder was obtained by art exhibits, rummage sales, and donations. Bonds were issued for ten years without interest.

The King's Daughters Hospital Incorporated Co. was formed July 22, 1904. Members were Mrs. Lee (W.F.) Bryce, Mrs. Anne Harbison, Drue Smith, Lizzie Willis, Willie Mae Beard, Josephine Matthews, and Bettie Meriwether. With faith like that which moves mountains and energy worthy of any cause, a few good women worked and the result was a new hospital at a cost of $7,000 which opened September 19, 1906. The hospital's purpose was "to help all men and women, Protestants, Catholics and Jews, to alleviate suffering, lift the dull load of care as much as it can, comfort the sick and weary and soothe the dying."

In 1907, another circle was formed with Mrs. Willis, president; Miss Harbison, secretary; Mrs. Cowherd, treasurer. Members were Maude Middelton, Willie Mae Beard, Bettie Allen and Cornelia Hale. To raise needed funds a $1,000 touring car was raffled away in 1912. It was quoted as being the most valuable thing ever given away in Shelby County.

The Steadfast Circle was organized December 19, 1914, at the home of Mrs. R. Lee Shannon. Officers were Lola McClure, Lulie Harbison, Jane Shannon, and Martha Weakley. The Circle grew to a membership of 61. Its main accomplishments were operating the hospital and helping to start and build the new hospital at the west end of town. It merged with the Jennie Benedict Circle in 1992.

There were three African American circles—Looking Up, Cheerful Helpers, and Amanda Smith. Pioneers of the Amanda Smith Circle were Mrs. Lula Ellis, president; Mrs. Pearl Taylor, vice-president; Mrs. Mary Catherine Ellis, vice-president; Mrs. Crevella Newton, vice-president; Mrs. Mildred Saffell, secretary; and Mrs. Nettle Mickie. Their most notable deed was the purchase of a creamery located on

Tenth Street for $2,000 in 1914. They turned this into the Daisy M. Saffell Hospital. It had two wards and two private rooms. Operation of the facility ceased in 1954 due to integration.

The Jennie Benedict Circle organized on November 18, 1942, as an outgrowth of the Steadfast Circle. Mrs. Dick Prillamen and Mrs. E.J. Paxton (Steadfast members) initiated 16 members. The Circle was very active printing three cookbooks, conducting a Spring Style Show and luncheon, etc. Membership grew to sixty-five and under the leadership of Helen Montgomery another Circle, The Kingsway, was formed.

Nineteen people signed the Kingsway charter on December 8, 1953. Officers installed were Mrs. E. H. Searcy, president; Mrs. Howard Logan, vice president; Mrs. T. C. Long Jr., secretary; and Mrs. Harry Smith Jr., treasurer.

Two other Circles, the Silver Circle, which merged with the Kingsway, and the Lora Sams, which was short lived, are no more.

The Shelby County Union was formed in 1991 to administer funds for a scholarship, which is $5,000 per year for four years given to a person with a physical handicap or learning disability. Requests for other needs are also granted through this group.

The largest venture undertaken by the combined efforts of all Circles was the building of the new King's Daughters Hospital. It was dedicated September 26, 1954.

Suffering the pangs of the small rural hospital the board voted to sell to United Medical Center in 1974, thus relinquishing the operation of the hospital to an organization outside the jurisdiction of the King's Daughters.

The funds received from the sale are handled by Fiscal Court. A board consisting of Fiscal Court and the Circle's awards funds, from the interest only, to those who are in some way connected to the medical field. There are usually ten to twelve people who receive help annually. As a result of the sale Circle participation declined but the ministries which the Circles sponsor are still a very vibrant part of their activities. The support of The King's Daughters and Sons Home in Louisville and sponsoring Chautauqua scholarships continue to be the main goals of the present-day Circles. The Circles still have input to what is now Jewish Hospital

ISAAC SHELBY CHAPTER KSDAR

By Mary David Myles

The Isaac Shelby Chapter of the Daughters of the American Revolution was organized November 16, 1898, and was named for Kentucky's first governor, Isaac Shelby. It was the eleventh chapter organized in Kentucky and was formed just eight years following the National Society's organization in 1890. The founding Regent was Mrs. Anna McClarty Harbison (Mrs. Howard). The chapter has a copy of the charter, which contains the names of the other organizing officers. The charter members were: Mary Virginia Thomas Guthrie (Mrs. James Guthrie) #1; Mary Phelps Smith (Mrs. L. Theodore Smith) #2;

Anna McClarty Harbison (Mrs. Howard Harbison) #3; Miss Nannie Peyton Ballard #4; Miss Florence Effie Ballard #5; Miss Eliza Louise Winlock Davis #6; Georgiana Winlock Davis (Mrs. Richard Davis) #7; Margaret Lyle Hocker Higgins (Mrs. John K. Higgins) #8 Annie Stuart Logan (Mrs. John I. Logan) #9; Kate Jarvis Potter (Mrs. DeLaMotte Potter) $10; Annie Caldwell Escott (Mrs.-Wilson Haldeman Escott) #11; Elise Todd Sampson (Mrs. George Leslie Sampson) #12, Miss Katherine Shelby Todd (great-grand daughter of Colonel/Governor Isaac Shelby) #13; Jane Hardin Bell (Mrs. John Wilson Bell) #14; Martha Hardin Frederick (Mrs. D.A. Frederick) #15. Officers were: Regent— Mrs. Howard Harbison; Vice-Regent—Mrs. George Sampson; Secretary—Miss Florence Effie Ballard; Treasurer— Mrs. James Guthrie; Registrar—Mrs. DeLaMotte Potter; Historian—Mrs. John Logan.

Offices held at the state level have been State Treasurer 1911-12 Mrs. Wilson Escott; Vice-Regent 1924-25 Mrs. Lowry Beard; State Historian 1929-32 Mrs. Graham Lawrence; State Regent 1932-35 Mrs. Graham Lawrence; State Historian 1941-44 Mrs. John Fulton Davis; State Historian 1992-95 Mrs. Robert F. Matthews Jr.

On October 15, 1938, the first marker was erected by the Isaac Shelby Chapter. It honored Captain William Shannon who donated an acre of land for public purposes around which the town of Shelbyville grew. This marker is located at Fifth and Main Streets. In 1940, the chapter placed a bronze plaque on the front of the Shelby County Court House containing the names of all the Revolutionary War soldiers known in Shelby County. Historic markers on millstones were erected on KY 55 North for Boone Station (Painted Stone Station) and on U.S.60 East for Tyler Station. The Chapter members have marked many Revolutionary War soldiers' graves.

On September 17, 1987, the chapter led a service at the First Presbyterian Church to celebrate the 200th anniversary of the Constitution of the United States. After a patriotic program, with the assistance of the Boy Scout Troop, the church bell was rung 200 times. In 1992, the chapter, in conjunction with the Shelby County Historical Society, hosted an open house and tea at the Stanley-Casey house to celebrate the bicentennial of the state and county.

The chapter has given good citizen awards to the outstanding senior at the Shelby County High School, good citizenship medals to middle school students, honored the American history essay winners in the middle school, given ROTC medals at Shelby County High School, and had entries in the JAC contest.

Members have been active and volunteered time in their churches and satellite operations. They have assisted with the library, the literacy program, the Shelby County Historical Society, nursing home visits, Sunday devotions, the hospital and related support and auxiliary groups, the International Order of the King's Daughters & Sons, and other civic and patriotic organizations. DAR related projects are supported—historic, patriotic, and educational. The chapter stresses Constitution week, Flag Day, and visiting historic sites in the commonwealth. Revolutionary War soldier's graves have been located, inscriptions copied and recorded. Also copied have been Bible records, wills, and graveyards.

KIWANIS INTERNATIONAL

By Lise Sageser

Kiwanis International began in 1915 in Detroit, Michigan. The Kiwanis club of Shelbyville was granted its charter on April 12, 1946, and has continually been in existence as a service club.
The motto of Kiwanis is "We build," and youth has always been its first and most important area of service. However, it has since moved into other areas and is an active community service organization. Any time there is a need, Kiwanis has been there to help. While many services have been performed, none would have been possible without help from the entire community.

Some services carried out on a continual basis are: three scholarships totaling $2,500 given each year to county senior high school scholars; Christmas baskets for needy families; glasses provided for many who are unable to afford them; Big Brothers and Sisters Christmas party; and help for people who have experienced fires. Each year the Kiwanis club joins with Rotary for the farm-city banquet where farmers from Shelby County are invited and served a meal with a guest speaker. The Kiwanis hosts a prayer breakfast each year and more than 200 attend from throughout the county. To raise money needed for community services, work projects are carried out each year.

The Shelbyville Kiwanis Club is in division 13 of the Kentucky-Tennessee District of Kiwanis International. The members of Kiwanis come from all areas of the community. They include men and women from different races and religions with one central theme "to do their best to improve their community and world."

MASONS

By O.J. Simpson

Masons are members of what is generally regarded as the oldest and largest fraternal organization in the world. The earliest document, which refers to ancient Masonry, is the Regius Poem, or Halliwell Manuscript. Scientists have concluded from the type of parchment, language, and lettering that this document was written in approximately 1390 A.D.

Masonry, or more properly Freemasonry, is believed by many scholars as having evolved from the medieval craft guilds on the British Isles and throughout Europe. Four of these early lodges joined together in 1717 to form the first " grand lodge." The Grand Lodge of England was formed on St. John the Baptist's Day, June 24, 1717, at the Goose and Gridiron Ale House in London. The Grand Lodge of Ireland dates from 1730 and the Grand Lodge of Scotland from 1736.

The fraternity was in existence in America by 1730. However, the first properly constituted lodge was St. John's Lodge of Boston, Massachusetts, which was founded on July 30, 1733. This lodge is still in existence.

By 1800 there were lodges in Lexington, Paris, Georgetown, Frankfort, and Shelbyville. In September 1800, these lodges met to organize a grand lodge for Kentucky. On October 16, 1800, the Grand Lodge of Kentucky, Free and Accepted Masons was organized. The founding lodges were named and numbered; Lexington Lodge #1, Paris Lodge #2, Georgetown Lodge #3, Hiram Lodge #4 (Frankfort), and Solomon's Lodge #5 (Shelbyville).

From its earliest beginnings, Masons have taken care of their own. In 1867, Kentucky Masons established the Masonic Widows and Orphans' Home in Louisville. This was the first Masonic Home in North America. In 1901, the Old Masons' Home was established in Shelbyville. This tradition of philanthropy has continued. In 1995, major North American Masonic philanthropies contributed $750 million or over $2 million per day, of which 70 percent went to the general American public.

There were three lodges in Shelby County with a membership, as of 1997, totaling 432 members. They are Solomon's Lodge No. 5, Shelbyville; Wingate Lodge No. 161, Simpsonville; and Shelby Lodge No. 662, Waddy.

In addition to symbolic lodges, Shelbyville has been the home for several "appendant" Masonic organizations collectively called the York Rite. Shelbyville Chapter No. 2, Royal Arch Masons, was established August 28, 1816. Harry F. Walters Council No. 101, Royal and Select Masters, was chartered February 29, 1952. Shelby Commandery No. 32, Knights Templar, was chartered May 10, 1908. Also, Shelbyville is home to a sister organization, Shelby Chapter No. 170, Order of the Eastern Star.

The Old Masons' Home on U.S. 60 East.

Courtesy of Katherine and Henry Cleveland.

LOYAL ORDER OF THE MOOSE

By Linda N. Whitaker

The Loyal Order of the Moose is a fraternal organization. The Shelbyville Moose Lodge was organized in 1967. Its charter was instituted on December 10 at the Shelbyville High School gym with 264 members. The first two life members were Col. Harland Sanders and John Buckner. The Shelbyville Lodge had the largest instituting class in the state of Kentucky.

The first Moose Lodge, located at the present site of Plantation Inn, opened in February 1968. In 1971, Gayle Stivers donated seven acres of land located on Frankfort Road just west of the bridge at Guist Creek for a new lodge. This property will continue to belong to the Moose Lodge for as long as it is the Loyal Order of the Moose.

In 1993, the Women of the Moose Chapter was instituted with 45 members. It is for women with a male affiliation in the Moose. The Moose Lodge and Women of the Moose donate to several local and national Moose charities. Some are as follows: Sheriff's Boys Ranch, Scholarship at Shelby County High School, Shelby County Multi-Purpose Center, Girl Scouts, Operation Care, a local family at Christmas, Tom Lincoln Golf Scramble, Michael Long Charity Golf Scramble, Crusade for Children, Trooper Island, Project Graduation, and Cancer Relay for Life.

OPERA HOUSE ENTERTAINMENT

By Bobbie Smith

Finding a place for entertainment purposes has long been the mission of Shelby Countians, especially when it comes to young people. Local records indicate that the Layson Hall at 632 Main Street was at one time the epitome of top entertainment. Known then as the Layson Opera House, the featured opening night program was a performance by Charles Kinkle on December 10, 1871. Greek Revival in style, the commercial building had been constructed in 1870 by Robert M. Layson for use as his undertaking and furniture business on the lower level with the opera house on the second floor.

In 1903, The Shelby Record indicated that a new, more modern "Shelbyville Opera House" was to be built at once. Apparently a group of investors were brought together, Articles of Incorporation were drawn up, and officers were elected. They came to be known as the Commercial Club. A vacant lot at Eighth and Main Streets was selected as the site.

An article from The Shelby Record dated November 14, 1904, told of Layson Opera House property being sold for $9,500. Owners W. J. and B. A. Thomas sold the property to Captain Ben F. Pemberton and W. Morris Goff, both former stockholders in the proposed "Shelbyville Opera House." At the time of sale, the property consisted of two store rooms on the ground floor, one occupied as a grocery and the other by the Shelbyville Steam Laundry. The upper story was Shelbyville's only hall where public entertainment could be had. The two new owners had been the manager and treasurer of the part of the

Courtesy of the Kentucky Heritage Council.

Layson Hall, also known as the Opera House, still stands at the southeast corner of Seventh and Main Streets.

building known as the Opera House for several years, and more than any other two men knew how to make money with it.

The new owners decided, along with the Commercial Club, to abandon the idea of a new opera house and try to work with the one in existence. The article indicated that "The new owners had already begun to remodel the building and when it is completed there will be few, if any, more convenient, safer or prettier opera houses outside of Louisville in the State." Messrs. Gruber and Sons completed the remodeling work.

The description of the building as it was to be remodeled was as follows: "There will be a lobby of considerable dimensions in the front, from which a stairway to a hall, that will be made on the east side of the building, will give ingress at the side of the building, about forty feet from the front. There will be a gallery for the exclusive use of the colored people, and they will have an entrance that is separate and distinct from the one to be used by the white people. There will be a private box on either side of the stage, and there will be a balcony that will extend entirely across the pavement. There will be three exits leading to the main entrance and fire escapes at every window."

"Fully $2,000 will be expended in remodeling the building, and the contractors have agreed to complete the work by January 18. In addition to this, new opera house chairs of the latest improvement will be put in, the decorations and scenery will be up to date, the whole going to make a house for entertainment that will be an honor to the city."

"Messrs. Pemberton and Goff have tendered one of the private boxes for the opening night to the King's Daughters and this will probably be sold, the proceeds to go to their Free Hospital Fund. A number of the members of the Commercial Club, who agreed some time ago to pay $5 each for seats on the opening night in a new Opera House here referred to. They think the owners deserve to be encouraged in their undertaking and it is probable that all of those who signed that agreement will do likewise."

By December 1904, the Shelby Record announced that the newly named "Crescent Theater" had closed contracts with the Do Do Comic Opera Company and decided to have their opening night on Friday, January 6, 1905. The work was delayed and the opening night was actually held on January 12, 1905. The Shelby News reported that a moderate sized crowd attended the opening to see "Happy Hooligan." Nearly all of those in attendance arrived early and spent their time saying nice things about the Theatre, the new owners, the handsome souvenir program, and the many features that made it a gala occasion.

There didn't seem to be any notable entries regarding the Crescent until 1906. Amazingly enough, more than three hundred people were present at an opening of a skating rink at the Crescent Theater! This argued well for the success of the enterprising gentlemen, Will McGrath, Harry McCreight, and Ben Pemberton who were managers of the rink. The management had determined there would be no rough housing on the floor and that no objectionable characters were to be admitted. Seventy-six pairs of skates were all in use on the opening evening and many more were ordered as they ran out so quickly. In using the rink accompanied ladies were given the floor for a period of time, then ladies who were unaccompanied, then gentlemen who were without ladies and then the children would have their regular turn. Ladies were admitted free, gentlemen were charged 10 cents. There was a charge of 15 cents to rent skates.

At least a year after the skating rink opened, a city ordinance in 1907 provided for licensing of amusements and entertainment. It apparently included exhibitions of dramatic performances, lectures or any other entertainment where a charge of admission was made. The Opera House had a $50 annual license fee and the skating rink a $15 fee.

The ground floor of the property was leased to Shelbyville Filter Company which sublet the room to Ben J. Figg, who conducted a moving picture show. The arrangement between the Filter Company and Mr. Figg was made during the absence of Mr. Goff. When he returned he learned that the picture show was going full blast and because of it the insurance on the building had increased. Goff wanted Figg to vacate and Figg said he had the contract with the Filter Company behind him. One night, Goff and some of his friends apparently went to a show and got into a "discussion" with Figg. A lawsuit ensued with Figg bringing a $5,000 suit against Goff for damages and assault and a warrant was also issued against Chief of Police Thompson, charging him and Goff with disorderly conduct. Ed Figg was found guilty of engaging in business without a license, Morris Goff was fined $10, and Chief Thompson was acquitted.

By late that same year, the Crescent Theatre was again under new management of Harry McCreight and Company and reportedly was doing a good business. The crowds were large each night and the price of admission was only 5 cents.

One interesting visitor who came to the Crescent that year was the notable Carrie Nation. In October 1907 The Shelby News reported that "She came to Shelbyville, spoke in the Courtroom and at night in the Crescent Theater. On Sunday afternoon her 'for men only' talk was coarse of course. On Monday afternoon she spoke at the Christian Church. By the sale of her small hatchets and books and subscriptions to her paper she took in about $50. Whether she did any good or not is a question open to debate." The newspaper editor of that day concluded by saying: "Just to be agreeable, we will say may be she did."

The Shelby Record in November 1907 indicated that under new management the name had again changed and would now be known as the "New Electric Theatre". It would provide the latest up to date, illustrated songs, stereopticon, and moving pictures.

The last newspaper reference regarding the theater was in July 1915. Apparently it had been closed a year or so before. The reason was condemnation due to safety hazards. The article referred to the owners hiring Joseph and Joseph Architects in Louisville to review the building and decide what kind of restoration would be possible. (These were the same architects that built the new courthouse in 1913.)

Other theaters whose names cropped up include the "Green Dragon" in 1915 offering a moving picture theater next to Hollenbachs in the Hartford Building. Admission had gone to 10 cents for adults and 5 cents for children. Later it was sold and came to be known as the Majestic Theatre. Another theater was located at 610 Main Street known as the "Bon-Ton." One other was the "Strand" located in what is today Shelby County Trust Bank at the International Order of Odd Fellows building front.

SHELBYVILLE-SHELBY COUNTY PARKS AND RECREATION BOARD

By Clay Cottongim

Recreation in Shelby County prior to 1970, when the joint Shelbyville-Shelby County Parks and Recreation Board was formed, consisted of several efforts made through the generosity of local residents and city government. The major recreation facility was the Shelbyville City Pool, which was constructed in 1948 and opened in the summer of 1949. This facility served as the community's recreation hub along side the Shelbyville High School and its football and baseball field. Prior to that time, residents of Shelby County had to travel to Crescent Hill Pool, Tuckers Lake, Cox's Lake in Louisville, or possibly the Kentucky River in Frankfort. However, most people found Clear Creek their best bet for a swimming hole or Picketts Dam in Finchville.

The Shelbyville city pool's main program in its early years was Red Cross swim lessons which Bill Shannon, then Shelby County American Red Cross Director, helped organize. Youth as well as adults from around Shelby County were able to get free swim lessons with a paid admission to the pool.

Competitive swimming in Shelby County got its start at the Shelbyville Country Club pool in the early 1970s under volunteer coach Bill Shannon. Boys and girls competed with other country clubs and swim teams in the area. The first school team was put together with representatives of the old Shelbyville High School.

With the strong support and push for year round competitive swimming and other aquatic programs at the local level, in 1988 the city pool was covered with an air support structure known as the "Bubble." It was made possible through the efforts of Bill Shannon and swim coach John Graham, along with the support of the Parks Board, Shelbyville City Council, and many individuals in Shelby County. The bubble opened in October 1988, and the first full-time aquatic director was Mary Hayes-Smith.

On February 10,1970, the Shelbyville-Shelby County Parks and Recreation Board was formed as a joint agency of the Shelbyville City Council and Shelby County Fiscal Court. The budget allotment from the city and county was a 50/50 match consisting of $6,000. Also, in November 1971, the property owned by the Louisville & Nashville Railroad on Union Street was donated to the Parks Board for a mini-park, which was then developed with Bureau of Outdoor Recreation Funds and named Mose Dale Park. In

February 1972, the Parks Board approached Dr. A.L. Birch about acquiring his property on Snow Hill for a community park, now known as Clear Creek Park. In June 1972, the Parks Board voted to purchase the Birch property, which consisted of 132 acres. Land was also donated in 1972 for what is now James Burnett Park on Thorn Street and Elmo Head Park on Third Street, and in April 1973, $19,700 in federal funds through BOR were granted to the Parks Board to develop all three mini-parks.

In May 1974, Ronnie Perkins was hired as the first full-time park director. He was succeeded by Mitch Bailey and in 1978 by the present director Clay Cottongim. In June, Fiscal Court purchased the Birch property for $190,000. Lake Shelby was officially leased to the Parks Board, and the facility was opened to all Shelby County residents as a public park. Development of the south end of Clear Creek Park began. Dr. Ron Waldridge, who spearheaded the initial efforts to build the park, is known as the father of Clear Creek Park.

On October 29, 1977, Clear Creek Park was dedicated. Construction began on the Clear Creek Park Driving Range and softball fields in April 1978. In August, construction began on two basketball courts at Clear Creek Park. The Parks Office was moved from the courthouse to Clear Creek Park in December 1978.

In March 1980, it was announced that Mrs. Marguretta Henderson had left half of her estate to the Parks Board which amounted to over $169,000. In September, Col. Harland Sanders donated $10,000 to the Parks Board for the construction of the Col. Sanders Shelter.

The lower shed of the original horse barn at Clear Creek Park was renovated into a youth activity center in 1982. The center was used for dances, movies, birthday parties and other rentals. The miniature golf course was constructed at Clear Creek Park in June 1984. Lake Shelby was closed to RV camping for reorganization of the facility. The golf shop was built. The new Clear Creek Golf Course was dedicated and opened Memorial Day weekend 1989, thanks to the efforts of Robert Doyle, Bennett Roach and W.R. Long. A $40,000 LWCF grant was awarded for a new bathhouse and electrical upgrades at Lake Shelby.

The 1990s have brought rapid growth for the Parks System beginning with the addition of the golf course and a year-round swimming facility in the late 1980s. The Parks Board received donations and grants to build the Dr. Birch Amphitheater. The Board had the Clear Creek Park master plan redrafted. It was instrumental in the purchase and renovation of Weissinger Hills Golf Course by the city in 1992. Robbie Hart completed his Eagle Project at Lake Shelby, which began the primitive camping area and nature trail along Lake Shelby. Danny "Kac" Newton was hired on 1995 as the parks first full-time athletic director. The Parks Board also voted to allow the Dorman Preschool to locate in Clear Creek Park next to the Waldridge Center. In return, the park was allowed to use the Dorman Center in the evenings and on weekends for meetings and programming. In 1997, the Parks Board hired its first full-time Park Ranger, Gena Johnson.

After ten years of planning, doing studies, and urging local government to finance it, ground was broken in January 1999 for the $5.1 million/ 39,000 square foot Family Activity Center. A facility with two indoor pools, a gym, fitness room, game room, indoor walking track, concessions, an outdoor pool, and an administrative area was attached to the existing Waldridge Center and Dorman Center. Clear Creek Park presently contains over 140 acres. Its many programs serve over 3,000 people each year.

The original Board was formed on February 10, 1970, and the first Board meeting was held on February 26, 1970. The following members of the Parks & Recreation Board were named:

Casting contest at the Lake Shelby boat dock, 1954. Mark Scearce at right foreground in boat; Jim Guthrie leaning against building; Ben Allen Thomas II, far right, fishing from dock; D. I. Cooper, wearing suspenders and seated in boat.

Shelby County Public Library, Shelby News photograph.

ORIGINAL BOARD MEMBERS

City Appointments	Joint Appointment
Harry Long	Dr. Ronald Waldridge - 4 years
Moses Dale	
Howard Pearce	Parks Board Chairmen
Lloyd Pollard	Harry Long Feb. 1970-Sept. 1970
	Dr. Ronald Waldridge Sept. 1970 - Dec. 1982
County Appointments	Tommy Webb Jan. 1983 - Dec. 1994
Roy Foster	Hubert Pollett Jan. 1995 - Present
James Merchant	
Hubert Briscoe	
Arnold Thurman	

INTEGRATION OF CITY POOL

By Duanne Puckett

When the city pool opened on Washington Street it was patronized by white swimmers only. It was not integrated until 1963 when 14-year-old David Spencer Jr. and two other African American children arrived at the pool and were allowed admittance. The Shelbyville weekly and the Louisville daily newspapers discussed the June 24 incident triggered by what reporters called "Negroes." Mayor Jesse Puckett, according to the *Courier-Journal,* was primarily responsible for the integration. "We knew we couldn't keep them out and City Council agreed beforehand to let them go in when they tried," said Puckett who served as mayor for twelve years and city clerk for fifteen before his retirement in 1987.

The repercussion of the "Negro" swimmers was devastating to the city pool economically. There had been an average daily attendance of about 200 before June 24 with admission cost being 25 cents for children and 50 cents for adults. On the day David Spencer and his friends swam, receipts dropped to $41.50. The mayor said the typical $100 day business even dropped to $2.50 one day during the desegregation period.

"The change in policy was dictated by economics," said Mayor Puckett in announcing a July 1, 1963, agreement that he worked out with attorney Willie Fleming, an African American. On each Monday, Wednesday, Friday and Sunday, the pool was limited to white patrons and swimmers only. On each Tuesday, Thursday and Saturday, Negro patrons and swimmers used the pool only.

Within 20 days, some of the 17 blacks who had signed the agreement with the City Council changed their minds and garnered support from groups in Louisville. When about forty blacks attempted to use the pool on a Friday, they were refused admittance by Mayor Puckett, Councilman Harry Long, and three city policemen who stood in front of the door. The matter remained unresolved until Memorial Day 1964 when the pool opened to both white and black bathers any day of the week.

PORTIA CLUB

By Lea McMullan Anderson

In January 1936, ten women college graduates who were interested in continuing their education and broadening their minds as their lives changed and developed through the years joined together and formed the Portia Club. Some of these women were wives, homemakers, and mothers; some pursued careers as teachers along with homemaking and motherhood; some pursued other careers. They established the club through the interest and encouragement of Agnes Hanna Guthrie and Lucy Mapes, members of a sister club, the Chautauqua Club. Charter members of the club were Elizabeth Guthrie, Ruth Willis, Florence Dudley Jesse, Ann Hays, Helen Hays, Mary Goodman, Jane McCoy, Sally Davis, Jane Gilbert, and Margaret Kirk.

The object of the club was to pursue steadfastly the yearly programs planned by the program committee for the promotion of higher education, personal improvement, and social progress. Each woman was responsible for extensive research on a topic and a presentation of the material at a meeting. The meetings were held twice a month with two topics presented each evening. The topics were current and included a variety of subjects, usually covering the areas of history, science, the arts, sports, medicine, people, education, industry, economics, a current play or book review, and whatever else expanded their minds.

Through the years the number of women in the club has fluctuated and the types of careers have varied. Topics are still researched and presented at monthly meetings in the homes of the members, and the format is essentially the same. The officers encourage attendance at all meetings, and the program committee still assigns the programs. In addition to the programs, members are encouraged to read as they share and rotate books each month. The pursuit of education in many fields and the continued expansion of the mind are still the main objectives of the Portia Club in Shelbyville.

ROTARY CLUB OF SHELBYVILLE

By William Shannon

The Rotary Club of Shelbyville (Charter #2623) was sponsored by the Frankfort Rotary Club and was chartered May 20, 1927. It consisted of 18 members: B.B. Cozine, E.H. Rothchild, Pryor R. Beard, Turner Bright, John E. Brown, John R. Butler, H.H. Carter, Matthews Hall, W.C. Hannah, R.A. Hoover, Albert Hollenbach, H.B. Kinsolving, Carl D. Matthews, H.O. Moxley, Moses Ruben, S.R. Skinner, L.G.Smith and A.C. Weakley. By 1950, the Club had grown to 80 members. At the time of its 50th anniversary, membership had leveled to 54.

The Crippled Children's Organization (now Easter Seals) was espoused by Frankfort Rotarian Harry V. McChesney at the charter meeting. Its support has been a part of the club ever since.

During the early years, Rotary support was given to many projects: Boys Scouts, Cub Scouts, Red Cross, Shelby County Community Chest, local hospitals, and sending students to "World Affairs Institute" in Cincinnati. The Club decided in 1937 to give an annual award to a graduating senior boy at Shelbyville High School. This was done from 1937 through 1974. When all county high schools were merged, the Rotary Club began giving the award each year to a Shelbyville High School student and a Shelby County student. Shortly before high school merger, the Rotary Club voted to make similar awards in the five county high schools of Gleneyrie, Finchville, Bagdad, Simpsonville, and Waddy, for the years of 1949 through 1953.

In the years since 1952 several new projects were started: "Fireside Information Meetings" in member's homes; distribution of the Rotary Magazines throughout the community; family picnics; Past Presidents' Nights; two "Rotary Ann" meetings each year; special meetings such as "Competitors, Employers, & Buyers and Sellers Nights," and the gift to each Rotarian of a 4-Way Test Plaque. Handicapped children's work under the leadership of Briggs Lawson and Easter Seals continued, as did support for Camp KYSOC, Camp Green Shores, and Cardinal Hill

In the year 1953-54, members raised and sold a tobacco crop with the proceeds going to Easter Seals. This project attracted worldwide attention. During the early 1950s the club started handling the gate at the Shelby County Fair and continues to do so. Farm-City Week began in 1954 and local Rotary & Kiwanis Clubs joined to sponsor this event with a special community banquet.

During the second twenty-five years, the club sponsored a little league team, an invitational tennis tournament, a high school booster night, athletic team banquets, and awards for 4-H and FFA members at the county fair.

In the early 1950s the club raised over $3,000 to help establish a playground. In the years 1953-54, the club provided leadership and labor in the construction of two all weather tennis courts, which are still in use at the West Middle School. For a short time (1976-79), it joined with other service clubs to provide $500 scholarships to deserving high school seniors.

One of the biggest changes was the addition of female Rotarians. The first lady Rotarian was Joyce Dudley, the Director of Nursing at United Medical Center.

In the Rotary year 1978-79, the club sponsored and the district awarded a graduate scholarship to Harriet Ballard to study in Portugal. Other projects included rejuvenation of the student loan program, golf scrambles, weekly jackpots, pancake breakfasts, cruise raffles, four Rotary-community sponsored rental signs.

Up to the present time the club has supported five Rotary Paul Harris Fellows: Colonel Harland Sanders, Briggs Lawson, Stewart McBrayer, Bill Shannon, and George Brinkhaus.

PAST OFFICIALS OF THE ROTARY CLUB

PRESIDENTS
1927-28 B. B. Cozine
1928-29 Matthews Hall
1929-30 A. C. Weakley
1930-31 M. E. Lee
1931-32 L. G. Sullivan
1932-33 C. B. Caudill
1933-34 W. M. Hannah
1934-35 J. M. Tydings
1935-36 David Bell
1936-37 Coleman Wright
1937-38 J. W. Holland
1938-39 C. W. Elsey
1939-40 Phil Moesser
1940-41 Forrest Smith
1941-42 Milton Fullenwider
1942-43 W. R. Reasor
1943-44 Lawrence Hughes
1944-45 W. Boyd Roe
1945-46 Briggs Lawson
1946-47 Howard Pearce
1947-48 Paul Schmidt
1948-49 Bernard Davis
1949-50 Tom Watson
1950-51 Hayden Igleheart
1951-52 N. E. McKay
1952-53 W. L. Shannon
1953-54 J. G. Goodman, Jr.
1954-55 Ralph Mitchell
1955-56 Auldon Edwards
1956-57 Ray Weller
1957-58 J. Edward Cayce

1958-59 Edwin Hall
1959-60 Purcell Lee
1960-61 Henry Bell
1961-62 Roy Miller
1962-63 Roy D. Ratcliffe
1963-64 Stewart F. McBrayer
1964-65 French Smoot
1965-66 June Davis
1966-67 Ted Igleheart
1967-68 William Pettus
1968-69 William E. Matthews
1969-70 Guthrie Goodman, III
1970-71 Tom Dawson
1971-72 Leroy McMullan
1972-73 John R. Davis
1973-74 John S. Mathis
1974-75 Dennis Liptrap
1975-76 Steve Rapp
1976-77 James Davis
1977-78 William H. Underwood
1978-79 David Mathis
1979-80 Tom Tucker
1980-81 Joe Paul Simpson
1981-82 Todd Davis
1982-83 William Lancaster
1983-84 Sherman Riggs
1984-85 Max Avery
1985-86 Bill Hundley, III
1986-87 Albert Linder
1987-88 David Bemiss
1988-89 George Brinkhaus
1989-90 Shelby Riner

1990-91 Charles Clifton
1991-92 Lee Shannon
1992-93 Robert Pearce
1993-94 Rob Schorering
1994-95 Jeff Miller
1995-96 Wade Hembree
1996-97 Mark Stivers
1997-98 Joe Piccini
1998-99 Gordon Griffin
1999-2000 Chuck Cicchella
2000-2001 Ryburn Weakley
2001-2002 Lindsey Logan
2003- Lynn Williamson

SECRETARY-TREASURERS
1927-28 P. R. Beard
1928-46 L. G. "Pop" Smith
1946-47 W. Forrest Smith
1947-69 W. Coleman Wright
1969-71 William H. Underwood
1971-72 John S. Mathis
1972-92 Stewart F. McBrayer

SECRETARIES
1992-99 Judy Hickman

TREASURERS
1987-91 Lee Shannon
1991-92 Mike Tipton
1992- Leonard Ballard

Ruritan Club

By Julian K. Wood

The first Ruritan Club in Shelby County was organized on November 5, 1953, at Bagdad. Wesley Newton was its first president, and there were twenty-four charter members. The McKinney Ruritan Club of Lincoln County, Kentucky, sponsored this club. Seeing what Ruritan could do for a community, Waddy formed a club on July 14, 1955, with 35 charter members and was sponsored by the Bagdad Club. The first president was W. K. Hedden.

Cropper also saw the need for a Ruritan Club. On June 14, 1960, Bagdad sponsored a club of 29 members headed by Henry G. Rowlette as president. On October 26, 1961, Bagdad sponsored a club at Mount Eden. Mount Eden had 43 charter members with James A. Gordon as the first president.

Shelby County Ruritan Clubs continued to grow in numbers and members. On November 8, 1965, Cropper sponsored a club at Chestnut Grove. This new club had 32 members and selected Walter Wilborn as its first president. Although this club started out very strongly and did much good for the community, members began to lose interest and the rolls dropped. Finally, in 1990, the club ended.

After several visits to the nearby community of Peytona, the Waddy Club sponsored a new club on May 20, 1971. The first president was Carl W. Masters, and there were twenty-three charter members. Unfortunately, this club also lost members and finally was dropped in January 1979.

A club was chartered Finchville on July 19, 1990, with 63 members. The first president was Mike Whitehouse.

All the clubs in Kentucky are patterned after Ruritan National which is headquartered in Dublin, Virginia. The first Ruritan Club was organized in Holland, Virginia, May 21, 1927. It was organized for the small, rural communities. The name Ruritan came from the Latin words "ruri" which means open country and "tan" which means small town. Ruritan expanded in Virginia and entered Kentucky on May 27, 1930. It was soon in other states and thus grew into a national organization.

Ruritan National has certain guidelines, but each club follows a local constitution in addition to national's guidelines. When Ruritan was first organized, women could not become members. This practice was discontinued some years ago. Since then women are welcomed into any club that votes them in as members.

There is the usual slate of officers and directors in each club. There are District Governors in each district. All of Kentucky makes up District 21. Shelby County has provided the following District Governors:

1957, Wesley Newton, Bagdad

1967, Buddy Yount, Cropper

1970-71, Charles Turner, Chestnut Grove

1976, Richard Floyd, Bagdad

1985, 1996-97, Carl Moore, Bagdad

Charles Turner of Chestnut Grove was elected National Director for 1973, 1974, and 1975.

Shelby County Ruritan Clubs have received many awards for community service, recreation programs, welfare, education, attendance, environment, business, and citizenship. The Blue Ribbon awards are given for outstanding community service and over 90 percent attendance rates. Only about 10 percent of all clubs ever receive this award and they include Bagdad and Cropper.

As of 1999, there were 158 club members in Shelby County.

OPTIMIST CLUB, OPTIMIST INTERNATIONAL

By Lise Sageser

The Shelby County Optimist Club was formed in 1993 with 32 charter members. There were two known Optimist Clubs in this area prior to this organization. Glenn Sageser, charter President, along with his wife, Lise, were instrumental in bringing this "Friend of Youth" organization into the community once again. The organization promotes Optimism, not only as a philosophy of life, but as an inspiration to Shelby County's young people. The members have one goal in mind, namely to make a difference in the lives of Shelby County's youth.

As a community service club, the Optimist Club requires minimal yearly dues. Once dues are paid, the club requires no additional monetary contribution from members. The club obtains funds through fund-raising events, and then spends those funds on the children and events in the community. Following is a brief list of the projects, which have been sponsored by the Shelby County Optimist Club—past and current:

Essay and Oratorical contests resulting in up to $1,500 scholarship provided by Optimist International. These contests reach children through high school age.

Tri-Star Basketball is a free, non-contact event sponsored each January by the club and involves all children between ages 8 and 13. This is a skill contest—dribble, pass and shoot—in which a trophy is awarded to one boy and one girl in each of the six age brackets.

Sponsorship of basketball and soccer teams through the Shelby County Parks Department.

Academic scholarships have been presented since 1997 to graduating Shelby County High School seniors. Each year one man and one woman receive a $250 scholarship to further his or her education in the vocational field.

Bicycle Safety Program is a cooperative program with the Shelbyville Police and Shelby County Sheriff's Departments to provide a free program which instructs local children in bicycle safety. Each year a free bicycle is the top prize for children visiting the event.

The Club sponsored "The Entertainers" which raised money for the building of the current Dorman Center.

The Club has been responsible for the Christmas Dinner at Operation Care. This is one of the highlights of the year for not only Optimist Club members, but for all of the volunteers who join in the effort.

The Club has become involved in volunteer after school programs at West/East Middle Schools.

SHELBYVILLE HORSE SHOW

By Edward Bennett and R.H. Bennett

The first annual Shelbyville Horse Show was held in August 1990. For several years prior, Edward "Hoppy" Bennett and his brother, R.H. Bennett, had discussed the possibility of having a first class saddlebred horse show in Shelbyville. Because they believe that Shelby County has the best saddlebred horses in the United States, the best horse trainers, and a community willing to support such an event, their dream became a reality. R.H. Bennett was the owner of Rich Field Video and Review Video Magazine. Both businesses deal exclusively with horse shows and exhibitions. Hoppy Bennett was the owner of Undulata Farm.

The Bennetts approached Redd Crabtree, a horse trainer in Simpsonville, with their idea. Both Redd and his wife, Nancy, were enthusiastic. With Nancy's encouragement, Jean Logan and Jean Matthews were enlisted and that small group formed a cadre of community supporters to spearhead development of the first horse show and what has become known as the "tent committee." In addition, the Shelby Development Corporation (SDC) joined the effort and their involvement throughout the years produced the Shelbyville Horse Show Jubilee, a festival that includes activities that incorporate the entire community with the horse show.

The horse show has continued to grow. In 1990, the Horseman's Club was a small tent event with hors d'oeuvres and drinks prepared at the homes of the "tent committee" and delivered to the fairgrounds. Today, the Horseman's Club is a catered event in a new two-story pavillion with a spectacular view of the show ring.

Attendance has increased significantly. In 1999, approximately 15,000 people turned out for the four-night event held in August. A vendor area featuring booths with antiques, jewelry, clothes, gifts, and food was added along the road behind the grandstands. Exhibitors from as far away as California, Texas, and Maine participated with approximately 400 horses competing in fifty-nine classes.

In its short history, the Shelbyville Horse Show has become nationally known. The United Professional Horseman's Association (UPHA) elected Shelbyville their National Honor Show in 1993 and again in 1999. In addition, the show has been named UPHA Chapter 9 (the state of Kentucky) Honor Show for eight years. In 1993, R.H. Bennett was named the UPHA Horse Show Manager of the year.

SIMPSONVILLE LIONS CLUB

By J. C. Smith and Sue Hall

The night of June 12, 1949, marked a big occasion in Simpsonville when the South Oldham Lions Club chartered the Lions Club with 29 members. International Director William Wilson presented the charter. The charter members were Fulton Smith, Jack Frazier, Bruce Sweeney, Estes Snider, Jack Perry, Hobart Henninger, Sr., William B. Sledd, Vernon Jones, James Golden, Wilson Herrick, James Perkins, Chris Bryant, Walton Buckman, James Eddington, Mack Walters, William S. "Red" Proctor, Walter Perry,

Allen Webb, Lillard Watson, Fred White, Lloyd Johnson, Herbert McDowell, Claude Moss, Roy Pearce, John Young, Sr., Frank Jones, C. H. Gabbhart, Sr., Ralph Howerton, E. B. Noland, Vernon Hulett, Maurice Miller, C. W. Brittain, Bob Hanser, Lee Druin and Charles Bastin. They included men in business, education, and farming. Some owned their business or farm while others worked for businesses or on these farms.

The original meeting hall was the Simpsonville Christian Church recreation room and the Gleaners Sunday school class served a meal. The club met for awhile at the Simpsonville Volunteer Fire Department. It now meets at the Simpsonville Community Center and meals are prepared by the food committee and occasionally by each member bringing items for the meal.

In the first nine years the club grew to a membership of fifty-seven for several reasons. The growth was primarily due to the exceptional qualities of those officers in positions of leadership who gave of their time and effort regardless of sacrifice. The second reason was the members themselves. They constituted a congenial, cooperative group of men who were willing to work together when called upon. The third reason was the wholehearted response by the people of Simpsonville and Shelby County. The fourth reason for success has been the activities, the lifeblood of any organization. They include the organization of the volunteer fire department, the care of the cemetery along with the Masonic Lodge building, the scouting program, organizing and chartering the Eastwood and Spencer County Lions Clubs, supervising the summer recreation program until the early 1970s, starting a coed youth basketball program with about 124 youth from ages 6 to 16, co-sponsoring with other civic clubs a scholarship program at Shelby County High School, delivering baskets of food and toys to needy and underprivileged families in the western Shelby County area, building and equipping the Lions Eye Foundation at the University of Louisville (a $6 million project), buying hundreds of pairs of eyeglasses, and providing other eye care for Shelby County needy. Every year the club contributes to the All State Band, Camps Crescendo, and Trooper Island, diabetes awareness, all star basketball, youth camps and other Lions' activities that deal with the sight and hearing impaired. The club also makes donations to those who need help with medical bills, funeral costs, food, clothes, etc. Each year the club presents a Citizen of the Year Award to a person involved in the Simpsonville area who has contributed in some way to help the community.

After about seventy years women could become members of Lions Clubs rather than the traditional Lioness Club. They make up a large and hard working percent of all clubs. Several women are and have been presidents of their clubs and district officers including District Governor. In 1962, the Lions of District 43N of which the Simpsonville Club is a member elected Bruce Sweeney to the office of District Governor. District 43N is one of six districts in Kentucky and includes forty-two Lions Clubs in thirteen counties. In 1977, J. C. Smith was elected District Governor.

The Presidents from chartering to date are: Bruce Sweeney, Fulton Smith, Maurice Miller, J. L. Coots, Walton Buckman, Herbert McDowell, James Golden, William Miller, Wilson Herrick, Charles Miller, Harvey Duvall, Jack Perry, Lee Druin, Thomas Lincoln, Middelton Phillips, Marvin Harris, William Shouse, James Carpenter, William "Red" Proctor, William Houchin, J. T. Clemmons, Jimmy Chappell, J. C. Smith, Bill Willard, Jim Smith, Leroy Fredricks, Mike Gee, Paul Mahuron, Larry Williams, George Hines, Bobby Griffin, John McCray, Bill Bohannon, Jerry Miller, Jesse Harper, Weldon Palmer, Forest Washburn, J. B. Martin, David Geoghegan, Chuck Danison, Bill Smith, Opal McGee, Jim Janes, and Sue Hall.

VETERANS OF FOREIGN WARS POST

By Earl Sorrels Jr.

The first V.F.W. Post after World War II was started in 1947. It was named Maddox-Yeary Post 6939. This name was chosen because Maddox was the first soldier killed in the war who lived in Shelbyville, and Yeary was the first soldier killed who lived in Shelby County.

The first meeting place was in the small courtroom at the courthouse with about eight members. It was moved from there to Harris Café located at Eleventh and Equity Streets. Later an army barracks was bought and placed on a lot at the intersection of Benson Road and U.S. 60 East. Membership grew until there were 180 members. Later moves were to the old skating rink and from there to the old Adams Camp on U.S. 60 West. The post disbanded.

Post 1179 is the second V.F.W. Post in Shelbyville. It was started in 1984 with about 25-chartered members. The first meeting was held at the Army Reserve Center at 524 Second Street. During the next few years, the membership increased to more than 150. After a couple of years the V.F.W. Post building was bought in the 600 block of Main Street, where it is today.

With WW II Veterans getting older and dying at a high number each day, it is very difficult to enroll members and keep the old ones active. However in 1999 there were about 100 members. The Post engages in many local projects of a charitable nature. The V.F.W. Post 1179 provides a color guard, firing squad, and members for funeral services.

COMMANDERS POST 1179

Daniel Moffett	1984-85
Bobby G. Powell	1986
Ludlow Cook Jr.	1987
Samuel G. Kovach	1988
Bobby G. Powell	1989, '90, '94
Thomas D. Bowman	1991, '95, '97
Earl Sorrels Jr.	1998-2000

SHELBY COUNTY WOMAN'S CLUB

By Delores Odenweller

The Shelby County Woman's Club held its organizational meeting on February 4, 1975, and became state and nationally federated in April 1975. The club was established through the efforts of Debra Magan who moved to Shelbyville from Frankfort where she had been a member of a Woman's Club. Twenty-three charter members were recruited, and the first president, Pam Evans, and other officers were installed at the 1975 state meeting.

The mission of Shelby County Woman's Club has been to support worthwhile causes and to recognize needs in the community, which can be adopted as projects. Often, civic-minded individuals and businesses are asked to help fund major undertakings. The Woman's Club has attempted to include all age groups, from newborns to senior adults in its service to the community.

Noteworthy accomplishments of the Shelby County Woman's Club include the following:

1976 - Started Dairy Doll and Dandy Contest for June Dairy Month

1977 - Published a Newcomer's booklet in conjunction with Chamber of Commerce; began presenting the "Poynter Cup Award" to an outstanding senior orchestra student; conducted the first "Holiday Home Tour" as a fund-raising project

1978 - Sponsored the first Shelby County Junior Miss Scholarship Program

1980 - Began awarding a vocational scholarship to an outstanding senior; hosted "Breakfast with Santa"

1981 - Sponsored a health fair; hosted a Morrocan teacher through an International Exchange Program; organized a political forum for local candidates; donated toward Shelby County Community Theatre Building Fund 1982 - Shelby County's Junior Miss, Cathy Montgomery, won the Kentucky Junior Miss title; added scholarship money to the Poynter Cup

1983 - Showed child abuse prevention films from Rape Relief Center to 3,650 school children; held a Celebrity Auction to raise funds to furnish a pediatric room for local hospital

1984 - Fingerprinted pre-school and elementary school children; sponsored the Martha Layne Collins doll at KFWC First Ladies display at State Capitol

1985 - Increased amount of vocational scholarship to $500

1986 - Began support of Project Graduation; co-sponsored with Jaycees the Dream Car Dinner raising $6,000 for Senior Citizen Building Fund

1988 - Financially supported the Nature Center at Shelby County High School and the Bubble for the city pool

1989 - Began supporting Hugh O'Brien Youth Foundation; gave proceeds from Dream Car Dinner to Rescue Squad for Jaws of Life; started selling spring flowers as a fund-raiser

1990 - Began helping with the Shelbyville Horse Show; began supporting Habitat for Humanity

1991 - Adopted the sale of poinsettias as a fund-raiser

1992 - Supported Shelby County Bicentennial Celebration; changed Poynter Cup Award to SCWC Scholarship for an outstanding female senior

1993 - Supported Big Brothers/Sisters, Dorman Center, Shelby County Educational Foundation; and granted community need requests

1994 - Started major playground project for Shelby County Park

1997 - Dedicated new playground equipment (total cost, $25,643); contributed to Youth Advisory Council; increased amounts of Junior Miss scholarships; discontinued state affiliation, donated to Dorman Center

1998 - Adopted a grant application process for community needs; donated $3,000 to Claudia Sanders Women's and Children's Wing of Jewish Hospital; donated to Children's Library and Dorman Center

1999 - Awarded grants totaling $3,000 to the Center for Women and Children; the North Central District Health Department; the Shelby County Preschool Family Resource Center; the Shelby County Family Resource and Youth Service Centers; and the Shelby County Education and Literacy Center.

By the year 2000, the club had awarded over $90,000 in scholarships to local students, over $28,000 to the Shelby County Parks, and over $35,000 to other community causes and organizations.

Shelby County Woman's Club was chartered by the Kentucky Federation of Woman's Clubs, April 1975. Clockwise from lower left: Betty Rose, Judy Burk, Pam Evans, Margaret Wilborn, Kathleen Thompson, Rosemary Riggs, Debby Magan, and Brenda Richardson.

Shelby County Public Library, Shelby County Woman's Club Collection.

SPORTS

By William Matthews

I t all began, according to newspaper records, in 1895 when teams from Shelbyville and Finchville first battled for local pride on the football gridiron. Since then there have been many individuals and teams from Shelby County which have achieved not only enduring county fame, but, in some instances, recognition upon the state and national sports scene.

Ben Allen Thomas II, Dan McGann, Mike Casey, Herbie Kays, Lee Tinsley, John Lyle Miller, Bill Shannon, Jack Green, Cindy Baker, Reggie Hicks, Charles Hurt, Jack Byrd, Montez Allen, Josh Buffolino, Vince Chambers, Tracy Driver, Kim Cunningham, Greg Gundlach, Scott Jones, Terry Davis, Chris Lancaster, Howard Logan Jr., Ron Ritter, Ken Slucher, Mike Stoner, Leonard Sullivan, Archie Ware Jr., William White, Adam Henson, Lisa Goodman Tipton, Lucien Kinsolving, Bruce Logan, Scott Wilson and Junior Jones are among those whose records reached near legendary proportion during their time in the spotlight.

MCANN is the only native Shelby Countian to have played in a World Series. He was born in Shelbyville on July 15, 1871. He played 12 years in the major leagues, and had a career batting average of .285. He appeared as the first baseman for the New York Giants in the 1905 World Series.

CASEY led the Shelby County Rockets to the 1966 State High School Championship. He scored 23 points in the 62-57 finale against Male, and became a standout at the University of Kentucky where was named to the All-Southeastern Conference team.

KAYS was considered by Coach Evan Settle perhaps his greatest performer on the hardwood, and was a leader on the coach's 1956 team that went to the state tournament. He scored 26 points in the team's hard-fought opening round loss to King Kelly's Wayland team. Kelly scored 50.

TINSLEY, originally signed by the Oakland A's, became a well-respected hitter for both the Seattle Mariners and Boston Red Sox in the 1990s; he was a three-sport standout at Shelby County High School

MILLER was an All-State fullback on Shelbyville's first unbeaten, untied football team, in 1947.

SHANNON captained Shelbyville High School's first unbeaten football season in 1936.

HICKS led the Rockets to the State High School Football 4A title in 1987, scoring the winning touchdown to upend heavily favored and unbeaten Boone County.

HURT, along with Norris Beckley, was the driving force on the Rockets' 1978 State Tournament Championship team. His turn-around shot at the buzzer tied the game in regulation, and

Lee Tinsley played for both the Seattle Mariners and the Boston Red Sox in the 1990s.

the team went on to defeat Covington Holmes, 68-66, in the tournament's first overtime game. He later starred at the University of Kentucky.

BYRD won the state high school tennis tournament three straight years (1939-41) and teamed with his brother Ryland to also win the doubles title.

THOMAS was captain, center, and a hard-hitting All-State player on the Transylvania College team of 1911 that tied with University of Kentucky (then Kentucky State) and Centre College for the state championship.

GREEN is Shelby County's only member of the National College Football Hall of Fame. After starring at Shelbyville High, he captained Army's national championship teams of 1944 and 1945.

BAKER was a standout on the 1977 Lady Rockets team, and became the first Rocket to gain a college basketball scholarship.

ALLEN was named an All-American at Centre College after starring on the gridiron for the Rockets.

BUFFOLINO won the AAA Cross-country title in 1995, and set an 800-meter record at the Boys State Track Meet in 1996.

CHAMBERS was named to the All-State team in both football and basketball.

DRIVER was voted the Most Valuable Player in the 1979 State Baseball Tournament, the Rockets' only state title in this sport.

CUNNINGHAM is the all-time leading scorer among both Shelby County boys and girls, tallying 2,761 points and being named first team All-State.

GUNDLACH was Kentucky's top-ranked and All-American pole-vaulter at Shelby County High; and All-SEC at the University of Tennessee.

SCOTT JONES was an All-American at Shadron State, and was on the Olympic Gold Medal Softball Team.

LANCASTER was an All-American hurdler, and four-time state champion in both high and low hurdles and the only athlete to win four state championships in the same event at the state level. He set the national record for the 300-meter low hurdles and was three time NCAA All-American and Division I indoor and outdoor champion

HOWARD LOGAN JR. won the Kentucky State High School Golf Championship in 1976.

RITTER was a standout basketball and softball player who signed a baseball contract with the Pittsburgh Pirates National League Baseball Team.

SLUCHER led the Bagdad Tigers to the Kentucky State High School Basketball Tournament in 1952. An All-State Honorable Mention, he starred at Georgetown College where he set the KIAC record with a discus toss of 146 feet.

STONER was an All-State football player at Shelby County High School, and signed a professional baseball contract with the Anaheim Angels.

SULLIVAN starred in both football and basketball at Shelby County, and was All-State in football. He was the first and only player to run for more than 1,000 yards in consecutive seasons. He was a four-year starter at the University of Louisville.

WARE won the State Golden Gloves Welterweight title in 1950 at the age of 19. He later excelled at Eastern Kentucky University in track and was also a member of the rifle squad.

WHITE was a two-time state champion in the long jump, and was named an All-American sprinter and jumper.

HENSON was captain of Shelby County's first ever cross-country state championship team. He was named to the All-Metro conference while attending the University of Louisville.

DAVIS was named Mr. Kentucky Basketball at Shelby County in 1968. He averaged 35.5 points per game, and later starred at Western Kentucky University.

KINSOLVING won the Shelbyville Golf Club Men's Championship 14 times.

BRUCE LOGAN won the Shelbyville Golf Club's Women's Championship 14 times.

WILSON won All-State honors at Shelby County High School, and in 1980 was named to the Gatorade All-American team.

TIPTON, Shelby County High School swimmer, was ranked No. 1 in the nation, and swam in the Junior Nationals in 1980-81 and the Senior Nationals in 1982-83. She qualified for the Olympic Trials in 1984. The All-American swam for Florida State University.

JONES was a standout, All-State flanker at Shelby County High School, and later starred at the University of Louisville.

And there are many others, including Joe Bowles, Norris Beckley, Lowell Ashby, Chris Armstrong, Ray Bailey Jr., Bill Busey, Bill Clements, Martin Deim, Richard Greenwell Jr., Curtis Head, Bill Manica, Dennis Morton, Daryl Roland, Shawn Stone, and Mike Williams who brought honor and glory to Shelbyville and Shelby County high schools over a period of many years.

There has been an exceptional number of winning coaches in many sports at both the city and county schools, men and women who not only knew how to win on the field, the diamond or in the gym, but were recognized for their integrity, leadership, and commitment to their students first, and athletes second. These include, but are not limited to, C. Bruce Daniel, Bill Harrell, Richard "Puss" Greenwell, Tom Creamer, Hubert Pollett, Eddie Mason, Tom Becherer, Elmo Head, Jim Wiley, Arnold Thurman, Larry Wingfeld, Charlotte Chowning, and Mitch Bailey. Special mention must be made of Harry Lancaster who coached at both Gleneyrie and Bagdad before going to the University of Kentucky where he eventually became the university's athletic director.

FOOTBALL

Long before football was played as an organized high school sport in Shelby County, there were football games between various club teams from towns such as Pleasureville, Carrollton, Versailles, Frankfort, Lexington, and Shelbyville. Teams also represented various American Legion posts around the Bluegrass area.

The ages of the players were not too important; what mattered was whether a potential player could run, block, catch the ball, and hit hard. Passing the ball didn't gain much prominence until well into the 1920s. Local games were played at what was then known as Coots Park, adjacent to the creek and just north of Washington Street between 1st and 2nd streets. In the summertime the field was used for baseball

One of the authorities on early 20th century football was Temple "Pete" Bird, who worked for many years as Shelbyville's Railway Express Agent. He recalled that Shelbyville's first American Legion team consisted of Gayle Carter, Joe Casey, Jim Ray, Howard Mayhall, Guy Morton, Coats Peak, Hatchett Burge, Johnny Green, Pryor Hower, Irving Snider, Jack Hughes, Middelton Jesse, Wesley Shawhan, Jack Letcher, and William Shinnick.

Later, in 1920, Shelbyville's American Legion team rolled up 144 points and held the opposition scoreless. The lineup included Albert Hollenbach and Paul Long at the ends; Roger Wells and Pogue Coffman at tackle; Roy Money and L. Henderson at guard; "Pete" Bird at quarterback; Clyde Coots and Isadore Sanders at halfback; and Jake Coots at fullback.

American Legion and club football faded away with the coming of high school football in the late 1920s and early 1930s.

Always known as a good football town, Shelbyville gained statewide prominence in the sport during the long tenure of Bruce Daniel, teacher, principal, and coach.

Daniel was a remarkable story in himself, being, to the best of anyone's knowledge, the only Georgetown, Ky., College graduate who lettered in five different sports: football, basketball, baseball, track and tennis. He arrived at Shelbyville High School in 1928, and in his first year coached all of the sports, taught five classes, and was paid $1,700 for the year.

Daniel's 1934 Red Devils were the first high school team in Kentucky to play under the lights.

Daniel, who served as high school principal for 20 years, was a pioneer in Christian leadership in athletics, and was a pivotal figure in the development of the Kentucky High School Athletic Association. He and his wife, Hildreth, were among the founders of the Kentucky Retired Teachers Association.

Daniel's teams reached their zenith from 1935 to 1938 when they won 30 games, lost three and tied one. The Red Devils were CKC champions in 1936 and 1938. The 1936 team was captained by running back Bill Shannon, and included Johnnie Milton and Vivian Harp at the ends, Edwin Hall and Ed "Bud" Stratton at tackles, Herman Whitaker and Kenneth Tipton at the guards and Hayden Igleheart at center. Bill Gregg was the quarterback, Jerome Ritchie and Shannon at halfback, and Jesse Floyd at fullback. Receiving All-State honors were Whitaker, Igleheart, Shannon, Gregg, and Harp.

The 1938 squad included Bobby Roberts and Clyde Rayburn at the ends, Joe McMillan and Norman Abraham at the tackles, Byron Green and Jack Green at the guards, and Fielding Ballard at center. The backfield included quarterback Harp, running backs Mac Moore and Bill Burnett, and fullback Floyd. Floyd and Harp were on the All-State squads, and All-Conference honors were conferred on Roberts, Rayburn, Abraham, McMillan, and Byron Green.

Daniel had many outstanding players, but the one he remembered most fondly, and the only Shelby Countian in the National Football College Hall of Fame is Jack Green. Green was a four-year letter winner, and is best remembered for the punt that he blocked in the Red Devils' 14-7 win over Lexington Henry Clay on Tobacco Festival Day in 1941. It was one of the few victories that Shelbyville ever recorded over the Blue Devils, and marked the team's high-water mark that season. Green was named All-State First Team Quarterback and Elliott Igleheart gained honorable mention honors, while Clyde Marshall, Winford Thomas, Green, and Igleheart were named to Henry Clay's All-Opponent team.

Jack Green, one of 10 children, was one of five brothers to play for Daniel. He began his college career at Tulane before receiving an appointment to the U. S. Military Academy. There he lettered three years, and was named an All-American in 1944 and 1945. The 1945 team, which Green captained, was voted among the best in U.S. football history.

After coaching at the Academy, Tulane, and Florida State, he was named head coach at Vanderbilt in 1963.

Later, he was an assistant at Kansas and Baylor before retiring from the coaching field. He died in 1981.

As head coach, Daniel compiled a record of 82 wins, 43 losses, and 5 ties. Richard "Puss" Greenwell, who had served as his assistant both before and after World War II, succeeded him as football coach. He stayed on as Greenwell's assistant for a number of years.

In the 125th anniversary edition of *The Shelby Sentinel*, Daniel named his all-time team. It included: Courtney Wadlington, Wilson "Pug" Hardesty, Bobby Roberts, and Paul Briscoe at ends; Bernard Whitehouse, Russ Ethington, Marshall "Speedy" Puckett, Ben McMakin, and Bill Adams at tackle; "Puss" Greenwell, Elliott Igleheart, Herman Whitaker, and Powell Puckett at guards; Fielding Ballard and Byron Green at center; Jack Green, Bill Gregg and Allie Kays at quarterback; Vivian Harp, Bill Shannon, Cecil VanNatta, Bill Burnett, Hubert Briscoe, and Mac Moore at halfback; and R. C. Travis and Jesse Floyd at fullback. Igleheart and Puckett also excelled at the college level, at Tulane and Murray State College respectively.

Daniel said his Honorable Mention team would include Carole Sanders and Charles Whitaker at end; Ed Coombs and Clyde Marshall at tackle; Carole Smith at Guard; Jimmy Scearce and Paul Sharp at center; and Jim Guthrie, Garland Shuck and Howard Logan in the backfield.

Greenwell's first team, in 1946, won six, lost one, and tied one. The following year, in 1947, Shelbyville High School produced its first ever unbeaten, untied team and the Central Kentucky Conference title. The team was led by hard-charging fullback John Lyle Miller who scored 11 touchdowns in only seven games; the quarterbacking of Bobby Owen Collins; a high-powered offense which rolled up 238 points; and a tenacious defense which limited eight opponents to a total of 26 points.

The first team included Ben Pollard and Bill Matthews at the ends, Bill Acree and Sid Krieger at the tackles, Mac Catlett and Martin Deim at the guards, and Jackie Sherrard at center. In addition to Collins and Miller, the backfield included running backs Bob Logan, Leslie Shuck, and Johnny Buckner. R.C. Brummett, Sammy Harrod, Jake Brummett and Bill Humston were also key components, either on defense or offense. Miller was named to the Louisville Courier-Journal's All-State team, while Collins, Matthews, Deim, Brummett and Catlett received Honorable Mention.

Greenwell also had undefeated teams in 1951, 1955 and 1957. CKC champs included the '47, '49, '55, and '62 squads.

Greenwell's final CKC championship came in 1962. That team included Jess Settle and Cam Scearce at ends, Butch McBride and Mike Simpson, at tackle, Hite Hays and John Hackworth at guard, and Tommy Bemiss at center. Charles Bradbury was the quarterback, with Mike Saunders, Dennis Morton, and Jerry Gordon in the backfield. Receiving All-State honors were Bradbury, McBride, Bemiss, and Morton.

What is particularly memorable about that year is that during the height of the Cuban Missile Crisis, Shelbyville won the title by defeating Danville, 6-0, on a touchdown pass from Bradbury to Scearce.

In 20 years of coaching, from 1946 through 1965, Greenwell's team won 132 games, lost 51 and tied 6. His All-Time team, as revealed in the 1965 Sentinel, included Jess Frazier, Jack Roberts, Joe Tennill, and Chester Ethington at end; Don Ethington, Foley Bustle, John Brown, and Jerry Aldridge at tackle; Bill Clements, John Hackworth, Martin Deim, and Bill Ellis at guard; and Richard Greenwell Jr. and Bobby Hubbard at center. The backfield included Bobby Jo Arnold, Charles Bradbury, Bobby Owen Collins, and Herbie Kays at quarterback; Donnie Swigert, Jake Brummett, Dennis Morton, Joe Bowles,

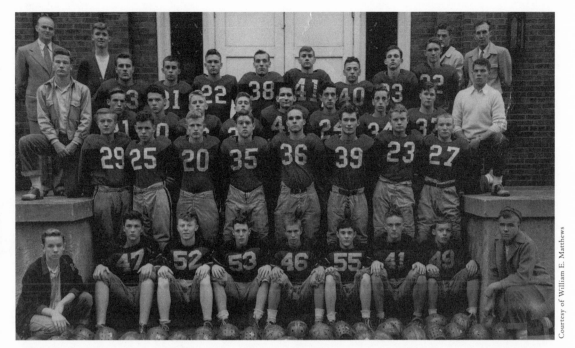

Courtesy of William E. Matthews

1947 Shelbyville High School team. The first unbeaten, untied team in Shelbyville High School history was represented by this squad, coached by Richard "Puss" Greenwell and C. Bruce Daniel. The team won eight games and the Central Kentucky Championship. In the first row, left to right, are manager Ralph Howser, Elmer Rounds, Howard Bright, Eddie Hayes, Roe Miller, Jimmy Lee, Edgar Vaughan, Ryan Blakemore, and manager Ollie Miller; second row, Kenneth Brooks, Charles Ray Ferguson, Jackie Sherrard, Bobby Owen Collins, John Lyle Miller, Ronald Miller, Bo Cowherd, and Charlie Ethington; third row, Bob Logan (kneeling), Jake Brummett, Jimmy Harris, Bo Moesser, Billy Humston, Sidney Krieger, Sammy Harrod, Art Landers, Willard Igleheart, and Bill Green (kneeling); fourth row, C. B. Daniel, manager Ray Miller, Bill Acree, Leslie Shuck, Johnny Buckner, R. C. Brummett, Mac Catlett, Martin Deim, Bill Matthews, Ben Pollard, Charlie Turner, and coach Richard Greenwell. Assistant coach Elmo Head not pictured.

Jerry Gordon, and Buddy Marshall at halfback; and John Lyle Miller and Sammy West at fullback.

Tom Becherer, who continued as head coach when the Red Devils and Rockets athletic teams were combined as a part of the school consolidation in 1975, succeeded Greenwell at Shelbyville High School in 1972.

Becherer's outstanding career as head coach at Shelby County was punctuated by the Rockets' 1987 victory over Boone County, 17-14, in the 4A state finals. Shelby County was a heavy underdog to the unbeaten (13-0) team from northern Kentucky, but a stout defense and opportunistic offense enabled Becherer's squad to prevail. Quarterback Reggie Hicks ran for 125 yards on 11 carries, and scored the game-winning touchdown on a 21-yard dash in the third period. While the team as a whole earned the title, it was Hicks, along with fullback Charles Warfield and tailback Marcus Stoner, who provided the offense which enabled the Rockets to win their only 4A-football title in the 20th century. Warfield scored the team's other touchdown, and Lee Hankins actually provided the margin of difference with a 22-yard field goal. What made the game especially memorable is that Boone County had handed the Rockets their worst defeat of the season, 28-0, several weeks previously. At that point in the season Shelby County stood 6-4. But it was a different team, a championship team, that showed up for the playoffs.

Courtesy of Tom Becherer

The 1987 Shelby County High School State Football Championship Team, coached by Tom Becherer, included, in uniform, left to right, Donnie Mason, Chris Waldridge, Ron Simmons, Chad Schott, Herb Fletcher, Mike Stoner, Ray Marshall, Reggie Hicks, Chris Waford, Steve Hall, Matt Crockett, Monty Wood, Darryle Hicks, Nelyon Robinson, and Steve Russell; 2nd row, Jeff Hayden, Tom Bailey, Mark Wilson, Shawn Riley, Melvin Hall, Monty Walker, Mickey Perry, Matt Kebrt, Tony Griffin, Ralph Stone, Gary Harrison, Geoffrey Manica, Greg Young, Keith Owens, and Edmund Becherer; 3rd row, Darrell Perry, Don Marshall, Jeff Conan, Eric Sutherland, Chris Cottongim, Brian Stivers, Chad Adams, Marcus Stoner, Tommy Thompson, Charles Warfield, Lee Hankin, Dan Druin, Chris Chanda, Mack Rayburn, Mike Rogers, Brent Wilson, Scott, Lawson, and Brian King. The assistant coaches were Hubie Pollett, Phil Bell, Mike Breidet, and Boyd Phillips.

Becherer remained head coach at Shelby County through the 1999 season, his teams compiling an outstanding record of 174 wins and 119 losses. Earlier he had posted winning records at Maysville (24-21-1) and Shelbyville (15-13-1).

The field house at Shelby County High School is named in honor of Becherer whose teams were also runner-up to the state champion on three occasions.

Becherer, with assistance from several individuals who served as assistant coaches during his stints at Shelbyville and Shelby County, named the following individuals to his all-time team:

Offense: Ends, "Pee Wee" Sullivan, Frankie Page, Mark Lafeir, Todd Willard, and Roy Bailey; Tackles, John Wilson, Kevin Wright, George Cottrell, Eric Beach, and Danny Hughes; Guards, Joe Meese, Jeremy Craig, Edwin Thomas, and Jeff Conn; Center, Ricky French, Chris Silverhorn, and Chris Waldridge; Quarterback, Reggie Hicks, Mike Brooks, Tommy Marshall, and Matt Casey; Fullback, Charles Warfield, Melvin Hall, Vince Chambers, and Bill Manica; Tailback, Leonard Sullivan, Marcus Stoner, Lee Tinsley, William White, and Shane Bolin; Flanker, Junior Jones, Montez Allen, and Kevin Armstrong. Defense: Tackles, Avery Marshall, Tim Roberts, Brian Stivers, Darrell Perry, Mike Harrod, Joey Woods and "Poochie" Cottrell; Ends, Bruce Moore, Chris Chands, James Allen, J. J. Pritchett, Scott Wilson, and Dale Chappell; Inside linebackers, William May, Doug Hall, Ben Nutter, Jeremy Craig, and Tommy Vogel; Outside linebackers, Marcus Stoner, Kelly Moore, Donny Sutherland, and Sam Cox; Safeties, Steve Brooks, Steve Seidel, Lee Tinsley, and Marcus Robinson; Cornerbacks, Junior Jones, William White, Timmy Sullivan, Darrel Hicks, Reggie Hicks, and Chris Waford; Punters, Curtis Head, Roy Bailey, Marcus Stoner, and Joe White; and Placekickers, Lee Hankins, and Bill Manica.

Todd Shipley took over as head football coach at Shelby County and after winning only 3 of 10 in 2000, the team bounced back to win 6 of 12 in 2001.

BASKETBALL

Few schools in Kentucky have won as many state titles in so many sports as Shelby County High School. Perhaps the two best-known state championship teams were the basketball squads of 1966 and 1978.

But long before those teams achieved statewide prominence, basketball was the principal, if only organized sport, for the several county schools that came into existence in the early 20th century. There were the Simpsonville Bobcats, the Mt. Eden Gamecocks, Henry Clay Wildcats, Gleneyrie Panthers, Waddy Warriors (originally Red Jackets), Shelbyville Red Devils, Cropper Yellow Jackets, and the Finchville Bulldogs.

These schools played many a hard-fought game in their small bandbox-like gyms and as the 1920s gave way to the 1930s, rivalries intensified and many outstanding players took to the courts in their quest for victory.

Jimmy Sampson at Henry Clay, Bobby Stratton and Carlisle Barrickman at Bagdad, Paul T. Perry and Ralph Hatchell at Waddy, Jack Veech at Finchville, Roy Abrams at Mt. Eden, "Red" Proctor at Simpsonville, Tom Long, Earl Hall and the Fraziers and Walter Maddox at Gleneyrie, and Thornton Johnson Jr. and Maurice   Johnson at Cropper are but a few of the many outstanding players who were continually bringing loyal fans to their feet.

James Sanford followed them at Henry Clay, Jimmy Tingle at Finchville, "Puss" Eddington at Simpsonville, Harvey Sutherland at Bagdad and many others who kept the fans brimming with excitement.

Retired Circuit Judge Harold Saunders, who played at Henry Clay, said he believed that Jim Brown from Cropper and Barrickman from Bagdad were perhaps the finest pre-World War II athletes to emerge from the county schools. Barrickman lost his life during that conflict.

Evan E. Settle Jr., a man who had played three years on the varsity for the legendary Adolph Rupp at the University of Kentucky, arrived in Shelbyville in 1938 to take over the basketball program and teach math in the classroom.

The veteran mentor actually began his career at Henry Clay High School in eastern Shelby County in 1934. There he coached a young man named Jimmy Sampson whom he considered the "best" during his three years at the school. Settle spent one year at Bedford High before coming to Shelbyville in 1938. Settle made his presence felt in the classroom and in the gym before leaving for the U. S. Air Force shortly after the United States entered the war.

Following six years in the service, Settle returned to the classroom and continued his success on the hardwood with the 1948 Shelbyville Red Devils. This team, led by Bob Logan, Johnny Buckner, Martin Deim, Jimmy Mac Ratcliffe, and Mac Catlett, defeated Valley High School on a lay-up in the final seconds to win the school's first ever trip to the Kentucky State High School Basketball Tournament at the old Armory in Louisville.

After defeating Garrett, 58-50, in their opener, the team fell to the Brewers, 57-34, in the second round. Brewers (36-0) won the title and, as of 2001, remained the only undefeated team in tournament history. In addition to the five starters mentioned heretofore, the 10-member tournament team also included Bill Green, Bill Matthews, Bo Moesser, Bill Humston, and James Martin. Buckner and Logan were named to the All-Regional team, and Buckner received All-State Honorable Mention.

Settle took teams to the state tournament in 1951, 1953, 1955, 1956, 1958, and 1967.

The 1951 team included Jake Brummett, Bobby Kemper, Homer Petrou, Muir Gene "Bubbie" Howser, Joe Bowles, Ray Baker, Bill Dawson, George Catlett, Jimmy Lee, Pete Raymond, Bill Catlett, and Bill Hardesty.

Included on the 1953 team were Bowles, Bill Clements, Paul Wilson, John Cowherd, Maurice Willard, Achille Biagi, "Skippy" Connell, George Catlett, Charles Mischler, and Clarence Raymond.

In 1955, Settle's state tournament team included standouts Bobby Swindler, Bobbie Carter, Mac Weaver, Herbie Kays, Jerry Gering, "Bubbie" Howser, Bill Clements, William "Shug" Hickman, Jess Frazier, and Sammy West.

The 1956 team lost to Wayland and "King" Kelly, 87-76, in the opening round of the state tournament, with Herbie Kays scoring 26. Kelly tallied 50. That team featured Bobby Carter, Lewis Mathis, Herbie Kays, Bobby Swindler, Billy Clements, "Shug" Hickman, Sammy West, B. J. Wright, Chester Ethington, and Jess Frazier.

The 1958 team beat Shepherdsville in the opening round behind Buddy Marshall's 21 points, then lost to Bowling Green in the quarterfinals. The 1958 team included Marshall, Johnny Chandler, Jimmy Swigert, Frankie Cowherd, Roger Chandler, John Brown, Charlie Mark Blakemore, Bobby Jo Arnold, Bill Frye, Chester Ethington, Don Ethington, and Donnie Swigert.

Settle didn't return to the state tournament until 1967 when one of his winningest squads (26-4) defeated Carrollton, 57-54, to win the 8th Region Title. That team, which lost to Monticello in the first round at Freedom Hall, included "twin towers" Herbert Johnson and Bernard Brown, as well as Charlie Matthews, Grant Hays, Randy Head, William Lewis, Howard Burley, Bob Montgomery, James Ellis, and Charles Marshall.

Later that fall, in 1968, Matthews set the all-time single game scoring record at Shelbyville when he tallied 46 points in a 79-73 season opening game loss at Owen County.

Settle, who retired in 1972, remembers most fondly Herbie Kays, considered his best all-time player; Joe Bowles, killed along with the rest of his family in an auto accident while he was in the midst of an outstanding career at Eastern Kentucky University; and Johnny Buckner and Bobby Cook, both of whom served as assistant coaches. Cook succeeded Settle as head coach, remaining in that capacity until the school closed as part of its consolidation with Shelby County High School.

Settle's All-Time team, as published in the 1965 Shelby Sentinel, includes Herbie Kays, Joe Bowles, Bobby Swindler, Jim Arington, Jimmy Mac Ratcliffe, Buddy Marshall, Martin Deim, Jerry Gering, Johnny Buckner, and Charles Blakemore.

Bobby Cook, who served as Settle's assistant during the 1970 and 1971 campaigns, took over head coaching duties in 1972, and enjoyed outstanding success during his brief stint at the helm. His winning record was highlighted by his team's appearance in the state tournament in 1975, the final year in Shelbyville High School history. That team went 27-6, and lost in the quarterfinals after upsetting the state's No. 2 ranked Owensboro Red Devils in the opening round. The starting five included Robert Jones, Vince and Dean Chambers, Mike Beach and Donnie Mason. Marcus Robinson was the first sub off the bench. Also on that team were two young men who would figure prominently in Shelby County High School's state tournament title a few years later. They were freshman Norris Beckley and 8th grader Charles Hurt.

The 1966 State Champion Shelby County Rockets Basketball Team included, front row, left to right, manager Bobby Burchfield, Johnny Edington, Gene Witt, Jobie Miller, Bill Busey, Terry Hall, and Keith Stratton, manager; Back row, Assistant Coach Arnold Thurman, Larry Glass, Hugh Smith, Jim Simons, Gene Edwards, Mike Casey, Mike Popp, Jamie Pickett, Ron Ritter, Bill Moffett, Dave Bohannon, Assistant Coach Mitchell Bailey, and Head Coach Bill Harrell.

Shelby County began producing championship teams almost at its opening in 1960 through the consolidation of county high schools located at Waddy, Simpsonville, and Bagdad.

Bill Harrell was the "Man of the Hour" when he took the Rockets to the state tournament for the first time in 1965. The team (31-2) was ranked No. 1 in the state, and Harrell was named Coach of the Year. All-Stater Mike Casey averaged 23.8 points for the season.

But excitement gave way to disappointment when Breckinridge County, in the tournament's quarterfinals, eliminated the Rockets 70-60. Butch Beard's 34 points led Breckinridge County. Beard later became an All-American at the University of Louisville.

At the beginning of the 1965-66 season, the Rockets were ranked No. 4 in the state behind Hazard, Ashland, and Louisville Male.

Just one loss, to Louisville Central, 67-65 in the finals of the LIT, marred Shelby County's record as it completed a record-setting season. The team thrashed Lincoln Institute, 124-57, to win the 30th District title before romping over Georgetown, 89-58, to win the 8th Region title.

So again the Rockets were favored to win it all at Freedom Hall in 1966. Evidently the team took its first opponent too lightly because a late game rally by Knox Central cut the final score to 71-70. Casey scored 20 points, while Terry Mills for Knox Central tallied 34 in a valiant but losing effort.

After such a narrow escape, the Rockets might have expected an easier road to victory in the quarterfinals. But it was not to be. It took a final seconds free throw by Hugh "Turk" Smith to enable the Rockets to prevail, 63-62. Again, Casey led the Rockets with 20 points, but it was Smith's free throw that would be remembered for a long time afterward.

After two close calls, and victories by a total of two points, the Rockets scored seven straight unanswered points at the end of the game to prevail over Louisville's Thomas Jefferson High School, 79-72, in Saturday morning's semi-finals.

The Rockets came out roaring in the championship game against Louisville Male. Jumping out to leads of 18-9 and 43-20, Shelby County seemed poised for a runaway victory. But the tide changed in the second half, and Male closed to within 47-44.

But the Rockets steadied behind the scoring of Casey and the ball handling of Bill Busey and Jobie Miller, and finally secured a 62-57 victory and the state championship. Casey and Busey were named to the All-Tournament team.

A crowd estimated at between 3,500 and 4,000 welcomed the team's motorcade as it proceeded from its starting point in Simpsonville and continued through Shelbyville and on to the county high school. Principal Bruce Sweeney gave the official welcome, and many locally elected and appointed officials mentioned their pride at what the team had accomplished.

Casey was named Kentucky's Mr. Basketball, and for the second year in a row, and the only time in Kentucky High School basketball history, Harrell was named Coach of the Year. In only six years at the school, Harrell's record was a remarkable 140-38, and 86-8 for the 1964-66 seasons.

Harrell's All-Time team, as reported in the Shelby Sentinel, included Casey, Busey, Simpson, Don Turner, Woody Fields, Jobie Miller, Jimmy Shaw, Tony Price, Daryl Floyd, Bill Willhite, Wayne Goins, and Bob McDowell.

Shelby County didn't reappear in the state finals until 1978 when Coach Tom Creamer deftly managed his No. 1-rated squad through a difficult schedule that included only three losses, all to either nationally or state-ranked teams, DeMatha of Maryland, Lexington Henry Clay, and Owensboro Apollo.

The 30th District tournament provided little challenge for the Rockets as they discharged Henry County, 107-43, in the title contest. The 8th Region tournament was somewhat more difficult, but the

The 1978 Shelby County High School Boys State Champion Rockets included, front row, kneeling, Arthur Sullivan, James Rockwell, Don Murphy, Mark Ashby, Gerry Davis, and Kevin Armstrong; back row, Coach Tom Creamer, Mike George, Norris Beckley, Austin Lee, Robert Davis, Charles Hurt, Pat Marshall, Maurice Way, Charlie Lecompte, and Dale Kennedy. Coaches Marnel Moorman and Ron Kuhl are not pictured. (Photo taken from the Rocket Yearbook.)

team had relatively little trouble in disposing of Bullitt Central, Oldham County, and Scott County. Norris Beckley scored 25 points in the finale against the Cardinals.

The opening game in the state tournament boded poorly for the Rockets as they had to contend with an unbeaten (35-0) Apollo team that had edged them previously. But the Rockets kept their poise down the stretch, and rode Charles Hurt's 23 points to victory, 62-55.

The quarterfinals provided more excitement, with Beckley's last second shot enabling Shelby County to slip by Lexington Henry Clay, 63-62, and gain the semi-finals. Beckley scored 24 points.

The semi-finals proved to be the Rockets only easy victory in the tournament. Inspired by Hurt's 26 points, Shelby County pounded Louisville Central's Yellow Jackets, 78-54, to gain a berth in the championship game.

What turned out to be the state tournament's only overtime championship game up to that time, and perhaps its most exciting finale in history, found Hurt throwing in a 15-footer with one second left to send the game against Covington Holmes into overtime, 64-64. Beckley and Don Murphy scored the Rockets two field goals in overtime, while Holmes got only two free throws. The final score, 68-66, gave the Rockets their second state title.

Mike George, Beckley, and Hurt were named to the All-Tournament team. Other key players on the team included Maurice Way, Mark Ashby, Don Murphy and James Rockwell.

Again, there was a joyous celebration at the high school, and a second banner went up proclaiming the Rockets Kentucky's best boys basketball team.

Creamer compiled an outstanding record from 1975 through 1987, winning 274 and losing just 81 for a winning percentage of slightly better than 77%.

Edwin "Eddie" Mason succeeded Creamer in 1988, and remained as head coach through the 1992 season. Mason's teams played hard, disciplined basketball as a strong tradition of winning continued at the school. Looking back over these years, Mason included Dwayne Crittenden at center, Mike Clark and Tom Hayes at forwards, and Chris Armstrong and Greg Mason on his all-time team.

Gary Kidwell succeeded Mason in 1993. Curtis Turley and Champ Ligon, in turn, followed him.

There is one other remarkable story to be told of Shelby County basketball. But it involves neither Shelbyville nor Shelby County, but, rather, the fighting Tigers of Bagdad High School.

Of all the county schools in existence prior to the merger of the high schools at Bagdad, Simpsonville, and Waddy to form Shelby County High School in 1960, only Bagdad ever appeared in the "Sweet Sixteen" or, as it is more properly known, the Kentucky High School State Basketball Tournament.

Longtime county sports historian Bill Young recalled the magical year of 1951-52. He noted that, until that season, county schools had always had difficulty getting by their Shelbyville "cousins" in District or Regional action. But that season turned out differently for the Tigers and their first year coach, Gayle Taft.

Led by Kenneth Slucher, Bagdad won 17 of 24 regular season games, and was anxious to take on all comers in post-season action.

As tournament time approached Slucher, Robert Gray Early, Clay Young, Bronston Hardin and Ed Thompson were fast becoming heroes to Bagdad basketball fans.

Bagdad dispatched Waddy, 72-38, in the District opener before losing to Simpsonville, 56-54, in overtime in the 30th District championship game.

But because both finalists were eligible for Regional action at Carrollton, Bagdad fans weren't disheartened.

After Milton, 54-43, in the Regional opener had eliminated Simpsonville, Bagdad parlayed 13-points by Slucher to a nail-biting 42-40 decision over Carrollton on the Panthers' home court.

Having stunned Carrollton, the Wildcats turned it up a notch in crushing Milton, 89-62, as Early scored 24 points and Earl Young chipped in with 22.

Bagdad opened with a rush in the championship game with LaGrange, winning handily, 60-46, behind Slucher's 26 points and Gray's 15.

So, finally, Young recalled, the jinx had been broken, and a team from Shelby County other than Shelbyville was state-tournament bound.

Unfortunately, the Tigers left their top game in the dressing room and fell to Pikeville, 46-34, in the tournament opener. But Bagdad fans still loved their boys, and numerous dinners followed throughout the spring of 1952.

That was Bagdad High School's final shot at glory because a few short years later not only would the high school be vacated because of consolidation, but the building itself was razed in order to make way for the Bagdad Ruritan Building.

Finally, before leaving basketball, it must be noted that the county high schools produced many winning girls teams, and, in fact, the girls enjoyed more success in the 1920s and early 1930s than the boys' teams. While an absence of records makes it impossible to chronicle even a few of their successes, teams from Bagdad, Waddy, Henry Clay, Shelbyville, and Simpsonville were frequent participants in local and state tournaments.

BASEBALL

The 1979 Rockets won the Kentucky State High School Baseball Team under the direction of head coach Hubert Pollett and his assistants, Mitch Bailey, and Phil Bell.

Tracy Driver was the team standout, wining the tournament's Most Valuable Player honors, and slugging a 350-foot homer as the Rockets beat Murray, 7-5, to win the title. Mark Chandler and Perry Joe Nutt excelled on the mound, losing just one game between them.

Shelbyville's American Legion team, directed by longtime coach Jim Wiley, won state championships in 1983, 1991, and 1992.

The 13-year-old Babe Ruth team won the state championship in 1986, followed in 1993 by the 15-year-olds winning another Babe Ruth State title.

Shelbyville also has a "big league" connection in baseball. The colorful, Hall of Fame Manager Casey Stengel played his first professional game in Shelbyville as a member of the Maysville team in the old Bluegrass League. The year was 1910, and Casey's team edged the locals in a game which ended in a near-riot because of Casey's shenanigans. The Maysville team had to be escorted out of town with a police escort.

Courtesy of Hubie Pollett

The 1979 State Champion Shelby County Rockets Baseball Team included, front row, left to right, Mike Rogers, batboy, Norman Minch, Kerry Whitehouse, Scott Clifford, Charles Clifton, Mark Chandler, and Scott Corn, manager; middle row, Billy Reese, Keith Waford, David Bodine, Cody Tipton, Rusty Harrod, Greg Stratton, and Lindsey Allen; back row, Phil Bell, coach, Mitchell Bailey, coach, Mike Marshall, Perry Joe Nutt, Greg Jennings, James Ray Wiley, Joe Long, Tracey Driver, Brian Mitchell, and Head Coach Hubert Pollett. The Rockets won 18, lost only 2. The team won the regional tournament by defeating Frankfort, 8-4, the semi-state by rolling over Connor, 5-0, and the state title by edging Murray, 7-5, on Driver's decisive home run.

SOFTBALL

Probably the best slow-pitch softball team in Shelby County was coached by Charlie McIntosh in 1970. Called Omer's Boys in honor of McIntosh's father, who sponsored the team, the club went to the national championships in Detroit, Michigan, where it won three out of five games. Three brothers played on the team: Ron "Bird" Ritter, pitcher, Allen Ritter, left field, and Gary Ritter, catcher. Other brothers on the team included Elmo Thomas and Billy Thomas. Mike Casey of All-State basketball fame played shortstop, and Jimmy Kinser was the centerfielder.

GOLF

The two names most associated with golf in Shelby County were Lucien Kinsolving and Bruce Logan. Kinsolving won the Shelbyville Country Club's Golf Championship a record 14 times starting in 1951 and ending in 1976. Logan won the Country Club's Ladies Title also a record 14 times, beginning in 1955 and ending in 1971. Her son, Howard Logan Jr., won the State High School Golf Championship in 1976. Men's winners and the years in which they won the title include: Kinsolving (1951, 1955, 1958, 1959, 1960, 1961, 1962, 1963, 1964, 1965, 1967, 1968, 1969, and 1976), William "Boopy" Gibbs

(1932, 1933, 1934, 1935, 1937,1938, 1948, 1949, and 1950), Doug Logan (1972, 1975, 1980, 1982, 1983, 1986, 1987, 1988, 1993, and 1997), Briggs Lawson (1931, 1932, 1936, 1941, and 1947), Dennis Long (1970, 1971, 1979, 1996, 1998, 1999, and 2001), Howard Logan Jr. (1981, 1985, 1989, and 1992), Lloyd Brown (1990, 1991, 1995, and 2000). Bob Logan (1953 and 1973), Tommy Settle (1977 and 1978), Paul Schmidt (1939), B. C. Coffman (1940), Steve Wakefield (1946), John Eddington (1966) Evan Settle (1974), and Dave Buffolino (1994). There was no men's championship tournament in 1984.

Ladies winners included: Bruce Logan (1955, 1956, 1957, 1958, 1959, 1960, 1962, 1963, 1964, 1965, 1966, 1968, 1970, and 1971), Catherine "Toddy" Miller (1946, 1947, 1948, 1949, 1950, 1951, 1952, 1953, 1967, and 1969), Carolyn Kinsolving (1989, 1991, 1992, 1994, 1996, 1997, 1998, 1999, 2000, and 2001), Jean Logan (1973, 1974, 1975, 1976, and 1978), Dorothy Davis (1932, 1933, and 1934), Burnett "Sunny" Wallace (1935, 1938, and 1939), Margaret "Deanie" Logan (1936, 1937, and 1941), Ermin Herrick (1980, 1982, and 1986), Liddie Harper (1985, 1988, and 1990), Helen Moberly (1972 and 1977), Kim Scott (1979 and 1981), Jeri Johnson (1983 and 1984), Clara Sutherland (1993 and 1995), Zerelda Matthews (1940), Jane McCoy (1954), Doris Kinsolving (1961), and Cherry Settle (1987).

TRACK

Shelby County won the 1984 State AAA Track Championship under the direction of Larry Wingfeld. All-Americans Chris Lancaster and William White carried the top-ranked Rockets to victory. Lancaster won the 110 and 300-meter hurdles, while White won the long jump. Lexington Lafayette finished a very distant second.

Jerry Gordon was the state track champ in both the 220 and 440 meters in 1963.

CROSS COUNTRY

Again with Wingfeld providing the leadership, assisted by Robert Belwood, Shelby County High won cross-country championships in both 1989 and 1990. The Rockets were led by twins Josh and Adam Henson in 1989, and by Jason Acree in 1990.

The 1989 team was ranked No. 3 in Class 3A, but gained enough points to win because of the twins strong showing at the Kentucky Horse Park in Lexington. Sophomore Jimmy Hatter was the hero. In 64th place with less than a mile to go, he made up 24 places and passed eight runners. His 40th place finish gave the Rockets just enough points to win. The following year, in 1990, Hatter finished 14th as Acree led Shelby County with his seventh place finish.

TENNIS

The name Byrd must be called to mind when anyone brings up the subject of high school tennis in Shelby County. Jackie Byrd so dominated the state scene that he won the state titles in 1939, 1940, and 1941. He also teamed with his brother, Ryland, to win the doubles title.

For years, the only tennis courts in Shelbyville were located behind the private homes of the Byrd family on Clay Street, the Fielding Ballard home on Main, and the George Armstrong home, also on Main Street. During the 1920s, and even earlier, there was a tennis court behind Science Hill School.

Each year, young men in the community would vie for the Byrd Cup, awarded to the winner of the annual tournament. Billy Gfroerer won the first Byrd Cup in 1932, and it was eventually retired by Bob Matthews who won the tournament three straight years, from 1955 to 1957.

A tennis court beside the Shelbyville High School gym was put into service after World War II, and again an annual tournament was held. Jimmy Burnett, who had been a longtime principal at Finchville High School, and his son Vance were familiar figures in helping to maintain the court over many years.

AIR RIFLE TEAM

Shelby County High School's Precision Air Rifle Team won the 1995 state championship. Sgt. Gerald Lyons was the coach.

CHEERLEADERS

Shelby County High School cheerleaders took first place honors in the nation in the U. S. Cheerleading Association competition in 1977-78. Monica Fleming was named National Cheerleader of the Year. Others on the team included Ann Aukerman, Janie Biagi, Sally Borders, Jennifer Imel, Sheri Goodridge, Lisa Ratcliffe and Karen Ruble. The coaches were Joy Lynn Quire and Patti Griffin.

Perhaps the most prominent and dedicated cheerleading coach in the state of Kentucky was Jane Meyer, who sponsored the Shelbyville cheerleaders from 1948 to 1975. Meyer, who died in 1999, helped organize the Kentucky Association of Pep Organization Sponsors (KAPOS).

As a result, cheerleading became a sport, and cheerleaders, along with other athletes, compete during tournament time for various championships, both individual and team.

One Shelbyville High School cheerleader who made state history was the daughter of Everett and Mary Hall. As Martha Layne Collins, she was inaugurated as Kentucky's first and only female governor in 1983.

The 1975 Shelbyville High cheerleading squad won the state championship the last year of the high school's existence. The highlight of the squad's performance was a five-tiered pyramid entitled "Devils Last Stand." The squad was composed of Captain Kim McCarthy, Gladys Igleheart, Karen Harrod, Sheryl Greenwell, Mary Stratton, Sherree Martin, Debbie Denton, and Lisa King.

MASCOT

"Rockets" was the name suggested by longtime, retired school superintendent George Giles when Shelby County High School was officially opened in 1960. At the time, the United States was unveiling an ambitious space program, which included putting a man on the moon. Giles reasoned that "Rockets" would denote a school that was soaring toward new heights of learning and achievements

The Benjamin Washburn house, built circa 1791, was demolished in the 1970s.

CHAPTER TEN

ARCHITECTURE

Log cabin at Second and Washington Streets when it was being demolished in the 1970s.

A two-story log cabin still standing on its original site at 1025 Main Street.

ARCHITECTURE

By John David Myles

The architecture of Shelby County closely resembles that of much of the central or Bluegrass area of Kentucky. The first habitations built by settlers were little more than tents made of felled trees whose branches were used for a roof. These structures were more often built to mark land for patent purposes than for permanent shelter. The first structure of substance was the Painted Stone Station on Clear Creek, north of Shelbyville, although its exact location remains subject to debate.

When settlers left the early stations and began constructing homes on their land and in settlements, they used the materials at hand—logs and stone. Log houses or cabins in Shelby County followed the models of other areas. Many were a single room in plan with a loft above. Logs of poplar and chestnut were smoothed on two sides and notched at each end to construct a box into which doors and windows were cut. The first permanent chimneys were built of limestone presumably quarried or retrieved near the site. In Shelbyville, two cabins stood until the late 1970s on the north side of Washington Street between Second and Third Streets, one of which was moved and rebuilt at the corner of College and Seventh Streets by Dr. and Mrs. Donald Chatham. A third, recorded by Otho Williams when it was being demolished, stood on the northeast corner of Second and Washington Streets and is recorded as having been a stage coach stop and toll house. The two-story cabin at 1027 Main Street is believed to have been built between 1806 and 1810 and to have served as a school run by David Locke. Even the first courthouse, built by William Shannon on land he donated to the city of Shelbyville, was log and is recorded to have cost 15 pounds.

While these structures were usually small and utilitarian, that was not always the case. A cabin on Pea Ridge Road was built upon a stone foundation with beautifully detailed chimneys and beaded ceiling beams. A later four-bay cabin owned by the Miracle family for many years and believed to have been built by David Owen had four full rooms, a central hall and a pair of 48-foot tie beams across the top. Originally located in what is now the Shelby Industrial Park, it was reconstructed in Christiansburg in the 1980s. Dr. John Knight's two-story home of cherry logs still stands within a much larger farmhouse just north of Finchville. Another large log home was owned for many years by the Money and Scearce families near the site of the Buck Creek Baptist Church on a now nonexistent stretch of Buck Creek Road west of Finchville. The only true "dogtrot" cabin known to survive in the county is the Bohannon-Redmon House on the Elmburg Road north of Bagdad.

Most cabins featured exterior stone chimneys but one saddlebag cabin survived until the mid-1990s at the southeast corner of KY 44 and KY 148 and another forms the rear ell of the later house at Highlander Farm south of Waddy. The David Burton house on Burks Branch Road features one interior and one exterior stone chimney as a result of attaching a second pen to the chimney end of the original. Many other cabins survive around the county as the nucleus of larger, later houses. In fact, if one sees a clapboard house with an exterior stone chimney, the smart money says there is a cabin under there.

Log construction was also used for early farm buildings. Double pen log barns survive at the Sleadd house on Hempridge Road, near the Thomas Threlkeld house off Benson Road and at the Pemberton-Tucker farm on the Clark Station Road west of Finchville. The log portions of these structures were presumably used to store field crops. The first two are topped by single gable roofs and are surrounded by shed or lean-to roofs, which have been enclosed to provide shelter for animals. The third now has stalls within the log pens. Similar single pen barns are found on the Basket farm on the Elmburg Road and the Froman Fry farm.

A double-pen log barn at the Pemberton-Tucker farm on Clark Station Road.

Courtesy of the Kentucky Heritage Council.

The other building material at hand in the earliest days was stone. While Shelby County never had as many stone houses as the counties in the inner Bluegrass, it was well represented in this area. The best known surviving stone building of course is the Old Stone Inn in Simpsonville. The Benjamin Washburn

Shelby County Public Library, Williams Studio photograph.

Three-bay, side hall plan stone house identified as "Joe Schooler's old house," in this photograph by Otho Williams taken in the 1890s.

house was reputed to be the earliest (ca. 1791). This two story, three-bay house was located on the Washburn Road eight miles northeast of Shelbyville and stood until the 1970s when, because of its advanced deterioration, it was demolished. Its stone was reused and some of the woodwork was installed in the reconstructed log home of Mr. and Mrs. James Oppel on Webb Road west of Simpsonville. Perhaps its most unusual features considering its early construction were the large windows with 12-over-12 sash on the first floor and 12-over-eight sash on the second entitling the house to the distinction of the only recorded building in Shelby County which could claim title to the description, Georgian.

At least two, two story, three bay stone houses were built in the county which featured side halls. One is known only from a photograph in the Otho Williams collection labeled "Joe Schooler's Old House." Another belonged to A. F. Scearce according to the 1882 Atlas. It had been added to a log structure and stood on the hill above Fox Run at the junction with KY 53 until the early 1980s.

The best-preserved stone house in the county is the Jacob Fullenwider house on Anderson Lane. Originally a four bay house of three rooms with lofts, it features an arched fan above the entrance door and unusual stone lintels rather than the typical jack arch above the twelve-over-twelve windows. Jacob (1767-1848) purchased the land on which the house was built in 1807 from Charles Lynch. It is assumed the house was constructed the next year. Jacob and his wife had

Courtesy of Mrs. Ben Matthews

The Jacob Fullenwider house, built about 1808, on Anderson Lane.

sixteen children. The house was abandoned for many years until Mr. and Mrs. Ben Matthews superbly renovated it in 1985 with the assistance of various craftsmen trained at Pleasant Hill and advice from Clay Lancaster.

Three three-bay, single story, hall-parlor stone houses survive in various states of dereliction. The Shelby Ware house near Waddy continues to serve its intended purpose despite unsympathetic additions and renovations. A rear stone wing of the Wells house on the Bellview Pike overlooking Clear Creek ignominiously shelters

The Wells house before the main block of the house and the kitchen wing disintegrated.

cattle who are doubtlessly as unimpressed with its splayed window reveals, carefully fitted stone jack-arches, six panel door, and box cornice as are its present owners. The main block of the house and an attached kitchen to the right of the entrance has disappeared except for remnants of their foundations.

The third lurks in a grove of trees on the Gaylord property between Shelbyville and Simpsonville south of U.S. 60. Shown as belonging to L. Conner in the 1882 Atlas, it is built of beautifully coursed stone and two-piece stone lintels capped its nine-over-six windows. It appears to have had a most unusual floor plan with doorways leading from the end walls either to the outside or to long lost wings. On the other hand, the rear or south facade appears to have been built with three windows (the central one of which retains its original pegged sash) and no door. Access to a later ell on the south was achieved by lowering one of the original windows. This charming and early house today hangs on by the grace of its superb construction, its isolation, and a rusty corrugated metal roof.

Stone was also the material of choice for early dependencies. Stone kitchens at Cross Keys and at the B. C. Harbison house off the Vigo Road have disappeared in recent years despite their individual listings on the National Register. Another survives attached to the rear of the Montgomery house. It was also the material chosen for construction of the first county jail. According to the specifications for its construction, it was to be 15 feet by 15 feet with one door and two windows. If it had been provided with a wide hearth it could have passed as one of the stone kitchens. Stone icehouses, cellars, and walls were also plentiful.

Outbuildings at the rear of Cross Keys Inn in 1934. The stone kitchen is the third building from the right.

Two surviving exceptions to the general rule that stone chimneys bespeak a log interior are a pair of remarkable houses built along the waters of Tick Creek. Overlooking the eastern reaches of Guist Creek Lake, the Thomas Threlkeld house survives, hidden at the rear of a farm, reachable only by foot from the Benson Pike. It is likely the earliest clapboard house surviving in the county and certainly one of the most sophisticated for its early date. Rather than covering log, the clapboard conceals post and beam construction, infilled with mud.

Near Guist Creek Lake is the Thomas Threlkeld house, a clapboard structure with stone chimneys and a stone addition.

The single story, three bay, hall-parlor home features exterior stone chimneys and, contrary to the usual order of construction, a stone addition was built to the left of the facade. A porch with chamfered posts spans the rear of the house and a separate log kitchen was located in the rear yard.

The builder of this frame house is unknown, but Anthony Middelton's family lived here in the 19th century.

A similar house was constructed north of the Clay Village Baptist Church. Also three bay, the hall-parlor structure faces west and now sports a heavy Greek Revival porch on square posts. At a very early date, it appears to have received an addition on the east and north sides which more than doubled its size. Fireplaces in finely wrought exterior stone chimneys heated both the original structure and the addition. The builder is unknown but the Anthony Middelton family resided on the farm for most of the 19th century. Anthony (1808-79) was born and spent his youth at his father's adjoining Cross Keys and one suspects that the porch with heavy cornice and pediment was added at the time Cross Keys was expanded and received its two similar porches. Anthony's daughter Bettie, who married Confederate veteran James H. Rice, lived in the home through the end of the century.

Brick was not far behind stone as a building material. By 1796, the County Court was drawing specifications for construction of a brick courthouse which was to be 36 by 42 feet with a steeple, bell spire, and weathercock. In all likelihood, it closely resembled a one-story version of the surviving courthouse in Washington County. The new inhabitants also constructed many brick homes in all areas of the county, which in most respects echoed the homes in Virginia and North Carolina where many were from. These structures ranged from one story, three bay, hall-parlor structures to two story, five bay, central hall designs and various configurations between and beyond.

The earliest brick structures are often described as being built in the "settlement vernacular." Put another way, their dimensions, heights, gable roof configuration and slope, and interior and exterior detailing differed little from that

The Brackett Owen house on Old Seven Mile Pike.

of the log cabins and small stone buildings, which were their contemporaries. One of the most interesting is the Brackett Owen house on the Old Seven Mile Pike. It is recorded that the first meeting of Shelby Quarterly Court was held at the home of Brackett Owen on October 15, 1792, and further that Brackett died in 1802. Whether this is the actual building in which the court met is subject to some doubt but this is clearly a very early house. A two-story, three bay, hall-parlor, its south facade is laid in Flemish bond and features a box cornice. A much later one-story wing extends to the east. Early mantels are still located in the second floor where the windowsills rest on the chair rail.

The Basket house on the Elmburg Road south of Bagdad is virtually identical in conception. While it retains more of its original detailing, its south wall has been completely rebuilt. Martin and Thomas Basket are said to have purchased the property in 1806, at which time the house is believed to have been built. A later ell extends from the northeast corner. The Basket house, the original Buffalo Lick Baptist Church, and the one-story, three bay, hall-parlor house of William Blades on the Vigo Road are said to have been built by Augustine Barnett. In all likelihood, Watch Hill on Aiken Road was built in this form although the first pictures of it show that it had long since begun its transition from pioneer homestead to latter day Tara.

Ashland was built for Thomas Weakley between 1812 and 1814 near the corner of Benson Road and Beard Lane. In addition to the basic hall-parlor plan, an original one-story room extended to the south. Although this room has been raised by a second story and has lost its chimney, the remainder of the house is remarkably complete, retaining paneled wainscots and reveals, reeded woodwork, and separate stairs to the original second floor rooms. The wainscot is particularly noteworthy. Only one other example of this feature is known to have existed in Shelby County. Its location, the Scearce house which stood nearby to the southeast, has recently been demolished. Ashland's primitive Greek Revival porch is a much later addition and should not mislead anyone from appreciating Ashland's age and architectural interest.

The Thomas Weakley house and its paneled wainscoting and reeded mantel are shown in these three photographs.

Three bay, side hall houses were common in Shelbyville but rare in the county. In town, the original Methodist parsonage at 231 Main Street is an excellent example of the type although it has been modified in certain respects over the years. Under the stucco, the old Saffell Funeral Home at the southeast corner of Fourth and Clay, earlier the home of the Goodman family, features lintels with bull's eye corner blocks above the exterior windows, one of two known examples of this refinement in the County.

Cardwell House, on the south side of Main between Third and Fourth, is actually two-thirds of a row consisting of three, three bay, side hall houses. Together these three buildings give the best glimpse of early Shelbyville and provide the closest architectural link between the frontier settlement and the port

The Cardwell house (the two central buildings pictured) may have been built in 1811. They were renovated in 1991.

cities of the East Coast. Believed to date to 1811, the two eastern structures were renovated in 1991 by the Shelby Development Corporation. Although marred by a plate glass window on the first floor, the western building still sports its original window frames and ogee sills on the second floor.

The Schofield house at 301-303 Main Street.

This configuration was particularly suited to the narrow deep lots into which the town was originally divided. In fact, the Schofield house at 301 and 303 Main is two, two bay, homes. Under their current Italianate decor, the Flemish bond brick indicates that they were built in the same era as the Cardwell houses. A photo from the Otho Williams collection at the Shelby County Public Library shows yet another variation, which stood on the northeast corner of Fourth and Main. It was a four bay, side hall structure with a single chimney for the front section. From the photo it is impossible to determine whether the parlor was two or three bays wide and whether the Greek Revival aedicule around the entrance is original or a later addition. The photo indicates that when taken, the home was the residence of John Ballard and was otherwise known as the "Old Winlock property." A photo taken in the 1850s

John Ballard's house was on the northeast corner of Fourth and Main Streets. Later the Pearce Motor Company was on the site and now the U. S. Post Office is there.

The old firehouse on the public square in an early photograph.

of the north side of Washington Street between Second and Third gives a wonderful indication of the feel of the oldest residential areas of Shelbyville before they were lost. Finally, an old photo of the firehouse on southeast side of the public square shows a Palladian window in the gable, which must have been the equal of any early window in the Commonwealth.

Out in the county, the early three bay, side hall house was rare. The Conner house or "Midland Trail Inn" at the junction of Conner Station Road and old U. S. 60 has been much altered but shows the proper proportion of early window frames prior to the Italianate improvements which changed so many of the remaining homes of the period. President Truman's maternal grandmother, Mary Jane Holmes, lived in another in the 1840s. Located west of the intersection of

The Holmes house was probably built in the 1820s.

Locust Grove and Zaring Mill Roads, the house was as much as thirty years old by that time and was a most refined building. Its sash on the first floor was nine-over-nine and the double front door was topped with a transom. The newel and rail of the stairway were mirrored on the wall of the staircase and the stringer brackets featured a tulip. Still in excellent structural condition in the mid-1970s, this gem now stands as a roofless shell with its front wall collapsed.

View of the North side of Washington Street between Second and Third in the 1950s.

Although shrouded by an enclosed one-story porch, a wonderful house stands on Beard Lane. It was likely built by Thomas King, possibly for his daughter Jane who married John Hanna in 1825. King bought the land in 1808 from the heirs of John LaRue to whom it had been granted in 1786. John ultimately had to defend King's title in 1859 when LaRue's daughter, Marguerite, sued alleging that she had never properly conveyed her title because she was a minor at the time of her father's death and married before acknowledging the deed. John ultimately lost the suit and a portion of the property was partitioned.

Over the years it was home to the Beard and Maddox families for extended periods. It remains a lovely and intriguing home. The two-story section is flanked on the north by an addition which is two rooms deep. An interior chimney on the north wall heats each and a broad gable spans them creating a substantial room on the second floor. This wing has an unusual cornice consisting of four rows of brick, the second and fourth of which are angled to produce the impression of dentil blocks, a design sometimes referred to as a "mouse tooth" cornice. On the interior, door and window reveals are reeded as are simple mantels.

Even more hidden and more interesting is Jonorochqua. Woodford Hall built it and the accepted date of its construction is 1812. If accurate, Woodford built the house at age 19. He gave

The "mouse tooth" brick cornice on the King-Hanna house, later home to the Beard and Maddox families.

it an Indian name, which is said to translate "do as you please." A pair of projecting two bay rooms flanked the original central section of the house and a detached kitchen was located to the southwest. Hall died in 1875 and the property passed to David Harbison, in whose family it remains. In 1902, the old house was enveloped by additions to the front and rear although little of the original building was disturbed. Will Speed of Louisville designed extensive gardens with a pool and pergola.

Three bays were not always enough and five were sometimes too much. Four bays left one wondering what to do with the front door. Sometimes the answer was simply to double it. Several early houses feature two front doors although the reason for their use may be no more complicated than outlined above. Though much altered, the two story, four bay brick on the Clore-Jackson Road originally had two front doors. It was built around 1828 by Samuel Booker to replace the home his father, Richard, had built on the property after purchasing the land in 1798. This home remained in the Booker family until 1974. A virtually identical house in a far better state of preservation is the Neal-Hamblin house on Hinkle Lane. Presumably built shortly after James Neal married his second wife, Jane Kinkaid in 1815, the house retains its reeded doorjambs and corner blocks throughout, glass-paneled cupboards, and a sunburst mantel.

A similar but slightly later house is located on Ritter Lane. John Morton conveyed the property to J. C. Burnett in 1835 and the house may have been built at that time. It originally had six-over-six windows and transoms over the doors, allowing the jack arches to follow the same line across the facade. A one story, four bay version clings to life in a barnyard on the La Grange Road near the Oldham County line. One of the most interesting two door houses was lost in the 1970s. The Bayne house stood immediately behind the Village Plaza prior to its demolition. Its two story central block was

J. C. Burnett may have built this brick house with two front doors about 1835.

spanned by a one-story porch, which connected projecting two bay wings on either end, an arrangement similar to the original Jonorochqua, and again seen in the later Shannon house on Zaring Mill Road.

The Charles Ware house on Pea Ridge Road was built in the 1820s and "modernized" in the 1890s with the addition of two front gables.

Sometimes four bays and two doors were not enough and a final variation was constructed. Charles Ware built a one story, six bay house with two front doors on the west side of Pea Ridge Road in the 1820s. While the house retains its original Federal woodwork on the first floor, it became even more unusual in the 1890s when two large gables were added to the attic giving the house a slightly Gothic feel. A very similar home was built by James Myles south of Finchville on the east side of Taylorsville Road sometime after he began purchasing property in the vicinity in 1833. While six bays seem to have been the limit in the county, the Stout-Buckman house on Van Dyke Mill Road features three windows and three doors. It also features batten doors throughout and a reeded mantel in the main parlor whose architrave is supported by deliciously naive Ionic columns.

Ultimately, the five bay, center hall composition won out and became the dominant floor plan for domestic architecture in Shelby County until the War Between the States. This is not to say that there were not attempts to make a center hall plan out of a four bay house. The Swindler-Smith house on the Mulberry Pike is the only known brick house of this type. The five bay form seems to have hit its stride in the early 1830s. Along with it came what Clay Lancaster called the "Geometric Phase" in which the basic structure was embellished with pediments, round and elliptical fan windows, and Palladian windows. The more sophisticated geometric floor plans of houses such as Farmington in Jefferson County and Rose Hill and the William Morton House apparently never made it to Shelby County.

Perhaps the earliest two story, five bay house in Shelby County is the Mareen Duvall house on Buck Creek Road. Tradition holds that it was built by a Mr. Hall in 1811 but some place the date closer to 1830. If it was built in 1811, it was exceedingly prescient and if it was built in 1830, its embellishment bordered on the anachronistic. Either way, it remains, the quintessential Kentucky farmhouse. Laid up in Flemish bond above a full stone cellar, the facade

Photos courtesy of the Kentucky Heritage Council.

The Mareen Duvall house has a façade laid in Flemish bond brickwork, and a twelve-panel front door.

features nine-over-six windows on both floors. The fascinating twelve panel front door is unusually wide and relatively short, falls below the top line of the first floor windows, and has no transom, begging the question of whether the house had a single bay porch when it was built. The interior has six-panel doors, reeded reveal panels, and the stair features carved stringer brackets. The property was purchased by Mareen Duvall in 1871 and remains in his family which has since lovingly cared for it.

Courtesy of the Filson Historical Society, drawing by Walter H. Kiser, ca.1950s.

The Hume-Bischoff house on U. S. 60 at the Jefferson County line.

Several other fine houses of this type survive in various parts of the county. The 1834 Foree-Maddox house is best known for the superb elliptical fan and sidelights around which it is designed. The Hume-Bischoff house on U. S. 60 at the Jefferson County line is best known for having been moved from its original location straddling the line near the road to a new site some 280 feet north in 1981. Unlike the previous two examples, it has nine-over-nine windows on the first floor to accommodate a semicircular fan above the door. After surviving the move, the house was subjected to two rounds of massive, unsympathetic additions and is now known as New Estate Farm.

The Fields house on Fields Lane is now only a shell. The Guthrie house on the south side of the Eminence Pike above Mulberry Creek was eventually demolished by Clear Creek Properties after nothing was left but its fine brick walls, which were Flemish bond on the gable ends as well as the facade. The Drane home on Drane Lane was lost to a tragic fire while undergoing restoration in 1978.

In town, the Stanley-Casey house is the only early house which presents five bays to the street. It is also one of a small number of examples in the county where the central bay projects from the line of the

Courtesy of the Shelby County Historical Society.

The Stanley-Casey house on Washington Street is now the headquarters of the Shelby County Historical Society.

facade. The other two story house sharing this feature is the singular Charles Stewart Todd house, the only surviving building in Shelby County pre-dating the Greek Revival with a hip roof. Both houses date from the early 1830s.

Two slightly later two-story houses of this type hint at the advent of the Greek Revival while maintaining unembellished flat facades and gable roofs. The Froman Fry house east of Southville features six-over-six windows and a rectangular transom over the main door and sidelights. It also retains what is considered the earliest "slave house," a two room brick cottage with a chimney at each end. The Allen house at the end of Parent lane in one of the bends of Brashears Creek closely resembles the Fry house and is notable for its doorway with pilasters and the introduction of windows into the north gable end.

The list of one-story, five bay, center hall structures is longer and unfortunately was longer still in days past. One of the best preserved, the Lawson Zaring house on Old Brunerstown Road, had been lived in by members of the Zaring family for over 160 years prior to its sale and demolition in 1998. The Booker

Drawing by John David Myles.

The Lawson Zaring house on Old Brunerstown Road was demolished in 1998.

house on Lucas Lane believed to date to 1816 is in the last stages of decay. A house virtually identical to it survives remarkably intact but uninhabited on the waters of Jeptha Creek on the south side of Rock Bridge Road. It appears to have been owned by Mildred Nolan in 1882. Dr. Birch's house in Clear Creek Park, shown as Dr. Cheatham's in the 1882 Atlas, was built in this form prior to receiving a second story around 1900. The Scott house on the Herrick farm on Scott's Station Road, the Paxton house on Pea Ridge Road, the Hedden house on Ditto Road, and the George Boswell house on Olive Branch Road are also examples of this very popular form and survive in various states of preservation. The John Simpson house on Zaring Mill Road south of its intersection with Popes Corner Road is one of the latest of the group, dating to 1850. Indistinguishable in form and layout, its detailing is Greek Revival.

The house on Pope's Corner Road owned by Miss Garnett Allen in the 1870s and later by the McMakin family was dismantled with plans for its reconstruction. It is interesting in several respects. It presumably dates to the 1830s but its facade is not laid in Flemish bond and it has no jack arches. Relieving arches built within the walls supported all openings in the house. Its interior woodwork can only be described as schizophrenic. In the parlor, a fine mantel with shaped shelf is supported by twin columnettes and the door and window frames are heavily reeded with bull's eye corner blocks. On the other hand, the only remaining door in the front section of the house has six panels. At the dining room fireplace the plain architrave and mantel shelf are supported by deeply fluted impost blocks which sit atop a surround with crossets, a design element dating back to the 1750s.

Perhaps the most interesting feature of the house is its molded brick cornice. Similar cornices are found on the Courtney house at the end of Pope's Corner Road and the Nathan Scearce house on Mount Eden

Drawings by John David Myles.

The Courtney house on Pope's Corner Road and a detail of the molded brick cornice.

Road. The Courtney house, a four-bay, hall-parlor plan, is also the only house outside Shelbyville with lintels and corner blocks above the openings on the facade. The Scearce house is a three bay, hall parlor building with jack arches above the openings. Both of these buildings are believed to date from around 1825.

Several five bay, one-story houses reflect the influence of the Geometric Phase and as a group are some of the most charming buildings ever constructed in the County. The best known is the Clayton-Holmes house in Old Christiansburg. It is usually remembered as the site of the marriage of President Truman's paternal grandparents, Anderson Shipp Truman and Mary Jane Holmes on August 13, 1846. Mary Jane was the sister of Catherine Holmes Clayton whose husband, Dr. James Clayton, purchased the house from its builder J. L. Flood. Some portion of the house was used as a landmark when the town of Christiansburg was platted in 1821. The house features a brick gable-end pediment above the central bay which projects from the line of the facade. The main section of the house also has a mouse tooth cornice similar to the King house on Beard Lane.

Courtesy of the Kentucky Heritage Council.

The Clayton-Holmes house in Old Christiansburg where President Truman's paternal grandparents were married.

Perhaps the most sophisticated is the house at the end of Blaydes Lane. For such a fine house and one which remained in the family of the builder until the 1980s, remarkably little is known for sure. It is said to have been built in 1833 and is attributed by some to Francis Blaydes. Francis is buried on the place and died in 1833 at the age of 42. Sarah F. Blaydes (1799-1883) may have been the key actor in the story. One suspects that Sarah was Francis's wife. Whether she continued to live in the house her husband completed before he died or replaced the earlier log home with the current home after his death is unknown. Everyone agrees that William Blaydes modernized the house in 1884, the year following her death.

Courtesy of The Filson Historical Society, drawing by Walter H. Kiser, ca. 1950s.

Perhaps built by Francis Blaydes, this brick house near Bagdad has an elegantly simple façade.

Regardless, the house was built with a gable atop a three bay projection on the facade. This unusually wide gable allowed room for a Palladian window above the half circle fan of the entry. This composition, both restrained and imaginative, is the best example in Shelby County of a style which was developed and perfected in Kentucky rather than having been imported from the fashion centers of the East. Unfortunately, William could not resist the fashions of the 1880s. He lengthened the windows on the facade using two-over-two sash and added a pair of steeply pitched gables to the front and rear to increase the available space in the attic rooms. The result is even more incongruous than at the Charles Ware house. Retaining its isolated position and many old trees in its lawn, the house, even as altered, is one of the finest early houses in the county.

A similar but much less successful attempt at the same style was built closer to Shelbyville on the Benson Road. It now forms the rear ell of a much larger house built by a Mr. Graham around 1880. In the old portion of the house, the projecting pavilion and gable above are limited to the central bay. As a result, the Palladian window in the gable appears almost a miniature and has none of the vertical impact of the one at the Blaydes house.

At the Snook house on Mulberry Pike, the central gable extended to become the roof for a porch supported by four free-standing and two engaged Tuscan columns. The tripartite window in the gable is missing the central half circle but must have originally had it. The entry features an elliptical fan, sidelights, and four engaged columnettes. The fan has either been replaced or features a unique arrangement of two rows of square panes sandwiched into the ellipse. While the pitch of the gable is too steep to qualify as Greek, this porch is the point of departure from the Federal to the Greek Revival. Once a pediment supported by columns was seen, the tide was sure to turn.

The Snook house is on Mulberry Pike.

One other similar porch survives and there is evidence of at least two others in the county. The survivor still graces the front of the Thomas house at the intersection of Mulberry Pike and the Cropper Road. This unusual two-story clapboard, four bay, center hall building appears to have been added to an earlier cabin some time in the early 1830s. Its one-story portico appears to be original and was supported by six Tuscan columns, four of which have been replaced. These columns were turned from single timbers and rested on pedestals at the height of the railing. The roof and pediment were somewhat heavy for the size of the columns and the height of the pediment caused the builder to use a shorter window above it. An early photo of the Leonidas Webb house on Webb Road shows a classic five bay, two story brick with a charming one-story porch over the central door. This porch appears to have been supported by four Ionic columns. The house is said to date from 1824 and to have been built by John Dale, a Baptist minister in Simpsonville, whose daughter sold it to Webb whose family still owns it. If this porch were original, it would be one of the earliest uses of the orders in the county. Ghosts of a similar porch with Tuscan columns can be seen on the facade at Stockdale.

The Leonidas Webb house on Webb Road may have been built in 1824. The porch was replaced by a 20th century wrap-around porch, which has since been removed as part of a renovation.

Perhaps the most imaginative early house in the county is the home known as the Montgomery house on Buzzard Roost Road. Besides having an attached stone kitchen, it is entered through a remarkable recessed porch supported by slender turned columns and pilasters. These divide the arrangement into three sections with elliptical spandrels and a half circle fan rests above the central section. The walls of the porch are plastered above a paneled wainscot. The door and sidelights are separated by engaged columnettes. The remainder of the facade features a three brick cornice. The house was apparently built around the time William Montgomery married Jane Todd in 1819. William was still the owner at the time of the 1882 Atlas. Members of the Sleadd, Stout, and Stratton families have since owned the property.

Depending upon one's point of view, the Greek Revival can be seen as the healthy outgrowth of Thomas Jefferson's desire to establish an American architecture appropriate for the agrarian republic or it can be viewed as fad which allowed anyone to feel lordly in a temple simply by attaching some columns to the front of whatever was handy. There is probably some truth to both points of view but it cannot be argued that when it arrived, it took Shelby County by storm and led to the construction of some of the finest buildings ever built here or anywhere else. Sadly, the finest of them can now be known only from ancient photographs. For example, Cross Keys, the finest Greek Revival building outside Shelbyville, was the only Shelby County structure included in Rexford Newcomb's "Old Kentucky Architecture" in 1953, by which time it had burned.

Built about 1819, the Montgomery house has an unusual recessed porch with paneled wainscoting.

The five bay, center hall plan was particularly well suited to the Greek Revival because the center door presented the perfect opportunity for the columns and pediment necessary for a temple. At first the temple was confined to the central bay and when used in this manner gave a strong vertical thrust to the facade of the building. This also allowed the continued use of five bays. In fact at houses such as the John Proctor Robertson house south of Waddy, the basic house to which the monumental portico is attached is virtually indistinguishable from the Federal form.

Chevy Chase, the earliest two story, four square or double pile house in the county, became a Greek Revival house when James and Salvisa Chase added the second floor to an existing single story, five bay Federal house and the additional four rooms and spiral stair behind it around 1840. A two-story porch on square posts completed their work.

Calvin Carpenter built another transitional house on the north side of the Finchville Road near the Jefferson County line in 1848. Clapboard over post and beam frame, the house had an unusual gable roof which became a hip at the east corner where the ell extended to the rear. On the exterior, the only hints of the Greek were a one story, one bay porch supported by two posts and the transitional cornice. Inside, its detailing was pure Greek Revival. The house remained in the Carpenter family until after

Bird's Nest, the Philemon Bird house, was demolished after a fire in the 1980s.

1882 and was the site of the Shouse Academy in the 1890s. The property was bought by John Tucker in 1915 and remains in the hands of one of his descendants who burned the house to the ground in the mid-1990s.

In addition to the return of post and beam construction, the Greek Revival heralded larger windowpanes in six-over-six windows. The Federal box cornice was replaced by the much deeper Greek entablature. The aedicule or surround for door and window openings became one of the primary decorative elements inside

Courtesy of the Kentucky Heritage Council.

The George Robertson house on Bardstown Trail is an impressive Greek Revival style house.

and out. The hip roof also made a brief appearance. The superbly maintained Helmwood Hall with its four Ionic columns was the finest example of this type. The facade of Philemon Bird's circa 1850 Bird's Nest on the Cropper Road differed only in having two paneled posts rather than four columns, no sidelights, and a window rather than a door above the entry. Bird's Nest was demolished after a devastating fire started by lightning in the 1980s.

The George Robertson house on Bardstown Trail is one of the most impressive of the Greeks. Although built of brick, the jack arches have given way to wood lintels. Its gable roof is supported by a full entablature with dentil blocks. The pediment, which rather naively carries the full entablature as well, is supported by two sets of square posts. Those on the first floor are also crowned by a full entablature requiring them to be shorter than those above and emphasizing the horizontal elements of the facade. A similar porch was built on the west facade of the John Knight house as it made its architectural odyssey from log home to 1890s farmhouse.

Another motif of the Greek Revival was the pilaster and once adopted, it was used to great effect to increase the verticality of the buildings on which it was used. Applied to the corners and on either side of the central bay, it distinguishes the exterior of the 1856 house of carriage maker Reunah Randolph at 1113 Main Street in Shelbyville as the walnut woodwork distinguishes the interior. The James V. Harbison house on Harrington Mill Road is very similar in design and its original one story porch featuring two exterior paneled posts and two interior Ionic columns is likely similar to the now missing original porch on the Randolph house. In all likelihood, the Randolph house had a door and sidelights in the central bay above the original porch similar to that on the Joseph Silcox house at 822 Main Street. This five bay house is said to date from 1850 and served as Elks Hall for many years. The hoods above its windows and ornamental iron porch are later additions.

Courtesy of the Kentucky Heritage Council.

The Reunah Randolph house at 1113 Main Street was built in 1856.

Courtesy of the Kentucky Heritage Council.

Porch detail of the Greek Revival James V. Harbison house on Harrington Mill Road.

The combination of the pilaster and monumental portico began to crowd the facade of the Greek Revival temple so a number of builders returned to the three bay facade while maintaining the room layout of the five bay center hall plan. The Martin house on Mount Eden Road and the John Hansborough house on Burks Branch Road are virtually identical in their presentation. Each is white painted brick with a gable roof supported by a full entablature above by

Ellis McGinnis Collection, courtesy of Michael McGinnis.

The cast iron porch and hoods above the windows are later additions to the Joseph Silcox house at 822 Main Street.

corner pilasters. Each features a monumental portico with four brick Doric columns. The distinguishing feature between the two is that the windows of the Martin house are a pane wider than those of the Hansborough house, a seemingly minor variation that has considerable impact on the overall impression of the facades.

The Martin house on Mount Eden Road is a Greek Revival house with a three-bay façade.

A clapboard version of the Martin house, Woodlawn was built by Robert Crockett and featured the most spectacular and elegant spiral staircase ever built in the County. For all its grace, Woodlawn has been allowed to fall into total decrepitude by its current owners. A much more pleasant fate has befallen John Crockett's Montrose across Trammell Lane from Woodlawn which is distinguished by its low hip roof and unusual floor plan. Perhaps the last gasp of the monumental Greek Revival in the county came at the Sleadd house on Hempridge Road. Its facade, although unpainted and featuring wooden posts rather than columns, is strikingly similar to that of the Hansborough house. However, the severe Greek entablature has been ornamented with paired brackets. The machine age has arrived and purity has fallen by the way.

Virtually identical to the Martin house, the John Hansborough house on Burks Branch Road also has four Doric columns.

The Greek Revival houses described above were all constructed as the centerpieces of substantial farms when the agricultural economy of the county was thriving in the twenty years prior to the War Between the States. However, the style reached its height in Shelbyville where its monumental qualities lent themselves to the construction of large, public buildings of the sort Jefferson had envisioned. Far and away the most elegant edifice in Shelby County, before or since, was the St. James College which was located on College Street between Eighth and Ninth Streets until it was replaced by the current Northside School in the 1930s.

The building appeared to be a two-story structure, eleven bays wide by three bays deep. Each bay of the building appears to have been separated by a two-story pilaster. It was actually three stories tall and was crowned by an astronomical observatory. The third story had small windows concealed in the full entablature which ran on all sides of the building. These small windows also appeared below the pediment of the massive two story, hexastyle Ionic portico on the south facade. There was a single story tetrastyle Ionic portico with flat roof on the east and likely a mate on the west. The observatory facade featured ten Ionic columns and the dome above housed a telescope said to have been nationally known. A far grander building than Olde Centre or Giddings Hall at Georgetown College, it was in a league with Old Morrison at Transylvania and Gideon Shryock's Old Capitol.

Stuart's Female College at the northwest corner of Seventh and Main Streets ran it a close second. Equally articulate but far more imaginative in its application of the Greek architectural vocabulary, it was also three stories with the windows of the third located in the entablature which bore a low hip roof. Rather than a portico, its facade featured four, two story Doric columns in antis. The bays on either side of the recessed porch were framed by pilasters between which the walls projected in a graceful curve, an element apparently unique in the annals of early architecture in Kentucky. The final note in the composition was a balustrade at the ridge of the roof which appears to have spanned the three central bays.

Little but what can be surmised from old photographs is known about the interiors of these buildings. In all likelihood, the three central bays of St. James were devoted to hall and stairs and the building appears to have been bisected by a cross-hall running end to end. There were likely eight classrooms on each of the main floors. The Stuart College was a considerably smaller building and is far more difficult to decipher. One suspects that it had two rooms per floor behind the porch and two more, one in back of the other behind the curved bays or a total of six per floor. Before it was demolished to make way for the old post office, the building suffered a possibly greater indignity. Professor J. E. Nunn added a full third floor and the graceful curved bays were turned into turrets with pyramidal roofs on either side of

Courtesy of Charles T. Long.

The old First Presbyterian Church was built in 1845 at the corner of Seventh and Main Streets. It was demolished for a new church in 1888.

a central gable. It is amazing to think that buildings of the size and sophistication of these two schools were built in Shelby County. It is sad to know them only from photographs.

Across Seventh Street, the Presbyterians built a new church in 1845. Their previous building had been located at the site of the Shelby County Public Library. From surviving photographs, the church appears to have been a substantial Greek Revival building with a recessed porch supported by two Doric columns in antis surmounted by a pediment created by the main roof gable. An octagonal steeple rose from a square base with corner pilasters. It was built with two doorways but was demolished in 1888 to make way for

a new church on the site. The recessed porch was little used here although popular in certain areas such as Danville. It was used on at least two clapboard Greek Revival houses in the county, a derelict two story house on the Nutter farm on Drane Lane and on the one story Payne cottage where it was surmounted by a gable with a stepped tripartite window. Both houses feature corner pilasters and pilasters on either side of the porch.

Courtesy of the Kentucky Heritage Council.

The recessed porch on the Payne house was a feature not often used in Shelby County houses.

In form and detailing, the 1845 Presbyterian Church very closely resembled the Olive Branch United Methodist Church, a beautifully preserved building erected around 1861. While it lacks the columns and steeple, it is a delightfully proportioned brick building with two entries between the outside bays which are separated by pilasters supporting the gable end which forms a pediment. Forty feet wide and 65 feet deep, four windows on each side light the nave. The Olive Branch church is in turn virtually identical to the Rockbridge United Methodist Church as constructed.

Returning to Shelbyville, mention must be made of the finest Greek Revival residence constructed in the city or the county. It is located northeast of Seventh and Washington Streets on Lot 2 of the original plat of the city which was conveyed by Samuel Shannon to John M. McGaughey in 1810. McGaughey at one time owned lots 1, 2, 3, and 4. McGaughey sold Lots 1 and 2 to Henry H. Martin in 1845 for $400. Henry was from New Orleans and in 1836 married Arrabella Clement Hieronymus,

Ellis McGinnis Collection, courtesy of Michael McGinnis.

Henry Martin probably built this elegant Greek Revival house about 1845. Shown in a circa 1909 photograph, it still stands on Washington Street near Seventh Street.

a sister of Julia Tevis. It is assumed that Henry built the house shortly after purchasing the property, so that he and his wife could be near the Tevises whose cottage still stands on Lot 4. Henry sold the property to William M. Rogers in 1858 for $3,900. Rogers' son Dr. William S. inherited the property. Dr. Rogers' wife Annie was organist at the Methodist and Presbyterian churches in Shelbyville, taught from her home, and boarded students from nearby Science Hill. Annie sold the property in 1938 to John Fawkes Sr., in whose family it remained until 1959 when it was sold to Louise Chatham whose husband still owns it and has allowed it to reach an advanced state of deterioration.

Henry Martin's New Orleans background may explain the unusual sophistication of his clapboard house. It features a tetrastyle portico of fluted Doric columns over the central three bays. Its full entablature with box gutters spans the main facade and the east and west facades. It is the size of a double pile house but

appears to have been built in the shape of "u" with parallel ells extending to the north from the east and west sides. The east ell has a one-story extension which appears to be original. A third presumably later gable now fills the gap between the outer two. On the interior, it features an entry hall without stair and a transverse stair hall behind, an arrangement only found elsewhere at Stockdale. There was likely a balcony of some sort above the entry as a door with transom and sidelights remains in place on the second floor. There is no evidence

Courtesy of the Kentucky Heritage Council.

The Tevis cottage at 607 Washington Street.

of anything ever having been attached to the columns at the second floor level. Henry and his house were likely the inspiration for the portico at Tevis Cottage and the porch at Science Hill, which also feature fluted Doric columns.

Mention must also be made in passing of the commercial building that stood adjacent to the northeast quadrant of the public square. Built on a narrow lot, presumably only twenty feet wide, its facade was divided into thirds by two story pilasters. The most interesting feature was the fenestration on the second floor. Tripartite windows giving this modest storefront a highly sophisticated and unusually modern appearance filled the spaces between the pilasters.

Courtesy of Duanne Puckett.

The commercial building at the extreme left of the photograph has a façade divided by two-story pilasters.

Other notable Greek Revival buildings in town included the third courthouse, a five bay, and three-story affair whose middle floor was taller than that above or below. The windows on the second floor were either twelve-over-twelve or sixteen-over-eight and those on the first and third were eight-over-eight. The primary embellishments were a two-story, tetrastyle Doric portico without pediment and a three-tier

The third Shelby County courthouse was an imposing Greek Revival structure, circa 1909 photograph.

cupola. The Armstrong Hotel stood for many years at the southwest corner of Sixth and Main Streets. In Simpsonville, the Masonic Lodge, although it has been covered in stucco and its second floor windows have been blocked, is an excellent example of the vernacular use of the Greek Revival for institutional purposes.

Earlier reference was made to the Sleadd house and the advent of the bracket. A remarkable group of houses, at least a dozen of which survive, are distinguishable from those discussed earlier because, while they retain the basic Greek Revival form, they feature brackets in their cornices. They may be distinguished among themselves in various ways, primarily the type of window used. All but two have hip roofs and all are three bay. All feature plain lintels above their windows although some of them are wood while others are stone. Several feature elegant plaster cornices and ceiling medallions in their primary rooms. Most predate the War Between the States, most of those just barely, and one was completed in 1865 to replace a log home burned by Union troops during the War. One has a traditional date of 1837, another 1840, both of which are probably too early, but it is clear that this style was being used at the same time when many of the monumental Greek Revival houses discussed earlier were built.

Four of these houses feature single six-over-six windows. The given date for the Sturgeon-Gregg house, 1840, makes it one of the earliest of the group. It does not have pilasters and has undergone numerous changes over the years so it is possible that its brackets were acquired after its construction. The Henton-Scearce house remains in the family of its builder but its entry has been altered over the years. Sylvan Shades, site of the Doolan Academy, has the most interesting brackets. At all the other examples of this sort, the brackets were applied to the frieze board of the cornice.

Thomas Doolan owned this house, Sylvan Shades, and had a school, the Doolan Academy, in a building on the site.

Often, larger brackets were used above the pilasters and smaller ones imitated modillion blocks in between. At Sylvan Shades, the frieze board and smaller brackets were eliminated leaving the unusual impression that the roof floats, supported only by the brackets atop the pilasters. Sylvan Shades also has chimneys on either side of the main hall, allowing the placement of windows on the narrow ends of the main block.

Woodbower is the youngest of the group and features an unusual floor plan although its other elements would suggest an earlier date of construction. The main block of the house faces west and two story ell projects from the northwest corner. However, the ell is offset to the north creating an unusual junction of two hip roofs. This placement allows a window facing west in the first room of the ell and complements the use of chimneys on the hall walls to allow as much light as possible into the interior. Woodbower is also unusual in that it is the only house of the group which retains its original one story, one bay porch. This property remains in the family of its builder.

Two of these houses feature tripartite windows in the outside bays of the facade. This feature, associated with earlier Federal houses in other parts of the state seems to have found limited application in Shelby

County. When used, it allowed a wider expanse of window that the single and added two vertical lines to the facade, increasing the sense of height as at Oxford, the James Knox Logan house on the Brunerstown Road.

This double pile, two-story house appears to have been built around 1860 by a grandson of pioneer Benjamin Logan who operated a gristmill on Bullskin Creek and lived in an earlier house on the site. An elegant home in all respects, it has an unusual recessed entry, highly detailed plaster medallions in the hall and double parlors on the east side, and a lovely spiral staircase with cherry banister. Perhaps its most unusual feature is the tripartite window in the north wall of the rear parlor which was built with hinged panels below, allowing access to the rear porch from this room. The property remained in the Logan family until 1890 when it passed to Patrick Joyes who built Joyes Station Road to connect Brunerstown to U.S. 60 and allow access to Joyesdale Station on the nearby railroad. He sold the property in 1904 to Charles Ware, whose family owned it until 1970.

The other house featuring tripartite windows is Grasslands, the Joseph Hornsby house on Clark Station Road. The given date of its construction is 1837. It does not have pilasters and retains a gable roof. This house is a single pile structure with ell. Although its brackets have been removed, it, like Oxford, retains a significant collection of early farm buildings. It has been in the Trumbo family since the 1890s.

Grasslands, the Joseph Hornsby house, was built about 1837 on Clark Station Road.

The more fashionable fenestration for the facades of these houses was the double window composed of paired four-over-four sash. Perhaps the first surviving house to employ this arrangement was Tarry Long on Zaring Mill Road. Built in 1851, it was also one of the first houses in the county to employ ornamental iron work, having been built with a three part, one story cast iron porch which spanned the central bay. With this adornment, the central pilasters were apparently deemed unnecessary although they were used at the front and rear corners of the house. The Temple of the Four Winds columns now spanning the front of the house are an unfortunate addition made in the 1960s.

The James Fullenwider house on Anderson Lane is a very similar double pile structure said to date from around 1860. Built on a knoll facing east, it is unusual in having a separate entrance and stair on the south. A pediment above the central bay and another fascinating variation of the use of brackets distinguishes the facade. In the other houses discussed, a simple wooden Doric capital is used at the top of the pilaster. Here, the capital has been superseded by two small brackets located immediately below those in the cornice, visually connecting the cornice, which features elongated dentil blocks, and the pilasters in a way not otherwise observed.

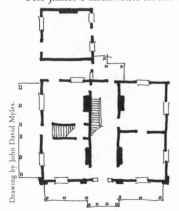

The James Fullenwider house on Anderson Lane has a double pile plan.

The final group of houses of this sort originally presented virtually identical facades. In fact, tradition holds that they were built by the same builder, one after the other. Traditionally, the R. P. Hanna house on Hanna Road is the first of the three and was built with an ell to the left of the entry hall. Although some mantels are mid-20th century replacements in the "colonial" style, it retains much of its original woodwork and the roof of its one bay, one story porch appears to be original. The next was said to be Pine Grove. Pine Grove's original ell was built immediately behind the central stair hall and had two-story porches on either side. A later ornamental iron porch spans the first floor of the facade.

The unknown builder is said to have perfected the form at Booker Brook Farm, the Joseph Hornsby house on the Clore-Jackson Road. A double pile house with chimneys similar to Sylvan Shades and Pine Grove, it also bears a close relationship to the Logan house. Like the James Fullenwider house it features a secondary entrance on one side. Although its main entry porch has been replaced, the house retains original porches on the south side and across the rear. These are one story and are supported with square posts with capitals similar to those on the pilasters. The cornice features paired brackets above each post with modillion blocks between the pairs of brackets, an arrangement similar to the main cornice. A notable group of farm buildings survives at Booker Brook.

Although it is difficult to determine today, the house at Golden Creek Farm probably belongs in this category. It is said to have been built by Basil Hobbs Crapster after he began acquiring property on Little Bullskin on the south side of U.S. 60 in 1864. Long known as Marlbank, the property has had many owners who have added to and altered the basic farmhouse which lies beneath. The neoclassical entry, portico with Ionic columns, and the west wing were likely added during the ownership of Dorothy Doe from 1928 to 1966. Mrs. Doe's family owned the Honey Crust Bread Company and many people still know the property as the Honey Crust farm. Joe and Maymie Gregory, owners of the Louisville Colonels basketball team, bought the property in 1966 and added the east wing and undertook extensive renovations. The Dunn family owned the property from 1970 through 1973 but lost it in the Prudential Building & Loan debacle. Mr. and Mrs. Robert Denham, owners of Mother's Cookies, owned the property from 1973 until 1985 when it became the centerpiece of the Gaylord saddlebred operation and acquired its current name.

While the houses described above were originally part of large working farms and all remain so except for the Sturgeon-Gregg house, they have one sister in Shelbyville. The Broadbent house on Clay Street is virtually identical to the R. P. Hanna house except that the paired windows are repeated over the entry. Formerly the residence of judges Peak and Pickett, it is currently beautifully maintained by Judge Pickett's grandson, George Broadbent. Tradition holds that Clay Street carries that name because Henry would regularly water his horse at the spring in the front yard when traveling between Lexington and Louisville.

Finally, it was in town that the Greek Revival breathed its last. The only remaining commercial building in this style is the Layson Hall at the southeast corner of Seventh and Main. Built in 1869, this three-story building with modillioned cornice and round louver in the tympanum of the pediment formed by the gable has been considerably altered over the years but still dominates its location.

The other "revival" style of the nineteenth century was the Gothic Revival. For whatever reason, it appears to have little impact here except in the ecclesiastical setting. The first manifestation of the style seems to have been the First Baptist Church building which is said to have been constructed in 1859 and stood on the southwest side of the public square. In plan, a rectangle with four windows on either side of the nave, it differed little from the Greek Revival churches discussed above. However, buttresses

The old First Baptist Church is thought to have been built in 1859 in the Gothic Revival style. It burned in 1909.

divided its side bays and it featured lancet windows and a tall pointed steeple. It burned in 1909. Although taller, it bore a very close resemblance to Trinity Church in Danville.

The Roman Catholics erected a similar structure at the northwest corner of First and Main in 1861. Known since as the Church of the Annunciation, its primary element of Gothic detailing was its lancet windows with stone arches and sills. Its steeple, chancel, and exterior cornice were added some years later. Another similar but smaller structure was erected by the Episcopalians at the southeast corner of Third and Main in 1868. St. James has never had a steeple but it was likely the first building in the county where the pitch of the roof exceeded a 45 degree angle. The interior is extremely plain and decorated only by the structural beams which support the roof and the colors from its old stained glass windows. The windows above the altar are likely the oldest in Shelbyville and are certainly the most brilliant.

If a primary feature of the original Gothic was the achievement of height, the original was best emulated by the First Assembly Presbyterians who constructed their church on the southwest corner of Ninth and Main in 1871. In shape and detail, it was simply a larger version of St. James to which were added a one story vestibule at the center of the facade and an elegant tall spire at the northeast corner. This tower had doors facing both streets. After these Presbyterians reunited with their brethren at Seventh and Main, portions of this building were converted into a residence which the Citizens Union Bank replaced with a parking lot in the 1970s.

In 1875, the Simpsonville Christian Church moved from its prior location on Antioch Road and built a 60 by 36 foot church on the southwest corner of U.S. 60 and Old Veechdale Road. The sides are divided into five bays, reflecting the narrower lancet windows. The

The First Assembly Presbyterian Church was built in 1871 at Ninth and Main Streets. It was demolished in the 1970s.

brick corbels on the facade and a unique variation of the pilaster theme which separates the side windows distinguish this church. Each pilaster widens near the top with twice-repeated quarter circles which emphasize the Gothic arch of the windows.

The Simpsonville United Methodist Church was built in 1876 and the building is a fascinating combination of elements. The nave has four bays separated by buttresses built over pilaster-like elements similar to those at the nearby Christian church except that they feature only one-quarter circle on each side. It is topped with a brick cornice. The tall tower and spire are above the central entry but access to the nave is reached through two doors which are reached from arches on either side of the tower. The most interesting feature of the building is its multi-color slate roof, the only one of the sort extant in the county. It is laid in five horizontal bands, the first and fifth of which are solid and dark, the second and fourth of which are light with a chevron pattern, and the middle of which is again dark, relieved by diamonds.

Both of the largest Gothic churches in Shelbyville have been rebuilt in their current form after disastrous fires. In 1888, the First Presbyterian Church decided to replace its Greek Revival building with a new Gothic structure. The members constructed a beautifully detailed building with a corner tower and a cross plan with large gables facing south and west. This form allowed semicircular seating and the chancel was placed on the east wall with a pipe organ behind. Single, large windows fill the corresponding positions on the west and south walls. The building had extensive stone and molded brick detailing and combined Norman with Gothic elements. Three years after being built, the building burned and was duplicated in 1891.

A similar fate befell the Centenary United Methodist Church which was built facing the northeast quadrant of the public square in 1897. Very similar to the Presbyterian Church in conception, its tower is larger at the base and hence a more dominant part of the structure. The stone detailing of the building is more restrained and less eclectic than that of the Presbyterian Church and, possibly because of its position, this building appears much more firmly grounded. This church was gutted by fire in 1978. The exterior was restored to its pre-fire appearance but the roof was suspended above the original walls from new laminated beams and the chancel was reoriented to the southwest corner of the building, allowing expanded seating area. The Bagdad Baptist Church is similar in design and layout to both of these Shelbyville churches.

Other churches were built with or received later Gothic embellishments over the years. The Christiansburg Baptist Church and the Rockbridge United Methodist Church were altered to accommodate the prevailing style over the years and when the Salem Baptist Church was rebuilt in 1894 after a fire, it too received lancet windows and an arched door on the façade. The Bethel A.M.E. Church on Clay Street in Shelbyville also has Gothic elements added at various dates.

The only extant house in Shelby County to have been built in the Gothic style is the home between New Christiansburg and the Bagdad Road which was owned by Anna White in the 1882 Atlas. The two bay, side hall building is clad in board and batten and the second floor roof has equal gables with overhanging eaves and highly decorative bargeboards on the front and sides. The entry features an original transom and sidelights but the first floor window has been altered.

The most interesting use of the Gothic in domestic architecture in the county occurred in the rebuilding of the James Drane house at the Henry County line on the Eminence Pike. Originally a three

An example of the Carpenter Gothic style, the Anna White house is in Shelby County.

bay, double pile Greek Revival house built in 1842, it lost its roof and second floor after a tornado in 1889. It was rebuilt with seven Gothic gables, three on the facade and two on each end. Only the gable over the front door had a window that opened into the upstairs hall. The second floor rooms were lit by four dormers, two between the gables on the facade and one each on the ends. All of these gables rise to a flat roof over the center of the house. The house retains a beautifully laid stone fence at the road which is surmounted by a short iron railing. Prior to its reconstruction after the widening of the highway, stone obelisks marked the entry. Commonly known as the house of seven gables, it is truly unique.

To underline the limited influence of the Gothic Revival and to make the transition from the Greek Revival to the Italianate which became the dominant style in the years immediately following the War Between the States, one should take a brief look around Science Hill. In the fields of architecture, education, culture, commerce, and preservation, it has been a dominant force in this community for almost as long as there has been a community to be dominated. From an architectural standpoint, it includes features of every style in the nineteenth century except the Gothic.

The original building is a five bay, two story, brick structure surrounded by a porch supported by fluted Doric columns. In the south parlor, reeded arches with bulls eye corner blocks frame the mantel. The south parlor and library featured handsome built-in bookcases with glass doors in the Greek Revival style. The dining room to the north also features substantial Greek Revival woodwork. The court was formed by two rows of class and dormitory rooms. Its second floor balcony is supported by posts with brackets and leads to the floor above the chapel, a large, two story Italianate building at the eastern extreme of the complex originally entered only through great doors at the end of the court. Eventually the court was enclosed and capped by a cupola. Over the years, other rooms were added to the north of the original building.

The courtyard at Science Hill School after it was enclosed. Undated photograph probably by the Williams Studio.

Science Hill was never a sophisticated structure like the St. James or Stuart academies. However, having grown like Topsy over its 125 years of operation, it is a far more interesting and complex building. More to the point, it survived. After the demise of the school, Mark J. Scearce ultimately purchased the building and it became a booming commercial complex anchored by the Wakefield-Scearce Galleries, an importer of fine English and European antiques and silver. Mr. Scearce received the Ida Lee Willis award for his preservation efforts at Science Hill in 1993, shortly before his death.

The Italianate style prevailed for a number of years after 1865. It reached its zenith early in the First Christian Church building which stood at the southwest corner of Fourth and Main Streets from its construction in the early 1860s until it was destroyed by fire in 1969. Far and away the finest Italianate building ever constructed in the County, it is on the short list with the St. James Academy, the current courthouse, and Stockdale vying for first place across the board. It is sadly ironic that this beautifully preserved building fell victim to a fire started during maintenance work on the cupola.

The plan for the building was an ordinary rectangle. However, there was nothing ordinary about the exterior detailing. The corners of the building and projecting entry bay had stone quoins and the windows were set within relieving arches. The same relieving arches, inside which a second arch was set, articulated the two outside bays of the facade. A dentil cornice, topped by heavy brackets which were repeated in the shallow pediment over the entrance bay, supported the low hip roof. The entry itself was composed of paneled double doors surmounted by another stationery pair which were in turn sheltered by a curved pediment supported by a pair of brackets which measured five feet tall and carried two beautifully carved acanthus leaves each. A four-sided cupola with eight Corinthian columns crowned the entire confection and proved its undoing.

Some mention must be made of the Methodist church which stood on the north side of Washington Street between Fourth and Fifth from the time the Methodists sold their property further west to John Tevis in 1858 until a later building was constructed. It is included here because it was a contemporary building with the Christian church although it can only be described as peculiar and fits no known

architectural category. A rectangle four bays deep, it had arched windows with heavy semicircular hoods. Pilasters, which on the front ran through the cornice and were topped by brick finials most closely resembling French chimney pots, separated the bays. The middle bay of the facade featured double doors behind a bold surround upon which a slightly shorter arched window sat. The doors were atop a wide flight of eleven steps with iron railings and, as the lot sloped to north toward the creek, the building sat upon a full lower story.

The old Methodist Church was an unusual structure which stood on the north side of Washington Street between Fourth and Fifth Streets.

One of the earliest and most unusual houses was the Henri Middleton home near Peytona. In plan the central block closely resembled Booker Brook, being a double pile with four chimneys in the hall walls. Instead of having a full second floor over the main block, it was built with two story wings at each end which were heated by two additional chimneys located against the walls of the main block, a total of six chimneys. Each wing had a concealed stair to its second floor room. The high ceilings of the central section and the comparatively low ones in the wings allowed the entire structure to be spanned by a single gable roof. The house featured paired four-over-four windows and a bracketed cornice. The recessed entry had decorative iron trim. An attempt to restore the house in the 1990s failed and it has subsequently been demolished. The grandest Italianate house ever built in the County was the Guthrie home which stood at the head of what is now Colony Drive until it burned in 1932.

The Henri Middleton house near Peytona was demolished in the 1990s.

In addition to brackets, the Italianate style which flourished in the 1870s and '80s came to be identified with ornamental hoods over tall, narrow windows (often two-over-two), irregular floor plans, and ornate wooden porches, often supported by narrow posts with more brackets. The brackets themselves were an outgrowth of the steam powered saw and larger panes of glass resulted from increased technical ability to make large sheets or plates of glass. Many window hoods, porch elements, and mantels were cast iron, a material whose possibilities were

The James Guthrie house was a grand Italianate structure until it burned in 1932.

fully exploited in domestic and commercial architecture. In the interior, wood graining and marbleizing were popular. These technical advances allowed a level of creativity not previously seen but also led to the demise of the simple, handmade embellishments of the earlier era.

Many Italianate houses were built with a "T" plan which refers to an arrangement where there are generally three rooms of similar size on one floor in addition to the stair hall. The "T" is formed when one room is generally beside the stair hall which is the same depth and the other two are placed on the other side of the hall and by necessity project forward from and to the rear of the hall. The space in front of the single room and hall provided the perfect spot for a one-story porch.

Of course, the most elegant example of the type had a modified "T" plan where the stair rose to the left of the entry and the single room was behind it. This fine house stood for many years near the intersection of the Cropper and Vigo Roads and was also distinguished by two first floor oriels. At the time of its demolition in the 1970s, it still boasted marble mantels and splendid ceiling medallions. A brick barn of much earlier date remains at the site.

The Tribble house facing Hedden-Imel Lane also features a modified plan and an oriel. The oriel reached its fullest form at the James A. Pickett house south of Finchville on the Taylorsville Road. A one-story version is located on the advancing bay to the right of the entry and a two-story version with five windows lights the dining room and a rear bedroom above.

The James A. Pickett house near Finchville has typical Italianate details.

Out in the county, brick, two story, houses such as the J. B. Allen house on La Grange Road, Fox Run Valley Farm, and the Stephen Hanna house on Mulberry Pike featured "T" plans. The James Lee Yeager house, which stood on the farm that became Eastview Subdivision, was also in this category. In Shelbyville, the John Ballard house at 927 Main Street and the William C. Hall house at 1204 Main Street with their ornamental iron porches and the Dr. Pratt house at 708 Clay, now missing its porch, are excellent examples. The Italianate was also a style which encouraged variation, likely in direct response to the rules of order and proportion which had governed the Greek Revival. Once

The William C. Hall house, 1204 Main Street, has a cast iron porch.

the rules were thrown out, there was no end to the variation. The wonderful Samuel Harbison house on Zaring Mill Road features a totally irregular floor plan, ornate cast iron window hoods, an extra gable, heavy cornices, an iron porch on the front, and its original two story wood porch on the rear which features a railing with balusters cut from flat boards rather than turned.

Cast iron window hoods and an elaborate iron porch are Italianate features of the Samuel Harbison house on Zaring Mill Road, now owned by Willard and Sadie Igleheart.

The Samuel Ellis house features "Monk bond" brickwork on the façade.

The variations went even further at the Samuel Ellis house on the La Grange Road. One bay of the ornamental iron porch has given way to a projecting entry whose door is topped by a pediment on brackets. The primary windows are topped with cast iron semicircular hoods and an oriel projects from the west end. A new variation in bricklaying also appears here. The facade is laid in Monk bond, a variation on Flemish bond which uses two stretchers for every header. As a result the headers appear as vertical stripes adding to the verticality of the facade.

Monk bond was also used at the John H. Wright house on Buck Creek Road. The plan of the house is very straightforward with rooms on either side of the stair hall with an ell extending from the right. To this plan a two-story projecting pavilion has been added over the entry. On the first floor, this pavilion has arched openings to the ground on three sides. On the front, the arch is constructed of three rows of corbeled brick and springs from carved stone corbels which rise over stone quoins. This unusual feature, in combination with the bond, heavy bracketed cornice, and bricks incised with John's initials argue for a construction date soon after the death of John's father, Lemuel, in 1884.

In town, several Italianate houses were built to the tried and true three bay side hall plan. One of the most elaborate is the Jeptha Layson house at 1005 Main Street. Here the first floor windows have been extended all the way to the

The John H. Wright house on Buck Creek Road is a more restrained Italianate structure, probably built in the 1880s.

floor. The Presbyterian Manse at 627 Main Street is a simpler version of the form and features a hip roof rather than the projecting gable of the Layson house. The prize in this category goes hands down to the Cowles house at 726 Clay Street. Tradition holds that it was built in 1850. However, Shinnick records that a house on the site owned by George McGrath burned in 1863. Everything about the existing house with the exception of its current six-over-one sash argues for a date near the time McGrath sold the property to George Smith in 1871. Beneath its massive and unfortunate wraparound stucco porch lies a remarkable house. The left block is a three bay, side hall. The hall is divided into a foyer and a separate rear hall which houses the circular stairway with turned balusters. The house is laid in the unusual Monk bond and features heavy hoods over the windows, including the arched window in the

A 1909 photograph of the Eugene Cowles House shows a bit of the original cast iron porch at the right amid the trees.

projecting gable. During the ownership of the Cowles family, guests visiting Science Hill were often entertained here, Carl Sandberg being notable on the list. Regardless of its date, it is one of the finest houses in Shelbyville and is now the home of Joseph E. Burks II and his family.

The most exuberant Italianate in town is the Jesse Glass house at the foot of Ninth Street at 834 Clay Street. Its facade is similar in arrangement to the Simpson house although its detailing is heavier and its windows are not arched. Its entry is recessed and the double doors retain beautifully etched glass panels. J. N. and Mary L. Funk transferred the lots upon which the house was built to Jesse Glass in 1863 for $4,500, a sum that would indicate that some building was on the property at the time of transfer. Glass owned the property until 1905 and must have built the house around 1880.

After Glass's death, the house was owned by Anna Harbison and later purchased by James Heady Wakefield in 1927. Wakefield was a developer whose family had at one time run the Armstrong Hotel and who was heavily involved in the subdivision of St. Matthews. From 1970 until 1983, Colonel Walter B. Smith owned it. After a period of decline, it was refurbished by Bill and Barbara Porter in 1999 and is again a showplace, now owned by John Marshall.

Courtesy of the Kentucky Heritage Council.

Houses of the Italianate style were also built of clapboard. A particularly notable example is the Charles Collins house on Aiken road. Its facade is very similar to that of the Samuel Harbison house and to the Walters house at Kingbrook Farm at Simpsonville. It has all of the usual decorative features plus an oriel on the projecting block and an unusual band of fishscale weatherboarding between the first and second floors. Two other fine clapboard Italianate houses have been

The Charles Collins house is an Italianate house built of clapboard.

lost to fire, the home on the Shields farm at the intersection of Mount Eden Road and McMakin-McMullan Roads and the Brown house north of Waddy on the Waddy Road.

The Italianate style was also chosen for the jailer's house which was constructed in 1864 when the second jail which was attached to it was enlarged. The enlarged jail was subsequently demolished and its stone used in the construction of the fortress behind it. Built in 1891 by McDonald Bros. of Louisville, it is a strange cross between a Norman keep and a garden folly. Conditions inside were doubtless closer to medieval. It served the County until replaced by the Shelby County Detention Center which opened in September 1997. The new facility, located on Snow Hill is modern and in every way a vast improvement over the bastille it replaced. However, a one story, concrete block affair, it lacks the "charm" of its predecessor, now a dispatch office.

The old jail was as close as anyone came to another of the late nineteenth century styles, the Richardson Romanesque. However, in 1899, plans were afoot to construct a new courthouse in the style. "The Headlight," a publication of the Louisville &

Ellis McGinnis Collection, courtesy of Michael McGinnis.

In 1891 the medieval-like county jail was designed and built by the McDonald Bros. Jail Building Co. of Louisville.

Nashville Railroad about the people and places of Shelbyville at that time, included a photograph of a three-story, rough stone building with a tall central clock tower bearing the caption, "Proposed Court House." It was further reported that the city was to occupy the first floor and the county the upper two and that there was substantial agreement on the design which bears a striking resemblance to the 1898 courthouse in Lexington. It is not known what became of this fashionable design or the nascent attempt at city-county cooperation.

The Headlight, 1899, courtesy of William Matthews.

A "Proposed Court House" for Shelby County was pictured in The Headlight in 1899, but it was never built.

Once popularized, the clapboard house on the "T" plan became the basic form for substantial farm housing across the county until the advent of the American four-square and the ubiquitous bungalow. Along the way, the various farms around the county were supported by a number of accessory buildings, primarily barns. Some are notable mainly for their size, such as the Weissinger Mule Barn which now serves as the clubhouse for the city golf course and was said for many years to be the largest

Ellis McGinnis Collection, courtesy of Michael McGinnis.

The old Weissinger mule barn at Undulata Farm, shown in a 1909 photograph, is now the clubhouse for the city golf course.

barn in the state. The barn at the Guthrie farm on the Eminence Pike, and the barns at the Painted Stone farm further out the Eminence Pike, were also notable for their size and construction. The barns, fences, and other buildings constructed by Sallie Henning at Allen Dale to house the prized Jersey herd can only be described as remarkable.

The octagonal mule barn at Birdland farm was built in the 1880s and was unique to the County. As built, it had stalls for forty mules and was so arranged that all could be fed from the center at one time. It was bulldozed, cupola, decorative barge boards and all, along with the Victorian home and a log cabin on the farm, the lane leading to it which was home to Mrs. Tate Bird's peacocks, and the fence rows along the Cropper Road, which were home to thousands of daffodils. A fascinating pair of barns survives at Sunny Meadows Farm on the Mount Eden Road. Said to have been built by Amish craftsmen for Hugh Collins in the 1930s, they have stalls on the ground level but their lofts are completely open under high curved roofs.

The agricultural buildings which have been major facts of life in Shelby County for most of the 20th century have been the tobacco warehouses. Originally concentrated in Shelbyville on the rail lines, a number were subsequently built on the east end of town when truck transportation overtook rail as the primary form of moving tobacco. Built for seasonal use, they were in many ways quintessential

Courtesy of the Kentucky Heritage Council.

The octagonal mule barn at Birdland farm, built in the 1880s, was demolished in recent years.

twentieth century buildings. They were built for their specific purpose and were totally devoid of any accoutrement unnecessary for the sale or processing of tobacco. Their sole purpose was to cover as much space as possible with a roof and to do so as cheaply as possible. In this respect, they are indistinguishable from an architectural standpoint from our Walmart Superstore. Having been built with a very specific

Ellis McGinnis Collection, courtesy of Michael McGinnis.

The Equity Tobacco Warehouse in a 1909 photograph.

purpose, it will be a challenge to find other uses for them if they are no longer needed for tobacco.

Any discussion of "agricultural" buildings should also include reference to the amphitheater and Floral Hall at the fairgrounds, the first of which succumbed to fire and the second to the Fire Marshall. The incarnations remembered by all but a few living Shelby Countians were built in to replace their predecessors which burned in 1903. The amphitheater surrounded the show ring and provided covered seating with exhibit space below similar to that still standing at the Mercer County fairgrounds.

Courtesy of the Sentinel-News.

Floral Hall was a cruciform confection which was open in the center to a large octagonal cupola.

Quilts were often displayed over the railings on the second floor, brightening the otherwise unfinished wood inside. For those who remember the celebration of the fair's hundredth anniversary before both of these structures were lost, the present Floral Hall is a sad mockery of its predecessor, regardless of its increased utility.

From the period of the War Between the States until 1912, L.H. Gruber & Sons carried on much of

Floral Hall, with its octagonal cupola, was built at the fairgrounds after 1903.

the commercial building and distinguished residential construction in the County.

During this time, two High Victorian or Queen Anne houses managed to be built in Shelbyville by someone other than the Grubers. The Jack Glenn house at 804 Main and the John Logan house at 700 Clay are noteworthy not only for their turrets but also for their abundant exterior detail and stained glass windows. The Glenn house is said to date from 1894 and the Logan house dates from 1890. In 1923, Oscar Kaltenbacher who served as city judge for 33 years purchased it. Another notable house, the E. J. Doss home at 830 Main Street demonstrates how quickly styles could change. Long owned by the McCormack family, it was clad in stucco and had wide overhanging eaves. The parlor and dining room were lit by large simple Palladian windows, the arch of which was repeated on porches at either end and at the columned entry. By comparison to the Logan and Glenn houses, it is positively stark.

The turn of century saw the advent of the beaux-arts style of architecture growing from the widely influential World's Columbian Exhibition held in Chicago in 1893. Richard Morris Hunt's administration building was white and composed of four Doric corner pavilions and an open Ionic colonnade topped by a 250-foot-high dome. It stood in stark contrast to the heavy, dark, eclectically ornamented buildings of the late nineteenth century and caused a revolution in American public building.

Four prominent buildings in Shelby County were built in this style, the courthouse, the First Baptist Church that faced it across the public square, the Shelby County Public Library, and the original portion of the Old Masons Home. The courthouse and church were completed in 1912 and strongly resembled each other in mass and detail. The church replaced the congregation's earlier Gothic building which burned in 1909. Built with a five bay facade and monumental tetrastyle Ionic portico, it was entered through doors at the sides of the recessed porch. It was pulled down after its roof collapsed in 1958.

The courthouse is a larger and grander version of the same building. Designed by Joseph & Joseph of Louisville, its first floor offices are arranged around a cruciform hall which allowed entry from all four sides. The walls in this hall are faced with white marble and the floor is laid in a similar marble in a running bond pattern. Both are trimmed in a dark green marble. The Circuit Courtroom spans the central portion of the second floor and originally had a balcony on the third. Three arched windows on each side light it and the walls are articulated by Ionic pilasters above an oak paneled dado. An unusual lion's head motif is located in the panel of each pilaster. The room retains its original ornate light fixtures, bench, and bar.

The building rests upon a raised basement, which opens to ground level at the rear. The first floor is reached by a high granite stair which leads to a recessed porch below a truly monumental hexastyle portico of stone Corinthian columns in which the two outside columns on each side are paired. The tympanum is adorned with paired cornucopias and the scales of justice. The cornucopias are repeated below circular medallions above the second floor windows under the porch and the entry is topped by a pediment with a carved cartouche. The east or Fifth Street side of the building is also fully ornamented, the primary difference being that Corinthian pilasters separate the Circuit Courtroom windows. This facade is rarely viewed directly but, lacking the almost forced monumentality of the Main Street portico, it is actually a more pleasing elevation.

The pediments on the south, east, and west of the building are on the gable ends of a roof system which spans the Circuit Courtroom and is covered in clay tile. An anthemion border presumably made of tin crowns those on the east and south. The projecting blocks at the corners of the building are only two stories tall and have a heavy cornice supported by paired consoles and crowned by a pierced parapet.

The library was built in 1908 through the generosity of Andrew Carnegie. In its original form, it was an almost perfect Palladian villa, brick on a raised basement, with stone tetrastyle Ionic portico and a dome above. The interior consisted of a vestibule, a hall separated from the two end rooms by Ionic columns and a semicircular room to the rear. The library has been expanded on three occasions. The most recent has been the most sympathetic in materials and detailing but completely masks the pristine proportions of the original. The Old Masons Home on the other hand is today a case study in the progressive styles and methods of building in the twentieth century.

It could be said that architecture in Shelby County reached its zenith with the completion of the courthouse in 1912. Given the onslaught of World War I, the Great Depression, World War II, the

International Style, and the automobile, one could certainly understand if nothing had been built thereafter. However, building continued. In 1916, Joseph & Joseph designed the Shelbyville High School. A building of similar size and layout was constructed at Clay Village. Both were built on raised basements and classrooms were arranged along transverse halls. Both are also notable for their ornamental stone trim which is particularly imaginative at the Henry Clay School.

The Northside Elementary School, built on the site of the St. James Academy in 1931, and the old Coca-Cola Bottling building are virtually the only things built in the modern styles of the first half of the twentieth century. The Bell Telephone office at Seventh and Washington and the old post office at Seventh and Main were constructed at about the same time. The rear of the post office bears a strong resemblance to Northside but the facades of both the Seventh Street buildings are embellished with carved stonework in the classical manner.

Most homes constructed after World War I were either American foursquare or bungalows. There were a few notable exceptions between the wars, particularly on Main Street in Shelbyville. The Slater house, now Hall-Taylor Funeral Home, is an elegant brick Italianate Revival house with tile roof bearing considerable stylistic affinity to the Doss house. Its first floor windows are arched and surrounded by stone trim and the second floor windows rest on a stone stringcourse. A wide terrace spans the front of the home. Its neighbor to the west was built for Paul F. Schmidt in 1930 to plans by Louisville architect Arthur Tafel. A brick and stone Tudor Revival with slate roof, it is distinguished by its circular stair which is reflected in the stone wall with ascending windows which fills the inside angle of the "L" shaped plan.

The Tudor Revival house built in 1930 for Paul F. Schmidt was designed by Arthur Tafel of Louisville.

At about the same time, O. L. Moore built a substantial two story stone home at Cedarmore in the Colonial Revival style. The home featured a columned entry and French doors on the first floor of the facade. Perhaps the finest home built in this style is the R. L. Shannon house at the southwest corner of Main and Ashland Avenue. A throwback to the days of the five bay, two story brick, it has a finely proportioned gooseneck pediment over the entry door and sidelights. Soon thereafter, noted Louisville architect Stratton Hammon designed a home for Mr. and Mrs. Walker Gibbs which was to have been built on a lot in the curve of Alton Road. The one and one half story brick house with Colonial details and two large bay windows overlooking what was to have been an entrance court was ultimately built on the bluff overlooking Mulberry Creek on the Cropper Road near Cozy Corner.

The house built at Cedarmore by O.L. Moore.

Few late Colonial Revival homes were built outside of Shelbyville. Those constructed were substantial residences. The Mack Walters home on the south side of U.S. 60 between Shelbyville and Simpsonville has a classic facade with a two story Doric portico and wings on either side of the central block. However, the rear of the house is predominantly glass, through which a wonderful view to the south can be enjoyed.

The other is the Girdler house designed in 1932 by Louisville architect William Arrasmith to replace the Guthrie house at the head of Colony Drive which burned shortly after being purchased by the Girdlers. In its first iteration, the brick house was painted white and had a full height porch across its entrance facade. A subsequent owner, Mrs. Hugh Caperton, decided to eliminate the porch, white paint, and cupola in the mid-1950s. Today it is a lovely federal house with paneled library and spiral staircase. All principal rooms open off the central hall which is lit by fine leaded sidelights.

For the first half of the twentieth century, the automobile had little immediate effect on the development of the county except for the construction of the necessary gas stations and car dealerships. Early stations remain at the northwest corners of Beechwood and Main and Tenth and Main. Early auto dealerships survive at Fifth and Clay and Fifth and Washington, the latter now serving as the courthouse Annex. Another stood for many years at the northwest corner of Fourth and Main. Residential development continued to follow the basic grid of the town. Although in the 1970s it appeared that much of the county might become an airport, the only one to be built was for ultralight planes. Designed by Taliesen West, it survives on a ridge off Grubbs Lane, its original lines obliterated by a later roof.

Ellis McGinnis photograph, 1950s.

Built in the 1920s as the Owen-Moore Ford dealership, this building is now the county courthouse annex.

The nineteenth and early twentieth century commercial buildings in downtown remained the primary retail space and a trip to Louisville to shop was still a special event. However, construction of the Winn-Dixie store near the fairgrounds was a harbinger of things to come. The Shelby Motel and the Jerry's Drive-In were soon constructed further west to accommodate customers with automobiles to park. The trend continues today with the Citizens Union Bank leaving downtown for a large suburban building. A Kroger store and an A&P were built on the east end of Main Street in what had been residential areas since the founding of the City.

In the late 1950s, two things arrived which have dramatically changed the landscape, culture, and physical appearance of both Shelbyville and Shelby County: I-64 and the industrial park. Many of these changes have been overwhelmingly positive and others unfortunate. When the first grocery stores became too small, they were abandoned and new, larger ones were constructed further from the center of Shelbyville, beginning a leapfrog process most recently followed by Walmart whose current superstore is clearly the retail center of the county. I-64 was also crucial in bringing industry to Shelby County.

With the arrival of Briel Industries and Roll Forming Corp. in the 1950s, a new form of industrial architecture arrived in the County. Today, factories dot land on either side of Dry Run near the KY 55 exit from the interstate. The largest and most prominent is the Budd Company whose massive white building can be seen from Simpsonville where the Kingbrook industrial complex is currently being constructed. One hopes it will not be considered too unkind to observe that the aesthetic appearance of the buildings that house important employers has not been the number one priority of those building them.

Other major buildings of the second half of the twentieth century include the Jewish Hospital in Shelbyville and the Shelby County High School, both of which have seen major additions since their original construction. The high school was one of the last to be built on more than one floor. Since then, schools have been built on one level, often closely resembling tobacco warehouses, especially those built when it was believed energy efficiency demanded eliminating windows. All those built since the Cropper school have been constructed with concrete block and brick veneer and the gymnasium has been the only element to relieve the monotony. The most recent, the West Middle School completed in 2000 and designed by Nolan & Nolan of Louisville, follows the pattern although in recent years there has been a resurgence in the use of windows.

It is heartening that the design of the recently completed Shelbyville City Hall seeks to reincorporate some of the ideals which went into the construction of the library and the courthouse. Perhaps best described as Post-Modern, at least the suggestion of the portico and dome from earlier and greater public buildings has been incorporated. It also takes advantage of its location overlooking Clear Creek and care was also taken in completing its interior with materials appropriate to a building which should engender public respect. One can only hope that this is the beginning of a new trend in public architecture.

There have been some delightful additions to the landscape. Native architect Quintin Biagi designed several modern homes in the 1950s and '60s, including his home in Todd's Point and his current office on west U.S. 60. His redwood and copper storefront for the Biagi appliance business on Main Street merits study by those who pass. The home he designed for Ben Allen Thomas Jr. on the Cropper Road overlooking the Bellview Pike is a particularly interesting combination of modern and traditional architectural styles taking advantage of the scenic setting. Quintin's son David, now on the faculty at the University of Kentucky School of Architecture, has built a home for himself on the Todd's Point farm which has received international acclaim. David's recently completed addition to the Church of the Annunciation

is a delightful abstraction of the earlier building as seen through the prism of Vatican II. Another of Quintin's sons, also Quintin, has recently completed a new shingled home on Brown Avenue which demonstrates that modern architecture of the proper scale can live gracefully amid much older homes.

Other prominent Louisville architects have added to the traditional housing stock of the County. The Robert Logan home on Sequoyah Drive designed by Neal Hammon is one of the most delightful exercises in classic design ever built in this or any other

Architect Quintin Biagi, Jr. designed this house on Brown Avenue for his family.

Courtesy of John David Myles.

county. Hammon's own home on Fox Run Road demonstrates the continued practicality and grace of the traditional foursquare plan. Hammon also designed the John Sanderlin home further out Fox Run. The current First Baptist Church is the work of Peyton Davis and although unfortunately altered on the interior since its completion in 1969 and minus one section of its steeple after a tor-

The Robert Logan house on Sequoyah Drive was designed by Neal Hammon.

nado, it remains an elegant building with its stone aedicule at the entrance and windows salvaged from the 1912 building in its transepts. Davis also designed the Hayden Igleheart home on Washington Street in 1960, one of many replications of Lexington's Rose Hill, including the Ted Igleheart house at 181 Wedgwood Drive by Neal Hammon.

Architect Neal Hammon designed his own house on Fox Run Road.

Over the past two hundred years, much has been built in Shelby County and much has been lost. A rich inventory of fine buildings remains today but many are endangered and Shelby Countians have been careless with this rich resource. They have also fallen victim to the modern desire to build as quickly and cheaply as possible without much care for aesthetics or posterity. Buildings tell stories and some of almost every description will survive. The story our early buildings tell is of a people who, even with limited resources on the edge of a wilderness, were concerned about the appearance and longevity of what they built. As Shelby County continues in its third century, some thought should be given to the story that will be told in the future by what we are building today.

The present First Baptist Church on U. S. 60 was designed by Peyton Davis and completed in 1969.

L. H. GRUBER & SONS

By John David Myles

If our city and county were named for the men who left the most indelible mark upon the landscape, we would without question be living in Gruberville, the county seat of Gruber County. Who, you may ask, was Gruber? There were several Grubers who left a remarkable legacy in our community. The first was Lewis Henry Gruber, a Baltimore native who was born in 1823. When he died in 1911, the Shelby Record reported the event, without apparent irony, under the headline "The Oldest Citizen of Shelbyville Dies of Old Age."

Courtesy of Dorothe Gruber Roulston.

Lewis Henry Gruber in a photograph from the 1890s.

Gruber the elder came to Shelbyville in 1840 after crossing the mountains on foot and stopping in Cincinnati and Louisville. He apparently made a hit upon his arrival. The story goes that a crowd was assembled in the public square to erect a liberty pole in celebration of William Henry Harrison's election as president. When those assembled were unable to accomplish their goal, Gruber rigged a crane with ropes and timbers and the celebration was on. His first job was at Allen Dale farm and he later worked as a baker, a candy maker, a rope spinner, and a carpenter. It was as a carpenter that he achieved success.

He was employed from 1846 to 1848 in constructing the courthouse which was demolished to make way for the present structure. Around the same time, he was involved in construction of Montrose Hall, the brick Greek Revival home on Trammell Lane which survives today. In 1859, he constructed the Armstrong Hotel which stood at the southwest corner of Sixth and Main. Gruber was also involved in the original construction of the Church of the Annunciation in 1860.

The magnificent First Christian Church, which burned in the late 1860s, is also credited to Gruber. This building featured marvelous brickwork and a remarkable frontispiece capped by an arched pediment supported by brackets which were five feet tall. A graceful cupola which proved its downfall topped the building. Probably the first major structure in Shelbyville to employ the Italianate style, it must have been truly revolutionary when built and certainly demonstrated that Gruber was willing to try something new with boldness and panache.

During the War Between the States, Gruber served in the Home Guard. However, family tradition holds that he was a lover, not a fighter. As head of the home guard, he is supposed to have led the locals east to the county line to meet a group of John Hunt Morgan's famous raiders. Rather than tangle with the raiders, he convinced them that they could make a much more productive foraging expedition if they would go south of Shelby County. That they did. Gruber's other Civil War service was through his blacksmith shop where he shod over 400 Union horses, for which it took him twenty years to be paid. Maybe because they wouldn't name the town for him or maybe because shoeing horses for free didn't feed the family, the Grubers moved to Illinois in 1864. By 1867, he was back and ready to build. One of the best known of his buildings is the Italianate home he built in 1872 for James David Allen. The home, now owned by Mr. and Mrs. William Shannon features an original cast iron porch, tall, narrow windows with ornate hoods, a low hip roof, and interior chimneys - two of which warm a grand double parlor. A similar home was built for the Guthrie family at the head of what is now Colony Drive. In downtown Shelbyville, Gruber was responsible for the Cresent Theater, also known as the Layson Opera House, which still stands at the southeast corner of Seventh and Main.

Along the way, Lewis Henry Gruber found time to marry Lucy Catherine Dear of Clay Village in 1858. They had two sons, Lynn Thomas born in 1859 and Henry Calvin born in 1863. In 1882, Lewis, Lynn, and Henry formed L. H. Gruber and Sons. At that time, the Shelbyville we know today really began to take shape. It and they were poised on the brink of a great building boom which would change the face of our city and give our county some of its most imposing domestic landmarks.

The center of the empire was the block bounded by Main, Clay, Second, and Third Streets. In 1871, Gruber the Elder began acquiring property in the block and by the time of the firm's demise, members of the family owned almost all of the block except for St. James Episcopal Church. Their planing mill, the old blacksmith shop, and at least three houses were located there.

Prior to the formation of the firm, Lewis Henry was building in the Italianate style embodied by the Allen-Shannon house at 1122 Main Street. Although incorporating the latest architectural details, that house is built in a traditional foursquare plan with central hall. Even more anachronistic is the Pemberton house at 810 Main Street. But for the detailing, the basic form of this house could have been built in 1825 as well as 1875.

Courtesy of Dorothe Gruber Roulston.

L. H. Gruber's two sons are pictured in this tintype. Lynn Thomas Gruber is at the left and Henry Calvin Gruber is on the right. The man standing is unidentified.

The winds of change that had been blowing through the architectural world since the 1840s eventually began to be felt on the banks of Clear Creek. The irregular or picturesque style became a factor here after the War Between the States. Probably the best example of the style built in the county was the Van Dyck house which stood at the intersection of the Cropper and Vigo Roads. Complete with asymmetrical facade and oriels, marble mantels and exuberant plaster ceiling medallions, it was demolished in the 1970s. However, it stood quite long enough to influence dozens of other farm houses which imitated its flat "T" layout, although many of these retained a central hall.

Asymmetry seems to have first arrived in Lewis Gruber's work in the home he built for hotelier George

The George A. Armstrong house, 1165 West Main Street in a circa 1909 photograph.

A. Armstrong at 1165 Main Street. Still basically Italianate with a low hip roof, the house features a recessed facade to the right of the central hall. Further variety is achieved by the use of double windows on the left, forward portion of the facade while those on the right are single. All have ornamental hoods supported by brackets and the house is wrapped by a porch and porte cochere supported by Ionic columns. A very fortunate house, it remained in the Armstrong family until 1947 when Mr. and Mrs. Charles Humston purchased it. Susan Scearce Burnett and her husband Pat now own the home. Although the formal gardens and tennis court have disappeared, the carriage house was lucky as well. Around 1950, it was converted into a charming residence by Mr. and Mrs. E. J. Reed and has long been the home of Mrs. William Andriot.

Once Lewis Henry got the hang of asymmetry and the boys joined the firm, the building boom began. The firm built Brown Lea on the Eminence Pike around 1885 for Cameron Brown. Originally an ornate Queen Anne Victorian, this home was remodeled between the World Wars to have a more classical appearance. Now the home of Mrs. Logan Brown, it retains the flat "T" plan, wide porches and porte cochere. A similar though less ornate house was built for Samuel D. Glass further out the Eminence Pike at about the same time.

In town, they let their imaginations and the creativity of their mill take over. Although they have all succumbed to the indignities of aluminum or vinyl siding, a group of clapboard homes built on Main Street between 1885 and 1895 demonstrate the firm's dexterity with the high Victorian style. The Hocker house at 920 Main is a textbook example of the type. The high gables and complex foot print gave ample opportunity to display various windows (some leaded), turned balusters, brackets, and various designs executed in shaped shingles.

The Hocker-Glass house at 920 West Main Street in the 1890s.

The siding applicators were somewhat less destructive when they dealt with the Grubers' work at 1004 Main. The home was built for J. V. Goodman, a hemp buyer and trader back when that was an honorable profession. Now housing the offces for the H. B. Smith Company, the home features an interesting window on the east side and a wonderful sleeping porch. Viewed from the rear, it becomes evident that making all those gables meet neatly was sometimes more than even the Grubers could accomplish.

The home they built for the Chowning family at 1160 Main and old Baptist parsonage at 909 Main have been so stripped of their original exterior detailing that it is difficult to imagine their original texture. 909 Main was later the Harp Tourist Home for many years and has recently become another of the growing number of antique shops in town. One shudders to think what might happen to the local economy if most people followed Dr. Johnson's admonition that "Life is surely given us for higher purposes than to gather what our ancestors have wisely thrown away."

The Grubers did not limit application of new techniques and designs to asymmetrical residences. They also became heavily involved in construction of commercial buildings around the Public Square. They constructed the old, old post office (as distinguished from the merely old post office at Seventh and Main) on Sixth Street, now the home of Clark Printing. Here they employed the then revolutionary technologies of cast iron and plate glass. The cast iron supported the heavy masonry of the upper stories leaving room for the great sheets of plate glass on the ground level. This combination did for commercial buildings what the buttress did for the medieval cathedral. It also gave us the archetypal commercial structure that lines Main Streets everywhere and was the last great advance in building until Mr. Otis invented his elevator. Similar buildings were built by the Grubers in the Freeman block on the north side of Main between Fourth and Fifth and the Middelton block on the south side of Main between Fifth and Sixth which was rebuilt by them after a fire in 1900.

While these commercial buildings were innovative, the more interesting commercial buildings constructed by the Grubers were faced with Bedford limestone. The Grubers did fascinating things with this material. The old Shelby County Trust Bank, the International Order of Odd Fellows building immediately next to it, the lower facade of the former Bank of Shelbyville, and Dr. Buckner's office building on Sixth Street are all Gruber-built and are presumed to have been designed by Lynn.

Nothing but a few foundation stones of the original Shelby County Trust building remains but the others have survived in remarkable condition. Each is composed of arches with exaggerated keystones and employs at least two different stone patterns. Dr. Buckner's office, now Dottie's Beauty Shop, features two sections of rough stone laid in American bond, unremarkable in itself. However, the rows alternate between blocks 8 inches tall and blocks 3 inches tall. Between these two sections is yet another separated above by a stringcourse upon which the second story windows sit and a stringcourse below from which the arches for the door and triple window spring. This section is a checkerboard pattern composed of alternating rectangular blocks of smooth and rough stone. This motif is also used on the facade of the Bank of Shelbyville building where the blocks are much smaller and square.

Two other stone buildings are known to have been built by the Grubers: Henry's home on Magnolia Avenue and the Chapel at Grove Hill Cemetery. The Chapel is the only known building by the Grubers in the Gothic style. Built in 1893, it was designed by Lynn Gruber and may have served as his initiation into stone masonry, the buildings described above having been built later. It features quoined corners, slate roof, lancet windows, and a charming portico composed of four columns on plinths supporting a pediment out of which is cut a Gothic arch. Complete with organ, two-tone slate floors, and stained glass windows, it was used for funeral services until the 1950s when it was relegated to use as the most elegant storage shed in the county.

In 1997, Mrs. Robert Matthews approached the Cemetery board and began a restoration campaign. Since that time, the masonry has been cleaned and tuckpointed, and the windows have been restored.

The building was rededicated in 1998 and is again available for public use even though many customs have changed since it was built as the centerpiece of the county's largest cemetery.

Illustrative of these changes was an account in the *Shelby News* reported on November 7, 1912. "Business in Shelbyville was entirely suspended Tuesday afternoon during the funeral. The service, which was conducted at Centenary Methodist church at two o'clock, was attended by the largest concourse of people ever at a funeral in this city. As a mark of respect the pupils at the public schools were dismissed for the day. Members of the Howard Lodge of Odd Fellows, Tasso Lodge of Knights of Pythias, members of the city council, the Police and Fire Departments and the Boy Scouts attended the funeral in a body." Having had an additional day before going to press, the Shelby Record reported on November 8, 1912, that the City Council "...ordered the engine house bell to be tolled every half hour on Tuesday."

The bell in question now hangs long silenced in front of the Armstrong Agency on Main Street but in 1912, its mournful peal announced the passing of Lynn T. Gruber. While serving his third year as Mayor of Shelbyville, he succumbed to an attack of colitis complicated by pneumonia. One week short of 53 years old, he had been ill for less than a week, prompting the News to proclaim that the "End Comes With Shocking Suddenness." Thus, with appropriate pomp and observance, the saga of the Grubers in Shelbyville came to an end.

House built by the Grubers for Mayor Luther Willis at 1108 West Main Street.

Such an end of the saga could hardly have been foretold as the 20th century unfolded. L. H. Gruber & Sons was going great guns. Lewis himself was still very much alive and the Colonial Revival was gripping the nation. Over the next decade, the Grubers built a number of houses on the outskirts of the city on either end of Main Street.

The first was the Luther Willis house at 1108 Main Street. Mr. Willis was a lawyer and mayor and his house, built before the turn of the century, took its present form after a fire. It is quintessential Southern Main Street. The symmetrical three bay facade features a central door with sidelights and transom surmounted by a balcony and matching door and sidelights. Shelter is provided by a two-story porch supported by Corinthian columns. The pediment is fully developed in the classical mode. The entablature forms the cornice for the entire house and is topped with a hip roof. Corinthian pilasters close the composition at the corners. Six over six windows harken back to colonial times although they are much larger than their predecessors. A terrace with wooden railing originally spanned the front and connected to the porte cochere on the left side. Completely exposed to the elements, it is one of the few features of the house which has not survived.

The Robert A. Smith house, 1124 West Main Street, circa 1909. It is now the location of Shannon's Funeral Home.

Around 1900, the Grubers built a house at 1124 Main Street for Robert A. Smith which subsequently became the Shannon Funeral Home in the 1940s. Of similar size and also arranged around a central hall, this house has five bays and a steep hip roof with three dormers. Its porch, originally a one-story affair supported by four columns and topped with a wooden balustrade, was extended prior to purchase by the Shannons. On the other end of town, a three bay version of this house was built at 37 Main for L. G. Smith. It was demolished in the early 1970s.

Sitting to the east of that property, the lone holdout is the stately J. C. Burnett house long owned by the Riner family. Built in 1905, this brick home is best known for its semicircular portico which is supported by four Corinthian columns. Three bay, its gable roof is supported by a modillioned cornice and features dormers similar to the Smith house.

The stately house award goes to the Samuel Monroe Long house at 1217 Main Street built in 1909. A synthesis of the various elements of the others, it is a brick, three bay, two story house with a hip roof. It also features a modillioned cornice, four Corinthian columns, and corner pilasters. The porch features a full pediment although the modillions follow the angles of the pediment rather than maintaining perpendicular sides. Wide sidelights and a fan window surround the central door. The son of the builder lived in this beautifully maintained residence until his death at 101 in 2000. It retains its original carriage house and full lot extending to Washington Street.

The Grubers also built the Tudor home at 1116 Main Street and Henry's stone house on Magnolia, which have similar layouts. The physical evidence would indicate that they also built the Hall home on the corner of Magnolia and Linden, its neighbor to the north, now home of Mr. and Mrs. Bob Walters, and the Biagi home across the street, although the connection is undocumented. If others built these residences, it seems certain they followed Lynn Gruber's plans and purchased their millwork from the same source.

The most remarkable group of houses built by the Grubers was not in town. Between 1900 and 1910, they constructed a group of country houses which remain landmarks today. The first of these was the home on the Cropper Road at Chenoweth Farm constructed for brothers William John and Ben Allen Thomas. Built for two families, this is a massive clapboard house and the Grubers seem to have thrown the pattern book at it, maybe in an attempt to please everyone involved. Why stick with a hip roof when you can have gables too? Why not throw in a couple of dormers as well? Why choose between a straight porch spanning the facade when a bow can be added to emphasize the entrance (as if the sidelight and balcony combination were not enough)? Why stick with rectangular windows when there is a spot for a couple of oval ones? Even the arrangement of the six Ionic columns on rough stone bases which support the front porch is unusual. There are recessed balconies on the east side along with the ever-present porte cochere. It is not your average duplex in which the fourth and fifth generations of brother Ben Allen's descendants now reside.

What do you do to top that? You build Undulata for Col. Harry Weissinger on Zaring Mill Rd. in 1903. The most academically classical of any of the Gruber buildings, this three story brick home was

House at Undulata Farm built for Col. Harry Weissinger by the Grubers in 1903. Designed by McDonald and Sheblessy of Louisville.

Courtesy of the Kentucky Heritage Council.

designed by the Louisville architects, McDonald and Scheblessy. Its two story semicircular Ionic portico seems almost diminutive against the stark, facade topped by a wide modillioned cornice and low hip roof. Single story porches on the sides frame the central block which is backed by wider extensions on either side. Approached through the gates which feature the best ironwork for miles and sitting in a park with many mature trees, this is a showplace in the best sense of the word. What do you expect from a man who built the largest barn in the state for his mules? For many years the home of Jane Meyer, the home and its remarkable set of barns and outbuildings fell into disrepair after she sold the property. The house and its remaining acreage were saved from development by Ed Bennett who has since lavished love and resources to restore the property to its original grandeur and provide a fitting home for his saddlehorse operation.

From there, the Grubers built the stone house at Allen Dale for Betty Allen Meriwether. Reminiscent of an English cottage and strongly influenced by the Arts and Crafts style, it is unique in Shelby County. Long, comparatively low, and only one room deep in some parts, it is a complete break from the traditional layout. Composed around a single story porch with four stout Tuscan columns, it is dominated by a pair of projecting gables. The drive passes through the gable at the left, providing a porte cochere and separating a service wing from the main house. Along the way, the house provided the backdrop for the social and farming exploits of Mrs. Meriwether's daughter, Sue Henning, becoming the centerpiece of interminable litigation, and stood empty for years. In the early 1970s, Brig. Gen. (Ret.) and Mrs. R. R. Van Stockum returned to the farm and began the process of restoring the house and grounds. Along the way, the General found time to research and write the story of his wife's family, published as *Kentucky and the Bourbons*.

In 1905, Col. Weissinger's brother, Phil, decided to build his own home on the back of the property which extended from Zaring Mill Road through to the Mount Eden Road. Long known as the Plantation Inn and long neglected, this was a more neoclassical house in its details, if not its composition, than Undulata. Its small portico supported by thin columns welcomed visitors into an abode said to have had silver and cut glass hardware. Unusual features include the angled bay on the northeast corner, stucco exterior walls, and the casement windows. The house was demolished in late 2002.

The last of the Gruber's country houses was the Muir House, built in 1910 on a bluff overlooking the old Clear Creek Bridge on Zaring Mill

The W. C. P. Muir house, built about 1910.

Courtesy of the Kentucky Heritage Council.

Road. Symmetrically massed with a projecting entry and wrap-around porches on both sides, the first floor is stone and the second is sheathed in shingles. Said by some to have been built to resemble a boat by Commander W. C. P. Muir, the formal rooms of the house flank an elegant staircase leading to a landing with a Palladian window. The rustic exterior belies the elegance of the interior woodwork and formality of the plan. Local lore placed tales of ghostly sounds in the home in the 1960's. Always approached from the rear, the house is no longer seen from the front because of the relocation of the road and bridge in the late 1970s. Having had a long and varied list of owners over the years, it is now the home of Mr. and Mrs. R. H. Bennett whose three daughters will likely give the legendary ghost no peace anytime soon.

By January 1911, Lynn and Henry had built what remain some of the county's finest houses and their parents were celebrating their fiftieth wedding anniversary. However, change was to come and come swiftly. By February, Lewis Henry was dead. Soon thereafter, Lynn and Henry disbanded the firm and Henry moved to Louisville. However, Lynn had his greatest project awaiting him.

It is an ill wind turns none to good and as ill as it may have seemed at the time and as evil as it seems today, the wind which required separate education for blacks and whites at the beginning of the century blew Lynn Gruber to good. It forced Berea College to cease educating blacks and whites together and prompted the college to found the Lincoln Institute. The site chosen was Simpsonville and the contractor was Lynn Gruber. His last buildings were by far his largest and most imposing. The centerpiece of the campus was the administration building, Berea Hall. A three story brick building on a stone foundation, it prominent feature is the six story tower which aligns with the entrance road. Its design relies on many of the same sources that produced the Collegiate Gothic style prevalent on many college campuses. A balancing wing to the east of the tower was originally contemplated and structural connections were left exposed in anticipation. If it had been constructed, this would have been a truly imposing edifice. Gruber was also responsible for the original men's and women's dormitories, Eckstein Norton Hall and Morris B. Belknap Hall.

It is fascinating to contemplate what Lynn Gruber might have accomplished in architecture, in construction, and in public office if he had not been felled at an early age. War followed soon after his death and that war wrought many other changes. When one reviews the legacy of the family, it is easy to understand why this city was so struck by Lynn's passing. It is rare for a family to leave such a mark on a community. Theirs is a legacy we should cherish and preserve, even if we don't change the name to Gruberville.

Berea Hall at Lincoln Institute, built in 1912.

Courtesy of John David Myles.

HELMWOOD HALL

By John David Myles

William S. Helm built Helmwood Hall, which faces the Eminence Pike midway between Shelbyville and Eminence, around 1840. He was born in 1806, the son of Joseph Helm Jr., of Lincoln County. Joseph and his wife gave William 193 acres in Shelby county in 1830, likely on the occasion of his marriage to Rebecca Henton on February 23 of that year. William purchased 82 more acres from his parents in 1831 and later added to the farm until it contained 432 acres when sold by him in 1874.

Helmwood is a superb Greek Revival farmhouse. Tradition holds that John F. Hagan designed and built the house. Whether Helm had help from Hagan or a plan book, his home is a beautifully proportioned five bay, two story clapboard structure with a low hip roof, interior end chimneys, six-over-six windows, and a two-story tetrastyle porch over the main entry. Fluted ionic columns support the porch, complete with pediment, and its entablature continues around the house signaling clearly that the porch was no

afterthought. Sheltered by this porch, the front door is topped by a six-pane transom and a dentilled cornice and has narrow three-pane sidelights and pilasters. An ell extends from the right side of the house and a single story, originally detached, brick kitchen is located behind the ell. A single-story porch follows the inside of the ell.

The interior of the house is completed in the same restrained but carefully executed

Courtesy of the Kentucky Heritage Council.

Helmwood Hall, built about 1840 by William S. Helm, is a fine example of a Greek Revival farmhouse.

detail as the exterior. These elements include door surrounds with pilasters and full entablatures, reeded casings with corner blocks, eleven-foot ceilings, and a cherry stair rail on straight balusters, which curves around a turned newel. The house has four-panel doors and the mantels are simple, reflecting the overall Greek Revival design.

Helm and his first wife had two daughters who lived long lives and three sons who each died before their second birthdays. The first Mrs. Helm died in 1854 and William married Ann Collier in 1856. Mr. Helm served as one of Shelby County's representatives in the General Assembly in 1842 and in 1871 was a county magistrate. Helm, a Southern sympathizer, sheltered John Hunt Morgan during his flight South after escaping the federal prison in Chillicothe, Ohio, in December 1863, disguised as a cattle buyer.

In 1874, Helm traded half the farm for other land on Bullskin Creek and sold the other half and the house to Hagan, the reputed builder. It appears that Helm moved to Eminence where he died in 1885. Hagan owned the property until his death in 1902. In 1914, his heirs sold the property to James S. Hays whose family lived there until the early 1950s. Passing from the Hays family to Dr. and Mrs. Donald Vandertoll, the farm was subsequently sold to Dee and Robert Ellis who sold the house and 25 acres to Kelly Scott Reed and Mark E. Dennan in 1984.

HORNSBY HOUSE

By Frederika Clore

The Hornsby house sits on a cattle and horse farm on the Clore-Jackson Road. The main house was designed by William Gill and built by Julia Ann Booker about 1860. Two duplex servant's cabins were built as well. The house was built in the Greek Revival style. It is one of only six two story double-pile brick houses to be identified in Shelby County from the 1840-65 period. The bricks were made on the farm. It is two stories, three bay, brick double-pile, center passage plan with low hipped roof, interior chimneys, sash windows on each floor, twin parlors, and a front hallway with plaster floral crown moldings. It contains twelve rooms, two wide halls, a front hall winding cherry stair case, ceilings twelve feet tall and rooms 20 feet x 20 feet. The foundation contains unusually long blocks of hewn stone. The stones were quarried on the farm near Fox Run Creek.

The house and farm have been in one family for five generations. On December 27, 1988, the house was placed on the National Register of Historic Places. It is a Kentucky landmark.

The Hornsby house at Booker Brook farm was built around 1860 and has remained in one family for five generations.

BENJAMIN LOGAN HOUSE

By Arlene Redinger

The farm upon which the Benjamin Logan house sits consists of 263 acres and is located about five miles west of Shelbyville. The principal buildings include the frame smoke house, the two room brick house, separated by a large brick fireplace, brick kitchen, and the 20 foot deep stone icehouse. All are registered on the National Register of Historic Places.

It is the house that is noteworthy and which sets this farm apart from many others. This remarkable old house is a two-story brick home of Greek Revival architectural style. Like many of the distinguished older homes its bricks were made on the farm and the foundation is made of stone. The interior is characterized by 13-foot ceilings, upper and lower, center halls, and ten rooms with fireplaces in each one. The three plaster ceiling medallions enhance the beauty of the center hall and the double parlors, now the living room and the dining room respectively. A large flat archway separates these rooms with wide moldings decorating each side, containing sliding doors, which can separate the two rooms. Off the dining room, the tripartite window has a hinged apron in the central opening to form a door to the back porch. The back porch has been brought back to the original design of two story square columns supporting the upper porch. The back stair descending from the upper porch has been relocated to enter the kitchen.

On the formal side of the house are double parlors. Two fireplaces have arched pilaster mantels with large open hearths one in each room. The other fireplaces on the opposite side of the hall have plain pilaster mantels with large open hearths. The rooms are 18' x 20'. The floors are of wide plank ash with large molding 14 inches in width surrounding the walls. The doorways are 10 feet tall with transoms above two doorways and one above a bookcase in the family room. A winding staircase of cherry descends from the upper to lower hall ending in a turned banister. Near the top of the staircase is a large

stained glass window, which was inserted in 1990 in an original back window revealing the Logan Crest. There is a sunroom, which was added on to the existing kitchen built from the foundation of an original side porch. Slave labor was used in construction of the three layer outer brick walls with crude plaster made of sand, hog's hair, and narrow wood slats covering walls. All interior walls are made up of two layer brick with plaster cover.

The front portico was researched and returned to its original design by architectural historian Clay Lancaster. It consists of one-story square wood pillars supporting a second-story porch with surrounding

The Logan house, on the Brunerstown Road, was built about 1860. Noteworthy are the tripartite windows and the pilasters at the corners and on the front façade.

wrought iron railing on its top. Early stone steps from the original porch remain in front of the existing porch. There are two end and two center brick pilasters and two centered doors lower and upper. Tripartite windows flank the doors. The lower entry door has floral cut glass sidelights and is topped by a transom. The upper door has plain glass sidelights and is also topped by a transom. All windows of the house have wood lintels above and stone sills. The roof has wide overhanging wooden eaves with deep bracketed cornices on fascia boards bordering the hipped roof with its original turned metal cover. A smaller similar covered roof covers the sunroom and kitchen.

TARRY LONG

By John David Myles

Tarry Long on the Zaring Mill Road may well be the largest ante-bellum house built in Shelby County. Four-square with a perpendicular ell, it features eight rooms and two immense halls in the front block. The house was built in 1851 by Nathan Howell who imported the original three-arch cast iron porch and furnishings for the house from New Orleans. He also embellished his home with white marble mantels.

For its date, the house was on the cutting edge of the change between Greek Revival and the Italianate. The only vestiges of the Greek Revival in the original construction were the corner pilasters and the shallow hip roof. The narrow double windows, bracketed cornice, and door and sidelight configuration were all very much Italianate in design.

The interior is truly immense. The hallway is a full two rooms deep and has a spiral staircase running up the left side. The hallway and double parlor to its right feature superb plaster cornices and center medallions. A large doorway separates the two rooms of the parlor.

The house passed to the Wells family in 1890. Ghosts of two sons of this family are said to inhabit the house. As the story goes, a quarrel broke out between them and one took a gun to the stable to settle the quarrel. In the waning light he mistook his father for his brother and upon learning that he had killed his father, shot himself. Thereafter, the farm was sold to Oliver Goss who sold to the Fairleigh family of Louisville. In 1920, it was purchased by the Duff family which lived there until 1942. Passing to the Wakefield brothers and later to Howard Pearce, Dr. and Mrs. W. E. MacGregor bought it in the late 1960s.

The MacGregors undertook various renovations including removal of the original porch and its replacement by the current monumental portico featuring four Temple of the Four Winds columns. In the early 1970s, the MacGregors moved on to another project and Mr. and Mrs. G. L. Lentini, a noted Louisville restaurateur, purchased the farm. The Lentinis continue to operate the farm which includes a large portion of the Clear Creek bottom south of Shelbyville. Mr. and Mrs. Robert J. Ehrler purchased the house in 1994. The Ehrlers, a lawyer and dentist respectively, have undertaken various renovations to this grand old house including repair of its superb stone fence which is one of the most finely laid in the county.

Tarry Long is shown here with its original cast iron porch imported from New Orleans. A four-columned portico replaced the porch in the late 1960s.

Sentinel-News photograph.

FOREE-MADDOX HOUSE

By Lucille Fry Gray

The Foree-Maddox House is located twelve miles northeast of Shelbyville in Christiansburg. William P. Foree (1785-1849) of New Castle and his wife Elizabeth Major Foree built it from 1832 to 1834. He resided also in North Carolina and Virginia. It was constructed of brick made on the grounds. The two-story house has a fan light and side lights for the front door. It was constructed in a Federal style with windows nine over six, and six main rooms measuring 20 feet by 20 feet. It was once used as a stage coach stop. In the front field is the Foree family cemetery.

Drawing by John David Myles.

The Foree-Maddox house, built about 1834, has an impressive double front door with fanlight and sidelights.

At the time of William P. Foree's death, the farm passed to his son Judge Joseph M. Foree. From the Foree family the farm passed in 1875 to the ownership of Greenup Maddox (d. 1891) of Owen County and his wife Fanny Sacra of Shelby County. When their five-year-old daughter and only child died, they reared a cousin James Pendleton Maddox (1855-1902) as their own. He married Mattie Belle Maddox (1875-1928). James was willed the farm and reared a son Jesse Pendleton Maddox and daughter Mary Eleanor Maddox (1884-1967) who married Ernest Malcom Davis (1874-1958). They bought the farm in 1917 along with Allen Davis his brother and his wife Beulah.

The farm has passed to many owners: the Clark Brothers (1924-61); Boo Ford and Charles Davis (1961-72); Murray Armstrong (1972-74); and James A. Gray and Lucille Fry Gray (1974-). The farm now consists of 49 acres where hay is grown for Black Angus cattle. Only the original house and root cellar remain, but the Grays have added a brick garage, barn, farm office, holding pens for cattle, log cabin, swimming pool, tennis court, gazebo, and patios where flowers are grown. It was commissioned a Kentucky Bicentennial Historic Farm in 1992.

PINE GROVE

By John David Myles

Richard Booker, a descendant of the holder of the original land grant, built Pine Grove on the Smithfield Road. It superseded a single story brick house believed to have been built about 1816. Mr. Booker and his daughter are said to have moved into the house before the plaster dried causing him to catch pneumonia and die shortly thereafter. As the War Between the States came to an end, a team of horses was stolen from the farm by Union troops for which the family was later compensated. However, no other damage was done to Mr. Booker's new home.

Miss Booker married Seldon Lard in 1866 and they occupied the home until 1881 when the property was sold to Zack Head. He had two daughters, Flora and Margaret, who married William H. and R. R.

Ellis McGinnis Collection, courtesy of Michael McGinnis.

Pine Grove, built before the Civil War, was modernized in 1905 by Flora Head Giltner and her husband, R. R. Giltner. They added the cast iron porch on the façade and made extensive interior changes. Photograph circa 1909.

Giltner, descendants of W. S. Giltner, an early Campbellite minister and founder of the Eminence College, who had performed the wedding of Miss Booker and Mr. Lard.

As originally built, the house was a simple two story brick with four-over-four double windows on either side of the central front doors on each story of the facade. Pilasters separated the three bays and a small porch sheltered the first floor door and provided a balcony for that on the second floor. A bracketed cornice supported the shallow hip roof. The house was built to a T plan and consisted of six rooms, two halls and two stairways. The separate brick kitchen had four rooms and a massive fireplace.

The chimneys of the main house are built on the interior walls allowing room for windows on the outside end walls. The central hall features a spiral staircase and the front three rooms have plaster cornices with egg-and-dart moldings and Acanthus medallions.

In 1905, Flora Head Giltner (Mrs. R. R.) decided the house was not large enough and that the simple facade needed some decoration. The area of the left back verandah was enclosed and a dining room and fourth bedroom were added. The original rear staircase was removed and a rear hall and stair were added directly behind the front hall. The area between the house and the old kitchen was also enclosed.

On the front of the house, Mrs. Giltner added a one-story New Orleans cast iron porch which extends almost the entire width of the facade. The second-story door was given importance by a Mansard canopy decorated with fish-scale shingles. A porte cochere was added to the right side of the house. In 1912, lovely parquetry floors were laid in the front three rooms. Many of the fine trees, including gingkoes, spruce, hemlock, and the eponymous pines in the lawn were planted at this time.

During this time, the farm was well known for its Hereford breeding operations. In the 1940s, a private airstrip was maintained on the farm and two dairies were operated until the 1980s. The property passed to Flora and R. R.'s son, Robert Marion, and to his son William Fairleigh upon his death in the late 1960s. Bill Giltner was a noted banker and farmer much involved in the introduction of the computer into agricultural practice in Shelby County. He was also a dedicated member and lay reader at St. James Episcopal Church for many years.

In 1992, his son, Robert Carlton Giltner undertook extensive renovations to the house which included removing many of Flora's exterior additions and simplifying the floor plan of the ell. In 2001, the house and farm were sold to Mr. and Mrs. J. Paul Keith, III, of Louisville.

ROCKWALLS

By John David Myles

Much like the daffodils which dot fields and roadsides, remnants of old stone walls often peek from beneath tumbles of honeysuckle, poison ivy, and other miscellaneous brush when nature stands briefly naked before the riot of spring. The daffodils and the walls often speak to those who will listen of long vanished habitations, roadways lost to disuse, and the care our ancestors took many years ago to define, protect, and enhance the properties they were carving from the wilderness. Also like the daffodils, or narcissus, or jonquils, the walls go by many names —stone walls, rock walls, stone fences, rock fences, and even the usually inaccurate slave fences.

In Shelby County remnants abound and a few stretches of wall survive in remarkably good order. Fences or remnants are most prevalent along Old Finchville Road, Old Mount Eden Road, the Kentucky Street-Old Taylorsville Road-Zaring Mill Road area, and the Eminence and Bellview Pikes. Perhaps the best known wall is the one in front of the Shelby County High School which lent its name to Fieldstone Acres. Remnants of what must have been a magnificent line can be found between Guist Creek and Cross Keys where old U.S. 60 made a wider curve than the now fifty-year-old "new road." A similar fence now vanished ran along the south side of U.S. 60 west of Shelbyville until the new road became four lane.

These were the areas of some of our community's earliest settlements. The fences at the corner of Old Mount Eden Road and Old Seven Mile Pike were likely built when that property extended to the home of Brackett Owen where the first sessions of court in Shelby County were held. Near the railroad track, another piece of this fence still stands behind Owen's house. The Zaring Mill Road area was not only the site of the Zaring Mill, the predecessor of the Climax Mills, but was also the site of the early Red Orchard settlement. The wall fronting Tarry Long contains some of the finest rock work in the state. The Eminence Pike and Bellview Pike areas were the scene of Squire Boone's Painted Stone Station. A piece of the wall on the south of the Painted Stone tract is today falling victim to the widening of Eminence Pike. U.S. 60 itself is supposed to have begun life as a buffalo trace, became the Midland Trail, evolved into the primary carriage road from Louisville to Lexington, and served as a major federal highway until surpassed by the interstate. Rock walled springs and ponds and enclosed graveyards can be found throughout the county.

Where did these walls come from? Who built them? Why were they built? How were they built? Can they be saved? Can those

Louis Payne, next to his rebuilt dry-laid stone fence in 1990.

which have fallen from neglect be rebuilt? Answers to many of these questions are found in the fascinating book *Rock Fences of the Bluegrass* by Carolyn Murray-Wooley and Karl Raitz published in 1992 by the University Press of Kentucky. Murray-Wooley and Raitz divide dry-laid fences into two types: plantation and turnpike. They contend that most of the fences of either type were built by Irish stonemasons rather than slaves and trace their roots to similar walls or fences in areas of Ireland, Scotland, and England whence many of the settlers and masons hailed.

Murray-Wooley and Raitz posit that the bulk of the fences were built by Irish masons or masons of Irish descent. On the other hand, their list of stonemasons includes D. Brannock, H. Brannock, B.W. Brawner, John Burks, James Carpenter, William Cheek, John Cook, Allen Dernasir(?), Ephraim Earnspiker, James Fairweather, Presley Jacobs, D. Martin, William Moreland, E. Pearce, and George Ritter (?), all of whom were working in Shelby County in 1850 and all of whom were Kentucky natives except Mr. Brawner who was born in Virginia and Mr. Fairweather who was a Scotsman. These gentlemen would have been working at the height of the turnpike construction in Kentucky.

Plantation fences were most often built to serve as property boundaries and to contain livestock on farms. Turnpike fences were most often built as new roads or turnpikes were constructed in the mid-nineteenth century and judging from the change in construction, their primary purpose had by then become appearance rather than strength. Murray-Wooley and Raitz distinguish the plantation fences from turnpike fences by noting that, "Turnpike fences employ some of the same features as plantation fences: double walls, battered sides, and upright coping." However, while the plantation fences were constructed with the long side of a rock facing into the wall to provide a stronger bond with the other side of the fence, turnpike fences often had the long side facing out, thereby covering more area with a single stone.

For both types of construction, two walls were built facing each other with tie rocks holding the two together. As no mortar was used, the weight of the rock above held the rock below in place. These facts form the basis for the first of the three rules the gentleman from Bourbon County relayed to Louis Payne when he rebuilt Mr. Payne's fence along Zaring Mill Road when the bridge over the interstate was constructed in the early 1960s. First, each rock must rest on two others. Second, a rock should never be hit with a hammer. This rule was likely important to Mr. Payne's project as it involved rebuilding an old wall, and rock exposed to the elements for years tends to shatter when struck. The final rule was don't ever put a rock down after you've picked it up. While the first two relate to preservation of the fence, the third relates to preservation of the builder. It seems clear that Murray-Wooley and Raitz would add fourth and fifth rules: always place the long side of a rock into the wall and add as many tie stones as possible.

Can someone armed with this history, these rules, and a missing or crumbled wall restore one of these treasures? Yes, if he is patient and willing to indulge in sometimes backbreaking work.

STOCKDALE

By John David Myles

Stockdale, the federal house on the Eminence Pike, was built between 1831 and 1833 for Charles Stewart Todd and his wife Letitia on land given Letitia in trust by her father, Governor Isaac Shelby. Charles was the son of U. S. Supreme Court Justice Thomas Todd and attended the College of William and Mary. He served as a military aide to William Henry Harrison, Secretary of State under Governor George Madison, state representative, and envoy to Columbia and Russia. He was also a noted farmer and editor.

Drawing by John David Myles.

Stockdale, built in 1831-33, in a drawing that depicts a portico based on the ghost imprint of an early portico.

Given the background of its builders, it is no surprise that the house is by far the most sophisticated early dwelling to survive in Shelby County. The five bay, two story brick house features an unusual hip roof and interior end chimneys. Rubbed jack arches crown its six-over-six windows. The central bay projects from the plane of the facade the depth of one brick and is topped by a pediment with lunette. The facade is laid in Flemish bond above a dressed limestone foundation. The detached sidelights on either side of the front door and the window above it are similar in arrangement to those at Federal Hill and feature bull's eye corner block surrounds. The symmetrical arrangement of the entry hall's four doors is facilitated by location of the stair in a separate hall behind the entry. Blind windows on the chimney ends of the main block maintain the symmetry of the facade and are unique in Shelby County. Interior woodwork includes bull's eye corner blocks, sunburst mantels, and paneled cupboards. In addition to the main house, an original square brick smokehouse has been rebuilt as a guesthouse and a very old corncrib with decorative bargeboards survives in tact, as do remarkable herringbone brick sidewalks lined with limestone.

Despite other successes, Todd was plagued by debt and eventually left Shelby County for Owensboro and died in Baton Rouge in 1871. Letitia's children sold the property in 1858 to Joseph Bird. It was subsequently sold at public auction to Cameron Brown around 1900 in whose family it remained until Dr. and Mrs. Lawrence Jelsma purchased it in 1984. Their renovation of the National Register home received the Ida Lee Willis Preservation Project Award from the Kentucky Heritage Council in 1987.

The Jelsmas continue to run the dairy on an adjoining farm started by his father in the 1930s. Dr. Jelsma is a noted neurosurgeon, as was his father before him, and Mrs. Jelsma is a former Chairman of the Jefferson County Board of Education and Secretary of the Arts and Humanities Cabinet during the administration of Governor Brereton C. Jones.

Drawing by Walter H. Kiser, courtesy of The Filson Historical Society.

Stockdale as it looked in the late 19th and early 20th centuries after an Eastlake style front porch had been added.

STURGEON-GREGG HOUSE

By John David Myles

The story of the Sturgeon-Gregg home begins in 1803 when David Gregg bought 208 acres of land in far western Shelby County on the Midland Trail. In 1804, Simpson Sturgeon bought an adjacent 230 acres. Sturgeon first built a log cabin which was restored near its original site by Mr. and Mrs. James Reed in the late 1960s. This property, now owned by Mr. and Mrs. Maurice Moorman, is about a quarter mile closer to what eventually became Simpsonville. Before he died in 1822, Sturgeon built a two story, four room brick house which now forms part of the north wing of the Sturgeon-Gregg House.

Sturgeon married Polina Logan and she inherited the house and 65 acres as her dower at his death. She lived in the house until 1837 when David Gregg's son, William, purchased 208 acres of his father's land and Mrs. Sturgeon's dower interest. In 1838, William signed his sister Harriet Louisa's marriage bond and she wed Solomon Young. Harriet and Solomon left Shelby County for Missouri where they had a daughter, Martha Ellen, who had a son named Harry S. Truman.

Around 1840, William Gregg added the two-story, three bay Greek Revival structure now seen from Shelbyville Road. The six-over-six windows have stone lintels and the facade and chimney ends are laid in modified Flemish bond. Shadows indicate the existence of a columned portico over the front door. This door and its mate above have transoms and sidelights with double-paned clear and red glass. Gregg's addition sits on a full cellar. He also added a one-story gallery to the west side of the ell and a two-story gallery carrying the same bracketed entablature as the facade on the east.

William also increased the size of the farm which by the time of his death in 1870 included 1,500 acres. His slaves built the nearby Long Run Baptist Church in 1845 and a brick schoolhouse south of the highway which stood until 1984. He, his wife Elvira, and three of their children are buried in the family

The Sturgeon-Gregg house as it looked in the 19th century after the Victorian porch and bay window were added.

Courtesy of Violet Stalker.

James Leander Hardin, who married Vinette Gregg, modernized the façade of the house probably in the late 1870s.

cemetery north of the house. A fourth child, Vinette, inherited the property upon her father's death.

Vinette married James Leander Hardin, a descendant of pioneer and Revolutionary War soldier, Colonel John Hardin. James, a lawyer, was educated at Transylvania University. As a Captain in the Union army, he was wounded at the Battle of Chickamauga. The couple modernized the facade of the house, adding a one-story Victorian porch topped by a bay window. James shared his father-in-law's interest in the brick schoolhouse and went to Louisville by train on September 8, 1881, to buy desks for it. On his return, he was one of seven men killed when the Anchorage to Shelbyville train hit a bull, jumped the track, and fell into Floyd's Fork.

The interior of the house also survives intact. The Greek Revival section has "eared" casings at the doors and the tall windows which feature panels below. The stair rail is cherry and the two parlors have beautifully detailed plaster medallions in their ceilings. These ceilings are also decorated with brightly colored geometric designs. This embellishment was added by a German prisoner of war, August Knorr, who stayed at the property during World War I.

Today, the farm consists of 55 acres. However, the house and several outbuildings have survived in fine condition and in the hands of Gregg's descendants. The brick quarters built by Sturgeon, a brick smokehouse with diamond-patterned vents, and a root cellar survive on the grounds.

WOODBOWER

By John David Myles

Thomas Chiles came to Shelby County to settle land granted to his father, Walter, by Governor Patrick Henry in 1775. He built a large, double log cabin on a hill east of the Peytona Road near Bagdad. He and his three children lived in the log house until 1863. Tradition holds that Union troops destroyed it that year and that daughter Sarah saved her brothers by kicking down the door of the burning house.

To replace the log house, Thomas built the large Italianate home which passed to Sarah. She married Harrison Bailey and the farm passed to their son, Thomas Chiles II. His wife was a professional vocalist, one of many Shelby Countians to have an early fascination with Chautauquas. Appearing under the stage name of Cecelia Eppinghausen Bailey, she performed, taught, and kept a notable circle of friends, including William Jennings Bryan. Thomas Chiles' niece, Mrs. Ben Allen Thomas II, purchased the farm. She in turn willed the farm to her granddaughter, Dr. Betty Thomas in 1984.

Construction of the house apparently was completed in 1866 as that date appears on a brick in the house. It consists of eight rooms and two halls, reflected in its three bay facades. The exterior was designed to allow the maximum amount of light, each room featuring a window on three walls. The two rooms meet only enough to allow a door between them. The front hall is wider than usual with a flat landing running the width of the room. The front door retains its original frosted sidelights and small stoop, which appears to be original.

The rear hall houses a small stair and, until renovations in the 1980s, an original bathroom. The old bathtub was a long, narrow tin affair encased in wood. The toilet was also constructed of wood and the room featured a tank, which stored rainwater piped from the roof.

The woodwork throughout was typical of the period. The exterior embellishment of the home is also typical of the period, combining Greek Revival pilasters and six-over-six windows with Italianate cornice brackets and an arched door above the front door. The interior chimneys are elegantly laid up and feature another Italianate motif, a blind arch between the flues. A one-story porch spans the ell shaped by the wings and has entrances to both halls.

Dr. Thomas, a veterinarian, undertook necessary renovations upon inheriting the property, although the house remains remarkably unchanged since its construction. Under her guidance, Woodbower remains a working farm.

Courtesy of John David Myles.

Woodbower, a brick Italianate house, was built by Thomas Chiles and completed in 1866.

WOODLAWN

By John David Myles

John Crockett inherited 1,000 acres on the headwaters of Guist Creek in the Mulberry community. Two log houses were constructed on the property.

Crockett was the father of two sons, John Edward and Robert Y. John Edward died at an early age leaving his property and four daughters in the care of Robert Y., his bachelor brother. In 1848, the family began building a Greek Revival home on the Logan Road. One of the daughters, Margaret, married Joseph Alexander Logan who lived at Montrose across the road. Woodlawn passed to the Logans in 1889. Joseph and Margaret raised four children at Woodlawn. In 1974, the property was still owned by two of their children and the estates of the other two.

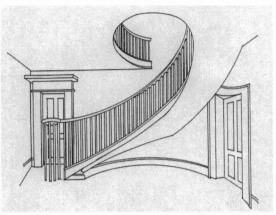

The elegant staircase in Woodlawn, circa 1848. The house is now a shell and the staircase has lost its stair rail that curved from the newel to the second story wall.

Drawing by John David Myles.

Tradition holds that it took Robert Crockett several years to complete the home. The level of refinement reflected such patience and the influence of Minard Lafever's "The Modern Builder's Guide," published in 1833. The superb staircase was very similar to designs in plate 40 of the Guide to Greek and Gothic architecture in the then modern taste.

The exterior of the house was clapboard over post and beam construction. Built to a T plan, each of the front rooms was lit by large eight-over eight windows, one front and one rear. The facade was accented on the ends by pilasters, which matched the four portico columns. These supported a full pediment and a balcony outside the second floor door. The four-panel doors on both floors featured transoms and sidelights.

The elliptical staircase was a work of art. The octagonal stair rail formed a continuous curve from the newel to the second floor wall above. The rail unwound from a tight curve which formed the newel and was supported by square balusters which were anchored directly into the floor. A parallel panel which hid the risers of the steps heightened the effect.

The mantels and door facings consisted of modified side pilasters and entablatures typical of the period. The woodwork in the front two rooms and hall retained its original faux bois finish. The interior chimneys of the front block provided space for doored cabinets in the front rooms. The rear ell was typical of the period, featuring a rear staircase between rooms and a double verandah on the right side.

In its heyday, Woodlawn featured a magnificent lawn and a tennis court. The property passed from the last of the Logan heirs in the 1980s, and the house has since been cannibalised for its materials and is now in an advanced state of decay.

Decorating graves in Grove Hill Cemetery during the Grand Army of the Republic Reunion, May 31, 1887.

CHAPTER ELEVEN

WARS

REVOLUTIONARY WAR

By William E. Matthews

Shelby County has suffered what would appear to be a disproportionate number of losses among men who fought and died in the nation's conflicts, dating back to the Revolutionary War. In 1992, Betty B. Matthews, then president of the Shelby County Historical Society and State Historian, Kentucky Society of the Daughters of the American Revolution, presented the following account of Revolutionary War soldiers based on old records of the Isaac Shelby Chapter, DAR.

She wrote that a list of all Revolutionary soldiers who finally settled in Shelby County would never be complete because Kentucky did not become a commonwealth until 1792. Consequently, records from the war itself were from the original 13 colonies.

The names of Revolutionary War soldiers that we do have include Thomas Weakley, John Lyle, Lt. James Holmes, Capt. Robert Tyler, George Boswell, William Harris, Col. Brackett Owen, Richard Booker, Nicholas Blankenbaker, Lt. Joseph Winlock, William Crawford, David Harbison, Benjamin Stout, George Shillideay, Lt. Daniel Wilcoxson, Bland Ballard, Joseph Thompson, Kendrick Banta Sr., Rev. Peter Fullenwider, Corp. William Long, Col. John Hardin, and Bland Williams Ballard.

A list of Revolutionary soldiers from Shelby County pensioned under the Act of March 18, 1818, reads: Jesse Alvis, Charles Ballew, John Callett, Sgt. Amos Chapman, John Dougerty or Doherty, Thomas Fitzsimmons, Daniel Hartley, James Johnson, 1st, and James Johnson, 2nd, William Morgan, John Millikin, Thomas Petit, Henry Randolph, Seth Stratton, Isaac Sampson, James Sacrey, Levi Wentworth, Joshua Wayland, and Samuel Yager.

Pensioners under the Act of May 15, 1828, were Samuel Holley, Thomas Jones, Surgeon John Knight, William Long, Elliott Rucker, and Lt. Joseph Winlock.

Pensioners under the Act of June 7, 1832 were Nicholas Blankenbaker, John Blakemore, William Brown, Martin Baskett, Benjamin Brevard, John Blackwell, Pete Bryant, Peter Brumback, James Christie, Peter Carnine, Charles Caset, Benjamin Conyers, Obadiah Clark, Samuel Farra, Elisha Ford, William French, James M. Franklin, Joseph Foree, Robert F. Gale, Benjamin Grisby, Elisha Gibson, Edmund Graves, George Hawkins, Sgt. James M. Holland, Sgt. Thomas Higgason, William Heppard, George Herring, James Hickman, Archibald Johnson, Thomas Kelso, Sgt. William Kendricks, John Knox, Hugh Lemaster, Wilson Maddox, Daniel McCalister, Capt. Daniel McClelland, Abraham Moore, Charles Mitchell, Alexander Morse, Micajah Neal, Robert Paris, James Rowe, John Riley, Capt. Benjamin Roberts, Sgt. Godfrey Ragsdale, Joshua Richards, Paul Rayzor, Reuben Stout, Reuben Sanders, Henry Smith, Sgt. Evan Thompson, William Tinsley, Joseph Thompson, John Thompson, John Travis, Lt. Van Swearingen, Peter Watts, Benjamin Washburn, Robert Woolfolk, Lt. Daniel Wilcoxson, and Henry Wiley. Pensioners living in Shelby County in 1840 were Bland Williams Ballard (81), Nicholas Blankenbaker (82), Samuel Burke (84), William Crawford, Meshack Pearson (86), Joseph Reeves (73), John Riley (79), Nancy Davis (widow, age 81), and David Harbison.

Betty Matthews concludes that "these patriots, given land grants, established new frontiers, opened up new lands and contributed to the beginnings of several new states."We are thankful for the sacrifices made by the patriots of all wars. Their hardy spirit shaped our country and made this a great nation."

In 1940 the Isaac Shelby Chapter of the DAR remembered the Shelby County patriots who fought in the Revolutionary War by placing a plaque on the front, outside wall of the county courthouse. The names contained on the plaque are Nicholas Blankenbaker, Sgt. Bland Williams Ballard Jr., Col. Bland Ballard, Richard Booker, Col. William Boone, George Boswell, Thomas Bradshaw, William Crawford, Jacob Fullenwider, Capt. George Hopkins, William Harris, Lt. James Holmes, David Harbison, Col. John Hardin, Gen. James Knox, Dr. John Knight, Gen. Benjamin Logan, William Long, Presley Carr Lane, Col. John McGaughey, Brackett Owen, Godfrey Ragsdale, Lt. John Riley, Capt. William Shannon, Benjamin Stout, Augustine Shelburne, George Shillideay, Sr., Robert Thurston, Capt. Robert Tyler Sr., Lt. Van Swearingen, William Tinsley, Gen. Joseph Winlock, Samuel Wells, Lt. Daniel Willcoxson, and Thomas Weakley.

While other records of those who served in the Revolutionary War are very sketchy, we do have a partial list of men who served in Squire Boone's Company. This company was stationed at what was then Painted Stone Fort near Shelbyville. They include: Capt. Squire Boone, Alex Bryant, John Buckles, Richard Cates, Charles Doleman, John Eastwood, Joseph Eastwood, Jeremiah Harris, John Henton, Abraham Holt, Morgan Hughes, Evan Hinton, John McFadden, John Nichols, Peter Paul, John Stapleton, Robert Tyler, Abraham Vanmeter, Adam, Jacob, and Peter Wickersham, James Wright, and George Yunt.

WAR OF 1812

While many Shelby Countians undoubtedly served in the War of 1812 between the United States and Great Britain, there is almost no local information available, either in history books or in newspapers of that era. Descendants of Bland W. Ballard discovered muster rolls in the 1960s containing the names of men who served under Ballard in the War of 1812 in the 1960s. The poor condition of the documents rendered many of the names illegible.

THE MEXICAN WAR

By William E. Matthews

Kentucky historians have written extensively about the War with Mexico, and have made much of the perseverance, valor and gallantry of those who served as volunteers from the commonwealth. We know from these history books that American troops followed victory after victory, and finally marched into Mexico City and dictated their own peace terms which made the Rio Grande from its mouth northward to the Pacific the boundary line between the two nations. This treaty gave the United States not only the empire-like territory of Texas, but also New Mexico, Nevada, Utah, California, Arizona, and Colorado.

But as with all wars and great victories, there were substantial losses in human lives. On the battle monument at Frankfort are the names of many heroic sons of Kentucky who gave their lives in this conflict. These casualties whose bodies were brought home from Buena Vista are among those immortalized by Theodore O'Hara, whose eulogy, "Bivouac of the Dead," is used in most military cemeteries around the world.

Shelby County suffered the loss of several dozen men in the Mexican War. *The Shelby News* (later renamed *The Shelby Sentinel*) lists the names of the following 22 killed in battle or died of disease in its issue of July 26, 1848: 1st Sgt. W. E. Boothe, Sgt. Warfield Bright, Corp. James B. Ashby, Privates John C. Drake, Nathan M. Pifer, Adam C. Sill, James B. Tilley, M. R. Garnett, C. W. Doss, J. J. Williamson, J. W. Berry, Ezekiel Brown, John Z. Truel, J. J. Thurman, George Steele, Sanford Harris, Isaac Jacquette, David A. Love, John Mitchell, Isham O. Smith, Charley Wise, and Musician James Sullivan.

Earlier, in its edition of Dec. 8, 1847, *The Shelby News* listed the names of the Shelby Guards, Company I, 3rd Regiment, Ky. Infantry, who had boarded the ship Palestine, ready to sail for Mexico. This was an all-volunteer group under the command of Col. Thomas Todd.

The company included H. P. Johnson, John N. Logan, W. C. Whitaker, William E. Boothe, Joseph C. Dear, Harrison Eubank, James Sullivan, John Mitchell, C. W. Doss, John C. Roswell, Bland McCarty, William Eakin, J. W. Taylor, William Teasley, A. T. Ragland, David Ashmore, James B. Tilley, James Webb, William Ashby, William H. Thompson, James L. Vaughan, William G. Neel, William F. Thompson, Fred Jones, John Easton, J. J. Thurman, William Cosby, John Branfield, Joseph D. Davis, William J. Livingston, Allen Demaree, J. H. Moore, Hiram McDonald, Joseph Lake, H. Y. McLamore, M. B. Garnett, S. G. Myles, George Wise, J. J. Williamson, E. G. Dear, George W. Gregory, A. C. Still, and William Miller.

Also in the Company were William Morris, J. Jaquette, Sanford Harris, D. K. Stockton, Thomas A. Tyler, Charles Wise, Warfield Bright, John W. Berry, James M. Thompson, James W. Daugherty, James B. Ashby, Charles Jones, J. R. Gore, Allen Thomasson, Benjamin Robinson, William Lawell, J. J. Smith, John Z. Truel, Silas McClung, Richard James, George Steele, P. D. Tinsley, Brandford Brasham, John C. Davis, Joshua Gibbs, C. C. McGruder, David A. Love, John M. Ball, James M. Long, James Thompson, J. O. Smith, Benjamin Switzer, James Kelley, Ezekiel Brown, Benjamin Baker, William A. Thompson, N. M. Pifer, James O'Bannon, John C. Drake, David Wayne, George G. Maddox, Michael Hilbert, and James Corley.

The Shelby News carried a letter from Camargo, Mexico, dated April 4, 1848, from Lt. J.H.D. McKeen to Calvin Sanders of Shelby County, which reads, in part:

"It was the fate of J. F. Ellingwood and John Sanders of Shelby County to fall on the memorable field of San Juan de Buena Vista on Feb. 23. It was in the last charge of our cavalry against a large body of the enemy's lancers. We can assure their friends at home that, however much they lament the loss of their noble young men, it cannot be felt more sensitively than by their comrades in arms.

"They went to the charge like every true Kentuckian should -- to conquer or to die. These men now sleep together in a common grave with their fellow soldiers who perished in the line of fire. That noble state has good cause to mourn the loss of so many brave men. Their fate will ever live in the brightest pages of her history. Their names are to be cherished by every true lover of Shelby County."

The "Unknown Soldier" who is buried in Frankfort's Eternal Camping Ground was a young man from Shelby County. Distinguished Frankfort attorney-author L. Frank Johnson, in his book in 1929 about the Mexican war, wrote: "When Captain Benjamin Milan was organizing his Franklin County company of cavalry for the Mexican war, a young man from Shelby County made application to become a member of the company.

But on account of his extreme youth, the young man was refused permission to enlist. A few days later the young lad appeared with his widowed mother who implored Capt. Milan to change his mind. Subsequently, he was enrolled.

"He manfully bore his part in the toil and hardship of the campaign. When Capt. Milan was ordered to charge the Mexican lancers at Buena Vista, he directed the boy to remain in a safe place. But the lad begged to participate and said he would be called a coward if he did not do his part.

"Capt. Milan very reluctantly yielded his consent and, after the battle, the boy's body was found on the battlefield, pierced through by a Mexican lance. His body was returned with the other members of the company who lost their lives in that battle but, due to an oversight on the Captain's part, his name was not provided with those of the other bodies, and, hence, he was buried in an unmarked grave. No one ever came forward with information that would help mark his grave, and it is assumed that his mother believed he perished in battle and was buried in Mexico. Consequently, he became Shelby County's 'Unknown Soldier' of the Mexican War."

A letter from Col. Todd to Henri F. Middleton, publisher of *The Shelby News*, and reprinted in the newspaper said that, "The Shelby Guards were mustered out of service on July 17, 1848. He said that, "The Company brought with them the corpses of William E. Boothe, John C. Drake, James B. Ashby, James B. Tilley, and Dr. Joel D. Sublett.

"These were all who died with the Company and were buried by their comrades. The others died in hospitals and were buried by hospital officers; their places of interment were not marked. It was impossible to distinguish their graves amongst the hundreds which environed the American hospitals in Mexico.

"The Company regretted exceedingly that it was impossible to give their deceased comrades sepulcher in American soil, but they had to yield their wishes to necessity."

THE CIVIL WAR

By William E. Matthews

The sympathies of Shelby Countians lay strongly with the Confederacy during the Civil War, but, somewhat contradictorily, a majority of those who went off to fight did so as soldiers in the Union army. The reason is that, while many adults enjoyed the southern way of life, they were opposed to the idea of secession.

The census in 1850 placed Shelby County's population at just over 18,000. But of these 18,000, more than 6,000 were slaves, slaves representing the single largest source of tax revenue for county government.

Accordingly, most slaveholders favored the south, while non-slave-holders were overwhelmingly pro-Union.

The gallant 15th Ky. Infantry, which fought for three years on the Union side, enjoyed the allegiance of many Shelby Countians.

In fact, Companies A & B of the infantry consisted almost entirely of Shelbyville and Shelby County residents. It was commanded by Capt. Abraham Rothchild who lived in the Southville area. It was Capt.

Rothchild who, after the war, founded what became a statewide-known clothing store on Main Street in Shelbyville.

His units contained many "sharpshooters" from the Mt. Eden area. For most of the war, the companies were part of a regiment commanded by Col. Marion Taylor, distinguished attorney-soldier from Shelbyville. Earlier, he had been a captain in Company A.

Shelby County soldiers battled from Perryville to Atlanta, and took part in Sherman's famous "March to the Sea."

Casualties from the regiment were horrific. Of 888 men in the regiment, including over 100 from Shelby County, over 400 were killed or wounded.

The regiment was organized in Louisville during August 1861, and at first consisted of 80 raw recruits from the Louisville area. They botched their first mission which was to intercept arms being shipped through Lexington, Ky., to the Confederacy.

Later, a group of men from Shelbyville was formed into the "Shelby Zouaves." These union soldiers were basically farmers, farmers' sons, and clerks. Most Shelby County men started as privates or non-commissioned officers, but, later, many gained battlefield commissions. These men included George Dearing, Richard Whitaker, Joseph and Henry Lyle, Joseph Atherton, Don Spaulding, Jourdan Ballard, George Petry, John and Harry Tilden, Harry Baker, Joseph McClure, Frank Todd, Irvine McDowell, Ezekiel Forman, Lud Luckett, and D. N. Sharp.

The officers of Company A of the 15th Kentucky included Capt. Marion G. Taylor, 1st Lt. James A. T. McGrath, 2nd Lt. Frank A. Winlock, 2nd Lt. John Marche, 1st Sgt. John S. Churchill, 3rd Sgt. John McCarty, 4th Sgt. William Kelly, and 5th Sgt. H. Clay Daniel.

Officers of Company B included Company Commander Abraham Rothchild, Capt. J. R. Snider, 1st Lt. B. H. Hower; 1st Sgt. W. H. Gray, 2nd Sgt. J. J. Hardesty, 3rd Sgt. G. W. Reed, 4th Sgt. Robert Foster, and 5th Sgt. C. D. Brown.

In February 1862, the regiment marched to Bowling Green, and the Confederate troops fled as the Union troops moved in. Shelby County men remembered the occasion because they captured a large supply of rebel salt beef and rye bread which was a treat from their inadequate rations up to that time.

From there, they marched to captured Nashville where they found the bridges destroyed. They crossed by steamboat and some of the veterans, after the war, said this was one of the war's highlights.

Later, they moved to Huntsville, Alabama, where they stayed for six months before racing back to Louisville to challenge the invading force of Confederate General Braxton Bragg.

After checking Bragg, the two armies faced off at what became known as the "bloody battle of Perryville." Losses were extremely high on both sides. When the battle began, the young men from Shelby County and other soldiers in the regiment were lined up behind a rail fence and big barn.

Although the confederates mounted a savage charge, the 15th Kentucky regiment held despite heavy losses.   On this one charge alone, 63 Union troops were killed, and over 200 wounded. The dead included Lt. McGrath, commander of the "Shelby Zouaves."

The next battle, just as bloody, was fought at Stone River on December 31, 1862-January 2, 1863 in Mumfreesboro, Tn. where the regiment lost another 81 killed or seriously wounded, including the regimental commander.

In June 1863, Capt. Taylor was promoted to colonel and placed in command of the 15th. D. N. Sharp was made adjutant, and Woodford Hull, a Shelbyville private, was made quartermaster.

Shelby Countians continued to give their all, as well as their lives, in sharply-contested battles at Mission Ridge and Chickamauga.

After being out of action for a while, the 15th found itself locked in the siege of Atlanta where they "burrowed around" the city for 30 days. Following Atlanta's fall, they were called upon to accompany Gen. Sherman in his "March to the Sea."

Shelby Countians wounded at Atlanta included Col. Marion C. Taylor, Capt. Rothchild, Lt. W. Gray, Lt. Joseph H. Lyle, Ordinance Sgt. Thomas Baker, Corp. Henry Swindler, Frederick Green, Conrad Ritter, Gus Mullin, Robert Coombs, S. L. Graham, and James Pulliam. Lt. Joseph H. Lyle was killed in battle.

At Atlanta, the 15th had encountered Confederate General Joseph Lewis's Kentucky brigade, which enjoyed the services of several Shelby Countians. Later, near Jonesboro, Union forces overran the Confederate Kentucky unit, and many were captured. Men of the 15th Kentucky visited the prison where the prisoners were being held, and Col. Philip Lee of the Confederate troops shook hands with Col. Taylor. Col. Lee was from Shelby County and, after the war, served for many years as commonwealth's attorney.

After Sherman's trek to the sea, the 15th Kentucky saw little additional action, and, in fact, the unit returned to Louisville on Christmas Day 1864. They were mustered out on Jan. 14, 1865, three months before the war ended. Most had served three years, three months, three weeks, and three days.

Several Shelby Countians who found prominence or notoriety during the Civil War include Dr. Richard F. Logan, Walter C. Whitaker, J. W. Harrington, Ed Terrill, Richard T. Owen, Col. W. L Scott and Capt. G. W. Stewart.

Dr. Logan, great-grandson of famed pioneer leader Gen. Benjamin Logan, served as a surgeon for the 15th Kentucky regiment, but resigned shortly after the Battle of Perryville. For the rest of the war, he was in charge of a military hospital in Louisville.

Whitaker was a man whose sympathies lay with the South, but was totally opposed to secession. He was the grandson of the famed pioneer Aquilla Whitaker. Whitaker turned out to be Shelby County's most famous soldier during the war, and was a general when hostilities finally ended in 1865. When the war broke out, he was a state senator. He soon joined the 6th Kentucky Volunteers and on Nov. 21, 1861, Col. Whitaker's regiment departed for Eminence, Ky. After the regiment had battled Confederates at Pittsburg Landing in Tennessee, where the unit came face to face with the 2nd and 7th Confederate cavalry units, Whitaker rushed back to Frankfort and a crucial senate debate on secession. Whitaker and several others claimed credit for keeping Kentucky in the union because there was strong pro-southern sentiment in the legislature.

Later, Whitaker's regiment fought at Shiloh, Chattanooga, and Chickamauga. After a bullet entered his chest at Chickamauga, and he fell from his horse, apparently fatally wounded, Whitaker remounted his animal and said, "If I have to die, I can't think of any better time than when I'm fighting." He tore a piece from his shirt, stuffed it into the bleeding bullet hole, and returned to battle, sticking it out to the finish.

He was promoted to major general on March 13, 1865.

After the war, he moved from Shelbyville to Louisville where he became a noted criminal attorney.

J. W. Harrington served with great distinction as a colonel in the Confederate army, and died in California on March 10, 1906. He was the presiding judge in the famous Modoc County lynching case in California.

Ed Terrill was and remains Shelby County's most infamous criminal. He was reared near Harrisonville, and was known as a rounder from the time he was old enough to go to school. He joined the Confederate army, and killed two Union soldiers who attempted to detain him.

Later, he was cursed and struck by an officer in the Confederate army. Terrill promptly shot and killed him. He was court-martialed, and sentenced to die, but he tunneled out of the jail in Shelbyville and escaped to Louisville.

He then went over to the Union side, and was placed in charge of a group of scouts who had become proficient in hunting for Confederate marauders that infested Shelby, Spencer, Henry and Nelson counties.

While fighting the Confederates, Terrill and his hired band of killers darted about and around Shelbyville, killing the innocent along the way, and also committing any number of robberies.

Finally, a group of local citizens got fed up, and trapped Terrill and a friend, Charles Baker, in the old Armstrong Hotel on Main Street. The two men were asked to surrender, but, instead, both charged out into the street with their guns blazing. Merritt Redding, owner of the Redding Hotel on Main Street between 6th and 7th, was fatally shot. The citizens' group returned fire, and Baker was killed instantly. Terrill was badly wounded, and taken to jail. Later, he was allowed to return to his home at Harrisonville where he died.

Richard T. Owen died in 1909, and his obituary in The Shelby Record depicts him as a man of "strong character who enjoyed immense popularity during his lifetime." Owen was Shelbyville's Town Marshal when the Civil War broke out and he, his brother Bob and longtime friend John R. Deering joined the Confederacy, and were posted to Mississippi initially. He served in an infantry unit in the 2nd Battle of Manassas, and won a battlefield promotion to captain. He was badly wounded at the Battle of Antietam, and walked with a very pronounced limp the rest of his life.

After the war he served as Shelby Circuit clerk, and as both county and city tax assessor. He was particularly active in Confederate army reunions. His funeral was preached by his friend of so many years standing, the Rev. John R. Deering, by now a well-known Methodist minister in Lexington.

Gen. John Hunt Morgan named Scott's Station in western Shelby County after Col. W. L. Scott, who served as a colonel under the Confederate army commander. Both before and after the war, Scott enjoyed a reputation as a champion breeder of fine animals. He was particularly known for his herd of Jersey cows, and for many years he won renown for not only the number of cows he owned but for the many blue ribbons which they won at state fairs in many states.

G. W. Stewart was a real "captain" in more ways than one. At the age of 18 he was already captain of a flatboat on the Ohio River. A few years later, he was recognized as one of the finest captains on either the Ohio or Mississippi rivers.

Because the Civil War knocked out the commercial steamship trade, Stewart was put in charge of the "New Uncle Sam," a military transport which carried Stewart into action at Belmont, Ft. Donelson, and Shiloh.

Shelby County Public Library, collection of Lou B. Finnell.

A group of soldiers, probably in the Kentucky Militia, circa late 1890s. Two men from Shelby County are indentified: back row, at left, Paul Crane; third from left, George Petry.

At Belmont he viewed the battle with U. S. Grant. He was considered a man of "iron nerve and a perfect stranger to fear." After the war, he was a passenger on a steamboat that blew up on the Mississippi due to a faulty boiler. It is said that he personally saved at least a dozen people who were struggling in the water.

Stewart settled down in Shelby County in 1868, and spent the rest of his life farming. He died on April 30, 1887.

Union and Confederate units in which Shelby Countians served suffered severe casualties. But no Confederate unit endured the pain and suffering of what became known as the "Orphan Brigade."

When the few survivors of this brigade held their annual reunion in 1900, three men from Shelby County attended. They were G. W. Weller, William Newton, and James Scroggins. Two other local soldiers, Col. J. F. Davis, and James Johnson, had been with the brigade but had transferred.

On May 7, 1864, this brigade of 1,140 men under the command of Gen. Joe Johnson left Dalton, Ga. They fell back toward Atlanta to face an overwhelming number of troops under the command of Gen. Sherman. In the next 100 days, the brigade battled Sherman's men without let-up. By the end of August when the fighting stopped, more than 1,000 men in the brigade had been either killed or wounded. "Trial by fire" was perhaps first used by a southern newspaper to describe the harsh circumstances which befell this brigade.

After the war Union and Confederate veterans visited with their comrades in the annual reunions which took place not only on the national and state level, but in virtually every small town and city whose citizens had paid such a high price. In Shelby County, men who had fought for either the Blue or the Gray became prominent farmers, businessmen, and office-holders. Others became factory workers, store clerks, and government employees.

WORLD WAR I

Company K, the World War I unit from Shelbyville and Shelby County, saw several changes in officers and men during its three years of service. A roster at one time would not list all who were enrolled for its entire existence.

However, the roster at the time of its organization and oath-taking ceremony when the National Guard unit was inducted into the U. S. Army reads: Howard P. Rives, Captain John Dawson Buckner, 1st Lt., Frank S. Wright, 2nd Lt., Clarence R. Heady, 1st Sgt., and Estes D. Barnett, quartermaster sergeant, Louis Ruben, Philip Sleadd, Will Booker Owsley, and John D. Dugan, line sergeants; and Orville Barrett, Harry D. Powers, Dan O'Sullivan, Frank Gruber, Lawrence T. Harbison, Andrew Meehan, and Howard Williams, corporals.

Privates were Thomas Duncan, Frank L. Duncan, Davis I. Estes, Homer H. Eichler, Joseph French, Willis Froman, McIntire M. Haley, Simon S. Hill, Oris Harlow, John (Jack) Hughes, Edwin E. Haley, John William Hundley, Clifton Hedden, Hugh Johnson, Daniel Long, Roger L. Long, Edwin McCandless, Leonard Malmeran, Pryor Marshall, Jesse Miles, John P. Morris, Thomas Perry, William Price, Myley Proctor, Oris E. Rodgers, Edward R. Rice, Charles Redman, Frank Reardon, Edward Shelton, John P. Snydor, Charles M. Taylor, John M. Turner, Robert B. Tracy, Frank Whitman, Benjamn R. Warfield, Charles Whitman, and Robert C. Whisman.

Also, Augustus Whisman, Lea Wallace, Ira K. Watts, Charles Murphy, Charles O. Low, Frank (Doc) Bruce, N. Burkhead, Jerry Baker, G. (Nick) Blackeby, Henry Cozine, Palmer Craig, Maurice Craig, Calvin

A group of Shelby County soldiers in 1918, probably at Camp Meade, Maryland. Standing: Roscoe Webb, Clay Cornelius, ___Davidson, William Ethington, Arthur Radcliff, Orval Florence. Kneeling: Salem Redman, Shelby Sharp, Walter Morgan, Roy McMullen, Herbert Neal, Horace Pearce, Eddie Mullins. Sitting: Fred Harrington, Cecil Money, Judiah Gill, George E. Hanser, Caldwell Bird, Guy Duvall, Edwin Coots.

Crim, Samuel R. Caldwell, Oscar Douthitt, Lester Devine, Henry Harris, and Orville B. Tracey.

Musicians (buglers) included Rodger Bemiss, Lewis Frederick, Joseph Dawkins, Robert Wood and Lester Samples. James O'Sullivan and C. G. Chandler were listed as mechanics.

(Resources which made this article possible include *The Shelby News, The Shelby Record*, and the *Shelby Sentinel*.)

J. FRANKLIN BELL POST #37 AMERICAN LEGION OF KENTUCKY

By Harold Saunders

In 1919, soon after World War I, a group of war veterans held an organizational meeting in Paris, France, resulting in the National Organization of the American Legion. On September 16, 1919, the United States Congress granted a charter for the organization and the first national convention of the American Legion was held on September 18, 1924, in Minneapolis, Minnesota.

On May 10, 1924, a charter was issued for a post in Shelby County, Kentucky, and the number 37 was assigned to it. By action of the membership, the post was named "J. Franklin Bell Post No. 37, American Legion of Kentucky."

Brigadier General J. Franklin Bell was born in Shelby County on January 8, 1856, and died on January 8, 1919, after distinguished service in the Philippines and in World War I. For his bravery he was awarded the Congressional Medal of Honor, only one of two ever given to a Shelby County resident. The other was awarded to Private John H. Callihan in 1861.

The fifteen charter members of Post 37 were: Herbert B. Kinsolving Jr.; Daniel O'Sullivan; Lucien Harbison; Sidney S. Smith; Robert L. Shannon Jr.; Wesley L. Burk.; R.L. Stout; George L. Willis; Henry B. McAfee; Philip R. Sleadd; Gerhard Epping; John D. Buckner; W. B. Hawkins; and John M. Turner. Other members of the post include J. Michael Casey, Orval Florence, Hubert Briscoe, Ben Staples, Callie Beard, and H. V. Tempel. Harold Y. Saunders, a 50-year member of the Post served as State Commander of the American Legion in 1965-66. In 1946 Post #37 had its all time high in membership, with a total membership of 367.

Courtesy of Charles Long.

Post #37 was named for Shelby County native Gen. James Franklin Bell. Gen. Bell is pictured at the George A. Armstrong house on Main Street after his return from serving with the Philippine Expeditionary Force, 1898-1901.

WORLD WAR II

By William E. Matthews and Mary David Myles

World War II was brought home to Shelby Countians immediately with the attack on Pearl Harbor when local newspapers reported that Roger Allen Palmer was reported missing following the sinking of the battleship U.S.S. Oklahoma.

Fortunately for Seaman Palmer and his family, he survived the sinking of the Oklahoma, but 57 other Shelby Countians would not be so lucky. They were among the 400,000 Americans from all walks of life and in all branches of the service who did not survive the war, dying in either battle or from accidents, diseases, and miscellaneous other causes.

The clouds of war had begun forming as far back as the mid-1930s with Adolf Hitler's bellicose posturing, followed in 1938 with the Nazis takeover of Austria, and on Sept. 1, 1939 with the invasion of Poland.

As country after country fell in Europe, President Franklin D. Roosevelt and the U. S. Congress, despite many expressions of isolationism from around the country, began expressing a concern that war was imminent.

Consequently, in 1940 a conscription bill was enacted in congress, and on Oct. 16, 1940, it was announced that 16.5 million men between the ages of 21 and 35, would be asked to register with their draft boards across the land. It was expected that the first 75,000 men would be in uniform by mid-November

Shelby County Clerk Lucy L. Ford was designated to provide the forms for the potential draftees, and a countywide committee was named to serve as a draft board. William Calvin Beard became the first (and, as it turned out, longtime) draft board clerk, and his face became very familiar to literally hundreds of Shelby County men.

A county-wide Civil Defense Committee was established in the fall of 1940 at the direction of the Governor of Kentucky, with Shelbyville Mayor Robert F. Matthews chosen as chairman, and W. Boyd Roe as vice-chairman. Other members of the committee included Roy S. Jones, anti-sabotage chairman; Winifield Baker, committeeman for incendiary devices and general fire safety; Mrs. Charlton Nash, health representative; Mrs. Sid Hundley, assistant health representative; and Reed Webb, chairman to detect un-American activities.

By the end of the war, 1,580 men and women from Shelby County had served in the various branches of the U. S. Armed Forces

On V-J Day, August 14, 1945, there were 1,082 Shelby County men and women in the service. The U. S. Army claimed 886, including 746 white and 140 colored. The U. S. Navy had 168 servicemen, including 149 white and 19 colored. There were 24 white U. S. Marines, and four colored. One white was serving in the U. S. Coast Guard. There was an additional 168 regulars, including 82 in the Army, 69 in the Navy, 15 Marines, and two in the Coast Guard.

Prior to the end of the war, 315 had been discharged beginning as early as January 1945.

While war was being waged on two fronts by the U. S. Armed Forces, citizens were busy in Shelby

County collecting scrap paper, metal, and rubber, raising Victory Gardens, participating in air raid drills, saving their food rationing and tire coupons, and reading the local newspapers for war news and information about local citizens who had been drafted, or had voluntarily stepped forward to serve their country.

Under the leadership of Shelby County Salvage Committee Chairman Briggs Lawson, the biggest collection of scrap metal occurred at Henry Clay High School where an estimated 50 tons of metal were estimated to have been collected in a single pile. The boys of the school, under the direction of Principal H. V. Temple, made a farm-to-farm canvas with a collection of trucks, some of which dated back to the 1920s. Fulton Smith of Simpsonville directed the unloading of trucks not only at Henry Clay, but also at other schools in the county and in Shelbyville itself.

German prisoners of war were brought back to this country on troop ships and were used to help with a severe labor problem in Shelby County. Labor was particularly scarce since so many young men had been called into service. A Shelby County Labor Committee formed to oversee the German prisoners was composed of Ben Allen Thomas, Calloway Bright, Harry Bird, Clarence Miller, George T. Kent, Judge William R. Reasor, County Agent J. W. Holland, and E. C. Alexander.

This committee's assignment was to spread the German prisoners over as wide an area as possible to get the maximum number of crops harvested.

Overall, the POWs proved very satisfactory in saving the tobacco crop in 1943, and 1944, but there were a few exceptions. One farmer reported that the prisoners, consisting principally of older men who had fought with Rommel in North Africa, objected to getting the tobacco gum on their hands, and insisted on wearing gloves.

The first German prisoner encampment was in the middle of the Eminence Fairgrounds. Later, it was moved to a location on East U. S. 60 across from where the Shelby County High School now stands. There were about 300 prisoners in the camp, which was enclosed by barbed wire. In order to provide water to the camp, prisoners were obliged to dig a waterline by hand. They were paid $3.00 per day by any farmer who received water as a consequence of their efforts. This money was then turned into the U. S. Army, which provided the POWs with spending money and personal items. The POWs were particularly adept at filling silos.

Many of the farmers provided food to the prisoners. Clarence Miller said his mother made potato salad for the prisoners who worked on the Miller farm. The POWs would pour vinegar into the water and then drink it. This was about as close as they would ever get to the Schnapps which they remembered, from Germany. Miller remembered the men as being good workers who told him that he was supporting the wrong side. The POWs worked in groups of 10, watched over by a U. S. soldier armed with a machine gun.

For several of those who stayed at home, the Kings Daughters Hospital held a Nurses Aid Class under the direction of Miss Burnice Holmes. Those who graduated included Mrs. Maurice Montgomery, Mrs. Ike Lee, Mrs. Robert Marshall, Mrs. J. B. Hudspeth, Mrs. Earl Stucker, Mrs. King Walters, Mrs. Henry Bell, Mrs. Leo Gibbs, Jane Agee, Nancy Jane Buckner, Helen Hanser, Mary Fortner, and Lee Tinsley Collins.

Three women who had served together at the Kings Daughters Hospital in Shelbyville were decorated for their coolness and bravery under artillery fire and threats of air attack. They were on the beaches at Normandy a scant 0660 hours after the D-Day Invasion began on June 6.

Courtesy of Ben Allen Thomas.

The Shelbyville War Memorial, dedicated November 11, 1983, was promoted and funded by the local Veterans of Foreign Wars post. It contains the names of men who were killed in World War I, World War II, the Korean War and the Vietnam War. The Fund-raising was headed by C.L. Love and George Pigg.

The women were 1st Lt. Margaret Hornback, daughter of Mr. and Mrs. S. R. Hornback, 1st Lt. Ora White, of Taylorsville, and 1st Lt. Gladys Martin of Mt. Eden, all of whom had enlisted as a team. They worked in an evacuation hospital in France with pre-operative and post-operative shock patients. They assisted in more than 1,800 operations during the first 16 days in France. Before being sent to France, where they were among the first nurses to land, they served in the North African and Sicilian Campaigns. On a rain-soaked field in Belgium, each of the three nurses received the Bronze Star for their extreme devotion to duty.

It would be impossible to tell the story of each of the 57 men who gave their full measure of devotion to their country in World War II. While most died as the result of enemy action, there were some who were claimed by accidents or disease. Perhaps it is good to mention several of the men as being representative of those who cared so much.

Pvt. Arvil Yeary, son of Mr. and Mrs. Neal Yeary, was the first Shelby County boy to lose his life in World War II. Arvil was the youngest of three brothers who served in the U. S. Army. He was only 20 years of age at the time he was killed in action in the southwest Pacific. His brothers, Hubert and Jasper Lloyd Yeary, survived the hostilities.

The death of Technical Sergeant Jesse G. Maddox, son of Mrs. J. G. Maddox Sr., affected the community deeply because he had been such a popular young man. The Shelby Sentinel reported that his parents were now proudly displaying a Gold Star Flag in the front window on their home.

Sgt. Maddox's plane crashed in Switzerland after being forced down by German fire following a raid deep into Nazi Germany. He had been a radio operator on a B-17 Flying Fortress participating in what was the largest raid on Munich up to that time in the war.

He and his crew were buried in Switzerland with the highest military honors. The American Ambassador to Switzerland attended, along with his wife, and other members of the consulate.

A graduate of Shelbyville High School, Sgt. Maddox had been a member of the First Baptist Church, and of the Upper Room Bible Class at the First Christian Church.

After the war, the Swiss government decided not to maintain the small beautiful cemetery in which Maddox and his crew had been buried, so Maddox's remains were brought back to Grove Hill Cemetery in Shelbyville.

Among the other losses of life were those of Joe Gordon, son of Rev. Angus and Mrs. Gordon. Rev. Gordon had been minister of the First Presbyterian Church in Shelbyville. Another loss that affected the community deeply was that of Gregory J. Biagi, killed during the last few days of the war in Europe. Young Gregory had excelled at Shelbyville High, and undoubtedly had a brilliant future ahead of him.

Also lost was Benjamin McMakin, who died when an American submarine torpedoed a Japanese vessel carrying prisoners-of-war. McMakin had been captured during the early days of the war.

Another casualty of the war was Paul Barnett, son of Mr. and Mrs. Victor Barnett of Bagdad. An instructor in instrument flight training, Barnett lost his life in a training accident in Texas. His first cousin, Lt. W. Thompson Kent, a ferrying pilot, was lost on a flight from Great Falls, Montana, to Alaska.

These are but a few of the very personal losses which Shelby County suffered during the war.

Several others from Shelby County were luckier. One of those was George N. Busey Jr., also from Bagdad, who narrowly escaped death when his P-51 Mustang collided with another plane over Bradenton, Florida. Both pilots bailed out, and Lt. Busey was injured when he landed. But he survived the war to become one of Shelby County's leading farmers and citizens.

African-American citizens also made a significant contribution to the war effort. Among those were the four sons of Jim Wooten, a tenant farmer living on the farm of Steve Hornback. Leonard Wooten was an Army Mess Sergeant in Louisiana, Austin and George saw action in New Guinea, and William, the youngest, served in the U. S. Marine Corps. All four returned to Shelbyville after the war, and all are now buried in the Saffell Cemetery on North 7th Street.

Among ministers who served during the war, none was more heroic than Chaplain Thomas N. Giltner, who had served the First Christian Church in Shelbyville as Minster prior to volunteering for service.

Giltner was singled out by the U. S. War Department for his efforts during the Saipan Island invasion. His citation stated, "Of his own volition, Chaplain Giltner went forward to the front line to bring comfort and aid to the wounded and dying, and to locate and recover the bodies of the dead, despite the fact that he was constantly under heavy sniper and machine gun fire. The conduct of Chaplain Giltner throughout the entire operation was a source of inspiration to all persons and reflects great credit on himself and the military service." Chaplain Giltner was in the front lines on 18 of the 24 days in which his comrades saw action.

In a dramatic message to his wife Margaret and to members of the church, Giltner wrote, "Seeing starving, dirty, and wounded women and children, day after day, trapped by opposing fire, thank God the war is here and not at home. This is a devastated island, destruction is complete. I'd give a million to be in Shelbyville tonight." Giltner was awarded the Bronze Star for his bravery.

Another man who saw extensive service during the war was Edwin W. Hall, who would come home and become one of Shelby County's most influential businessmen and civic leaders. Hall was seriously wounded in action in France during D-Day, being among the first troops to hit the beach.

Corp. Robert Proctor, son of Mr. and Mrs. Clarence Proctor, was another hero of the European fighting, wining the Silver Star for braving extremely heavy enemy fire and land mines to render aid to the wounded and dying.

The names of the 57 men who did not come back from the war included Paul T. Barnett, Carlisle Barrickman Jr., Julius Beecham, Gregory Biagi, William P. Brooks, Walter Brown Jr., Francis M. Carpenter, James M. Coleman, William D. Collings, Samuel Collins, L. Bailey Cowherd, Forest W. Crider, G. Thurston Dawson, Howard C. Dempsey, William H. Edgar, Roy I. Figg, Raymond E. Floyd, Lewis S. Frederick, Jr., Homer Gaddie, Everett E. Goins. and William I. Goodrich.

Also, Joe Gordon, Joseph Greenwell, Charles E. Hawkins, Robert W. Hodson, Noble Hundley, James B. Jackson, W. Thompson Kent, Fred J. Kurtz, Rufus C. Litton, Jesse G. Maddox Jr., Boyd Mahoney, Garnett Martin, Louis G. Martin, James McBride, Earl T. McDonald, Benjamin L. McMakin, John G. Merchant, Marvin Murphy, Robert G. Newton, Jesse T. Parido, Elmo D. Perry, Allen Phillips, Lawrence H. Rogers, Nevel Rodgers, Glen H. Roney, James V. Samples, Robert H. Scott, Herbert W. Shaw, E. Raymond Sorrel, Phillip Sleadd Jr., William I. Temple, Roy P. Tindall, John W. Wheatley, and J. Arvil Yeary.

THE PRISONER OF WAR PROGRAM

By Clarence L. Miller

One of the less known accomplishments of the Shelby County Farm Bureau was the Prisoner of War Program. With World War II in full swing in Europe and the Pacific, just about all the manpower of the country was engaged. Shelby County farmers found it difficult to find labor to fill silos and cut hay and tobacco when ironically the United States Army came to the rescue.

In 1942-43 the Nazis were defeated in North Africa, and thousands of prisoners fell into American hands. They were the pride of the German army. Far too dangerous to be left anywhere near the battlefield, they were brought to encampments at Fort Knox, Kentucky, and other army compounds in the South.

Idleness spelled trouble so the operators of these encampments conceived the idea of putting prisoners of war to work on farms. However, these men could not be left alone to wander about unguarded and the army could not actually supervise their work. Some responsible agency had to be found to provide the necessary supervision.

The farmers' own organization, the Farm Bureau, was the answer. The army contracted with it to do the job. It furnished the enclosed compound, equipped it with shelter (in the form of tents), supplied water, electricity, food, and the necessary guards. The prisoners themselves did all the housekeeping and cooking. Farmers paid the Farm Bureau about $1.50 per day per man. In turn, the Farm Bureau paid the army, and it paid a small part of this sum to the individual prisoner.

In 1943, a central compound or prisoner of war camp was established at the Eminence Fairgrounds to serve all the surrounding counties. Calloway Bright, the President of the Shelby County Farm Bureau, committed it to utilize at least 10 groups consisting of 10 Prisoners of War ("POWs" as they came to be known) each.

A farmer had to furnish transportation from the compound to his or her farm, usually in high-sided cattle trucks. Ten POWs had one guard with a submachine gun. The guard was to be the interpreter, for none of these Germans spoke English, or so it was thought. Some POWs spoke it, although they did not want it known.

The first day of operation was in late-August 1943 at tobacco suckering time. Although it was difficult to explain what needed to be done and how to do it, the prisoners quickly learned to cut tobacco, house it, and later to fill silos. The experiment lasted only the one season, but while it did, it was a great success.

KOREAN WAR

By Roger Green Jr.

For years known as the "Forgotten War," coming on the heels of World War II and followed quickly by the Vietnam War, the Korean War has often been overlooked by the American people. However, the Shelby County community once again answered the call of this nation and provided many young men to the military.

On June 25, 1950, around Kaesong, the ancient Korean capital, the North Korean Army poured across the border and began pushing the under equipped South Korean troops southward. By June 28, the North Korean troops had captured Seoul, the South Korean capital, and had the South Korean Army retreating.

President Harry S. Truman, realizing that South Korea desperately needed help, ordered United States troops into Korea on July 1. The United Nations with the support of the United States organized a multi-national army, commanded by General Douglas MacArthur to stop the attack by North Korea. However, by the end of July, the UN forces had nearly been pushed into the sea around Pusan. Within this Pusan area there were some 140,000 troops making a last ditch effort to save South Korea. In September, General MacArthur launched a counterattack at Inchon that finally resulted in recapturing Seoul and pushing the North Korean Army back to the 38th Parallel. The UN forces continued to advance into North Korea and pushed to the Yalu River, the border between North Korea and China.

On November 25, the Chinese attacked and forced the UN forces to retreat to the port of Hungnam. Fighting continued throughout the winter and into the spring of 1951. Peace talks began in July 1951 and lasted for more than two years. Fighting continued along a stationary battlefront near the 38th Parallel. On July 27, 1953, after two years of peace negotiations, the armistice was signed.

By nationality, the military deaths were United States, 54,246; South Korea, 415,004; other UN members, 3,094. Of the 5.72 million United States troops that served in the Korean War, 123,000 were from Kentucky. In addition to the 868 Kentuckians killed in battle, 157 died of other causes, and 2,545 received nonfatal wounds.

Eight young soldiers of Shelby County died for their country in this conflict. Their names are etched on the war monument in Veterans Park, across from the Shelby County Courthouse.

Pfc. Edward Julian Wilson was Shelby County's first Korean War casualty. Serving in the U.S. Army with the 9th Infantry Regiment, 23rd Infantry Division, he was killed in action on September 24, 1950. His father, Lewis Wilson of Bagdad, and his grandparents, Mr. and Mrs. Robert Wilson of Hatton, survived him.

Corporal Charles Lindberg Miller lost his life on November 4, 1950, while serving with the 70th Tank, 1st Cavalry Division. His wife, the former Jeane Scearce of Finchville; his parents, Mr. and Mrs. G.W. Miller, Snow Hill; two brothers, Roe and Ollie Miller; two sisters, Mrs. Eddie Berry, Louisville and Mrs. Wallace Kent, survived him. Cpl. Miller had graduated from Shelbyville High School in 1947 where he had been a member of the football team and was active as a scout leader with Troop 161.

Spfc. Charles H. McAtee was listed as missing in action on December 1, 1950, and subsequently presumed dead by the Department of Defense as of December 31, 1950. PFC McAtee arrived in Korea on October 25, 1950, and served in the 503rd Artillery Battalion (155mm), 2nd Infantry Division. He was a graduate of the Shelbyville Colored School, Lincoln Institute, and attended the Paducah Trade School. He was the son of Mr. and Mrs. Clarence McAtee of Shelbyville.

Pfc. John William Payne, serving with the 8th Cavalry Regiment, 1st Cavalry Division, was killed in action on January 1, 1951. His parents, William and Lucille Payne of the Chestnut Grove area, survived him.

Madison B. McAtee, a member of the 15th Infantry Regiment, 3rd Infantry Division, was killed in action on February 3, 1951. He was the second son of Mr. and Mrs. Clarence McAtee to die in the war. He enlisted in the Army on May 23, 1950.

Pfc. Willie Beckley, a member of the 159th Artillery Battalion (105mm), 25th Infantry Division, was killed in action on May 24, 1951. His mother Katie Beckley survived him.

Lieutenant Robert Hardin Giltner lost his life in Korea in an aircraft accident on November 15, 1952. He was the son of Mr. and Mrs. Robert M. Giltner. Lt. Giltner was also a veteran of World War II.

First Lieutenant Harold Egbert Rogers, flight instructor, lost his life on February 22, 1954, in a flight training accident at Webb Air Force Base, Big Springs, Texas. A Korean War veteran with over nine years of military service, he was decorated with the Distinguished Flying Cross and had over 120 combat missions. He was a graduate of Gleneyrie High School. His wife Fay Lurine and three children survived him.

VIETNAM WAR

By Roger Green Jr.

The Vietnam War was the longest in our nation's history. The 1954 Geneva Accords divided the Southeast Asian country of Vietnam into North and South Vietnam. Soon thereafter, Communist North Vietnam began a guerrilla war against South Vietnam. The Republic of South Vietnam sought American advice and assistance in the mid-1950s, and Americans were soon involved. The first two Americans died on July 8, 1959, and the advisory effort, which grew rapidly in the early 1960s, led to full-scale deployment of American armed forces by order of President Lyndon B. Johnson in 1965. The Vietnam War increased in intensity from an advisory effort to a limited conventional war involving more than 2.7 million Americans who served in the war zone. More than 58,000 lost their lives; 300,000 were wounded, with approximately 80,000 severely wounded. Of the casualties, about 2,400 remain missing. America never formally declared war, and the resulting ambiguous political nature of this conflict created uncertainty at home, as well as in Vietnam.

Negotiations to end United States involvement began in 1968 and were concluded in January 1973. The resulting treaty, or Peace Accord, was signed by representatives of the United States, the Democratic Republic of Vietnam (North Vietnam), the Republic of Vietnam (South Vietnam), and the Provisional Revolutionary Government (Viet Cong). By its terms, an in-place cease-fire was ordered on January 28, 1973, and all American troops (except those assigned to the U.S. Embassy) were withdrawn two months later. In the spring of 1975, the North Vietnamese Army (NVA) launched a full-scale conventional armor and infantry attack on the South. On April 30, 1975, NVA tanks entered Saigon and the Republic of Vietnam had fallen.

Approximately 125,000 of Kentucky's sons and daughters served in the United States Armed Forces during the Vietnam era. 1,068 Kentuckians either gave their lives or are still missing. The first two Kentucky deaths occurred in 1961 and the last Kentuckian was killed during the American evacuation in 1975. Shelby County lost fourteen young men in the war. Some were born and raised here and others had moved to the community with their families. They were part of this community and their sacrifice to their nation will never be forgotten.

The following gave their lives in the Vietnam War:

Sgt. Paul J. McGaughey Jr., the first Shelby County soldier to die in Vietnam, was killed by sniper fire on December 5, 1966. He was serving as a tank commander with M Troop, 3rd Squadron, 11th Armored Cavalry on an operation in the Xuan Loc Province.

Sp4 Benjamin Luther Barrick, 21, was killed about 1:30 p.m. Sunday, April 16, 1967, when the light truck he was driving ran over a land mine. Barrick was a bulldozer operator with C Company, 1st Engineer Battalion, 1st Infantry Division, who was working on a landing strip about sixty miles north of Saigon. He enlisted in the Army in July 7, 1966, and took basic training at Fort Knox and later was sent to Fort Leonard Wood, Missouri for his engineer training. He attended Shelbyville High School and worked as a flower arranger and delivery person for Bowles-Martin Florist.

Pfc. Charles Ira Carter died in the U.S. hospital in Japan on Sunday, July 16, 1967. The 20-year-old soldier suffered head injuries when the tank he was driving struck a land mine near Saigon on May 18, 1967. He was participating in "Operation Junction City," at that time the largest military operation to occur in Vietnam. While under treatment in a Vietnam hospital he developed encephalitis and was transferred to the hospital in Japan on June 8. Pfc. Carter developed pneumonia and died from this illness. Pfc. Carter attended Henry County High School and later worked at Briel Industries in Shelbyville. A rifleman in the Headquarter Company, 2nd Battalion, 2nd Infantry, 1st Infantry Division, he entered the Army last August 1966 and received his basic training at Fort Knox, Kentucky.

Cpl. James Leonard Travis Jr. died November 22, 1967, as a result of gunshot wounds received during hostile ground action. He was assigned to A Company, 3rd Battalion, 22nd Infantry, 25th Infantry Division, Vietnam. Cpl. Travis was a 19-year-old graduate of Shelby County High School class of 1966. After graduation he was employed at General Electric Appliance Park in Louisville until called to active duty on March 15, 1967.

Sgt. Hubert E. Waford, 20, was killed April 12, 1968, while on a night patrol with his unit in Vietnam. He was assigned to D Company, 3rd Battalion, 22nd Infantry, 25th Infantry Division. He enlisted March 15, 1967, and received his basic training at Fort Knox and began his tour in Vietnam August 22, 1967. In November 1967 he escorted the body of Cpl. James Leonard Travis back to Shelbyville. They had enlisted on the buddy plan. The first of December 1967 he returned to Vietnam where he served with honors until his death. He was a graduate of Shelby County High School. Sgt. Waford was awarded posthumously the Silver Star Medal for heroism and gallantry, the Bronze Star Medal for heroism, the second award an Oak Leaf Cluster for heroism, the Purple Heart and the Good Conduct Medal. He had previously been awarded the Combat Infantryman Badge, the National Defense Service Medal, Vietnam Campaign Ribbon, Vietnam Service Medal and the Sharpshooter Badge.

1stLt. Stanley Garfield Lawson, 25, a Marine Corps helicopter pilot, was killed September 21, 1968, in Quang Tri Province, Vietnam. He received multiple wounds to the body sustained when his aircraft received hostile rifle fire while departing a hot landing zone causing the aircraft to crash and burn. He graduated from Shelbyville High School and Union College, Barbourville, Kentucky, where he received his B.S. degree. He entered the Marine Corps in October 1966. He received his flight wings from Helicopter Training Squadron Eight, Elyson Field, Pensacola, Florida, on March 26, 1968.

Pfc. Douglas Melvin Allen, 18, United States Marine Corps, was killed in action on Monday, December 9, 1968, while on patrol in Quang Nam Province, Vietnam. Born in Shelbyville, he moved to Washington, D.C. in 1958 and attended Cardozo High School. Burial was in Arlington National Cemetery.

Sgt. Edwin Howard Hardestry Jr., 22, was killed in action on February 16, 1969, while serving as a machine gunner with C Company, 4th Battalion, 47th Infantry, Stn Infantry Division, in the Mekong Delta region of Vietnam. He had recently been awarded the Bronze Star Medal for heroism in combat against a hostile force, and the Combat Infantry Badge. He had returned to Shelbyville the previous year as an escort for the body of his brother-in-law 1st Lt. Stanley Lawson, killed in action on September 21, 1968. Sgt. Hardesty had graduated from Shelbyville High School and attended Western Kentucky University before entering the Army.

Pfc. William Porter Thompson Jr., 23, was killed in action on March 27, 1969, while serving as a rifleman with C Company, 2nd Battalion, 3911 Infantry, 9th Infantry Division, in the Mekong Delta region. He graduated from Shelbyville High School and from Centre College in Danville in 1968. Pfc. Thompson entered military service August 12, 1968, and arrived in Vietnam on January 19, 1969. He was married December 21, 1968.

Pfc. James (Jimmy) Yates, 20, was killed in action in Vietnam on September 9, 1969. He entered the Army March 1969 and arrived in Vietnam in August 1969. He was a graduate of Taylorsville High School and a member of Briar Ridge Christian Church.

Sgt. Troy Hillis Batterton, 21, was killed in action on April 8, 1970, while serving with B Company, 6th Battalion, 31st Infantry, 9th Infantry Division, in the Mekong Delta region of Vietnam. He entered the Army April 14, 1969, and arrived in Vietnam on March 15, 1970.

Sp4 Lanny Wilson Banta, 22, died January 29, 1969, from wounds he received while in a combat operation with B Company, 2nd Battalion, 3rd Infantry, 199th Light Infantry Brigade. He entered the Army July 14, 1967, and arrived in Vietnam on April 5, 1968.

Commander Robert Donald Kemper, 37, was killed on March 3, 1971, in a flight training accident near the Naval Air Station, McCain Field, Meridian, Mississippi. Commander Kemper graduated from Shelbyville High School and the U.S. Naval Academy in 1956 and received his Navy wings in September 1957. He also did graduate work in engineering at George Washington University. He was a veteran of Vietnam with 256 missions over that country. As a result of his missions in Vietnam, he had won 46 citations for his bravery and service including 2 Distinguished Flying Crosses, 27 Air Medals, 7 Navy Commendation Medals and 3 Vietnamese Air Crosses for gallantry.

Cpl. Phillip Scott Glass, 20, was killed in action May 14, 1971, while serving with A Company, 3rd Battalion, 20th Infantry, 23rd Infantry Division (American). Cpl. Glass was a graduate of Shelby County High School, the class of 1968. He entered the Army on August 3, 1970, and took his basic training at Fort Knox. He later went to Fort Polk, Louisiana, and was sent to Vietnam on December 29, 1970.

Shelbyville native Barney Bright in his Louisville studio.

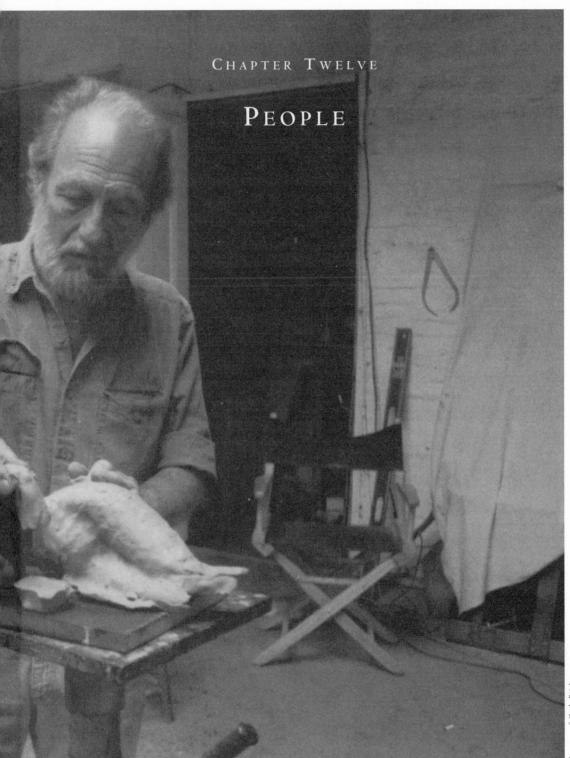

CHAPTER TWELVE

PEOPLE

Courtesy of Gayle Bright.

COLORFUL CHARACTERS OF SHELBY COUNTY

By Byron Crawford

T he colorful characters of Shelby County have been so numerous that if all were given a page in its history, they would likely fill this book. Space constrains us to offer the following brief sketches of some of the county's more colorful personalities who, by nature of their nicknames or particular eccentricities, have ascended to folk-hero status.

Insufficient information was available for profiles of some deserving characters, and at least one living character was omitted at his request. The sketches presented were compiled from interviews with, or statements from, friends or acquaintances of the characters profiled. In many instances, ages and dates of people and events could not be recalled with clarity and were estimated by our sources.

MARSHALL THURMAN "DANGER" CRAIG. Craig lived in northern Shelby County in a cabin near Six Mile Creek for many years during the early and mid 1900s. Danger's range was generally in the area around Bagdad, Christiansburg, Elmburg, Jacksonville, Shelbyville, and occasionally Frankfort.

The origin of Danger's nickname was a mystery to most who knew him. The late Rufus Harrod, whose family lived near Danger during the 1930s, could never get Danger to reveal how he came to have the nickname. But Danger did tell Harrod that he had a brother in Frankfort whose nickname was "Lightning."

Danger subsisted mostly by hunting and fishing, and by the generosity of neighbors who often shared with him their garden and farm produce. He was of muscular build and had exceptional strength.

Julian K. Wood, the former postmaster at Bagdad, who lived just up Six Mile Creek from Danger, remembered that Danger came walking down Six Mile Creek one day with a wringer type Maytag washing machine tied on his back.

"He had carried the washing machine nearly three miles over rough terrain, and he stood there and talked to us for I don't know how long and never did set the washing machine down," Wood said.

Rufus Harrod recalled having seen Danger on numerous occasions tie large shocks of fodder on his back and carry them back to his place—just over one mile away from their farm—to feed his cow. "It was something to see, because you couldn't see anything but just his legs. Cars would stop to let him by," said Harrod.

Although Danger was not inclined toward steady work, he took some pride in digging wells and cisterns around the community, and earned a reputation for his trade.

He was digging a cistern for his half-brother, Tom, one day when Rufus Harrod and his father heard a commotion and rushed to investigate. They found that part of the cistern wall had caved in burying Danger almost to his shoulders. In an effort to rescue him, Tom had looped a log chain around Danger's neck and was trying to pull him out with a mule.

"Danger would plead and pray for a while, then he'd cuss a while," said Harrod. Finally, rescuers placed a large bucket over Danger's head to prevent him from suffocating if there was another cave-in, then they dug him out.

Harrod could recall that Danger once built a model of an unsinkable lifeboat, and might have patented the idea had not the identical design already been patented some 60 years earlier.

Julian Wood remembered that Danger experimented extensively with a contraption that he built on Six Mile Creek that he claimed was a perpetual motion machine. "The first time the creek got up, it washed away the contraption, and the perpetual motion dream never materialized," Wood said.

Wood remembered that Danger had a large, antique, handmade "dough tray" or "bread bowl," made of buckeye, that everyone who saw it tried to buy. But Danger would never sell the heirloom.

"That was my mother's, and I'm going to keep it," Wood could recall Danger saying. "But one cold morning he got up and didn't have any wood to start a fire with, and he chopped up that dough tray to start a fire. He would grab anything available to start a fire," said Wood. "He chopped up every one of his chairs and what little furniture he had for kindling, and wound up sitting on old beehives."

Danger was married twice and had three daughters. He eventually moved to Frankfort and became a street preacher in later life. His date of death and place of burial could not be found.

OLD FOLKS. Chester "Old Folks" Eden of Bagdad was a small man, but a tough one. During his early years he had worked on a farm and at stores around Bagdad. But for about the last 20 years of his life, he helped with wrecker runs and other odd jobs around a service station in Bagdad and salvage yard near town that both were owned by Clarence Yount.

Although Yount tried to keep "Folks" warmly dressed and well-fed, Old Folks was his own man, and his misadventures with strong drink often caused him some difficulty. He often slept in the service station or in a room at the salvage yard. One winter two of his toes froze and had to be removed. He carried them around with him in a paper sack for a while, showing them to anyone who would look. One night at the salvage yard he riddled the door with a shotgun blast, thinking someone was trying to break in.

Old Folks didn't talk much, but he could be witty on occasions, and most everyone around Bagdad liked him.

Clarence Yount said he never found out how Old Folks got his nickname. A stranger in Bagdad, looking at a piece of property nearby, saw Old Folks sitting on a doorstep in the middle of town one summer afternoon and stopped to ask some questions. He noticed the train tracks ran right through the middle of town and asked Folks if the trains blew their whistles much while passing through. "Hell no, they don't blow," Folks replied. "When you see the (SOBS) coming, you've just got to get out of the way." Old Folks died in 1984 at about age 69. He is buried in the Bagdad Cemetery.

FLETCH. Fletcher "Fletch" White was among Southern Shelby County's most well known characters from the early 1950s to the early 1990s. He was of medium height and build with sharp features. He wore glasses, and usually dressed in clean bib overalls, work shirts buttoned at the neck, work shoes, and a cap, and he generally carried a good pair of work gloves with him.

Gloves were important to Fletch. He mentioned them often in conversation, and he liked to wear them. Years before he died, he would tell friends that he had put aside six new pairs of gloves for his pall-bearers to wear when they laid him to rest. He said he wanted to be buried in a Hart-Shaffner & Marx suit.

Funerals were also important to Fletch, and he often showed up at one of the funeral homes in Shelbyville for the funeral of someone he didn't know. He dressed in a suit when he went to funerals, and he either walked or depended on someone giving him a ride every place he went. Those with whom he caught rides could always expect the conversation to touch on gloves and funerals at some point. Fletch once remarked to his friend, artist Whitie Gray, that he'd sure like to go to cowboy star Gene Autrey's funeral; that he bet it would be something to see.

Often, Fletch would review the funerals he had been to in recent weeks, with particular emphasis on the crowds. If he went to a funeral that was poorly attended, he would be disturbed about it for months. He loved old marbles, particularly the stone variety, and kept hundreds of them hidden in socks, boxes and cans.

Almost all the local population knew Fletch and liked him, so it was never much trouble for him to catch a ride to Shelbyville or home to Southville. From the early 1950s for almost forty years Fletch lived with Jay and Bessie Mae Carriss who farmed and operated the store in Southville. Fletch helped Jay some on the farm and was treated as a member of the family by the Carrisses. He was never married.

When Fletch died in 1991, though he had virtually no family left, hundreds of people turned out either to pay their respects during the visitation at Shannon Funeral Home or for the funeral at Salem Baptist Church near Southville, where he is buried in the church cemetery. Six pallbearers wearing new gloves laid him to rest in a Hart-Shaffner & Marx suit.

ERNEST "WALKING" FORD—a.k.a. "Kentucky" Ernie Ford. Ford moved into Danger Craig's old cabin on Six Mile Creek after Danger had moved away to Frankfort, probably in the late 1960s or early 1970s.

Ford was of medium build, with dark complexion. He kept a menagerie of poultry, livestock and pets, and was often known to hitch rides with people in the community while carrying a goose, a pigeon, or some other bird or animal he had acquired in his travels.

He walked almost everywhere he went, often pulling a cart loaded with odds and ends, or carrying his day's acquisitions in coffee sacks on his back. One day in Shelbyville he got two large sacks full of coal, which he attempted to carry back to his place on Six Mile Creek some 13 miles from Shelbyville.

"He couldn't carry both sacks of coal at the same time, so he'd carry one sack a little piece and set it down, then he'd walk back and get the other sack, and carry it a little piece and set it down," said Wood. "He finally got home with both sacks of coal."

During one December tobacco stripping season, when farmers were paying $2 a day for strippers, Ford worked a few days, then decided he had a better idea for making $2 a day.

He began cutting cedar trees on the surrounding hillsides and taking them to Shelbyville, two trees at a time, pulling them in the cart and selling them for 50 cents apiece in town. Then he would return to Six Mile, get two more cedars, take them back to Shelbyville and sell them for 50 cents each. "He thought that was a better way to make $2 than standing in the same spot stripping tobacco all day," Wood said.

During a television interview in the mid-1970s, Ford insisted that he was a cousin of the late Tennessee Ernie Ford, a popular singer and television personality of the 1950s and `60s, but most of his neighbors didn't put much stock in his claim.

Occasionally, Ford would offer the *Sentinel News* in Shelbyville an article that he had written about his adventures or life on Six Mile Creek, several of which the newspaper published.

Ford was married and had children. He moved to Franklin County in later life and died in 1984 at age 76. He is buried in the Bagdad Cemetery.

JIMMY HEDDEN. Hedden and his red bicycle were nearly inseparable. Over the years they came to be a familiar part of street life in Shelbyville. Jimmy was of heavy build with a round face. He wore glasses and, in later years, a helmet while riding his bike. Not surprisingly, pranksters often hid his bike.

If he had not suffered brain damage from rheumatic fever as a child, Jimmy might well have turned out to be a motorcycle policeman. Instead, he patrolled Shelbyville's streets on his bike, usually carrying with him something resembling a policeman's ticket book, which he used for writing "tickets" to parking violators. He often tipped police with information concerning crimes in the area and wrote down the license numbers of parking violators for the police to cite.

Among his favorite assignments was directing traffic at busy intersections when a funeral procession was passing through town or church services let out, or sometimes when the fire truck was leaving the station. He always joined in parades, making sounds like a siren, for people to get out of the way. One of his favorite places to loaf was at the fire station. If the fire wasn't too far away, he often rode his bike to the fire scene.

Several years before he died, friends around town rallied to keep him from having to move to Pittsburgh, Pennsylvania, to live with his sister. Jimmy's mother, with whom he had been living, died, and Jimmy understood that his sister was to be his new guardian. He cried when he learned that he might have to move, and told several of the town's people that he didn't want to go. Circuit Judge William Stewart intervened in the matter and arranged for Jimmy to remain in Shelbyville. He died at Colonial Hall Manor in Shelbyville in December of 1996 at the age of 60.

ELLIOTT "WILDMAN" LOWERY. Lowery was a colorful personality in the Simpsonville community during the mid-1900s. There was in those days a tavern located between what later became the entrance to Purnell Sausage Company and the nearby Old Stone Inn. "Wildman had been known to ride his horse into that tavern," recalled Hobie Henninger who remembered Lowery. "He rode a motorcycle in there once, too, I was told."

Wildman was a self-employed carpenter and painter during most of the years that Henninger knew him. He rode a motorcycle with a sidecar for several years, and carried his ladders tied to the sidecar.

In appearance, he was remembered as resembling the typical western cowboy—slender and weather-beaten, with graying hair in the 1950s.

Henninger's grandmother taught Wildman in Sunday school—probably in the 1920s before Lowery earned the nickname, "Wildman."

Henninger used to talk with him during the 1950s at an appliance store across from the old Simpsonville High School. Henninger had a part-time job at the store after school.

"Wildman was well known, and did get a little rowdy at times, but he was always employed and always worked, and he always had a good time," said Henninger. "I heard about him shooting up a place one time." "Wildman was all I ever heard the other men call him when I was a kid, but my mother called him Elliott," said Henninger. Circumstances of Wildman's later life were not available.

AMOS MURPHY. Amos Murphy was the janitor at Shelbyville Elementary School during the mid-1900s and was described by Shelby County artist, builder, designer and historian W. Whitie Gray as an incurable practical joker. Gray was a student at the school and witnessed many of Murphy's jokes firsthand. As he grew older, he often acted as an accomplice.

Murphy was tall and slim and walked with a limp. He did not drive an automobile, and lived across from the school. He and his friends would pitch horseshoes in the schoolyard during good weather. Murphy had a cluttered workshop in the school's furnace room where he made doo-dads out of wood scraps and planned many of his pranks.

He loved to startle people, and he took delight in tying a black fishing line onto an old dirty rag, looping the line around a nearby post or tree, then hiding in the distance and dragging the rag across the sidewalk in front of unsuspecting passersby.

"One of his favorite pranks," Gray recalled, "was to place a garden hose in the grass beside a sidewalk, in a dark area under a tree. When the passerby reached that spot, Amos would make a sound like a mad dog in his end of the hose, where he lay hidden. There were different reactions, but generally the frightened person would jump off the curb and take to their heels."

Amos liked to play jigs on a fiddle and would often dial phone numbers at random, Gray remembered. "He would say, 'Hello, if you'll hang on a minute I'll play you a little tune.' And he'd play 'Old Joe Clark' or 'Back Up and Push,' or some other old fiddle tune," said Gray. "He never signed off, just hung up the phone. I wondered if anybody ever listened."

A pioneer cemetery was located in a corner of the library yard, and Amos and Gray decided they'd play a prank on people walking through the yard near the cemetery at night. They made a life-sized dummy out of burlap and fixed a strong line around its neck to lower the dummy from a tree above the cemetery path. Then they hid some distance from the path and waited.

Finally, a couple known for their roughness came walking up the path, arguing with each other as they walked. Amos and Gray waited until the two were almost under the dummy, then dropped it from the tree. It swung onto the shoulders of the man, who was walking a few feet behind the woman. He let out a moan and stumbled backwards.

But the woman turned with a loud profanity, pulled up her dress, drew a knife or straight razor from her stocking top and began cursing and slashing at the dummy's head and upper body, yelling for the pranksters to show themselves so she could give them the same treatment.

"We never used the dummy anymore after that," Gray said. "It would have probably taken two days to have sewed him up anyway."

AFRICAN-AMERICANS

By Duanne Puckett

The majority of African-Americans have always experienced discrimination, hardship, and hurt. Yet, they stuck together as a community because of their faith, their families, and their desire to be better than those who went before them. In Shelby County that desire stemmed from growing up in areas such as Martinsville, Bradshaw, Johnsonville, Henry Clay, Bunker Hill, Cabin Town, Buck Town, and Montclair. They were all-black neighborhoods, some of which were built on former dumps and most of which were without indoor plumbing or electricity for many years. But in those places they were like one huge family, an extended number of caregivers who kept a watchful eye out for youngsters. Their stories, recorded at the end of the twentieth century, reveal a place of segregation, hope, and fear.

One 90-year-old who was born in the Finchville area has vivid memories of the Ku Klux Klan. "There would be times they simply wouldn't let us have food or burning wood," he said of the town's storekeepers. "And my folks never went out past dark." As a result his family moved to Shelbyville to escape such hardships.

Once they moved, the tension seemed to ease but the discrimination did not. One woman never darkened the door of the Shelby County Public Library until she was 69 years old because of an incident that occurred when she was a child. There were no reference books in the all-black school, so she went to the library where she said "they refused to let me in, said my people were not welcome there. That was a hurt I never got over."

All remembered walking to Bohn's Creamery at Second and Washington Streets for ice cream, knowing they could not stay inside to eat it. Similarly a 53-year-old remembered the Chatham Clinic on South Sixth Street awarding good patients with coupons for free ice cream at Begley's Drug Store at Sixth and Main Streets. "We could get the ice cream but never eat it at the counter like everyone else."

Even the downtown movie houses had their segregated seating areas for blacks located in the balcony where the springs punched through the cushions and there were no vents for the air conditioning. "We even waded through trash because they didn't clean it as regularly as they did the downstairs," said one African-American recalling those days. However, movies were an escape for blacks and whites. One woman remembered an elderly gentleman going to his first picture show. "He always carried a revolver and when the cowboy Buck Jones lost his gun during a shoot-out, the man stood up in the movie and yelled, 'Here, Buck, take mine!' "

A family of six girls lived within one block of the city school, yet they had to attend Lincoln Institute near Simpsonville. They waited in the Byrd Coal Company yard for the bus, rain or shine, heat or cold. "I think the only reason we were allowed inside when it rained or snowed, though, was because our daddy bought coal from Mr. Byrd. I can remember going right by that white school every day, knowing I could not go in," recalled one student.

Riding the bus didn't seem much of a luxury either since a kerosene heater sat in the middle of the aisle. "It's a wonder we didn't all burn up," a classmate said. That school bus would have been a luxury

Shelby County Public Library, Williams Studio photograph.

A cakewalk competition at the Shelby County Fairgrounds sponsored by the African-American community, n.d.

to most blacks in the early days because very few had any form of transportation. One man walked from Johnsonville to town once a week on Saturday. And church was the only form of entertainment and education for others. "My mother was blind so I had to stay home," said one 90-year-old woman. "I cried to go to school but I learned more in those years I did go than some who went to higher grades. They taught me Roman numerals, geography, and penmanship."

Ironically, the majority of those who experienced school integration called it "the worst thing that happened to blacks." Among the many comments supporting this belief are the following: "We didn't have black teachers who cared about you or understood you. And black students today are at somewhat of a disadvantage because some teachers went during those early integration days when relationships were not so good. Then there are those parents who did not have a good experience in school, so they pass along that negativity to their children." "Some teachers were simply cruel to us. Some students spit on us, called us "nigger" and told us to go back where we came from. Then when we did go back home after school, some blacks said we were simply trying to be white." "The guys seemed to get along better in school because they played sports. And those with lighter complexion and more money were more accepted too." "When we went to join clubs, the clubs surprisingly were canceled. I was eligible to win the Latin award and they didn't give one that year. Then I was up for the French I award but they only gave French II." "In all my years of going to city schools, I can remember only one white parent who invited me to their house when we were seniors in high school."

The one 90-year-old mother whose eight children went to Lincoln Institute made sure they could all count to 100 and write their name and alphabet before they ever stepped foot inside a classroom. "We prayed about it and I kept a broomstick with me to scoot them onto the bus every day. I didn't stand for any excuses," she said.

A much younger woman who attended Lincoln remembered "getting a tanning if I arrived at school without my satchel. Yet, my father could not read or write. He wanted better things for me."

Education meant better living conditions and better jobs than those traditionally opened to African-Americans. Most agreed that blacks were known for their domestic positions. The 90-year-old laughed and said she got a job ironing dresses for 50 cents apiece because a white woman saw all these clothes hanging on the line in mint condition. "She didn't know they belonged to my six sons! I'd do all the wash at night and pour the water out on the street to not get caught. Then wait for the sun to get hot the next day to dry all those thirty pair of underwear. I'd pay a $1 round-trip to ride the bus to Louisville to a second-hand shop on Walnut Street (now Muhammad Ali Blvd.) where all the rich people would bring in their discards. I'd wash and boil them, iron them, fold back the collars, make them look brand new. So that's how I got a 50-cent job that I thought was big money!"

Others said, "Black men and women played a major part in domestic work and nurturing other people's children. White teens were better and contributing to that were the many black women in their homes."

Yet, the sting of white versus black runs deep as one woman remembers her father helping with the mortar, clay and brick to build the swimming pool knowing his own children could not swim there. One man could take the mail from Louisville to the depot because he owned a wagon, yet he could not deliver the mail to a person's house because he was black. If blacks had serious illnesses, they were treated at King's Daughters Hospital on Henry Clay Street. Otherwise, they received treatment at the Daisy M. Saffell Memorial Hospital.

Most blacks came to Shelbyville despite the prejudices because of the work that was available. Some even started jobs at the age of 9. "I had to stand on a box to hand out items" in the grocery store, said one. "I learned to cook, keep house, stock coal furnaces before I eventually finished high school and went to work at the Old Mason's Home farm. That's the worse job I ever had, milking those cows," he said.

Others went to work in the homes, restaurants, tobacco redryers, and even the handful of black establishments. Some remembered the Lucky 8 Club where dances attracted Chuck Berry and Ike and Tina Turner before they were famous.

Black tenant farmers ended up in Detroit to make money in the factories during the Great Depression. "They would send money back here to keep the family afloat," one remembered. Some remembered others being escorted to the county poor farm. But the primary memory for those blacks interviewed for this scenario was the church. "We went from church to church to church to keep off the streets," said one. The 90-year-old woman remembered with fondness her ties to the original St. John United Methodist Church, which was bulldozed in 2000. Others mentioned Bethel A.M.E., which reportedly had ties to the Underground Railroad. And others beamed with pride over Clay Street Baptist Church, which has the largest structure in town for a black congregation and which opened a day care and Christian life center in 1999. They talked about the first youth choir formed with 149 members in 1940.

They remembered fish fries. They recalled outdoor revivals where the men would stretch tobacco canvas from tree to tree to fan away the flies from the baked goods and homemade ice cream. They knew which church their schoolteachers attended. They commended Betsy Hanna (Schmidt) of the First Presbyterian Church for offering Vacation Bible School to the black children. And admired Hazel Vaughan for inviting the black youngsters to see "Scrooge" during Christmas at the First Presbyterian

Church, even if the black party was separated from the white children. "It was so instrumental to our learning, our loving, our families. God has been good to us."

The countless number of blacks who achieved "first" status in various walks of life felt that goodness in the community. Some continue those walks:

Willie Fleming was one of the first African Americans to graduate from the University of Louisville School of Law in 1954. Fleming graduated from Shelbyville Colored Junior High School in 1944 and went on to Lincoln Institute where he was valedictorian of the class of 1947. While at the all-black high school, he was president of the junior and senior classes and lettered in football and basketball. At graduation, he received more awards than any one student in the history of the school.

Fleming graduated with honors in 1951 from Fisk University in Nashville with a Bachelor of Science degree in business administration. He was the first in his family (one of eight children of William Newton and Bessie Payne Fleming) to go to college. While there he was president of his senior class and lettered all four years in football, earning the nickname "Hard Rock" Fleming.

Back home in Shelbyville, Fleming was the first African-American to develop a subdivision. It was Monica Gardens, named after his daughter who was among the first black cheerleaders at Shelbyville High School, and is located on U.S. 60 East. He worked hard during the Civil Rights movements to bring about better conditions for the black citizens in Shelbyville.

When Mitchell Howard Payne entered Southside Elementary in 1957 as a second-grader, he was among the first blacks to integrate the school system. He set out to get involved and leave a mark. After graduating from Shelbyville High School in 1968, the son of Llewellyn and Hattie Payne went on to Western Kentucky University where he majored in government and minored in history. He attended graduate school at WKU where he received degrees in public administration and urban affairs. He received his law degree from the University of Louisville. Payne pooled all those resources to make his mark: serving on various state government committees, working in Washington, D.C., for U.S. Rep. Romano Mazzoli, working as director of the Office of Minority Affairs at U of L, working as principal assistant to Finance Secretary Gordon Duke, and being named the first black finance commissioner for the commonwealth, and only the second black commissioner in the history of state government. Payne became an administrator at U of L. His accomplishments there caused Governor Martha Layne Collins to appoint him finance commissioner. She said there were many qualified candidates but "Payne (has) a combination of efficiency, education and energy that ensures success..."

Brenda Jackson became the first black to be elected to the Shelby County Board of Education. As a 1964 graduate of Shelbyville High School, she was among the first to integrate the school system and feel the discrimination by white students and teachers alike. Yet, she used those hardships to move forward and attain a degree in accounting, now holding a position with the state government as an auditor in the Administrative Office of the Courts. She relies on her difficult days as a black student to help make decisions and implement programs in today's school system to support black students and to close the achievement gap between minorities and the general student population.

(Source: Martha Mason, Elnora Harris, Inez Harris, Vanessa Harris, Stella Lee, Brenda Jackson, Sam Beckley, Vivian Overall, Mary Lee Sullivan, George Lee Stone, Willie Fleming, and Mitchell Payne.)

DAVID ALEXANDER

By William E. Matthews

In his Literary History of Kentucky, William S. Ward, writes that, "while there were a half-a-dozen mystery writers in Kentucky who wrote a respectable whodunit, there was only one, David Alexander (1907-73) who was a true professional."

Alexander was born in Shelbyville on April 21, 1907, to David Catlin and Effie Buckner Alexander. He moved to Louisville as a small boy, and later attended the University of Kentucky (1926-28). He then began his writing career with the *Lexington Herald*. He was early attracted to horse racing and breeding, and in 1930 he went to New York to begin working on the *Morning Telegraph*, one of the country's early turf publications.

At the age of 26, he became managing editor of the *Morning Telegraph* and remained in that capacity for 10 years. After a stint in Lexington where he wrote for the *Blood Horse* and the *Thoroughbred Record*, he returned to New York where he became racing editor for the *New York Herald Tribune* until it ceased publication.

Alexander was considered one of the top turf writers in America, and his *The Sound of Horses, from Eclipse to Kelso*, is rated among the top horse racing books ever published.

He spent some time in the U. S. Army (1943-45), and then graduated from the New York Institute of Criminology. He wrote his first mystery, *Murder in Black and White* in 1951, and this was followed almost immediately by *Most Men Don't Kill*. Overall, he wrote 15 mysteries, including his last one in 1962. The Saturday Evening Review called his *Shoot a Sitting Duck* (1955) his best effort yet.

Ward claims that Alexander was an even better short story writer than novelist. His 13 stories in the volume *The Man Who Went to Taltavul's* won second prize in the Ellery Queen Mystery magazine competition, and he also won the Edgar Allen Poe award from the Mystery Writers of America. His best stories, it was generally agreed, focused on Broadway and Times Square in the 1950s, with the celebrated detective Bart Hardin getting the best of the bad guys.

The New York Times called *Die Little Goose* (1956) his best. Other books which won acclaim included *Death of Humpty-Dumpty* (1957) and *Hush-a-bye Murder*, (1953). Alexander married Alice LeMere in 1930. He died on March 21, 1973.

BLAND W. BALLARD

By William E. Matthews

While there is no doubt that Daniel Boone and his brother Squire Boone contributed much to the opening of the West, their fame was enhanced greatly by John Filson's book *The Discovery, Settlement and Present State of Kentucke* published in 1874, which prominently featured Daniel Boone and his exploits.

Certainly, in comparing the records of the more famous Daniel with his brother Squire, one might reasonably conclude that the latter did indeed contribute more to the "opening of the West," and in making Kentucky a safer place for the new arrivals than did brother Daniel. Of his reported exploits, Daniel, who was somewhat embarrassed by the publicity he received, once commented, "If I'd done half the things they attribute to me..." Ahh, but the story telling around campfires—thus legends are born.

There's another pioneer personage who, while well known to state historians, is hardly a household name in the classrooms around the commonwealth. He was Bland Williams Ballard. Legend has it that, at the ripe old age of 92, shortly before his death, he had an opportunity to take one last shot at an Indian. The story goes that a hungry Indian came to the door begging for food. While Mrs. Ballad was bustling around the kitchen getting him something to eat, the old Indian fighter, said, "I smell an Indian," raised up out of his bed, got his rifle and fired a shot through the window. The shot split the top rail of the fence across which the frightened Indian was making a speedy retreat.

In 1853, there were no Indians left in the area, and that account of Ballard's final effort seems highly questionable. But it made for good story-telling down through the years. What made Ballard the subject of so many stories, both true and fictitious, was his knack for killing Indians. No one on the frontier had his kind of reputation when it came to tangling with native Americans. Perhaps his proficiency grew out of witnessing his own family's slaughter in what became known as the "Tick Creek Massacre." There is little doubt, according to several historians, that Bland Williams Ballard was far more proficient in battling and killing Indians than either of the Boones, Simon Kenton, George Rogers Clark, or some other notable figures. And though the general public may have forgotten him, he enjoyed quite a reputation in his time.

Z. F. Smith's 1889 *History of Kentucky*, which devoted four pages to Ballard, identifies him as a premier soldier, scout and spy, especially in the Wabash expeditions of Col. George Rogers Clark, Col. Charles Scott, and Gen. James Wilkinson. He also fought alongside "Mad Anthony" Wayne at the Battle of Fallen Timbers. Wilkinson described him as "a fearless prudent, sagacious and reliable spy."

Ballard also participated in the settlers' defeat at Long Run, and was captured at the Battle of the River Raisin during the War of 1812.

Bland Williams Ballard was born on October 16, 1761, in Spotsylvania, Virginia, the third child and eldest son of Bland Ballard and his wife whose name has been lost to history. There is no record of what happened to his mother, but when Bland Williams Ballard was a young man of 18, his father, and two sons moved to Kentucky where Bland W. joined the militia and became an active participant in defending the western frontier. At that time, young as he was, he had already served in the Revolutionary War. He was described as being six feet tall, "a strong, raw, bony man who weighed up to 200 pounds, passionate and quick."

When young Bland came to Kentucky in March 1779, this was about seven years before Davey Crockett was born, and 10 years after Daniel Boone's first glimpse of Kentucky. The Indians were making a last desperate effort to stem the swelling tide of white men into their hunting grounds.

Besides his father and brother, with Bland W. were cousins James and Proctor Ballard. From these men have descended the numerous Ballards of Kentucky, including one-time U. S. Senator Thruston Ballard Morton. Bland Ballard, his son Bland W., James and Proctor had all been Revolutionary War soldiers, having enlisted with Capt. Benjamin Roberts' Virginia Company. After coming into Kentucky

Portrait of Bland W. Ballard attributed to Chester Harding.

under the command of Gen. George Rogers Clark., they assisted in building the first forts at Lexington and Bryan's Station. They also spent two weeks at Harrodsburg, helped plant a crop of corn at Boonesboro, and assisted in building the forts at Beargrass and Ft. Jefferson, down the Ohio River.

The two Blands and James accompanied John Bowman on his unsuccessful expedition against the Indian towns at Chillicothe, Ohio. Although forced to retreat, the company captured 163 horses and killed two Indian chiefs.

In 1780, they and others of Clark's men built several log houses at an advanced base on the very spot where John Filson, eight years later, named Losantiville, now Cincinnati. When not engaged in regular campaigns, Ballard served as a hunter, scout, and spy for Gen. George Rogers Clark, who was stationed at Louisville.

During this time he had several encounters with Indians. One of these scouting occasions found him exploring the Ohio from the mouth of Salt River to the Falls of the Ohio, just below Louisville. He was near what is now known as the town of Westport when he detected three hostiles moving along the shore on the other side of the river. Soon, they got into a canoe and headed straight for his position on the Kentucky side. When they got close, he opened fire, killing one Indian instantly. He then outdueled the other two in hand-to-hand combat. Upon reporting the successful conclusion of his mission, Gen. Clark presented him with a linen shirt. This was the only shirt he owned for many years except for those made of leather.

At the time, Ballard was living at Linn's Station on Beargrass Creek when he was asked to assist some families who were trying to move from Squire Boone Station, northeast of Shelbyville, to more secure stations along the Beargrass. They were well on their way when a large group of Indians firing rifles and brandishing battle axes mounted an all-out attack. Some of the women were thrown from their frightened horses. Ballard assisted them, and in the confusion some of the settlers managed to escape. The rest held their ground, vigorously defending their families. But many were killed. Getting behind the Indians, Ballard began picking them off one at a time. But the Indians then turned on Ballad, who knew he had to get away and summon help. Having lost his horse in the battle, Ballard hid in the bushes and jumped one of his attackers, took his horse, and made his escape. The number killed at what became known as the Long Run Massacre has never been accurately established, but the settlers suffered a resounding defeat.

Afterwards, the settlers learned that the Indians who attacked them at Long Run were the same ones who had intended to attack Squire Boone Station. Later, Ballard was among Col. John Floyd's band of 37 men who chased after the Indians in an effort to "teach them a lesson." Unfortunately, the Indians were waiting in ambush, and 16 of Floyd's men were killed.

A few years later, on March 31, 1788, a band of Delaware Indians planned to attack a tiny fort at Tyler's Station on Tick Creek, about six miles east of Shelbyville. There were about 15 to 20 Indians in the party when they came upon Bland Ballard's small log cabin located a few yards from the fort. The younger Ballard, fortunately, was not in the cabin at the time, but was at the nearby fort when he heard shouts and shooting. The first to die was his brother, Benjamin, who was killed as he was returning to the cabin with some wood.

The elder Ballard, his second wife Diane, and the children were in the cabin and barricaded the doors and windows. But the Indians soon broke open the door and murdered the father and stepmother, and young Ballard's sister and half-sister, and scalped the youngest sister, Thursia, who recovered and lived to old age. As the Indians were fleeing the scene, Bland Williams Ballard went to work with his rifle, and later told an interviewer, Samuel Graham, of the State Historical Society of Wisconsin, that he killed at least three Delawares.

In later life, Ballard told historian Lyman C. Draper that he figured his guns and knives had accounted for at least 30 to 40 Indians, "maybe more," during his lifetime. There are in the Draper manuscripts at the State Historical Society in Wisconsin many more accounts of the adventures of Bland Williams Ballard by men who knew him and fought by his side. His fearlessness and daring commanded the admiration of both friends and foes.

When Gov. Isaac Shelby called for volunteers during the War of 1812, Bland W. Ballard was 53. Still, he offered his assistance in the struggle against the British and Indians, and commanded a company in Col. Allen's regiment. He fought at Tippecanoe, and brought back with him a battle ax which, according to legend, was used in scalping famed Indian Chief Tecumseh. It is a false story since Tecumseh was not even present for that battle. This battle ax remains in the possession of Ballard's descendants in Shelby County, as do several land grants issued to Bland Williams Ballard in April and July 1785 by the respective governors of Virginia, Edmund Randolph and Patrick Henry. Presumably these grants were for his service in the Revolutionary War.

In the Battle of the River Raisin, Ballard fought gallantly, was badly wounded, and taken prisoner. At the close of the War of 1812, he returned to Shelby County where he took up residence about four miles west of Shelbyville. His home was a log cabin which he later weatherboarded. Over his fireplace hung a buckskin string containing six or seven Indian scalps, and over his front door hung his favorite gun. In the stone doorstep were carved the initials B.W.B. Not only was he the era's best known Indian fighter, but Ballard also was credited with many other accomplishments in civilian life. In 1792 he was a leading force in making the road which is now U. S. 60 the primary road from Shelbyville to the Falls of the Ohio. In 1798, he was appointed a trustee for Shelbyville Academy. Although Ballard could not have been considered an educated man, since there is little, if any, record of his school days, he was remarkably persuasive as an orator and legislator. He was elected to Kentucky's General Assembly in 1800, 1803, and 1805. When he died in 1853 at his home in Shelbyville, he was buried close by in the family cemetery.

A year later, his remains, along with those of his first wife, Elizabeth Williams Ballard, were re-interred in the Kentucky heroes section of the cemetery in Frankfort in a ceremony attended by many notables from around the state. Bland Williams Ballard and his wife, Elizabeth had seven children, James, Mary, Dorothy ("Dolly"), Susan, Sally, Martha, and Nancy. Ballard's second wife was Diane Matthews (d. August 17, 1839), and his third Elizabeth Weaver Garrett Matthews (d. 1841). He had no children by either Diane or Elizabeth.

Bland Ballard Matthews of Shelbyville is a great, great, great, great, grandson of Bland Williams Ballard and his first wife, Elizabeth. It was their daughter Susan who married John Matthews, and the line was continued through Absalom T., Benjamin F., Robert F., William E. and Bland Ballard Matthews.

Remarkably, a significant honor was bestowed on this Kentucky hero.

In 1842, while Bland Williams Ballard was still living, Ballard County in western Kentucky was named for him. (Author's note: The foregoing account of Bland Williams Ballard is based, on part, on an article by Margaret Bridwell, which appeared in the Louisville *Courier-Journal* on Oct. 21, 1957.)

LLEWELLYN BALLARD BAXTER

By Vivian Overall

Llewellyn Ballard Baxter was born September 12, 1872, in Shelbyville. He was the fourth of seven children born to Elizabeth J. and Thomas S. Baxter. A meticulously kept record of births in the family Bible, in fact, places the time of his birth at 10:00 P.M. Unfortunately, the 1880 United States Census for Shelbyville is not nearly as meticulous, listing Llewellyn as a nine-year-old "daughter" named "Louise." No doubt Assistant Marshall W.H. Ballard, who compiled the statistics on June 2, had an ear infection on that day. The family's home, at that time, was on Clay Street. Later, the Baxters would move to Equity Street in the heart of the tobacco warehouse district.

Education was important in the Baxter family, and, as corroborated by census material, all the Baxter children received schooling. Llewellyn's father, Thomas, had originally come to Shelbyville sometime before 1870 as a schoolteacher. Llewellyn was a product of Shelbyville schools, but it is not possible to say with any accuracy which ones he attended because records are spotty. In 1880, there were seven schools for black children in Shelby County; in 1885, there were about twelve. These schools met principally in churches; but no doubt all the Baxter children received some formal education from their

Courtesy of Betsie Lou Baxter Collins.

Llewellyn B. Baxter, known as "Sarge," in his World War I uniform.

father. Llewellyn also attended Fisk University in Nashville, Tennessee, and, subsequently, received his Shelby County Teachers Certificate, signed by County Superintendent James H. Barnett on September 29, 1894. He was twenty-two at the time, and for the next three years he taught in Shelby County.

After teaching, he joined the United States Armed Forces, where he served in the Ninth and Tenth Cavalry, as well as the Twenty-fourth and Twenty-fifth Regiments of the Infantry. The U.S. Army was strictly segregated throughout Baxter's career, and all these units were designated "colored." His professional military career spanned more than 30 years, and in addition to the United States he was posted to Cuba, during the Spanish-American War, where the Ninth and Tenth Colored Cavalry participated in the battles of Santiago and San Juan Hill; The Philippines, during the Philippine Insurrection of 1899-1902, where the Twenty-fifth Infantry, Colored, fought in the battle of Mt. Arayat (January 1900); and, along the Mexican border, where between the years 1911-16 the entire U.S. Cavalry was used to protect the border from the activities of Pancho Villa.

At retirement, he returned to Shelbyville with his wife, Sidney Ann Davis Baxter (1877 – 1956), and their daughter, Betsie Lou Baxter.

"Sergeant," as his friends affectionately knew him, was for many years very active in community politics. He was the Secretary-Treasurer of the Republican County Committee and worked closely with Chairman Harry D. Martin. He was also a committee member and office holder in the United Brothers of Friendship, a national and international benevolent fraternal order of African-Americans, founded in Louisville in 1861.

Llewellyn Ballard Baxter died on April 1, 1946, at the U.S. Soldiers Home of the Veterans Administration Hospital in Washington, D.C.

THOMAS S. BAXTER

By Vivian Overall And Kevin Collins

All records indicate that Thomas S. Baxter was born into slavery on May 7, 1843, in Fayette County, Kentucky. Although it is often difficult to know with any certainty the male parentage of slaves, we can be reasonably sure that, among the few Baxters then living in Fayette County, Thomas B. Baxter of Lexington, District 1, was the father, and a thirty-something year old unnamed female slave owned by him, was the mother of T.S. Baxter.

The 1850 Kentucky Census shows Thomas B. Baxter to be a fifty-one year-old white male clerk, born in Scotland in 1799, living in his own home (valued at $2,500) with Mary Baxter (nee Kinnear), his thirty-year-old wife, also from Scotland. Newlyweds, relatively speaking (married May13, 1848, in Millersburg, Bourbon County) it seems probable that Baxter had bought his unnamed female slave in the early 1840s, before his marriage. The 1840 census shows the forty-one year old bachelor living in Lexington without slaves. However, the Lexington Slave Schedule of 1850 indicates that Thomas B. Baxter owned three slaves, a female of perhaps forty, and two children, perhaps eleven and nine. The age and sex of children listed in Slave Schedules was often, out of lack of interest by the compiler, guessed at or sometimes, for reasons of propriety, falsified. The eleven-year-old female child cited here in the 1850 Schedule is almost certainly the male Thomas S. Baxter.

The 1860 Fayette County Census makes no mention of any of the aforesaid Baxters, but with the coming of the Civil War years it is possible that clerk Baxter was in military service. At about sixty years of age, however, he is more likely to have died. In 1860 his wife Mary is then shown living in her own home valued at $3,000, in Millersburg. Her personal estate has also increased, suggesting, again, that her husband was dead and she has benefited by inheritance. Mary, at this time, owned one female slave, age seventeen, and the Schedule shows that she had manumitted one other slave, probably our Thomas S. Baxter.

The 1870 census shows, for the first time, a T.S. Baxter living in Shelbyville. It is noted that Baxter is thirty years old (not his true age of twenty-seven), which would be in agreement with the age listed for him in the 1850 Lexington Slave Schedule (eleven years old). His profession in Shelbyville is entered as schoolteacher. No wife or family is listed as living with him at this time. It appears, in fact, that he may have roomed with another schoolteacher, also a man aged thirty named J.D. Mumford (or Minnford), originally of South Carolina. This is a bit mysterious, since other records show that by 1870 Thomas Baxter had a wife, Elizabeth J. (a former slave from Virginia), and was the father of two daughters, Mary and Isabella. Perhaps the rest of the family was then living in another county, and Baxter has come to Shelbyville for work, with the remainder of the family to follow at a later date.

Whatever the explanation, it is known that at the age of 27 he was an educated former slave, something of a rarity that reinforces the idea he was owned by someone like a clerk, in a household where he might be positioned to receive some education, as opposed to being a field slave, for instance, where the opportunity for lessons in reading and writing would have been almost non-existent. Secondly, we know, as a result of a family Bible in the possession of Baxter's granddaughter, Betsie Lou Baxter Collins, of Indianapolis, that T. S. must have been a proud man possessed of a joyous personality with a taste for accuracy and precision. His family Bible neatly lists, in his own hand, the names, dates, and hour of birth of his seven children.

1. Mary L. Baxter b. May 1, 1868   6a.m.   (d. no information)
2. Isabella J. Baxter b. March 17, 1870   12 a.m.   (d. Sept. 4, 1871)
3. Thaddeus S. Baxter b. May 4, 1871   5 p.m.   (d. Oct. 4, 1871)
4. Llewellyn B. Baxter b. Sept. 12, 1872   10 p.m.   (d. Apr. 1, 1946)
5. Cora Belle Baxter b. Jan. 9, 1875   12 p.m.   (d. June 27, 1875)
6. Elizabeth W. Baxter b. March 24, 1876   12 p.m.   (d. no information)
7. William H. Baxter b. June 3, 1882   2:30a.m. (d. no information)

We know other things about Thomas S. Baxter. In 1869, he organized the first Republican Club and served as its president for many years. In later years he would become a power (as much as the racial attitudes of his day would permit) in the Republican politics of Kentucky, and would serve, for over thirty years, as a member of the Shelby County Republican Committee.

A History of the United Brothers of Friendship and Sisters of the Mysterious Ten, a negro benevolent and fraternal order, reports Baxter to have been the Treasurer in 1871 on the Committee of Permanent Organization for the formation of a Kentucky state-wide Grand Lodge. Subsequently, he would be elected the State Lodge's Grand Secretary. He also served an organizer for the Order, and by 1877 had formed, among others, a branch of the UBF in Memphis, Tennessee. At Mt. Sterling, Kentucky, in 1877, Baxter was elected Grand Master of the Order, only the third person to receive this honor since the Order's inception.

In 1880, the Baxter family resided on Clay Street. In the coming years they would move to 1121 Equity Street, in the heart of the tobacco warehouse area of Shelbyville. This area would become the Sixth Ward of Shelbyville, and Thomas S. would represent it on the Shelbyville City Council. Much later, his youngest son, William, would also live on Equity Street and would, with his wife, Malinda, operate there, for over thirty-five years, the first integrated restaurant in Shelbyville. Of the surviving Baxter children listed in the 1880 Shelby County Census (Isabella, Thaddeus and Cora Belle had died), Mary and Llewellyn were in school. Elizabeth was only three years old. Mrs. Baxter was listed as a housekeeper and Thomas as an editor. He was, in fact, one of four editors for the *Ohio Falls Express*, the influential UBF newspaper that published from 1879 to 1904.

The entire United States Census for 1890 was destroyed by fire, and so one of the principal sources of information on the Baxter family for the preceding decade is lost. We do know, however, that the Baxter's youngest son, William H., was born in 1882, and that he would, with his wife, remains a life-long resident of Shelbyville. We know that Thomas S. continued his commitments to the United Brothers of Friendship, and he is listed as an appointee to a Past Masters' Council Committee that met in Galveston, Texas, in 1884; to the Kentucky Republican Party he would shortly be a party candidate for the City Council.

Thomas S. Baxter was a Shelbyville City Council member from 1892-1910.

The Shelby Record (quoted below) dates the beginning of Baxter's service on the Shelbyville City Council at about 1892 and its end in 1910. No local records seem to have survived to corroborate this 1890s date. Certainly Baxter's election from the Sixth ward coincided with the formation of wards in Shelbyville, but there is also no fixed evidence for when this happened. A History of Blacks in Kentucky, Vol. 2, authored by George C. Wright says,

"In all likelihood, the first election of blacks to office (in Kentucky) occurred in Hopkinsville and Christian County in November 1897. . . . They were Edward W. Glass, elected to the city council of Hopkinsville, James L. Allensworth, county coroner, and John W. Knight, constable in the North Hopkinsville district. . . . Of the three, Edward Glass served longest, remaining on the city council for the next twelve years. . . .

Afro-Americans also served on the city councils in several other cities in the early 1900s. Though details are sketchy, Shelbyville had a councilman by the name of Baxter for many years."

If the *Shelby Record* of January 21, 1910, is accurate in its exultant utterance, as quoted below, then it would seem that Thomas S. Baxter was both the first and, among those early pioneers, the longest sitting African-American elected to office in Kentucky. To appreciate both Baxter's commitment and his courage, one must remember that, although his entire Shelbyville life was spent in an atmosphere of racial discord the years from 1891 through 1911 were particularly violent, encompassing three lynchings (in 1891, 1901, and 1911) involving six black victims.

But more subtlety, two points in the public record of that time paint well the devalued and marginalized condition of blacks in general, and of a black political officeholder in particular. The 1900 census for Shelbyville lists the occupation of all males in the Baxter household as "day laborer" at a time when T.S. Baxter was, and had been for seven years, a city councilman, an editor, and an educator. All females in the Baxter household were designated "washwoman." The second piece of information is, perhaps, even more telling. In the entire span of Baxter's political career, between eighteen or twenty years, there are almost no references to him, or his position as Councilman, in the local newspaper, *The Shelby Record*. Even granting the fact that the paper was Democratic and Baxter was a Republican; the situation is still mind-bending. There are years when the activities of the City Council are reported on a weekly basis. Baxter is never mentioned, except on the very rare occasion when he is listed among those who have been absent from a meeting.

The Shelby Record of January 21, 1910 reported the end of Thomas S. Baxter's tenure as a City Councilman:

"For the first time in twenty years the Board of Council of the City of Shelbyville is composed of white men exclusively. T. S. Baxter, who has been in the Board for eighteen years, was ousted last Thursday night and a white gentleman, Mr. Curtis P. Hall, is now the Councilman from the Sixth ward. It was easy enough and the wonder is that the idea had not suggested itself sooner. The laying off of the boundaries of the wards at any time is a privilege of the Board, and those who may be aggrieved by its action are without recourse: as what it may do is in accordance with the Constitution, under which Fourth class cities are conducted.

The Fourth, Fifth, and Sixth wards were redistricted, all of that part of the city which heretofore constituted the Sixth being thrown into the Fourth and Fifth, and the territory recently added to the city and parts of these two wards, now constitute the new sixth ward. By the change made in the boundaries, Baxter is no longer a resident of the Sixth and consequently ineligible to serve as a Councilman. The Sixth, as it was, contained colored voters almost exclusively, and at every election Baxter was always a winner. To defeat him was as impossible, as it was for either of the few white men living in that ward to have a chance to get into the Board. Baxter had a vote on every question that came up, and at one time when the white members were "split," being three to three, he held the balance of power. As more than 981/2 per cent of the property of Shelbyville is owned by white taxpayers, a large majority of them believed that their affairs should be in the hands of reputable white men exclusively. This was the argument, and Baxter was ousted. The Fourth and Fifth, as they now are, are both hopelessly Republican, and the Negroes could carry them, but there will not be an election until nearly two years yet. By that time the boundaries will be changed again, and if another colored man is elected, the wards will be redistricted again.

It is not a matter of politics at all. Simply a question of Shelbyville's Board of Council being composed of white men. Should the Republicans elect a respectable white man he will serve the same as the rest, but the colored brother's day, as a City Father, is passed. The ordinance redistricting the wards was approved and published, and at the meeting Thursday night Baxter was informed that he was no longer a member of the Board. He asked for the pay that was due him and a warrant for his salary was drawn. He then vacated his place and upon motion Mr. Curtis P. Hall was unanimously elected."

The 1910 Census, compiled four months after the gerrymandered removal of Baxter from elected office, listed his occupation as U.S. Storekeeper at a distillery. At this time a grandson, Julias Freeman, age 14, also lived in the household. Like all Baxter children before him, he was enrolled in school.

Thomas S. Baxter died on July 26, 1917, at the age of seventy-four, of arterial-sclerosis complicated by chronic nephritis. He was buried from the Saffell and Saffell Funeral Home three days later, on a Sunday. On August 2, *The Shelby News* published an obituary in which they said, among other things, that Baxter was "at one time one of the best known Negroes in the State . . . was a power among his race in Republican politics . . . and when in his prime was considered the best parliamentarian of his race in Kentucky." The remaining years of Mrs. Elizabeth Baxter were spent living with her son, William, and his family on Equity Street. She died March 23, 1926.

HENRY WALTON BIBB

By Kevin Collins

Born in Shelby County in 1815, Henry Walton Bibb was the son of a slave mother who bore the name of Mildred Jackson, and a white father, most likely James Bibb, a landowner and politician. The knowledge of a slave's male parentage in those times was often problematic, given the fact those female slaves had no legal standing or protection of any kind in cases of forced or unwanted sexual attention. Thus Henry, like many slaves, had no knowledge of his father. James Bibb had died before Henry's recollections, but Henry possessed his mother's testimony on the subject of parentage, and there is no reason to discount it.

Henry was a very light-skinned slave, the oldest of his mother's seven boys. Their owner was David White, Esq., a judge in Shelby County who had come into possession of Mildred before Henry was born. As a child, Henry was separated from his mother and leased out for cash to farmers, both in Shelby and surrounding counties. This experience of being "shadow-labor" for the advancement of the "twice white" girl left an impression on Bibb.

In 1833, at the age of 18 Henry met a mulatto slave named Malinda, who lived in Oldham County about four miles from Judge White's residence in Shelby. In 1834, Henry Walton Bibb, the legal property of Albert G. Silby, married Malinda, a slave owned by William Gatewood of Bedford, Trimble County. Since slave marriages were not religiously or legally sanctioned, the "marriage" ceremony consisted of a simple promise of fidelity while holding hands. In time Bibb was sold to Gatewood, for $850. Some months after the sale, a daughter, Mary Francis, was born. But the child was often shaken and beaten by Mrs. Gatewood.

In the winter of 1837, Bibb resolved to escape slavery. Having hidden a suit and some money, he made his attempt during the Christmas season. On holidays, slaves were sometimes permitted by their keepers to work for wages for themselves and the support of their families, but only for small amounts of money. So, with the excuse that he wanted to work in a slaughterhouse during Christmas, Henry got permission to walk from Bedford to the Ohio River. Once there, he put on the suit and, because of his light skin, was able to pass for white. He crossed the river to Madison, Indiana, and there boarded a Steamboat to Cincinnati.

In Cincinnati Bibb was helped by a black man named Job Dundy. There for the first time he learned about the Underground Railroad. After walking for days, he arrived in the village of Perrysburgh, Ohio, a settlement that included fugitive slaves. He stayed there and, working through the winter chopping wood, managed to save $15 for the passage to Canada. On the first of May 1838, against the advice of friends, he began the return trip to Kentucky to get his wife and child. Arriving in Bedford in a mid-week of June, Bibb was able to contact his wife (who had been told that her husband had been sold off to New Orleans by "lying Abolitionists"). He gave her money for the escape, which was planned for the next Saturday when slaves were free to visit other slaves without arousing suspicion. It was not safe, however, for Henry to stay in Bedford, so he made his way back to Cincinnati to await his family.

While in Cincinnati, Bibb was betrayed by two men posing as abolitionists. Each man gave Henry 50 cents to aid him in his escape effort, thus gaining Bibb's confidence. They asked him questions about his former owner, and then, returning to Kentucky by boat, informed the Gatewood family of Henry's whereabouts. For their efforts they collected a $300 reward.

Bibb was taken into custody and sent to Louisville, where it was determined that he would be sold in order to recoup the cost of his recapture. He was taken, for appearances sake, to a hotel instead of the city jail, locked in a room, and guarded by the notorious Louisville "negro hunter" Dan Lane. But when Lane became ill in the livery stables, Bibb escaped. It took two nights, hiding in the daytime, to walk the forty miles from Louisville to Bedford. Remaining in Bedford for several days, Bibb was able to contact his family. Together they made escape plans, which would have them meet in Ohio in two months time. Then, as pressure for his recapture mounted, Bibb left for Perrysburg, and safety.

After months of waiting in Ohio without word or appearance from his wife, Bibb once more resolved to return to Kentucky. It was now July 1839 when he made his way back to Bedford and his mother's house. In quick succession, however, he was again betrayed. He was surrounded and captured by an angry, armed mob. He was bound in irons and taken to the Bedford jail. His wife and child were collected and, after three days, the Bibb family was taken to Louisville to be sold. A Kentucky slave dealer, Madison Garrison, bought the entire family for resale on the New Orleans slave market. They were then taken to the Louisville workhouse, on Payne and Lexington Streets, to work under lock and key, until Garrison had bought enough slaves for the trip south.

In December 1840 Bibb was separated from his wife and child, never to see them again. Whitfield, as punishment for Bibb's escape attempts, split the family and sold Bibb separately to two gamblers. They, in turn, shortly sold him, to cover gambling debts, to a wealthy Cherokee Indian slaveholder for nine hundred dollars. When his Indian owner died, he escaped yet one more time. In January 1842 he traveled to Michigan.

In May 1844, Henry Bibb gave his first antislavery lecture to an audience in Adrian, Michigan. In 1845, the antislavery Friends of Liberty in Michigan employed Henry to lecture throughout the state. That same year, on a trip to Indiana, Bibb learned that his wife and daughter were no longer the property of Whitfield. The Deacon had sold them both, and Malinda had become the concubine of her new master.

Bibb continued to lecture, particularly in the Northeast. In 1847, he met Mary E. Miles, of Boston, at an antislavery meeting in New York City. After one year's betrothal, the couple, in June 1848, was married in a Church service and according to law.

On May 1, 1849, the narrative of Henry Bibb, of Shelby County, was completed. It was published in New York in 1850. That same year, because of the passage of the Fugitive Slave Act, Bibb moved to Ontario, Canada. There, continuing his writing, he published a small antislavery newssheet, The Voice of the Fugitive. Appearing semi-monthly, the paper extolled the efforts of the Underground Railroad and often listed the names, as well as the former owners, of slaves who had successfully escaped to Canada.

In addition to his writing, Henry Bibb organized The Refugee Home Society near Windsor, Canada. With contributions from antislavery groups in the United States, the Society bought a large tract of land on which each black refugee family was to receive 25 acres. By 1854, the incorporation date of Windsor, there was, perhaps, 250 people of color living there. The Society had bought 2,000 acres of land; about 20 families worked homesteads totaling 500 acres. Both a school and church were maintained. Henry Bibb died in 1856 at the age of 41. His widow, Mary, devoted her years to teaching school in Windsor.

A. L. BIRCH

By Robert T. Swanson

Dr. A. L. Birch graduated from Iowa State College in 1921. Upon graduation, he worked for the Los Angeles Livestock Veterinary Department. He returned to his native Worthington, Minnesota, and practiced as a partner in the veterinary clinic there.

In 1946, he and his family moved to Shelbyville to practice veterinary medicine and raise and race thoroughbred racehorses. They lived on the farm across from the Old Mason's Home that became Webb Transfer and is now the Shelby County School Bus Garage.

In 1950, Dr. Birch bought 139 acres (maybe at auction) which was part of the Dr. Sonne farm. The farmhouse is said to be made of handmade bricks, supposedly sitting on a log foundation buried in the ground. In addition to tobacco, thoroughbred horses were raised on the farm. He raised the thoroughbred Timely Tip that won the Arkansas Derby, the Ohio Derby, and ran in the Kentucky Derby. This horse is buried near the family home at the park and has an inscribed gravestone.

Sentinel-News photograph.

Dr. A. L. Birch, local veterinarian, is shown in a 1973 photograph as he gave rabies vaccine to a milk cow on the J. R. Sanderlin farm after several rabid foxes were killed on area farms. Dr. Birch vaccinated some 500 cows in the Sanderlin herd on that day.

Dr. Birch was an excellent athlete in his youth. He was on the high school champion football team in Worthington in 1920. He also played high school basketball. He participated in football, and was captain of the wrestling, and boxing teams in college. He was an outstanding polo player as well. This interest made him later start a Boy's Athletic Club in Worthington. Dr. Birch was also involved with student athletics in Shelbyville. He would give members of the football and basketball teams silver dollars at the end of their respective seasons and bought athletic shoes for needy students. Little was known about this as he kept it rather quiet. When the Shelby County Fiscal Court wanted his farm to build a park, Dr. Birch made an offer stating that he would donate one half of the property if the county would buy the other half and establish a county park that would serve the youth and families of the county. The offer was accepted. Clear Creek Park is in the result of that gift.

Dr. Birch was an active Mason in Shelbyville. He retired in 1975 and moved to Boone County, Kentucky. He died in 1979 and is buried in Grove Hill Cemetery.

SQUIRE BOONE

By R.R. Van Stockum Sr.

Historians, including Willard Rouse Jillson, have concluded that Squire Boone, having been overshadowed by his older brother Daniel, has not been accorded his proper place in history.

Daniel, ten years older than Squire, singled out by Kentucky's first historian John Filson, gained international fame as the prototypical frontiersman. Just as James Boswell magnified the image of 18th Century literary giant Samuel Johnson, so Filson created an image of Daniel Boone that was larger than life. This he did in his small book *The Discovery, Settlement and present State of Kentucke*, first printed in Philadelphia in 1784 and soon thereafter in France, Germany, and England. Filson accepted Boone's story as entirely factual and edited it in such a way that Boone was seen to have literary accomplishments to match his skill as Indian fighter.

Squire, about five feet nine or ten inches tall and 160 pounds, had the muscular build of a smithy. From his brother he had learned how to survive in the wilderness, how to cope with nature, and how to deal with the Indians. He was fond of hunting, but not so much as Daniel. While he did not demonstrate the diplomatic talents of his brother in dealing with the Indians and in explaining these dealings to his fellow pioneers, he was more active as an Indian fighter than Daniel.

Squire Boone's father, also named Squire, was born in 1696 in Devonshire, England, emigrated to Pennsylvania in 1713, and in 1720 married Sarah Morgan. Of eleven children of this union, Daniel, born in 1734, was the sixth child; and Squire Jr., in 1744, the tenth. Their father maintained a good standing in the Friends Society (the Quakers) until 1748 when, following the marriage of a second child outside the faith, he was expelled.

In late 1751, when Daniel was 17 and Squire a young lad of seven, the family settled at the Forks of the Yadkin River in North Carolina where Squire Boone Sr., had already purchased the first of two 640 acre tracts of land. Certainly ownership of two sections of land indicates that the Boones were a reasonably affluent family for the times.

About 1759, Squire Jr., who had developed a great interest in guns, was taken by his mother to Pennsylvania where he spent five years as an apprentice to his first cousin Samuel Boone, an accomplished gunsmith. Squire obviously developed a fondness for Samuel, eight years his senior and more a contemporary of Daniel's. He developed skills in working with iron and an inventiveness that later made him a valuable companion on the frontier. Samuel, like Daniel, became a role model. Squire was to remain close to both and each had the effect of enlarging his life, Samuel at the forge and Daniel in the wilderness.

In August 1765, soon after returning from his apprenticeship, Squire, at his family's Yadkin home, married Jane Van Cleve, not yet sixteen, whose father was of Amsterdam Dutch descent. Shortly after his marriage and following the death of his father, Squire accompanied Daniel and several other companions on a hunting and exploratory trip to the panhandle of east Florida. John Mack Faragher, a Daniel Boone biographer, characterized this trip as " . . . an extended bachelor party, featuring a good deal of flirting and cavorting with pretty serving girls and Seminole Indian Maidens." Despite the general agreement of most historians that Squire Boone was a preacher, there are serious doubts that this was true. This statement of Squire's son Enoch is remarkable for what it does not say: "Jonathan, George & Samuel Boone, brothers of Col. Danl. Boone, were all Baptists. Squire Boone, son of Samuel, who had a thigh broken in the Blue Licks battle, was a Baptist preacher."

The party was disappointed in Florida and returned home on Christmas Day 1765 to hear overblown reports and rumors of the beautiful and productive land to be found in Kentucky. One frontier preacher years later exclaimed "O my dear honeys, heaven is a Kentucky of a place."

In 1767, Squire probably accompanied Daniel and William Hill when they crossed the Blue Ridge and Alleghenies to reach a salt lick a few miles west of present day Prestonsburg. Daniel, who did not describe this trip to Filson, would not have realized that he had reached Kentucky.

In the winter of 1768-69 John Finley, peddler and horse trader, while a guest of Daniel's in the upper Yadkin, spoke glowingly of Kentucky to the Boone brothers, and knew where the gap in the mountains was. On May 1, 1769 Finley, Daniel Boone, Boone's brother-in-law John Stewart, and three others left the Upper Yadkin for Kentucky with their equipment and supplies packed on 10 to15 horses. Squire remained home to help with the crops. As Daniel described this trip to Filson: "We proceeded successfully, and after a long and fatiguing journey through a mountainous wilderness, in a westward direction, on the seventh day of June following, we found ourselves on Red River, where John Finley had formerly been trading with the Indians, and, from the top of an eminence, saw with pleasure the beautiful level of Kentucke." Each year the Kentucky Historical Society commemorates this day, the seventh of June, as "Boone Day."

Not mentioned by Boone to Filson was their passage through the Cumberland Gap, which was to become the gateway to the West. This famous gap, associated by many with Boone, had provided ingress into Kentucky for many years, even before it was used in 1750 by famed explorer Dr. Thomas Walker, who had named it after the Duke of Cumberland.

For the next six months Boone and his companions took advantage of the abundance of game to hunt and to trap, anticipating the arrival of Squire Boone with supplies. Near the end of December 1769 Boone and Stewart, hunting together, were captured by Indians but managed to escape without furs, hides and horses, but with their lives. After several days of hard travel they reached their base camp on Station Camp Creek only to find it abandoned. Nearby, however, Boone found his brother Squire who, with Alexander Neeley, had come over the mountains with horses and supplies. Jillson has described this rendezvous as being remarkable: "Many deeds of bravery and heroism mark the pages of early Kentucky history, but none can compare with this spontaneous, intelligent and perfectly timed expedition designed and executed by Squire Boone to bring relief to his brother Daniel. Historians generally, from John Filson to the present time, it must be agreed, have failed to see the full significance of this action and Squire Boone's fame has suffered accordingly." Squire said years later he had come "in search of the Western world and my brother Daniel Boone."

Daniel, Squire, Stewart and Neeley remained in Kentucky; the others returned home. Shortly afterward, while hunting with Daniel, John Stewart was killed and Neeley, alarmed, left alone in an unsuccessful attempt to reach the Yadkin. Thus Daniel and Squire found themselves alone in a vast wilderness. They hunted every day and spent the winter of 1769-70 in a "little cottage," in the prose of Filson, probably a lean to or a primitive log cabin. On May 1, 1770, a year after the party's departure from the Yadkin settlements, Squire returned home for horses and ammunition, leaving Daniel alone. The Warriors' Path followed by Squire through eastern Kentucky was especially dangerous at that time of year, the weather being conducive to incursions of Indian hunters and war parties.

On July 27, 1770, Squire Boone, to Daniel's "great felicity," rejoined Daniel, as planned at their old camp on Station Camp Creek. (There are credible reports that Squire later made a second round trip to the settlements for resupply.) Not thinking it safe to stay at their camp longer, they proceeded to the Cumberland River, reconnoitering that part of the country until March 1771, and returning home to the Yadkin in April. Accepting the dates of this long hunt as related by Daniel to Filson, we can calculate that while Squire did not accompany the party when it departed, he did spend nearly 15 months on this hunt, most of this time being alone on the trail or with only the company of his brother.

FRONTIER KENTUCKY

On September 25, 1773 Daniel Boone, having sold his farm on the Yadkin, guided his family and five others, undoubtedly including Squire's, in an aborted attempt to settle in Kentucky. Two weeks later, discouraged by the loss of six of the party, including Daniel's oldest son James, in a Shawnee attack, they turned back to the settlements.

The story of Daniel Boone's trail blazing party into Kentucky in March 1775 is so well known that it is not necessary to recount it in detail. It should be emphasized however that this expedition to found the Colony of Transylvania was under the command of Judge Richard Henderson, a partner in the Transylvania Company. Boone led the advance party only; Henderson followed a few days later with the main body.

On March 24, while camped three miles south of present-day Richmond, Kentucky, only fifteen miles from their destination, the party was rudely awakened by an attacking party of Shawnees. "Once in safety, Squire Boone found that he had seized his jacket instead of his powder horn and shot pouch. Half naked, and with no means of defense, he crawled about in the darkness with his useless rifle until he could find his brother and borrow ammunition." Delayed by the attack, Boone continued his advance, on April 1, arriving at the chosen site near the confluence of Otter Creek and the Kentucky River. This was not strange land to Boone and his brother Squire who had explored this area during their long hunt of 1769-71. It is surprising that historians have not emphasized this fact. When the fort at Boonesborough was completed, Squire Boone's house was located inside the compound with his gunshop adjoining. Again we are reminded of the contribution made on the frontier by Squire as a gunsmith.

Henderson lost no time in establishing legislative and judicial bodies. The journal of the proceedings of a convention that he called in May 1775 is remarkable for the formal legislative processes it records. One of the early actions, appropriately on the motion of Daniel Boone, directed the bringing in of a bill for preserving game. Later in the session Squire Boone was given leave to bring in a bill to preserve the range.

Daniel and Squire, once Boonesborough was thought to be secure, returned to the settlements and brought out their families. Also, like other pioneers, they were seeking to claim land for themselves and their families. Squire stated years later in a Shelby County deposition:

"In the summer of the year 1775 I came to the place where Boone's Station on Clear Creek was since

Built... I then made a small improvement. . In the spring of the year 1776 I came again to the same place and took a stone out of the creek and with a mill pick picked my name in full and the date of the year thereon, and I painted the letters & Figures all red from which this Tract of land Took the name of the painted Stone tract."

In May 1776, Squire Boone, then with his family in Harrodsburg, turned when he heard the call "Boone," only to receive a shot, which broke one of his ribs in two places. In another action one of Squire's companions was killed while both had taken shelter behind a bag of corn. When an Indian rushed up to scalp his victim, he was startled by Boone who ran him through with the small three-edged sword. The sword was broken and Boone, being cut on the forehead, carried a scar for the rest of his life. He later described this as "the best little Indian fight he ever was in both parties stood and fought so well."

Squire was involved with his brother in the Great Siege of Boonesborough in September 1778. Daniel, after his initial conversation with Chief Black Fish, who had adopted him during his recent captivity, brought back the terms of surrender. Squire responded that "he would never give up; he would fight till he died." The rest were of the same opinion. "Well, well," remarked Daniel philosophically, "I'll die with the rest." However, in order to delay the Indian attack until anticipated reinforcements could arrive from Virginia, the garrison agreed to negotiate.

Following the parlay that ensued, terminated by the famous hand-shaking incident, the settlers extricated themselves from the grasp of the Indians and ran for the fort. All except Squire Boone, who entered through a camouflaged cabin door after the big gate had been closed, escaped without serious injury. Later, Daniel Boone cut a ball out of his brother's shoulder and Squire's wife Jane dressed it. Limited physically because of this wound, Squire was still able to exercise his considerable talents as artisan and gunsmith. Squire directed the construction of two wooden cannon from black gum trunks, banded by iron wagon tires. One burst, but the other, loaded with 20 or 30 one-ounce balls was fired with a terrifying effect, at least upon the morale of the attackers. Squire is also credited with the idea of inserting pistons into old muskets to create improvised squirt guns to throw water on the cabin roofs when they took fire.

The settlers withstood the siege, suffering few losses but exacting heavy casualties on the besiegers. Daniel Boone was later court-martialed for his suspicious actions in surrendering to the Indians months before the siege but was completely exonerated and subsequently promoted.

The lengthy and complex Virginia Land Act of 1779 established a "settlement right" to 400 acres for any settler who had raised a crop of corn prior to January 1, 1778, or had lived in Kentucky for as long as a year prior to that date. Anyone who could qualify for a settlement was also eligible for an adjoining 1,000 acre "preemption," but for this he had to pay $40 per hundred acres. To implement this law the act established the Virginia Land Commission, headed by Colonel William Fleming, which during the "Hard Winter of 1779-80" braved the extreme cold and the Indians to travel between the stations to adjudicate claims.

The late Dr. Mary K. Bonsteel Tachau, noted University of Louisville historian, has written that the Virginia Land Commission "journeyed to Kentucky and reviewed more than 1,400 claims . . . . they confirmed 1,328 of them (representing approximately one-eighth the area of the state) declared their work completed and the conflicts resolved, and returned to

Virginia. Seldom has a public commission been more industrious, optimistic, or naive."

Squire appeared before the Fleming Commission, while it was sitting in Louisville in November 1779, securing a certificate for a settlement of 400 acres and a preemption of 1,000 acres, known as "Painted Stone," on Clear Creek in the name of his brother-in-law Benjamin Vancleve. He was a signer of the early petitions of 1779 and 1780 to the Legislature of Virginia, requesting that Louisville be formally recognized as a town.

During the "Hard Winter of 1779-80," Squire, accompanied by his friend and fellow hunter Evan Hinton, while reconnoitering the Painted Stone property, became snowed in. In the spring of 1780 he brought thirteen families to this tract where he built a large station, picketed in, nearly an acre in size. On June 28, 1780, Squire, as captain of a company of militia stationed at "Painted Stone," reported that he had a strength of 23, although the list he submitted contained only 22 names, including his own.

During the winter of 1780-81, Evan Hinton had a contract to lay in and cure a large quantity of buffalo meat for Colonel George Rogers Clark. Returning from Louisville on February 6, 1781, with salt to cure the meat, Hinton and his party were captured 3 miles from Boone's Station and the salt was either taken or destroyed. This was a logistical disaster of significant proportions, described by County Lieutenant Floyd to General Clark as an event "which I fear will embarrass & perplex you exceedingly."

In April 1781 Boone's Station was attacked and when Squire Boone, in his shirt tail, and a dozen others seized their guns, and ran out at the alarm, about 20 Indians waylaid them. Squire, while trying to cover the retreat, received two gunshot wounds, one breaking his right arm just below the elbow, and the other in his right side, but was able to get back inside the stockade. Simon Girty, "the Great Renegade," who was with the Indians, later boasted that he had made Squire Boone's white shirt fly. Squire's arm was shattered and when it healed was an inch and a half shorter than the other; afterward splinters of bone would occasionally work out. The ball was cut out from his side and it took several months for his recovery.

The Painted Stone Station continued to be harassed. Over the next few months small raiding parties of Indians killed several more settlers. Isolated as it was, the fort was held with great difficulty. The hunters had to steal out at night, hunt by day and return by night with their game. Squire Boone was confined all the spring and summer as a result of his wounds.

LONG RUN MASSACRE AND FLOYD'S DEFEAT

These Indian raids caused a group of families to decide to depart for the relative safety of Linn's Station, the nearest settlement, about 21 miles away, necessitating the abandonment of the under-manned station. Early in the morning of September 13, 1781, accompanied by a militia escort that Squire had arranged, nearly all the families, including Squire's eight year old son Isaiah, departed. Squire Boone, so weak from his wounds that he could barely creep around, and his twelve year old son Moses remained with widow Hinton and her family to await the return of pack horses to evacuate them. The fleeing families soon became scattered along the trail and many in the military escort fell behind to attend an ill militiaman.

At midday as the group approached the main ford at Long Run, about half way toward their destination, the Indians suddenly attacked. The men scarcely had time to cut off the packs, and mount the women and children on the horses. Young Isaiah Boone, running through Long Run, stumbled and fell into the stream. As he scrambled out, he saw an Indian on the opposite bank but his gun was wet and would not fire. George Yunt shot the Indian, who rolled into the water, and told Isaiah to run. "What shall I do with my gun?" said the lad. "Throw it away," said Yunt. This, Isaiah was not disposed to do and he clung to it for a while before reluctantly throwing it away.

Vince Akers, who has studied this tragic event, known as the "Long Run Massacre," states that no more than 15 were killed, possibly as few as eleven were. Even so, it seems appropriate to describe this small engagement as a "massacre" because of the fury of the attack and the slaughter of women and children.

As soon as the stragglers started to drift into Linn Station, Colonel John Floyd, as County Lieutenant, the commander of the militia of Jefferson County, hastily gathered a small force and left the next morning with 27 mounted men. They were intent on burying the dead, punishing the Indians and thwarting any attack on Painted Stone, defended now only by the critically wounded Squire Boone and his son Moses. That Floyd was willing to undertake such a hazardous mission on his own volition speaks volumes about his leadership, his courage and his initiative.

Immediately following the Long Run Massacre the Indians that had attacked the fleeing settlers were reinforced by their main party, attaining strength of some 200. They camped near the site of the massacre to await the American's reaction, which was not long in coming. Floyd's small company, advancing as fast as possible, arrived at the massacre scene before the Indians, still intent on plunder, were able to set up an ambush. However, they quickly pulled back from the section of Boone's Wagon Road between Floyd's Fork and Long Run, east of present day Eastwood, to allow the relieving force to ride through. They then closed in behind to surround Floyd's company and commenced firing from both sides of the road. Surprise was complete and the effect catastrophic. Colonel Floyd, at 10:30 P.M., immediately upon his return to Linn's Station wrote the following dispatch to General Clark at the Falls of the Ohio (Louisville): "I have this minute returned from a little Excurtion against the enemy & my party, 27 in number, are all dispersed & cut to pieces except 9 who came off the field . . . .I don't yet know who are killed. . . . A party was defeated yesterday near the same place & many Women & Children wounded. I want satisfaction: do send me 100 men, which number with what I can raise will do. The Militia have no good powder do send some."

Floyd's defeat was a tactical disaster; only four Indians were killed, but one was a chief who had been a great supporter of the British efforts to keep the Indians organized for this campaign. Satisfied with their plunder and discouraged with the loss of their chief, the Indians returned north across the Ohio to their villages. Later Floyd wrote: " . . . this country was Invaded by a very considerable number of the enemy, and . . . it is my opinion that if the Defeat . . . had not have taken place that before a Sufficient number of Men could have been Embodied to repel the Enemy that Boons Station or some of the Stations on Beargrass would have been reduced by them."

A day or so after Floyd's defeat, about 300 men from the Falls and nearby stations, marched to the battlefields, buried the dead at both places over a mile apart and proceeded to Boone's Station where Squire was in great suspense, a number of the cattle having returned following the first Indian attack.

From May to December 1782 Squire Boone served as a representative of Jefferson County in the House of Delegates in Virginia. Jillson writes of this experience: "In the unhealed wounds of his body, Squire Boone, with his backwoods manner and plain hunter's garb of doeskin and leatherstocking bore to the Virginia Assembly an appeal for the settlers of the west more eloquent and touching than the mouth of man could utter."

When Squire returned from Virginia in the fall of 1783, he brought a large number of settlers with him. He attended the first Kentucky Convention in December 1784 as a delegate from Lincoln County. With several of the new settlers, including his cousin Samuel, the gunsmith, he visited his old station on Clear Creek, which he found burned down. Although the Indians continued to be troublesome during 1784, he rebuilt the station, and erected a gristmill and a sawmill on the creek.

Squire became one of Shelby County's largest landowners, largely by acting as a land locator for wealthy men who did not relish the hazards of the frontier. He would accept their Virginia treasury warrants, make entries for land, arrange for surveys, and obtain title, acquiring half the land for his efforts. According to his son Judge Moses Boone, owing to losses from conflicting and interfering land claims, he was compelled to sacrifice his property, including his station, which he left in 1786. Said Moses: "Boone did not go to law yet felt not a little vexed that others who never settled the country nor aided in its defense should have ousted him . . .."

Land locators and speculators came into Kentucky on the heels of the pioneers; in fact many of the pioneers like Daniel and Squire were engaged in buying and selling land for profit. Squire Boone, however, was primarily involved in the early days, not in land deals, but in hunting and defending himself and his family against the Indians. He had little interest in administrative matters, little knowledge of the proper legal procedures, and little time for such mundane activities. Like his brother he was restless, constantly in search of new lands, new areas and new interests. Thus, it can be argued that his financial and land problems were not entirely due to avaricious land sharks, but due, at least in part, to his own inattention to administrative detail.

In later life Squire was frequently called upon to give depositions in conflicts involving land claims. In one, given in Squire's own house in Shelby County on May 18, 1804, he said, "he was principled against going into the town of Shelbyville [Site of the Shelby County Court] upon any business whatsoever." This lament of the old Indian fighter would have been elicited by remembrance of the many suits brought against him in land disputes, one resulting in his being imprisoned for debts in Louisville for a time before his friends could secure his release. (Gen. George Rogers Clark was there, too.)

Squire said in later life that while serving in the legislature, he had once been invited to dine with the governor, and "that is as high a grade of honour as I ever rose to." Only a few years later he was so poor that he had to steal hominy from a slave, and "that is as low a grade as I have ever been reduced to." And "every place between these two extremes I have experienced."

Discouraged by his land losses and ever the wanderlust, Squire in 1787, accompanied by his son Isaiah and his cousin, gunsmith Samuel Boone, attempted a settlement at Chickasaw bluffs near present-day Vicksburg, Ms. where he opened a gunshop under the protection of Spanish authorities. He eventually lost that protection and returned to Kentucky with no possessions except his gun. In 1791, he went to St. Simon's Island in Georgia, then returned to Pennsylvania by boat where he remained for three years. He returned to Kentucky in 1795, but then in 1799 joined his brother Daniel who had settled in Missouri, remaining there for a year or two. He then returned to Shelby County, but left discouraged for the last time in 1806 with his family for Harrison County, Indiana, twenty-five miles from Louisville, where he established a settlement, built a small mill and again took up gunsmithing. Here he died in August 1815 and at his request was buried in a cave on his property not far from Corydon, in a place now advertised as "Squire Boone's Cavern."

How can we evaluate the life of this remarkable frontiersman? Admired and respected by his fellow pioneers, he was more inclined to fight than to explain and negotiate. Certainly his Indian adversaries had reason to fear him. He had a penchant for invention and innovation, witness his wooden cannon at Boonesborough; everywhere he lived for any length of time, he built a mill or a forge. While his qualifications as a frontier preacher are suspect, he certainly had a strong sense of religion as reflected by his attempt at crude verse carved into stones in the foundation of a mill he built in Indiana where he died in 1815:

"I set and sing my soul's salvation and bless the God of my creation." "For God my life hath much befriended, I'll praise him till my days are ended." But above all he shared with his brother awe and appreciation of the great out doors, impatience with the mundane, an urgent need for new experiences and, until his declining years, a distaste for settling in one place. Perhaps Squire Boone himself best summarized his life on the frontier in a petition for an allowance.

"To the Honorable the President of the United States and the Rest of the members [of] Congress Assembled, Living on the Frontier caus'd many misfortuns to befal me, in indeavouring to support the Country, and no [ ], that your petitioner had Rec'd Eight Bullet Holes through him and has been in seventeen engagements with the Indians in support of his Country and lost his property by unforeseen accidents and Indian afore said and the many wound that your Petitioner has Rec'd render him incapable of Labour for a suport."

BARNEY BRIGHT

By Gayle Bright

Jeptha Bernard (Barney) Bright was born on July 8, 1927, in Shelbyville, the second child and only son of Jeptha and Deanie Wakefield Bright.

When he was quite small, his mother, to keep him amused, gave him some dough to play with, and that's when his love of sculpting began. Bright graduated from Shelbyville High School, and attended one semester at Davidson College in North Carolina. After a stint in the U. S. Navy, he married Sally Cook, and they had four children, Leslie, Becky, Jep, and Michael.

Bright moved to Louisville in 1948 and became a student at Louisville's Art Center Association. He won the sculpture prize from the Art Center in both 1948 and 1949. In 1949 he earned his first commission, a small terra cotta for the lobby of Louisville Children's Hospital.

Bright worked briefly at General Electric before being laid off. He then purchased his studio at 2031 Frankfort Avenue, and those doors stayed open until his death. The studio was a "magic shop" for Bright. The building dated back to the Civil War. To walk on the wooden floors was threatening. Bronzes, clay models, plaster models, welding tools, posters, and various memorabilia cluttered every foot of space. There wasn't a flat surface in the whole studio that didn't have something on it.

In the back was a large area where he cast his bronzes. Rickety steps led up to a tiny two-room apartment where he stayed for several years after he and his wife separated. Years later Bright taught his son Jep the foundry business, and a foundry was set up at a different location.

In the 1950s Bright sculpted a beautiful fountain for Mrs. Thomas Bullitt. It consisted of three slender female nudes surrounding a small pool. In 1958 he created a large female nude for the Brownsboro Road branch of Citizens Fidelity Bank. In 1963 he modeled "Cock" for Louisville's Presbyterian Seminary, symbolic of Christ's admonition to Peter that he would betray Christ three times before the cock crowed. In 1965 Bright had to sell his beloved studio for financial reasons, but in the 1970s he was able to buy it back.

Bright sculpted the "Winged Man" found in the WAVE gardens in Louisville in 1968, a lead garden piece for Mrs. Barry (Mary) Bingham in 1969, and a fountain for the lobby of WHAS in Louisville in 1968. In 1969 he created silver figurines of small female nude figures and children in various poses. He placed the sterling silver figures on black rocks found on Swan's Island, an island about 30 miles off the coast of Maine. Bright loved Maine, and from 1967 until his death in 1997 he went to Maine almost every year. It was in Maine that Bright married his second wife Gayle.

Bright produced several outstanding works from 1970 to 1973, including "The Animal Tree" for the Louisville Zoo, "Pamela Brown" for Actor's Theatre, "Ab Russell" for the University of Louisville Law School, "Truth and Justice" for the Legal Arts Building, and "The River Horse" for the Louisville's Federal building.

Already well known in Louisville and state circles, Bright's popularity perhaps reached its greatest renown with the design and production of a clock for downtown Louisville. After his first design was rejected, he produced a clock in the form of a race track, with the historical figures in the gazebo. The five racers were Daniel Boone, King Louis XVI, George Rogers Clark, Thomas Jefferson, and the Belle of Louisville. On December 3, 1976, the first race was run, with the Belle of Louisville coming home first.

Bright has several beautiful pieces in Cave Hill Cemetery, including Sandra Twist, Jody White (a nude boy reaching for three birds in flight), three birds in flight with their wings touching, a memorial to Sherri Applegate, and Mr. Magic, the magician who bows for eternity.

Bright did his share of public figures (John Y. Brown, Col. Harland Sanders, Thruston B. Morton). Unfortunately, only one piece of Bright's public sculpture is in Shelbyville, a figure of the Risen Christ done in 1989 for the Church of the Annunciation.

Bright reached out nationally in 1975 when he was commissioned to do a life-size figure of "Dr. J." (basketball legend Julius Irving) which stands outside The Spectrum in Philadelphia.

In 1989 Bright did a portrait of Hall of Famer horse trainer Woody Stephens and Forty Niner. He also did a small but realistic rendition of the 1933 Kentucky Derby called "Fighting Finish." In 1994 Bright did five female figures for the lobby of the Women's Pavilion Health and Resource Center in Louisville's Alliant Medical Pavilion. The focus is on women at various stages in their lives. Bright also did a firefighter's memorial in 1996. It is of a fireman carrying a baby and holding a little girl by the hand. This piece stands across from the Hall of Justice in Louisville.

In 1996, Bright completed what many consider his most moving piece. Called "The Holocaust Memorial," it is awesome in its bleakness and simplicity. If one looks closely, one can see the tortured hands and faces in the flames that rise over the fence, and through the barbed wire. The piece is prominently featured at the Jewish Community Center in Louisville.

Barney Bright was a unique, charming, handsome and talented man. He lived life very much as he desired to do. He died of lung cancer on July 23, 1997.

THOMAS E. C. BRINLY

By Betty B. Matthews

Thomas Edward Cogland Brinly was born near Middletown, Kentucky, on June 10, 1822. He was the son of John W. and Mary (Bradbury) Brinly, the former a native of Jefferson County, Kentucky; the latter of Manchester, England.

The father of Mary Bradbury Brinly was John Bradbury, a noted botanist, who came to this country at the invitation of American botanists, and devoted the remainder of his life to scientific labor and research in this field. He spent much time among the Indians of the West, and was at New Madrid, Missouri, at the time of the terrible earthquake, which destroyed that town in 1811.

His many thrilling experiences were published in a book giving an account of his life, travels, and botanical work. He was a distinguished Mason, and helped organize Abraham Lodge at Middletown, one of the first five lodges organized in Kentucky.

Mary Bradbury Brinly was born on March 3, 1799, and died December 9,1856. She is buried in the Masonic Cemetery at Simpsonville beside her father.

Thomas E.C. Brinly began manufacturing plows at Simpsonville. He was the first manufacturer of steel plows in Kentucky. A demonstration of the first plow made by Thomas E.C. Brinly was on the farm of John Hall, three miles east of Shelbyville. The business moved to Louisville and became known as the Brinly-Hardy Mfg. Co., of which he was president until his death in 1902. Its plows were sold nationwide, especially in the Deep South in the years immediately before and after the Civil War. The business continued to prosper and remained in operation into the twenty-first century, although it removed to Indiana.

Thomas E.C. Brinly married first Jane McDowell. Their son was John Lyle Brinly. Jane McDowell Brinly died July 1853. In December 1854, Thomas married Catherine A. Goodknight of Shelby County. Thomas E.C. Brinly third marriage was to Eliza Thomas.

John Lyle Brinly married first Victoria Goodknight, a sister of his father's second wife. Thus he and his father became brothers-in-law. Victoria was the niece of Isaac Goodknight, the first white child born in Kentucky. She died leaving children: William Brinly, Hardy B. (of Louisville), Laura Brinly (who married Rev. S.J. Cannon of Louisville), Maud (who married Joseph Beall of Oldham Co.), Henry M. of Louisville, and Clifton who died young. John Lyle Brinly married a second time, a Mary Blackman of Washington County, Indiana.

JOHN EDWIN BROWN

By Kevin Collins

John Edwin Brown, a prominent banker and seminal figure in the development of the farm cooperative movement in Kentucky, was recognized as one of Shelby County's leading citizens, with an active and abiding interest in all its civic organizations. Born August 11, 1883, the son of Cameron and Mary King Brown, Mr. Brown resided his entire life in Shelby County at his family home Brownlea Farm three miles north of Shelbyville on Eminence Pike.

A product of the local school system, Brown matriculated at Kentucky State College (now University of Kentucky), and graduated in 1903 with a degree in agriculture. In his many years of active association with his alma mater, he was an Alumni Trustee; President of the Alumni Association; and Director of the Thomas Poe Cooper Agricultural Foundation. In 1951, the University of Kentucky, in recognition of his service to both agriculture and to the university, awarded Brown an honorary doctor's degree.

Brown was concerned with the problems of farming and farm marketing. At the age of twenty-three, he represented Shelby County on the board of directors of the Burley Tobacco Growers Co-operative Association at Winchester. From 1923 to 1925, he would be the director of the Burley Tobacco Growers Co-operative in Lexington. From 1911 to 1913 he was president of Shelbyville's Star Warehouse Company, a loose-leaf tobacco sales house. It was also in 1911 that Brown began his banking career, becoming a director of the Citizens Bank of Shelbyville, a position he would hold for twenty-one years. During World War I he also served as a chairman for both Liberty Loan and Red Cross drives. At the age of thirty-nine, while serving in the Kentucky House of Representatives, Brown introduced and helped to enact the Bingham Cooperative Marketing Act, which authorized the formation of non-profit cooperative associations to encourage the orderly marketing of farm products. This act subsequently served as a model for similar legislative acts in other farm states. Brown also introduced legislation to permit the establishment of credit unions in Kentucky.

In 1932, during the Great Depression, Brown left his position with Citizens Bank of Shelbyville to assume management of the Regional Agricultural Credit Corporation for Kentucky and Tennessee. The corporation was responsible for financial aid to distressed farmers in these two states. Then, with the formation in 1933 of the Louisville Bank for Cooperatives, Brown began an eighteen-year tenure as bank president. During these years he administered the Commodity Credit Corporation's price support system, as well as other agricultural loan programs. During the 1930s Brown also served as the President of the Kentucky Farm Bureau Federation (1932); Director-President of the Emmart Packing Company of Louisville (1933), where he was a presiding official from 1932 to 1952; and, Director of the Bourbon Stockyards Company in Louisville (1937-51). From 1947 until his retirement in 1951, Brown also served as general agent of the Farm Credit Administration of Louisville, a district that in fact included, in addition to Kentucky, the states of Ohio, Indiana, and Tennessee. In all, Brown served twenty-two years in the Farm Credit Administration. In 1949 Mr. Brown was named a trustee of the American Institute of Cooperation.

Brown was married to the former Sarah Elizabeth Logan of Danville. He was a member of the First Presbyterian Church in Shelbyville, and served many years both as a deacon and an elder. Brown held memberships in the Pendennis Club and the Filson Club Historical Society. He died on October 3, 1952, and is buried in Grove Hill Cemetery.

Betty Jean Chatham

By Sarahbeth Chatham Farabee

Betty Jean Chatham, a native of Somerset, Kentucky, moved to Shelbyville with her husband Don in 1953. Don, a family doctor from Louisville, was setting up a medical practice and he and Betty Jean wanted to raise their family in a small town.

From the very beginning Betty Jean was very involved in many aspects of Shelby County life and activities. A gifted pianist, organist, and composer with a B.A. from Georgetown College in piano performance (graduating cum laude), a Bachelor of Music from the University of Louisville (with honors), a Masters of Music (with honors) in organ performance and thirty credit hours toward a doctorate degree, she wanted to share her musical talents with her new community. Her mother, Bernice Lindle, a gifted pianist and organist herself, had instilled in Betty Jean both the appreciation and love for music and the desire to share her talents.

She gave piano concerts for the benefit of the Shelbyville High School Orchestra and Band. She taught private piano lessons to children and young people for many years. She traveled extensively around the world doing piano concerts, revivals, a Billy Graham Crusade (working with Cliff Barrows and the late Ethel Waters), recitals, and accompanying a variety of well-known sacred singers. She also worked with the late comedian, Grady Nutt. She performed concerts at forty different colleges, universities, and seminaries around the United States.

She has often played in conjunction with the Baptist Church. She was the pianist at numerous national Southern Baptist conventions. She played piano for the Baptist Women's Missionary Union's 100th Anniversary in Richmond, Virginia, and was the featured pianist at the dedication of the new Baptist Hymnal (used in Baptist churches through the nation) in both 1975 and 1991. For four years Betty Jean was the pianist for religious retreats sponsored by the chaplaincy of the U.S. Air Force including one at Clark Field in the Philippines.

In the summer of 1999, she was to write all the music, do the orchestration, and conduct the orchestra for the Shelby County Community Theater's world premiere of the original musical "Science Hill, 1919." In addition, she has done over 300 arrangements and compositions for organ and piano and children's songs. She has had 80 compositions published.

From 1991 to 1993 she was the artist in residence at St. Catharine's College in Springfield, Kentucky, working with former Governor Martha Layne Collins, the college's president.

Chatham founded and directed an interdenominational community choir of young people in Shelby County. This group presented many city and county programs singing both secular and sacred music. They also went on several concert tours, including ones in Hawaii, New York, Canada and eleven different states.

Chatham was the manager and co-owner of Chatham Station, an antique, gift and bridal shop for 16 1/2 years. She is a member of the Chautauqua Club. She founded and performed in the command performances benefit programs at the Shelby County Community Theater. She founded the Children's Choirs program at First Baptist Church, Shelbyville. She alternated as pianist and organist at First Baptist since 1956. For all her work, in 1973 she was named the "Outstanding Young Woman of Shelbyville."

SHELBYVILLE CITIZENS OF THE YEAR

By Ted Igleheart

Mayor Neil S. Hackworth soon after his election in 1982 inaugurated an annual award recognizing Shelbyville's Citizen of the Year for distinguished contributions to the community. The selection is made by the City Council. Included in the list are ministers, volunteers, teachers, businesspersons, coaches, physicians, journalists, agriculturists, etc.

Those recipients are as follows:

1983: Charles Hurt	1993: Sam Beckley
1984: Sam Chandler	1994: Jean Logan
1985: Jane Bailey	1995: Marnell Moorman
1986: Mark J. Scearce	1996: Marvin Byrdwell
1987: Briggs Lawson	1997: Donald Chatham
1988: William Lee Shannon	1998: Mary Helen Miller
1989: Emma Ellis	1999: Betty Matthews
1990: Bennett Roach	2000: Hubert Pollett
1991: Deborah Magan	2001: C. Thomas Craig
1992: Randy Brown	2002: Mary Simmons

FRANK COCHRAN

By Duanne Puckett

In 1967, Shelbyville Mayor Jesse Puckett hired Frank Cochran, the first African-American to work for the Shelbyville Police Department. Born on April 7, 1931, at Taylorsville in Spencer County, he was the son of Atlee and Geneva Cochran. He spent his early childhood in Spencer County but attended high school at Lincoln Institute in Simpsonville in Shelby County. He entered the Armed Forces in 1950 and served three years during the Korean War. Cochran served on the police force until poor health caused him to retire in 1989 at age 50. He died on December 9, 1989.

Commendations that he received during his police career included congratulatory letters from President Ronald Reagan and William Webster of the Federal Bureau of Investigation. He received the Lieutenant Governor's Award from Martha Layne Collins and awards from the Kentucky Law Enforcement Council and Martin Luther King Equality Celebration. A Kentucky Colonel, Mr. Cochran also received a Letter of Distinction from Shelbyville Mayor W.B. Porter.

MARTHA LAYNE COLLINS

By Frances Smith

Two 12 year-old boys were perched in a maple tree on Frankfort's Capitol Avenue, watching the inaugural parade of Kentucky's fifty-second governor.

"It'll be different," said one, gazing down on the state's first woman governor. "It'll be nice." Thinking it over, the other responded, "It will give everyone a chance to see which will be better—a boy or a girl." It was not whether Martha Layne Collins could be a better governor than a man, but whether a woman was equal to the task of managing the affairs of Kentucky's highest elective office. Governor Collins was not only Kentucky's first woman to serve as chief executive, but she was only the third elected in her own right in the United States.

Aware of the scrutiny that would follow, the poised blonde leader spoke of her historical significance in her inaugural address. "If I am to be a symbol, then let it signify the kind of individual freedom and opportunity precious to typical Kentuckians from whom I come, and with whom I remain."

The typical Kentuckians from whom Martha Layne Collins came are found in the heritage of Shelby County. She refers often to her early roots in Bagdad and the influence the people in this small farming community of 250 had on her life. It was fitting, then, that on December 14, 1983, the first step of her new journey began with a service at Bagdad Baptist Church--which she attended the first twelve years of her life. As her motorcade left for the trip to the state capitol, more warm memories of her childhood flashed through her mind when she saw the throng of smiling children shyly waving to her from the yard of her elementary school.

The daughter of Everett and Mary Taylor Hall, Collins was born in Shelbyville on December 7, 1936. Her father came from a family of four children and her mother was one of ten children. Everett Hall, a native of Owen County, graduated from Georgetown College and served as teacher, coach, and principal at Bagdad High School and later at Cropper School. Mary Taylor was born and reared in Spencer County but completed high school in Bagdad where she fell in love with her basketball coach. They married the

Martha Layne Hall (later Collins) was the 1954 Burley Tobacco Festival Queen. She is on the far left in this photograph.

Ellis McGinnis photograph.

summer following her graduation and made Bagdad their first home. Eventually, the couple expanded their partnership into the business world and became co-owners of Hall-Taylor Funeral Home located in Shelbyville. Growing up in a funeral home gave their daughter great respect for life but it also taught her first hand its uncertainty and the importance of public service and duty to others.

At the age of 12 Martha Layne had to leave behind the many freedoms and familiarities unique to rural living for her new life in Shelbyville. She remembers the tentative acceptance she felt as she started her junior high and high school years and her disappointment when she was not chosen for some of the things she wanted to do. She spoke of the strong influence her mother had in getting her through those times. "If I went home and told my mother someone else had been elected class president and maybe I was a little upset, she would say, 'Now you've got this job. It may not be as big as president, but you do a good job here and maybe next time you'll be elected president.'"

She took the small jobs, was a leader in her church group, helped start the Youth Center at the Public Library, worked at the swimming pool, and was elected cheerleader. In 1954, she became the Shelby County Burley-Tobacco Festival Queen and in 1959 was the Kentucky Derby Festival Queen.

Martha Layne went to Lindenwood College before transferring to the University of Kentucky where she majored in home economics. Her focus was demonstrating products, whether agricultural in nature or newly developed technology such as refrigerators. She laughingly says those were her Betty Furness days. Little did she know how helpful this training would be when, as governor, she traveled throughout the nation promoting markets for Kentucky's products.

In the summer after her sophomore year in college, Martha Layne Hall worked at Shelby County's Cedarmore Camp and met the camp's lifeguard Bill Collins, a quarterback for Georgetown's football team. They were married two years later. While he was in dental school at the University of Louisville, Martha Layne taught in Jefferson County. Their two children, Steve and Marla, were born during those years. Bill set up his dental practice in Versailles and Martha Layne began teaching at Woodford County Junior High School.

Asked to help Wendell Ford in his 1971 gubernatorial campaign, Martha Layne Collins began at the level of precinct committeewoman but soon was selected as the state's National Democratic Committeewoman and served from 1972 to 1976. When Ford was elected governor, Collins took a leave of absence to work for the state Democratic Party. "I went to work with women's groups. And soon, people around Kentucky were saying. 'Why don't you run for office?'" she said.

In her first bid for elective office, Martha Layne Collins became clerk of the Court of Appeals, which promptly became the Kentucky Supreme Court after a sweeping judicial reform. This thrust her into the state spotlight and provided her with a chance to become lieutenant governor. She went on to win the lieutenant governor's seat in 1979. Then, less than a decade after she entered politics, Martha Layne became the first woman to win a Southern governorship without following her husband into office.

In the 1983 general election, she defeated Jim Bunning, 561,674 to 454,650, after defeating Harvey Sloane and Grady Stumbo in a hard fought primary. One of her major accomplishments came when the Japanese company, Toyota Motor Sales, USA, decided to establish a large automobile plant near Georgetown. As a result, a record number of new job opportunities were brought to Kentucky under Collins' national and international economic development programs.

Leaving office in 1987 she became an international trade consultant. She taught at the University of

Louisville in 1988 and at the Institute of Politics at Harvard University in 1989. In June 1990, she became president of St. Catharine College in Washington County, a position she held until June 1996. She then became director of the International Business and Management Center at the University of Kentucky, and in 1998 went to Georgetown College to work in the president's office.

Former Governor Ned Breathitt summed up the human being who had occupied the Governor's office for four years when he characterized her as "very down to earth, and warm, which was the character of her whole public life. She didn't overstate anything."

But, perhaps the best compliment came from one of the typical Kentuckians that Governor Collins swore to serve: "It was not like government [when she was Governor]. It was more like being a Kentucky family."

CHARLES LOWELL COOK

By Charles Lowell Cook Jr.

Charles Lowell Cook was a breeder, trainer, exhibitor, and dealer and one of America's foremost authorities on saddlebred horses. He was registered as a senior judge with the American Horse Show Association. It was said of him, "They like Cook because they know he judges the horse on its merits, and not on who owns it. They know he judges it on the way it looks and handles in the ring that day, and not on the number of blue ribbons taken in times past that hang in the tack room of its stable." Cook established a reputation for breaking horses so that amateurs could ride them. With his "million dollar hands," he could transform a "bad acting" horse into a steady performer with gentle manners. Shelbyville became a popular town for hunting finished saddle horses with buyers from all over the country stopping at the Charlie Cook stables.

This remarkable man was born February 2, 1889, in Shelby County the son of Isaac Marion and Mary Elizabeth Cook. He was a horse lover from the start and, at the age of ten, prepared a suckling colt for the Shelby County Fair. Thereafter, he won every boy's riding class in which he showed until he was fourteen. For the next five years, he worked on his father's farm training young horses for the show ring, and at the age of nineteen opened a training stable in Shelbyville. On June 5, 1913, Cook was married to Sallie Thomas Lee, at "Maplewood," the home of the bride's parents, Mr. and Mrs. George Thomas Lee, Shelby County. They had two children Mildred Louise and Charles Jr.

Early in Cook's career he managed Otto W. Lehman's Chesney Farms, Lake Villa, Illinois, and his brother E. J. Lehman's Longwood Farm, Lake Villa, Illinois, where he brought out the champions Ella May, Baby Vampire, Personality, and such contenders as Brilliant Scandal, Prince Pal, and Silver Gale. Under his management and showmanship these stables became prominent in America's show stables of saddle horses.

Cook returned to his hometown of Shelbyville and opened a public training stable. He discovered Easter Star, a chestnut gelding, 15.2, with two white feet, and a small star, foaled on Easter Sunday in 1915. Most of the good judges of horseflesh, at one time or another viewed Easter Star but he was passed over until Charlie Cook saw him. After watching his unusual speed and hock action, Cook lost no time in buying him for $600.

Closing out the season of 1921 as a five-gaited horse, Easter Star won the open gelding class and finished third in the Gelding Division of the $10,000 Stake at the Kentucky State Fair. In the World Grand Championship Stake with Cook in the saddle, Easter Star was tied second to the famed Mass of Gold. Susanne (Emily Ellen Schaff) writing in Volume II, Famous Saddle Horses says, "Charlie Cook made one of the greatest shows with Easter Star that has ever been witnessed in any ring, a performance that was so brilliant, so inspiring and thrilling that it caught the fancy of the crowd and there was vociferous shouting from all points of the amphitheater for 'Number 9', the designation of Easter Star." After Charlie sold Easter Star in May of 1922, the gelding went on to win the Gelding Division of the $10,000 Stake at the State Fair in Louisville and was resold on the morning of the night when the finals were held. Easter Star brought the highest price ever paid up to that time for any saddle stallion, mare or gelding. That night Easter Star won the finals of the World Grand Championship Stake and Charlie Cook had made a World Champion which had been his lifetime ambition.

Another champion was Jonquil. She was a golden yellow mare, 15.1 1/2 hands, with three white feet, black legs and a small star. Jonquil was entered in the 1926 Championship Three-Gaited Stake at the Kentucky State Fair carrying number 13. After one solid hour of showing, in the third workout, she won the stake over a field of 23 horses. Jonquil was the first horse to ever win the Three-Gaited Championship at Louisville for four consecutive years.

This was during the period when the stake included both over and under fifteen two horses. Charlie Cook, who understood her every move, rode Jonquil to victory each time. She was conceded to be the best three-gaited saddle mare in the world.

A darling of the horse fanciers in 1940 was Sweet Compernelle, the first three year old to win the Three-Gaited Grand Championship Stake at Madison Square Garden, New York City, trained and ridden by Cook. A New York sportswriter wrote, "Sweet Compernelle's color as that of a cloth of gold; she has a small star, flowing cream colored tail and both rear ankles white, while her motion both fore and aft, her air, poise and determination, together with her faultless confirmation, make of her just that which she has proven to be a 'freak of the saddlebreed'."

In 1939, V.V. Cooke, owner of Meadow View Farm near Louisville, and owner of the third largest Chevrolet dealership in the south, persuaded Cook to leave his hometown and become the manager of his saddle horse nursery. It did not take long for him to have Meadow View Farm well represented at the Kentucky County Fair horse shows and the State Fair. Some of the popular winners were Commentator, Meadow View Mist, Commander In Chief, Smart Trick, Genius Jewell, Dixie Bell, Midnight Rose, and War King. When World War II stopped the manufacture of automobiles, Cooke was forced to disband his show horse stable.

Once again, Charlie Cook returned to Shelbyville and reopened a public training stable at the Shelby County Fair Grounds. Soon after returning he began to experience health problems and at the same time was faced with the terminal illness of his wife, Sallie, who died February 5, 1943. His saddle horse business was dissolved in 1944 and he lived with his daughter for eight years. In spite of poor health, he returned to training saddle horses on several occasions. Charlie Cook died in Shelbyville's King's Daughters Hospital on May 3, 1964. His obituary said, "Mr. Cook was a gentlemen with high ideals, strong in his convictions, devoted to his family and loyal friends."

LUDLOW COOK

By Ted Igleheart

Attached to the wall outside the Fiscal Courtroom in the Shelby County Court House is a bronze plaque which reads:

In Memory of Magistrate Ludlow Cook who served this court 40 years, longer than any other Kentuckian held a single office.

Born in Shelbyville in 1897 the son of George F. and Lydia Franklin Cook, Cook made a name for himself at an early age when he handled a pack of bloodhounds for a Captain V.G. Mullican of Lexington, who provided the dogs in criminal investigations. Cook took the dogs to eastern Kentucky in the aftermath of the Hatfield-McCoy feud to hunt down fugitives from the law. After burglaries in Shelby, Spencer, and Anderson Counties, his dogs hunted down the criminals who were then arrested and tried. The dogs were also used to locate elderly missing persons and young runaways. Cook and his dogs found a baby girl in southern Indiana who had been missing for three days. Stories of his exploits appeared in magazines all over the country.

In 1917, Cook married Sadie Dean and lived to celebrate his golden wedding anniversary in 1967. He was elected to the office of Magistrate in 1937 from the Waddy-Harrisonville District and served out his last term in 1977. Cook was well known in the farming communities for his quick wit, fiery temper, and storytelling. Among other accomplishments, he was elected as president of the Kentucky Magistrates and Commissioners Association in 1957, was a director of the Shelby County Farm Bureau and the Shelby County Board of Health, a member of Moriah Baptist Church, a charter member of the Waddy Ruritan Club, chairman of the East Shelby Volunteer Fire Department, an Army veteran of World War I, member of the American Legion, and a Kentucky Colonel. He was widely known not only in Shelby County but also over the state among county officials.

Cook died on October 13, 1980, and left surviving five daughters and one son: Lucile Briscoe of Waddy, Cecil Jewell of Simpsonville, Elizabeth Cook of Shelbyville, Catherine Collins of Mocksville, N. C., Betty Nethery of Louisville and Ludlow Cook, Jr., of Shelbyville. He also had four sisters: Gertrude Skelton of Southville, Lorena Shelburne of Mount Eden, Jannie Crafton of Waddy and Ethel Casey of Louisville, as well as two bothers: Alvia Cook of Shelbyville and Hubert Cook of Mount Eden.

HELEN CRABTREE

By William E. Matthews

Relatively few people were honored as much in their lifetime as Helen Kitner Crabtree who changed the image of the saddlebred industry from a professionally oriented, male-dominated industry to an owner/amateur/juvenile/ladies industry during her lifetime.

From the time that she and her husband Charles began operating a stable near Simpsonville in the late 1950s, Helen Crabtree knew no limits. Crabtree Farms became known as one of the finest and most revered saddlebred breeding and training centers in the United States.

Her fame brought horse owners and riders from across the land to Simpsonville to not only admire her horses, but study her riding techniques which garnered so many championships in ring after ring, state after state. What she did, most importantly, was change an industry which had been almost entirely male-dominated to one that now favors more female than male riders.

Her love for horses was revealed at an early age. She began her show career at the age of four, and was riding professionally at age 12.

Crabtree was also an accomplished author, writing the *Sports Illustrated Book of Gaited Riding* in 1962 and in 1970 Saddle Seat Equitation for Doubleday Publishers, still considered the "bible" for equitation instructors and riders. Additionally, she also wrote regularly for *Saddle and Bridle* and *National Horseman* for many years.

While she and Charles were noted trainers, Helen Crabtree was even better known as a riding instructor, teaching hundreds of young women the art of riding saddle seat. She also had a knack for picking the right mount for each of her students, and she also stressed the idea of good sportsmanship to one and all. Her style of riding became so widely adapted that her young pupils became known as the "Crabtree girls." She also helped develop her own saddle, now known as the Crabtree Saddle.

Crabtree was a graduate of McMurray College in Jacksonville, Florida, where she got the position as head of the riding department the day after her graduation. The college team was undefeated during Helen's tenure.

The Crabtrees came to Shelby County in the late 1950s and began constructing a stable near Simpsonville. That started an era of unexcelled accomplishments, including 75 World Championship Saddlebred Horses, and 22 National Equitation Championships. At the peak of its success, Crabtree Farms was operating on almost 200 acres, and had as many as 100 horses in training at any one time. In one year alone, the stable had 58 horses showing at the Kentucky State Fair.

In 1980 Helen and Charles were invited by President Ronald Reagan to participate in his first inaugural parade, and she remembered riding up Pennsylvania Avenue with 16 of her best horses. "I was overcome with patriotism and pride in our group," she recalled.

She traveled the globe to teach clinics and judge shows in England, France, and South Africa.

Space does not permit enumerating all her awards and honors, but among the most notable were her designation as the American Horse Show Association's Horsewoman of the year in 1964; her induction

Helen Crabtree on "Popular Time" in 1980.

into the St. Louis Horse Show Hall of Fame in 1975; Trainer of the Year designee by the United Professional Horsemen's Association; and Lifetime Achievement Award by the AHSA. She and Charlie were inducted into the World Championship Horse Show Hall of Fame in 1989. USA Equestrian honored her with a 50-lb. bronze trophy in Helen's likeness riding the horse Warlock.

Helen Crabtree received her first license in 1950, and went on to hold licenses in Hackney and Harness, Morgan, National Show Horse, Parade, Roadster, Saddle Seat, Equitation, Saddlebred, and Shetland.

In 1989 at the age of 74, Helen Crabtree rode in competition for the final time at the Lawrenceburg Horse Show. Following her retirement from the ring, she and Charlie continued to make their home on 13 acres of the original farm property near Simpsonville.

Helen Crabtree was always quick to credit her success to the two men in her life, husband Charlie and son Redd Crabtree, who won many Kentucky State Fair Horse Show Championships in his own right. She said, "My husband and my son, without them, their inspiration, talent and kindness, I couldn't be Helen Crabtree." Helen Crabtree died on January 4, 2002, at Jewish Hospital in Louisville.

ALFRED DEADERICK DOAK

By John Hunt Doak and Kevin Collins

Alfred Deaderick Doak, the eldest child and only son of the Reverend Doctor Alexander Hunt and Day Von Albade Deaderick Doak, was born on June 8, 1907, in the manse of his father's church. The Rev. Doak was a minister from 1906 to 1913 at the Mulberry Presbyterian Church, located on the Bagdad road in northeastern Shelby County.

In 1913 the family moved to Wilmore, south of Lexington, where Alfred attended grade school. The family relocated to Georgetown in 1921, where the red-haired "Rusty" Doak, as his classmates called him, attended and graduated in 1924 from Georgetown High School. He subsequently enrolled in Georgetown College and graduated cum laude in 1928 with a degree in chemistry. He was a member of the Pi Kappa Alpha fraternity and president of his senior class.

In 1929, after a short spell teaching high school chemistry and biology, Doak matriculated at Harvard Medical School. Summers were spent as a medical apprentice assisting doctors in sundry Kentucky coalfields. After graduating medical school in 1933, he did his internship and residency in internal medicine at Duke University Hospital. In 1936, he completed another internship in pediatrics at Johns Hopkins Hospital.

In November of the same year Doak opened his medical practice in Shelbyville. His first office was above Hall's Drugstore in the 500 block of Main Street. Subsequently, from 1938 to 1941, Doak shared office space with Dr. Caspar Hayes, a dentist. They were located on Main Street across from the post office.

During World War II Doak served in the U.S. Army Medical Corps. After flight surgeon training in Texas, First Lieutenant Doak was assigned to the staff of the Chief Flight Surgeon, 12th Air Force. He participated in the invasion of North Africa and the Italian campaign. He was promoted to Lieutenant Colonel and was the recipient of the Purple Heart.

After the War, Doak returned to his medical practice in Shelbyville. With an office on Washington Street, across from Science Hill, he ministered to patients in every conceivable medical and financial condition. A dedicated "country" doctor, who made house calls and saw the practice of medicine as his Christian calling, Doak perhaps found his greatest joy in his pediatric practice. He estimated that he delivered some 2,500 babies during his years in Shelby County and once told his son that, "there is no greater excitement and nothing more gratifying than delivering a baby and seeing the joy it brings to a mother's face."

In 1938, Doak married the former Evelyn Marie Cowan, a music teacher at the Science Hill School. They had four children. In addition to the demands of medicine, Doak also served on the Shelbyville school board and was, for 20 years, a member of the Rotary Club. He was also a Deacon and an Elder of the First Presbyterian Church of Shelbyville.

In 1966, Doak sadly left Shelbyville to accept a position with a Veterans Administration hospital in Johnson City, Tennessee. In 1977, at the age of 70, he retired. He died in 2002.

CHARLES WILLIAM ELSEY

By Kevin Collins

The Reverend Dr. Charles William Elsey, former pastor of the First Baptist Church of Shelbyville, was born, June 10, 1880, in Laurel County. The son of Alex and Sarah Mourn Elsey, the Rev. Elsey's pastorate in Shelbyville spanned 31 years, from March 1, 1926, until January 1, 1957.

A product of the public school system of Fayette County, graduating in 1897, Elsey, at the age of 22, was ordained a minister of the Baptist Church on June 29, 1902. Following his ordination he became a pastor with the Fifth Street Baptist Church in Lexington, which he served until 1908. It was during these years that he also earned a Bachelor of Arts degree from Georgetown College in 1905. He completed his theological studies at the Southern Baptist Theological Seminary in 1907.

In 1908, the Rev. Elsey assumed the pastoral duties of the First Baptist Church in Cynthiana. He served that congregation for thirteen years. During this pastorate he published the first of two well-received spiritual books *Journeying with Jesus* (Gotham Press, Boston). In 1913 he also received his Doctorate of Divinity from Georgetown College. From 1921 to 1925, the Rev. Elsey served as President of Cumberland College in Williamsburg.

In addition to his work at the First Baptist Church of Shelbyville, the Rev. Elsey was a member of the Kentucky Baptist State Board of Missions; the Home Mission Board of the Southern Baptist Convention; one of the Board of Managers of *The Western Recorder* (the weekly newspaper of the Kentucky Baptist Convention); chairman of the committee of founders of the Kentucky Baptist Foundation; a past moderator of the General Association of Baptists in Kentucky; a director of the Historical Society of the Southern Baptist Convention; and, a trustee of the Kentucky Baptist Children's Home at Glendale. In addition, he was also a member of the Board of Trustees of Georgetown College. In 1937 his second book, *The Prodigal's Father* (Broadman Press, Nashville), was published.

The Rev. Elsey was married to the former Birdie Young. He died in 1964, at the age of 84, and is buried in Grove Hill Cemetery.

Courtesy of First Baptist Church.

Dr. Charles W. Elsey was pastor of the First Baptist Church in Shelbyville for 31 years. He also wrote a history of the church spanning the years from 1819 to 1962.

WILLIE FLEMING

By Duanne Puckett

In 1968, when the black community was mourning the death of Dr. Martin Luther King Jr., Willie Fleming felt positive about the steps being taken in Shelbyville: the integration of public facilities, the election of a black council member, the hiring of a black police officer, the increasing role of blacks in community affairs. At the same time, Fleming saw a stark contrast between the opportunities available in Shelbyville to those in Louisville where blacks had already been employed as bank tellers, secretaries, receptionists and plant superintendents.

It was because of that lack of opportunity in Shelbyville that Mr. Fleming practiced law in Louisville, even though he and his wife reared their family in Shelbyville. Their children graduated from integrated schools and one of their daughters was named Miss Teen Cheerleader and was among the first blacks to make the high school cheerleading squad.

Fleming graduated from Shelbyville Junior High School in 1944 and went on to Lincoln Institute where he was valedictorian of the Class of 1947. While at the all-black high school near Simpsonville, he was president of the junior and senior classes, and lettered in football and basketball. At graduation, he received more awards than any one student in the history of the school.

In 1952, he graduated with honors from Fisk University in Nashville where he received a B.S. degree in business administration. He was the first in his family (one of eight children of William Newton and Bessie Payne Fleming) to go to college. While there he was president of his senior class and lettered all four years in football, earning the nickname "Hard Rock" Fleming.

His "first" status continued when he enrolled at the University of Louisville School of Law, becoming one of the first two African-Americans to receive a law degree in 1954. He passed Kentucky's Bar Exam in 1955 and has been in practice ever since.

In Shelbyville, Fleming was the first African-American to develop a subdivision. It's called Monica Gardens and is located on U.S. 60 East. He joined Bethel African Methodist Episcopal Church on Henry Clay Street at an early age, based on what he said his parents instilled in him: Christian values, love for God and church, and a strong quality of perseverance and persistence, essential for succeeding in every walk of life. For his church, he has been general counsel and trustee board member for more than 20 years.

He also made improvements for the black community in 1949 when he and other African-American leaders pressured the City School Board to replace what had been the Negro Elementary School. The facility on Bradshaw Street burned in 1945 and the Shelbyville Independent School Board sold the property. For a makeshift school, the School Board rented the United Brothers Lodge Hall adjacent to the old school property. It was a two-story frame building, heated by coal stoves and without indoor plumbing. After Fleming and other blacks voiced concern, a new $100,000 Shelbyville Colored School was built at Eleventh and High Street. He continued his interest in the education system by holding meetings with the City School Board to have integration in 1957 of the elementary and high schools.

The Shelby County Civic Organization was formed by Fleming and other African-American leaders in 1963 with the assistance of the Rev. Horace Taylor, pastor of Bethel AME. One accomplishment was having the Shelby County Board of Education integrate its schools that year and the high school for the 1964-65 term.

Turning their attention to the community, Fleming and his counterparts forced Mayor Jesse Puckett and Shelbyville City Council to fully integrate the city swimming pool beginning with the 1964 season. He also had meetings with Mayor Puckett, beginning in 1963, about the need for public housing. Two years later, the Shelbyville Municipal Housing Commission was formed and in 1969, a 100-unit apartment complex was built north of U.S. 60 with funds from HUD. The complex is called Bondurant Heights, after Puckett's mother.

Fleming and the Civic Organization persuaded Lee Nor Mack in 1964 to run for a seat on Shelbyville City Council. He won the election to become the first black city councilman in more than 60 years.

MARY LOUISE FOUST

By Mary David Myles

Mary Louise Foust was born on October 15, 1909, in New Albany, Indiana. Her parents were Reverend David T. Foust and Mary Margaret (Rippel) Foust. Her family moved to Shelbyville where she graduated from high school. She earned a degree from Georgetown College and worked at a Shelbyville bank while she attended Georgetown. She later received a law degree from the University of Louisville.

Mary Louise Foust started in state government in 1938 as a filing clerk in the Department of Revenue. She served three terms as the state auditor. After her first term as auditor, Foust resumed her law practice. In 1969, she was elected to fill the unexpired term of the late Clyde Conley. She was then elected to another full term from 1971 to 1975. She was the first woman in Kentucky to be a licensed attorney and a certified public accountant. And in 1963, she became the first woman in Kentucky to run for governor.

Known as a political maverick because she was not aligned with the established political "machine," Foust was an outspoken critic of Governors Wendell Ford and Julian Carroll.

Courtesy of Mary David Myles.

Mary Louise Foust served three terms as state auditor for the Commonwealth of Kentucky and practiced law in Shelbyville and Lexington.

Foust practiced law in Shelbyville and in Lexington and was licensed to practice law before the Supreme Court of the United States. In the private sector she was with Bittner and Clark, Certified Public Accountants in San Francisco; United States Steel Corporation in New Albany, Indiana; and Humphrey Robinson and Company in Louisville.

Foust was a member of the First Baptist Church of Shelbyville where she was received for baptism on October 1, 1922, a member of the Isaac Shelby Chapter of the Daughters of the American Revolution for 50 years, an honorary member of the Shelbyville Business and Professional Women's Club, and the Democratic Womens Clubs of Fayette County and Frankfort. She also was a President of the Kentucky Branch of the International Order of the Kings Daughters and Sons.

Georgetown College established the Foust Co-Curricular Series in 1985-86 in honor of her endowment to the school's concert, lecture and arts program. The college also bestowed upon her the Doctorate of Laws Degree on May 14,1988.

RALPH WALDO GILBERT

By Kevin Collins

Lawyer, judge, U. S. Congressman, state legislator, and leader in Kentucky Democratic politics, Ralph Waldo Gilbert was born January 17, 1882, in Taylorsville. A descendant of an old pioneer land-grant family that migrated to Kentucky about 1785, Ralph was the youngest of three children born to George Gilmore and Elizabeth Hinkle Gilbert. The family moved to Shelbyville in 1886 when the elder Gilbert became an attorney for the Cumberland Ohio Railroad Company.

Gilbert's predecessors had a long tradition of public service. His grandfather, James Gilbert, had served in the General Assembly in 1846 as a representative from Spencer County. His father had been a state senator (1884 to 1890) as well as a four-term U.S Congressman (1898 to 1906).

Ralph Gilbert attended local schools followed by undergraduate work at the University of Virginia, graduating in 1899. He studied law at the University of Louisville and graduated in 1901, at the age of nineteen. He then began his legal practice in Shelbyville and appeared before the local bar extensively throughout his life. Gilbert was a commanding presence and a persuasive speaker both in front of a jury and, as in later years, on the radio as a political candidate. His most memorable local court appearance may have been as a defense attorney in the October 1938 trial of the Garr brothers, accused of murdering General Denhardt in front of the Armstrong Hotel.

Gilbert began his thirty-year public career in 1910 with his election to the office of Shelby County Judge. He served two terms from 1910 to 1918. In 1920, he won election to the U.S. Congress and served four consecutive two-year terms. He was again elected to the Congress in 1930, following a single term in Frankfort in the Kentucky House of Representatives. He served in Washington until March 1933, when he once again returned to the Kentucky General Assembly. As a U.S Congressman his interest and expertise was farm legislation, but he was also a member of the Insular Affairs Committee, where he championed Philippine independence.

In 1935, Gilbert was elected to represent the Twenty-first District in the Kentucky State Senate. During his career as a state legislator, both in the lower and upper house, Gilbert, among other things, co-authored the Brock-Gilbert Honest Election Act, chaired the Judiciary Committee and was senate majority leader. He twice sought to run for Governor, but reconsidered. In 1939, he was a candidate for Lieutenant Governor.

Gilbert resided on his farm, bought in 1908, a few miles east of Shelbyville on U.S. 60. He was twice married and had three daughters by his first wife, the former Jane Thompson of Shelby County, who pre-deceased him. In 1935, he married the former Victoria M. Vodila of Pennsylvania, who was his secretary when he served in Congress. He was a member of the Methodist Church of Shelbyville. He died July 30, 1939, and is buried in Grove Hill Cemetery.

GEORGE WILLIAM GILES

By Kevin Collins

George William Giles, superintendent of Shelby County Schools from 1940 to 1961, was born December 12, 1904, in the town of Gratz in Henry County. He was one of seven children in the family of George William and Helen Dennis Giles.

A graduate of Southwestern College in Winfield, Kansas, Giles also attended Kentucky Wesleyan College and completed post-graduate work at the University of Kentucky. A resident for many years of Cropper, Giles began his commitment to education there, serving as a teacher, principal, and basketball coach for most of the 1930s. His love of sports, particularly baseball, led him to organize and manage teams in a tri-county baseball league composed of Shelby, Henry, and Oldham Counties. After the formation of Shelby County High School, it was Giles who suggested a name for the school's athletic teams, the "Rockets."

As superintendent of Shelby County Schools Giles completed a major consolidation when eight county high schools became a single entity, Shelby County High School. The new school just east of Shelbyville on U.S. 60 opened in the fall of 1960. Concomitant with this consolidation Giles implemented significant changes in the school transportation system. During the twenty-one years of his administration the school system maintained attendance levels that ranked within the top 10 percent of schools in the state.

Giles was a member of the Cropper Methodist Church. He married Nell Catherine Underwood and they had two sons, Dennis and George William III. He died October 25, 1961, at the age of 57, and is buried in the Dutch Tract Cemetery, Pleasureville, Henry County.

HORACE HENRY GREENE

By Duanne Puckett

Horace Henry Greene was born in Louisville on April 12, 1907. He was the eldest of ten children. His father, George, was an employee of Standard Manufacturing Company, and his mother, Muriel, was the daughter of W.H. Bloomer, who was a Methodist minister.

A relationship of love and support prevailed in the home, which served as background for Dr. Greene's preparation for a full life of Christian service to humanity.

The Reverend J.H. Ross baptized Dr. Greene at the New Coke Methodist Church in Louisville. In 1918, he joined the church on profession of faith under the pastorate of the Rev. H.W Simmons.

He graduated from Louisville's Central High School in 1926, and a few months later, in August, was licensed to preach. In 1929, Rev. Greene graduated from Gammon Theological Seminary and was ordained by Bishop W.M. Clair. He was

Dr. Horace Henry Greene served as pastor of St. John United Methodist Church, 1969-1986.

admitted to the Lexington Conference in 1930. In 1932, he was received into full connection and ordained an elder.

Greene married Daisy Mae English on June 11, 1931. Two sons, Horace Henry Greene Jr. and Elwood Lamont Greene, were born to this marriage.

Greene served in the following capacities: Clair Methodist Church, Irvington, Kentucky (1929-31), New Zion Methodist Church, Lexington (1931-39), Gunn Tabernacle Methodist Church, now included within Wesley United Methodist, Lexington (1939-48), District Superintendent of the Louisville District, Lexington Conference (1948-52), Calvary Methodist Church, Cincinnati (1952), R.E. Jones Temple Methodist Church, Louisville (1953-64); District Superintendent, Louisville District and Lexington District of Tennessee/Kentucky Conference 1964-68), Director of Church and Community Planning, Louisville Area (1968-73).

When he retired in 1973, Dr. Greene continued to be active as pastor of the Shelbyville Circuit in the Frankfort District of the Kentucky Conference of the United Methodist Church. The Shelbyville Circuit includes Wesley United Methodist Church at Chaplin, Kentucky; Allen Chapel United Methodist Church; and St. John United Methodist at Shelbyville. He also served as a member of the Chaplin's Clergy group serving the Good Samaritan Hospital of Lexington. The center on Tenth Street run by St. John is known as the H.H. Green Center.

His interests were community oriented. He served as a member of the executive board of the Old Kentucky Home Boy Scouts Council, a member of the Lexington and Fayette County boards of education, a member of the Good Samaritan Hospital board, chairman of the Community Action Agency in Lexington/Fayette County, director of the Wesley Foundation at Kentucky State University, and a member of Union College board of trustees.

Greene received an Honorary Doctor of Humanities Degree from Union College in 1971. He held many important positions in his church and on boards. This made him one of the best known African-Americans in the state. Rev. Greene died August 22, 1986, and was buried in Greenwood Cemetery in Lexington.

SUE THORNTON HENNING

By R.R. Van Stockum Sr.

Born in Shelby County on August 14, 1866, Sue Thornton Henning was a descendant of John and Ann (Polk) Allen of Frederick County, Virginia. On September 6, 1887, at the home of her mother Bettie Allen Meriwether in Shelbyville, she married James Williamson Henning Jr., a successful young Louisville financier and son of Joshua Fry Speed's business partner James W. Henning Sr.

During the period 1907-28, following the failure of her husband's brokerage firm in New York City, Mrs. Henning returned to Allen Dale, her ancestral farm that had been in her family since 1795. Here, as owner and breeder, she displayed to the end the grace, dignity, and aplomb that had been hallmarks of her career. She established a prize-winning herd of registered Jersey cattle. In 1914, the farm produced the national grand champion Jersey bull. Under her direction, Allen Dale Farm became nationally and internationally renowned and Henning became the first woman to serve on the board of the American Jersey Cattle Club.

In 1909, Mrs. Henning's daughter, Susanne, despite the adamant opposition of her mother, married Marquis Antonie de Charette, scion of a distinguished French military family and a descendant of Charles X of France. Before her death, Henning was dispossessed of her farm because of financial insolvency. She died on June 29, 1933, in Washington and is buried in Grove Hill Cemetery in Shelbyville.

Courtesy of R. R. Van Stockum, Sr.

Sue Thornton Henning is at right in this ca. 1908 photograph; her mother, Bettie Meriwether is in the center, and her daughter Susanne Henning is on the left.

MARGARET HORNBACK

By Duanne Puckett

In 1965, the *Shelby Sentinel* selected the twenty-five most influential citizens in Shelby County as part of the weekly newspaper's centennial celebration. Among the handful of women was Margaret Hornback.

Born in Anderson County, Kentucky, on December 18, 1910, Hornback left her mark as a vital member of the medical community. From childhood, she had dreams of becoming a doctor. But upon graduation from high school she decided to go to school during the day and work in the hospital laboratory at nights. That caused her to change her career plans from physician to laboratory technician. Shortly after beginning that career at the King's Daughters Hospital on Henry Clay Street in Shelbyville, she learned of a need for someone to work in the operating room. This sent Hornback to nursing school--a decision she never regretted.

When World War II began, Hornback shared her nursing skills with those who needed them most. As a first lieutenant in the U.S. Army, she served in the North African and European theaters. Stationed there three and a half years, she nursed many soldiers from the front line. By the time of her discharge, she had reached the rank of captain and received a Theater Ribbon, one silver battle star, and three bronze battle stars along with six overseas service bars.

When she returned to Shelbyville after the war, she worked with the local health department as a public health nurse. For a little over eighteen months, she traveled around the county, visiting homes and saw that everyone received the required inoculations. In September 1947 Hornback returned to King's Daughters Hospital where she was hired as director of nursing "until they could find someone else," she once said.

Apparently, no one else was found with the qualifications and dedication that she exhibited because she remained in that position 27 years. During that time, her responsibilities were to "provide skilled care for patients in the hospital and to develop capabilities in the staff to care for the sick." Before she retired, she spent one year as in-service coordinator, which involved teaching nurse's aides the proper approach to patient care and the techniques of bedside nursing.

During the 1950s, Hornback helped to improve the overall health-care provisions in Shelby County. Along with countless other volunteers, she was instrumental in seeing that King's Daughters expanded to a new facility on the west end of town. It is known today as Jewish Hospital Shelbyville.

Hornback retired from the hospital, but she did not hang up her nursing cap. She worked as a volunteer nurse at a hospital in the Gaza Strip in Israel, which was the site of many Egyptian-Israeli terrorist attacks.

She was an active member at Shelbyville First Baptist Church, and it was because of her strong faith she became a missionary nurse. She believed nursing was her calling: "We all have an area for which we are designed for divine providence. I believe nursing was mine," she said. Hornback died in April 1998.

BENJAMIN FRANKLIN HUNGERFORD

By Duanne Puckett

Benjamin Franklin Hungerford was described as a symbolic picture of Uncle Sam; an erect, peppery, little man in frock-tailed coat, a black silk hat, well-groomed with chin whiskers and a knowing smile. He was born in Sparta, New York, in 1825 and came to Shelbyville in 1859 to succeed the Rev. J.W. Goodman as president of what was called the Kentucky Female College. When the Civil War forced the closing of the school, he took up preaching—a career that spanned 50 years.

Hungerford left New York for his health. Carrying $300 in his pocket he crossed the Great Lakes by steamer where he was robbed of all his cash except for a $10 gold piece. He met up with a kinsman who encouraged him to settle in Owen County where Hungerford founded the New Liberty Female College in 1851. Two years later he married Rosa Ann Allnut with whom he moved to Shelbyville.

Hungerford ran a private academy in Rockbridge, a community just southeast of Little Jeptha Creek on KY 714 for 11 years. Then he returned to Shelbyville and was associated with Rev. George Scearce in a school for boys at Third and Washington (the Stanley-Casey House). His own home was a two-story white mansion overlooking a rise on the east end of town at what is today KY 53 South and U. S. 60 East.

He died in 1916 but Shelby Countians became familiar with Brother Hungerford through extensive diaries that he wrote in ink in hardbound school notebooks for about 50 years. Permission to publish the diaries was given to the Shelby News by his grandsons, Guthrie and Frank Jesse. The notebooks are now on microfilm at the Southern Baptist Theological Seminary.

In the diaries, he jotted down each day's happenings, including the hard times of the Civil War, which brought financial disaster to the Baptist preacher. On July 22, 1864, he wrote: "Today, 25 guerrillas attacked Shelbyville, intending to rob the town. But through the bravery of two citizens, four were killed and the rest hastily decamped. May God protect us while we sleep." The Union Army confiscated his school for a hospital along with two blocks of land he owned in the vicinity. His journals didn't reflect bitterness from the war; instead they manifest sorrow over the frightful horrors of the conflict.

His pastorates included Little Mount, Pigeon Fork, Mount Moriah, Taylorsville, Elk Creek, Burks Branch, Dover, Buffalo Lick, Salem, Graefenburg, Lawrenceburg, and at Clear Creek in Woodford County and Salem in Indiana. Hungerford recorded that he baptized 2,000 converts, married 2,000 couples, and preached about that many funerals.

Rev. Benjamin F. Hungerford, a Baptist minister in Shelby County, kept a journal of his daily life for many years.

Shelby County Public Library.

577

WILLIE JENKINS

By Duanne Puckett

Football at Shelbyville High School was the responsibility of Richard "Puss" Greenwell for 36 years. However, he gave credit to a valuable assistant for keeping the program running smoothly. That assistant was not a coach but the team manager, Willie Jenkins. Greenwell remembered how the petite-framed black man "always hung around" and then finally one day asked if there was anything he could do. The rest was history.

Willie, as players and fans fondly called him alike, handled all the equipment, took care of the players' personal belongings and washed the uniforms. He once called himself "an all-around fellow. I do anything they want done."

His work did not go unnoticed. Coach Greenwell remembered one football game in Harrodsburg when the host team lost every personal article out of its locker room. None of the Red Devils' belongings were disturbed. When the police questioned the coaching staff why, they pointed to Jenkins and said, "That's why."

Not only did Jenkins care for the boys' material items; he also kept their morale close to his heart. Tom Becherer, who took over the Devil's coaching job when Greenwell retired in 1972, remembered how he would sometimes give a player a push as he left the locker room if he thought the athlete was moving too slowly.

In 1972, Jenkins was recognized for his years of service to Shelbyville High School when he was the second letterman to ever receive an honorary jacket. Jenkins often said about his own red wool coat with a large "S" on the chest, "It's beautiful! I hardly ever wear it but I want it with me when I die." It was displayed near his casket when he passed away less than ten years later. The other person to receive an honorary letter jacket was Jane Meyer, the cheer leading coach from 1943-74.

CHARLES KINKEL

By Bobby Smith

Writing music compositions for local women to perform, Charles Kinkel became quite noted for his abilities. He taught at Stuart's College and then later at Science Hill Female Academy for 20 years. The *Handbook of American Music and Musicians* notes that his compositions were almost all piano pieces, many of which were designed for teaching purposes. Among the more popular listings were: "Pearl and Daisy Polka;" "Polymnia Polka;" Postillion d'Amour;" "Mabel Marurka;" "Angel of Night;" and "Lover's Serenade."

A sketch in the *Handbook* indicates that he was born in Rheinpfatz, Germany, in 1832. Though not especially educated in music, he always felt a great love for it. The Revolution of 1848 produced such an unsettled state of things in Germany that he resolved to leave, and the following year he arrived in the United States and settled in Shelbyville.

Although a musician, Kinkel was chosen as the president of the new Citizens Bank in 1888. He designed the plan and arrangement of the interior of the building. One finds an entry about Mr. Kinkel in the *Shelby News* in 1888. It indicated that he was one of the 11 incorporators of the new financial venture, and said:

"Serving as president, Prof. Kinkel is a German by birth, but he has been a resident of the United States since 1850, and since 1858, with the exception of temporary absence, Shelbyville has been his home. He is known far and wide as a musical composer, and his long service as a professor in Science Hill School, years ago, placed him in the front rank of the educators of the land. It is a generally received opinion that musical composers are dreamers-not so in the case of Prof. Kinkel. Not only does he possess the divine afflatus, but he is also a levelheaded, practical business man—an able financier— a gentleman who holds the confidence and esteem of the community. To him we shall have occasion to refer more than once in this review."

Charles Kinkel married Florence Norvell on December 1, 1864. Norvell was born of Virginia parents. Kinkel is listed in the 1865 Science Hill Girls School Catalogue as the Professor of Music. Mrs. Kinkel is listed as his assistant.

The 1870 Shelby County Census reflected a growing family. They had a four-year-old daughter, also named Florence, and a one-year-old son named Karl. It is apparent from this record that Kinkel had some financial means as he had four servants in his employment.

Kinkel and his wife attended the St. James Episcopal Church. Mrs. Kinkel died in 1878 and Charles died in 1891. Apparently, their residence was located either at 611 Main Street or just to the east of it.

MARQUIS DE LAFAYETTE

By Bennett Roach

The thriving village of Shelbyville got hoisted to the national social scene almost overnight when Gen. Marquis de Lafayette and his entourage visited, dined, and danced here in 1825.

It was a countrywide return to the young republic for the noted Frenchman, a sentimental return to the country which he had fought for, and helped create 50 years previously.

It was quite a feather in Shelbyville's cap since Lafayette had primarily visited the nation's larger cities, rarely stopping at what were much smaller villages. In 1825, Shelbyville had a population of 1,201, about one-fourth of the number who were residents of Louisville.

The visit here was on May 13, 1825. Lafayette and his party were en route to Frankfort and Lexington. Traveling by stagecoach and on horseback, the entourage included the governors of Florida, Indiana, and Tennessee. Henry Clay and Judge John Rowan were in the party. An honorary guard of Lafayette cavalry accompanied the procession out of Louisville and east on the old road through Middletown to Shelbyville. Adverse weather or difficult roads probably caused the overnight stop in Shelbyville.

Whether intentional or not, the arrival of this international figure was taken in stride by local citizens. Being on the main line from Louisville to Lexington, Shelbyville was used to sheltering travelers of all sorts, from important personages in fine carriages down the scale to hog drovers and assorted pedestrians.

Tradition says that the town rolled out the red carpet in welcome to the famous visitor. It has been established that he stayed at Megowan's Tavern on the corner of Sixth and Main Streets. Later, it became the location of Hasting's Stagecoach Inn.

That night a reception and banquet was held in the large hall in the McGrath building next to the courthouse. Miss Eliza Bullock, afterward Mrs. Petitt, and Miss Jane Hardin, after Mrs. Logan, mother of J. M. Logan, were the belles of the ball. Newspaper accounts of the evening report that Gen. Lafayette spoke in very complimentary terms of the beauty and charming manners of the Shelbyville ladies.

The town of Shelbyville expended $30 for powder to fire salutes on the arrival and departure of Lafayette's party.

Some delightful local legends grew up over the visit, especially the ball and banquet. Old newspapers of the day are available on microfilm, but only a scant amount of space is devoted to Lafayette's visit to Shelbyville. Souvenirs of the Shelbyville reception and ball have been preserved over the years, including one or two dresses worn by ladies who attended and danced with Lafayette.

Tradition says that Lafayette and his party spent the night at Cross Keys, the stagecoach stop about six miles east of Shelbyville. But Major Hume, noted author of that era, says almost conclusively that Lafayette spent the night at Megowan's Tavern.

For the 175th anniversary of Lafayette's coming to America to help Washington, a party of French diplomats re-enacted Lafayette's visit of 1825. They traveled from Louisville to Lexington and stopped in Shelbyville where the Shelbyville Kiwanis Club treated them to dinner.

Lafayette, according to local observers, tried to look and act "American." He described himself as "plain and Republican," in the extreme. He wore plain brownish trousers, and a plain blue coat with covered buttons, Lafayette had been through the French Revolution, and had renounced his title as Marquis. "I am an American General," he said. He also appeared to have a "winning sense of humor," according to a local newspaper at that time.

Speaking with a line of soldiers, he would shake hands with the individual and say, "Are you married?" If the soldier answered, "Yes," Lafayette would respond, "Lucky man." If the soldier said, "No," then Lafayette would again respond, "Lucky man."

When Lafayette reached Lexington, Transylvania accorded him an honorary degree. Earlier he had been a contributor to the college's endowment, along with George Washington, John Adams, Aaron Burr, Robert Morris, and other famous men of the 18th and early 19th centuries.

THE LATINO COMMUNITY

By Marcia Biagi

If someone were to ask in the year 2000 what is one of the most noticeable changes in Shelby County in the past twenty years, one might agree that it has been the appearance and influence of a whole new culture. It is the reality of the Latina migration being discovered and discovering new life and growth, even as the new immigration laws make it almost impossible for Latinos and others to come to this country and to this county where their help is desperately needed. And the changes are obvious.

If one is of school age (whatever level), one notices that a few new students may be darker in complexion, with dark eyes and hair, and most strikingly may be very quiet, but at times can be heard talking animatedly in a different language which one might recognize as Spanish when with others who speak the same.

If one works in a social service sector, one perhaps notices that persons who apply for appointments, whether medical, dental, educational, legal, or other, have names which are a bit difficult to spell and pronounce; and one hopes that when they appear they'll either speak English or have an interpreter along.

If one shops at Kroger or Walmart, one definitely has seen or heard men, some women and children, carefully searching through the stores for some goods or products that they will recognize as part of their Latino way of cooking and eating, and many times searching also for words to express themselves in English at the check-out-line, or as they purchase telephone cards, or money orders to send to their families in Mexico, Guatemala, or Honduras.

If one is a farmer, particularly in tobacco, one probably has been looking for Latinos to work at certain times of the year; or maybe to stay and work all year while one trusts they will be around when help is

Workers setting tobacco on a Shelby County farm.

needed. It seems more and more that there are fewer and fewer local workers who want to do manual labor. So, it is understandable that the recent influx of Latinos is due in a great part to the needs in Shelby and other counties.

Before the late 1980s most of the need for increased labor during tobacco harvesting time was supplied by farm families, by hiring students or factory workers who were looking for a second job. Harvesting of tobacco begins, depending upon seasonal variables, by August. The harvesting and stripping continues till about the Christmas season, again, depending on weather. Migrant Latino labor became important to the county's tobacco industry by the late 1980s.

Rosa Martin from Puerto Rica grew up in New York City and came with her Anglo-American husband for work. They settled in Henry County near Sulphur. She recalled feeling alone with no one to speak her native Spanish. She only knew of two other Latino women who were also married to Anglo-Americans, one of whom is Elsa Matheney.

Martin recalls being contacted by the Extension Office and asked to teach Spanish to about 25 farmers and fruit growers. (Jean McIntosh of Annunciation Church said she remembers that some of the first Latino migrant workers were hired to work in the peach and other orchards in Trimble County). She enjoyed the opportunity, and later worked as a volunteer to teach the actual migrant farm workers "Consumer Education."

What began in Trimble and Henry Counties happened in Shelby County as the migrant workers arrived and found farmers desperate for help. Each year more Latino migrants appeared, as by word of mouth and telephone the news was getting around that there was work in Kentucky, and the pay, especially for tobacco farms, was like a gold mine for hard working individuals who could earn up to twenty times for cutting tobacco here as compared to wages in their own countries.

Sister Lupe Arciniega of the Loretto Sisters lived and worked in South America, and then in 1987 came to offer her services to the Catholic Archdiocese of Louisville to serve Spanish speaking migrants in the rural areas. Arciniega soon learned of the migrants arriving in the Henry County area to work in tobacco. She visited them and eventually organized a place for them to meet. She got a grant to hire Rosa Martin to do more local outreach in Henry County, then eventually a grant to also hire Sister Gia Therese Mudd of the Ursuline Sisters for six months (who later was given a salary by the Annunciation Church of Shelbyville and St. John's Church of Eminence to continue). Sister Mudd's talents and commitment to be an advocate for the Latino migrants soon made her known in many circles, especially in the Shelby County area as she began to organize a Resource Center in Shelbyville for the Latino community with the help of many volunteers, church groups, and organizations. A "Centro Latino" was inaugurated in April 1997 on the grounds of the Catholic Church and continues to serve the Latino population in a non-discriminatory manner in emergency assistance (donations of food and clothing), counseling, and accompaniment for health, education, work, social, and legal needs.

About the same time, in the early 1990s, other church related groups sought to aid the growing Latino population. The Baptist churches made it possible for one of their own, Jesus Pachato, to begin an active ministry, helping many in their physical, social, educational, legal, employment, and spiritual needs. Several other churches have shown great compassion in reaching out in ministry including the Assembly of God Church, the Centenary United Methodist, the First Presbyterian, the God of Prophecy Church, and others.

Latina children performing traditional dances in costume.

Perhaps because of the lack of education and the manual labor they willingly do, many Latinos are mistreated, and/or exploited. This is a serious problem and there are examples where local citizens have taken advantage of Spanish speaking persons who are too afraid to speak up.

Still, Shelby County seems to be a magnet for many Latinos who feel they have been treated kindly, and appreciated. Migrating workers continue to arrive looking for ways to provide for their families in Mexico, Guatemala, Honduras, El Salvador, Ecuador, and other countries in spite of the new 1996 Immigration Laws, the higher and more fortified walls constructed on the border, and the increased enforcement by police.

What we are witnessing and experiencing in these recent times is a movement toward globalization that is unprecedented in its effects on populations. Our Latino neighbors contribute not only to the needed work force, and to Shelby County's economy, but also in many other ways.

Have you dined in one of the popular Mexican restaurants lately? Have you enjoyed hearing Latino music which is gaining in popularity nationwide? Have you had the chance to meet and have a moment of sharing something together with one or more of the Latino folks? Have you experienced the faith and devotion of Latinos on Good Friday as they publicly reenact in a prayerful and powerful way the passion and death of Jesus through the streets of Shelbyville?

Along with their deep faith which is ingrained into their culture and in their being, the Latinos/Hispanics are known for deep family and community values. Family members are expected to help one another. Older brothers and sisters are expected to help take care of younger ones. They can be great organizers around a need in the community. Many times a tragic death or accident of a Latino will mobilize family and other community members to start collecting funds in areas where other Latinos live or work, even reaching out to those in other towns, and almost always there is a positive response, their hand goes to their pocket for a donation.

When a culture is assimilated into another, difficulties are bound to arise. Economic and social pressures within the Latin community have resulted in some instances of conflict with the law enforcement community. Members of the police department and civic leaders were concerned enough by 1997, that a grant was applied for by the police ("COPS" program) and civic agencies. They received a $59,000 "Problem Solving Grant" from the Department of Justice and hired a Latino Community Liaison, who began in July 1998 to work in various ways. The work involves serving as a translator and facilitator, and as a teacher of Spanish to police who are interested and to persons of other professional offices, along with other services. It has been commendable for agencies to take action like this.

One problem area that contributes to economic pressures is the difficulty of finding housing. There is the fact that there is very little "affordable housing" for local residents, much less for persons who work hard but want to spend very little on housing so that they will have more to send to their families in Latin America. Thus the reality is that many Latinos will live together to decrease what they pay individually for rent, and at times there are problems that arise from living in close quarters.

This account could not be complete without a recognition of the encouraging welcomes that have been extended to the new neighbors through various health, education, and social departments in Shelby County. Due to staying on to work (after tobacco season), or more recently because of getting work in the growing number of factories, Latinos have sent for or are coming with their families. Whether these demographic and cultural changes are considered problems or challenges, it has been to the credit of the Shelby County school system and the Departments of Health and Social Services that great efforts have been made to absorb and help the Latino community.

There are many other positive responses to receive, appreciate, and help our Latino neighbors and friends, too numerous to mention. One effort is a coalition of various persons and agencies that formed in October 1997 as a result of Annual Health Fairs organized for the Latino Community. The "Regional Latino Network" meets monthly and has done a lot to raise issues of importance for the Latinos. One of their first projects was to do a Survey of Needs as felt by Latinos in the area in early 1998. Results of the questionnaires showed that the persons felt their greatest needs in: 1) learning English; 2) dental attention; 3) was a close tie between having work and getting legal status.

Family literacy in Shelby county has been funded through the Ohio Valley Educational Cooperative since 1990. Family literacy is a family based approach to learning. Adults and their children receive educational services together. From 1990 through 1997 the program was homebased. Teachers made weekly visits to families in the comfort of their own homes. This program is free for qualified families. Eligibility requirements include one parent working toward their GED or learning English as a Second Language, and there must be a child between birth and age 8 in the family. During this time approximately five Latino families received services. This was a very small percentage of the total number of families served during these years. Over 5,000 Latinos live in the county.

Since fall 1998, the family literacy program has been a center based program at the Henderson House. Transportation is provided to the center. Adults attend classes two to three times per week with their child. While the adults are learning parenting, employability skills, adult education and

English as a second language, their children are learning preschool skills in the early childhood classroom. We also have a special time for parents and their children to play together.

During the 1998-99 school year the family literacy program served approximately 25 Latino families. For the 1999-2000 school year we have served approximately 45 Latino families. This number represents approximately 90% of the total number of families in the family literacy program in Shelby county.

The Migrant Education Program serves migratory workers and their families who move to Shelby County in search of "temporary or seasonal work in farming, fishing, or timber harvesting". The program provides services to individuals between the ages of 3 and 21. Since the program's beginnings in Shelby County in 1995, the number of participants grew steadily during the first three years, but has leveled off during the past two years. As the total number of participants in the program increased the first three years, so did the number of Latino participants.

There is a Latino liaison for the city of Shelbyville. The job is one that assists the Shelbyville Police Department, establishes a better understanding of the diversity that exists between the Latino community and its counterpart the Anglo community, and assists Latinos that have problems with housing, work, education, and child care.

The work immigrants do is often dirty and dangerous. This has always been the case for newly arrived migrants. Yet they continue to come for economic opportunity and because life here is better than the harsh conditions at home. In time, as with earlier groups, they not only contribute to the richness of the American mosaic, they become an ingrained part of it. In time, they too will see the benefits of opportunity and move up the ladder in Shelby County and everywhere.

ZACHARIAH LEE

By Elsie Butler

Zachariah Lee was born in North Carolina in 1786. His father was Daniel Lee who brought his two sons Zachariah and Rowland and two daughters Rebecca and Lucretia to Kentucky in the late 1700s. They lived for a while in Madison County and later moved to Shelby County.

Zachariah Lee served in the War of 1812 and was with other Kentuckians at the River Raisin. He was one of a few who survived that terrible battle with the British and Indians. He volunteered again in 1813. He was described as being 5'9" tall with blue eyes and fair complexion. Later he lived on the Lebanon Road in Franklin County, Kentucky.

Zachariah married Hannah Lewis, daughter of Joseph Lewis, on August 13, 1815, in Shelby County. Zachariah and Hannah had four children—William Henry, Mary, Sarah Jane, and Rowland. Hannah died about 1824. On June 30, 1827, Zachariah married Levina Burns in Franklin County. They had eight children plus the four stepchildren, all of whom Levina cared for. William Henry Lee married Nancy Ann Chadwich, granddaughter of Benjamin B. Penn, Jr. who was a Revolutionary War veteran and who later lived and died in Franklin County, Kentucky.

William Henry and Nancy's daughter Mary Frances Lee married Willis Lindsey Watkins. They later became the grandparents of William Chester Watkins, Arnett Lee Watkins, and May Watkins Rodgers of Franklin County, Kentucky.

Zachariah Lee lived to be 75 years old and died July 17, 1862. Levina died on June 21, 1881, at 71 years of age. Both are buried in the Lebanon Cemetery, which is located within a few miles of where he lived when he volunteered for the War of 1812. The cemetery is in Franklin County, Kentucky.

BENJAMIN LOGAN

By Ted Igleheart

One of the first settlers to fight for and occupy the "Dark and Bloody Ground" of Kentucky was Benjamin Logan, who must be included in the illustrious ranks of the Boone brothers, Simon Kenton, George Rogers Clark, John Floyd, Isaac Shelby, Bland W. Ballard, and James Harrod.

Logan was born in 1743 to David and Jane McKinley Logan in Orange County, Virginia. He married Ann Montgomery in 1772 and had nine children: David, William, Jane, Mary, Elizabeth, John, Benjamin, Robert, and Ann. His son William studied law in Shelby County and served in the General Assembly, on the Court of Appeals, and in the U.S. Senate, but was defeated for governor.

Logan gained valuable experience in Indian fighting when he was appointed a sergeant under Colonel Henry Bouquet in the British Army. Logan and James Harrod participated in the battle of Bushy Run on August 6, 1763, in which the Indians were defeated and pushed back from the frontiers of the Upper Ohio Valley. The Indians, under the leadership of the fierce Ottowa and Ojibway chieftain, Pontiac, had taken one British fort after another until defeated at Bushy Run.

Logan planted corn in the vicinity of St. Asaph's Station (later to be called Logan's Station) in the spring of 1775. He brought his wife, their young son and four slaves from Virginia in the spring of 1776. The Virginia Assembly appointed George Rogers Clark a major and made him the ranking military authority in Kentucky County of Virginia. Serving under him were Daniel Boone, Benjamin Logan, John Todd, and James Harrod, who were made captains of the militia. Concerted attacks by the Shawnee Indians under Chief Blackfish were made on Fort Harrod in March 1777 and each was repulsed.

Logan was appointed Sheriff of Kentucky County at its first court session at Harrodsburg in April 1777. He was later placed in command of the Lincoln Militia and helped raise troops to serve under General George Rogers Clark for an invasion of Indian territory to put an end to the frequent raids. Logan had been promoted to the rank of colonel when Lincoln County was formed and was appointed one of its first magistrates. During its second session in February 1782, Logan offered the Lincoln County Court ten acres of land at Buffalo Spring near Logan's Station as the site for a courthouse and public buildings and fifty acres nearby for use by the Court, which was accepted in August 1783.

Colonel Benjamin Logan raised two battalions of men from Lincoln to fight under General Clark in a raid on the Shawnee stronghold at Old Chillicothe. Eager to avenge the disastrous defeat at Blue Licks on August 19, 1782, 1,050 men joined in the march against the Indian settlements. The campaign was a great victory scattering the Indian armies, demoralizing their warriors, and ending large organized raids on Kentucky territory.

Colonel Logan led an expedition on the Wabash Indian villages in October 1786 after uprisings there had again raised fears of raids on the settlers. Ten of their villages containing 200 houses were destroyed, 15,000 bushels of corn were burned, and many Shawnees were killed or taken prisoner. The aged Shawnee chief, Moluntha, who had often befriended the settlers, was taken prisoner. In spite of instructions of Col. Logan not to molest the prisoners, Col. Hugh McGary, who had often committed violent acts of barbarousness, seized an ax from a squaw and killed Moluntha. McGary was court-martialed and suspended from active service.

Resentment at Virginia's failure to provide adequate protection from Indian raids had risen to fever pitch by 1787 and a convention of representatives from the seven counties met in Danville. Benjamin Logan and Isaac Shelby were among the delegates. The sentiment was for separation from Virginia and, in spite of some efforts to form an independent state, the consensus was to become a part of the United States.

On February 4, 1791, the Congress voted favorably to admit Kentucky into the Union and set the date for official statehood as June 1, 1792, with an estimated population of 75,000, the largest city, Lexington, with a population of 1000. Isaac Shelby was elected the first governor. In its first session, the General Assembly established Shelby County in honor of its first governor.

General Logan purchased the 1,000-acre preemption of Jacob Myers and the 1,400-acre preemption of Thomas Gibson on Bullskin Creek in Shelby County. In 1794, he built some cabins and a grist mill on Bullskin and began the construction of a house at a nearby spring. He was now the owner of 14 slaves, 10 horses, and 70 cattle. With completion of the house, he moved in March 1795 from Lincoln County to Shelby County, where he felt he would have a better chance of waging a successful campaign for the governor's office, since Isaac Shelby was also from Lincoln County. On May 5, 1795, the people of Shelby elected him Representative to the General Assembly. He had served earlier as representative from Lincoln County.

Logan did not have the education or polish of his two opponents for governor, James Garrard and Thomas Todd. The question in 1796 was whether a poorly educated pioneer could hold his own against his well-educated and seasoned opponents. Was his illustrious career as a military leader and Indian fighter, builder and defender of Logan's Station, revered statesman in the statehood and constitutional conventions lost on the newcomers who settled Kentucky after the Revolution? Many of his contemporaries were gone. The Boones and Kenton had moved out of the state. James Harrod had disappeared, probably killed by Indians. John Floyd had been killed outside his station. George Rogers Clark was a broken man, deeply in debt and an alcoholic. However, Logan received a plurality of 21 of the electors' 53 votes. Without a majority for any candidate, the electors, without a constitutional sanction, took a second ballot, after leaving off Todd and John Brown, who had not been an announced candidate. On this ballot, Garrard received a majority of the votes, having made a deal with Todd supporters. Todd was appointed to the Court of Appeals. Since the Constitution did not provide for a runoff when no majority was obtained for a candidate, the election was disputed but the Senate, which was authorized to intervene in disputed elections, refused to disturb the decision of the electors. Logan, in an effort to prevent a crisis in the young government, finally acquiesced in the decision, against the urging of his supporters, who continued to argue that Logan was the rightfully elected governor, having received in the first poll a plurality of the votes. This dispute probably caused the abandonment of the Electoral College system in the second constitution.

General Logan was a delegate from Shelby County, along with Abraham Owen, to the Second Constitutional Convention held in Frankfort in July 1799. Fifty-five delegates attended from twenty-five counties. The new constitution went into effect before the election of 1800, providing for election of a governor and lieutenant governor by direct vote of the people and again Garrard was elected over Logan, this time without dispute. He served in the first, second, third, fourth, sixth, and seventh General Assemblies.

General Benjamin Logan died in his 60th year on December 11, 1802. He had attended a sale at the home of Bracket near Shelbyville. While seated at the supper table there, he suffered a stroke and died instantly. He was buried with military honors on the hill overlooking Bullskin Creek. The General Assembly, which was in session, passed a resolution in mourning of his death and in memory of "the firm defender of his country." Logan County was named in his honor.

LEE NOR MACK

By Duanne Puckett

In the midst of the civil rights movement of the 1960s, Lee Nor Mack sought election to the Shelbyville City Council. His was a bold step and a successful one since he was the first African-American in many years to hold such a position.

He was elected from the district which included the majority of the black community. Yet when the city division lines were lifted and council members were elected at-large, Mack continued to be the top or among the top vote getters. Mack served for 18 years (1967-85).

Mack was born in Shelbyville in 1914. He grew up on a farm near Bagdad where his parents were tenant farmers, and attended school in Shelbyville. He worked as a shipping clerk at the Lee-McClain Clothing Factory. A Navy veteran, he served in World War II.

During his terms on the council he was particularly pleased with the rehabilitation projects started for Martinsville, an all-black neighborhood north of Washington Street. It was in that area that he made his home with his wife of 49 years, the former Margaret Jackson. One street leading to the neighborhood bears his name—something that made him extremely proud.

Mack was also singled out to work to help create what became the Shelbyville/Shelby County Parks and Recreation Department. He later served as city representative on the Parks Board for a number of years.

When Dr. Martin Luther King Jr. was assassinated in 1968, Mr. Mack said Dr. King's principles represented the most effective means of achieving the goals of blacks to be integrated into American life. He noted that those who turned to violence were young black people and the more underprivileged who had become particularly embittered at what appeared to be a bleak future. But Mack believed if there was a change in public attitudes and more opportunities were created for advancement, regardless of a man's color, then that despair could change to hope. "You have to be a Negro to understand this predicament," he said in 1968. "Unless you've experienced the insults and deprivation, there's just no way you can imagine how we feel. Fortunately, we are a people of pride and that pride is beginning to pay off in better racial understanding and future opportunities."

Mack's other interests included his church, Bethel A.M.E., where he was a trustee. He died December 7, 1985, and was survived by a son, daughter, and his widow.

ELIJAH P. MARRS

By Kevin Collins

Elijah Marrs, slave, Union soldier, educator, Baptist minister, Republican politician and early advocate of African American civil rights, was born in January 1840 in Shelby County. His father, Andrew, was a freeman, but his mother, Frances, was a slave. Elijah and his brother, along with thirty others, were the property of Jesse Robinson, whose farm lay just two miles outside Simpsonville. In his autobiography, Marrs recalls that the farmer Robinson, who was also a deacon of the Baptist Church, was "not hard on us, and (he) allowed us generally to do as we pleased after his own work was done, and we enjoyed the privilege granted to us."

In his twenty years as a slave, Elijah worked first as a dining-room boy; then as a stock boy with the dairy herd, and finally as a field hand. But through all of this, his passion was to learn to read and write. An elderly slave on Robinson's farm, Ham Graves, gave instruction at night, and both Marrs boys surreptitiously began their lessons. At the same time Elijah also learned alphabet-letters from the white children his age living on the Robinson farm.

Then, when he was eleven, the Rev. Charles Wells of the Colored Baptist Church of Simpsonville baptized Elijah. This Christian conversion persuaded Robinson to let Marrs attend Sunday school and also learn to read, so that he might better know the Holy Bible. Ten years later this literacy would permit Marrs to read news of the Civil War to the slaves on Robinson's farm and to read and answer correspondence written from colored Union soldiers to their Shelby County families. Marrs was known locally as the "Shelby County Negro clerk," a title that, as his owner pointed out, served to put Elijah's life at risk to possible violence from local rebel sympathizers or others affronted by the literacy of a slave.

On September 26, 1864, Elijah Marrs, with twenty-six other Shelby County slaves, enlisted in the Union Army, having led them from Simpsonville to the recruiting office in Louisville. He was assigned to Company L Twelfth U.S. Colored Artillery, and posted to the Taylor Barracks on Third Street. Because he was literate Marrs was made a non-commissioned officer. He became the Third Duty Sergeant of Company L. After three weeks at Taylor Barracks, his unit was marched to Camp Nelson, in the rolling hills of Jessamine County along the Kentucky River.

In his eighteen months of military service, Marrs, served in Russellville (Logan County), Bowling Green (Warren County), Munfordsville (Hart County), Glasgow and Cave City (Barren County), Elizabethtown (Hardin County), Hardinsburg (Breckinridge County), Columbus (Hickman County) and Paducah (McCracken County). His unit engaged rebel forces in Glasgow on Christmas 1864, but miraculously escaped entrapment without injury. They were, however, captured on January 8, 1865, at Big Springs, by a Confederate force under the command of General Williams. Marrs and his unit were treated humanely and, after giving up their weapons, were paroled. Under escort, they were marched back to their regiment in Hardin County.

At both Bowling Green and Fort Nelson Sgt. Marrs was detailed to look after the hundreds of black refugees (the wives and families of slaves who had enlisted in the Union Army) driven from their homes by their former masters.

In the winter of 1865, with the war over, Marrs was promoted to Regimental Quartermaster. While in Paducah, in charge of a supply train, he contracted smallpox. After his recovery he was granted furlough home to Shelbyville and traveled there with his brother,

A photograph of Rev. Elijah P. Marrs from his autobiography, The Life and History of Rev. Elijah P. Marrs, *published in 1885.*

Henry, who had just recently mustered out of the Army (in Arkansas) with the rank of Sergeant Major. Marrs described his three-week furlough in Shelbyville in his memoirs; "I went on to Shelbyville, where I met my father, mother, sisters, and brother. You may know we had a happy reunion. We talked and cried, and friends gathered from all parts of the city to greet me.... I enjoyed myself to my heart's content. The ladies and gentlemen showed me every attention, and entertainments were almost nightly given in honor of my presence."

Marrs, almost unconsciously, counterbalanced this very positive remembrance of Shelbyville by a recitation of two violent incidents that also happened on the same furlough. He was attacked at knife-point by three white men who objected to "a Negro officer of the army," and an incident in which Marrs, at the point of his gun, forced the retreat on Main Street of another white man intent on doing him harm. Such were the mixed blessings of Shelbyville for a black soldier in 1865.

On April 24, 1866, Marrs mustered out of the Union Army at Louisville. Returning to Shelby County as freedmen, Elijah and brother Henry worked together in a partnership. They formed a cartage business, which Henry ran while Elijah farmed 25 acres of rented land. In the ensuing eight months they realized eight dollars a day from the hauling business, and reaped an abundant harvest from their farming efforts.

A second of the brothers' entrepreneurial efforts involved the formation of a Colored Agricultural and Mechanical Association in Shelby County. About 1870, with Henry as President and Elijah as Treasurer, a company was formed, $750 in subscription money raised, and about 42 acres of land purchased near Dry Run Creek aside the Louisville-Frankfort Turnpike. This location (near the intersection of U.S. 60 and KY 55 South) became the fairground for an annual Colored A & M Fair, at that time a novel idea. An easy walk from the black neighborhood of Drewsville, the first fair netted $3,000. Succeeding fairs were also profitable. In 1874, the Marrs brothers sold the enterprise to Silas Ford of Shelbyville and the Colored Agricultural and Mechanics Fairground continued until some time near the turn of the century.

In September 1866 Elijah, at the request of friends, opened a school in Simpsonville. Despite several dangerous incidents with the Ku Klux Klan, Marrs taught more than one hundred students that first year. In 1867, Marrs began teaching in La Grange in the first school under the protection, physically and financially, of the Freedman's Bureau. Then in 1870 he took charge of a school in New Castle. Through 1874 he continued teaching in these two counties despite, especially in Henry County, difficulties with the Klan.

In 1874, Elijah briefly left teaching to study at Roger Williams University in Nashville, Tennessee. But by January 1875 he returned to teach his fifth and final term at Henry County. Then, from September 1875 until June 1878, Marrs taught in Shelbyville. He taught more than three hundred pupils, some of whom became teachers.

In 1879, responding to a letter from his brother Henry, Marrs was drawn to Louisville to help found the Baptist Normal and Theological Institute. This was to be the crowning achievement of the Marrs brothers' legacy as educators. The school opened, at Seventh and Kentucky Streets, on November 29, 1879. Elijah Marrs was its first President. By March 1880 the school had thirty-three students, ten of whom were students of ministry. Recognizing their limitations as educators, however, the Marrs brothers recruited William J. Simmons in 1880 to be the school's next President. Simmons, a graduate of Howard University, remained President until 1890. In these ten years the Institute vigorously expanded. It was renamed State University. In 1918, to honor his contributions, State University was renamed Simmons University. In 1930, the University of Louisville purchased most of Simmons University to establish the Louisville Municipal College for Negroes. Theological studies, however, continued to be taught by Simmons College (in a single building on the same site) until 1934, when the renamed Simmons Bible College moved to its present day location of 18th and Dumesnil Streets.

The Reverend Marrs began his calling as a preacher in the early 1870s. From his earliest years as a teacher he had also taught Sunday school. During the war he had sometimes been invited to preach in military camps to gatherings of colored soldiers and refugee families. On August 22, 1875, Marrs was ordained a Reverend in the Colored Baptist Church and took up full ministerial duties. In that same year he was elected a messenger to the General Association of Colored Baptists of Kentucky. In time he would become the Association's Treasurer.

In 1878 the Temperance Movement (called the Murphy Movement) began to gather recognition and converts in Shelbyville. Marrs, working with other ministers from white Baptist Churches, led an integrated effort to promote it. He served as President of the Temperance Society for three years, and led integrated meetings in both Shelbyville and Simpsonville. In 1880, the Rev. Marrs helped found the Beargrass Colored Baptist Church at Crescent Hill in Louisville, and served as the Church's pastor until his death in 1910.

Elijah Marrs also led an active political life. He was a delegate to every major statewide Republican convention that Kentucky blacks held in the post-Civil War era. He was a tireless public speaker, influencing black voters and parishioners on those issues that advanced equality.

In Shelby County, in 1869, he helped elect Republican lawyer Zacharia Wheat (1806-77) to a judgeship on the County Court. In 1869, he was the first colored man elected to the presidency of the Republican Club of Oldham County. Marrs was very active in voter registration campaigns, especially in 1870 the first year in which Kentucky blacks voted. In 1871, Marrs and W. L. Yancey formed the Loyal League in Henry County, a society designed to protect the local black population from Ku Klux Klan attack. Elijah served as the League's first secretary. On August 3, 1871, Marrs married Julia Gray, daughter of Harriet Gray of Shelby County. They lived on Main Street in Shelbyville in a two-story frame house that Elijah had built just previous to the wedding. Julia Gray Marrs died after a lengthy illness on April 9, 1876. She is buried, as a member of the Mysterious Tens No. 1 (an adjunct of the United Brothers of Friendship), in the Shelbyville Cemetery. Elijah Marrs, also a Member of the UBF, died August 30, 1910, and is buried in Greenwood Cemetery in Louisville.

ROBERT MATTHEWS JR.

By Betty Matthews

Kentucky's only Attorney General from Shelby County, Robert Foster Matthews Jr. was born in Shelbyville on September 14, 1923, the eldest son of Robert Foster Matthews and Zerelda Baxter Matthews. After graduating from Shelbyville High School in 1940, he obtained a B.A. degree in economics from the College of William and Mary in Williamsburg, Virginia. Following graduation in 1943, he enlisted in the midshipman program of the United States Navy and served in the Atlanta and Pacific theaters of World War II.

Matthews was discharged in 1946. One year earlier he married Betty Buntin in Atlanta. She was also a graduate of the College of William and Mary.

After obtaining a law degree from the University of Virginia, Matthews returned to Shelbyville and worked in state government as an attorney in the Revenue Department. A 2-1/2 year interim was spent in Amarillo, Texas, working with a great-uncle, Charles Killgore, on his cattle ranch.

Again returning to Shelbyville in 1953, Matthews later resumed his career in state government as administrative assistant to Governor Bert T. Combs. He became Commissioner of Finance and served as Attorney General from 1964-67.

One year later, he became a partner in the Louisville law firm of Greenbaum, Grissom, Wood, Doll & Matthews (now Greenbaum, Doll & McDonald). Following retirement he practiced privately and did pro bono work as administrator hearing officer for the city of Louisville, hearing appeals of persons charged with offenses against the city.

The Matthews are parents to two sons and have four grandchildren.

BENJAMIN L. McMAKIN

By R.R. Van Stockum Sr.

Benjamin L. McMakin, born in Shelbyville on November 26, 1913, was a popular member of the 1931 Shelbyville High School football team, coached by Bruce Daniel, and president of his class. Upon graduation from VPI in 1935, he was commissioned directly into the regular Marine Corps as a second lieutenant. The writer first met McMakin when serving with him in the Sixth Marine Regiment in San Diego in 1939. Then First Lieutenant McMakin was a promising young officer whose capabilities had been recognized by his assignment to the important position of regimental adjutant. Obviously he was a promising young officer destined for a very successful career. Quietly confident, he possessed the important military quality, command presence.

Less than three years later, at the outbreak of World War II, then Captain McMakin was serving in the Philippines with the Fourth Marine Regiment. After a tenacious and heroic defense during which McMakin was wounded, he and the out-manned marines were captured in early 1942. He survived as a prisoner of war for nearly three years only to die of wounds near the end of the war when a Japanese ship, the Brazil Marti, carrying prisoners from the Philippines to Tokyo was bombed. The Japanese death certificate gave his date of death as January 16, 1945, but this was later corrected to January 18, 1945, by a fellow prisoner who kept a personnel roster of those aboard the ship. He was buried at sea. While the monument in his memory at Grove Hill Cemetery in Shelbyville shows his rank as captain, he had been promoted posthumously on March 20, 1946, to the rank of Major.

NICHOLAS MERIWETHER

By R.R. Van Stockum Sr.

Nicholas Meriwether was a pioneer settler, land locator, and entrepreneur in early Kentucky. He was born in Louisa County, Virginia, June 4, 1749, to Nicholas Meriwether (1719-58) and Frances Morton. He and his brother George married sisters who were their first cousins, daughters of Captain William Meriwether (1730-90). Meriwether first arrived at the Falls of the Ohio in 1779 or possibly a year earlier. While not an officially appointed surveyor, he became one of the early Kentucky land locators, running private surveys through the virgin land of Kentucky for himself and his family, and for others from whom he extracted a fee.

Meriwether, who frequently used the Ohio River for his travels to Kentucky, left many letters describing the threats of Indian attack along this route and how best to avoid them. "By no means take any Stock on Board the Boat your family comes in. Sail all night unless exceedingly dark & be upon the way early in the mornings when you do stop, & stay but little time at a place."

Between October 4 and November 27, 1784, while living on one of his lots on the north side of Main Street between Sixth and Seventh where he kept one of the first houses of public entertainment in Louisville, Nicholas lost through natural causes his wife and four of his sons. While family papers or public records do not reveal the cause of these tragic deaths, it is reasonable to suspect that it may have been smallpox.

On October 12, 1786, he married Elizabeth Daniel, sister of Walker Daniel, first attorney general for the court for the District of Kentucky who had been killed in an Indian ambush in 1784. A year later he purchased Squire Boone's old "Painted Stone" tract in Shelby County, which he called "Castle Hill" after the Meriwether estate in Albemarle County, Virginia. In 1804, the year after his cousin, Meriwether Lewis, departed the Falls with William Clark on the "Voyage of Discovery," Meriwether took his family down the Ohio and Mississippi to settle in West Bank, Mississippi, returning later to Kentucky to die in Shelby County on April 28, 1828.

Meriwether was an active and imaginative man who involved himself in many land deals and commercial ventures, creating enemies in the process, some real and some imagined; but through his drive and ambition he contributed significantly to the development of the Kentucky frontier.

JANE MEYER

By Duanne Puckett

Hundreds of cheerleaders lost their "Other Mother" when Jane Wellhouse Meyer died in June 1999 at age 83. Miss Meyer had been the cheerleading sponsor for Shelbyville High School from about 1944 until 1974 when the school closed.

Meyer came to Shelbyville from Eau Claire, Wisconsin, in 1942 when her parents, Mr. and Mrs. Eli Meyer, bought Undulata Farm where they raised show horses. A trophy is still given at the Shelby County Horse Show each year in honor of Meyer's horse farm. Meyer was a graduate of Bryn Mawr College, a member of the Shelbyville First Presbyterian Church, the Shelby County University of Kentucky Alumni Club, and the Shelby County Boosters Club.

Because of a shortage of teachers, Miss Meyer became a member of the high school staff under an emergency certificate to teach health and physical education. It was in that role that she became cheerleading sponsor and the number one fan for the Red Devils. Not only did she serve as chauffeur to the cheerleaders for every football and basketball game, but she also sponsored the annual athletic banquet in her Undulata mansion for 25 years. Every football and basketball player, as well as each cheerleader, received a trophy on his or her place setting engraved with Jane Meyer Banquet and the appropriate year.

When Shelbyville merged with Shelby County Public Schools in 1975, Miss Meyer switched her loyalty to the Rockets and became one of their biggest boosters. She was a regular at every athletic event and was a fixture at the Booster Bingo games at Floral Hall on Thursday nights. She was responsible for statewide competitions for cheerleaders after founding the Kentucky Association for Pep Organization Sponsors in 1954. She held every office in the association and remained active long after her retirement with other sponsors.

When the field house was built at Shelby County High School, the room set aside for cheerleaders was dedicated in Meyer's honor. The 1997 homecoming was proclaimed Jane Meyer Night in honor of her years of devotion.

In true testimony to her school spirit, Miss Meyer was buried at Grove Hill Cemetery wearing her Red Devils cheerleading sponsor coat. The school fight song, "Loyalty," was also played during the funeral.

Courtesy of Duanne Puckett.

Jane Meyer, owner of Undulata Farm, hosted every Shelbyville High School athletic banquet from 1943 to 1973.

W. T. MILLER

By Ann Frederick Miller

W.T. Miller, born in 1877, was a young country man who came to town and started building houses in the east end of Shelbyville. The Miller lumber business was located behind the Growers Warehouse on Linden Avenue.

W.T. would build a house and move in his family, sell that one, build another, and again the Millers would move. W.T. and his brother, John, built the large two-story brick houses on Bland Avenue. He also built the "telephone building" at the corner of Seventh and Washington.

When building began developing in the west end of Shelbyville, W.T., Mary, and their six surviving children, Forrest, W.T. Jr., Mary Grace, Lynn, Ralph, and Jack spent their growing up years in their two-story yellow brick on Main Street, four doors up from Plainview Drive.

Miller built many apartments, too. W.T. and the "well" children used the stone duplex on Plainview when a child caught smallpox and the big house had to be quarantined. He had a hand in developing Snow Hill subdivision.

When Tom Craig of Craig Realty would sell a house he would always say, "Remember this is a Miller built house." Craig developed Bayne Acres and named Miller Avenue after W.T. Miller. Miller died in 1961.

MARNEL C. MOORMAN

By Maureen Ashby

Marnel Clay Moorman was born on May 14, 1943, in Owensboro, Kentucky. His life of service throughout the Shelby County community was based on the philosophy "Children are our greatest resource."

Moorman received his primary education at Central City Grade School in Central City, Kentucky, and his secondary training at Drakesboro Community High School. After graduating from Western Kentucky University in 1965 with a B.S. degree in science and biology, Moorman was offered a teaching position at High Street School in the Martinsville community, by the principal of Shelbyville High School, Bill McKay. In a school designated for African-American children, Moorman taught mathematics and science, and coached basketball. In 1966, he moved to Shelbyville High School. In 1975, the merging of the Shelby County Public System led Moorman to teach and assist in the basketball program there.

Moorman earned an M.A. degree from Georgetown College in secondary education. In 1986, he was elected the first African-American vice president of the Kentucky Education Association. He was re-elected to the post in 1988 and 1990, and in 1992 Moorman became the first African-American president of the Kentucky Education Association. He successfully ran for a second term in 1994. He served eight years as a member of the Kentucky Education Association's board of directors, chaired numerous committees, which included Program and Budget, Human Relations, and the Minority Affairs/Affirmative Action Committees.

Serving as a delegate to the Kentucky Education Association for more than 24 years and a delegate to the National Education Association's Assembly for 21 years, Moorman was instrumental in implementing education reform procedures in Kentucky. Also, he represented Kentucky's teachers on various task forces, including the Council on Teacher Education and Certification and the Kentucky General Assembly Task Force on Educational Funding.

Moorman's professional affiliations were numerous. In 1986, he received the prestigious Smith-Wilson Award, which recognizes civil and human rights in education. In Shelby County, Moorman's support of organizations to serve others were evidenced from his association with Shelby County Big Brothers/Big Sisters, Shelby County Association, Shelbyville Improvement Organization,

Marnel C. Moorman, Shelby County educator, was the first African American vice president and president of the Kentucky Education Association, serving several terms in each position.

Shelby County Parks and Recreation Board, Miss Black Shelby County Pageant, and the Shelbyville Boys Club. On a state and national level, Moorman was a member of the Fifth District Education Association, Kentucky Education Association, and the National Education Association.

He was married to the former Laura Loving of Shelby County. They had two daughters, Tolya and Elizabeth, and a son Marnel Jr. A third daughter, Alison, died in 1993. Moorman's untimely death happened in an automobile accident on October 14, 1994. Clay Street Baptist Church, located in Shelbyville, dedicated a family life center as a memorial to him.

BRACKETT OWEN

By Catharine Hays Owen Ellis and Thomas A. Courtenay

The Owen name is an ancient Welch patronymic, which started as a personal name, Oen, meaning lamb. The first recorded member of the Owen family in America was Thomas Owen in 1632. He was an early Virginia immigrant, arriving from London in the ship Susan, and settling in Jamestown.

Thomas Owen's son John married Phoebe Brackett. They moved to Sandy River, Virginia, in 1749, where he died in 1767. John's will was made on February 24, 1764, and listed his children as Mary; Lydia; Jemima; Kesiah; Lucy; John William; Thomas; Brackett; Jessie and Agnes.

Brackett was their eighth child. He was born in Henrico County, Virginia, August 9, 1733, and died in Shelbyville, Kentucky in 1802. In 1760, Brackett Owen married Elizabeth McGehee. She was born

September 5, 1744, and died November 18, 1800. Brackett and Elizabeth had eleven children, among them Abraham for whom Owen County is named.

Brackett Owen was administrator of his father's will. He lived on Mountain Creek, Virginia. Family tradition has it that Owen moved to Kentucky in the summer of 1785, and built a fort on the land he received as a Land Grant from Patrick Henry, Governor of Virginia. The fort was known as Owen's Station, and located at the northwest corner of Highway 53 and Seven Mile Road. Grove Hill Cemetery is believed to be part of his land. Thomas Courtenay later owned the farm.

The first Court in Shelby County was held at Brackett Owen's farm on October 15, 1792, in a brick building near the present intersection of Seven Mile Road and old Mount Eden Road. The house is still standing.

On December 11, 1802, a sale was held at the Owen house and attended by Benjamin Logan and others who stayed for supper. While seated at the table, Logan suffered a stroke of apoplexy and died instantly.

Brackett Owen's son, Jacob, married Emily Martin, an active member of Centenary Methodist Church. The large stained glass window, forerly on the Fifth Street Side of Centenary Methodist Church before the fire, was given in memory of Emily and J. M. Owen. Jacob also owned and operated J. M. Owen and Company selling drugs, hardware and groceries. He was also a partner in the R. S. Owen and J. M. Owen Mill.

CHARLES ELIJAH PALMER

By Kevin Collins

Charles Elijah Palmer, prominent Shelbyville veterinarian of forty years, was a native of the Hoosier State, having been born June 14, 1889, in Patriot, Indiana. The son of Ezra and Mary Fox Palmer, he was a graduate of the Cincinnati Veterinary College. Following graduation, Palmer practiced several years in Ohio before entering the military.

During World War I Captain Palmer served in the Veterinary Corps, First Cavalry, U. S. Army, and after his discharge served with the Kentucky National Guard in the 138th Field Artillery. He settled in Shelbyville in 1919.

Palmer held many positions and honors in his chosen profession, and was well known throughout Kentucky. He was a member of the American Veterinary Association as well as a member and past president of the Kentucky Veterinary Association. He was official veterinarian of the Kentucky State Fair. For over thirty years he was a member of the Kentucky State Board of Veterinary Examiners. In Shelby County he was a director and past president of the Shelby County A & M Association and for fifteen years supervisor of the Shelby County Fairgrounds.

An avid fisherman, conservationist and sports enthusiast, Dr. Palmer was active in fish and wildlife conservation in the county. He worked to promote the construction of Pickett's Dam in Finchville. Built in the 1930s, it was named in honor of George Pickett, commissioner of Fish and Game, and was built by local farmers for conservation and recreational purposes.

Palmer was also a banker, and worked for 17 years as both a director and a vice-president of Citizens Bank. He was also a president and member of the Shelbyville Rotary Club; a charter member and second commander of the J. Franklin Post of the American Legion; and a member of the Honorary Order of Kentucky Colonels. Palmer was also active in the Boy Scouts of America.

Palmer was married to the former Jean Small and had one son, Charles E. Palmer Jr. He was a member of the First Presbyterian Church of Shelbyville. He died October 30, 1960, and is buried at Grove Hill Cemetery.

MITCHELL HOWARD PAYNE

By Duanne Puckett

When Mitchell Howard Payne entered Southside Elementary in 1957 as a second-grader, he was among the first blacks to integrate the school system. When he looks back at those times, he has said, "I was just a student who had self-motivation and luckily was surrounded by a good group of competitive peers - close friends, an interracial group - who all wanted to achieve at our fullest."

He also decided to "set an example of being totally involved." After graduating from Shelbyville High School in 1968, the son of Llewellyn and Hattie Payne went on to Western Kentucky University where he majored in government and minored in history. He attended graduate school at WKU where he received degrees in public administration and urban affairs. He received his law degree from the University of Louisville.

Payne pooled all those resources to make his mark: serving on various state government committees, working in Washington, D.C., for U.S. Representative Romano Mazzoli, working as director of the Office of Minority Affairs at the University of Louisville, working as principal assistant to Finance Secretary Gordon Duke, and being named the first African-American finance commissior (for the commonwealth, and only the second black commissioner in the history of state government). Payne's most recent position at U of L has been in administration.

In his role in the Office of Minority Affairs, he was charged with fostering racial harmony in all university activities, and to ensure equal educational opportunity for everyone at U of L. However, Payne saw his most important task as counseling students on their lives in college and afterwards. His advice was to "establish goals—short-term goals and long-term goals—and to develop their skills, including their decision-making skills." He also said, "The opportunity is there. It's a matter of looking where your resources are."

Payne considers himself fortunate to have had a number of adults around him as a child to teach him those very lessons. He named his parents, extended family members, teachers, coaches, ministers, professionals and other role models with whom he came in contact from the all-black school known as Lincoln Institute.

He also believes the civil rights movement of the late 1950s and early `60s probably had something to do with his ability to achieve. Payne's graduating class from high school was the first that never experienced racial segregation in schools.

His accomplishments in administration for 12 years at U of L are what attracted the attention of Governor Martha Layne Collins to appoint him as finance commissioner. She said there were many qualified candidates but "Payne (has) a combination of efficiency, education and energy that ensures success..."

As commissioner, Payne was primarily responsible for state procurement services; centralized, statewide accounting requirements; surplus property disposal; the state's postal system, which handled about 5 million pieces of mail; a statewide record keeping system; and state printing services.

SALLIE DEMAREE PETTY

By Duanne Puckett

Sallie Demaree Petty was a familiar figure in Shelbyville where she was often found at the Post Office chatting with customers or through her columns about the community's past that were published in the county's newspapers. The petite woman always wore a hat, carried a handbag clutched under her arm, and walked with a brisk stride. She died July 21, 1977, at the age of 97-- alone at Colonial Halls Nursing Home on Henry Clay Street. Her husband, Charles, died in the 1940s; her only child, Charles Luther Petty, died unexpectedly at the age of 56 in 1959 after serving as a Louisville postal carrier.

Mrs. Petty managed alone until the winter of 1972 when she became so feeble and her once bright mind dimmed that she was forced to abandon her living quarters on Washington Street. D.C. Poe, who had run a downtown business, took charge of Mrs. Petty's affairs because of their acquaintance through the

Courtesy of Duanne Puckett.

Sallie Demaree Petty in Shelbyville in 1969.

Centenary United Methodist Church. He even made pre-arrangements for her funeral at Shannon Funeral Home and with owner Bill Shannon, picked out the casket, flowers and dress she was to wear. She was buried at Grove Hill Cemetery.

BEN POLLARD

By Duanne Puckett

When a truce and cease-fire was announced for the Vietnam War in January 1973, some Shelby Countians thought of the plight of Ben Pollard, a graduate of Shelbyville High School whose plane was shot down in May 1967 and who had been listed as a Prisoner Of War for six years.

The town rallied around the Pollard family when positive identification was given of his whereabouts and his return to the United States. A homecoming celebration was held March 27, 1973: "Ben Pollard Day " at Shelby County High School where about 2,500 gathered. With him were his wife, Joan, and two children, Mark and Ginny, who were 8 and 3 respectively, the last time they saw their father.

All stood as Lt. Col. Pollard entered the gym with his wife holding onto his arm. There were several tears being wiped away as the high school band played "God Bless America." Others taking part in the service were Pollard's former classmate, Bert Smith, then minister of Paris Christian Church; his former football coach, Bruce Daniel; and Martha Layne Collins, who represented Governor Wendell Ford.

Classmate Paul LeCompte co-chaired the celebration with DuAnne Puckett, a reporter for the *Shelby News*. LeCompte was accompanied to the homecoming by who he called "hoodlums" - Pollard's fellow classmates from the class of 1950 from Shelbyville High School. In gratitude for their presence and gift of a silver tray, Pollard teased, "You see standing before you the first man (in our class) to go to prison and I didn't even have any time off for good behavior."

Pollard's time in Shelbyville High included five years of football, five years of basketball, one year of baseball, four years in band, two years in the Airplane Club, and three years in Key Club. He was a member of the 1948 basketball team that made the first trip for Shelbyville to the State Tournament. He went on to graduate from Purdue University and was serving as a professor at the U.S. Air Force Academy when he was shipped to Vietnam as a F-105 fighter pilot.

"You don't know what it's like to be behind a door you can't open" is how Pollard described his ordeal in 1973's homecoming. When he spoke to the Shelby County Historical Society in 1999, he revealed more details about his ordeal. When his aircraft was hit May 15, 1967, he had to bail out, along with his navigator who he would not see for six years... six years of hell in the Hanoi Hilton as a Prisoner Of War. When he bailed out of the plane, he knew he was seriously injured during the descent. As he hung from a tree from his parachute harness, he fainted from the pain. When he came to, he realized he was paralyzed and the morphine that was in his pack six feet away "might as well have been on the moon." He did manage to reach the ground and begin to crawl down the mountain... after nine hours of the grueling journey, he was discovered by Vietnamese who turned him in.

"They stripped me to my shorts and tied my arms behind me," he recalled. Realizing he couldn't walk, the soldiers made a makeshift stretcher on which Pollard was carried from village to village—the nightmare began as he was stoned and beaten and kicked throughout the process.... Which was followed by a 60-90 mile ride in the back of a truck over the roughest terrain possible. It was 24 hours later when he ended up in Cell 18 at the prison camp where the torture began and "went on and on and on."

In the fall of 1969, conditions changed when more food was allowed, the torture ended and some packages were received. The biggest relief was larger cells so the prisoners finally became cellmates and could communicate. Pollard wrote his first letter home in September 1970 and received his first in October—a five-line letter that had the best line he could ever have read, "I can still see it today: `the kids are happy, healthy and normal and we love you."

His wife was planning a trip overseas in May 1967 when she received word her husband was missing in action. It wasn't until 1970 that the government went public with the torture the POWs were enduring. It was then she joined forces with Ross Perot and other Air Force wives to protest the treatment through a letter-writing campaign, a campaign that her son Mark and his friend Mark Vaughan of Shelbyville participated in. She realized she could do more good in Colorado she so left Shelbyville and became active in the National League of Families.

It was November 15, 1970, when she received the first letter from her husband...a letter a communist woman brought back from Hanoi and broadcast over national television before dropping it in the mail to Mrs. Pollard, The entire community of Colorado Springs waited its arrival, along with the media. When it did arrive, she went in a room alone and after seeing that six-line letter in his handwriting she knew he was alive. Despite the horror stories she had heard about POWs returning, she knew "the Ben Pollard I knew and loved would be coming home."

MAURICE RABB

By Duanne Puckett

"Dr. Maurice Rabb fought much of his life for civil rights and the social revolution he helped to engineer will be the stuff of history books one day." That's how the *Courier-Journal* eulogized Dr. Rabb after the 80-year-old died in November 1982.

Rabb practiced medicine in Shelbyville and Louisville for more than 50 years, but not without prejudicial struggles. In 1948, he was the first African-American to train at Louisville's General Hospital. Five years later, he was the first black to be admitted to membership in the Jefferson County Medical Society. His membership came only after two attempts and only after the society dropped the word "white" as a requirement for membership.

His own education was controlled by the word "white" when he lived in Columbus, Mississippi. When Rabb asked his father why there wasn't a high school for Negroes, his father asked a member of the board of education. The Rabbs were told Negroes could only go to the tenth grade because "that's all they need."

He obtained more education than that as he attended Fisk University in Nashville, where he met his wife, Jewel, whom he married in 1930. He went on to Meharry Medical College, also in Nashville. Upon graduation, the Rabbs moved to Kentucky, his wife's home, and he practiced medicine in Shelbyville for 16 years before moving to Louisville with their son, Maurice Rabb II, in 1946. There Mrs. Rabb taught at Central High School. Their son followed in his father's footsteps and became a physician.

Dr. Rabb was a spearhead in the civil rights movement in addition to his medical practice. He served 12 years on the national board of directors for the NAACP and was saluted for his service at the national convention in 1982.

Other awards included the Louisville Urban League's Equality Award; The Louisville Defender's Outstanding Kentuckian Award; a Kentucky Colonelship signed by Gov. Edward Breathitt; and a Louisville Ambassador of Goodwill certificate signed by Mayor Kenneth Schmeid.

One of his prized possessions was a black-and-white photograph taken with President John F. Kennedy at a White House reception for the National Medical Association in August 1963.

WILLIE C. RAY

By Duanne Puckett

If you were a student in the Shelbyville school system from 1930 to 1960, you were passenger on a "tight ship" run by a firm captain, Mrs. Willie C. Ray. That is how one student described the former school superintendent who took over the Shelbyville Independent School System in 1930, the same year that Bruce Daniel was hired as coach. He became principal of Shelbyville High in 1934 when his office was next door to Mrs. Ray's in the building on West Main Street. He remembered "that within an hour after the bell rang, she knew who was absent and went to check on them. She believed in attendance!" Ray stressed attendance contests in homerooms to try and reach 100 percent marks. Daniel said she would even go to the pool halls, a popular hangout at the time, and round up students. She vowed, "When they close the pool halls, we'll close the schools." Bennett Roach owned and operated the Shelby News during Mrs. Ray's tenure. He remembered one year when it snowed and there was a question about closing schools. She said at the time, "Are the Greyhounds running? If they are, the school buses will run too."

Ray was born Willie Cassell Hughes on April 1, 1892, in Bloomfield, Kentucky. She moved to Lexington where she attended private schools and lived with the family of a professor at Transylvania University where she graduated in 1913. She started her career in education in 1913 at the old Graded School on College Street in Shelbyville. She transferred to Simpsonville High where she remained as principal until her promotion to city superintendent.

Willie C. Ray was a teacher, school principal, and then served as superintendent of the Shelbyville Independent School System from 1930 until 1960.

Ray was active in the schools, attending every athletic event and even coaching the girls' basketball team. But academics and the importance of education came first in her life. She set out to make Shelbyville schools the best she could. Science Hill School on Washington Street in Shelbyville was quite popular in the 1930s so a rivalry developed between the prep school for girls and the city high school. Because of the improvements she made at Shelbyville High, it gained in stature.

She would attend National Education Association conventions and bring home programs to implement that cost nothing or very little, She was quite frugal with the city's tax money. However, when she decided Shelbyville needed a gym, Mrs. Ray went to the community to get it completed by 1934. Before that, the games were played outdoors.

Also during her tenure, Northside Elementary was built in 1939 and Southside Elementary was built in 1957. The east wing at the former high school was also added. (The school became West Middle in 1975 with the merger of the city and county school systems. A new West Middle School opened in August 2000 off La Grange Road.)

Ray had leadership roles with the Kentucky and National Education Association and was even appointed to a national education committee by President Harry S. Truman. She traveled to Washington, D.C. for lobbying efforts and after her retirement she enjoyed traveling for pleasure to the Orient and Moscow.

However, education was her biggest pleasure, having said during an interview in 1975, "I've been interested in schools all my life; I always played school as a child. So when I became superintendent, I wanted to be very, very close to the school," referring to her home at 1134 Main Street, across from the city high school where she lived with her husband James Ray, a longtime county clerk, farmer and tobacco warehouseman. She later moved to Crestview Health Care Center where she died at the age of 101 on November 30, 1993.

ALICE HEGAN RICE

By Zena B. Jesse

Alice Hegan Rice was born in Shelbyville on January 11, 1870, at the home of her maternal grandfather Judge James Caldwell. Judge Caldwell's home was located on East Main Street where a car wash now stands. Her parents were Samuel Wilson Hegan and Sallie Caldwell Hegan.

In 1800, her great, great grandfather, Adam Middleton, came over the Wilderness Road from Virginia and built a house about six miles east of Shelbyville. Streams of pioneers passed his door who needed rest and refreshment so he hung two huge, brass keys on a tree in front of his house and turned his home into Cross Keys Tavern. As the years went by the house and grounds were added to and the Inn became known to all who traveled to the western territory. Records show that between 1800 and 1825 the inn sheltered over ten thousand travelers.

During her childhood, Alice enjoyed visiting her relatives at Cross Keys, which she found to be a delightful old house but it was her grandfather Caldwell's house in Shelbyville where she spent most of her childhood. Every summer and every Christmas Alice's family and all the cousins, aunts and uncles gathered at the big, friendly house nestled among the trees, glowing with lights and ringing with laughter.

In the summer Alice and her cousins enjoyed wading in Clear Creek. On hot summer evenings the adults moved the piano out to the front porch and along with a violin, guitar, and mandolin gave concerts. An enthusiastic audience of neighbors hung over the entire length of the front fence and enjoyed the concerts with the family. Alice enjoyed making up stories and plays to entertain her young cousins, and she considered these summers to be nothing short of paradise.

Alice's grandfather Hegan graduated from Maynooth College in Dublin, Ireland, and came with a brother to America. With his young wife, he traveled to Louisville and opened a business place that he called an "Art Emporium." It was the first establishment of its kind in the South and boasted the first plate glass windows in Louisville. Wealthy Southern planters came by boat and stagecoach to buy pictures and pier glasses. Located behind the store was a factory where massive gold leaf frames were manufactured. Throughout the South today frames can be found bearing the signature "T. Hegan".

Because of delicate health, Alice received her early education at home. When she was ten years old her family moved to Louisville where she entered Miss Hampton's School for Girls. While there she wrote articles for the school newspaper. When she was fifteen she submitted an unsigned article to a Louisville newspaper and to her astonishment it was published.

Alice was a life-long member of the First Christian Church in Louisville, which sponsored a mission Sunday school in a slum neighborhood known as the Cabbage Patch. When she was about sixteen she and a friend visited the mission. The service was disturbed by the shenanigans of a gang of boys outside. So Alice offered to go out and try to hold their attention until Sunday school was over. In the midst of spitballs and jeers, Alice began telling a story that finally grabbed the boy's attention. Her efforts were so successful she was asked to teach a boy's Sunday school class. Peace reigned and Alice learned a lot about little boys and slum conditions.

Alice Hegan Rice, noted author and Shelby County native, is perhaps best remembered for her novel, Mrs. Wiggs of the Cabbage Patch, published in 1901.

After finishing school, Hegan made her debut into Louisville society. She continued to engage in charitable work and became a member of the Author's Club of Louisville. This was a group of young women, all of whom aspired to be authors. With their encouragement, Alice wrote her first novel, *Mrs. Wiggs of the Cabbage Patch*. The story revolves around a woman who, in spite of her poverty, met her problems with courage and a sense of humor.

The book was published in 1901 by the S.S. McClure Publishing House and made Miss Hegan famous overnight. In the next forty years, it sold over 500,000 copies and was translated into French, German, Swedish, Danish, Chinese, and Japanese. The book was also made into a stage play and a movie. It is still in print today.

In 1902, Hegan married the poet Cale Young Rice. Their permanent home was in the St. James Court area of Louisville but they spent their summers in Maine. They traveled extensively in Europe and the Orient and their travels provided material for Mrs. Rice's books and her husband's poetry.

Alice Hegan Rice was one of the most famous authors of her day. In all she had twenty novels and numerous short stories published. Mrs. Rice's favorite among her novels was *Mr. Pete and Co.*, the story of a junk dealer she met on the Louisville waterfront.

Although Mrs. Rice somewhat romanticized the poor and their problems in her novels, she had a genuine lifelong concern for the poor. In 1910, Mrs. Rice and Louise Marshall founded the Cabbage Patch Settlement House to help the people in that area. This ministry grew to include a paid staff and one hundred volunteers. Also, Mrs. Rice's book Calvary Alley was written in hopes of shedding light on the intolerable housing conditions of the poor and stirring up indignation in the community that would lead to remedying the situation.

Mrs. Rice's books were unpretentious, unassuming, and wholesome. They were filled with real pathos, keen humor and a kindly understanding of human nature. Her characters are fresh and vivid and her books were drawn out of her own experiences. Mrs. Rice received honorary degrees from Rollins College and the University of Louisville. She died at her home in Louisville in 1942 on her seventy-second birthday and was buried in Cave Hill cemetery.

MOSES RUBEN

By Duanne Puckett

When Moses Ruben died on November 23, 1962, the editorial headline in the Shelbyville newspaper said, "Moses Ruben Will Be Remembered." It spoke of his integrity, talents, and devotion to public service. It wasn't until later that the public learned of Mr. Ruben's will in which he left his entire estate, following the death of the last member of his family, to King's Daughters Hospital in Shelbyville. When the hospital was sold to a for-profit company, Louis Ruben, his brother, contested the will and won, establishing the Moses Ruben Fund which has awarded more than $500,000 in grants to Shelby County projects since 1990. Louis Ruben died in 1989 at the age of 97. Their sister, Bessie Stern, died in 1972.

The Ruben parents were immigrants. In 1882, Nathan Ruben and his young wife Rebecca left their native Russia and came to America. They settled in Danville where they opened a store and began rearing a family: Mark, Moses, Bessie, and Louis. The family moved to Shelbyville in 1896 where Nathan Ruben founded a department store, the forerunner of Ruben's women's wear operated by his sons, Mark and Moses. Louis owned and operated a dry cleaners.

Ruben's Dry Goods was at 602 Main Street in a building next to what was Farmers & Traders Bank, which is now the Biagi & Associates engineering firm. Moses ran the store while Mark was on the road buying and selling. This setup continued through the 1940s and World War II until Mark died in 1945. Moses didn't retire until 1957, completing 50 years in his department store. He was 77 when he died in 1962.

Ruben was an organizer of the Shelby County Building and Loan Association, a City Councilman, and a chairman of the Shelbyville Water & Sewer Commission. He worked in the movement to convert the city's inadequate water supply from Clear Creek to Guist Creek Lake. He was a charter member of the Adath Israel Temple in Louisville where he was buried along with his brothers and sister.

Terms for the Moses Ruben Fund call for it to be administered by a committee of three: one appointed by Fiscal Court, one appointed by the Ministerial Alliance, and one appointed by the Rotary and Kiwanis Clubs. The charter committee members were Bob Walters, the Rev. J. Howard Griffith, and Bill Shannon. In 1998, Chuck Hickman replaced Mr. Shannon for the civic clubs. The fund is now administered through the Shelby County Community Foundation.

Sentinel-News photograph, 1992.

Moses Ruben owned Ruben's women's clothing store in Shelbyville and endowed the Ruben Trust Fund, which makes grants to local charities.

GEORGE WILLIAM SAFFELL

By Duanne Puckett

"Professor Saffell has been a great inspiration to his people, always striving to hold before them ideals of the highest citizenship and principles of true Christianity" is how the March 1953 newspaper article announced the death of George William Saffell. .

Born May 10, 1876, in Frankfort, he was the son of George and Addie Saffell. He was educated at the Frankfort public schools and the Kentucky Normal School after which he moved to Shelbyville where he taught school before deciding to become a mortician. He began the Saffell Funeral Home located at Fourth and Henry Clay Streets where his wife, Mildred Stone Saffell, continued the business long after his death.

His committment to the community is seen in bequests that established a non-profit foundation to accept and provide funds for upkeep and maintenance of the Daisy M. Saffell Hospital and the Saffell Cemetery. It also provided for the maintenance of a recreation center for "colored" children to be established in the Mammoth Skating Rink on Henry Clay Street. Additional money was left to local churches and $500 set aside as a student loan fund for worthy students on the basis of competitive exams to be given by Kentucky State College (now University). Only graduates of Lincoln Institute who had lived in the state a minimum of one year were eligible.

Professor Saffell was a member of Bethel African Methodist Episcopal Church where he taught Sunday School for 30 years. Among the many organizations to which he belonged were the Masons, Knights of Pythias, Odd Fellows, and United Brothers of Friendship. He was also a life member of the National Funeral Directors Association which he served as president for many years.

He died March 22, 1953, and was buried in Calvary Cemetery on North Seventh Street.

CLAUDIA SANDERS

By Henry Cleveland and Kevin Collins

Claudia Ellen Leddington Sanders was born in 1902 on a farm in Knox County, Kentucky, one of fourteen children. In 1930, she went to work for Harland Sanders at the Sanders Cafe in Corbin, Kentucky. In 1948, she married Sanders, and along the way helped her husband build Kentucky Fried Chicken (KFC) from its humble beginnings of two restaurants in 1952 to more than 600 franchises in 1964, when the company was sold.

Harland Sanders once described his wife as "my packing girl, my warehouse supervisor, my delivery person—you name it. She worked like a Trojan." Mrs. Sanders would package herbs and spices and deliver them to the railway station or the post office—sometimes at midnight—to get them to a restaurant that needed them in a hurry. She often traveled with the Colonel as a hostess for KFC, and in the early days of the company would wear an ante-bellum gown as she greeted diners in restaurants that sold the chicken.

In 1997, David Novak, president and chief executive officer of KFC and Pizza Hut, said, "We could not have been the company we are now without Claudia's contributions. Her commitment to Kentucky Fried Chicken and her work as goodwill ambassador inspired our franchisees and employees alike."

Shelbyvillians remember her as "elegant, gracious, straight forward, and charming." Mrs. Sanders was also inspirational to many Shelby County businesswomen. She was an active member of the local Professional Woman's Club for more than twenty years. She was a member of the board of directors of Union College in Barbourville, as well as a member of the board of directors of Colonel Sanders Kentucky Fried Chicken Ltd. in Canada. She was an honorary chairwoman of the National March of Dimes.

In 1969, she and her husband opened the Shelby County restaurant that would later bear her name—Claudia Sanders-The Colonel's Lady. Together they ran this establishment until 1973 when they sold it. Today, even after her death, it is still called the Claudia Sanders Dinner House. In addition to her many business interests, Mrs. Sanders found time for Shelbyville friendships. For many years she was a regular at Dottie's Beauty Shop. She found this small two-person hair salon, founded in 1940 by proprietor Dottie Gordon, both comfortable and convivial to good conversation. Occasionally, she would enjoy shopping trips and lunch at Stewart's in Louisville. She was particularly fond of shopping for hats.

After Colonel Sanders' death in 1980, Claudia Sanders sold their thirty-two acre farm on Smithfield Road and moved to 1321 St. Andrews Drive in the Brentwood Subdivision of Shelbyville. She resided there until her death on December 31, 1996.

Among the Sanders' many philanthropic endeavors was a charitable trust which the couple set-up in Toronto in 1965 using shares of the company that franchised KFC restaurants in Canada. Until 1997, the trust distributed millions of dollars over thirty years to fourteen institutions, eleven of them in Kentucky.

Claudia Sanders had two children by a previous marriage: Elvis Ray and Billie Jean. She is buried alongside her husband in Louisville at Cave Hill Cemetery.

HARLAND SANDERS

By Henry Cleveland and Kevin Collins

Harland David Sanders was born September 9, 1890, in Henryville, Indiana. The son of Wilbert D. and Margaret Ann Sanders, Harland was only six years old when his father died. When his mother remarried in 1902, Harland left home to lodge with relatives. His formal education ended shortly thereafter with the completion of the sixth grade. At the age of sixteen he found himself an enlistee in the U.S. Army. Then, over the next twenty years, he held a variety of jobs in and near the Louisville area. But by the age of thirty he had settled in Corbin, Kentucky, as the proprietor of a Shell Oil station on U.S. 25 with a small eating facility, called Sanders Cafe. His fried chicken developed a reputation with the motorists and truckers, and he soon relocated across the street to a motor court with a larger restaurant.

In 1935, Governor Ruby Laffoon made Sanders an honorary Kentucky Colonel, and by 1939, with its inclusion in the Duncan Hines Adventures in Good Eating book, the Sanders Court motel and restaurant had begun to gain some national exposure. Between the end of World War II and 1955 business grew and the restaurant expanded to accommodate 142 customers.

The planned construction of I-75, however, was designed to bypass Corbin by about seven miles. Realizing the impact of this on his business, Sanders sold it in 1955. Nearly broke, he chose now to pursue more vigorously the franchising of his regionally famous chicken recipe. At the age of sixty-six, Sanders began to recruit restaurant owners to become Kentucky Fried Chicken franchisees. The first franchise was sold to The Do Drop Inn in Salt Lake City, Utah. The first "take home" store—a major innovation in its day that would revolutionize the fast food industry and become the prototype KFC franchise—was built in Jacksonville, Florida. The first franchisee in Louisville was Kaelin's Restaurant on Newburg Road; in Shelbyville, the first franchisee was the Chicken Villa on U.S. 60 West.

By 1949, Sanders had received a second honorary commission as a Kentucky Colonel and from then on he recognized and began to cultivate the image that would eventually become one of the most recognized marketing icons in the world. The signature "Colonel Harland Sanders," with the sculptured picture of an aristocratic-but-down-home, courtly, Dixie gentleman in white suit and string tie, a head of rich white hair, with meticulously-trimmed mustache and goatee, would, in time, become— with the exception of Louisvillian Muhammad Ali—the world's most recognized Kentuckian.

In 1960, Colonel Sanders established his residence and his new company's headquarters in Shelbyville, on U.S. 60 West. By 1960, there were more than 200 KFC franchises in the United States and Canada. By 1964, when Sanders sold the company, there existed more than six hundred KFC outlets. Throughout its subsequent ownerships, Sanders always remained active in the company as a goodwill ambassador, often traveling as much as 250,000 miles a year.

In 1969, Colonel Sanders and his wife, Claudia, opened a restaurant west of Shelbyville. Originally named Colonel Sanders Kentucky Inn, by 1972 it had been renamed Claudia Sanders- The Colonel's Lady. In 1973, they sold the business to Cherry and Thomas Settle, and by 1976 it had acquired the current name, Claudia Sanders Dinner House. Located at 3202 Shelbyville Road, the establishment suffered a devastating fire on May 10, 1999. The Settles rebuilt completely, however, and on September 26, 2000, they reopened for business.

In 1976, after living a few years in the Hurstborne area of Jefferson County, the Sanders again took residence in Shelby County, buying a 32-acre farm on Smithfield Road, just outside the city of Shelbyville. Here the Colonel spent much of his time gardening or in his alfalfa fields. He continued, as in the past, his good will trips on behalf of KFC. For many years his driver-companion in travel was Dick Miller, a native of Shelby County. Sanders, a member of the First Christian Church, on Fourth and Main, was a close friend of Pastor Ed Cayce. In fact, it was through the intercession of the Colonel that the Reverend Cayce met his future wife, Eleanor. Another close Shelbyville friendship was with Paul Johnson, proprietor of a barbershop on the 400 block of Main Street. The much-traveled Harland Sanders would often return to Shelbyville specifically to have Johnson cut his hair. Occasionally, the Colonel would enjoy

Col. Harland Sanders in a Sentinel-News photograph.

fishing trips to Canada with Miller, Cayce, and Johnson. Along with other Shelbyville intimates, they would also be guests of the Sanders' at other social events, such as the annual birthday party for the Colonel, catered in Louisville and sponsored by Kentucky Fried Chicken. "I am happy to be a resident of this county," Sanders said in 1979, "there are some real nice folks here."

Colonel Sanders was very active in philanthropy. One of his favorite local causes was the Big Brother/Big Sister program. He contributed time and money to, among others, religious charities, hospitals, medical research, education, the Boy Scouts, Junior Achievement, and the March of Dimes— for whom he was national chairman for several years.

Harland Sanders was married to Josephine King in 1908; they had three children: Margaret, Harland Jr., and Mildred. They were divorced in 1947. In 1949, he married Claudia Leddington Price. Sanders died on December 16, 1980. He lay in state at the Capitol rotunda in Frankfort, and is buried in Louisville's Cave Hill Cemetery with his wife, Claudia. The monument at the gravesite is a bust of the Colonel executed by his daughter, Margaret, who died in 2001.

MARK J. SCEARCE

By Duanne Puckett

One of Shelbyville's most famous landmarks is Wakefield-Scearce Galleries and the community has one man to thank, Mark J. Scearce. The complex of brick buildings on Washington Street served as home to Science Hill School from 1825 to1939. Mr. Scearce and Mark Wakefield bought the property in 1947, converting the one-time chapel into a world-renowned antique establishment. Scearce had owned a jewelry store since 1940 on Main Street. He was inspired by his grandmother to appreciate silver since she bought him books to read on the subject while he was confined to bed with an illness for more than a year during World War II. His friend, Hayden Igleheart, supplied him with books on antiques and book collecting. He was influenced to pursue the interest further by Mr. Wakefield, who was 40 years his senior. Mr. Wakefield told Mr. Scearce at the time, "I've got the money and you've got the knowledge."

The Shelbyville native's first job, however, was with Walters & Thompson feed store after graduating from Shelbyville High School at the height of the Great Depression. He and his brother, James, also opened a grocery before Mark bought the Owen S. Kenny Jewelry store in 1940.

When World War II broke out, jewelry merchandise became difficult to obtain, and Scearce decided he would rather offer old silver than have empty showcases. He took advantage of every opportunity to study the various periods and makers. Wakefield encouraged him to attend the British Antique Dealers Fair in England in 1947. He returned with about two railroad carloads of silver and furniture.

He patterned his underground silver vault after those he saw in England. He also adapted another custom of English silversmiths by having the mint julep cups marked on the bottom with an American eagle and the initials of the U. S. President. He presented the first cup produced to each president starting with Eisenhower.

Mark Scearce (center) supervised unpacking a shipment of antiques at Wakefield-Scearce Galleries. Conn West is on the left and Jane Lane is at right.

Courtesy of Katherine and Henry Cleveland.

In 1961, Scearce began an extensive renovation of the buildings, starting with the Science Hill Inn, the dining room located in the complex. It was during that time that he also gave the courtyard a facelift, capitalizing on the New Orleans look by adding wrought iron furniture. In 1980, he took on another renovation project when the individual boarding rooms along the courtyard were converted into shops: linen, silver, women's clothing. The west wing was later opened to house a bookstore, children's clothing store, and men's apparel.

Scearce took a personal interest not only in the business but also in the building because he was a believer in historic preservation. For his work, he was presented the coveted Ida Lee Willis Preservation Award from the Kentucky Heritage Commission in 1993—three days before his unexpected death at the age of 76.

That was only one of numerous accolades bestowed upon the man during his life because of his commitment and involvement in his community, its clubs and his church. His first preservation honor came in 1980 when he was presented the Kentucky Heritage Commission's commercial award for preserving a landmark building: the former home of Science Hill School. His preservation project involved 58,000 square feet of space, took 13 months, and entailed 37 miles of new wiring and 14 miles of plumbing. When he accepted the silver bowl award, he said of the structure, "it might burn down or fall down but it won't be bulldozed down."

The Shelbyville City Council named him Citizen of the Year in 1986. It marked his initial involvement in what became the Shelby Development Corporation, an organization challenged to keep Main Street and the downtown environment alive and well in the midst of urban progress. Scearce took the first step in this rejuvenation when he installed brick sidewalks in front of his property in the 1980s—a pattern that became part of the Streetscape design a decade later throughout a five block area. Neil Hackworth, mayor of Shelbyville at the time, said the city created a Historic District in 1986 to "protect the historic resources developed by Mr. Scearce...."

Scearce showed his fondness for his hometown when accepting the Citizen of the Year plaque calling it "the nearest thing to my heart." That devotion to the downtown became obvious when he began a Christmas Gala each November to kick off the shopping season, a kick-off that still attracts close to 12,000 people annually, people who also visit other shops which benefit from the tradition.

Marcus Johnson Scearce was born October 21, 1916, into an 18th century Shelby County family, the second son of Sally Johnson and Shelby Scearce. His mother, who died three years later, was a day pupil at the Science Hill School that her son so nobly preserved years later. Their grandmother reared him and his brother.

His interest in education included a 25-year stint on the Shelbyville Independent School System board, participation in art contests and shows in the courtyard at the Galleries for students, donation of books and money to school libraries, and numerous awards for 4-H programs. He helped found the Shelby County Chamber of Commerce in the 1940s and served as president of the Kentucky Jeweler's Association.

His interest in the community included a thirty-year membership in the Shelbyville Rotary Club and membership in the Shelby County Historical Society, Shelbyville Country Club, and service on the board of the Shelby County Public Library and Jewish Hospital Shelbyville. He was also a director of the Shelby County Community Theatre for which he helped secure funds to buy property at Eighth and Main to house productions.

Not only was he a member of Shelbyville First Baptist for more than 40 years, but also was once chairman of the deacons. Mr. Scearce also served as chairman of the building committee when the building at Fifth and Main collapsed in the 1950s. It was his foresight and knowledge that salvaged many of the treasured stained glass windows and other artifacts that were incorporated into the new church structure on West Main Street.

He also served on the board of Kentucky Southern College in Louisville, Parents Board of Centre College in Danville, Associate Board of Georgetown College, and Board of Trustees of Georgetown College. The college was the recipient of funds from a book he published, *Stuff & Things* (1990), which was a collection of favorite tidbits he had saved through the years.

His favorite pasttime, though, was his family, starting with his high school sweetheart, Nancy Peyton Ballard, who was known fondly as Peytie. She often accompanied him on his buying trips to England and took up painting. Scearce often commended his wife for her support of his business, which was evident as the two stood side by side at the door to the Galleries to greet guests during the annual Christmas Gala.

During the presentation of the Kentucky Heritage Commission's medallion three days before he died, Mr. Scearce was described as "...always, first and foremost, a class act. Antique dealers, economic developers, leaders of all kinds and persuasions would do well to learn the maxims by which he ran his business: Integrity. Honesty. Keeping his word. Maintaining the highest quality in everything he does."

WILLIAM SHANNON

By R.R. Van Stockum Sr.

On June 23, 1792, during its first session, the General Assembly of Kentucky passed an act creating Shelby County (named after Governor Isaac Shelby) from part of Jefferson County. This act took effect September 1, 1792. The first officials of the new county were: David Standiford, sheriff; Martin Daniel, Benjamin Roberts, and Thomas Gwyn, judges of the Court of Quarter Sessions; and Thomas Shannon, Joseph Winlock, Daniel McCleland, and Abraham Owen, judges of the County Court (justices of the peace). The Shelby County Court began its first term October 15, 1792, at the house of Brackett Owen, a prominent early settler and father of Abraham Owen. William Shannon, brother of Justice Thomas Shannon, served as county clerk, pro tempore. One of the first matters of business was to establish the location of Shelbyville, the county seat. After giving careful consideration to the Painted Stone area, the court chose a site where the main road from Frankfort to the Falls of the Ohio crossed Clear Creek.

William Shannon, sometimes described as Shelby County's greatest landholder, owner of the land selected, was obviously influential in this decision. He pointed out the advantages of the site including the number of springs, but perhaps more convincing was his offer to donate an acre of land for the public buildings. He also offered to lay out fifty of his adjoining acres for town lots. His motives are difficult to evaluate so long after the event. However, even today landowners are willing to donate rights of way for roads in order to enhance the value of their adjacent holdings.

At the November 1792 session of the Kentucky General Assembly, in the first year of the commonwealth, an act was passed establishing the town of Shelbyville on William Shannon's lands. David Standiford, Joseph Winlock, John Knight, Abraham Owen, and Thomas Gwyn were designated as town trustees to lay out the land in lots and streets and sell the lots for the benefit of Shannon.

Ed Shinnock attempted to identify this "William Shannon" who played such a significant role in the establishment of Shelbyville: "There was a Captain William Shannon who served as quartermaster under George Rogers Clark in his western expedition, but it has not been ascertained whether it was this one or not." It can now be stated with certainty that the William Shannon who served as commissary and quartermaster for George Rogers Clark for a three-year period commencing in March 1779 was in fact the one upon whose lands Shelbyville was established.

At the meeting of the county court in January 1793 a contract was let to Shannon for fifteen pounds for the erection of a courthouse where the present Shelby County Court House stands. The session of March 19, 1793 was the first recorded as being held at the new courthouse in Shelbyville. James Craig, the first regularly appointed county clerk, served at that session.

In 1794, there were about 20 well-built houses in Shelbyville on the lots owned by William Shannon. There was also a tavern established by John Felty. In an altercation that year in front of the tavern, Shannon threw a stone at Felty and simultaneously was struck in a vital part by a dirk thrown by him. Shannon died instantly; Felty died a few days later. It is ironic that William Shannon, who in 1792 donated the acre of land for public buildings and built the first Shelby County Court House, also became the first person to have his will probated by the Shelby County Court.

ISAAC SHELBY

By Duanne Puckett

When Kentucky became a state in 1792, the first governor was Isaac Shelby, the man for whom Shelbyville and Shelby County are named.

His father, Evan Shelby Jr., was 16 when his family of five brothers and sisters left South Wales in 1732 with their parents Evan and Catherine Shelby and arrived in Philadelphia.

Evan Jr. married Letitia Cox. Isaac was the couple's third child, born December 11, 1750, when the family was living along the Potomac River near Hagerstown, Maryland. When his grandfather died the following year, Isaac Shelby's father inherited 2,500 acres. By 1754, the family had 24,000 acres in what is now Washington County, Maryland. They moved to western Virginia in 1772.

By the age of 23, Isaac Shelby was a lieutenant in his father's company of the Virginia Colonial Militia of Fincastle County. In 1777, the Cherokees signed a peace treaty so Isaac returned to his life as family man, farmer and cattleman, businessman and statesman.

In years to follow, he was a member of the local Commission of Oyer and Terminer, a high criminal court; elected a delegate to the Virginia Legislature; appointed a mayor in the escort of guards for the commission to run the western boundary between Virginia and North Carolina. Shelby was also a delegate to the North Carolina Legislature.

He purchased 400 acres of land in what was to become Kentucky in 1776 at about $2.25 per 100 acres along with a pre-emption, which allowed him to acquire 1,400 acres of the choicest land in the state for $409.

On April 19, 1783, he married Susannah Hart in a ceremony at Fort Boonesborough. In 1786, he completed the family homestead, called Traveler's Rest in Lincoln County, which remained in the Shelby name for four generations until it was accidentally burned in 1905 when the owner tried to burn down a wasp's nest. The fire made bigger headlines than when he became governor since a single paragraph noted the election results May 15, 1792.

The governor and first lady had 10 children; one died in 1801 less than 2 months old. The last child was born in 1804. One daughter, Letitia, born in 1799, married and ended up living in Shelby County. The home that she and Captain Todd occupied was known as Stockdale off Eminence Pike.
In 1812, Isaac Shelby was elected to a second term as governor even though he ran for office reluctantly. Upon taking office he became involved in the War of 1812. During the war the governor raised a large number of troops and joined General William Henry Harrison to fight the British in Ontario at the Thames River. Shelby returned to Kentucky a hero. He left office in 1816 and retired to Traveler's Rest. He died there July 18, 1826.

Courtesy of The Filson Historical Society.

Isaac Shelby, first governor of Kentucky, for whom Shelby County and Shelbyville were named.

AUGUSTUS OWSLEY STANLEY

By Ted Igleheart

The "Stanley-Casey House" located on Washington Street at the northwest corner of Third Street, restored and occupied by the Shelby County Historical Society, was the birthplace of Kentucky Governor Augustus Owsley Stanley on May 21, 1867.

Stanley's parents, Rev. William Stanley and Amanda Owsley Stanley, a niece of Governor William Owsley (1844-48), moved to Shelbyville where Rev. Stanley preached for the Christian Church. He had been a member of General John Hunt Morgan's Cavalry during the Civil War and entered the ministry following his discharge.

A. O. Stanley attended the Kentucky A & M College (now University of Kentucky) in Lexington and was graduated from Centre College in Danville. He read law after teaching for several years and was admitted to practice in 1894. He married Sue Soaper in 1903, with whom he reared three sons. Residing in Fleming County, Stanley was defeated for County Attorney

A.O. Stanley, governor of Kentucky during 1915-19, was born in Shelbyville in the Stanley-Casey House, present headquarters of the Shelby County Historical Society. This photograph was made in 1916 while he was governor.

in his first try for public office and moved to Henderson, where he was elected to six terms to the U.S. House of Representatives. He ran for the U.S. Senate in 1914 but was defeated by Governor J. C. W. Beckham.

In 1915, Stanley received the Democratic nomination for Governor and faced his close friend, Edward P. Morrow of Somerset, who had won the Republican nomination. The two men traveled together taking the stump across the state, first tearing each other apart in raucus debate, then praising each other in flowery oratory, and sharing a hotel room that night. Stanley was well known for his frequent imbibing of bourbon beverages. On one occasion under a hot sun, he vomited in full view of the crowd while Morrow was speaking. When Stanley took his turn to speak, he proclaimed in vigorous opening remarks: "That just goes to show you what I have been saying all over Kentucky. Ed Morrow plain makes me sick to my stomach!"

Stanley won the election by 471 votes in the closest governor's race in state history. But he resigned in 1919 after being elected to the U.S. Senate, serving until 1925 when he lost his bid for reelection to Frederic M. Sackett. He then opened a law office in Washington, D. C., where he died on August 12, 1958, and was buried in the Frankfort Cemetery.

During Stanley's term as Governor, prohibition was a dominant issue, failing in both houses of the General Assembly in 1916 but passing in 1918 after federal law mandated prohibition. He obtained a corrupt practices act, convict labor bill, antitrust measures, a workman's compensation act, and tried to reform the state's tax system. When he resigned as Governor, he had seen most of his programs adopted, including a new budget system.

BOBBY STRATTON

By Duanne Puckett

When Bobby Stratton became the second County Judge-Executive, he campaigned on the philosophy that money would not be the answer to all the county's problems. He said one of his first priorities would be fiscal responsibility. When he campaigned for re-election each time since 1982, Stratton pointed to the accomplishments that had occurred without damage to the county's fiscal budget or without an increase in taxes. When Stratton was first elected to office in 1982, the tax rate was 12.5 cents per $100 valued property. In 2001, it was 11.1 cents per $100.

The Shelby County native's business experience came from operating a grocery store and sporting goods store on the east end of Shelbyville for more than 20 years. He also helped create the youth baseball league in the community and was responsible for the American Legion Baseball League for about 30 years. Ballpark fields bear his name.

Stratton also served eight years on the former Shelbyville Independent School System's Board of Education. For his work, he was awarded the Friend of Education award in 1974.

The Bagdad High School graduate's other community involvement include being former Master of Solomon Masonic Lodge No. 5 F & AM, Chairman of the Masonic Board of Kentucky, and member of the Shelby County Farm Bureau and the Kentuckiana Planning Development Agency (KIPDA).

He also served in the 40th Infantry Division in the Pacific Theater in World War II. He and his wife, Helen, were married in 1946 and had four children and seven grandchildren.

In 1978, Stratton ran against incumbent Sammy Wood, farmer Sanford Roberts, and attorney Vic Brizendine. Other opponents included Mike Taylor in 1998 when Stratton captured 3,162 votes to Taylor's 2,434 in the Democratic Primary. He defeated Republican Charles Bates in the November General Election that year. Stratton believed his victory was because of the many projects that were completed during his terms.

Some of those projects included:

• Converting a former auto dealership at the corner of Fifth and Washington into the courthouse Annex, housing the county's clerk and the property valuation administration departments.

• Building a community center for meetings and other public use on Washington Street. It was named the Stratton Center.

• Building a senior citizens center, also on Washington Street, where the Multi-Purpose Community Action Agency is now housed to meet the needs of not only the elderly but the low-income as well.

• Expanding the parks department and helping secure funds to develop the Family Activity Center with indoor pool and gymnasium that opened in 2000.

• Building a new Emergency Medical Services complex near the hospital.

• Building a new jail on Snow Hill and converting the old stone jail behind the courthouse to serve as a dispatch center for the community.

• Establishing the Shelby Clean Community Program to reduce litter and the Convenience Center on

King's Highway for refuse collection, once the landfill, was closed.

• Converting the old county firehouse on Seventh Street into a second community meeting center and establishing a recycling center on the adjacent property.

Stratton was also proud that 277 miles of county roads were paved with county tax money.

He retired at the end of his term in 2002, ending a 21-year career as county judge-executive.

BEN ALLEN THOMAS II

By Kevin Collins and Duanne Puckett

Ben Allen Thomas II was a Kentucky pioneer in progressive farming techniques as well as farm cooperative movements. He was born April 20, 1890, at the family farm on Cropper Road, where he lived all his life. The Thomas family dates its farming history in Shelbyville back to 1795, when Thomas' great-grandfather traded a house and a lot in Harrodsburg for 1,500 acres of farmland in Shelby County (cf. Chenoweth Farm).

In a memoir written about the tobacco industry many years later, Thomas recalled a child's picture of Shelby County farm-life before the turn of the last century: "Our farm began growing tobacco in 1882, and I remember dropping tobacco plants when I was six or seven years old. They gave me a small basket and I went along and dropped the plants about 2 feet apart. The rows were about 3 feet apart, and our usual yield was about 1,500 to 1,000 pounds per acre."

In 1921, Thomas became one of the organizers and promoters of the Burley Tobacco Cooperative. He founded the Western District Warehousing Corporation in 1922.

He was also a pioneer in milk cooperatives. In 1923, he founded the first dairy unit. This effort would eventually lead in 1931 to the incorporation of the Falls Cities Milk Producers Co-op, still later known as Dairymen Inc. He was vice-president of this co-op for three years and president for seventeen. He was also the first president of the American Dairy Association of Kentucky, serving for seven years as well as a member of its national board of directors. In addition, he was president of the Central Dairy Council for ten years, and was later made a director for life.

His work forming cooperatives in the tobacco and dairy farming industries was augmented by his seminal efforts on behalf of both the wool industry and farm-resource conservation. For ten years he was vice-president and president of the Kentucky Wool Growers Co-op. In addition, Thomas' interest in conservation resulted in his appointment to the state committee of the Agricultural Adjustment Association, and out of this a co-op was organized that eventually terraced 3,000 acres of Shelby County farmland, an example for many more farms. The Co-op's construction of dams for farm reservoirs also contributed to water conservation. He was also an organizer of the Southern States Shelbyville Co-op, and somehow was able to keep the details of all of his cooperative work mainly in his head.

In addition to all of this, Thomas managed the family's Chenoweth Farm for 40 years, from his father's death in 1912 until his sons' ascendancy in 1952. Perhaps, on a personal note, his most satisfying experience in farming might well have been the fact that he had the Grand Champion Steer at the International Livestock Exposition of 1922.

On the financial front, Thomas was president of the Bank of Cropper from 1912 to 1921, as well as a director of the Deposit Bank of Pleasureville, the Shelby County Trust Bank, and the Hurst Home Mutual Insurance Company.

A former student and captain of the 1911 football team of Transylvania University, Thomas received an honorary Bachelor of Law degree from there in 1963. In 1978, at the age of eighty-eight, he was awarded the Morrison Medallion and Transylvania Medal from the University for his contributions to college life and programs.

Ben Allen Thomas II was a leader in agriculture, tobacco and dairy cooperatives, and managed the family farm, Chenoweth Farm, for forty years.

The Kentucky Farm Bureau gave lifetime achievement awards in agriculture to Ben Allen Thomas in 1959, by the University of Kentucky the Golden Sheaf Award and in 1961.

Thomas was an elder of the First Christian Church. He died December 17, 1985, at the age of ninety-five. He is buried at the Grove Hill Cemetery. His wife, Vestina Bailey Thomas, whom he married in 1919, died on December 28, 1984. They had two children: Ben Allen Thomas III, b. April 23, 1920, and Winford Bailey Thomas, b. May 4, 1924.

CHARLES STEWART TODD

By Sherry Jelsma

Charles Stewart Todd was born January 22, 1791, in Lincoln County, Kentucky, the son of Thomas Todd, Kentucky's first Supreme Court Justice, and Elizabeth Harris Todd. Beginning at age eight, he was educated by tutors and at schools in the Danville area and then at Translyvania. At age seventeen he entered the College of William and Mary in Williamsburg, Virginia, and graduated in 1809. He then studied law with his father in Woodford County, Kentucky, subsequently attending Judge Tapping Reeve's law school in Leitchfield, Connecticut. After being admitted to the bar in 1811, Todd established his law practice in Lexington, Kentucky.

In 1812, Todd joined Stewart Megowan's Company in Lewis' regiment and was appointed Acting Quartermaster in the Advance of the Left Wing of the Northwestern Army. He served in the army until 1815, gaining the title of Colonel, by which he was addressed the rest of his life. During the War of 1812, he served under General William Henry Harrison as well as Governor Isaac Shelby at the Battle of the Thames.

Resuming law practice in Frankfort after the war, the dashing Colonel Todd fell in love with Governor Shelby's youngest daughter, Letitia. They were married on June 18, 1816, in the Governor's Mansion in Frankfort. Newly elected Governor George Madison appointed Colonel Todd Secretary of State.

However, Madison died six weeks later and Todd resigned and was not reappointed by Governor Gabriel Slaughter. Todd ran for the state legislature and won in both 1817 and 1818, representing Franklin County. The Todds lived in Frankfort and had a son and a daughter.

The entire nation was suffering financial stress during the panic of 1819. Todd had lost money in land deals in Frankfort, and when his partner died suddenly, he was left holding a huge debt for a warehouse. He looked to the federal government for a job. President James Monroe offered Todd a four-year appointment to Colombia as Agent for Commerce and Seamen. Although it meant leaving his family, it was a certain income, and he accepted. Letters to Henry Clay from Todd indicate his debts were heavy and weighed on his mind. After one year in South America, Todd returned to Kentucky to regain his health. He returned in 1822 to Bogota to the newly independent Republic of Colombia, now recognized by the United States. His job required an excellent knowledge of geography, trade policy, tariffs, and laws of the sea. The duplicity of Pedro Gual, Foreign Minister in Bogota, irritated Todd to the point that he wrote directly to President Santander of Colombia with his complaints. When offered a second appointment to Colombia, Todd refused.

In 1826, Governor Shelby died and left to Letitia 500 acres of land in Shelby County. Charles and Letitia moved their family to the farm, called Stockdale, and built an elegant brick home. Colonel Todd began to clear the land and engage in agriculture. They grew hemp, grass hay, corn, and raised blooded cattle and hogs. Todd was vice president and then president of the State Agricultural Society. He promoted good farming practices, such as deep plowing, rotation of crops, and using manure for fertilizer.

Both Letitia and Charles became Presbyterians in 1828; nine years later and again in 1839, Charles would be sent as Commissioner to the Presbyterian General Assembly in Philadelphia. Cholera devastated the family in 1832. Three children died within a week and are buried in Grove Hill Cemetery. The twelfth and last of the Todd's children was born in 1838; four of those children died before adulthood.

Todd had been active in politics throughout his life. He was a great correspondent, speechmaker, conversationalist, and had friends all over the nation. In 1840, he went to Cincinnati as publisher and editor of the *Cincinnati Republican* and wrote the Sketches of the Civil and Military Services of W. H. Harrison. In November 1840, General Harrison visited Kentucky and is said to have visited Stockdale and the Todds. Called by one author the head of Harrison's campaign, Todd followed the General to the White House for the inauguration in 1841 and lived there with him until the President's death one month later.

Todd had expected a government appointed from Harrison, but with his death, Todd was dependent on President John Tyler for an appointment. Finally, this occurred in a four-year commission of Envoy Extraordinaire and Minister Plenipotentiary to the Court of Russia at St. Petersburg. Todd learned a great deal about Russia and helped Emperor Nicholas I by bringing railroad engineers from the United

Charles Stewart Todd, builder of Stockdale, in a photograph from 1864-66.

Courtesy of The Filson Historical Society.

States to develop the railroad from St. Petersburg to Moscow. Todd was a great success with the Emperor and his Court; his dispatches to the Secretary of State are detailed and informative.

On his return in 1846, Todd retired to Shelby County and continued to raise blooded cattle. His two sons helped him run the farm. Being a popular man, Todd was asked to run for the nomination for Governor in 1848 by the Whig party. He refused because he did not think he would win the nomination. That same year he began widely campaigning for General Zachary Taylor as President.

In 1850, he gained a commission to go west with General Robert Campbell and Oliver Temple to treat with the Indians. After completing the treaty, Todd went to Texas to work for the Southern Pacific Railroad and began speculating on land there. While he was away, the sons running Stockdale needed cash. The nation was in another financial depression beginning in 1857 and people were seeking land or gold in the West as a quick solution to their problems. Finally in 1858, Letitia sold Stockdale, the house, and 754 acres to Joseph Bird at auction. Their fifteen slaves were sold as well, and the Todds lived with their children in Owensboro and in Baton Rouge, and often visited the children in Shelby County.

When the Civil War began, Colonel Todd returned from the West and volunteered for the Union Army, but was refused. Son Charles Henry served as a doctor in the Confederate Army; grandson Charlie Stewart Todd was killed in Murfeesboro serving in the Union Army.

Letitia died in 1868 in Owensboro at her daughter's home. Colonel Todd continued to travel, write, and give speeches. His last speech was delivered at Lake Erie in 1869 at the anniversary celebration of Oliver Hazard Perry's victory in the War of 1812. He died of pneumonia in 1871 at his granddaughter's home in Baton Rouge.

MARY UNDERWOOD

By Walter Underwood

"The widow Underwood and family also of the first settlers," is the way Moses Boone made note of those brave pioneers who settled Painted Stone Station in 1780, including Marius Hansbury, who would become Mary Underwood's second husband and Evan Hinton who would leave his wife a widow later in the year.

Mary Underwood was the first female head-of-household in what is now Shelby County. She had five children: John, Nathan, Jacob, Polly, and Phoebe. Polly, the oldest, was about 15. How and why Mary got to Painted Stone isn't known, but clues suggest what may be the story.

Benjamin Underwood, Mary's husband, made a land claim in the spring of 1776 to the south of what is now Bagdad Road through which ran Mulberry Creek, several miles east of the Painted Stone site.

What happened to Benjamin Underwood is not known, but Mary was aware of the land claim and packed up five young children and headed off for the promised land in Kentucky. Family lore has Mary starting from somewhere along the Monongahela River, south of Ft. Pitt. Mary Underwood is believed to have loaded her five children and whatever belongings they could carry on two flatboats and started out into the unknown perils of Indian country for the journey down the Monongahela, then down the Ohio. According to John Floyd, "near 300 large boats have arrived (the Falls at Louisville) this spring (1780) with families."

John Underwood, as the eldest son and heir to Benjamin Underwood, represented the family before the Virginia Land Commission at St. Asaph's Station on April 25, 1780, and obtained a certificate for the 1,000-acre land claim in Shelby County.

Three young men, Thomas Hansbury and John and Nathan Underwood, left the safety of Painted Stone early one April morning in 1781 to clear ground for the early spring crop. They were attacked by Simon Girty led Indians who killed Hansbury and captured John Underwood. Nathan Underwood was able to reach safety in the fort. Squire Boone and others came out in their shirttails to try to rescue John Underwood. This was the famous incident in which Simon Girty wounded Squire Boone and later bragged to all who would hear that he made, "Squire Boone's shirttail fly." The story was often retold by Girty, according to the prisoner John Underwood after his release and return to Painted Stone.

Squire Boone was so seriously wounded he dispatched George Yount to Harrodsburg for a doctor. The doctor never came but Boone recovered enough to conduct a wedding of Yount and Polly Underwood in one of the earliest marriage ceremonies in Shelby County.

By September 1781 life had become too difficult in the remote outpost at Painted Stone which was abandoned by all of the settlers except the families of Squire Boone and the widow Hinton. Mary Underwood and three of her children were part of the party along with the newlyweds Polly and George Yount who left on September 13 or 14 for the safety of the Beargrass Stations closer to the Falls of the Ohio.

The journey was not easy. The Indian attack at Long Run was swift and deadly, enough to be called a massacre. Mary Underwood and family straggled in to Linn's Station after running from the Indians and fording Long Run Creek, which was swollen from a recent rain. "Many women and children were wounded," John Floyd wrote to George Rogers Clark. Marius Hansbury, who had lost a son when John Underwood was captured, lost a daughter at Long Run.

John Underwood was among a group of Revolutionary War prisoners released to go home July 18, 1783. He was about 15 years old when released at Ticonderoga and told to walk home to Shelby County. He rejoined his mother and family, likely returning to Painted Stone when it was resettled during the winter of 1783-84. By 1789, he paid taxes on the land claim which later he divided three ways among Mary's three sons: John, Jacob, and Nathan, all of whom married and raised families in Shelby County. By 1796, Mary Underwood and Morias Hansbury were married.

ALEX BOSWELL VEECH

By Kevin Collins

Alex Boswell Veech, farmer, pioneer promoter of rural electrification, agricultural and civic leader of Shelby County, was born October 11, 1888, the son of Emmett Cratton and Lizzie Boswell Veech. A lifelong resident of Shelby County, Veech had a farm near Finchville. He was a charter member of the Shelby County Farm Bureau and served as its director for twenty-five years before being succeeded by his son, Alex Jr. He was, in addition, both a past director of the Kentucky Farm Bureau, a position he held for three years, as well as a past director of the Louisville Livestock Marketing Association, a position he held for fifteen years.

Sentinel-News photograph.

Alex B. Veech was an early promoter of rural electrification and a prominent figure in agriculture.

Agricultural honors in Veech's life were plentiful. In 1942, the University of Kentucky Extension Service and the Progressive Farmer Magazine honored him with the designation of Master Farmer. In 1957, the Kentucky Farm Press and Radio Association designated him Man of the Year in Agriculture. In 1958, the University of Kentucky again honored Veech with a Golden Sheath Award for his contributions to agriculture. Finally, in 1960, at the age of seventy-two, Alex Veech received the Kentucky Farm Bureau's Distinguished Service to Kentucky Agriculture Award.

Veech was best known for his efforts on behalf of rural electrification and his work in and promotion of cooperatives. After the federal government established the Rural Electrification Administration (REA) in 1935 and the General Assembly passed the necessary legislation in 1937 to make Kentucky rural electrification possible, Veech was a guiding presence in several electric cooperatives. He was president from 1937 to 1970 of the Shelby County Rural Electric Cooperative, as well as president for twenty-one years of the Eastern Kentucky Rural Electric Cooperative. He was a former director of the Kentucky Association of Electric Cooperatives (established in 1948). In addition to his work with electric cooperatives, Veech was also a president and for twelve years a board member of the Southern States Cooperative, a farmers co-op based in Richmond, Virginia.

His commitment to rural electrification was honored first in 1970 with the dedication of the Veech Auditorium at the East Kentucky Power Cooperative Headquarters in Winchester; and later in 1973 when the boardroom of the Shelby Rural Electric County Cooperative building on Finchville Road was also named for him.

Alex Veech served for three years on the Shelby County school board. He was a member of the Solomon Masonic Lodge and a member and deacon of the Finchville Baptist Church. He was married to the former Marguerite Neel, who passed away in 1965. He died October 12, 1978, and is buried in Grove Hill Cemetery.

HARRY FRAZIER WALTERS

By Kevin Collins

Harry Frazier Walters, farmer, County Judge, member of the General Assembly, and State Commissioner of Agriculture, was born January 11, 1891, the son of M.R. and Maxie Frazier Walters. A resident of Shelby County all his life, Walters grew up near Simpsonville and was a product of the Shelby County school system.

A lifelong farmer, Walters had a large farm near Shelbyville. In fact he had just finished hand tilling his garden only hours before his fatal heart attack. The tobacco industry in all its phases was a principal agricultural interest of Walters, but he was also adept at dairy farming, and once distinguished himself by defeating the then-Governor Earle Clements in a milking contest. He was a charter member of and significant presence on the Shelby County Farm Bureau.

"Judge" Walters, as he was known to his friends, was a member of the Democratic Party, and his judicial career spanned two terms as a magistrate and then two terms as County Judge from 1933 to 1939. He was the presiding judge in the 1938 celebrated trial of Roy and Jack Garr. The Garrs were accused of the murder of General Denhardt in front of the Armstrong Hotel. In a controversial verdict, the jury found them to be not guilty. In 1939 Walters resigned his last year as County Judge and was elected to the General Assembly. In his eight years as a legislator, Walters served four sessions on the House Agricultural Committee, three of them as chairman.

Walters became State Agricultural Commissioner in 1947, and was an enthusiastic supporter of the State Fair Reorganization Act. As a member of the State Fair Board he was a vocal supporter for the creation of the new state fairgrounds and exposition center in Louisville. He also helped form the State Agricultural Production and Marketing Commission. In 1949, he was elected secretary-treasurer of the Southern Association of Agricultural Commissioners. He was also Kentucky chairman of an effort to distribute commodities to needy overseas institutions, such as orphanages, called the Christian Rural Overseas Program.

Walters was a member, deacon, and chairman of the board of the Simpsonville Christian Church. He was a member of the Simpsonville Masonic Lodge as well as a member of the board of directors of the Old Masons Home near Shelbyville. He was an ex-officio member of the board of the University of Kentucky and a member of the board of directors of Midway Junior College. He was a member of the Rotary Club.

Harry Walters was married to the former Fannie Bell Goodnight. He died on June 16, 1951, and is buried in Grove Hill Cemetery.

ADRIEL CLARK WEAKLEY

By Kevin Collins

Adriel Clark Weakley was born on December 12, 1887, in Shelby County. He was the son of Adriel V. and Annie Thompson Weakley. Educated in the Shelby County school system, Weakly received his B.A. degree from Georgetown College and his medical degree in 1912 from the Johns Hopkins Medical School.

Weakley began the practice of medicine in Shelbyville in 1914, and, except for two years of military service, he practiced continuously for 41 years. He was the family doctor to two generations in Shelby County, spanning the practice of medicine from the days of horse-and-buggy house calls to the era of modern hospital medicine. His office was in the Smith-McKenney building in Shelbyville with his residence on Adair Avenue. A member of several state and national medical associations, Weakley was a president of the Shelby-Oldham-Henry Counties Medical Society. In 1955, the Society honored the 68-year-old physician for his life's contributions to Shelby and the surrounding counties.

A veteran of World War I, Dr. Weakley served overseas in the Army Medical Corps. Subsequently, he would serve as Commander of the Shelby County American Legion. He was a president of the Shelbyville Rotary Club. He was a member and deacon of the First Baptist Church of Shelbyville, an amateur but excellent historian, and a dedicated conservationist and sportsman who loved to don waders and head to Lake Shelby for a day of fly-fishing.

Weakley was twice married. In 1916, he married the former Evelyn Guthrie. They had two children, a daughter Jule and a son Adriel Clark Jr. Mrs. Weakley died in 1948. In 1952, Weakley married the former Ruby Bowles Jamison.

He died June 14, 1973, and is buried in Bagdad Cemetery.

HARRY WEISSINGER

By Betty Matthews

Undulata is the idyllic name that Col. Harry Weissinger chose for his Shelby County farm. A leading citizen of Louisville and a wealthy tobacco manufacturer, Weissinger was born in 1842 on a farm that is now the site of Central Park in Louisville. His father, George Weissinger, was a journalist and co-founder with George Prentise of the Louisville Journal.

When he was barely 18 years old and preparing to attend college, the Civil War broke out. Weissinger enlisted and served in the Confederate Army in Gen. John Hunt Morgan's command. He was on a raid in Ohio when he was captured. He escaped imprisonment and served until the war's end. Returning to Louisville, he became a traveling salesman, then went into the tobacco business.

His firm was the Harry W. Weissinger Tobacco Co. It prospered and he originated and developed methods of processing plug tobacco that were adopted by the entire industry. Eventually he sold his business to the American Tobacco Co. in 1902.

At various times Col. Weissinger was president of Louisville's Board of Trade, a railroad vice president, bank director, and president of the Board of Aldermen. He built the Weissinger-Gaulbert apartment building and owned other downtown structures. He was active in Democratic politics.

Upon retirement in 1902 he turned to country life. He chose an area two miles south of Shelbyville where he purchased 1,600 acres fronting both the Zaring Mill Road and Mount Eden Road. The farm made him one of the largest landowners in Shelby County at the time of his death on May 9, 1915. He tended to spend the summers on the farm. He had two sons, Muir and Phillip, and three daughters Mrs. Stanton Tiffany, Mrs. S.T. Castleman, and Mrs. Julius Manger. He is buried in Cave Hill Cemetery.

Sentinel-News photograph reproduced in 1992.

Col. Harry Weissinger, founder of Undulata Farm, is shown on the steps of the house he built.

DAVID WHITE

By Kenneth A. Dennis

David White was born on November 1, 1749 in Amelia County, Virginia, the oldest in a family of five known children. On September 6, 1774, he took as his wife one Susannah (ca. 1753-1845) whose maiden name is not known. They were married by Parson Bromskill of the Church of England in Amelia County and were to have four children: David, Jr., whose death is recounted below; Polly, who married William Shanks on November 1, 1806; Benjamin, who became a cabinet maker and married Elizabeth Haiden on April 21, 1815; and Susan, who married John Wood on October 31, 1816. She would predecease both of her parents, dying on August 30, 1828. She was 44 years old, left an eight-year-old son, David James Wood (1819-1910), and is buried in Flat Rock Cemetery in Shelby County. The fate of John Wood is unknown.

In 1775, shortly after his marriage to Susannah, David White was drafted into the Virginia Militia for a period of six months. Under the command of Capt. Booker, his company crossed the James River and marched in the direction of Williamsburg, Virginia. Booker's company was largely engaged in guarding the coast against the British. After his discharge, White soon enlisted as a regular soldier in the Virginia Line. For approximately three years, until his discharge in 1778, White was attached to Col. Meade's Regiment and was again given the task of guarding the coastline, mostly in the areas of Hampton and Yorktown, Virginia. He was involved in numerous skirmishes but no general battles.

In the autumn of 1779, White, his wife, and two children moved to Kentucky. Bland W. Ballard (1761-1853) recalled seeing the White family at Boonesborough at that time. David White continued with his family to Martin's Station, but returned to Boonesborough periodically for corn and was there on March 7, 1780, the day before Col. Richard Callaway was killed by Indians.

White belonged to the Kentucky County Militia and was enrolled in the company of Capt. Charles Gatliff. He had come to Kentucky as part of a group that was under orders from Gen. George Rogers Clark to serve as scouts and defenders of the settlements. Martin's Station, where the Whites settled, was located in present-day Bourbon County on Stoner's Creek, a branch of the Licking River. John Martin had established it beside a well-used aboriginal path known as the Alantowamiomee Trail. Unfortunately, White and his family were not to remain long at the station.

On June 22, 1780, Capt. Henry Byrd of the King's 8th Regiment of Foot captured Martin's Station. The White family and the other captured inhabitants of the station were marched to the forks of Stoner Creek and Licking River where they were loaded into canoes to begin the long journey north to the British prison at Detroit.

It was in the early course of this journey that personal tragedy was to strike the Whites. In the descent, their canoe capsized and young son David, Jr., who would have been little more than five years old, was drowned. What few possessions and papers they had been allowed to bring were also lost. Grief-stricken over the loss of their eldest child and now devoid of any worldly goods, the Whites were forced on without delay toward Detroit and imprisonment.

From that time on, White would invariably sign his name "David White Sr.", in effect insuring that posterity would know that there had been a David, Jr. —a young pioneer boy whose grave was the waters of the Licking River in the Kentucky wilderness.

On August 3, 1780, after nearly a month and a half of what White would term "great hardships and privations", the prisoners arrived at Detroit. In the records of the Kentucky County Militia, pay was terminated for White and the other militiamen on June 26th.

Edward Tyler, Jr. (1767-1840) of the pioneer Tyler family of Jefferson County, Kentucky, stated that his sister, who was later brought to Detroit, shared a house with the Whites there. They were to be held as prisoners for more than three years. The signing of the Treaty of Paris on September 3, 1783, ended the Revolutionary War, and the captives were released on October 16 of that year. The Whites, Tyler's sister, and the others safely made their way south through Indian country by means of a pass issued by Maj. Arent S. DePeyster, the British officer in command at Detroit. By Christmas 1783, the Whites were back in Kentucky at Lynn's (or Linn's) Station.

On December 6, 1785, an 18-year-old orphan named Bartlett Asher was legally bound to White "to learn the art of a carpenter." It will be remembered that White's son, Benjamin, was to be a cabinetmaker. These were obviously skills that White possessed and was able to teach. Asher was to remain in Jefferson County after the Whites moved eastward.

On January 2, 1787, David White was appointed a captain in the Jefferson County Militia. He was much involved in local affairs, and March 6, 1792, found him on jury duty hearing the case of the Commonwealth vs. Bruner. The jury found for the plaintiff with 40 shillings damages.

By the beginning of the 1790s, the Indians had been driven from the area. On June 1, 1792, Kentucky entered the Union as the fifteenth state, and on June 23 of the same year, Shelby County was formed from a portion of Jefferson County. It was at this time that David White acquired 100 acres of land on Long Run Creek in the newly created Shelby County. He was to spend the rest of his long life there.

David White was engaged in agricultural pursuits and made occasional trips to the growing town of Louisville. Several of these trips were necessitated by his involvement in litigation concerning land claims. He and Susannah raised their three remaining children, saw them married, and watched them settle in Shelby County. In 1836, at the age of 87, White applied for his pension for service in the American Revolution. The application was approved, and he received $80.00 annually in two $40.00 semi-annual payments. He also received a one-time arrears payment of $520.00.

On July 27, 1838, after an illness of some two weeks, David White Sr. died in his home in Simpsonville. The old pioneer was laid to rest on his property, and a gravestone with the following inscription was erected: *Sacred to the memory of David White, Sr., Who was born Novr 10th 1750, Who departed this life, July 27th 1838, Aged 87 Years 8 Months and 17 Days, May he that rests, beneath this clay, Enjoy a blessing on that day, When all the dead shall arise, In glorious triumphs to the skies.*

Susannah White survived her husband by nearly seven years, dying in 1845 at the approximate age of 92. Benjamin White inherited his parents' home, which stood until 1992 when, being in an unstable condition, it was demolished. The surrounding land has been subdivided, and only the location of the old well is evident. The grave of David White Sr. is on the front lawn of one of the homes built on the property.

R. S. SAMMY WOOD

By Duanne Puckett

The first order of business for R.S. "Sammy" Wood as the first County Judge-Executive under the new court system was questioning the limit of $10,800 placed on his salary by the previous magistrates. He brought up the issue with the new Fiscal Court at the January 5, 1978, meeting - four days after he took office.

Wood was not the only one new to his post in 1978. All the magistrates except one were newly elected. Joining the men during Fiscal Court meetings was newly elected County Clerk Sue Carole Perry, who replaced Ruth Vawter.

The habit of the magistrates in the 1970s was to discuss various matters downstairs before the formal meetings in the courtroom began. And after each meeting, there was always a vote where to have lunch together.

Wood was the only man to be elected to two terms as sheriff 1954-57 and 1974-77. He was also a two-time deputy sheriff 1946-53 and 1963-73.

Wood and his wife, the former Lucille Ethington, celebrated their 65th wedding anniversary June 8, 1994. The couple lived in the Elmburg community where he was a member of the Elmburg Baptist Church where he was a deacon. He also served on the board of directors at the Central Bank and was a farmer and lumber dealer. The couple had three children: Martha Jean Wood, Nancy Lou Proctor, and Billy Joe Wood. At the time of Wood's death, they also had five grandchildren and four great-grandchildren.

Wood died July 13, 1994, at The Forum at Brookside in Louisville. To the end he was known as a soft-spoken man who was proud to have accomplished all that he did with an eighth-grade education. He was also known in the community for wearing loud sport coats and driving a Cadillac.

WILLIS COLEMAN WRIGHT

By Mary David Myles

The elementary school on Rocket Lane was named for W. Coleman Wright, a former Shelby County Circuit Judge. Wright was born in Simpsonville on February 6, 1907. He received his law degree from the University of Kentucky on June 20, 1930, and was admitted to the Bar on June 20, 1930. He had a private practice until he was elected Shelby County Attorney.

In 1940, Governor Keen Johnson appointed Wright to fill a vacancy as Shelby County Judge. He served in that position until 1952 when he was elected and commissioned by Governor Lawrence Wetherby as Circuit Judge, a position, except for a period during World War II, he held until his death. His Circuit, the Twelfth, included Anderson, Shelby, Spencer, Henry, Trimble, and Oldham Counties. The Kentucky Bar Association named him Judge of the Year in 1968. Wright was the first attorney for the Shelby Rural Electric Co-op Corporation and helped obtain the easements for the electric lines. In 1939, he became a Director of the Farmers and Traders Bank and in 1968 he became its President. He held this office until his death in 1970. In 1955, Governor A. B. Chandler appointed him to the Parole and Probation Committee. He helped to write the Parole and Probation Act of the Commonwealth of Kentucky.

Judge Wright was active in community service. He was chairman of the American Red Cross Chapter from 1936 to 1962, served two years as vice president of the Louisville Area Boy Scouts of Americas, trustee of the Lincoln Institute in Simpsonville, and a director of the Old Masons Home. Wright was a member of the Centenary United Methodist Church where he taught the Young Adult Sunday School Class and served as chairman of the Board of Trustees for many years.

In 1942, Wright entered World War II as a private and advanced to captain before his discharge in 1946. Judge Wright was a delegate to the National Democratic Convention in Philadelphia in 1948 and Chicago in 1952. Wright had no children but he loved them. His wife, Bess, said, "I don't think anything would have been more wonderful than to name a school for him. It was a gift from Heaven."

W. Coleman Wright, Judge of the Twelfth Circuit Court of Kentucky from 1952 until his death in 1970.

WHITNEY M. YOUNG

By Duanne Puckett

African-Americans had been attending Berea College's elementary schools since 1866. In 1869 seven black students became part of Berea's first college class. That successful experience in racial relations came to a halt in July 1904 with the passage of the Day Law by the Kentucky General Assembly. State Representative Carl Day had visited the Berea campus in November 1903 and was shocked to see blacks and whites living together in the same dormitories. He immediately introduced the bill which was passed preventing the education of whites and black together in all Kentucky schools.

Fighting back, Berea took the case all the way to the Supreme Court but lost. The school trustees then voted to help secure a school for blacks elsewhere. After successful fund-raising, 444 acres were bought near Simpsonville. It was to be called Lincoln Institute.

When the doors to the new school opened in 1911, Whitney Moore Young was one of the first to enroll. He was born at Paynes Depot in Shelby County on September 26, 1897, to Taylor and Annie Young. He attended Zion Public School, Male Underwood School in Frankfort, and the Chandler Normal School in Lexington.

After graduating from Lincoln in 1916, he moved to Detroit to work for the Ford Motor Company. Following service in the U. S. Army in France during World War I, he returned to Ford to work as an electrical engineer. When Lincoln Institute offered him a job in 1920, he left a high paying salary to head the engineering department for $68 a month. He was promoted to dean and later to president, becoming the first black to hold that position. Facing a $10,000 debt, Young held successful fund-raising and student recruitment campaigns to make Lincoln the leading black preparatory school in Kentucky.

He served on the staff of Lincoln from 1918 to 1935 and became president in 1936, serving in that role until 1964, when the school closed and he moved with his family to Louisville.

Young continued his own education while running the school. He received a bachelor's degree from Louisville Municipal College, a master's degree from Fisk University in Nashville, and an honorary doctorate in education from Monrovia College in Liberia. He served twice as president of Kentucky's Negro Education Association in the 1950s and served on four commissions appointed by various governors of Kentucky. He was also appointed to the Citizens Committee for the Implementation of the Civil Rights Law by President Lyndon Johnson.

In 1918, Young married Laura Ray of Lebanon, who was the first black postmistress of Kentucky at Lincoln Ridge and the second black postmistress in the United States. They had three children: Dr. Arnita Boswell, a professor at the University of Louisville and one of its first black deans; Dr. Eleanor Love, a professor at the University of Chicago; and Whitney M. Young Jr., nationally known civil rights leader.

Dr. Young died on August 18, 1975, and is buried in Lexington.

Shelby County Public Library, from Ann Patterson.

Whitney M. Young, front row at left, with other Lincoln Institute faculty members in 1929.
Front row, left to right: Young, Rev. Dean Kirk Smith, Dr. A. Eugene Thomas, Miss _____ Shaw, Mrs.
_____ Ellis, George T. Cordery. Second row, left to right: Mrs. Ruth Smith Seals, Miss Rachel Davis, L. M.
Scott, Gus_____, Miss Helen Hort, Miss Minnie Perry. Back row, left to right: _____Hight, Miss L.
Dollins, Clifton Holt, William Crutcher, and W. Taylor Seals.

WHITNEY M. YOUNG, JR.

By Duanne Puckett

Growing up on the grounds of Lincoln Institute in Shelby County, Whitney M. Young Jr. had a good childhood. But the worst lesson he ever received was when his parents took him to Shelbyville to see a movie. He was about 5 years old and rushed past his parents as they bought the tickets. He couldn't wait to get a seat down front. Young remembered vividly the encounter in a speech, "… I was literally grabbed by the usher, who called me 'nigger' and 'boy' and told me to 'get on out of here.' He also asked 'Don't you know where you're supposed to be? You're supposed to be in nigger heaven.' " That was the name for the segregated balcony section where patrons sat in a small, crowded area on wooden chairs compared to the downstairs area which was air-conditioned and had cushioned seats. Thus Whitney M. Young Jr., first tasted discrimination as the white usher escorted him to the stairs marked "For colored only."

Born July 13, 1921, at Lincoln Ridge in Shelby County, he was the son of Laura Ray and Whitney M. Young. His father was an instructor at and later president of Lincoln Institute, an all-black school in Simpsonville. Young graduated from Lincoln as valedictorian in 1936 and received a premedical degree from Kentucky State College (University) four years later, again graduating at the head of his class.

He taught mathematics and coached at Rosenwald High School in Madisonville before enlisting in the Army in 1941 when he was sent to the Massachusetts Institute of Technology where he studied electrical engineering for two years. Young became a first sergeant in the 369th Regiment Anti-Aircraft Artillery Group. While serving in the all-black unit under white officers, Young decided to make race relations his life's work.

He and Margaret Buckner of Campbellsville were married in 1944. She became a teacher and author of children's books about black history and civil rights. They had two children, Marcie and Laurene.

Denied admission to the University of Kentucky, Young attended the University of Minnesota from 1944 to 1947 where he helped organize a chapter of the Congress of Racial Equality. Remaining there, he became director of industrial relations at the Urban League in St. Paul, Minnesota, after he received a master's degree in social work. He was promoted and served as president of the chapter in Omaha, Nebraska, from 1950 to 1954. In January 1954 he moved to Atlanta University to become the dean of the School of Social Work, a position he held until August 1, 1961, when he was named executive director of the National Urban League.

An advocate of equal employment opportunity, improved housing and education as the means for social and economic equality for blacks, Young advanced the League's programs through support from corporate, government, and foundation entities. He redirected the organization, which had been focused entirely on socioeconomic issues. His work took the Urban League from a yearly budget of $250,000 to more than $20 million.

During the 1960s Young emerged as a national civil rights leader. He served on seven presidential commissions under John F. Kennedy and Lyndon Johnson. It was Johnson who presented Young with the Medal of Freedom in 1969. President Richard Nixon delivered Young's eulogy. The Shelby County native also served in official capacities with conferences dealing with social welfare and social work. His involvement in civil rights put him in contact with Dr. Martin Luther King Jr. Although his talents were mainly in the board room, he did help King with the 1963 March on Washington. He also spread his message of equality through two books, *To Be Equal* (1964) and *Beyond Racism: Building an Open Society* (1969), as well as a weekly syndicated newspaper column. He also started a program in 1968 to attack ghettos and the problems spreading there. Young died March 11, 1971, in a swimming accident in Lagos, Nigeria, while attending a conference to increase understanding between races. The school where he was born and where his father was on the faculty and where he graduated as valedictorian now bears his name. The Whitney M. Young Jr. Job Corps Center outside Simpsonville helps young people perfect their skills to become productive members of society. Several are minorities, which would please

Young whose goal was economically strong black communities that would be integrated into the general society without violence. It is a testimonial to his well known quote, "We must learn to live together as brothers or we will all surely die together as fools."

GEORGE YOUNT (YUNT)

By Juanita Hyatt Reason

A well-established custom in Kentucky was to never let an Indian invasion go unpunished. In early November 1782 Gen. George Rogers Clark led a group of 1,050 militia 130 miles north up the Miami River in what is now Ohio and took successful revenge on several Indian villages including the principal Shawnee town of Loramie's Store. The towns were completely destroyed, burned to the ground, including all provisions, and nothing was spared. The value of the property and provisions greatly surpassed all expectations. No large body of Indians ever invaded Kentucky again.

These early years in Kentucky were known as "breathless, bloody years." Yet during all the hardships and perils these pioneer men and women stood side by side, suffered, labored, and grew strong. And many of them prospered. George and Polly Yount (also spelled Yunt) were two of many settlers who experienced the fears and privations of wilderness life. George has been remembered as being one of the bravest of the pioneers in a time abounding with brave and daring men.

George Yount was born December 27, 1757, and died May 9, 1823. At age eighteen years he enlisted on August 13, 1776, into the Pennsylvania 8th Regiment of the Revolutionary Army Volunteers. This regiment consisted of seven companies raised from Westmoreland County and one from Bedford County. It was commanded by Col. Aenas McCoy and Lieut. Col. George Wilson, both of whom died during early spring 1777. The regiment was then placed under the command of Col. Daniel Broadhead, Lieut. Col. Richard Butler, and Major Stephen Bayard. During his three years service George Yunt was among the forces that fought at the Battle of Trenton, the Battle of The Brandywine, the Battle of Paoli, the Battle of Cowpens, and several other skirmishes. On March 5, 1778, the regiment was ordered to Pittsburgh (Ft. Pitt) for the defense of the western frontiers. George was discharged at Pittsburgh in October 1779. Following his discharge he came to Shelby County. Besides being a soldier of the Revolution, he was also an Indian fighter, a farmer, and a true wilderness pioneer.

Polly Underwood Yount, whose full name was Mary Elizabeth, was born November 2, 1765, and died February 8, 1840. She is believed to have been a daughter of Revolutionary War soldier Benjamin Underwood and Mary Crow Underwood. Mary Crow Underwood came to Squire Boone's Painted Stone Station in 1780 as a widow. She remarried soon after to Marius Hansbury. It is believed her other children were Phebe, John, Jacob, and Nathan. On February 24, 1781, Polly married George. According to Bible records thirteen children were born to the couple. They were: John born 1781; William born 1783; Jonathan born 1785; Benjamin born 1787; Elizabeth born 1789; Nathaniel born 1791; Joseph born 1793; Rachel born 1795; Mary born 1797; Phebi born 1799; George Jr. born 1802; Jacob born 1804; and Sarah born 1807.

INDEX

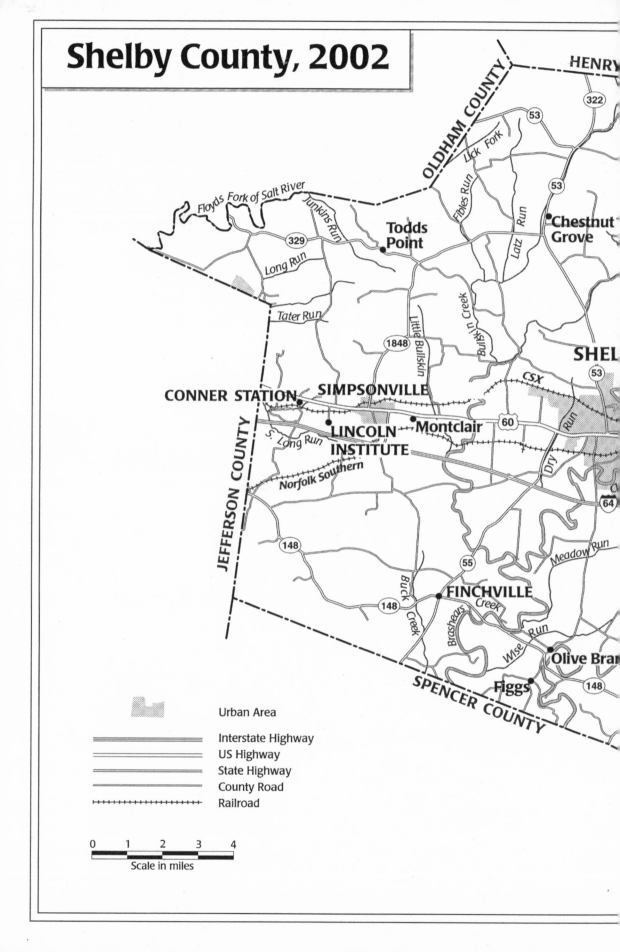

Shelby County, 2002

HENRY

OLDHAM COUNTY

322

53

53

Lick Fork

Fibles Run

•Chestnut
Grove

Floyds Fork of Salt River

Junkins Run

Todds
Point

Latz Run

329

Long Run

Little Bullskin

Bullskin Creek

SHEL

Tater Run

1848

53

CSX

CONNER STATION

SIMPSONVILLE

S. Long Run

LINCOLN
INSTITUTE

•Montclair

60

Dry Run

Norfolk Southern

64

148

Meadow Run

55

JEFFERSON COUNTY

Buck Creek

FINCHVILLE

Creek

148

Brashears

Wise Run

Olive Brar

SPENCER COUNTY

Figgs

148

Urban Area

Interstate Highway
US Highway
State Highway
County Road
++++++++++++++++++ Railroad

0   1   2   3   4

Scale in miles